MORAL ISSUES AND CHRISTIAN RESPONSE

MORAL ISSUES AND CHRISTIAN RESPONSE

Sixth Edition

Edited by

Paul T. Jersild
Lutheran Theological Southern Seminary

Dale A. Johnson
Vanderbilt University

Patricia Beattie Jung
Loyola University, Chicago

Shannon Jung
Center for Theology and Land
University of Dubuque and Wartburg Theological Seminaries

Harcourt Brace College Publishers

Fort Worth   Philadelphia   San Diego   New York   Orlando   Austin   San Antonio
Toronto   Montreal   London   Sydney   Tokyo

Publisher	Earl McPeek
Acquisitions Editor	David Tatom
Product Manager	Steve Drummond
Developmental Editor	Susan Petty
Project Editor	Jon Davies
Production Manager	Linda McMillan
Art Director	Garry Harman

ISBN: 0-03-018062-7
Library of Congress Catalog Card Number: 97-75099

Copyright © 1998, 1993, 1988, 1983, 1976, 1971 by Holt, Rinehart, and Winston

Photo credits: p. 1, © David Young-Wolff/PhotoEdit; p. 55, © John Curtis/OFFSHOOT Stock/Bonnie Kamin; p. 103, © Joel Gordon; p. 185, © N. R. Rowan/Photo Researchers; p. 269, © Jon Riley/Tony Stone Worldwide; p. 341, © Joseph Nettis/Photo Researchers.

Address for Orders:
Harcourt Brace College Publishers
6277 Sea Harbor Drive, Orlando
FL 32887-6777
1-800-782-4479

Address for Editorial Correspondence:
Harcourt Brace College Publishers
301 Commerce Street, Suite 3700
Fort Worth, TX 76102

Web site address:
http://www.hbcollege.com

Printed in the United States of America

7 8 9 0 1 2 3 4 5 6   067   9 8 7 6 5 4 3 2 1

PREFACE AND ACKNOWLEDGMENTS

For quite some time the work of Paul Jersild and Dale Johnson in their jointly produced editions of *Moral Issues and Christian Response* has been widely respected. It has been the best such introduction to contemporary moral issues that combines an overview of current events with Christian moral interpretation and, as such, is useful for undergraduate courses on Moral Problems, Christian Ethics, Church and Society, and Comparative Religious Ethics.

We are delighted to be involved in this sixth edition of *Moral Issues and Christian Response*. We are grateful and honored by Paul and Dale's invitation to join them in the editing of this work. (We have had a good time saying "Jersild, Johnson, Jung, and Jung," we admit. Sounds like a law firm or a pharmaceutical house.) We know a good thing when we see it and have not changed the format of this edition. As in previous editions, the book includes a survey of what Christian ethicists and others had been writing about many contemporary and often controversial topics. Included in each chapter are different, if not opposing, perspectives on the same issue.

While the basic philosophy and format of the book are the same, the sixth edition has been substantially changed in many ways. We have significantly increased the number of pieces from both women and Roman Catholic moral theologians and have broadened the range of opinions represented in that way. We still offer a variety of Reformed, Lutheran, Radical Reformation, and other Protestant perspectives.

Some seventy-five or eighty percent of the essays are new, most of them written since 1993, and the "Suggested Readings" (which might offer clues to research for term papers, response papers, or other additional research) have been updated. We have added two new chapters on immigration and on consumer lifestyles, and have cut the chapter on the legalization of drugs. It is difficult to keep the number of issues from getting out of hand.

This edition begins with two chapters that frame the moral issues constituting the balance of the book. The first considers theologically the ways in which the church is or should be related to politics and the moral realm generally; the second raises the topic of what sources of moral wisdom—women's experience, the Bible, guiding vision—should be considered in making such crucial moral decisions as are presented in the following pages. The book then turns to chapters centered on issues of sexual ethics, prejudice and discrimination, immigration, ecology, violence, the death penalty, economic ethics, and bioethical problems.

This sixth edition will be helpful in stimulating and delighting its readers in the invigorating game of moral reasoning. It will equip you in thinking about some of the major issues of our time and developing a discriminating, Christian response to them.

We wish to acknowledge in particular the assistance of those professors who use the text in class who were willing to share their opinions of student reaction to the various chapters. We have in many cases followed their suggestions.

There are many colleagues from the Society of Christian Ethics who have guided our selections. Very, very important has been the work of Patty Walker, the program assistant at the Center for Theology and Land in Dubuque, Iowa, who has helped coordinate this work and provided invaluable editorial suggestions. Other gifted people who worked with us include Ed Peck, graduate assistant in the Department of Theology at Loyola University, Chicago and now assistant professor at Neumann College, Philadelphia, and Jane Johnston, student at Wartburg Seminary and now pastor at Estherville (Iowa) Lutheran Church; they contributed to the collecting and first winnowing of an amazing number of articles, essays, and books. We wish to thank Ms. Mara Martini, secretary at the Department of Theology, Loyola, and Jill Stivers and Trish Schmidt, Wartburg, for their typing. Drs. John McCartney, Loyola, and Jeffrey Bullock, Dean at the University of Dubuque Seminary, were supportive and interested; that makes a huge difference.

We wish also to thank the people at Harcourt Brace who contributed to the sixth edition: David Tatom, acquisitions editor; Susan R. Petty, developmental editor; Jon Davies, project editor; Garry Harman, art director; and Linda McMillan, production manager.

Shannon Jung
Patricia Beattie Jung

CONTENTS

PART THREE
The Christian and Issues of Prejudice and Oppression   103

Chapter 5
RACISM: THE STRUGGLE CONTINUES   105

Chapter 6
FEMINISM IN CHURCH AND SOCIETY   132

Chapter 7
HETEROSEXISM   158

PART FOUR
The Christian and Issues of National Priority   185

Chapter 8
IMMIGRATION: CAN WE HAVE OPEN BORDERS?   187

INTRODUCTION

We all face hundreds of moral choices each day. Many of them are so common—Should I tell the truth? Should I betray a friend?—that we don't think about them. We simply tell the truth as a matter of course. We act toward our friends in ways that are trustworthy. We develop moral habits of honesty, trustworthiness, and integrity. These patterns of acting no longer require much reflection; we simply act morally out of habit.

During the course of our lives we experience a wide variety of disappointments—the dashing of a cherished dream, the breaking of a relationship, failures in professional life, family conflicts or even the death of someone close. How we respond to these experiences says a lot about our moral character or the kind of person we are. Our responses are based on our habits, but they are also more reflective; we decide—to some extent—how to respond.

Just as revealing of moral character is how we respond to the triumphs of our lives, our successes and achievements and the praise and adulation which they bring. Coping with success can be just as much of a moral challenge as coping with failure or disaster. Whatever the situation we respond either with grace, stamina, courage, humility—or with resentment, self-pity, despair, and false pride. More accurately, since most of us are neither saints nor rogues, we respond with a mixture of both morally admirable and morally questionable traits. Our lives reveal moral ambiguity more than pure goodness or pure evil. We think about our habits and our responses; thus, we critique the moral goodness or questionableness of those responses.

Both our individual character and our thinking about the morality of certain issues are important foci of moral discourse. This volume, however, is concerned with individual thinking and the thinking of a community of faith—the Christian church—and how it relates to issues of social morality. Not only individuals but a group like the church can reveal something of its character by how it responds to the moral issues and challenges of the day. It can respond with boldness, courage, and integrity, or with timidity or even apathy. Of course there are many churches—denominations we call them—and they relate to issues differently. Nonetheless, there are elements of our Christian heritage—shared beliefs—which all churches affirm and hold in common. This heritage embraces certain ideals and values which claim the allegiance of those who follow Jesus Christ, whatever their particular church affiliation. As with individuals, however, churches also reveal much ambiguity and tension in their corporate life.

These conflicts can often occur because of intense feelings caused by social issues. Christians can heatedly disagree over questions like abortion, the death penalty, and wars of intervention. They also disagree about solutions to social issues, so that while most churches repudiate racism, they frequently disagree about how to address issues caused by prejudice and discrimination. Sometimes these disagreements become so heated that they threaten the life and welfare of particular denominations. Many Protestant denominations are threatened by disagreements about the ordination of gays and lesbians, while the Roman Catholic Church finds increasingly divisive the question of the role and ordination of women in the church. Denominational positions on social issues are often the object of attack on the part of offended parishioners who disagree with the perspectives being espoused. Whatever ideological factors separate Christian people into factions labeled conservative or liberal, they are particularly divisive in the area of social issues.

THE CHURCH AS "GUARDIAN OF MORALITY"

As is true of other human organizations, there are weaknesses in the church which compromises its witness and voice in the public world. In addition, there are factors at work which threaten the church's effort to be faithful in its social witness. Primary among these is the expectation of public leaders and people generally that the church should function as a kind of moral police officer, exerting its influence on behalf of "law and order." This expectation may be strong among church members as well. Many in the church likely understand its primary purpose to be the guardian of the nation's morals.

This role gives the church a somewhat conservative cast, acting as defender of the status quo and protecting the public from anything new and questionable. To the extent that it accepts this role, the church can unwittingly become a servant of the dominant political ideology or party which has a vested interest in identifying the church with its own power. The church can lose its independent voice and become a means of shaping public morality in support of the dominant group's policies and set of beliefs. Thus, the church can lose its capacity to challenge political authority and suggest new directions. Although the church does not have as much moral authority today as it once did, it nevertheless exerts significant influence in shaping a common national morality. In an increasingly pluralistic society, the church continues to be the principal religious establishment and can on occasion speak with considerable impact.

Rather than bemoan the civil function of religion in which the church expresses the ideals and aspirations of American society, the church can celebrate its legitimate influence. The church does serve as a "glue" in maintaining the traditional ethos of a people. This function can be quite important in defining the moral foundations of a society and recalling the society to conserve its values or reform them if need be. At the same time, it is apparent to church leaders and members that the primary role of the church in the realm of social morality is to interpret its message with integrity as it relates to that morality. Sometimes the church is called by its own faithful ideals and values to take a prophetic, even unpopular, stance simply because that is the Gospel mandate. The church does have something distinctive and important to say, not simply in defense of cherished traditional values, but in pointing society to a more acute sense of justice and to the power of love in every human relationship.

There are many issues confronting church and society that move the church to speak out. These issues may be classified into three groups. First are all those that relate to Christian teaching and piety and the role of religion in the public life of the nation. These include church/state issues such as prayer in the public schools, the teaching of creationism, and Christian symbols in public places. Only two of our articles touch on these issues—the articles by Robert Rector and Franklin Gamwell. Second are moral issues relating to individual choice and lifestyle, such as pornography, conscientious objection to war, and the use of reproductive technologies. These are of course influenced by social dynamics and only present themselves as being more personal. Third are all those moral issues relating to corporate justice within a society and between nations, where individuals or groups of people are oppressed or victimized. This third group includes such concerns as the use of political and economic power, minority treatment, and war and peace. Often we are confronted personally by such broadscale social issues. In this book, we address a number of issues that fall primarily under the latter two categories. These two, personal and social morality, are actually interdependent, a part of the fabric of community. They are as inseparable as the way persons are formed by the church and then in turn form the church themselves, as inseparable as citizens and the nation.

If the church takes its own message seriously, it will find itself on the frontiers of social morality, addressing words of healing and understanding when difficult issues cause rifts between church and society, and exercising an intense concern for justice on behalf of those who are being victimized. The church's mission demands that it address every issue which involves the welfare of our society and the destiny of particular individuals. Sometimes, as in the case of homosexuality, that involves reconsidering a past judgment in light of new evidence and argument. Sometimes, as in the case of racism, that involves maintaining a concern for an old sin that remains very much with us.

HOW DO WE ARRIVE AT MORAL JUDGMENTS?

One answer to this question is that we should simply turn to the Bible. We might note that if there is one encapsulation of all of morality for Christians, it is Jesus' response to the lawyer who asked him which was the greatest commandment. Jesus said: "You shall love the Lord your God with all your heart, and with all your soul, and with all your mind. This is the greatest and first commandment. And a second is like it: You shall love your neighbor as yourself. On these two commandments hang all the law and the prophets." (Matthew 22: 37–40). This is an important perspective, but its generality requires that we understand it in light of other sources of moral authority as will be obvious in Chapter Two.

How *are* we to discern what Jesus' two great commandments mean in addressing particular moral issues? Such discernment and analysis is the task of

Christian ethics. Whether we speak of the church or of individuals who are seeking answers to moral issues in our society, there are several elements which contribute to a responsible moral stance. These elements can be discussed under three questions: (1) What are the relevant factual data? (2) How do we know what we ought to do? and (3) Is our judgment reflective of and consistent with our deepest convictions?

(1) WHAT ARE THE RELEVANT FACTUAL DATA?

Though it is obvious, it is nevertheless true that careful attention must be paid to the facts before meaningful moral judgments can be reached. For example, knowing the facts about world population growth may leave the impression that industrialized affluent nations have taken steps to control their impact on the environment. When one considers the level of consumption that those in affluent nations enjoy, however, their impact on the environment is considerably greater than less consumptive peoples. Getting the facts, and all the relevant facts, is a daunting but indispensable step in moral decision-making. In the areas of population growth and environmental impact as well as others, we may pay greater attention to the facts that support our impressions and particular points of view.

Relevant factual data are very much the issue in arguments which would justify or challenge the level of military spending in maintaining a strong national defense. Beyond the difficulty of determining the facts about when national security has been achieved, there is the tendency on the part of the Pentagon (and, of course, others) to exaggerate the continuing need for a strong armed forces to generate support for maintaining institutional strength. There is a common practice in many arenas to overestimate need in order to secure greater support. The "facts" tend usually to be intermixed with political motives.

Many investigations into the impact of the death penalty provide data which can influence one either toward acceptance or rejection of legal execution. If one believes that the only justification for the death penalty is the effect it has in deterring crime, then it is essential that one has access to responsible studies which can give accurate data on that question. There are studies which cite statistics showing that there is a deterrent effect and others which rule out deterrents altogether. Often the moral agent (you and me) has to decide where the preponderance of evidence lies.

When a church decides to issue a statement or study document on a particular issue, its first obligation is to assemble a group of persons whose knowledge of the subject guarantees an in-depth consideration of many viewpoints. Experts can be summoned to inform the group more fully and to bring balance to its deliberations. The reality is that the facts are always interpretations, never objective, even though particular interpretations may be more plausible than others. How, for example, can a church body decide whether a homosexual orientation is hard-wired biologically in a way that is beyond a person's control or whether a person's sexual orientation is always a matter of choice, when the experts disagree? Yet this is a highly significant fact when it comes to making moral judgments about homosexuality.

Because we bring our biases, our perspectives, and our dispositions to the consideration of any given issue, it is also necessary that anyone investigating the dimensions of a moral issue be open to competing perspectives and ideologies. When differences over social issues assume a strong ideological character, truth itself is often the victim as people close their minds to opposing points of view. We lose a spirit of self-criticism which tempers our inclination to claim absolute certitude and keeps us open to views which challenge our own. It is important for churches to be centers of moral discourse where those who disagree can do so with safety; they can know that their shared loyalty to Jesus Christ enables them to hear each other as those through whom the Spirit may be speaking.

(2) HOW CAN WE KNOW WHAT OUR RESPONSIBILITY IS?

STYLE

When we speak of what we ought to do, we are getting at the distinctive character of moral experience or human responsibility. It is our sense of responsibility or obligation (what we *ought* or *ought not* to do), which suggests that there are *norms* for human activity by which we can judge actions as being morally right or morally wrong. Whenever we speak of norms which would capture a sense of duty or a moral imperative (such as "I ought to pay my debts," or "I ought not destroy this artist's painting"), we are also revealing certain values that are implicit in our sense of responsibility. Whether we speak of duties, or values and ideals toward which we strive as worthy goals or ends, we are speaking the language of ethics, which seeks to analyze and make sense of our moral experience.

In the history of ethical thought, there have been two clearly distinguishable responses to the question, "How do we know what our responsibility is?" (In other words, "What ought we to do?") The first, called the *deontological* view (with an emphasis on duty), maintains that there is an objective moral order which is "built into" the structures of life lived in community. Some have maintained that we can perceive that order through the right use of our reason (a view found in the Roman Catholic tradition), while others have maintained that we discern that order through moral intuition. However aware one is of the moral order of things, to know it is to know one's duty or what one ought to do. The rules and commandments by which we live thus express our duties to each other, and the more generally recognized they are the more important they are as signals concerning the nature of the moral universe. The Ten Commandments, for example, include prohibitions ("Thou shalt not ...") which are not arbitrary or ephemeral but are essential to order and well-being wherever life is lived in community.

The second view is not convinced that there are absolute duties which must be carried out regardless of circumstances. It focuses on the ultimate good to which one's actions may lead and, therefore, looks at the ends or goals of one's actions to determine their moral value. Our responsibility, this view maintains, is to act so as to produce the best situation possible. This is called the *teleological* view, from the Greek word *telos*, meaning "end" or "goal." While the deontological view recognizes duties which one must observe regardless of consequences, the teleological view places the moral value of the act precisely on its outcomes and whether certain values are achieved. One prominent expression of this viewpoint is utilitarianism, which maintains that the supreme value is the greatest good for the greatest number.

Historically, Roman Catholic ethics has reflected the first view described, for its understanding of natural law assumes an objective moral order to which human action should submit. At the same time, the teleological view, which looks at the ends of human action, has also played an important role in Catholic ethical thought. In recent decades, Protestant ethics has more often stressed the contextual or situational character of moral experience. We can only know what our responsibility is in context, it asserts. In part this has been a reaction to legalism as well as a reflection of a greater awareness of the historical character of our moral experience. This has meant that we are more sensitive today to the fact that "absolutes" or "universal norms" are not untouched by historical conditioning and circumstance. Protestant ethics has thus become more value-centered rather than focused on hard-and-fast duties that are supposed to be obeyed at all times and places.

Both approaches are in fact utilized in our moral decision-making. There are times when we feel responsible to another person, and we know that we ought to act in a particular way in order to fulfill this responsibility. We are tempted many times to rationalize away this sense of obligation, but as ethical beings it is well for us to recognize that moral obligation is one of the distinctively human experiences that is absolutely essential to viable community life. This truth is worth noting in an age of individualism that stresses personal freedom, one in which we can rather easily discount moral obligations as guilt trips laid on us by parents or other authorities.

There are many times, however, when the course of action to be taken is not all that clear; the nature of our responsibility is blurred, and we find ourselves balancing one value against another. We ask ourselves what the result of our action will be in an effort to gain some clarity about what we ought to do. Thus values are related to a final goal which we think justifies the decision we make. The teleological approach is also a part of our moral decision-making.

How do these methods of making moral decisions relate to the social issues addressed in this book? The reader should examine the argument of each writer in view of these methodological considerations, and here we will examine one particular chapter for the sake of illustration. Consider the chapter which has to do with immigration policy and whether the borders of the United States should be closed to further immigration, or at least that immigration be severely restricted. There are several deontological arguments being made *both for and against tightened immigration.* One argument in favor of tightening immigration asserts that our first obligation is to those people who are already legal residents of the United States and to their children. Another, also deontological, line of argument suggests that we have an obligation to be the country which offers all of "the tired, the poor" a refuge no matter what. Both values could be appealed to on the basis of Christian warrants. Notice that there are several teleological arguments that are made in those essays that come down on *both sides of the immigration debate* as well. The teleological argument is made that if we allow whoever wants to immigrate to the United States to do so, we will be overrun and several negative consequences will result: further unemployment, overloaded social services agencies, increased taxes for residents. There are also teleological arguments on the other side: if we restrict immigration, we will be jeopardizing conditions which have led to the creativity necessary for technological advance and we will also be inviting violence and armed conflict on the part of all those who are prevented from entering the United States.

Usually arguments appeal to both deontological and teleological bases; they recommend acting on both the basis of duty and in light of the possible results of our action. Arguments may also take into consideration the motives of those actors being faced with a moral decision. Many times the motives or dispositions of moral agents do not receive the notice they deserve since motives are hard to discern. However, the moral quality of many acts rests on the intentions of the agent; notice how much more rapidly we are inclined to forgive someone who says, "I didn't intend to hurt him/her/them." In the area of social policy, it is hard to assign motive because social policy is a corporate creation. Nevertheless, even here, it is evident that engaging in morally problematic behavior with malevolent intent is considered more heinous an action than the same act committed either innocently or with good intentions.

(3) ARE OUR MORAL JUDGMENTS BASED ON OUR DEEPEST FAITH CONVICTIONS? DO THEY REFLECT THOSE CONVICTIONS?

Our moral decisions are shaped by our understanding of the facts of the matter and by the values which are important to us. But resting beneath our decisions is a perspective or outlook on life—what we might call a "life-orientation," or faith. We use the word "integrity" to describe the moral dimension of this orientation. It is actually a matter of expressing who we really are, for personal identity is essentially expressed in what we believe and to what and to whom we are committed as moral beings. This gets at the real "us" which is never disclosed simply by our race, gender, or economic status. The kind of morality that characterizes our lives reveals ultimately what we believe concerning the world in which we live and the meaning of our own lives, even if this credo may not be very well articulated.

Discussing these kinds of convictions gets us into religion. Religious belief gives meaning to life so that we live with a sense of purpose and direction. It addresses that most fundamental question, "*Why* should I be concerned with being moral?" Because religious belief provides a basis for our moral convictions, it has a bearing on our moral character. For the Christian this framework of meaning involves the conviction that we are creatures of God, not "thrown" into a meaningless universe but created with a purpose: to praise God by serving God's creation, which means in part to serve our fellow human beings. This orientation appears to be foolishness to the realists of this world, but it reflects the wisdom of Jesus who noted that it is in losing oneself for others one finds oneself (Matthew 10:39). Jesus' own life has always been the Christian's supreme model for what it means to live as a son or daughter of God.

Our Christian faith not only gives an answer to the question of *why* we are concerned about morality, it also enters into the content of morality. We understand that God's purposes, as expressed in Scripture and church tradition and the dynamic witness of the Holy Spirit, remain constant: the flourishing of all life, service of neighbor, witness to God's sovereignty, profound human happiness. How those purposes get lived out is a matter for human discernment, with God's ongoing help. While the motivation behind Christian action is distinctive and particular, the specific action that is engaged in may look exactly the same as that which the Zen Buddhist engages in for his or her own distinctive reasons. Though distinctive, our motives may overlap; we may both be committed to the worth and dignity of human and animal life, and to loving our neighbors as ourselves. Our motives, self-understandings, and purposes retain distinctiveness, however.

The Christian language of self-denial—or following the example of Jesus Christ—is somewhat idealistic. Given the self-centered character of our lives, we are not inclined to embark on a path of radical self-sacrifice. Nonetheless, the ideal is a prod and a reminder of what we are intended to be, and at times we are indeed moved by our convictions to "go the extra mile." It should be noted that to speak of this ideal does not provide Christians with specific answers to specific questions concerning what we ought to do. The fact that Christianity is a "religion of the book" has made it a temptation to find in sacred writings the final word on every conceivable moral issue. What the Bible does provide is the basis for an orientation of faith and compassion in addressing questions of morality. As is evident from several essays in this volume, Christians reading the same biblical material can disagree as to its specific implication (or whether it even *has* a specific implication) for a particular social issue in our time.

As with the individual Christian, the church as the community of faith is challenged to live in commitment and discipleship so that its witness in the realm of social morality has the ring of authenticity and truth. While the church cannot solve the world's problems, its message and reason for being make it impossible to divorce itself from those problems. Its mission in every age is not only to proclaim its message but to embody it, bringing a measure of compassion and a quest for justice which both inspire and challenge the larger society. If the church is to fulfill its social responsibility, it will have to become increasingly what one ethicist has called "a community of moral discourse." Particularly at the grassroots level—the local congregation—the church needs to address the issues of the day through both study and action. Especially in an era when moral decisions seem totally relative and choices impossible to justify, it is important that the church call Christians and other citizens to serious moral deliberation about the issues that affect our life in this world. Christians would assert that there are better and worse moral directions, ones that are more or less pleasing to God, and that these choices and policy directions deserve rigorous debate and decision-making. Involving itself in public life in this way constitutes one important answer to what the church is called to be, and makes more likely a "response" to moral issues that will indeed be "responsible."

MORAL ISSUES AND CHRISTIAN ETHICS

Ethics can be defined as the critical study of the moral dimension of life. Its task is not in most cases to give definitive answers but to raise issues and to give the community a way of addressing them, a way of discerning which courses of action are beneficent. The ethicist does not simply catalogue moral behavior, but investigates the values and principles and rules by which people live. If the subject is Christian ethics, the concern is to spell out the meaning of Christian faith for the moral life and to determine the distinctive nature of that life in view of its underlying convictions. This volume addresses a variety of moral issues and should be helpful in informing the reader about the nature of these issues. However, to fulfill its purpose, it should also provide readers with the opportunity to do some ethical reflection of their own. The issues themselves certainly merit considerable attention; but beyond this, reflection on these issues should generate discussion of the ways decisions are made and the kinds of fundamental assumptions and principles that shape these decisions.

Another factor which has entered into our selection of material is the conviction that we live in a pluralistic society and that dialogue with others outside of the Christian community is imperative. It is in recognition of our pluralism that the ethical norm is now often seen by Christian writers in "human" categories rather than in simply "Christian" ones. The overlapping moral concern of those who are Christian and those who are not is indicated by the use of phrases like those frequently occurring in the documents of Vatican II, which stress building for all persons a more truly human world and condition of life. Several of the articles in this volume are not written from an explicitly Christian perspective, but they assist the reader in understanding the issue being addressed and offer perspectives with which the reader may agree or disagree. That is also part of the learning experience.

The fact that opposing viewpoints will often be found in each chapter may be confusing and even distressing to some. Our intention, of course, in placing opposing views in juxtaposition is to encourage you to clarify the issue for yourself. The risk of confusing the reader seems worth taking in view of the fact that the complexity of moral issues today makes it unlikely that any one position will be able to convey all of an issue's dimensions. It is also important to recognize that the complexity of many of these issues will invite differing responses among Christians themselves. The challenge is that we take responsibility to understand these issues and to address them consistently in light of our convictions.

Moral Issues and Christian Response

PART 1

Taking a Stand

Chapter 1

POLITICS AND THE CHURCH'S RESPONSE TO SOCIAL ISSUES

Individual churches have quite different responses to social issues. Some have been very sensitive to issues of social justice and can be relied upon to make studied and well-reasoned responses to the prominent issues of the day. They see that as integral to their faith. Others may be preoccupied with the evangelistic mission of the church and have not seen their task as one of speaking out on social issues. Today there are few evangelical churches that do not understand their commission as involving both evangelism and social mission. Consider, for example, the way the religious right, and especially the Christian Coalition, has gotten into politics during the past two decades. There are still a few denominations that downplay the missionary and social aspects of Christianity; the zeal of other denominations in addressing these issues seems to rise or fall with the ethos of the culture, among other things. Currently we seem to be just coming out of a trough or low ebb of social concern.

What accounts for differences among churches? One thing that seems significant is what aspects of God's being and activity the particular church emphasizes. If the emphasis falls on God's salvation and God is conceived of as acting unilaterally to save whomever God chooses, then there may be a somewhat passive role for human agency and less attention paid to the role of the church in politics and in shaping the values of the culture. If emphasis falls on the covenant between God and God's followers, or if God's law is seen as a means of grace, then there will likely be greater emphasis placed on human agency and the significance of human action in the realms of politics and culture. It is easy to miss the impact that such foundational ideas about who God is can have in directing a church's witness in the world.

Though it is outside the scope of this book, it is nevertheless important for us to lift up the first of the two great commandments of Jesus Christ: "You shall love the Lord your God with all your heart, soul, and mind." The command to love one's neighbor is often seen to be the foundation of Christian moral concern; however, the command to love God is foundational to that second commandment. How does one love God? Some ways are the expression of gratitude for life and beauty and all wonders. Others are prayer and worship and singing. Yet another is to yearn passionately to please God in response for all God has done for us. The great mystics of the church often spoke of enjoying God, of being in communion with God, of finding their lives suffused with God's being. Others of us are often surprised by grace and overwhelmed with the greatness of God.

The pervasive obsession with spirituality in the past indicates many people's drive to discover transcendent meaning in their lives. Sometimes that involves God, sometimes not. However, the drive for a spiritually more profound sense of our lives does give us a clue to our need to love God, to be rightly directed toward God. That spirituality is the foundation of serving our neighbor, and indeed of our Christian response to moral issues.

Finally, the church's response to moral issues can never be equated with God's response. We human beings are finite and can only use the best of our reasoning, our openness to sources of wisdom like Scripture and church tradition and the sciences, and our responsiveness to the urgings of the Spirit to arrive at moral responses. Nevertheless, the church affirms that the Spirit works through moral deliberation, through faithful people striving to discern God's will even if the social issue under discussion is controversial.

This raises the question of who really speaks for the church. Can bishops or elected leaders of churches be expected to reflect the thinking of all the membership? Is there even likely to be a consensus that could be expressed? Though there is not likely to be a consensus, there ought to be a willingness to enter into conversation with other Christian viewpoints in a faithful process of deliberation. If those in leadership understand their roles to include enabling a process of moral deliberation rather than arriving at one correct answer, we might be able to say that all believers, entering into goodwill dialogue, speak for the church. That process depends on church leaders, on gathering the best available factual knowledge, and on being open to all sources of moral wisdom inside and outside the church. The church must remember to be true to Scripture, to tradition, to the voice of God from whatever source it comes.

Those who are convinced that the church must address the issues of our day have answers to several possible objections. They say it is not necessary for a church or its officials to find a consensus in the church in order to address a social issue. It may well be that no such consensus could be reached. Even if a majority opinion could be reached, that in no way guarantees that such an opinion most nearly reflects Christian values. Church leadership speaks *to* as well as *for* the church, helping to educate the members concerning the implications of Christian belief for particular social issues. There certainly will be room for faithful disagreement (disagreement that should be voiced), and this dialogue will usually help generate a more nearly Christian position.

Furthermore, it is not humanly possible to collect all the relevant facts on an issue before making a decision. Neither the church nor any other institution or group of people can delay a decision until all the facts are in; no one would ever decide anything if that were a prerequisite. It is necessary to make a decision after gathering and weighing the facts that *are* available. That does not lessen the church's responsibility to gather the best available information from many sources, especially those with which it is likely to disagree. Sometimes church statements have, in the past, seemed factually deficient.

The question of whether the church should be involved in social and political issues is not that difficult. The two more difficult questions are *why it should be involved* and *how*. The first article, by Edward Vacek, suggests an answer to the *why* question. He asserts that there has been an "Eclipse of Love for God" and calls the church and its members to return to their foundations: "In short, many contemporary Christians subscribe to Jesus' second great commandment, but not to his first." Vacek argues that our love for God grounds moral reflection, but that love for God and being in a relationship with God is essential for Christians for reasons that go beyond the moral. We cannot be fully human beings unless we love God. In saying this Vacek reiterates an ancient strand of wisdom, but one that seems quite contemporary to today's search for the divine.

Vacek challenges us to think about *why* Christians are involved in moral issues; Robert Benne helps us by offering four ways that Christians *have* been involved in public life—*how* they have conceived the relationship between Christianity and social issues. His article delineates four possible responses the church can make to the issues of public life—emphasizing character, conscience, corporate witness, and institutional power. Many Christians who are concerned about the impact of the church in the public arena would not regard Benne's first two options as genuine alternatives. These two options do not call on the church to address directly those in positions of political or economic power, nor do they result in any official word from the church on issues that confront the nation. These two options are, however, essential ingredients in whatever else the church might say or do. The third option—corporate conscience—is expressed in denominational social statements that attempt to influence public policy directly. This option is expressed in the expectation that the church will be the "guardian of morality," a position we discussed in the *Introduction*. The fourth option—the church with power—is direct advocacy, in which the church uses its institutional clout to influence public policy. While it is clear that Benne considers this the option of last resort, other ethicists and churchpeople would be more disposed toward acting in this manner.

The final two essays represent almost classic liberal and conservative positions in regard to one social issue: the so-called underclass, or people with low income. Both the articles recognize the Christian mandate to love one's neighbor and to assist those who are disadvantaged. *How* they would go about that differs in ways that can be correlated with Benne's typology of church-politics relationships. The piece by Robert Bellah, Richard Madsen, William Sullivan, Ann Swidler, and Steven Tipton is an excerpt from the new edition of *Habits of the Heart—Individualism and Commitment in American Life*. In it they bemoan the loss of community in the United States, and especially the sense of responsibility for neighbor. What is threatened is our sense of solidarity or mutual responsibility with others. Their concern is to renew the cultural capacity for community. Their recommendation is that the overclass act as a true establishment working for the good of the whole society. For the underclass, they call for a change in public policy, a recovery of self-respect, and the social reconstruction of local communities. The church, and the society at large, are to contribute to this effort. It is clear that this liberal position conceives of the relationship between church and society as one of corporate conscience or power advocacy.

By contrast, Robert Rector represents a conservative stance on "God and the Underclass." He is disturbed at the horrors that afflict the underclass and believes that such social "pathology, while most acute among urban blacks, is spreading relentlessly among whites." He focuses on the debilitating effect of welfare and concludes that, although economic incentives must not be minimized, we should also look at how character or "the habits of the heart" are formed. The weakening of traditional moral culture at all levels of society has promoted the burgeoning underclass pathology. Rector maintains that the institution most capable of transforming this behavior and helping individuals lift their lives out of poverty is the church. One way of doing this is through giving poor parents vouchers or scholarships that would enable them to enroll their children in the schools of their choice. Schools with a religious base would prosper and would arrest the present slide into moral chaos. The focus here falls clearly on the ethics of character and conscience in Benne's typology.

At one point the American establishment and Christianity (especially Protestantism) were often equated. Sometimes the church provided legitimacy to political positions. Those days are receding. It becomes even more important, however, for the church to retain its independence and to speak to U.S. society using its best available wisdom, secure in the knowledge that God wills the best for all people. The church is not the voice of God, but it can serve the invaluable role of calling all citizens to adopt a transcendent perspective on realizing the common good.

The Eclipse of Love for God
Edward Collins Vacek

When David Hare interviewed clergy as part of his research for his play, "Racing Demons," he ran into a problem: None of the priests wanted to talk about God.

"The Eclipse of Love for God," by Edward Collins Vacek, in *America* 174, no. 8, March 9, 1996, pp. 13–16. Reprinted with permission.

One of the disturbing questions his play raises is whether contemporary Christians, with the exception of a few fanatical fundamentalists, are concerned about loving God.

In my own conversations with Christians, I find that almost all of them talk approvingly about love for others, some talk confidently about God's love for us, but few are willing to talk about their love for God. When I press them to say what it means to love God, some of them in fact deny that we can love God directly, many admit that they don't give much thought to love for God and most deny that there is any ethical obligation to do so. They judge that it is wrong not to love people, but they have no such thoughts about neglecting God. In short, many contemporary Christians subscribe to Jesus' second great commandment but not to his first.

In the 17th century, some historians of spirituality point out, people thought the essence of Christian life was to draw close to God. After the 18th century, however, the point of Christian life became service of neighbor. Today, for example, people generally consider Mother Teresa a saint. But most people do so because of her devotion to the poor. Seldom does anyone say she is a saint because her love of God is so intense, though that once was the primary meaning of sanctity.

CONTEMPORARY OBJECTIONS

When I ask my students, "What do you mean by love for God?" they usually give one of four answers. Some volunteer that loving God means keeping the commandments, like not killing or stealing. Most say that loving God means helping one's neighbor. The more theologically educated add that it means taking care of the poor. Lastly, those steeped in our psychological age share that loving God means caring for one's own deepest self. All seem not to notice that atheists affirm these four practices.

Many theologians have also set aside Jesus' first great commandment. They do so for theological reasons. Some note, for example, that the perfect God has no need of us; hence our love for God does nothing for God. Indeed, love for neighbor rightly enjoys a certain advantage over love for God, since the former is good both for the neighbor and for us.

Other theologians, following the strand of Karl Rahner's thought that stressed anonymous Christianity, claim that the one necessary love is love for neighbor. In their view, Matthew 25 shows that we do not have to think about God; all we must do is serve the neighbor....

Furthermore, ordinary people recognize that, even though we can perform certain behaviors on command, we cannot will ourselves to have emotions. Emotions, including love, are not the sorts of acts we can just decide to have. Hence, many hold that while we are morally obliged to do the works of love, there can be no ethical requirement to love God.

Some theologians, following certain mystics, raise another difficulty. God is transcendent and utterly incomprehensible. But, since we cannot love what we cannot know, we cannot love God. These Christians are joined by others who hold that—in the darkness of this post-death-of-God and post-holocaust era—all we can do is to wait patiently for some new revelation from God. We should not expect ourselves to love the God who is uncanny, awesome, unfathomable mystery and who seems more absent than present.

Others argue that love for God is not really central in Christianity. Classical theological traditions have centered on obedience to God's will or on trust in God's promises, not on love for God. St. Paul, for example, speaks rarely of love for God. Instead he champions faith in God, and for him the whole law boils down to love of *neighbor* (Gal. 5:14, 6:2; Rom. 13:8–10). Pauline theologians note that it is God's love, not our own, that flows in our hearts.

Thus, theology encourages the current tendency to collapse the first great commandment into the second. Although John wrote, "those who love God must love their brothers and sisters also" (1 Jn. 4:21), thereby indicating that love for neighbor presupposes love for God, today a number of theological positions conspire to suggest that love for neighbor suffices. Where Jesus urged that we love God with our whole mind, heart, soul and strength, today we urge one another actively to love our neighbor and—harder for many—to love our own selves.

DIRECT LOVE FOR GOD

I want to argue that love of creatures is not enough. Just as we must eat and think and play, or else we wither and die, and just as we must develop good relations with other human beings if we are to develop as persons, so also we cannot hope to become fully human unless we love God. We are essentially relational beings. We are stunted when our relational potentials are unfulfilled. We have a native desire for God, and our hearts will shrivel up unless they beat for God. Hence, in order to become fully who we are, we must be growing in love for God.

The off-putting implication of this otherwise pious-sounding claim is that atheists or agnostics or even exclusively neighbor-loving Christians are living objectively unethical lives. That claim strikes many as too harsh. Let me offer three clarifications. First, I am speaking of what objectively ought to be the case. I do not say that sincere atheists, agnostics or neighbor-loving Christians are sinners. Presumably they are following their conscience. If so, they are morally good. Nevertheless, their consciences are mistaken. Their understanding of human life is incomplete. Their life is not all it *should* be.

Second, my fellow theologians, influenced by people like Rahner, doubtless will argue that atheists, if they are sincere and not just lazy, seek the truth. But, since God is truth itself, these atheists are in fact seeking God. All they get wrong, so to speak, is the name. To this position, I offer a personalist's response. Existentially, there is a great difference between seeking the truth and being in a personal relationship with God. Those who love God live differently. They engage in time-tested ways of developing this relationship, e.g., celebrating the Eucharist or participating in retreats. They pray and are attentive for a personal word from God. They contemplate and rely on Jesus Christ. Those who are not in a personal relationship with the Christian God will not do these sorts of things, and so they cannot similarly develop this most important dimension of human life.

Third, the lives of people without love for God can be morally right in other aspects. In one very important area of their lives, those who do not love God are deficient human beings. Just as a man can be good to his children but neglect his wife, so many people who are otherwise wonderful persons lack this demanding and uplifting relationship.

In short, it is not enough just to love our fellow human beings. Sincere conscience and anonymous theism are not enough. To give a parallel: Imagine that I put out food for a stray dog I happen to like, but that, unbeknownst to me, belongs to a rich but stingy woman I despise. Physically, one might say that I am serving the rich woman, but morally speaking that is not what I am doing. Similarly, giving water to a stranger is quite different from desiring to serve Christ. Our explicit intentions make a great difference in our moral life.

It is also not enough to love creatures explicitly as a way of showing love to God. At times, we can and must also direct our love immediately and directly to God. Of course, one way of expressing love for God is to care for God's creation. But much as taking the garbage out for sick neighbors is no substitute for directly developing an interpersonal relationship with them, so too doing good works to show love for God presupposes other activities devoted to directly loving God.

A CONTEMPORARY CHALLENGE

Every age has its central religious concept. At one time the question of faith energized. Today Christians often answer the question "Do you believe in God?" with little investment. The question "Do you trust God?" is more involving, but it still leaves in abeyance the way we live our lives. A question that will challenge all of us today is this: "Do you love God?" That question evokes the endlessness of our heart's quest as well as the incomprehensibility of God, and it gives us an absorbing center for our lives.

I imagine that when Jesus went off to pray he was not just gathering up energy to love his fellow human beings, nor was he simply purifying and developing his inner life. Rather, he chose to spend time with his Abba. He wanted and needed that time. He prayed, and in that prayer he united his mind and heart with God. Our love for God requires something similar.

How might such a relationship develop? The first step is one that, generally speaking, women seem to understand more quickly than men. That step is to accept God's love for us. In other words, our first response is *not* to return love to God, but rather to let God's love affect or change us. We deny God's transforming influence if we rush to return love to God or to spread love to our neighbor. Sitting with eyes closed and hands open, we let God's love touch and move us; there begins our salvation.

Thereafter, we can and should love God in return. Love means that we affectively affirm God's goodness. We want to be close to God, and we rejoice when we are close. At the same time our love for God will not long let us rest, but moves us to penetrate ever more appreciatively into God's goodness. Correlatively, we are disconsolate when we are alienated from God. We miss God when God no longer seems near.

Our love for God also makes us want to cooperate with God in doing what God wants to do. That leads us to be involved in creation. Hence love for God at one level moves us into the incomprehensibility of God and at another level moves us both to cherish the world and to want to overcome its ills and injustices.

Clearly, this love for God is not reducible to texts read, prayers said or gifts offered. It is not simply a matter of obedience or trust. Rather, this love for God can and should become the dominant, organizing emotional center of our whole lives. Moses Maimonides, the great medieval Jewish philosopher, argued that love for God should be similar to the passion a man has for a woman. For Aquinas, those who love like this constantly think of one another, constantly try to please one another. This process of attention grows and grows until it becomes a pervasive feature of one's whole emotional life. So it can be with our love for God.

There will be periods of rapid and intense growth in this love. Births of babies and failures in achieving goals are prime times for spurts in our love for God. Then come quieter periods in which we just maintain a good relationship. The quiet periods prepare the way for a deeper relationship that we cannot force, but for which we can hope. As we grow in love for God, this love becomes more a part of our very identity. It more and more informs who we are. For example, if asked to do a new job, one of the first questions that enters our mind is how this new task might affect our relationship with God. . . .

At the end of this essay, let me make it clear that in speaking of love for God, I do not mean to exclude love for neighbor or self or world. Rather, love for God leads us to cooperate with God's love of the world. Hence—strange as it seems— one of the reasons we want to love ourselves and others is that we want thereby to cooperate with God's love for us. In a profoundly religious sense, we are aware that the ordinary and usually best way that *God* can love creatures is through *our* love for them. Still, although love for neighbor and love for self are essential to the Christian life, my concern here is that we must not let these wholesome Christian loves eclipse our love for God. That love should be the sun of our lives.

The Church and Politics: Hot and Cool Connections
Robert Benne

The modern world is awash with examples of lively interactions between religion and politics. Sometimes it is politics or law affecting religion. The FBI attacks the Branch Davidians at Waco. Judges rule out prayer at local commence-

From "The Church: Hot and Cool Connections," by Robert Benne, in *The Cresset,* February 1996. Reprinted by permission of the Rockford Institute.

ments and order baccalaureate services off campus. The Justice Department pursues a local fundamentalist church that pays heads of household more than non-heads because St. Paul says so. An amendment is proposed that would give more freedom to religious expression. All these are examples of the public sphere affecting religion.

But religion also affects politics. Abroad we have conservative Muslim agitation for Islamic republics. Christians and Muslims fight for political power in Africa. Religion is used to sacralize nationalist causes in the former Yugoslavia. The Catholic bishops press for human rights in Mexico, Central and South America. Christians organize for more democracy in Korea. Stories are now unfolding that point out the importance of the Pope's role in the fall of Communism and the Lutheran role in assuring a peaceful transition from Communism to democracy in East Germany. Dramatic examples all.

The domestic scene is just as interesting. The issue of abortion simply won't go away, thanks to the passion of religiously based protest groups. The Republican avalanche of November 1994 is viewed in part as an effect of resurgent religious populism. Organizations like the American Family Association tenaciously challenge television and movies to clean up their acts. Mainstream Protestant denominations continue their advocacy efforts in national and state legislatures as they have been for many years. But, above all, there is the rise of the Christian Coalition, which has drawn much attention because of its political involvements on the conservative side. With over 1600 chapters and 1.7 million members, it is led by an attractive and sophisticated Ralph Reed.

The very effectiveness of the Christian Coalition has raised the hackles and fears of secularists and liberal Christians alike, though it is difficult to see how the Coalition's involvements are any different in principle from what liberal Christians have been doing for many years. At any rate, the church is taking on a vigorous new role in American political debate and action.

This profusion of "revolting religion," as a student of mine once put it to describe the Reformation, comes as a surprise to many of the elite centers of western culture. After all, one of the expectations of the more militant edge of the Enlightenment was that religion would be more and more relegated to the private sphere where it could not become a public nuisance or worse. That more militant Enlightenment party thought that reason, science and technology would lead us away from the oppression of kings and the obfuscations of priests toward a world of eternal progress.

Christianity, irrational and therefore dangerous in their view, would gradually disappear among the educated classes and would no longer play a role in education, politics, law, medicine or any other public endeavor. As the history of the West has unfolded, these desired outcomes were partially realized. The secularist hopes seemed to have become more plausible.

Wishing, however, did not make it so. Indeed, the ideological blinkers worn by secularists prevented them from even seeing the emerging role of Islam on the world stage. Islam as a publicly relevant religious movement was and is real. Secular intellectuals are only now catching on to the perennial relevance of religion to politics. Whether they like it or not, it is a fact.

No religion worth its salt lacks a public dimension. Great religions are comprehensive visions of life. Their themes are relevant for all of life, not just for the private sphere. Theistic religions affirm that God is the God of all life, not just of the inner recesses of the heart. Belief in God's universal law will have public repercussions for any society with a critical mass of serious believers. This is just as true of the United States as it is of Iran or India. The religious impulse for public relevance is irrepressible. Indeed, after long years of marginalizing the public relevance of religion, the West is now finding that the church is asserting its public face.

So, the question is not *whether* organized religion will affect politics, but rather *how* it will do so. Moreover, there are great stakes involved for both church and society in the manner in which this "how" is addressed and acted upon. Some kinds of interactions are dangerous for both church and society. Indeed, I will argue below that the greatest dangers with regard to this issue in this country regard the church, not the society. The American church has more to lose than American society if it does not attend carefully to how it involves itself in the political order.

In the following I will move through the two basic ways that the church affects politics—indirect and direct. Those two break into further subdivisions which I will explicate briefly. (Those who wish a more detailed elaboration of this topic might consult my recent book, *The Paradoxical Vision: A Public Theology for the Twenty-first Century,* Minneapolis: Fortress, 1995.)

By "indirect" I mean that the church as an institution does not become directly involved in political life. What political effect it does have comes through its laity who are involved in the political world. "Indirect" ways of connecting the church to politics are characterized further by their being unintentional or intentional. Let's look at the indirect and unintentional mode first.

THE ETHICS OF CHARACTER

The indirect and unintentional mode means that the church simply affects the deepest inward orientation of persons—their character—through its preaching, teaching, worship and discipline. When the church is really the church it has a profound effect on the formation of the outlook and character of its participants. In fact, when the church does indeed bring forth a "revolution of the heart and mind" of its members, it does have a powerful and deep-running effect on its surrounding society. It is arguable that this is the most powerful way a religious tradition affects public life. And it certainly is the least controversial.

There have been many historical studies of this mode. Weber, in his *The Protestant Ethic and the Spirit of Capitalism,* and Lindsay, in his *Essentials of Democracy,* showed how the church, without intending it consciously, had a powerful affect on economic and political life respectively. Weber argued that capitalism could not have emerged without the "this worldly asceticism" of Calvinism while Lindsay contended that the development of democracy in England would have been impossible without the dissenting communions that practiced democracy within their churches.

In a similar vein, Glenn Tinder, in his *The Political Meaning of Christianity,* argues that Christianity, through its millions of lay persons, has provided the spiritual center of democratic politics with its belief in the "exalted individual." We also have many contemporary examples of Christian laypersons who have been formed powerfully in their churches and who then act out their belief in the specialness of each human person in their public, political life. As voters or leaders they insist on just and humane policies. In the latter category one thinks of a Senator Paul Simon or a Supreme Court Justice William Rehnquist.

Interestingly enough, the Lutheran Church—Missouri Synod, has rarely moved beyond this indirect and unintentional mode. Yet it has been a powerful former of persons and has much indirect effect on public life through laity who have been shaped by its ethos. A surprising number of Missouri laypersons and clergy have entered formal political or associational life.

This mode of connecting the church and politics has much to say for it. It keeps the church from itself becoming politicized, it respects the ministry of the laity, and it focuses the church on its primary mission of proclamation. While many, if not most, laity would like to stop with this level of church-political connection, it is to my mind insufficient. For one thing, the church as church is entrusted with the whole Word of God for the world; it must articulate the Law and Gospel to the public world, not just to individuals. Second, laity often fail to connect their faith and their daily life in the public world. Third, the task of formation is not being done so well these days. The laity's character is not shaped so decisively by the church as we all would like. We cannot simply rely on unintentional influence.

THE ETHICS OF CONSCIENCE

So we need a more intentional way of connecting the church with political life. We need an ethics of conscience to build on the ethics of character. This more intentional way aims at awakening the conscience of the laity by bringing the laity into a lively conversation with the social teachings of the church. Like the first indirect way, the institutional church does not become a direct actor, but unlike it, the church does try intentionally to connect the teachings of the church with the public life of the laity by stimulating their conscience.

The Evangelical Academies of Germany are excellent examples of what I mean here. The Academies were formed after World War II to guard against any future take-over of the public world by demonic powers, which had happened so disastrously in the Nazi time. The Academies brought together theologians and ethicists of the church for conversation with laity in specific callings. They also brought together diverse parties within large institutions who had natural conflicts of interest, e.g., union and management. The idea was to provide a grace-full context for working out connections between Christian values and worldly challenges. In the mutual conversations that ensued all parties became more aware of the teachings of the Christian moral tradition, the issues involved in contemporary challenges, and how the two related.

This sort of heightened moral deliberation can and does go on within our churches, but it needs much more disciplined attention than it currently gets. This "ethics of conscience" approach needs to be carried on at all levels of the churches' life if laity are to be equipped to make connections between their Sunday and Monday lives. This is not a simple task, of course, for many reasons. Many lay folks don't want their consciences stimulated when they come to church. Others invest their own social and political opinions with undue religious weight, making civil conversation well nigh impossible. Many local congregations lack materials and talent to pull off such moral deliberation.

But, nevertheless, it seems to me that this is a place for the church to direct far more attention than it has in terms of materials and training. This indirect and intentional approach really aims at equipping the saints for their ministry in the world. If done well, it promises far more than the more unintentional approaches to religion and politics.

There are several other indirect but intentional sub-categories that I will only mention in passing. One involves the capacity of the church to awaken the conscience of the laity and then encourage them to form independent voluntary associations of their own or to join other associations that have already been formed. One thinks here of voluntary associations like Bread for the World or the Christian Coalition. These independent voluntary associations are very numerous, e.g., Lutheran Peace Fellowship, Cry for Renewal, Catholic Worker and literally hundreds associated with the many denominations.

These organizations allow lay folks to band together to express an agenda that is so controversial or outright political that the churches themselves cannot properly handle it. They continue to be important conduits of Christian political witness, even as they provide significant voices for democratic political life. (In this regard, it is difficult to understand why so many secular and Christian liberals seem to regard the Christian Coalition's efforts as somehow an illegitimate religious incursion into political life. One can certainly criticize the Coalition's stance on the issues as well as its implicit claim that its stance is "Christian," but as an independent voluntary association it is a perfectly legitimate expression of a Christian voice in political affairs, just as, say, Bread for the World is another legitimate voice.)

Another indirect and intentional way the church can affect the public order is through its church-related institutions. If the church really has the courage to embody its vision and values in the institutional life of its related colleges, social service agencies, senior citizen homes, etc., it will make a strong public witness. Such "social pioneering," as H. R. Niebuhr termed it, has been and is one of the most effective ways of influencing public life. Institutional incarnations of religious values demonstrate the connections between church and world in a particularly persuasive way.

THE CHURCH AS CORPORATE CONSCIENCE

If the church were to take these indirect modes of connecting religion and politics seriously, it would have its plate full. And there would be less energy and time left for the direct ways of relating religion and politics. However, there are theological and ecclesiological reasons for more direct approaches to religion and politics. Theologically, the church is entrusted with the Word of God in both Law and Gospel; it is called to address them both to the world, not just to its own congregants. God's moral and religious claims are on the whole world, not just Christians. Ecclesiologically, the church is more than its dispersed laity. As an institution it too is the Body of Christ; it is called to act corporately, not only individually.

Thus, we have a warrant for direct and intentional approaches to the world. The best examples of these are Papal encyclicals, bishops' letters, and church social statements. In such instruments the church not only addresses its laity but also tries to influence public policy. In truth, Catholics have been far more successful along these lines than Protestants. Though every main-stream Protestant communion tries mightily to make an impact on the world with its statements, they are for the most part ignored by both its laity and the world.

There are reasons for this disparity. First, Catholics speak with moral weight because of the size of their communion and because the Pope and bishops have retained a measure of moral authority. Second, Catholics speak relatively infre-quently on carefully chosen topics. This gives them time to craft statements carefully and to take seriously the input and feedback they invite. Third, Catholics seem to argue from their own unique moral tradition. This gives them a certain immunity from the world's ideological divides and lends them an in-tegrity that is increasingly scarce in our fractured public world. Fourth, they carefully distinguish among levels of authority. Affirmations of core convictions that all Catholics should hold are distinguished from public policy options about which Catholics of good will and intelligence can disagree. Room is made for both consensus and disensus.

These characteristics are often lacking in Protestant attempts to influence policy by social statements. We need not go into the sorry catalog of shortcom-ings with regard to these qualities. Fortunately, there are signs that Protestants are beginning to come to their senses. The Evangelical Lutheran Church in America, for example, is currently re-thinking the frequency, kind, and manner of its social statements. Perhaps we can look forward to more effective means of expressing the church's corporate conscience.

It should be noted that historically one of the most effective means of pub-lic witness has been a prophetic "no" to certain political or social practices. The Confessing Church's direct refusal to capitulate to Nazi demands on the church is a case in point, as was the Norwegian church's resistance to Nazism. The Pope's denunciation of abortion as part of the "culture of death" is another. Often, when social practices move toward the demonic, a vigorous proscrip-tion rather than a presumptuous prescription is called for.

So, in spite of all, the church must act as the Body of Christ's conscience. It should do so wisely, sparingly and authentically. When it does so, direct and in-tentional influence is a legitimate and effective way that the church connects with the political sphere.

THE CHURCH WITH POWER

Some of the dramatic examples of the church's involvement with politics that I listed at the beginning of this essay demonstrate this direct approach to the political sphere. Under this mode the church moves beyond persuasion to more coercive types of involvement. It uses its institutional power—money, staff, troops—to sway public policy according to its will. This approach is the most controversial and debatable way of connecting religion and politics. It is controversial because it commits the institution, the Body of Christ, to partisan public policies about which the membership often has no consensus. It is debatable because it commits the church to the use of power, the "earthly sword," a practice against which the Reformers protested. God has given the church the power of the Word, they argued, not worldly power, and when the church gets too involved in political power it loses its integrity as the Body of Christ. It lends its sacred symbols to very worldly projects.

Protestant churches participate in "soft" forms of direct power when they operate "advocacy offices" in the national and state legislatures, when they use their pension and investments to induce businesses to follow policies the church endorses, and when church bodies commit money and leadership to "conflict-oriented" community organizations. The controversy surrounding each one of these activities bears witness to their borderline legitimacy.

A wise church, I believe, will use such means only when there are no other options for the church or the society. The church, for example, must inescapably invest its money, so it should do so on the basis of its own values. But it should do so within rather wide parameters; it should proscribe or support business practices only at the obvious extremes. It should not be overly aggressive and intrusive with regard to the vast majority of enterprises in the murky middle. With regard to society, the church may responsibly act directly if there are no other organizations to do so because they are absent or have been suppressed. The Polish Catholic church's support of Solidarity is case in point along those lines. The Catholic church's withdrawal of support for Ferdinand Marcos in the Philippines is another. But in both cases the church withdrew from direct political action when other options became available in the society.

CONCLUSION

It is clear that there are a number of options for connecting religion and politics. I have outlined a number of those options above and have commented on their legitimacy. I believe that the Lutheran tradition strongly prefers the more indirect connections, though it leaves room for judicious use of the direct. We would do well, I think, to focus much more attention on the indirect and intentional ways of making a public impact. The laity in the world and in church-related institutions are the foot-soldiers in the battle for a humane and justly ordered world. The church should heed its calling by preparing them more fully.

The House Divided: Meaning and a Renewal of Civic Membership

Robert N. Bellah, Richard Madsen, William M. Sullivan, Ann Swidler, and Steven M. Tipton

While the idea of community, if limited to neighbors and friends, is an inadequate basis for meeting our current needs, we want to affirm community as a cultural theme that calls us to wider and wider circles of loyalty, ultimately embracing that universal community of all beings of which H. Richard Niebuhr spoke. We should remember that when Jesus was asked, "Who is my neighbor?" he answered with the parable of the Good Samaritan (Luke 10:29-37), in which the true neighbor turns out to be a Samaritan, a member of a group despised in Israel. It is not that Jesus didn't think that a person living next door, or an inhabitant of one's own village, or a member of one's own ethnic group could be a neighbor. But when asked directly, he identified the neighbor as a stranger, an alien, a member of a hated ethnic group. Any community short of the universal community is not the beloved community.

Much of what has been happening in our society has been undermining our sense of community at every level. We are facing trends that threaten our basic sense of solidarity with others: solidarity with those near to us (loyalty to neighbors, colleagues at work, fellow townsfolk), but also solidarity with those who live far from us, those who are economically in situations very different from our own, those of other nations. Yet this solidarity—this sense of connection, shared fate, mutual responsibility, community—is more critical now than ever. It is solidarity, trust, mutual responsibility that allows human communities to deal with threats and take advantage of opportunities. How can we strengthen these endangered capacities, which are first of all cultural capacities to think in certain ways?

When we consider how to renew the cultural capacity for community and solidarity in each of the three classes into which our society is divided—the overclass, the underclass and the anxious class—it would be well to remember something we have already mentioned: that in American society religious associations have the strongest hold on their members and almost alone have the capacity to reach individuals in every class. We can formulate the need for a fundamental reorientation toward community and solidarity as a kind of conversion, a turning of consciousness and intention. In the biblical tradition conversion means a turning away from sin and a turning toward God. An idea of turning away from preoccupation with the self and toward some larger identity is characteristic of most of the great religions and philosophies of mankind. Conversion cannot come from willpower alone, but if it is to be enabled we must recover the stories and symbols in whose terms it makes sense.

If we think first of the overclass, the thirty-year critical assault on the dominance of white Euroamerican males in our society has not greatly dented that dominance in practice, but it has been used to justify a decline in civic responsibility on the part of the powerful and a selfish withdrawal into monetary aggrandizement. In an open society we can work to make room for more inclusive leadership without derogating the contributions of older elites. We need at least a portion of the overclass acting as a true establishment (that is, elites seeking their own good by working for the good of the whole society, i.e., noblesse oblige) if we are to deal with our enormous problems. If the members of the overclass can overcome their own anxieties they may realize that they will gain far more self-respect in belonging to an establishment than to an oligarchy (that is, when elites seek their own interests by exploiting the rest of society). They may come to see that civic engagement—a concern for the common good, a belief that we are all members of the same body—will not only contribute to the good of the larger society but will contribute to the salvation of their own souls as well. Only some larger engagement can overcome the devastating cultural and psychological narcissism of our current overclass. A return to civic membership, to commitments to community and solidarity, on the part of the overclass would be good not only for society as a whole but also for its individual members.

It would be well to point out that the majority of the people we interviewed in *Habits* belong to the lower echelons of the overclass, to what is commonly called the upper middle class, however much they (and we, who belong to the same class) would be uncomfortable with that terminology. Of course these are not the people who make the big decisions or who profit most from our current economy. They could even be called, in Pierre Bourdieu's pointed phrase, "the dominated fraction of the dominant class." But, as we argued in *Habits,* they are the symbolic center of our society, their style of life is that to which most Americans aspire, and they do indeed prosper more than 80 percent of their fellow citizens. Their resources are far greater than those of other classes: they have the cultural and social capital and the civic skills to influence the direction in which our society goes. The question is, can they recover a coherent view of the world which will allow them to use these resources for the common good rather than for their own aggrandizement?

The anxious class faces equally serious challenges, for its problems are not only cultural and psychological but sharply material. The average income for a white male has slowly drifted down from an all-time high (in 1992 dollars) of $34,231 in 1973 to $31,012 in 1992. Even worse than that income decline, which in considerable degree is offset by increasing female participation in the workplace (though that creates its own problems), is the concomitant rise in economic uncertainty. We are becoming a society of what has been called "advanced insecurity." Downsizing, part-timing, and a loss of benefits have become a way of life.

The anger and fear generated by acute economic anxiety are easily displaced onto "welfare queens" and illegal immigrants. These feelings also contribute to the decline of voting and associational membership, even union membership, as well as to the rise of divorce. While economic anxieties are real and must ultimately be dealt with structurally, the resulting decline of civic engagement in the anxious class only deepens its cynicism and despair. Renewed engagement with the larger society—for many, through churches first of all, certainly through labor unions, and then through civic organizations—is the most likely way to meet the very real problems that face society's largest group. And on top of its material problems the anxious class shares more than a little in the psychological and cultural problems of the overclass, for which a renewed sense of meaning giving coherence to ideas of solidarity and community would be the best antidote.

Meeting the problems of the underclass and attempting to reincorporate its members into the larger society is the most challenging task of all. The basic problem stems from economic developments that have simply rendered the twenty or thirty million members of the underclass superfluous (and, we should not forget, have rendered much of the anxious class merely marginally relevant). Only a fundamental change in public policy will begin to alter the situation, and in the present atmosphere such a change is hardly to be expected.

But even indispensable changes in public policy cannot alone meet the situation. Where social trust is limited and morale is blasted, one of the most urgent needs is a recovery of self-respect and a sense of agency that can come only from the participation that enables people to belong and contribute to the larger society. Participatory justice asks each individual to give all that is necessary to the common good of society. In turn it obliges society to order its institutions so that everyone can work to contribute to the commonweal in ways that respect their dignity and renew their freedom. Not by transfer payments alone or the compassion of social workers will the problems of the underclass be solved.

In responding to the problems of the underclass, perhaps we need to turn to the principle of subsidiarity, which is derived from Catholic social teaching. The idea is that groups closest to a problem should deal with it, receiving support from higher-level groups where necessary but, wherever possible, not being replaced by those higher-level groups. This principle implies respect for the groups closest to the persons in need, but it does not absolutize those groups or exempt them from the moral standards that apply to groups at any level. A process of social reconstruction of the underclass would require massive public resources, but these should be brought to the situation by third-sector agencies, local so far as possible. Today subsidiarity language is, in contradiction to its basic meaning, used to justify cuts in government spending. In truth, subsidiarity is not a substitute for public provision but makes sense only when public provision is adequate.

Ultimately what the underclass needs is not so different from what the overclass or the anxious class needs. Its social capital is more depleted and its morale more thoroughly shattered, but, like everyone else, what its members most require is a clear sense of solidarity and community and a future shared with the rest of society.

In conclusion it may be helpful to put our present situation into relation to two earlier moments in American history. The first is the crisis of the republic in the 1850s, during the dark years that would lead to the Civil War. David Greenstone has suggested that the American politics of the day were divided between what he calls a reform liberalism represented by Abraham Lincoln and a utilitarian liberalism represented by Stephen Douglas. The Lincoln-Douglas debates, which took place during the Illinois senatorial campaign of 1858, were a defining moment in American history. The issue was whether slavery should be extended to the territories in the West. Douglas took the line of popular sovereignty: if they want slavery, let them have slavery. In other words, freedom to do what you want was, in this case, freedom to do what the white majority wanted. The basis of Douglas's position was a utilitarian liberalism that asked only for the summing of preferences, not about the moral quality of the preferences.

But Lincoln said that slavery was wrong, that it contradicted the nation's most fundamental principles and should not be extended to the territories no matter what the majority there might want. In other words, freedom is the right only to do that which is morally justified. The basis of Lincoln's position was a reform liberalism that had its roots in New England Puritanism. It drew upon biblical and republican sources and was committed not only to the notion of an objective moral order ("the laws of nature and of nature's God") but also to the notion that individuals live in a society that has a common good beyond the sum of individual goods. It was this moral politics that led Lincoln to his great "House Divided" speech in Springfield, Illinois, on June 16, 1858. "A house divided against itself cannot stand," Lincoln said. "I believe this government cannot endure, permanently half *slave* and half *free*."

If we apply Lincoln's words to our situation we can say that the house today is divided not by slavery but by deepening class divisions. Douglas had no problem with a house divided, since he saw society as nothing more than the sum of individual choices and their consequences. Lincoln, however, judged certain conditions to be objectively wrong and held society accountable for changing them. Our situation today is historically linked to what Lincoln was talking about, for though slavery has been abolished, equality for African Americans has not been achieved. But we believe that it is not so much race discrimination that is the problem, though that continues to be serious enough, but, rather, the racialization of the class hierarchy—the Brazilianization of America, as Michael Lind calls it.

Race differences are real in our society, but we should not let them obscure how much we have in common. Jennifer Hochschild in *Facing Up to the American Dream* has recently analyzed the ways in which Americans differ by race. She shows that black and white Americans share most of the ideology of the American dream—by which she means not only material but moral aspirations—

though they differ as to how far African Americans have realized it. Focusing exclusively on race differences obscures an important truth about our society: race differences are rooted in class differences. Class differences transcend race and divide all Americans.

We believe the degree of class difference today is wrong in the same sense that Lincoln believed that slavery was wrong: it deprives millions of people of the ability to participate fully in society and to realize themselves as individuals. This is the festering secret that Americans would rather not face. Many nations have persisted while divided into a small elite that lives in luxury and a large mass in various stages of insecurity and misery, but this nation, with the ideals and hopes of the last 200 years, cannot permanently so endure.

This brings us to our second historical reference: John Winthrop's sermon "A Model of Christian Charity," delivered on board ship in 1630 just before the Massachusetts Bay colonists disembarked. In that sermon Winthrop warned that if we pursue "our pleasure and profits" we will surely perish out of this good land. Rather, what Winthrop, paraphrasing the Apostle Paul, tells us is that we must "entertain each other in brotherly affection, we must be willing to abridge ourselves of our superfluities, for the supply of others' necessities . . . we must delight in each other, make others' conditions our own, rejoice together, mourn together, labour and suffer together, always having before our eyes . . . our community as members of the same Body."

Under the conditions of today's America, we are tempted to ignore Winthrop's advice, to forget our obligations of solidarity and community, to harden our hearts and look out only for ourselves. In the Hebrew Scriptures God spoke to the children of Israel through the prophet Ezekiel, saying, "I will take out of your flesh the heart of stone and give you a heart of flesh" (Ez. 36:26). Can we pray that God do the same for us in America today?

God and the Underclass
Robert Rector

Like the script of a horror film, the underclass nightmare lurches through the pages of every major urban paper.

- In Queens, a heroin-addicted mother with AIDS murders her four-year-old daughter, stuffs the body in a laundry bag, and with the help of her current boyfriend—also a drug addict—tosses the bag from a bridge into the East River. The woman is "mother" to four children through a succession of drug-numbed boyfriends.

- In Philadelphia, two commercially successful "gangsta rap" artists realize their fantasies, gunning down a female police officer during a holdup.
- In Chicago, police raid the apartment of five sisters on welfare. The apartment swarms with cockroaches and is chilled by a winter wind pouring through broken windows. In four rooms are 19 children, the youngest 12 months old. Feces and garbage cover the floor; hungry children share food in a dog bowl with several dogs. Dazed, one of the kids asks a policewoman, "Can you be my mommy?"
- In Detroit, a five-year-old is thrown from a 14th floor window of a public-housing complex because "he refused to steal."
- In Washington, D.C., a gunman empties a semi-automatic into a swimming pool crowded with young children.

The statistics are numbing. In Cleveland, the black illegitimate-birth rate has hit 85 percent. In Washington, D.C., nearly half of all young black men are in jail, on parole, or under arrest. Young men in Harlem are more likely to die of violence than were soldiers in Vietnam.

While underclass pathology is most acute and devastating among urban blacks, it is spreading relentlessly among whites. As Charles Murray warned in his seminal *Wall Street Journal* article, "The Coming White Underclass," the illegitimate-birth rate (harbinger of all underclass problems) is rising steadily among whites and now approaches 25 percent. The white illegitimate-birth rate now almost equals the black rate in the mid 1960s when Daniel Patrick Moynihan first issued prophetic warnings about black family collapse.

Conservative explanations of the growth of the underclass have focused on the destructive impact of welfare. As an underclass community starts to emerge, increasing numbers of young women become married to a welfare check rather than to the father of their children. Marital disruption starts transforming other behaviors. Young boys raised without fathers grow up wild. Deprived of the role model of a working husband and father, young males look to other role models—amoral, self-destructive, and violent. As marriage is no longer seen as a necessary prerequisite to childbearing, the behavior of young women also changes; self-control shrinks; promiscuity and early sexual activity flourish.

Welfare's deconstruction of marriage is thus behind the whole tangle of underclass pathology: eroded work ethic, dependence, illegitimacy, drug abuse, crime. This thesis, developed largely by Charles Murray in *Losing Ground* and subsequent writings, is accurate and compelling. But it is important to note that Murray has never argued that welfare is the sole cause for the growth of the underclass. Moreover, even in the implausible event that the entire government welfare system were obliterated overnight, it is unlikely that this would promptly produce renewed and viable underclass communities. The social equivalent of the second law of thermodynamics holds: it is far easier to destroy social order than to re-build it.

Still public debate on the underclass remains preoccupied with manipulating external economic incentives to alter behavior. Liberals focus on providing well-paying jobs to encourage constructive behavior; conservatives seek to curtail welfare's rewards for self-destructive behavior. We seem to have forgotten that behavior is shaped not only by external economic incentives but also by cultural norms and internal character—"the habits of the heart." While economic incentives must never be minimized, we should also look to how character is formed: How the principles of virtue are planted and cultivated in the psyche.

Not surprisingly, the growth of the underclass since the mid-Sixties has coincided with a weakening of traditional moral culture at all levels of society: sexual mores have changed, the bourgeois family and the work ethic have been ridiculed, self has been exalted over family and community, passion and self-indulgence have been lionized over self-control. The weakening of traditional moral culture was as significant a factor as government welfare programs in the burgeoning underclass pathology. Any strategy aimed at putting the thousand anomic pieces of Humpty Dumpty back together must combine welfare reform with moral and cultural renewal.

To understand the cultural aspect of our problems, we should look to the past. A good place to start is Marvin Olasky's *The Tragedy of American Compassion,* which examines successful charity efforts in America's past. Olasky explains that charity workers in prior centuries saw the problems of idleness, drunkenness, crime, promiscuity, and marital desertion as emanating from moral culture and individual character. Historically, private charity organizations took as their central task the molding of character and self-discipline within vulnerable low-income communities. Efforts to deal with the economic aspects of behavior while ignoring the moral and spiritual would have been regarded as foolish.

Typical of these earlier anti-poverty efforts was the Young Men's Christian Association (YMCA), established in the nineteenth century, as an instrument for combatting urban crime. The YMCA saw its mission as molding the moral character of the young: it successfully undertook a struggle to win the hearts and minds of inner-city youth.

We can also learn from the life of John Wesley, the founder of Methodism. Wesley crisscrossed eighteenth-century England on horseback for nearly half a century, traveling thousands of miles over miry, nearly impassible roads, delivering countless sermons to a largely ignored and rootless urban population. Wesley and his followers transformed the mores, character, and conviction of England's lower and middle classes. Many credit him with setting the moral foundation for England's economic, political, and social progress over the next century.

Two hundred years after Wesley's death, we still find one institution that is overwhelmingly effective in transforming behavior and in helping individuals to lift their lives out of poverty and despair, self-destruction and violence. That institution is the church. The power of religion is amply documented. Investigating black inner-city youth, Richard Freeman of Harvard finds that boys who regularly attend church are 50 percent less likely to engage in crime than boys of similar backgrounds who do not attend church; they are 54 percent less likely to use drugs and 47 percent less likely to drop out of school.

My own research finds similar effects among all classes and races. Boys and girls who regularly attend church are two-thirds less likely to engage in sexual activity in their teens. Regular church attendance halves the probability that a woman will have a child out of wedlock.

The findings pile up. Children attending religious schools are two-thirds less likely to drop out than are nearly identical children who attend secular schools. Children aged 10 to 18 who do not attend church are a third to a half more likely to exhibit anti-social and dysfunctional behavior.

Finally, research shows that young people who attend church have a positive effect on the behavior of other youngsters in their immediate neighborhood. The positive effect of young people motivated by religious virtues is the exact counterpart to the heavily publicized negative peer pressure exerted by street gangs who suck the young into lives of aimless violence and alienation. What we need are more gangs of Sunday-school students as an antidote to the Crips and Bloods.

Religion is a social penicillin, lethal against a wide array of behavioral pathogens. Ironically, the modern liberal mind regards religion not as a medicine, but as a leprosy from which society must be quarantined. The issue is not merely the purging of religion from the public square, but the more critical expansion of the public square in the modern era, displacing the church from its essential roles in education and charity.

But despite liberal efforts to shove it to the sidelines, the church remains America's strongest weapon in the war against family disintegration, crime, drugs, and despair in low-income communities. Churches can clearly succeed in tackling these problems where government has clearly failed. What is necessary is to allow the church to resume some part of those functions in which it has been supplanted by the modern state. In particular it is crucial to break up the near monopolies over education and aid to the poor which the state has erected through its enormous coercive fiscal power.

How can this be done? The first step is school choice: giving poor parents vouchers or scholarships equivalent to the sum that is spent nominally educating their children in the public schools. These scholarships should be used to place children in schools the parents choose: public, private secular, or religious. If true choice in education were established in the inner city, thousands of parents, desperate to save their children from a rising tide of violence, drugs, and promiscuity, would flock to religious schools. New schools, affiliated to the most dynamic inner-city churches, would spring up.

The potent moral force of the churches would be magnified as they became interwoven with more aspects of the life of the inner city. Parents who placed their children in church-affiliated schools would themselves be drawn more closely to the moral authority of the church and to other parents who shared their values. Each church school would become a nucleus around which a community of shared norms could develop. The school would serve not only as a moral haven for children, but also as a moral beacon reaching into the surrounding neighborhoods.

This spring, legislation capable of sparking this type of moral renewal in the inner cities was introduced in the House. "Saving Our Children: The American Community Renewal Act of 1996," sponsored by black Oklahoma Republican J. C. Watts and by Jim Talent, Republican from Missouri, combines the older conservative concept of enterprise zones with a new moral dimension. Following the enterprise-zone concept, the bill would create economic opportunity by cutting taxes and red tape in up to a hundred urban areas. Its novel feature is that in order to qualify for tax relief the locality would have to agree to offer school choice; low-income parents in the community would be eligible to receive federal scholarships enabling them to send their children to private primary and secondary schools, including religious schools. The bill would provide up to a half-million such scholarships.

The Watts-Talent bill also creates a new tax credit intended to enlarge the role of private-sector charity in aiding the poor. It would allow individuals to deduct 75 percent of the cost of donations to private charities working directly with the poor: many, if not most, of these charities would be religious in nature. The credit would be available to federal-income-tax filers nationwide and could be applied to charitable gifts worth up to $400 each year. The Watts-Talent bill thus uniquely combines the economic and moral strands of conservative thought into a single vehicle to help the urban poor.

Liberals, passionate to preserve their current political quarantine of God, will argue that the bill violates the First Amendment's provisions on religious establishment. But the Supreme Court has repeatedly ruled to the contrary. As long as the individual beneficiary, not the government itself, determines where funds will be spent, there is no prohibition on government-derived money being spent for religious education. Just as a widow can endorse her Social Security check and place it in the collection plate at her church, a parent may use a government scholarship or voucher to enroll a child in a religious school.

Some conservatives will object that the bill continues and validates the Federal Government's role in aiding the poor. But the Federal Government currently spends almost $300 billion each year on a huge variety of programs for the poor. The "radical" welfare reform passed by Congress last year and vetoed by President Clinton did not cut this spending, but merely slowed its rate of growth. Conservatives cannot place the underclass on hold while they wait for the federalist's millennium when federal domestic spending will cease. As long as the taxpayers contribute hundreds of billions of dollars to federal coffers each year on behalf of the poor, we have an obligation to see that that money is spent in ways that heal rather than harm. It should become a conservative axiom that, as long as a single federally collected dollar is spent on poor children, that dollar should be spent in the way that has the greatest potential to help: education vouchers to allow poor kids to go to religious schools.

By unleashing the church's strength through school choice we can at least *begin* the struggle for the hearts and minds of the next generation. Of course, religion is not a magic bullet. But without religious-based moral renewal, the chances for arresting the present slide into chaotic violence are nil.

School choice is thus not a narrow education issue. It is, rather, a pivotal battleground in which the moral struggle for the soul of the underclass will, in a large measure, be fought. The weapons for this vital struggle are at hand if we choose to grasp them. Meanwhile the body count continues. In Chicago, a 12-year-old is gunned down on the way home from a Halloween party. In a Manhattan welfare hotel a mother deliberately scalds her two-year-old infant to death. In Los Angeles, a family with young children returning from a barbecue makes a wrong turn and is surrounded by a murderous ring of gang members who riddle the vehicle with bullets. Several family members are hit; a three-year-old girl dies. The abyss widens.

Chapter 2

FOUNDATIONS OF CHRISTIAN MORAL RESPONSE

In the first chapter we considered a variety of ways in which the church has related to public life and gave two examples of how different two reputedly Christian solutions to the same problem can be. In this chapter we focus on the basic sources of moral wisdom that give direction to the Christian church in addressing social issues. The Bible is the most prominent source of moral authority in addressing such issues, particularly among Protestant Christians. Its transmission through the various church traditions has resulted in an impact that has been truly profound. As "the Word of God," it bears an authority that no other source can claim. At the same time, this topic raises a host of difficult and intriguing questions that reveal significant divisions among Christians and their churches. What the scriptures are actually saying to the church about any particular moral issue, or what kind of authority they bear concerning a given issue, are matters that elicit quite different responses from one church's tradition to another.

Determining what the Bible has to say about a moral issue is not simple. Whenever one relates the content of a body of literature from some 2,000 years ago to contemporary issues, the interpreter has to understand the historical context in which that literature emerged. He or she needs an adequate understanding of the original language and of the authors' cultural mores. We must ask what the moral judgments of the authors meant in that context before we can meaningfully relate what they say to our own times. A formidable body of scholarship surrounds this enterprise, whose impact on historical investigations has reached well beyond the realm of biblical scholarship.

It should be clear that if one wants to know "what the Bible says" concerning a particular moral issue, one risks distorting and misunderstanding what it says by simply quoting chapter and verse. But beyond this common misuse, there remains considerable disagreement among biblical scholars as to what kinds of moral judgments the Bible brings to various social issues of our time. One has to remember that the Bible is not a moral handbook, written in order to provide answers to moral issues. It was not written at one time by one author, but over hundreds of years in a variety of religious and moral contexts. There is more than sufficient room for various interpretations concerning the judgments that different writers made about moral issues.

Another aspect of this subject relates to the differing assumptions that Biblical scholars bring to their study of scripture. Those of a more conservative bent tend to be more literal in their understanding of the text. They are more likely to find laws that may be seen as applicable to current issues. Those on the other end of the ideological spectrum are more likely to discover broad themes or directions for moral guidance rather than specific rules. Yet others suggest that living in accord with the spiritual and moral wisdom of the Bible shapes a person's character and enters into moral direction in that way. There is justification for all three understandings as well as others.

The first two selections in this chapter represent quite different approaches to scripture. John Jefferson Davis presents what he calls "evangelical ethics," approaching the scriptures as not only a trustworthy guide for our moral decision making, but as "the only infallible and inerrant rule of faith and practice." Davis is not satisfied with general values that people glean from scripture, such as the sacrificial love that characterizes the teachings of Jesus, but asserts that specific commands and precepts are to be found there that are valid for all time. He acknowledges that the Bible may not provide specific rules to apply to every moral situation we encounter today, but the groundwork is there that enables us by deductive reasoning to reach the right judgment on each issue. Davis reveals considerable confidence that the Bible can be used as a kind of handbook to arrive at the right answers.

An opposing view of the Bible and its role in relation to Christian ethics is found in the article by Robin Scroggs. Scroggs makes what appears on the face of it to be a radical suggestion: He argues that the Christian community should no longer speak of the "authority of the Bible" but should replace it with an understanding of the Bible as the foundational document of the Christian faith. Scroggs thinks the notion that the ethical prescriptions of the Bible are suitable to our lives today is a delusion. Those who argue for this form of authority (and he would doubtless include Jefferson here) are disguising the fact that it is the mood of contemporary society that picks and chooses what is suitable from within the Bible. It is not scripture, not society, that is finally authoritative. He thinks that frequently the adequacy of theological—as well as moral—claims are tested by our contemporary perspectives, which makes them, rather than scripture, authoritative.

The article describes four proposals within biblical studies that address the present impasse, critiques them, and offers a fifth. By proposing that the New Testament (what happens to the Old?) is the foundational document, Scroggs means that these writings are "those documents that have elicited, set the basic agenda for, and defined what Christianity means as a historical reality." The New Testament is absolutely indispensable in learning what it means to be Christian; while it can be subject to critical appraisal, the Bible always has to be a dialogue partner. As far as moral guidance goes, Scroggs' proposal seems to see scripture as setting directions, as exhorting us to discern the will of God, and giving us the "freedom to care." Is that finally enough to claim?

The third essay, by Sister Marie Vianney Bilgrien, speaks to another foundation of Christian moral response: human and religious experience, specifically, the experience of women. As a source of authority, experience includes both not explicitly religious experience and also religious experience, both of which involve God's activity. If scripture can be seen as the dynamic repository of historical revelation, contemporary human experience can be seen as God's current revelation. Sister Bilgrien argues that there are real differences between men and women, that these differences are theologically and therefore morally significant, and that the theological tradition that has been shaped primarily by men's experience could be considerably enriched and expanded by the consideration of women's experience. She takes up three models for understanding women's experience: first as being complementary to men's experience; second as an equally valid form of experience in addition to men's; and third with a stress on the mutuality, rather than equality, of relationships. The article details several ways in which incorporating the perspectives of women's experience deepens and opens up other dimensions of moral wisdom.

The final article by Stanley Hauerwas represents the foundational authority of theology that can also be seen as including the additional sources of reason, tradition, and conscience. Different traditions articulate these foundational sources in various ways; thus, tradition is an important source of moral wisdom for the Roman Catholic church. Theology can be defined as the study of God's activity in the world and the Christian beliefs that are the heritage of our tradition. It is based on human reason and guided by conscience and the Holy Spirit. Hauerwas maintains that if we are to speak of Christian ethics or moral theology, then our decisions must bear the imprint of faith in God—the subject of theology.

Biblical Authority
John Jefferson Davis

The teachings of Scripture are the final court of appeal for ethics. Human reason, church tradition, and the natural and social sciences may aid moral reflection, but divine revelation, found in the canonical Scriptures of the Old and New Testaments, constitutes the "bottom line" of the decision-making process. Informed ethical reflection will carefully weigh the various words of men, both

Reprinted by permission of Presbyterian and Reformed Publishing Company, publisher of *Evangelical Ethics*.

past and present, but the Word of God must cast the deciding vote. Evangelicals believe that the canonical Scriptures are the very Word of God, the only infallible and inerrant rule of faith and practice, and consequently are the highest authority for both doctrine and morals.

The Bible functions normatively in evangelical ethics through its specific commands and precepts, general principles, various precedents, and overall world view. Many of the specific commandments of Scripture (e.g., "Do not commit adultery") are directly translatable into our present context. General biblical principles such as the sacredness of human life made in God's image (Gen.1:26,28) have crucial implications for modern ethical issues not addressed explicitly in Scripture, such as in vitro fertilization and genetic engineering. Old Testament practices such as tithing, while not specifically commanded in the New Testament, can function as a precedent as the people of God seek to fulfill their stewardship obligations in the present age. By teaching foundational truths concerning the nature of God, man, good, and evil, and the meaning and destiny of human life, the Bible provides a basic *world view* within which the various data of the human sciences can be understood. It had been said that "good facts make good ethics," but these "facts" must be seen within the proper framework if their true ethical significance is to be understood.

The understanding of Christian morals being advocated here exemplifies the *prescriptive* and *deontological* (Greek: *deon,* that which is obligatory) tradition in the history of ethics. According to this school of thought, Christian ethics is to be not merely descriptive of human behavior, but prescriptive in the sense of discerning the will of God in concrete situations, and the specific duties that follow from it. Evangelical ethics is concerned not with personal preferences and feelings, but with obligations that command the conscience.

There has been a widespread tendency in modern biblical scholarship to minimize the prescriptive element in New Testament ethics in favor of generalized appeals to Christian "faith" and "love" apart from the specifics of law. As Rudolf Schnackenburg has pointed out, however, "Jesus was not concerned only with interior dispositions, but wanted his demands to be interpreted as real commandments that are to be converted into action.[1] W. D. Davies has noted that in the mind of the Apostle Paul, the exalted Lord was never divorced from Jesus the rabbi, and the Holy Spirit was never divorced from the historic teachings of Jesus. Likewise in I John there is constant appeal to the commandments of the Lord, and frequent echoes of them. The love of God shed abroad in the heart of the believer is indeed the dynamic motivation of Christian behavior, but this love demonstrates itself in harmony with, and not apart from, the specific commands and precepts of Holy Scripture.

EMPIRICAL AND DELIBERATIVE ELEMENTS

Harmon Smith and Louis Hodges have written that there are two poles between which all Christian decision making must be done: "the reality of God on the one hand and the concrete, contingent situation of the actor on the other."[2] Biblical authority represents the "revelational-normative" dimension of Christian ethics; human reason, applying the biblical norms to the concrete situation in light of the specific data at hand, represents the "empirical-deliberative" dimension. Good principles and good facts are both necessary for sound decision making.

In the classic language of the Westminster Confession of Faith, the "whole counsel of God, concerning all things necessary for his own glory, man's salvation, faith, and life, is either expressly set down in Scripture, *or by good and necessary consequence may be deduced from scripture* . . ." (I,6; emphasis added). In this formulation human reason has a legitimate role in extending the general principles of Scripture to analogous circumstances not explicitly addressed in the canonical texts.

Cocaine abuse, for example, while not explicitly addressed in the Bible, is certainly inconsistent with the teaching that the body is the temple of the Holy Spirit and is not to be abused (I Cor.6:19,20). The principles of medical ethics that the physician is to "do no harm" and is always to treat the patient as an end and never as a means only—so crucial in the treatment of comatose or incompetent subjects—are essentially applications of the spirit of the Golden Rule to the new challenges of modern medicine. This use of reason in evangelical ethics is similar to the deliberations of a civil judge, who, being faced with entirely new circumstances in a pending case, attempts to apply existing law in the light of precedents and all the relevent data in order to serve the cause of justice.

While human reason plays an essential role in evangelical ethics, that role is not an autonomous one, independent of the authority of Scripture. Human reason, being impaired by sin, is not to serve as a separate norm as over against Scripture, but rather as the servant of divine revelation in the application of biblical truth. Information from the social sciences, for example, may be relevant to discussions of homosexuality, but the evangelical ethicist will, in the words of J. Robertson McQuilken, maintain "a jealous commitment to the Bible first and last as the originating and controlling source of ideas about man and his relationships."[3] The Christian ethicist will seek all the facts relevant to the matter at hand, but will recognize the need to interpret those facts with a mind renewed by the Holy Spirit, and within a framework of meaning controlled by the teachings of Holy Scripture.

CASES OF CONFLICTING OBLIGATION

In a sinful world, believers may occasionally find themselves confronted with conflicting ethical obligations. In the early church Peter and the other apostles faced conflicting demands for obedience from the governing authorities and from God (Acts 5:27–29). After Rahab the harlot received the Israelite spies, she was met with a choice between telling the truth or preserving life (Josh.2). Corrie Ten Boom, when hiding Jews in her home during the Second World War and queried by the Nazi authorities, "Are there any Jews in this House?" faced a dilemma similar to Rahab's.

Some ethicists have distinguished between *prima facie* ("on first appearance") duties and *actual* duties. Prima facie duties are duties, *other things being equal.* Actual duties are duties, *all things considered.* Is such a distinction biblical? In a sinful world, is it always possible to find a course of action that is thoroughly pleasing to God, or is it sometimes necessary to choose between the lesser of two sins? Are there general principles from Scripture that can furnish guidelines for resolving cases of conflicting obligations? These and related issues will be addressed in the analysis that follows.

One unsuccessful answer to the problem of conflicting moral obligations is known as "situation ethics." In this approach there can be no real conflict between two or more absolutes, because presumably there is only one absolute: "love." In each and every situation, one's moral obligation is to take the most "loving" course of action, even if that should mean discarding traditional ethical standards.

Joseph Fletcher, the leading proponent of this school of thought, has little use for codes and rules. "Christian situation ethics," he says, "reduces law from a statutory system of rules to the love canon alone."[4] Universal rules and principles are treated as love's servants and subordinates, "to be quickly kicked out of the house if they forget their place and try to take over."[5]

This "situational" and incipiently antinomian perspective was not entirely new to Fletcher, but had been anticipated by earlier trends in neoorthodox theology. Emil Brunner, for example, in the widely read *The Divine Imperative,* had written that "we are united to our neighbor by the Command of love, which excludes all legalistic rules and every attempt to stereotype human relationships."[6] A protest against legalism in the Christian life can easily become a rejection of the binding moral authority of the specific precepts of God's written Word.

The fundamental difficulty with the "situational" approach, of course, is the absence of a definite criterion for what constitutes a "loving" course of action in any given situation. Harmon Smith asks, "How does a person know that he is doing (or has done) the loving thing in the situation?"[7] The question is very much to the point. Apart from the abiding norms of divine revelation, the moral agent is left to the vagaries of personal preference, and the constantly changing "spirit of the age" to discern the "loving" thing.

The Bible clearly indicates that human beings, who possess sinful and fallen natures, cannot be left to their own devices to discern the will of God; the ability to rationalize selfish desires in the name of high sounding principles is all too real. Paul Lehmann, for example, attempts to legitimize extramarital sex by appealing to the "fulfillment of human wholeness" and "free obedience to what God is doing in the world."[8]

James Gustafson relates a conversation with a student at a liberal seminary during the late sixties—a conversation that illustrates how "situationism" can lead to the trivialization of serious moral principle. "I get up in the morning and look out the window," the student said, "to see what God is doing in the world. I read the *New York Times* to find out where he is doing these things today. Then I get with it."[9]

Evidently it did not occur to the student that reading (and obeying) the Bible had anything to do with discerning "what God was doing in the world." The serious reader of Scripture is confronted by the statement of Jesus that *authentic* love for God is demonstrated by keeping his commandments (John 14:21). The Bible points the moral agent away from the short-term rationalizations of personal preference toward the long-term perspective of eternity—the perspective that alone provides the proper framework for evaluating man's true and lasting interests.

The view advocated in this work regarding conflicting moral obligations could be termed "contextual absolutism." According to this perspective, there are many moral absolutes, not just one absolute of "love," as in situation ethics. Examples of moral absolutes are provided by the Decalogue: idolatry, murder, blasphemy, adultery, stealing, and so forth are always morally wrong.

Contextual absolutism holds that in each and every ethical situation, no matter how extreme, there is a course of action that is morally right and free of sin. God promises that in every situation of temptation or testing there will be a way of escape so that the believer will be able to endure it (I Cor.10:13). This position differs from the "lesser-of-two-evils" position, which holds that in some circumstances any course of action open to the believer will be sinful to some degree.

In some cases the right course of action may require suffering or even martyrdom. Jesus Christ, who is presented as the believer's moral ideal in the New Testament, did not commit any sin, but always obeyed the Father's will, even to the point of suffering and death (cf. I Pet.2:21,22). Daniel and his friends were willing to be martyred rather than compromise their convictions by committing an act of idolatry (Dan.3:17,18).

Following the course of action that is well pleasing to God may not always be easy in a sinful and fallen world, but such obedient and even heroic options can, by the grace of God, be found and followed even in the most extreme conditions. Such unswerving commitment to discerning and obeying the will of God—including a willingness to pay the "cost of discipleship"—is much needed in the twentieth-century American church, where believers are all too often tempted by the comforts and compromises of the surrounding culture.

The Bible as Foundational Document
Robin Scroggs

Whether the Bible speaks authoritatively for our own time is a question that cannot be decided by a single issue, even as crucial a one as sexuality. Rather, the

Robin Scroggs, "The Bible as Foundational Document," *Interpretation* 50 (January 1995): 17–30. Reprinted by permission of copyright holder.

problem of the Bible's understanding of sexuality is but one among many issues that have arisen throughout the centuries and that have called the claim of biblical authority into question. Since this is the case, I shall approach the question from broad historical and theological perspectives;[10] in fact, what I say here could be said without referring to the theme of sexuality at all. I do turn to this theme at the end of the paper to indicate how my position would inform contemporary Christian discussions about this most divisive dialogue in the church today.

THE PROGRESSIVE EROSION OF BIBLICAL AUTHORITY[11]

The erosion of scriptural authority has been constant since the Reformation and, especially, the Enlightenment (although the moves taken to avoid its authority are present from the earliest church). . . . Even a sweeping glance at this erosion should show how consistent the process has been.

The Purity of the Text.   That the text of the Bible was verbally inspired (including variations on the theme) came into question with the increasing awareness of the immense profusion of textual data, intensified by the sophisticated techniques of textual critics. Some theologians retreated into the position that the original autograph had been so inspired, but this was of little help when it became apparent that one could no longer have confidence in what that original autograph might have said.[12]

The Historical Accuracy of the Text.   That the text of the Bible reported accurately the events it described was already seriously questioned by the early nineteenth century, popularized by the then sensationalist findings of David Friedrich Strauss.[13] While opposing theologians struggled to defend such accuracy, the Enlightenment mood was too strong to arouse much sympathy in progressive circles. Theologians gradually learned to appeal to the claim that the texts never intended to be historical documents. They are, rather, expressions of faith, sometimes couched in myth, which present a claim upon allegiances.[14] From the scholars' perspective, these appeals are truer to the intentionality of the texts than to the view that had to be abandoned. Nevertheless, the obvious historical inaccuracies have been, for many, a serious obstacle to the acceptance of biblical authority.

The Ethical Prescriptions as Suitable.   The Bible's ethical norms for the lives of believers have been avoided since biblical times, in effect by ignoring them. Assault upon the Bible as a normative ethical code has become particularly apparent today. To oversimplify, it seems that where biblical culture has influenced the contours of the contemporary society, the biblical injunctions have been held to be authoritative—that is, they "fit" the present culture. Where the injunction does not seem to relate to a society's reality, the injunction is blithely ignored. The biblical injunction is then branded as "outmoded," fitting perhaps the context of its times, but not that of the contemporary society.

Thus, it is the mood of the contemporary society that judges what is held to be suitable and, therefore, perhaps authoritative.[15] . . .

Theological Claims as Normative to Beliefs.   Perhaps the most serious issue in the dispute about authority, because it is the one that calls most seriously into question the Christian religion itself, is that which judges theological claims in the Bible as inadequate or outmoded. This questioning is also as old as the church itself—even some New Testament authors disagree with Paul! The arguments about which documents should count as canonical is an obvious case in point. Luther, as is well known, belittled the theological insights of James, Hebrews, and Revelation.

These de facto denials of theological judgments—and thus biblical authority—have long been with us. . . .

The adequacy of the theology of the New Testament has come to be even more intensely critiqued in some contemporary scholarly and theological views. . . .

The question thus lies heavily upon us: Does the claim that the Bible has authority any longer make sense? If assessments about biblical faith and ethics are made from contemporary sensitivities about what is right or wrong, *then it is our contemporary perspectives that are authoritative.* Where the Bible agrees with those sensitivities, it is invoked to support what one already knows to be correct. Where the Bible disagrees, it is relegated to its historical context and becomes something we have overcome in our struggle for the truth. This is, I would argue, how the Bible is in fact used *by both evangelicals and liberals.*[16] What we need is a new understanding of the role of the Bible in the church today that acknowledges the actual reality of our situation—an understanding that takes the Bible as a foundational document but not as authoritative, that is, an understanding that does not assume that the Bible determines all that we are to think and do.

THE PRESENT IMPASSE

The hard fact of the matter is that, whether we like it or not, much of the Bible contains ethical and theological judgments that are considered objectionable, or at least questionable, by today's Christian cultures. The old view of the Bible as literally authoritative is clearly untenable, although it did have at least the advantage of clarity. Not surprisingly, those who attempt to hold on to some sense of the Bible as authoritative and to live in today's much different world must propose a view that is inevitably going to be much more complex and diffuse. The question is whether such proposals (we will look at three) have such cogency that they can have staying power, or whether they are simply way-stations on the road to a complete surrender of any claim for the authority of the Bible.

The Canon within the Canon.   All believers probably have certain biblical books that speak to them more than others. When pressed to define their faith, they may appeal over and over again to those books, whether the Gospels or Paul or some others. This is the simplest definition of the term "canon within the canon." As such, it probably is a universal phenomenon. Certain theologians, however, have stated the matter clearly and cogently.

Luther's view of the biblical books that are questionable, mentioned above, is a classic statement of this position. His judgment is based on what he considered the essence of the gospel, namely, that of "salvation by grace alone." Books that understand this (of course Paul is central) are acceptable; those that do not are at least peripheral. Bultmann's *Theology of the New Testament* represents a sophisticated scholarly treatment of this theme.[17] Paul and John lie at the heart of the gospel, and every other New Testament book is evaluated as to whether it measures up to the profundity of the essential myth producers.[18]

This approach has an advantage for those who wish to save the authority of the Bible. They can claim that their criterion for authority is found *within* some parts of the canon itself. Thus, while they may reject certain portions of the Bible as authoritative, they do this in the name of the authority of other portions. But this very approach has an Achilles heel. *By what criterion* is one part chosen as authoritative? Can that criterion itself be derived from the Bible? Or is it really the case that the decision is extracanonical, that is, derived from the contemporary experience of the believer? If that is the case, and I suspect it has to be, the real authority lies outside of the selected books. Rather, the books are selected because they "fit" the experience or beliefs of the one who selects.

The Word through the Words.   This view, often identified with Reformation theology, denies that authority lies in the words of the Bible, but can be found, rather, in the freedom of God to speak *through* the biblical text to reveal Truth. Christopher Morse has recently restated this perspective in trenchant ways that allow for contemporary critique of the biblical words.[19] His discussion can serve as an exemplar of this perspective and a test of whether this view is adequate to provide a basis for the authority of the Bible.

The biblical text is not in itself authoritative; it is only as God speaks through the words in the context of worship and proclamation that the words become the Word.[20] "Faith in the Word of God, therefore, proscribes the reification of God's communication in the words of any text.... What the church finds to be authoritative in the Bible is only that scripture within it through which God continues to speak currently in commissioning the church to hear and follow God's Word."[21]

This view provides two conclusions of importance for the contemporary situation. In the first place, it denies authoritative status to the words as Word. Texts can be interpreted in the context of their own time and place without any attempt to make them say what contemporary sensibilities would like for them to say. In the second, it provides for a dialogue with the words such that their ethical or theological conclusions can be questioned and, presumably, even rejected. To state the issue as provocatively as possible, this perspective would allow one to doubt whether the words of the texts are always consonant with God's Word.

How is this possible? Who or what is to be the judge of such matters? Inevitably, some acknowledgment of a legitimate subjective selection of appropriate critique is involved. . . .

Thus, it seems to me, we are back in the same dilemma of a selective, subjective judgment about when the proclamation of the biblical text is God's Word and when it is false prophecy. Our prominent sensitivities, for example, are to reject patriarchalism as theologically and ethically inappropriate. Yet it is not just the *reading* of the text that produces "false prophecy." The false prophecy has to be laid to the account of the writers of the texts themselves. In this view, it is not *illogical* to affirm that God can use false prophecy to proclaim God's Word. Yet there surely comes a point beyond which such a view makes less and less common sense.

Authority as Authorization of Communities.   In a provocative and passionate article, belying its location in a dictionary, Walter Brueggemann has argued for a different approach to the issue of biblical authority.[22] Rejecting earlier views, he turns authority into the power of the Bible to call liberated and liberating communities into existence. "Authority has to do with *issues of authorization,* i.e., how, in a pluralistic world like ours, concrete communities can be authorized to live, act, and hope in a manner which may at times oppose the accepted norm, a manner which can be justified neither scientifically nor experientially."[23]

With this move Brueggemann sweeps away all traditional approaches to the authority of the text, denies any primacy of propositional truth in discussions, and puts the "evidence" for biblical authority in the Bible's *power* to create and empower communities. The "burden of proof" thus resides in the communities authorized by the Bible, and the criterion for authority lies no longer in the adequacy of the "knowledge" contained in the Bible but rather in the quality of the authorized communities. The question now becomes what sort of community justifies the claim that the Bible is authoritative? It is a community which exhibits "obedient practice."[24] But from whence does Brueggemann get his criteria by which he measures *which* communities have "obedient practice" and thus evidence the Bible's authority? The proper, authorized communities are those which "will provide energy, courage, and legitimacy for action against the destructive tendencies embedded within our civilization."[25] Once again the criterion comes from contemporary judgments. Presumably there are communities that do *not* fit Brueggemann's understanding of obedience, however much they appeal to the Bible as their foundational document, and they would be rejected as authorized communities.

The Ambiguity of the "Inner Witness of the Holy Spirit."   I have pointed again and again to the constant, mostly explicit claim that the Bible is not authoritative in its words but rather that *some* words may *become* authoritative under certain conditions, under the right perspective of contemporary assessment. It would seem that all of these claims *could* fall under the rubric of the "inner witness of the Holy Spirit," that is, the believer's claim that a certain text (or in Brueggemann's analysis, a certain community) has, or is given, authority could be said to be guided by the Holy Spirit.

The claim that the Holy Spirit authorizes a particular reading of the Bible is, perhaps, an essential dimension of Christian theology. At the same time, church history is full of examples of such an appeal to justify every kind of theological and ethical claim dear to the heart of the claimer. Those who appeal to the Spirit for a certain view argue vehemently that those who make similar appeals for an opposing point of view are false prophets. Paul is probably not the first, and certainly not the last, to make such *ad hominem* arguments (e.g., II Cor. 11:13-15). The problem is that the claim to be an authentic interpreter of the Bible because of the action of the Holy Spirit is as fraught with ambiguity as is any "objective" reading of the text itself. For every claim, there can be—and usually is—a counter-claim and, ultimately, there is no test to determine the authenticity of the claim, an ambiguity that can lead to one sort of oppression or another against the opposing claim.

THE FINAL STEP: LAYING AUTHORITY TO REST

I have argued that there has been a gradual but constant erosion of the claims for biblical authority. In our current situation, in which biblical assertions are questioned in basic, not superficial, ways, the older views must be discarded. My judgment is that the recent attempts to save some meaning for the "authority" of the Bible are no more than way-stations. I propose instead that we forthrightly give up any claim that the Bible is authoritative (as I have defined the word) in guidance for contemporary faith and morals. This, I would argue, is the inevitable and *appropriate* final step in the long story of the erosion of biblical authority. In public discussions the Bible must be discussed as a human document from the past and our dialogue with it seen as a human process of the present.[26] The Bible has no "legal" authority to determine our "now."

This may seem like a radical—indeed heretical—proposal, but I would suggest that it is not as radical as it seems on the surface. *In practice* it may not be any different from the freedom claimed by believers of all ages—perhaps especially our own—who critique the Bible in the name of what seems to be ethically and theologically appropriate. In mainline circles today, certainly in that part of the circle inhabited by biblical scholars, the texts are exegeted as purely historical documents, located and interpreted in their historical contexts, without any appeal to a "supernatural" dimension in their formation and content.

What we need to do is to formulate how the Bible can be legitimately used in our situation, where it is and remains a book of the past. Such formulation would avoid two unacceptable extremes: a revisionism that distorts the text to make it say what we want it to say today,[27] and a tyranny that tries to take over our responsibility to think things through for ourselves. Theological imperialism would be overthrown by a common search for wisdom in an ambiguous situation. It would put us in our proper place.

THE BIBLE AS FOUNDATIONAL DOCUMENT

To relinquish the notion of biblical authority would also, I think, put the biblical texts in their proper place as well. I propose that this proper place is their essential value as the foundational documents of Christianity (here, I shall primarily refer to the texts of the New Testament). By foundational documents I mean that they are those documents that have elicited, set the basic agenda for, and defined what Christianity means as a *historical reality.* A Christian may disagree with what he or she reads in the texts; a Christian cannot refuse serious dialogue with the texts without calling into question the right of using the term "Christian" as a self-designation. This is not to let "legal" authority slip in by the back door. The same argument can be made for the importance of foundational documents in any movement. One cannot claim to be Marxist without serious dialogue with the writings of Marx, or to be a Platonist without intimate knowledge and appreciation of the dialogues of Plato. Marxist and Platonic tradition go beyond the foundational documents, just as Christian tradition throughout the centuries has gone beyond the New Testament. In no case, however, can the foundational documents be ignored.

The New Testament as Creator of Christian Faith.   To release the texts from an external, authoritative power releases the power *internal* to the texts to come to life and to function to change *by persuasion* our being, our thinking, and our action. The Apostle Paul himself sets the tone for our appropriation of Christian teaching in Romans 12:1–2. "I exhort you, members of the community, through the mercies of God to present yourselves as a living sacrifice, holy, well-pleasing to God, a sacrifice that is your reasoning service. Do not be conformed to this world but be transformed by the making new of your mind, that you may attest what is the will of God, that which is good and well-pleasing and perfect" (author's translation). Paul does not appeal in his *ethical exhortations* to the external claims of either the Hebrew scriptures or the teaching of Jesus (with one exception—I Cor. 7:10–11). He believes that the transformed self involves a transformed mind that is capable of coming to know God's will.[28]

When the Bible is freed from its prison as an external club, it can become the friendly persuader that draws us into the spell of the power of the earliest proclaimers. To use the language of authority for a moment, it would be possible to say that it is not because Paul is authoritative that I believe him; instead, Paul comes to have authority for me because what he says elicits my belief. The documents were "selected" as canonical because they were powerful in forming the new selfhood of persons. We need continuously to be addressed by these documents, not because they are canonical but because they are powerful.

The New Testament as Agenda Setter for Christianity.   By this, I mean that the early Christian documents ask the basic questions that they who consider themselves Christian must also ask. These documents also provide some basic answers to those questions. The questions asked are not the only questions one can ask. In fact, one frustration to beginning students of the New Testament is that it does not deal with some of the important questions they want to ask. Nor do the ways in which these early documents answer their own questions always please some Christians today. If the New Testament no longer holds as normative, then one is free to dialogue with both questions and answers.[29] One is *not* free, I would argue, to ignore those questions and answers. As the foundational document, the New Testament is due respect as a serious statement about what should count as important for Christians.

For example, the central focus of this foundational document is obviously the question of the importance of Jesus the Christ. Various answers are found in the documents themselves. One is, I would think, free to add one's own attempt to phrase an answer about this significance. One is *not* free to ignore the centrality of Jesus the Christ.

The New Testament as Definitional for Christianity. This means that just because the New Testament is the foundational document it provides the church with the basic definition of what it means to be Christian. Christianity simply cannot mean whatever anyone wishes it to mean. Definitions are, of course, expanded, contracted, or modified in the course of development; yet there are certain parameters given that limit what can be included. Marxism, presumably, cannot mean anything anyone wishes it to be, and the parameters of what counts as a Marxist expression are to be found in the foundational documents by Marx himself. Just as the term "Marxism" could not incorporate within it a laissez-faire capitalism, so the New Testament would exclude a definition of Christianity as an atheistic self-salvational system unrelated to Jesus the Christ. What any movement "means" is always set by the parameters of its foundational documents.[30] This is in no way to try to say that the parameters set by the New Testament are "true" in some objective, transcendent sense. In the eternal scheme of things Christianity may be "false," and a contemporary statement of what is "really real" may be "true." My conviction, however, is that any contemporary statement, if it differs significantly from the New Testament "definition," should not call itself Christianity.[31]

Thus, what I propose is a view of the New Testament as the foundational document of Christianity. As such, it is *absolutely indispensable* in learning what it means to be Christian. As foundational, the New Testament should be studied, preached, and set in dialogue with our contemporary struggle to be faithful to God in Christ. If I had my way, there would be more, not less, adult Bible education; there would be more, not fewer, expository sermons in worship. As the classic expression of Christianity, the New Testament includes writings that powerfully challenge all generations of believers, luring them into a transformed life that makes possible the noetic perception of God's will.

Foundational documents can be subjected to critical appraisal. Specific issues that obviously pertain to culture-bound realities are relatively easy to deal with. The hard problem is to decide just what the legitimate parameters are and whether one's own views have forced one to step outside those parameters. That problem has no sure method of solution, and people of good will will often take different views. It is here that listening is crucial, and it is imperative not to read others too quickly out of the kingdom of God.[32] ...

CONCLUSION

I have argued that it is now time to relinquish any claim that the Bible holds authority over our contemporary struggles about faith and morals. At the same time, I have argued equally strenuously that the Bible, as the Christian foundational document, must be engaged in a serious dialogue as we conduct our inquiry about what we are to think and do....

If Paul were here today, perhaps he would say something like this: Through Christ we learn that God is the gracious God who secures our selfhood without the anxious striving to create it by ourselves. Living out of this gift, we are freed to live a life of caring for others. In this freedom to care, we are exhorted to "attest what is the will of God" for our own time and place. The very basis of intelligent discussion about what is right in our present situation is this freedom to care. In so far as it is this posture that motivates us in our struggles to attest the will of God, we can have some assurance that our discussion is moving in the right direction. We, of course, have no proof that our contribution to the discussion is motivated by this freedom to care. There are, perhaps, certain hints: a willingness to listen, a certain diffidence toward our own proposals, a refusal to end the position by any appeal to authority, an awareness of our own ignorance and our willingness to dispel that ignorance.

In this discussion I would insist that the Bible be always a dialogue partner, especially when some of it says things we do not want to hear. As foundational documents the texts have, on the one hand, the power to transform and to lead us into new paths of thinking and, on the other, to speak caution to our eagerness to follow the secular world in the latest cultural passion. Removing the weight of legal authority from the Bible will free it to become a genuine partner in our search for God's will, a partner we can listen to without becoming resentful, a friend with whom we can respectfully disagree.

The Voice of Women in Moral Theology
Sister Marie Vianney Bilgrien

... Almost every feminist has her own definition of feminism. In simplest terms, it is the belief that women and men are equal in dignity as human beings. Most

Reprinted with the permission of Sister Marie Vianney Bilgrien and America Press, Inc. 106 West 56th St., New York, NY 10010. Originally published in *America*'s 173, no. 20, December 16–23, 1995, issue.

would also assert that equal dignity has usually been denied and that changes are needed in attitudes, concepts and structures to manifest this equality. A further step is yet needed. Feminism is not just a call for women to have an equal place in the current system; it challenges us to rethink the system itself in the light of women's experience. Women do not merely want equal access to what many consider a patriarchal or androcentric system. They want to remake the system.

Feminism is not defined by issues such as autonomy, pro-choice, rights in reproductive technology and so on. Women stand in various places on the spectrum of these issues. Feminism is truly defined by the foundational principles I have just enumerated: that men and women are equal, that equality has been denied and that the tradition is androcentric. It is important today for moral theology to admit that: (1) there are differences between men's and women's experience, (2) these differences are theologically and therefore morally significant, and (3) the theological tradition has been shaped mainly by men's experience.

Feminist theology is convinced that men and women are equal, but not the same. If men and women were the same there would be no need for feminism as a historical, theological movement. Revelation—God's self-communication—interacts with human experience. The question is, "Whose experience?" If it is true that theology has been based on a generic, inclusive human experience, then focusing on women's experience as distinct from men's would not make a significant difference. If, on the other hand, women's experience does make a significant difference, then we must consider that what was offered as universal was in fact a theology of a particular subset of humanity—that of men. It follows, then, that the full human condition, which involves more than the male condition, has not been and is not accurately accounted for.

Until now, men's experience has been accepted almost exclusively as the norm for the human person. Because women's experience has been left out, feminists claim that something distinctly human, not just something feminine, has been left out. Androcentrism distorts both human experience and theology. Both need to be corrected. The issue raised by the feminists should concern all, because it is a call to be truthful and faithful to God's revelation. It cuts much deeper than equality, power, inclusiveness and freedom. It affects how we know God and therefore how we relate to God.

Carol Gilligan, in her book *In a Different Voice,* challenges Lawrence Kolberg's standard work on moral development (a study of 84 boys, age 10–16). Gilligan found that girls' development differs from that of boys and hence affects their moral development. The contrasts are notable. The development of a male identity involves separation and individuation from the mother. The girl defines herself by relating to and identifying with the mother. Male identity is threatened by intimacy and finds relationships difficult. The female personality is threatened by separation and has problems with individuation. Males forfeit close relationships in order to foster freedom and self-expression. Connection, attachment and intimacy are more integral and necessary for the development of the female personality.

An important moral consequence of this development is that men struggle with selfishness and women with self-sacrifice—sacrifice that often militates against self-development. Using women's experience rather than some kind of generic human experience, one can then strongly question the androcentric concepts of sin and redemption. Sin has traditionally been defined as a form of pride, self-assertion, self-love, self-centeredness, the desire to be a god, not a creature. The concept of redemption is seen as a life modeled on that of Jesus: humble self-denial, a life of sacrificial love, abandoning the prideful will to dominate and putting God and others ahead of oneself.

Feminists reject this concept. Women typically have too little self; some have none. Through a life of nurturing and self-giving to husband and children, many women never achieve selfhood. Judith Plaskow, a Jewish ethicist, goes so far as to say that the temptations of women are not the same as those of men. Women are more likely to be tempted by such things as triviality, distractibility, diffuseness, lack of an organizing center or focus, dependence on others for one's own self-definition, underdevelopment and negation of self.

The distinctive feminine sin, then, is failure to become a self. The traditional description of sin as pride and self-assertion fails to recognize this. The parallel concept of redemption as self-sacrifice has similar problems. Redemption can be almost impossible to achieve because there is not a self to sacrifice, and the women's struggle to become a centered self and independent is looked upon as selfish and sinful. What can sound like good news to men, redemptive and liberating, can drive women deeper into their original temptation—the failure to become a self. It is important to be aware that women are not saying that the understanding of sin as pride is incorrect, but that this understanding of sin is limited and that this limitation goes unacknowledged. The characteristic male sin has been reified as the human sin, when in fact it is not. Women do not want women's experience to become normative in place of men's; they want the concept to be expanded to include both, not just for the sake of equality but for the sake of a better understanding of God's revelation and hence the possibility of a more complete relationship with the God who calls us to friendship.

Women warn that as the debate continues in church circles and among feminists themselves, we may fall into the trap of a dual anthropology. Do women share the same human nature as men, or is their humanity an essentially different mode of being human? This fundamental question is raised when one reads contemporary official church statements that invoke the "order of creation" from Genesis, Ch. 2 and 3, and the Pauline notion of "the headship of the male."

The complementarity of the sexes is put in such a way that women's roles and functions in church and society are seen to be of an essentially different nature from men's. Over and over one finds presuppositions and stereotypes that define women as particularly humble, sensitive, intuitive, gentle, receptive, passive. Implicitly or explicitly, these are contrasted with men's aggressiveness, rationality, activity, strength and so on.

Emphasizing the complementarity of the sexes, it seems, offers a new rationalization for the subordination of women. This dual anthropology is accentuated by our marriage symbolism. Christ's relation to the church and the sacrament of Eucharist are often explained in terms of the relation of male to female or activity to passivity. . . .

A further ethical issue along these lines arises in the dualistic attitude that both society and church entertain about virtue. Stereotypical feminine virtues such as gentleness, love, pity, honesty, simplicity and sensitivity are relegated to women and the private realm. . . .

Women's voices call us to deeper truth. If the complementarity of human nature continues to be stressed, the differences between male and female will become more and more exaggerated, and a dual anthropology will emerge. Questions about sin and salvation will intensify. Are there two human natures? How does the male Jesus save male and female? Is Jesus the model for the human person or only the male? What dangers lurk in upholding Mary as the model for women? Is Jesus the model for men and Mary the model for women? . . .

If the equality model is stressed, women's ordination cannot be ignored, nor women's place in the public arena of the church—even at its highest levels. If it is true that the human person attains self-determination and autonomy through the responsible use of freedom, then opportunities for growth have to be present for women in the life and movement of the church. To develop as mature persons, not just bystanders or dependents, we have to be part of the internal structure. But we are not. . . .

Carol Gilligan's research on moral development in girls indicates that women characteristically make moral decisions based on relating rather than autonomy. Accordingly, she has developed a feminist ethic of caring. She shows how women tend to orient themselves by responding to others. Moral decisions are made in a framework of relationships rather than of rights. Because women are more at home in relationships, they are more concerned with how we make commitments and how they are kept.

Women are doing a lot of study of the dynamics involved in commitments— study that sheds light on experience of marital fidelity, fidelity to God, the requirements of friendship and what makes it grow. They ask, "What ought we to love? To what should we commit ourselves? Who do I want to become?" These questions epitomize the moral life. All but the most fleeting, superficial relationships carry obligations. Women are looking deeper into the meaning of promises, contracts, covenants, vows.

Some examples: In *Personal Commitments* (1990), Margaret Farley notes that women's experience of commitment constitutes in large part our vantage point for understanding God's commitment to us and God's desire for commitment from us. Denise Lardner Carmody's *Virtuous Women* (1992) reminds us that Jesus is the paradigm of faithful commitment. Jesus laid down his life for his friends and for his God. Feminists will be Christian to the extent that they struggle with Jesus' self-sacrificing love.

Women wonder about Jesus' friends. Would his life and death have been different if his closest friends had been women? Women tend to have more friends than men do because of the importance of relationships to them. They challenge men to be aware that: (1) women and their concerns continue to be of marginal importance in men's perception, (2) males have more difficulty than females in understanding what the other gender means, and (3) men suffer and cause others to suffer from an inability or unwillingness to disclose themselves, to discuss feelings and to interact supportively.

Dialogue is the ground for building relationships. Women's voices call men to dialogue in society and in the church. We are not afraid of confrontation. It helps clarify issues and holds the possibility of ever deeper dialogue and relationship. Women know that a strong opponent is more confirming than one who politely listens but does not take your opinion seriously. When debate is not allowed on issues within the church, women ask if they are being taken seriously. Many believe they are not. Relationships cannot be one-sided.

More and more, women are stressing mutuality in relationships rather than equality. In the drive to help the other become equal in a relationship, there is the danger of slipping into paternalism or maternalism. Our relationships with developing countries and in the church have taught us that. In striving for mutuality, each one is held responsible and no one usurps the responsibility of the other. Mutuality in relationships is the feminist alternative to domination. Mutuality moves beyond equality to recognize the reciprocity of giving and receiving, caring and being cared for.

The implications of mutuality help us rethink such structural sins as racism and sexism. Both the racist and the sexist are diminished in spirit and lose some of their human dignity. Mutuality becomes destructive. Both the perpetrator and the victim are affected. The bad effects are mutual. Feminists want a new stress on mutuality along with a new respect for the place of women in all questions of social justice and discussion of social ethics. It is incomprehensible to women that they were not consulted in the writing of Pope John Paul II's encyclical *Sollicitudo Rei Socialis* (1988). In a world where the majority of the poor are women and children, where whole countries are made up of widows and orphans, where and when do they get to speak for themselves? More than likely the reality is not that they were actively excluded, but that it never entered the minds of the framers of the encyclical that they should even be consulted. The same is true for the writing of the encyclicals *Centesimus Annus* (1991) and *Veritatis Splendor* (1993).

Women are expected to be the repositories and safeguards of morality. Yet when women try to extend their moral consciousness into the wider political or religious world, their femaleness becomes a detriment. The drafters of church policy, in their teaching authority, assume that they know what is good for women because they assume that they know what is good for the human person always and everywhere. Until there is the recognition that women's distinctive voice has a role to play in understanding the human person, the shaping of social doctrine in the church will continue to suffer from myopic, one-sided and therefore ineffectual social policy.

Feminists are asking searching questions and challenging society in many areas of reproductive technology—a rapidly changing scene. Earlier women had asked: "Is in vitro fertilization acceptable from a feminist moral perspective? What is the situation with women's moral autonomy during the treatment? What about the child's interest?" They moved on to ask, "In what direction should reproductive technology be developed so that it can be applied in a humane and dignified way, worldwide?" Women are now critically examining the technology itself.

Feminists are concerned that more and more aspects of reproduction are being controlled by medical technology. Fertilization and selection techniques are beginning to overlap. Second, they are noticing that it is the reproduction experts, usually male, who decide which women will be considered for treatment. Third, as a result of medical improvement, more and more difficult decisions have to be made about couples unable to have children and about those with serious hereditary defects. Decisions are made by the medical profession without taking into account the fallout for those who are helped to have children or those who are rejected. With prenatal diagnosis and selective abortion, it will be less and less acceptable to bring a child with a hereditary defect to full term. Societies are already less and less willing to give support and monetary aid in the rearing of a defective child. So some women ethicists ponder whether it is wise or just to bring a child into a defective-child-free-world. Of course, it remains a value in a Christian society to teach people how to cope with suffering and handicap. Usually, though, this has been a question of coping with one's own suffering, one's own handicap. Now we have to struggle with such questions as: "Can I impose such suffering on my child? To what extent do I, the parent, share this with my child? Is it just and right?"

If immoral decisions have been made in these areas—and they have—the fact that feminists continue to raise such questions indicates that Christian values continue to be important and that the answers come only through continual dialogue.

The judgment about feminists seems to rise and fall on the issue of abortion. Yet when abortion is made out to be the only or the overriding issue, many women's voices are not heard. Different moral values play an important role in the pro-life, pro-choice feminists. Beverly Wildung Harrison, in *Our Right to Choose* (1983), looked at abortion not from a single focus on the act itself, but in light of the social reality in which women make the decision to have an abortion. Pro-choice feminists want us to consider all the social conditions, many of which force women into abortion: poor education, inadequate pre-natal and post-natal care, poor self-image, inadequate jobs and job opportunities, marital rape, inadequate food, clothing, school opportunities for the children they already have. Many women believe that the rate of abortion would decrease substantially if society worked harder to rid itself of these injustices.

Pro-life women are at their moral best when they stick to the morality of the act of abortion and focus on the moral value of the fetus. They are more effective in their approach when they base their arguments on a natural law ethic and less effective when they try to sway social policy. It seems to me that bishops, by trying to influence social morality through state and Federal legislation, have misplaced the real challenge of the church's wisdom and moral tradition. The church has a position that asks more of its members than the state can, and bishops should use that approach more often.

Women are saying many different things, many of which are contradictory. Issues that caused a flurry a few years ago have disappeared or are not as important. Feminists are criticizing each other, and the truer voices are coming to be heard. . . . The best of the feminists are asking truthful questions, want to work through truthful dialogue and arrive at whatever truthful answers are now possible—not because they are angry, not because they want to win, not because they want to trample on men's feelings, but because they are searching for the truth about themselves as women, so they can relate more lovingly to their neighbor and to God. . . .

Theology as Soul-Craft
Stanley Hauerwas

Theology is a minor practice in the total life of the church, but in times as strange as ours even theologians must try, through our awkward art, to change lives by forming the imagination by faithful speech.[33] Thus, I tell my students that I do not want them to learn "to make up their own minds," since most of them do not have minds worth making up until I have trained them. Rather, by the time I am finished with them, I want them to think just like me.

The strangeness of our times for Christians is apparent in the kind of response a paragraph like the one above elicits. "Who do you think you are to tell anyone else how to live? What gives you that right? You must be some kind of fundamentalist or a fanatic." I am, of course, a fanatic. I want, for example, to convince everyone who calls himself or herself a Christian that being Christian means that one must be nonviolent. In the process I hope to convince many who currently are not Christians to place themselves under the discipline of Christians who are trying to learn how to live peaceably.[34] I find it odd that in our time many people believe we can or should avoid telling one another how to live. From my perspective, that is but a sign of the corruption of our age and why we are in such desperate need of conversion.[35]

A more interesting challenge to my desire to change my readers' lives is that my focus on the imagination and language is insufficient to the task. Surely, being a Christian involves more than learning a language. But what could be more

Stanley Hauerwas, "Positioning: In the Church and University But Not of Either," *Dispatches from the Front: Theological Engagements with the Secular,* pp. 5–28. Copyright 1994, Duke University Press. Reprinted with permission.

important than learning a language and in particular one that, if I am to become a competent speaker, forces me to acknowledge my existence as a creature of a gracious God. That is why one must begin to learn to pray if one is to be a Christian. . . .

That Christians are odd, of course, will not be good news for most American Christians, including the smart ones who may be theologians. To suggest, as I do, that Christians should be suspicious of the moral presuppositions as well as the practices that sustain liberal democracy cannot but appear as rank heresy to most American Christians.[36] Most Christians in America are willing to allow fellow Christians to doubt that God is Trinity, but they would excommunicate anyone who does not believe, as I do not believe, in "human rights."[37] Not surprising, since most Christian theologians spend most of their time trying to show that Christians believe pretty much what anyone believes.

As a result, Christian linguistic practices cannot help but appear epiphenomenal. Why should one worry about Trinity when such language seems to be doing no discernible work? Thus, the agony of liberal Christianity, whose advocates seek to show that Christianity can be made reasonable within the epistic presuppositions of modernity, only to discover, to the extent they are successful, that the very people they were trying to convince could care less. Why should anyone be interested in Christianity if Christians were simply telling them what they already knew on less obscurantist grounds? Robbed of any power by the politics of liberalism, what remains for Christianity is to become another "meaning system." Accordingly, theology is seldom read by Christians and non-Christians alike because it is so damned dull.

By suggesting, therefore, that my task is to change lives, I am attempting to make what Wittgensteinians call a "grammatical point." Christian discourse is not a set of beliefs aimed at making our lives more coherent; rather it is a constitutive set of skills that requires the transformation of the self to rightly see the world. By suggesting that this transformation involves a battle for the imagination, I mean that it is more than simply a matter of "ideas." The Christian imagination resides not in the mind, but rather in the fleshy existence of a body of people who have learned to be with someone as fleshy as those called "mentally handicapped." Such a people have the resources to refuse to accept reality devoid of miracles. . . .

That I do Christian theology in such an unapologetic, radical manner will seem particularly offensive to those with liberal sensibilities.[38] Nonetheless, I hope that these exercises for the imagination may attract some to live as Christians. Living in a morally incoherent culture is a resource for such a task, since many continue, for example, to think that they ought to live honorably or at least strive to live lives of integrity.[39] They have little idea why honor or integrity is a good—or even what each might entail—but they still seem like "good ideas." I am willing, and I hope not dishonestly, to make use of these lingering ideals to suggest how some accounts of honor and integrity draw on Christian practices for their intelligibility. By doing so, I am not suggesting that non-Christians cannot lead lives of honor, but rather I hope to show the difference that Christian practice can make for how honor is understood. Equally, if not more important, is how the virtues of constancy and honor as practiced by Christians are integral to other matters we care about, such as love and politics.

Accounts of the moral life associated with honor, of course, are hierarchical and elitist. I have no wish to deny either characterization. I have little use for the democratization of our moral existence so characteristic of egalitarianism. Indeed, I regard egalitarianism as the opiate of the masses and the source of the politics of envy and influence so characteristic of our lives.[40] The interesting question is not whether hierarchies or elites should exist, but what goods they serve. A skilled sculptor or poet is rightly privileged in good communities because of his or her ability to help us be more than we could otherwise be....

ON THE POLITICS OF LIBERALISM AND THE UNIVERSITY

My relation to liberal politics is complicated, as should be clear by now, because I try to think and write as a Christian. Christian ethics, as a field, began as part of the American progressivist movement which assumed that the subject of Christian ethics in America is America.[41] I do not begin with that assumption, but with the claim that the most determinative political loyalty for Christians is the church. That claim, of course, creates the political problem of how the church is to negotiate the manifold we call the United States of America. I am not particularly interested in the compromised character of most American politicians; I assume the genius of American politics is to produce just such people. The more interesting political question for me is what is required of the church in such a society to produce congregations who require that a ministry exists which has the courage to preach truthfully.[42] ...

That the Christian tradition is intellectually and morally discredited for most people in universities robs Christian and non-Christian alike of resources for understanding our world. One of the difficulties we now confront in the university is the lack of any significant understanding of Christian discourse and practice by many secular intellectuals, some of whom may be Christian. Christianity for too many people simply appears as twenty impossible things to believe before breakfast. They are not to be blamed for such a perception, since intellectually powerful accounts of Christian convictions have not played any significant role in the culture of the university. Indeed, insofar as Christianity, or Judaism, has any compelling presentation, it is usually through the work of novelists and poets who do not bear the burden of "academic respectability." Given what I take to be the character of Christian convictions, I suspect that is the way it should be.

I do not expect any reappreciation of the work of Christian theology in the university in the foreseeable future. The disciplinary character of the knowleges that so dominates the university impedes any serious theological engagement. The loss of social power by Christians means fewer will be attracted to the ministry and/or the even less enticing work of theology. But what a wonderful time to be a Christian and theologian. Since no one expects Christians to make the world safe, since Christians are no longer required to supply the ideologies necessary "to govern," since Christians are not expected to be able to provide philosophical justifications to ensure the way things are or the way things should be, we are free to be Christians. If we make moral and intellectual use—which are of course closely interrelated—of the freedom that God has given us, we may find that we have some interesting things to say because we find our living such a joy. . . .

"BUT YOU ARE SO VIOLENT TO BE A PACIFIST— JUST WHO IN THE HELL ARE YOU?"

The image of withdrawal or retreat is all wrong. The problem is not that Christians, to be faithful, must withdraw. The problem is that Christians, particularly in liberal social orders like that of the United States, have so identified with those orders that they no longer are able to see what difference being Christian makes. I am not trying to force Christians to withdraw but to recognize that they are surrounded. There is no question of withdrawing, as all lines of retreat have been cut off. The interesting questions now are what skills do we as Christians need to learn to survive when surrounded by a culture we helped create but which now threatens to destroy us.

Of course, the image of being surrounded may be far too coherent to describe the situation of Christians. When surrounded, you know who the enemy is and where the battle lines are drawn. Most Christians especially in America, do not even know they are in a war. The "secular" I engage is not "out there" in a world that no longer identifies itself as religious, but it is in the souls of most people, including myself, who continue to identify themselves as Christian.[43]

Much of the battle engaged in this book is with my own troops. In effect, I try to help Christians see the radical challenges they present to a liberal culture, challenges that are intrinsic to their common practices and convictions—for example, that they can pledge fidelity to another person for a lifetime, bring children into a inhospitable world, pray for reconciliation with enemies, live lives of truthfulness and honesty. These dispatches are not being sent to a people safely back behind the lines, but to combatants who have not recognized they are in fact in a war.

From Barth I learned that theology is not just another "discipline" in the university. To be a theologian is to occupy an office, admittedly a lesser office, in the church of Jesus Christ. Accordingly, I am not in service to a state, or a university, but rather I am called to be faithful to a church that is present across time and space. To be in such service is a wonderful and frightening gift, since only God knows how one can be faithful to this most ambiguous calling. At least as a theologian I do not have the burden of being "a thinker"—that is, someone who, philosopher-like, comes up with strong positions that bear the stamp of individual genius.[44] Rather, it is my task to take what I have been given by friends, living and dead, some Christians and some not, to help the church be faithful to the adventure called God's Kingdom.

Yet for me to claim to be a theologian is not unlike my claiming to be a pacifist. I often make the claim to be a pacifist, even though I dislike the term; it seems to suggest a position that is intelligible apart from the cross and resurrection of Christ. Yet I claim the position even at the risk of being misunderstood. To be so identified not only is necessary to begin, but it creates expectations in others whom I trust to help me live nonviolently. I know myself to be filled with violence; by creating expectations in others, I hope they will love me well enough to help me live faithful to the way of life I know to be true. In like manner, I find that to the extent I am a theologian, it is because I have Christian friends whose lives make no sense if the God we worship in Jesus Christ is not God—they force me to try to think faithfully. . . .

Barth-like, (John Howard Yoder) simply begins in *The Politics of Jesus* to train us to read the New Testament with eyes not clouded with the presumption that Jesus cannot be relevant for matters dealing with what we now call social and political ethics.[45] In the process he helps us see that salvation, at least the salvation brought through God's promise to Israel and in Jesus' cross and resurrection, *is* a politics. As he says: "The cross of Calvary was not a difficult family situation, not a frustration of visions of personal fulfillment, a crushing debt or a nagging in-law; it was the political, legally to be expected result of a moral clash with the powers ruling his society."[46]

In this respect, Yoder presents a decisive challenge to the dominance of Reinhold Niebuhr's understanding of the Christian's relation to liberal democracies. The irony of Niebuhr's account of Christian social theory is that in the interest of justifying a "realist" perspective in the name of the Christian understanding of the sinful character of the "human condition," he depoliticized salvation. Because he was intent on justifying the Christian use of violence in the name of politics, Niebuhr, like so many Protestants, provided what is essentially a gnostic account of Christianity.[47] Thus, the cross, for Niebuhr, is a symbol of the tragic character of the human condition and that *knowledge* "saves" us by keeping us "humble."[48]

As one long schooled in a Niebuhrian perspective, I was helped by Yoder to see that the politics accepted in the name of being "responsible" gave lie to the most fundamental Christian convictions. In effect, he forced me to see that the most orthodox Christological or trinitarian affirmations are essentially false when they are embedded in lives and social practices which make it clear that it makes no difference whether Jesus lived, died, or was resurrected.

That Yoder continues to be dismissed by those in the Christian mainstream as "sectarian" appears a bit odd in light of the celebration of Yoder as a "postmodern theologian" by Fredric Jameson in his *Post-Modernism, or, the Cultural Logic of Late Capitalism.* Jameson notes that the central hermeneutic of theological modernism was posed by the anthropomorphism of the narrative character of the historical Jesus. Modern theologians assumed that only intense philosophical effort is capable of turning this character into this or that Christological abstraction. As for the commandments and the ethical doctrine, casuistry has long since settled the matter; they also need no longer be taken literally, and confronted with properly modern forms of injustice, bureaucratic warfare, systemic or economic inequality, and so forth, modern theologians and churchmen can work up persuasive accommodations to the constraints of complex modern societies, and provide excellent reasons for bombing civilian populations or executing criminals which do not disqualify the executors from Christian status.[49]

THE POLITICS OF FORGIVENESS, MEDICINE, AND WAR

It is Yoder who challenges such an accommodation by reminding us that Jesus is a politics....

Forgiveness and reconciliation name the politics of that community called church that makes possible a different way of being in, as well as seeing, the world. There is a danger in focusing on such themes, as generally forgiveness is seen as a "good thing" by most people. Yet I am not interested in forgiveness and reconciliation in general, but in that which is unintelligible if Jesus was not raised from the dead....

SUGGESTIONS FOR FURTHER READING FOR PART 1

Birch, Bruce C. *Let Justice Roll Down: The Old Testament, Ethics, and Christian Life.* Louisville, KY: Westminster/John Knox Press, 1991.

Birch, Bruce, and Larry Rasmussen. *The Bible and Ethics in the Christian Life.* Rev. ed. Minneapolis: Augsburg, 1988.

Boulton, Wayne G., Thomas D. Kennedy, and Allen Verhey, eds. *From Christ to the World: Introductory Readings in Christian Ethics.* Grand Rapids, MI: William B. Eerdmans Publishing Co., 1994.

Chopp, Rebecca S. *The Praxis of Suffering: An Interpretation of Liberation and Political Theologies.* Maryknoll, NY: Orbis, 1986.

Clark, David K., and Robert V. Rakestraw. *Readings in Christian Ethics, Vol I: Theory and Method.* Grand Rapids, MI: Baker Books, 1994.

Daly, Herman E., and John B. Cobb. *For the Common Good.* Boston: Beacon Press, 1990.

Drinan, Robert F. *The Fractured Dream: America's Divisive Moral Choices.* New York: Crossroad/Continuum, 1991.

Ellingsen, Mark. *The Cutting Edge: How Churches Speak on Social Issues.* Grand Rapids, MI: Eerdmans Publishing Co., 1993.

Fowl, Stephen E., and L. Gregory Jones. *Readings in Communion: Scripture and Ethics in Christian Life.* Grand Rapids, MI: Eerdmans, 1991.

Greenawalt, Kent. *Private Conscience and Public Reasons.* New York: Oxford University Press, 1995.

Hamel, Ronald, and Kenneth Himes. *Introduction to Christian Ethics: A Reader.* New York: Paulist Press, 1989.

Hauerwas, Stanley, and William H. Willimon. *Resident Aliens: Life in the Christian Colony.* Nashville: Abingdon Press, 1989.

Jersild, Paul. *Making Moral Decisions: A Christian Approach to Personal and Social Ethics.* Minneapolis: Fortress Press, 1990.

Kaye, Bruce, and Gordon Wenham, eds. *Law, Morality, and the Bible.* Downers Grove, IL: InterVarsity Press, 1978.

Neuhaus, Richard J. *America Against Itself: Moral Vision and the Public Order.* Notre Dame, IN: University of Notre Dame Press, 1992.

Porter, Jean. *The Recovery of Virtue: The Relevance of Aquinas for Christian Ethics.* Louisville, KY: Westminster/John Knox Press, 1990.

Sample, Tex. *U.S. Lifestyles and Mainline Churches.* Louisville, KY: Westminster/John Knox Press, 1990.

Schubeck, Thomas L. *Liberation Ethics: Sources, Models, Norms.* Minneapolis: Fortress Press, 1993.

Siker, Jeffrey. *Scripture and Ethics: Twentieth-Century Portraits.* New York: Oxford University Press, 1996.

Stivers, Robert L., Christine E. Gudorf, Alice Frazer Evans, and Robert A. Evans. *Christian Ethics: A Case Method Approach.* Maryknoll, NY: Orbis Books, 1994.

Thiemann, Ronald F. *Constructing a Public Theology: The Church in a Pluralistic Culture.* Louisville, KY: Westminster/John Knox Press, 1991.

Vacek, Edward Collins. *Love, Human and Divine: The Heart of Christian Ethics.* Washington, D.C.: Georgetown University Press, 1994.

Wallis, Jim. *The Soul of Politics: A Practical and Prophetic Vision for Change.* Maryknoll, NY: Orbis Books, 1994.

Wallis, Jim. *Who Speaks for God?: An Alternative to the Religious Right.* New York: Delacorte Press, 1996.

Wogaman, J. Philip. *Christian Moral Judgment.* Louisville, KY: Westminster/John Knox Press, 1989.

Wogaman, J. Philip, and Douglas M. Strong, eds. *Readings in Christian Ethics: A Historical Sourcebook.* Louisville, KY: Westminster/John Knox Press, 1996.

PART 2

The Christian and Sexual Ethics

Chapter 3

CHRISTIAN PERSPECTIVES ON SEXUAL INTIMACY, COMMITMENT, AND PLEASURE

During the past few decades, there has been an extensive reevaluation of Christian attitudes toward sexuality. Traditional perspectives have been challenged as being "antisexual," and considerable reeducating has occurred in developing a more positive attitude toward one's bodily self. This negative orientation toward sexuality is often traced to certain passages from the letters of Saint Paul or to the writings of Saint Augustine in the fifth century, both of whom had a profound influence in shaping Christian anthropology. The negativism in the tradition is epitomized by the fact that the two words "sex" and "sin" have been so closely united in our thinking that they are often regarded as synonymous.

Theologians generally agree that the "culprit" in this situation is the prevailing notion that humans are divided beings, consisting of a spiritual part (the mind or soul) and a physical part (the body). The spiritual part has been identified with the essence of the human person, which bears the image of God and which is therefore good. The body, on the other hand, has been seen as the physical "garment" in which the self is clothed, and from which the "evils" of desire and passion emerge. Against this dualistic view, Christian writers today are stressing the fact that the human being is a psychosomatic unity, a bodily self who cannot be divided without distortion. Moreover, if our *whole* being is essential to who we are as creatures of God, then we have reason to thank God for our physical as well as our spiritual being. It follows that our sexuality is essential to our being, to be celebrated as God's gift rather than mortified as an instrument of the devil.

These insights have had a salutary impact on current Christian anthropology and on the larger culture, but they have also encouraged a certain naivete or excessive optimism concerning our sexual selves. To "celebrate" our sexuality became the new imperative, with the accent on Christian freedom and the goodness of our sexuality encouraging a more open attitude toward sexual expression and experimentation. We have been embarrassed by the negativism in our tradition and have ridden with a vengeance the pendulum swing of reaction. At the same time, there have always been those who have sought a more balanced response, informed by both the positive affirmation of sexuality as God's gift and our capacity for the sexual exploitation of each other. The Christian doctrines of creation and fall express the fact that our sexuality is ambiguous; as sexual beings, we can establish beautiful relationships of mutual interdependence and support, but we can also reduce another person to an extension of ourselves.

Some contemporary Christians challenge the Church's traditional sexual ethic. Those particularly impressed with the potential goodness of sexuality are inclined to see restrictions—limiting sexual relations to heterosexual marriage and linking them inseparably to procreation, for example—as expressions of unwarranted fear and negativism. They argue that it is the quality of the relationship that will determine whether two persons are related sexually in a life-enhancing or destructive way. This is the argument of Jean Ponder Soto, who explores what spiritual meanings and moral implications might be associated with conjugal pleasures when they are disconnected from reproduction. Marvin Ellison also focuses on the substance rather than the form of sexual relationships, both within and outside of marriage.

Ellison's concern about the potential for injustice between sexual partners stems from his insights into the way patriarchalism and gender inequity structure sexual relationships in our culture. This leads him to call for the development of a new sexual ethic marked by "common decency."

Karen Lebacqz argues that women's experience of these links between sexuality and violence necessitate this development of a new sexual ethic under a different rubric. Since their very survival is at stake, heterosexual women must explore what it means for them to love an "enemy."

Elizabeth McAlister examines the question of the relationship between the form and substance of sexual relationships. She argues that it is precisely the marriage that enables sexual activity to be truly humanizing. Though it does not guarantee that relationships will be marked by either justice or love, she argues that apart from such a commitment, lovers will inevitably do violence—emotional if not physical—to each other and the wider community. Many Christians would not only disagree with some or all of the authors in this chapter, but would be greatly disturbed by what they are saying. For many, there is no question that Scripture expects abstinence before marriage and fidelity in marriage, with no questions asked. Many others would affirm those ideals, but are uneasy with the authoritarian or absolutist fashion in which they have been applied. The authors in this chapter have their own understandings about what it means to be faithful to the Christian tradition, yet they are concerned with finding a stance that also fully engages and speaks to the contemporary mindset. What does the current social construction of sexuality demand of Christians who would bring the wisdom of their tradition into fruitful conversation with the modern world?

The Church and Marriage:
Looking for a New Ethic
Jean Ponder Soto

During my lifetime, my own Roman Catholic tradition has undergone a major shift in its official thinking on marriage. The Second Vatican Council, in its document on *The Church in the Modern World,* proclaimed that there are two purposes in marriage: (1) the procreation and education of children, and (2) the mutual love and support of the spouses. The document broke with centuries-old teaching by refusing to prioritize these two purposes. Previously, the Roman church taught that the begetting of children is the primary end of marriage.

THE STAYING POWER OF PATRIARCHY

This understanding of marriage reflected the Roman society from which it sprang. In the Greco-Roman world, marriage and the begetting of children were considered a duty one owed to the Roman state. The survival of society depended upon the fertility of families. In the best of times, the population barely managed to replace itself. Further, the patriarchal family structure was the basic unit of that society. Men married (1) to establish a family, (2) to produce heirs and carry on the family name and fortune, and (3) to provide citizens to maintain the Roman state. In those early centuries, the church saw marriage as an almost entirely civil matter, which indeed it was.

After the barbarians invaded and the Roman empire slowly crumbled, the church took on the functions of the civil marriage courts. In time, the institution of marriage accumulated more church laws than anything else. Church law on marriage dealt with the rights and duties of the parties and with the conditions of validity of the marriage; church law treated marriage as a contract and modeled itself on civil contract law. Marriage was not considered a sacrament in the Roman church until the 12th century. There was little concern with the intersubjective relational aspects of marriage.

The Christian church inherited a body/spirit dualism and a Stoic philosophy that devalued the body, seeking the strictest possible control of it and of sexual activity. Augustine of Hippo set the tone for centuries when he taught that sexual intercourse was always sinful—even in marriage—because of the element of pleasure in it. He believed that sexual intercourse should take place within marriage only to conceive children: it was otherwise permissible (again,

From "The Church and Marriage: Looking for a New Ethic," by Jean Ponder Soto, in *The Witness,* December 1995, pp. 16–19. Reprinted by permission of *The Witness,* 7000 Michigan Avenue, Detroit, MI 48210.

within marriage) only when necessary to quiet the fires of concupiscence or to prevent a greater sin. When the Roman church reacted to the Protestant Reformation at the Council of Trent, it proclaimed again that celibacy was a state more perfect in virtue and closer to God than the married state. Trent declared that anyone saying otherwise should be declared *anathema*.[1]

Before the declarations of Vatican II, the "good" marriage was one that had been validly contracted by a baptized couple who agreed to have children (or to be open to that possibility) and who would remain united to each other until death.

NEW PERSPECTIVES

The early part of this century brought with it a number of new thinkers who emphasized the subjective aspects of marriage and the relationship between the spouses. One writer, Herbert Doms, a German priest, was especially influential. He believed and wrote that sexual activity in a marriage served chiefly to foster and express the mutual love between the spouses. This thinking was, at first, condemned by the Roman church—but was later incorporated, with qualifications, into the Second Vatican Council's teaching on marriage.

Today the sexual love of spouses is spoken of in a positive light—as a reflection of divine love and as caught up in divine love—but in the Roman church it is still inseparably linked to the procreation of children. The Roman church has maintained an official prohibition against "artificial" means of birth control and permits only the use of periodic abstinence as a means of regulating births. The Anglican Lambeth Conference had already moved past this stance and allowed birth control in some situations by 1930.

The reality, however, is that Roman Catholic women in the western world use artificial birth control. For the first time in human history, reliable and inexpensive means to prevent conception are widely available and used. What is not yet worked out is a solid, thoughtful, and comprehensive Christian vision of conjugal sexuality.

What is a vision of marital sex unlinked from the intent to bear children? The next important step is to hear from married couples themselves on the role of conjugal sexuality in their lives. Nothing can substitute for their lived experience. Couples can tell us of the concrete patterns of development within their marriage and their sexual expression. This information needs to be used to enrich a renewed theology of marriage.

Sexual intimacy "unlinked" from procreation forces a rethinking. If we agree—and not all would—that it is good, within a marriage, to unlink the intent to procreate children from the intent to engage in sexual intimacy for its own sake, then the question can arise about the role of divine mystery in such a sexual union: "What is God doing when a couple makes love?" The short answer is that God is making love too. One can say that God permits lovemaking, or gives lovemaking as a gift, or that sexual love is a reflection of God's love. But it is another matter, a further step, to say that God is present and active in sexual intimacy.

A spirituality of conjugal intimacy could call upon the Christian conviction that in Christ we become new creations, and that the Spirit is given so that we are co-actors with Christ; we live, suffer, rejoice, pray, and love joined to the Risen Christ. The life of married love—and its sexual expression—is not only a mirror of God's love, it is the very activity of the Trinity that lives in the marital relationship. The Vatican II document describes marital love as "caught up into divine love." Conjugal love is one of the best instances we Christians have of what the Incarnation means.

SEXUAL INTIMACY AS AESTHETIC

Like fine art, lovemaking can be undertaken for its own sake. Its value is intrinsic. The spouses, as artists, "make" love. With God, they become co-creators of their corner of the universe.

Conjugal love, like the dance, is ecstatic. The original context and meaning of *ecstatic* is "to be transported beyond oneself into the presence of God." Dance and lovemaking create a sacred space and arouse the ecstasy that pierces the boundary between the human and the divine.

Conjugal love is like an icon. Lover and beloved, by their touches and caresses, reveal and call forth the divine presence which each one possesses.

Christine Gudorf, in *Body, Sex & Pleasure: Reconstructing Christian Sexual Ethics,* makes a case for mutual pleasure as the purpose of marital sexual love. Her work is a corrective to the tendency to spiritualize marital sex excessively. It also aims at ending church "demonization" of pleasure. Far from being something to despise or fear, Gudorf notes that experiences of pleasure are necessary for human growth and wholeness.[2]

The notion of sexual union as an art work yields an ethic—just as the notion of procreation as the chief purpose of sexual union did. The ability to reveal God's love to one another, the gift of mutual self-donation, demands that the equal dignity of each spouse be recognized. The lovers in the *Song of Songs* are an example:

"The mutuality of their delight in one another, the totality of their self-giving, and the finality of the love itself, which seems in no way oriented toward the producing of children or the continuation of the tribe, are a celebration of equality between the man and the woman."[3]

Respect and appreciation, gratitude and awe—and all of the attitudes we associate as fitting in the presence of the holy—will also characterize sexual expression.

If procreation of children is no longer the primary end of sexual intercourse in marriage, the prohibition of same-sex unions seems superfluous. Same-sex relationships possess the same capacity for love as do heterosexual romances. In fact, aspects of the mutuality and equality operative in gay and lesbian couples at their best could well be a model for heterosexual couples that still labor under a dominant/submissive model.

Gudorf points out that a purpose of mutual pleasure in sexual intimacy creates an ethic that calls for sexual union to be free from any kind of violence or coercion, and requires the knowledge and circumstances necessary to give one another pleasure. Judith Wallerstein's *The Good Marriage: How & Why Love Lasts* (May 1995), the first in-depth study of successful long-term marriages, shows that sexual intimacy is central, but that other demands tend to crowd it out.[4] The time and place, then, for conjugal love must become sacred time and space and be protected. It is time that has the character of the Sabbath.

A couple's intimate life together needs the seasoning of time in order to grow in beauty and depth and strength.

When sexual expression truly is lovemaking, it is a journey into vulnerability. It is an aesthetic and ascetic discipline to begin the journey again and again with the same person. This is because the ability to disguise one's nakedness is ended by that repetition. Over time, the journey can lead from a desire to hide or protect oneself to the discovery of new dimensions in self and other.

A terrible tenderness can be found behind the layers that peel away. It is paradoxical, amazingly powerful, and almost too frightening; it reminds us of dying and rising.

Such a vision of married sexual love is one that lays full claims on the Incarnation. The making of an act of love is understood as a joint endeavor of the spouses and God. It is love—God's love and the spouses' love—that is revealed and expressed.

Through bodily pleasure, the Spirit touches and is touched. Such love can be transforming: for as the couple grow in their love for each other and in their recognition of the source of their love, they are changed. "God," the first letter of John tells us, "has loved us first." We respond in kind—loving spouse, and self, and God, with God's own love.

Common Decency: A New Christian Sexual Ethics
Marvin M. Ellison

It should come as no surprise to [C&C] readers that the church has lost its credibility where sex is concerned. It is also clear by now that if the church is going to regain any credibility, it has to take two immediate steps. It needs to acknowledge that a significant gap exists between official church teaching on sex and most people's lives, and it needs to clarify its theological and ethical mandate, especially where sexuality is concerned.

Even if these steps are taken, new pronouncements will amount to little if the church does not also become serious about developing an alternative sexual ethics—one that takes account of the changes of the last 25 years and gives concrete guidance for thinking about sex in everyday life.

Many of the most significant articles in [C&C] over the last few years have critiqued traditional teaching on sex and set forth a context and framework for a new sexual ethic. That crucial work now needs to be augmented by a willingness to talk about what the new context implies for "real life." This article takes first steps in that direction by presenting in capsule form a new context for sexual ethics and then going on to propose an ethic of common decency.

THE CONTEXT FOR SEXUAL ETHICS

- Not heterosexuality, not marriage, but responsibility should become morally normative for a contemporary Christian sexual ethics. The church's traditional ethic—well represented by the phrase "celibacy in singleness, fidelity in marriage"—is woefully inadequate. It denies the rich diversity of sexual experiences and relationships that bear moral substance, and it establishes uncritically the exclusive claim of heterosexual marriage to moral propriety and sexual maturity. It focuses on the form rather than the substance of sexual relations—asking about who does what with whom under what circumstances, instead of asking about the quality of honesty, care, and respect in sexual relationships.

  The church's lack of moral leadership on sex has in fact infantilized people, disempowering them to make responsible sexual choices. By defining a whole range of sexual experiences as sinful, the church has promoted guilt rather than sexual maturity; it has not helped people learn how to accept what they need, give and receive sexual pleasure freely, and direct their lives in order to enhance their own and others' joy and self-respect. If the church is going to be helpful here, it has to be willing to undertake a major shift in its ethical sensibilities.

- Loyalty to the God "of grace and glory" is the basis of the church's theological and ethical mandate to seek justice passionately, including sexual justice. In accepting this mandate, the church agrees to become a gracious place—a place of hospitality and safety, a kind of "unoccupied territory" where persons can experience and delight in loving and being loved.

  If it is going to become a gracious place, the church must honor the goodness of sex and the diversity of sexual experience; it must also transform its deep fear of sex and the body and, at the same time, admit its preoccupation, bordering on fixation, with both.

Christians have had big problems gaining a balanced perspective on sex. Doing so might enable us to "come out" and mature as *sexual persons,* to own that erotic power is intrinsic to our humanness, that it often (but *not* always) deeply enriches our connectedness to self, others, and God, and that in and of itself it is the source neither of our salvation nor of our damnation.

Accepting its mandate, the church also agrees to stand boldly with those afflicted by sexual injustice and oppression and to advocate their cause as its own.

Christians' integrity as a people of faith depends on our standing with and demonstrating genuine solidarity with those who suffer sexual oppression and injustice—whether they be gay men and lesbians, or sexually abused children and women. Only from real-life solidarity will we come to appreciate how much our lives are diminished by gender and sexual injustice, as well as by racism and economic injustice. If the church is going to help people critically assess their cultural context and the social forces that shape and misshape human sexuality, personally and corporately, it is also going to have to listen and learn, especially from those calling for a fundamental reconstruction of sexuality and sexual ethics.

■ All societies organize erotic life. Human sexuality is never simply a matter of "what comes naturally"; it is culturally encoded, given a distinctive shape that reflects certain values and social preoccupations.

Our own culture is patriarchal—built on gender inequality and the legitimacy of men's control over women, children, and men of lesser power. The gender of the person with whom we have sex is the standard used to determine whether persons are normal or abnormal. Beyond that, permission is granted only for sex between a man and a woman within the institution of a male-dominant marriage. More reluctantly, permission is given to sexually active couples on their way to marriage. At the same time, men are encouraged to gain sexual access to any woman, especially any woman not "possessed" or controlled by another man.

Under patriarchy, men are socialized to exercise power over others and to feel uncomfortable when they do not. Staying in control means controlling feelings and remaining "manly," detached and "rational." Women are socialized to accept dependency, emotionality, and powerlessness. Always operating within such differentials (never transcending them), patriarchal sex depends on a dynamic of conquest and surrender, of winning control over or of being placed under someone else's control. "Opposites attract." Inequality is sexy.

We learn, in other words, to accept sexism as natural *in our bodies,* as well as in our psyches, to believe that male gender superiority feels good and is beneficial to men and women alike. Patriarchal sex makes gender injustice appear pleasurable. Heterosexism complicates matters even more. It reinforces sexism by pressuring people to play their "proper" sex-stereotyped gender roles and to feel pain, fear, and guilt if they do

not. It enforces sexism by oppressing, if not punishing, sexual noncon-
formists. Heterosexism and homophobia operate to maintain gender injustice in our churches and throughout this society.

- The moral challenge before the church, therefore, is this: It must choose
between perpetuating a patriarchal ethic of sexual control and gender
oppression or pledging its commitment to an ethic of gender justice, of
mutuality between women and men, and of respect for sexual diversity.
Naming the sexual problematic accurately is a fundamental theological
and ethical task. The sexual problem the church must critique and challenge lies not in people, but rather in prevailing social, cultural, and ecclesial arrangements which stigmatize and devalue self-respecting persons who deviate from the sexist and heterosexist norm. Unless we
acknowledge this distortion of human equality and intimacy by sexism
and heterosexism, we will remain captive to a patriarchal culture's values
and loyalties.

   Therefore, we must not shy away from the following declaration: *Our
problem is not homosexuality or non-marital sex but conformity to the
unjust norm of compulsory heterosexuality and gender inequality.
This unjust norm must be altered, not those who question it.* What is
shaking the very foundations of church and society is the open call to
struggle for a nonsexist moral order in the family and throughout our
public institutions, including the church.

AN ETHIC OF COMMON DECENCY

Articulating a normative vision of sexual justice, applied inclusively regardless
of gender, sexual orientation, and marital status, has implications, most of them
controversial. The church can't avoid dealing with them as it begins to articulate an ethic of sexual empowerment. Such an ethic might best be termed an
ethic of common decency. It would look something like this:

   Not marriage, not heterosexuality (not homosexuality, for that matter), but
justice in sexual relationships is morally normative for Christians. Justice includes the moral obligation to promote one another's common decency and to
honor our need for intimacy and affection. Our sexuality is who—and how—we
experience this quite remarkable emotional, cognitive, physical, and spiritual
yearning for communion with others, with the natural world, and with God.
Sexual desire and passion ennoble our lives.

   Only by unabashedly reclaiming sex as intrinsic to Christian spirituality can
we begin to recapture a more earthy, sensuous, and concrete awareness that we
are created and destined to be lovers. We are invited to relish receiving and giving sexual pleasure. Affirmation and care are expressed with vitality and integrity
whenever we honor our capacity to touch and be touched with tenderness and
respect for our common dignity. Literally "staying in touch"—with our senses,
with one another, with whatever moves us in delight, horror, or curiosity—is an
open-ended sexual and spiritual project, full of surprises and challenges.

From a justice perspective, it is entirely fitting not to grant special status or moral privilege to heterosexual marriage, but rather to celebrate *all* sexual relations of moral substance whenever they deepen human intimacy and love. Marriage retains value and meaning not because it serves as a "license for sex" or a declaration of ownership and possession, but because it offers *one possible* framework of accountability and a relatively stable, secure place in which to form durable bonds of devotion, affection, and intimacy. Marriages should also be expected to strengthen persons to deepen ties of affection and friendship beyond, as well as within, the primary relation, rather than fostering control and dependency.

Some marriages may make room for additional sexual partners while others will thrive only by maintaining genital sexual exclusivity. Although justice requires relational fidelity—honoring and responding fairly to the demands of a relationship—the precise requirements for maintaining faithfulness cannot be predetermined in any formal fashion. Rather, the concrete "terms of endearment" can be detected and refined only as a particular relationship develops. For this reason, the most likely violation of the covenant bond will not be "outside" sex per se or collateral friendships, but the refusal to act in good faith, to remain mutually accountable, and to renegotiate the relations as needs and desires change.

Obviously, what I call "just" marriages require a high degree of moral responsibility and mutual commitment—not to mention a willingness to face the truth. Equally obviously, the right to participate in and receive community support for an enduring, formalized sexual partnership should be available to same-sex couples as well as to heterosexuals. For both alike, the question remains: When is a marriage properly "consummated," and how does one know that?

In this day and age, sexual activity alone does not mark the establishment of a marriage or authentic sexual friendship, nor should it. If sex does not "make" a marriage, however, neither does a church ceremony nor legalizing action by the state. As William Countryman has suggested in *Dirt, Greed, and Sex: Sexual Ethics in the New Testament and Their Implications for Today*, since the church does not constitute marriages but only offers its blessing, we need to clarify appropriate ethical criteria for knowing when a marriage has taken place.

Marriages "happen" only as persons committed wholeheartedly to empowering each other as genuine equals experience "mutual benefit arising from mutual devotion and affection." For this reason, as Countryman wisely notes, at least some divorces may signal less an "end to a marriage" than the public announcement that no genuine marriage has ever taken place. Therefore, in order to mark the moral significance, as well as the riskiness, of marriage as a sustained moral commitment, the church should be more discriminating about which relationships to bless. As Countryman notes, the church "would perhaps be better advised not to solemnize marriages at the inception of the relationship itself, but to wait a period of some years before adding its blessing." Then, at last, the church might get it right: Neither sexist nor heterosexist unions are "made in heaven."

AMONG AND WITHIN

An ethic of common decency will *celebrate the plurality* of intimacy needs and | ⌐ 2⟩
also *respect differences.* It will support persons in exploring their own sexuality
with tenderness and joy while deepening their respect for the sexualities of
others. This appreciation of diversity is essential because difference rather than
uniformity, and change rather than stasis, mark human sexuality as well as our
lives more generally—not only *among* persons and groups, but also *within* a
person's life.

Thanks largely to the feminist and gay and lesbian liberation movements,
few of us can now hold to rigid notions of gender. We have not only been challenged to stretch the boundaries of traditional gender roles, but many of
us have discovered new, often unexpected possibilities. For example, many
women report the delight of learning how to bring themselves to orgasm, thus
shattering the myth of the frigid, nonorgasmic female dependent on the male
for sexual climax; and some heterosexuals have found themselves attracted to
people of the same sex. The lesbian and gay communities include countless
people who have lived formerly (and contentedly) as self-identified heterosexuals. Our dominant sexual categories, in other words, simply do not do justice to
the realities and complexities of our lives. They also distract us from attending
to what actually matters to us as sexual and spiritual persons.

Living comfortably with change and ambiguity requires maturity and the
willingness to delight in difference and novelty. It also requires a measure of
confidence in our collective ability to discern meaningful moral distinctions, as
well as make morally responsible choices. The church has an important responsibility here to educate us about this "real" world of sexual diversity and, in particular, to facilitate the expansion of our moral imaginations.

No resource is more important to our common well-being than our capacity to imagine a radically different world. We also need the simple, yet morally
urgent awareness that not everyone lives and struggles as we do. To be able to
imagine the actual life-conditions of other people—whether the other is
"other" by gender, sexual orientation, race, class, culture, age, or physical or
mental condition—is indispensable to doing justice. The church serves us well
only when it encourages critiques of the present "frozen horizon" and stirs up a
more imaginative—and accurate—construal of the richly diverse human and,
therefore, sexual community.

TOWARD A MORAL PERSPECTIVE

3⟩

An ethic of common decency will encourage persons to *learn from failure.* It
will appreciate that failure is not the end of possibility and that people often
gain moral perspective by failing and then learning how to go on. An ethic of
grace is not an excuse for irresponsibility; rather, it welcomes and extends to
self and others, over the course of our whole lifetimes, the possibility of new
beginnings, of recovering from ill-considered choices or painful experiences,
and of retaining a sense of oneself as a responsible person whose task is not to

achieve perfection, but to "do the best one can" in light of real limits and sometimes forced options.

For example, attempts to prevent teenage pregnancy by prohibiting sexual experimentation or by instilling guilt and shame about sex are both inappropriate and counterproductive to young people's developing moral discernment and decision-making skills. Teenagers, too, need an ethic of empowerment rather than control. They need access to accurate, reliable information about human sexuality, encouragement to explore their own values and needs in a nonjudgmental and supportive environment, and recognition of their self-worth and ability to make genuinely life-enhancing decisions, as well as their fortitude to deal with the consequences of their choices.

For persons of all ages, becoming more responsible about sexuality includes learning how to assert one's own desires and needs while respecting others' integrity. It also means sharing insights, skills, and quandaries with others and, above all, asking for help. Breaking the silences around sex not only dispels myths and misinformation but also encourages us to ask critical questions and bolster one another in not conforming to unjust cultural norms and practices.

An ethic of common decency will not condemn out of hand any sexual relation displaying equality and mutual respect. *What is ruled out*, from the start, *are relations in which persons are abused, exploited, and violated.* Therefore, we must be empowered to protect ourselves, among other things, from abuse and exploitation, from uninvited touch and coercive sex, from disease and unintentional pregnancy. We must also be able to hold perpetrators of violence accountable and to insist that they alter their behavior, as well as make appropriate amends to those they have harmed. At the same time, we will need to challenge social structures that breed violence.

An adequate sexual ethic will do more than insist that "no harm be done." More importantly, it will serve to *strengthen people's well-being and self-respect.* Good sex is good because it not only touches our senses powerfully, but also enhances our self-worth and our desire to connect more justly with others. Sex is not something one "does" to another person or "has happen" to oneself. Rather, sexual intimacy is a mutual process of feeling with and connecting as whole persons. In having sex with someone, we don't "lose" ourselves as much as we relocate ourselves in the inbetweenness of self and other, as we receive and give affection, energy, and passion.

Such respect and pleasure can teach us how wrong it is to regard any and all self-interest as somehow morally tainted. As lovers and friends, we can be rightly interested in our *mutual* enjoyment and well-being. Being interested in others does not detract from but complements our self-interest, and vice versa. What harms or diminishes another can never be good for me. Positively stated, whatever enhances your well-being deepens the quality of my life as well. In a culture that has confused love with controlling others (or with giving over power to another), the church should educate each of us to know that we can connect with others only to the extent that we also stay genuinely present to ourselves, aware of our needs and feelings, and mindful of our obligation to honor ourselves, as well as the other person.

Finally, an ethic of common decency will *raise, not lower our moral ex-*
pectations. It will teach us how to demand of ourselves (and of others) what
we deserve: to be whole persons to each other and to be deeply, respectfully
loved.

GOOD EROTICISM

A gracious, liberating church will teach us to claim our right to a pleasurable
and good eroticism. It *may* also impassion us to invest ourselves in creating a
more just and equitable church and world. Desire for pleasure can authentically
include a desire for community and for a more ethical world. Contrary to many
voices inside and outside the church, sex and desire are not necessarily dangerous, selfish, or self-indulgent. Rather, erotic power can be an indispensable spiritual resource for engaging joyfully in creating justice.

And Christian spirituality *without* erotic passion is lifeless and cold. It is
also boring. More tellingly, the pervasive fear of sex and of strong passion, so
rampant in our churches, is deeply implicated in the difficulty many religious
people have in sustaining their passion for social justice.

Sooner or later, the church must face the conflict between a patriarchal and
a liberating paradigm of Christian spirituality and sexuality. Passionately challenging sexism and heterosexism is the necessary avenue to reclaiming an erot-
ically powerful, nonexploitative sexuality. And because justice lies at the heart
of any Christian spirituality worth having, we may stumble on a pathway to spiritual renewal as well.

Love Your Enemy: Sex, Power
and Christian Ethics
Karen Lebacqz

Dear Abby: A friend of mine was picked up and arrested for raping a 24-year-old
woman he had dated twice. He had sex with her the first time he took her out.
He said she was easy. The second time . . . she gave him the high-and-mighty act
and refused to have sex with him. He got angry, and I guess you could say he
overpowered her. Now he's got a rape charge against him which I don't think
is fair. It seems to me that if she was willing to have sex with him on the first
date, there is no way she could be raped by him after that. Am I right or
wrong?—A Friend of His[5]

From Karen Lebacqz, "Love Your Enemy: Sex, Power and Christian Ethics," *The Annual of the
Society of Christian Ethics* (1990). Reprinted with permission of Georgetown University Press.

This letter to "Dear Abby" highlights two problems. First, a young man has "overpowered" his date, forcing sexual contact on her. Second, the "friend" who writes this query is confused about whether such forced sex constitutes rape or whether it simply constitutes sex.

These two problems represent two dimensions of sexuality and violence in women's experience. First, violence in the sexual arena is a commonplace occurrence. Women are raped and experience forced sex with considerable frequency. Second, "normal" patterns of male-female sexual relating in this culture are defined by patterns of male dominance over women. Hence, "our earliest socialization," argues Marie Fortune, "teaches us to confuse sexual activity with sexual violence."[6]

In this essay I argue that an adequate Christian sexual ethic must attend to the realities of the links between violence and sexuality in the experiences of women. It must attend to male power and to the eroticizing of domination in this culture. Because domination is eroticized, and because violence and sexuality are linked in the experiences of women, the search for loving heterosexual intimacy is for many women an exercise in irony: women must seek intimacy precisely in an arena that is culturally and experientially unsafe, fraught with sexual violence and power struggles.

Typical approaches to sexual ethics are therefore inadequate because they presume an equality, intimacy, and safety that does not exist for women. Rather, heterosexual women need to operate out of a "hermeneutic of suspicion" that does not ignore the role conditioning or status of men and women in this culture. I will use the term "enemy" as a role-relational term to highlight the need to be attentive to the dangers built into heterosexual sexuality. The attempt to form a heterosexual relationship can then be seen as an exercise in "loving your enemy." From African-American reflections on living with the enemy, I then draw two norms for a heterosexual ethic: forgiveness and survival.

WOMEN'S EXPERIENCE: SEXUALITY AND VIOLENCE

Statistics on rape are notoriously unreliable, but most observers now agree that a conservative estimate suggests that at least one out of three women will be raped or will be the victim of attempted rape in her lifetime.[7] Rape and fear of rape are realities for many if not most women. Violence is directly linked with sexuality in the experience of many women.

What is particularly troubling is the *context* in which rape occurs. Popular images of the rapist perpetuate the myth that rape is an attack by a stranger. Indeed, the myth that rape is only committed by strangers may encourage men to attack the women with whom they are intimate, since—like the "friend" from "Dear Abby"—they do not believe that they can be charged with rape for forcing sexual intercourse on someone they know.

Rape is not committed only by strangers. In a study of nearly one thousand women, Diana Russell found that only 11 percent had been raped (or had been the victims of attempted rape) by strangers, while 12 percent had been raped by "dates," 14 percent by "acquaintances," and 14 percent by their husbands.[8] Thus, while roughly one woman in ten had been attacked by a stranger, more than one woman in three had been attacked by someone she knew. Rape or attempted rape does not happen just between strangers. It happens in intimate contexts, and in those intimate contexts it happens to more than one third of women. In a study of six thousand college students, 84 percent of the women who reported being attacked knew their attackers, and more than 50 percent of the rapes occurred on dates.[9] Moreover, these rapes are often the most violent: Menachem Amir found that the closer the relationship between the attacker and the victim, the greater was the use of physical force; neighbors and acquaintances were the most likely to engage in brutal rape.[10] Thus, not only are women not safe on the streets, they are not safe in presumably "intimate" contexts with trusted friends, neighbors, acquaintances, and even spouses.

The picture is even more complicated if we look not at the *number of women* who experience rape or attempted rape but at the *number of attacks,* the picture changes dramatically. Of the total number of rapes reported by Diana Russell, *wife rape accounted for 38 percent of all attacks.* Nearly two fifths of rape crimes are perpetrated within the presumed intimacy of heterosexual marriage.[11] Thus, it is not only in *public* places that women must fear for our safety: the nuclear, heterosexual family is not a "safe space" for many women. Moreover, while violent rape by a stranger is something that most women will not experience more than once in their lives, violent rape by a spouse is clearly a repeated crime. Some women live with the daily threat of a repeated experience of rape within the most "intimate" of contexts: marriage.

The net result is that sexuality and violence are linked in the experience, memory,[12] and anticipation of many women. Those who have experienced rape or who live with a realistic appraisal of it as a constant threat may eventually come to live with "a fear of men which pervades all of life."[13] Beverly Harrison charges that "a treatment of any moral problem is inadequate if it fails to analyze the morality of a given act in a way that represents the concrete experience of the agent who faces a decision with respect to that act."[14] If the concrete experience of so many women facing the realities of heterosexual sexuality is an experience of violence and fear, then any adequate Christian sexual ethic must account for the realities of rape, violence and fear in women's lives.[15] Heterosexual women must formulate our sexual ethics within the context of understanding the ironies of searching for intimacy in an unsafe environment.

EROTICIZING DOMINANCE: THE SOCIAL CONSTRUCTION OF SEXUALITY

The problem is not just that rape occurs or that women experience violence and fear in the arena of sexuality. A treatment of any moral problem must not only represent the concrete experience of the agent(s) involved, but must also *understand that experience in its social construction.*[16]

The problem is not just that a man raped his twenty-four-year-old date, though this is serious enough. The problem is not only that rape is common, though it is. The problem is that the rapist's friend, like many others in this culture, does not think that what happened was rape and does not understand the difference between sexual violence and ordinary heterosexual sexuality.[17] The "friend" who writes to "Dear Abby" is not alone. Of the college women whose experiences of attack fit the legal definition of rape, 73 percent did not call it rape because they knew the attacker. Only 1 percent of the men involved were willing to admit that they had raped a woman. In another survey, over 50 percent of male teenagers and nearly 50 percent of female teenagers deemed it acceptable for a teenage boy to force sexual contact on a girl if he had dated her several times or if she said she was willing to have sex and then changed her mind.[18] Thus, in circumstances similar to those reported to "Dear Abby," a large number of young people would not consider forced sex to constitute rape.

Nor is it only teenagers who think it acceptable for men to force sexual contact on women. In another study, nearly 60 percent of "normal" American men said that if they could get away with it, they would force a woman to "commit sexual acts against her will." When the vague phrase "commit acts against her will" was changed to the more specific term "rape," 20 percent still said they would do it if they could get away with it.[19]

In fact, men *do* get away with rape. Forcible rape has a lower conviction rate than any other crime listed in the Uniform Crime Reports.[20] A few years ago, a jury acquitted a man of the charge of rape even though the woman's jaw was fractured in two places as a result of her resistance; the acquittal rested on the finding that "there may have been sexual relations on previous occasions."[21] The confusion as to whether it is possible to rape a woman once she has consented to sexual relations therefore seems to be reflected in the law.[22] Given the attitude "I would do it if I could get away with it" and the fact that people do get away with it, it is no wonder that one out of three women will be raped or will be the victim of attempted rape.

Thus, violence has been structured into the system itself, structured into the very ways that we experience and think about heterosexual activity. Sexuality is not a mere "biological" phenomenon. It is socially constructed.[23] Sexual arousal may follow biological patterns, but *what* we find sexually arousing is culturally influenced and socially constructed. In short, there is a social dimension to even this most "intimate" of experiences, and in this culture sexuality, imbalances of power, and violence are linked. As Marie Fortune so pointedly puts it, "the tendency of this society to equate or confuse sexual activity with sexual violence is a predominant reality in our socialization, attitudes, beliefs, and behavior."[24] Thus, it is not only the actual experiences of violence and fear that we must address in order to have an adequate sexual ethic. We must also address the social construction of sexuality that creates the climate of violence and fear that permeates women's lives and confuses sexuality and violence.

Why is sexuality linked with violence in our socialization and experience? *The social construction of heterosexual sexuality in this culture has been*

largely based on patterns of dominance and submission in which men are ✓
expected to be dominant and women are expected to be submissive. Men are
expected to disregard women's protests and overcome their resistance. When a
man "overpowers" a woman, is he raping her or is he simply being a man in
both his eyes and hers?

Social domination is linked to cultural patterns in which men in general
have more power than women do. Men are not only physically larger in general,
but they also possess power to control social, legal, financial, educational, and
other important institutions. We are accustomed to male power because it surrounds us. However, the point of interest is not simply that men *have* power.
Rather, the key factor is that male power has become eroticized. Men and
women alike are socialized not only to think that being a man means being in
control but also to find male domination sexually arousing. The overpowering of
a woman is a paradigm for "normal" heterosexual relations at least among
young people and in segments of popular literature.

Studies of pornography demonstrate the eroticizing of domination in this
culture.[25] Andrea Dworkin, Nancy Hartsock, and others argue that pornography
is a window into one of the primary dynamics of the social construction of sexuality in this culture: "we can treat commercial pornography as . . . expressing
what our culture has defined as sexually exciting."[26] Pornography would suggest
that men are socialized to find both male power and female powerlessness sexually arousing.[27] In pornography, domination of women by men is portrayed as
sexy. It is the power of the man or men[28] to make the woman do what she does
not want to do—to make her do something humiliating, degrading, or antithetical to her character—that creates the sexual tension and excitement. Dworkin
puts it bluntly: the major theme of pornography is male power, and the means
to achieve it is the degradation of the female.[29] Since power-as-domination always has at least an indirect link with violence, this means that there is at least ✓
an indirect link between sexual arousal and violence in this culture.[30] In
pornography, women are raped, tied up, beaten and humiliated—*and* are portrayed as initially resisting and ultimately enjoying their degradation. No wonder
many real-life rapists actually believe that women enjoy sadomasochistic sex or
"like" to be forced;[31] this is the constant message of pornography.

Pornography is big business.[32] While pornography may not reflect the active *choices* of all men in this culture, it reflects a significant dimension of the
socialization of both men and women.

However, it is not only men in this culture who find male power or female
powerlessness sexy. Women in this culture (even feminist women, as Marianna
Valverde so devastatingly demonstrates)[33] are attracted to powerful men,
whether that power is defined in macho, beer-can-crushing terms or in the
more subtle dynamics of social, economic, and political power.[34] Women also
link violence and sexuality. In Nancy Friday's classic study of women's sexual
fantasies, "Julietta" gives voice to this pattern: "[W]hile I enjoy going to bed
with some guy I dig almost any time, I especially like it if there's something in
the air that lets me think I'm doing it against my will. That I'm forced by the

male's overwhelming physical strength."[35] Julietta is sexually aroused, at least in fantasy, by the thought of being overpowered. Nor is she alone. In *Shared Intimacies: Women's Sexual Experiences,* Lonnie Barbach and Linda Levine report that women's most frequent fantasies are "variations on the theme of being dominant and submissive."[36] Not all women link domination and eroticism, but the pattern is there.

Since men and women alike are socialized both to expect men to overpower women and to find the exercise of power sexually arousing, it is no wonder that the boundary between acceptable "normal" sexual exchange and rape has been blurred. The letter to "Dear Abby" exposes the confusion that arises in a culture that links dominance with eroticism and implies that sexual arousal and satisfaction involve a man overpowering a woman. The "friend" assumes that the woman secretly likes to be forced and that rape is acceptable on some level because on some level it cannot be distinguished from regular sexual contact.

CRITERIA FOR AN ADEQUATE ETHICS

It is plain, then, that to be adequate, Christian sexual ethics must deal not only with the realities of rape and fear in women's lives, but also with socialization patterns in which both men and women are socialized to find male power and female powerlessness sexually arousing. It must deal with the realities of the link between violence and sexuality in this culture, and it must understand the ways in which the social construction of sexuality contributes to the lived experiences of women and men. Only in this way will we truly link the personal with the political; only in this way can we bring moral reflection on sexual behavior into line with the fact that sexual relations are political and not merely personal.

To be adequate, Christian moral reflection must begin with real experience, not with romantic fantasies about love, marriage, and the family. We must name the realities of sexual violence in women's lives. We must take account of the fact that women often experience their sexuality in a context of rape, date rape, acquaintance rape, forced sexual contact and spousal rape. If nearly 40 percent of rapes happen within heterosexual marriage then a sexual ethic for heterosexuals must account for this real, lived, concrete experience of women. A Christian sexual ethic must have something to say to the man who raped his twenty-four-year-old date, to the woman who was raped, and to the friend and everyone else who is confused about what constitutes acceptable sexual contact between men and women.

To be adequate, Christian sexual ethics must carry out cultural analysis and mount a cultural critique. We must attend not only to the differences in power between men and women in a sexist culture, but also to the distortions that such differences in power have brought to the experience of sexuality itself. An ethic based on assumptions of mutuality and consent falls short of dealing with the social construction of sexuality in terms of the eroticizing of dominance and submission.

To be adequate, Christian sexual ethics must develop a role-based model of personal sexual relations because only a role-based model is adequate to the moral complexities that are exposed when we begin to take seriously the degree to which our sexuality and our sexual interactions are socially constructed. Women are not respected in the sexual arena, but are raped, attacked, and treated as objects. At the same time, heterosexual women seek to trust, love, and be intimate with those who have the power to rape, attack, and be disrespectful.[37] The twenty-four-year-old woman who was raped by her date must now struggle to find intimacy with those who will represent for her the violence in her memory and life. Other heterosexual women will "make love" to spouses who have raped them before and will rape them again. All heterosexual women seek partners from among those who represent the power of male domination in this culture. There are ambiguities and ironies in the search for intimacy in all these contexts. An adequate Christian sexual ethics must attend to these ambiguities and ironies.

A HERMENEUTICS OF SUSPICION

The first step for such an ethic will certainly be a "hermeneutics of suspicion." The distortions of culture must be exposed for what they are. This means that we ask first whether patterns of sexual arousal based on male domination and female submission are trustworthy patterns.

To say that women eroticize domination in fantasy is not to say what happens when women actually experience sexual domination. Since the issue of forced sex came up repeatedly in her interviews, Shere Hite finally asked women whether they were afraid to say no to a man's overtures, and if so, how they felt during and after the act of intercourse. Uniformly, the women indicated that they did *not* find sex pleasurable under such circumstances and that they experienced anger and feelings of powerlessness.[38] Whatever their fantasies may be, women do not in fact like being forced and do not enjoy sex when it happens against their will. Barbach and Levine put it bluntly: "What women enjoy in fantasy and what they actually find arousing in reality are two very different things."[39]

The famous "Hite report" on women's sexuality surfaced evidence that many women who are fully capable of orgasm and frequently do achieve orgasm during masturbation do not in fact have orgasms during heterosexual intercourse. Why, Hite asked, "do women so habitually satisfy men's needs during sex and ignore their own?"[40] Her answer is that "sexual slavery has been an almost unconscious way of life for most women." One of Hite's subjects put it bluntly: "Sex can be political in the sense that it can involve a power structure where the woman is unwilling or unable to get what she really needs for her fullest amount of pleasure, but the man is getting what he wants."[41] Hite concludes that lack of sexual satisfaction (perhaps better: lack of joy, pleasure, the erotic) is another sign of the oppression of women.

The first step toward an adequate Christian sexual ethics for heterosexual people, then, is to expose cultural patterns in which sexuality becomes a political struggle and in which domination is eroticized. The first step is an active hermeneutics of suspicion.

POWER AND SEX: THE NEED FOR A
ROLE-BASED MORALITY

If the first step for such an ethic is a hermeneutic of suspicion, I believe that the second step is a recovery of the significance of role and status. . . .

What we need is an approach to sexual ethics that can take seriously the power that attaches to a man in this culture simply because he is a man (no matter how powerless he may feel), the power that he has as representative of other men, and the power that he has for women as representatives of the politics of dominance and submission and as representative of the threat of violence in women's lives. . . .

I use the term "enemy" to indicate the man's role as representative of those who have power in this culture. I am aware of the dangers of labeling anyone as the "enemy." In her recent book, *Women and Evil,* Nel Noddings argues that when we label someone as the enemy, we devalue that person's moral worth.[42] It is not my purpose to return to a labeling and condemnation of men that often characterized the feminist movement a number of years ago; neither do I wish to devalue the worth of men.[43] Many men today are working hard to divest themselves of the vestiges of sexism that affect them. Not all men experience their sexual arousal along patterns defined by traditional pornography with its degradation of women. "Enemy" is a strong term, and to suggest that it can be used to designate the role of men because of the power of men in a sexist society is to run the risk of misunderstanding. Nonetheless, in the situation of the young woman who was raped, it is not unwarranted to suggest that her date has proven himself to be her "enemy," to be one who will vent his anger and use his power against her by using her for his own ends without regard for her person, her feelings, or her needs. Similarly, for the 25 percent of college women who also experience rape or attempted rape, we need a strong word. Precisely because the term "enemy" is strong, and even problematic, it will force us to take seriously the issues involved.

"LOVE YOUR ENEMY": TOWARD A
CHRISTIAN SEXUAL ETHIC

If we understand men and women to be in power positions that can be characterized by the role designation "enemy," then an examination of the meaning of "love of enemies" may contribute something to an ethic for heterosexuality. While I believe that the meaning of love of enemies can usefully illumine the moral situation from both the man's and the woman's side, I will focus here on the woman's plight and on what love of enemy might mean for her.

I will frame this discussion with two words drawn from reflections of black Christian ethicists. African-Americans in this country have had reason to struggle with what it is to be in relationship with those who stand in the role of enemy and to explore the meaning of "love of enemies." I will therefore take the words of a black man and the words of a black woman as each offering insight into the meaning of ethics in a context of "enemies."[44] These two words set boundaries within which a new approach to heterosexual sexual ethics as an exercise in "loving your enemy" might take place....

According to [Martin Luther] King, forgiveness means that the evil act no longer serves as a barrier to relationship. Forgiveness is the establishment of an atmosphere that makes possible a fresh start. The woman who has been raped and who then begins to date again—taking the risk that she will be able to find a safe space with a man, even though he represents the power of men and the very violence that she has experienced—is exercising "forgiveness." She is declaring her willingness to enter relationship.

In short, while forgiveness means that "the evil deed is no longer a mental block impeding a new relationship,"[45] the stress here needs to be on *new* relationship. To forgive does not mean going back to the relationship the way it was or accepting the evils perpetrated within it. Love of enemies, for King, begins in forgiveness, but forgiveness itself begins in the recognition of something that needs to be forgiven and, therefore, in the recognition of injustices that need to be redressed. Love of enemies requires justice.[46] Indeed, Paul Lauritzen argues that, in the absence of repentance, forgiveness may even be "morally objectionable" because it can involve "an unjustifiable abandonment of the appropriate retributive response to wrongdoing."[47] The stress in forgiveness is on recognition of the evil. The evil must be named for what it is, and the participants must be willing to establish a new relationship that does not incorporate that evil. Forgiveness means that we must be willing to set things right so that there can be a fresh start. Forgiveness is essentially restorative.[48] Where there is a concrete evil fact such as rape, forgiveness may require repentance; where the man is not himself one who rapes but simply one who represents the power of men in sexist society, forgiveness requires a willingness to establish a relationship based on justice....

This brings me to the second word, *survival.* Women who have been raped often speak of themselves as "survivors." This word then seems appropriate for a heterosexual ethics directed to women who are aware of the dynamic of male dominance and violence in their lives.

For an explication of survival, I draw on Katie Cannon's work. "Throughout the history of the United States," declares Cannon, "the interrelationship of white supremacy and male superiority has characterized the Black woman's moral situation as a situation of struggle—a struggle to survive...."[49]

Cannon's perspective seems important to me because it does not postulate what Hartsock calls "an artificial community of formal equals"[50] whose sexual relations can be described in terms of consent and mutuality. Rather, Cannon recognizes that all people do not have equal power and that issues of unequal power are central to ethical decision-making. Ethics must be done with attention to the social construction of experience and to the ongoing history of a community.

As forgiveness, with its implicit recognition of injustices that need rectification, is the first word to illumine love of enemies, so survival with its hard-nosed realism is the second.

The twenty-four-year-old woman who has been raped should forgive her attacker (enemy) only if he acknowledges wrong-doing, repents, and seeks a new relationship free of power, domination, and violence. She should seek relationship with those men who are actively struggling to combat the legacy of a sexist culture. She should love her enemies, both specific and representative, but she should not lose sight of the fact that she is dealing with "enemies," understood in a role-relational sense.[51] Her survival should be central to the meaning of love of enemies. . . .

Is Marriage Obsolete?
Elizabeth McAlister

In 1967, I was with the Religious of the Sacred Heart of Mary at our Provincialate in Tarrytown, New York. Jerry Murphy, a priest from Brooklyn, was beginning a sabbatical as our part-time chaplain. A parishioner drove him to Tarrytown. On their arrival, I gleaned this gem from their conversation: "The church in its teachings on divorce and remarriage is imposing a New Testament morality on pre-Christian people!"

Jerry's words have been building blocks in the formation of my conscience on marriage and divorce, sexuality and nonviolence. I understand him to say that if we could assume the parties were two committed Christians (or two people committed to the practice of nonviolence), they could surmount any obstacle with forgiveness, justice, truth, and love. The broken marriages and relationships howl to heaven—an indictment of our entropy, our willingness to remain infants in both nonviolence and the way of Christ.

Like whole generations, I was raised in the school of "Thou shalt nots!" To surmount that formation was no easy task. My exchange with Jerry Murphy occurred in the heat of the sexual revolution—a frenzied, fiery sea change that continues to impress itself on all aspects of our society. Friends engulfed by and burned in that cultural conflagration compelled me to seek the wisdom behind the church's precepts—a wisdom deeply rooted in an understanding of the human psyche and spirit. One of those insights was the need for sexual intimacy to be protected by a long-term commitment that we often call marriage.

But nonviolence and marriage (or nonviolence and sexuality) are virtually never talked about. The subject is too fraught with anguish. My own spirit becomes leaden when confronted with yet another divorce, separation, failed relationship among people I love. But I propose that we spur one another to reflec-

Reprinted with permission from *Sojourners,* 2401 15th St. N.W., Washington, DC 20009; (202) 328-8842; (800) 714-7474.

tion and dialogue, and risk examining the values of the culture in the light of basic truths about human relationships.

Perhaps, in so doing, we may be able to generate enough hope to counter the inertia and despair that overwhelm us. Perhaps we may even be able to give some witness to fidelity in marriage and nonviolence in relationships in a world that claims them beyond the capacity of human beings.

The churches are neither aid nor comfort. Jerry Murphy apprehended the disparity between the teachings of Jesus and of the church. Jesus (Mark 10) argued that Mosaic law permitted divorce because of the male's hardness of heart and mind. God never intended this, Jesus said, but "created persons as male and female" (Genesis 1:27). The Genesis passage to which Jesus referred is best translated as "the two persons—man and woman—enter into a common human life and social relationship because they are created as equals" (2:24).

With his intimate circle of friends, Jesus articulated a reciprocal formulation. On the one hand, if a man divorces and remarries, he commits adultery—in this he went beyond Jewish law, in which a man could commit adultery against another married man but not against his wife. On the other hand, a woman has the right to leave her husband—in this he contradicted Jewish law in which only the man could administer such proceedings.

Jesus recognized divorce as a spiritual and social tragedy, yet he acknowledged it as a given within which the fundamental issues of nonviolence (justice) must be nurtured. Both parties have the right to take initiative; both incur the responsibilities and limitations involved in the death of marriage. Jesus compelled his community to treat women as human beings, not as objects.

Half of all marriages today end in divorce, a profound spiritual and social tragedy. The conviction that marriage itself is at fault gains credence. Questions proliferate: How is it possible to bind one's self to another and commit to a future in which one's feelings will probably change? How is it possible for people to enter marriage with sincerity and integrity when they know that time will probably alter their sense of themselves and one another? If one pledges fidelity to another, doesn't one place oneself in danger of living in bad faith?

Our concept of marriage is profoundly corrupted when the images it invokes are all negative: possessiveness, property, rigidity, stubborn adherence to duty. This is a travesty, a betrayal of true fidelity. The gospel parable of the talents reveals that fidelity can't be identified with preservation of the status quo. No! Fidelity involves continuous vigilance against the inertia of conformism and the sclerosis of habit. Because authentic existence is a pilgrimage, faithfulness must be supple or it collapses into betrayal.

Marriage is an institution and as such shares in the corruption that befalls so many institutions; but marriage is also a form. Partners in a marriage accept a form that is not of their own making, a form that acknowledges the limits of creaturely life and urges the partners to live within their true orbit.

"The meaning of marriage begins in the giving of words! We cannot join ourselves to one another without giving our word!" Wendell Berry claims, with deep insight, that the form of marriage rests upon these immutable givens—words, bodies, characters, histories, places. He stresses that marriage is an unconditional giving.

When a writer determines to create a sonnet or a verse of haiku, she or he is limited by that form, but in a deeper sense is tapping a more mysterious level of creativity. So too, people can be challenged, enlarged, humanized by living with all the fidelity they can muster within the form of marriage.

I don't consider it extreme to suggest that the essence of marriage is a commitment to continue, through one's life, to struggle to become one in love and truth and freedom. When one or both parties abandon that struggle, the marriage no longer exists.

In stark contrast to the marriage form as challenging, humanizing, and nonviolent, I submit that sex apart from a committed relationship is violent—in at least three ways.

If sex is destructive of the humanity and individuality of oneself or one's partner, it is violent. The root of our bewilderment may be that sex is natural, but marriage is not. I can still hear a couple of young friends defend their sexual relationship: "It's natural!" But a third party was jilted and shattered in their coming together, and they were ignorant of and indifferent to her pain. All three were doing violence to one another, to themselves, and to all who cared for them.

How? Violence simplifies relations by denying the other's existence (or their existence as a person). Nonviolence pleads the question: What does it mean to be fully human? To enter into a relationship "for as long as it feels good, for as long as it is satisfying" risks reducing both partners to the vitality and lustiness of a particular moment or period in time. Their unity of being, their center, their humanity is threatened (and can be lost).

We learn too slowly that part of the struggle to become human is the realization that we derive a sense of our identity, we achieve unity, and we triumph over the corrosive acids of time through those relationships and friendships that enable us to integrate our past, present, and future—relationships that put us in touch with what is of lasting value in us. In pledging faithfulness to another, we aspire to nonviolence because we apprehend the other as a thou, not an it; as a presence, not an object; as a full human being, not simply someone who is fun to be with for a while.

If sex is acquiescence to cultural excesses, it is violent. If what distinguishes the human person are gifts of mind and heart, then the tools of nonviolence are truth and love. Truth announced or spoken without love is violence— no one can hear it. Love offered without truth is sentimentality, and rotten to the core. Together, truth and love constitute the two-edged sword that can heal as it cuts—deep into the person. Truth and love are geared to human community—to recreating, liberating, forming us into the people we are meant to be. As an end and a means, nonviolence is a constant struggle to be or become more loving and truthful. If there were ever a time when that process was supported by the culture, it is not now.

Ours is a cheap energy culture, assuming that everything desirable lies within easy reach. The articulation of the inalienable right to the pursuit of happiness has kindled terrible illusions in Americans, with perhaps obscure but nonetheless ruinous consequences. We seek happiness as an end in itself, rather than as a corollary of right living.

Truth, love, the struggle to become more human invite us outside the cheap-energy enclosure. As the traditional marriage ceremony insists ("for better or for worse, for richer or for poorer, in sickness and in health"), not everything in this venture of relationship will make us happy. The faith, rather, is that by staying with it we will learn something of the truth, that the truth is good to know, and that it is different and larger than we thought.

Truth, love, justice (nonviolence) imply (require) an attitude toward people that includes: absolute respect for the person—mind, heart, imagination; the conviction that every human being is, at least potentially, a sister or brother—that all are indeed one; and the resolution never to capitulate personal moral responsibility to any other person, group, or institution. Nonviolence is a refusal to do harm—in thought as well as in deed. It's a refusal of undue haste, of lying, hatred, wishing ill. This is impossible without a love that is grounded in truth and reality.

When our children were in inner-city public schools, their peers hankered after the culture without question. Classmates in the 7th and 8th grades had abortions and babies. Sex was raw, real, ruinous. The relationships they had with the younger adults in our community who regarded them as friends roused our children both to understand and repudiate the experimental relationships that prevailed among their schoolmates. Our daughter, Frida, put it this way:

When Jerry and I were in grade school, we were surrounded by children clamoring to be adults. In contrast, we found the company of adults liberated us to be young again. Liberated is a heavy word, but it is the word I mean. They gave us an alternative to the constant pressures to fit in—to be down, cool, in, hard.

We watched our classmates destroy themselves in an effort to be accepted. They forfeited respect in and for themselves; they abandoned the values imbued in them by parents and teachers; they settled for less than they deserved. We could have too; the pull to be a part of the in-group was very strong. It was in friendships with older people that we glimpsed real friendship, real belonging, real nonviolence in relationships. It was not about settling, or forfeiting, or losing ourselves—it was about becoming, being challenged, being valued, listened to, encouraged to grow, to be more fully human. It became clear to us that all that we would relinquish to be part of the in-crowd was not worth it.

In high school, our children and their friends learned to live levels of intimacy that were (and remain) wholesome, healthy, holy—relationships that enabled them to thwart the pervasive sexual mores. Now that they are collegians, their father and I continue to struggle with these issues with them, returning again and again to the considerations I'm trying to articulate here. Together we recognize these values as countercultural, and, more and more, maybe as true.

If sex is destructive to community, it is violent. This is a truth I unearthed and learned to embrace only because I was guilty of violating it. When Philip and I were trying to understand the gift of our love and how both to appreciate and be responsible for that gift, it was important to us to clothe it in secrecy. We did not yet understand the relationship between our love and our religious communities, though we knew that it would not be welcome there. And we were not ready to make our love the subject (or object) of the favorite indoor sport, later termed "bochinche" (loosely translated as "lifesharing with other people's lives").

Did we put a wall around our relationship and refuse to open it up to scrutiny or celebration? Had someone inquired about our relationship would we have bristled or labeled the inquiry invasive? For a time, yes—and for too long a time.

We used the pretext that our love was a private thing against the truth that the condition of marriage or a relationship like our own is worldly; its meaning communal. There is a profound tension between keeping something private to give it a chance to grow and knowing the moment when it needs to come into the light in the wider community.

As we learned more about nonviolence, we understood that nothing exists for its own sake, but for a harmony greater than itself which includes it. Our interdependence is so complete that even our thoughts have cosmic consequences. We all are one! And marriage is a sign and symbol of our relationship with all that lives.

I came upon *Living My Life,* the autobiography of Emma Goldman, on the shelf of a jail library. I was beginning a three-year sentence; she seemed an apt companion. What peacemaker hasn't been gladdened by Emma's, "If I can't dance, I don't want to be part of your revolution!"?

But Emma was an early believer in free love. I was offended by her musings about the ruptures that developed among comrades once they had been lovers and were no more. I was astonished by her astonishment. Her conduct was explosive, devastating others and herself with abandon, destroying the very community she was seeking to build.

Sexual relationships have profound consequences for the wider community. Who of us has not called for a meeting or an action or a party and found that friends we wanted to call together couldn't be in the same room because they were once lovers and were no more?

People are too important; when one is violated or abused, we are all affected. Until we learn to treasure each other, nothing is going to change—not for the better. Our communities are so small; those willing to consider serious issues and humane response to them are so few. Even in a healthy society the connections that join people, land, and community are complex and our society is far from healthy. But we cannot forever refuse to focus on the affairs that create such havoc among us.

If the principles I articulate here are valid, the question imposes itself: Where does this leave us? I think of Peter's amazed response to Jesus' instructions: "Who then can be saved?" And Jesus' response: "With people this is impossible, but not with God; all things are possible with God" (Mark 10:26–27).

Maybe Nietzsche understood the root of our malaise: "When God dies human relationships are reduced to the level of the will-to-power." He forces us to ask, Is faith in God the condition of fidelity in our relationships?

There is a hidden identity between faith and the unconditional love that people have for one other. Maybe fidelity is as entwined with faith as love of neighbor is entwined with love of God. Fidelity in human relationships is not something added to faith; it is the way a believer is faithful to God.

Those who live in fidelity create a climate in which belief can grow. Their love is a spring keeping the life around them free from despair, self-hatred, meaninglessness, by a testimony they do not necessarily articulate. Their fidelity is a participation in the mystery of being because it is the underlying significance of life that they experience within love. The mysteries of faith, which believers know as revelation, can be communicated only where the sacredness and mystery of being are still experienced in wonder. Where this sense of being is lacking, life ceases to be human and the word of faith falls on deaf ears.

In our marriage, Philip and I learn the good of living within the limits of our reality as creatures, as created, as responsible, as not totally "our own." Our marriage stipulates that we continually give our word (and not just that we gave it); that we welcome a future that may not seem desirable; and that we be generous toward it. At times, the word we have given to one another and the world may appear to be wrong, or wrongly given. But the unknown still lies ahead of us, so we can't finally say.

With the Jonah House community and the support and help of a lot of friends, we have recently been building a house in an abandoned cemetery here in Baltimore. When complete, we will move there and take care of that 22-acre piece of property. A friend, witnessing a disagreement between us on some detail of the project, reiterated the adage: "Build a house; lose a spouse!"

We understand the warning. In this project, as in so much of our lives, neither of us is in charge. Both of us, as well as the press of time, life, history, and the world itself are carving, cleaving, and crafting us and our love. Uncertainty dogs every effort. But that is real. What is unreal is the pretense of security, the projection of five-year or ten-year plans for our lives. Reality comes home—three times in the last months, Philip has faced yet another spell in prison; and still it hangs over us.

In our marriage we acknowledge that good is possible; it invites us to be alive, to hope for what is good, to await it, to prepare to welcome it, but not require it. We hope that our love, like the love of others who inspirit and inspire us, can be a witness against the prevailing gloom, against the deadly conviction of our futurelessness; against the hopelessness and faithlessness and despair of humankind.

Chapter 4

THE CHURCH AND FAMILY VALUES

As the articles in the previous chapter suggest, our discussion of sexuality inevitably leads us to consider our relationships with others, for we know ourselves as sexual beings in relation to others. The word "relationships" is apt not only because it is descriptive (sexual activity usually involves two people) but also because it is value-laden. It points to an aspect of what it means to be human, namely, to be in relationship with others in a way that respects and honors them, rather than exploits or oppresses them. The absence of meaningful relationships leads to loneliness, which can lead to depression and even to suicide, the ultimate denial of the person and the meaning of life. "Love," "fidelity," and "covenant" are terms that express ideals for human interaction.

A society such as ours that is torn by the fragility and pain of relationships—a continued high rate of divorce and growing understanding of the existence of physical and emotional abuse within families, for example—seems all the more desperate to nourish the ideal. So after some years of widespread public worry concerning the "crisis" or the "decline" of marriage and family life, there is emerging a renewed affirmation. Roman Catholic and some evangelical religious groups have taken the lead in constructing "marriage encounter" and "family life" focuses for their constituencies, but similar efforts have appeared in other quarters as well. Despite the apparently uncontroversial character of these activities, debates soon arise. One is about the need for discussions of the family to be realistic; its economic and parental, as well as cultural and social, configurations must not be ignored in the effort to shore up an ideal form. Another is about what should be done with those dimensions of human relationship that do not conform to or challenge the norm. Consider, for instance, the ongoing discussion in some denominations of the appropriateness of religious rites to acknowledge divorce or to affirm the value of fidelity in homosexual relationships. Still another topic of debate concerns gender roles in heterosexual relationships and within the parenting process.

Social scientists frequently suggest several reasons for the weakening of the institution of marriage, the difficulties—particularly for men—in moving

from a patriarchal to an egalitarian model, the new-found independence of women, economic pressures as well as opportunities that put additional burdens on a marriage, and sexual freedom and the attendant implications for commitment, to name just a few. Closely related to the state of marriage in our society is the state of the family, which has also generated widespread discussion in religious and political circles. There is extended debate over the fundamental question, "What is a family?" Some would address the issue by turning the clock back to a time when social relationships were simpler and traditional values more secure. Others have welcomed the "death" of the nuclear family and urge a departure from outmoded familial forms and expectations of the past.

Don and Carol Browning recognize the dimensions of crisis in the family but argue that neither of the above responses is adequate to reality. One must acknowledge that the social and economic conditions of life will not permit the luxury of a nostalgic look to the past; in a word, the traditional family is dying, if not dead. But if a postmodern understanding of the family must replace the traditional or modern family in our consciousness, the search for inclusive forms of family life should not obscure the importance of the intact nuclear family in the task of raising children. The Brownings contend that the churches have not only neglected the crisis but have also failed to discern at what points they could be helpful. Their recommendation is less for action than for articulation of a new love ethic that would fit the reality of the postmodern (two-income, more egalitarian) family and also provide a better moral foundation for the commitments of marriage and family. They call this an ethic of "equal regard," which avoids the excesses of self-sacrificing (potentially exploitative) and self-actualizing (potentially self-centered) interpretations of neighbor love. With a focus on raising children and on preparing children for their own opportunities for commitment, they put the family, often discussed within the churches as a matter of personal ethics, squarely on the social agenda.

Nicholas Peter Harvey raises a fundamental question about how Christians should respond to changing family values. He contends such changes should not evoke anxiety among the faithful. It is idolatrous he argues, to treat the family as the center of value by which people are identified and evaluated. This loyalty will be recognized as misplaced once the subversive implications of Christianity for the family are taken seriously. This alleviates the "crisis" mentality that plagues present day discussions of these issues.

In her response to him, Linda Woodhead appreciates Harvey's concern to relativize the modern church's defense of particular family forms. But she argues that concern about family affairs flows naturally from faith in Jesus Christ. Both the Incarnation and the Resurrection invite Christians to take their bodies, and the social institutions like the family that organize their bodily ties, very seriously.

The Church and the Family Crisis: A New Love Ethic

Don S. and Carol Browning

Are families declining or simply changing? This question continues to provoke heated debate in our society. Some say that while family forms are changing, families are not in trouble. These same people say that the problems of the family are temporary dislocations caused by evolutionary social change. Such a view implies that once church and society adapt to these developments, the health of families will improve. Our view is far more somber. We believe that the family is deteriorating.

TRADITIONAL AND NUCLEAR FAMILIES

Families are changing, yes. For instance, the so-called traditional family—families in which the father works outside of the home while the mother does the domestic chores and raises the children—is being profoundly altered. Proportionately far fewer of these families exist today than at the turn of the century or even 30 years ago. It is more accurate, however, to call the traditional family the "modern family." Its rise paralleled the emergence of modern industrial societies. This form of the family is decreasing in number primarily because more wives and mothers are joining the labor force. The traditional or modern family in this specific sense is only some 250 years old. In spite of the claims of certain fundamentalist and conservative religious groups, this family form is not God's ordained plan. Nor is it the family plan revealed in Scripture.

The idea of the nuclear family, on the other hand, refers to a bonded mother and father raising one or more children. Both mother and father may be employed, they might both work part time, they may both stay at home with the children, the mother might work while the father raises the children, or they may function together within an extended family or household. The so-called traditional or modern family was nuclear, but not all nuclear families are traditional.

Although the church need offer no special defense of the modern family, it has some strong theological reasons to defend and support the bonded mother-father team in its various forms. It is striking how the words of Genesis 2:24 that "a man leaves his father and his mother and cleaves to his wife and they become one flesh" recur throughout the Hebrew and Christian Scriptures. They are found on the lips of Jesus in Matthew and Mark, in the letter of Paul to the Corinthians and in the pseudo-Pauline letter to the Ephesians.

Since the traditional family was for decades the dominant form of the nuclear family, the two concepts get confused in people's minds. A speaker at one of the presessions at the "Families 2000" conference, sponsored by the National Council of Churches, after elaborating the problems of the traditional family, exclaimed at three points: "The nuclear family is dead. Thank God the nuclear family is dead." Knowledgeable members of his audience assumed that he was confusing the nuclear mother-father team with the traditional or modern family. Some of his listeners, however, suspected an even deeper agenda. They suspected that the speaker was radically relativizing the nuclear mother-father team in order to replace it by some vague model of the church as a new family surrogate. The distinction between the nuclear and traditional family was also blurred in the recent report on human sexuality by the Presbyterian Church (U.S.A.) titled *Keeping Body and Soul Together:* "Although many Christians in the post-World War II era have a special emotional attachment to the nuclear family, with its employed father, mother at home, and two or more school-aged children, that profile currently fits only 5 percent of North American households." This sentence seems to refer to all nuclear families; it really refers only to traditional families. Even then, this figure is the lowest we have seen quoted by any authority; it's probably more like 7 or even 9 percent. Actually, nuclear mother-father teams raising children make up about 25 percent of all households. Even this figure is misleading since it excludes older couples who have already raised their children. It also overlooks the large number of dual-income families in which the mother or father stays home during some of the preschool years.

THE DETERIORATING FAMILY

The idea that the family is declining refers to difficulties that families—traditional, nuclear, or otherwise—are having in fulfilling their principal tasks, especially in raising children to become healthy and responsible adults. Most everyone knows that the marriage rate is down, while the divorce and abortion rates have increased greatly. Less well known is the extent of out-of-wedlock births, up from 5 percent in 1960 to over 25 percent of all births in 1988. Over half of these were to teens between 15 and 17 years of age. Nor is it widely known that the number of children living with a single parent has grown from 7 percent in 1960 to approximately 25 percent today.

New evidence suggests that divorce, single parenthood and out-of-wedlock births are strongly correlated with one of the greatest social problems of our time—the feminization of poverty. Single mothers and their children make up the new poor of our society. One of every four children under six in the United States lives at or below the poverty line. Half of these children live with single mothers who are themselves poor. Some of these poor single mothers are divorced and some never married. Poor children are less healthy, less involved in school, more likely to drop out of school, more likely to get in trouble with the law, and much more likely to die prematurely. Poverty is often a result of marriages that did not work or did not take place.

Family disintegration imposes other costs on the emotional welfare of children. Although many children adapt to both divorce and living with single parents, life for them is on the whole more difficult. A recent study by the National Center for Health Statistics shows that one in five children under age 18 has a learning, emotional, behavioral, or developmental problem that can be traced to the dissolution of the two-parent family. By the time they are teenagers, one in four suffers from one or more of these problems, and among male teenagers the rate is nearly one in three (*Chicago Tribune*, December 9, 1990). According to researcher Judith Wallerstein, children of divorce display increased behavioral problems during the first two years after the marriage breaks up, and the effects of divorce on children can continue for many years. (See Judith Wallerstein and Sandra Blakeslee, *Second Chances*, 1989.)

We believe that these facts suggest a very grave state of affairs. They point to a situation that the mainstream Protestant churches have not wanted to face. For the past 30 years, these churches have been timid and inarticulate about the growing family crisis. They have let the family issue fall into the hands of reactionary political and religious forces to the right or radical cultural forces to the left.

Some Protestant leaders are striving to broaden the church's ministry to include the growing plurality of family forms—to include as coequals with the intact nuclear family all single-parent families, the divorced and remarried, blended families, childless couples, unmarried couples living together, and gay and lesbian couples with or without children. This effort often goes under the same banner of inclusiveness that justifies the church's outreach to members of different races, classes, and ethnic backgrounds. We do not wish to blunt this initiative. The church should do everything it can to minister to all people no matter what their family context, and it must do much to broaden its ministry to the new family forms. We believe, however, that these goals should not obscure the church's *central* support for the intact mother-father team dedicated to the task of raising children to take their place in the kingdom of God.

THE FAMILY'S PRIMARY TASK

We recommend a limited definition of the primary task of families: raising children. Research shows that none of the alternatives to the intact nuclear family (first marriages) performs this task as well. While families are certainly places of interpersonal intimacy, security, friendship, and mutual assistance, many other forms of human association perform these tasks. Only families are responsible for providing the security, stability, financial resources, stimulation, and commitment necessary to raise highly dependent human infants to adulthood. Furthermore, families are the primary carriers of the traditions, narratives, values, and the initial education necessary to raise children to be conscientious citizens and members in the kingdom. We're not suggesting that all married couples should have children. We do recommend that the family concept not spread to include every living arrangement that provides friendship, security, or mutual assistance. These arrangements doubtless perform an important function. Sometimes they even provide support—as does the church—for adults, single or married, raising children. But it is confusing to call them families except in a metaphorical sense.

For this reason, we also should be cautious about using the metaphor of family for the church. The church has familylike qualities, but it is not a family. It is as absurd to talk about the church functioning like a super-family as it is to speak of the state as a family. The church is probably only slightly more successful in raising children than is the state. Both institutions raise children only in emergency situations and only when there is no better alternative. During its plenary sessions the recent conference "Families 2000" came dangerously close to suggesting that in response to family disintegration, individualism and loneliness the church should become the new family surrogate, a warm and accepting replacement for the puny, broken, and disappearing nuclear families whose remains are strewn across the social landscape. However, "Families 2000" had little to say about how the church can support the postmodern, dual-income, mother-father team in its task of raising children.

Our point is that on the whole the nuclear mother-father team in intact first marriages does a better job of raising children than do single parents, stepparents, or unmarried couples. There are exceptions, of course. We are talking about broad but meaningful averages. (See Mavis Hetherington and Josephine D. Arasteh's *Impact of Divorce, Single Parenting and Stepparenting on Children,* 1988.) The intact mother-father team seems more invested in its children and has more success in raising children, measured by children's mental and physical health and their capacity to handle school, make friends, relate to the opposite sex, and have confidence about the future. If the church is interested in helping society raise strong, healthy, and self-directed children, the church must help produce as many intact first marriages as possible.

One of us studied for ten months a rapidly growing black Pentecostal church with a powerful family ministry. On the basis of that study, we concluded that special emphasis on the intact family can be formulated in ways that are inclusive of other family forms. The uniting elements must be a genuine concern for families and commitment to do what is best for children.

THE CHURCH'S TASK

We believe that the churches can do much to offset the family crisis. The churches and the Christian message can ease the transition from the traditional or modern family to the postmodern family and offer a vision of a new family ethic.

In the postmodern family, both mother and father will likely be employed outside of the home, either full or part time. Since both will earn salaries, wives will be far less dependent financially on their husbands than they were in the modern family. Mothers will spend less time parenting. If children are not to be neglected, fathers and other committed people will need to fill the gap. This is not happening now. Family, child, and education experts generally think that our children at all social levels are being neglected. The postmodern family will be more dependent on two incomes. Gender roles will need to be more flexible lest either the husband or the wife (most likely the wife) do a disproportionate amount of the family labor.

Family sociologist William D'Antonio has called for a new love ethic for this postmodern family. A Christian love ethic would arise from a more honest interpretation of the Second Commandment: "You shall love your neighbor as yourself." This principle of neighbor love is recognized by both Jesus and Paul as the summary and essence of the entire Jewish law. It is a vantage point from which to interpret other aspects of New Testament ethics, including its ethics for families.

The principle of neighbor love is difficult to interpret. Some understand it as a self-sacrificial love—a mandate to love the other at the cost of sacrificing the self. This extreme self-sacrificial interpretation of neighbor love has often been coupled with those passages in Ephesians, Colossians and 1 Peter that seem to advise women to submit to the spiritual authority of their husbands. This view of love is used to justify what sociologist Francesca Cancian calls the "duty family." Many fundamentalist Christian groups use this model of Christian love to legitimate male authority, the traditional family, and the submission of women. Extreme self-sacrificial models of love also can be manipulated to persuade oppressed people to endure passively, in the name of bearing their crosses, their situation of oppression.

The other extreme in interpreting the principle of neighbor love is what we call the independence or self-actualization model of love. In this view, loving your neighbor as yourself means that if you love yourself first, love of neighbor or spouse follows automatically. This interpretation often holds that love relations should be measured by how they contribute to one's self-fulfillment. This view of love is very popular both inside and outside of the church. It is the view of love held by what Cancian calls the "independence-type" family, where husband and wife view marriage as a means toward individual fulfillment. Both the sacrificial model and the self-fulfillment model contribute to the decline of families in our society

We propose a third model of Christian love, one that we believe is consistent with the core of the Christian tradition and can provide a love ethic for the postmodern working family. This model builds on the work of Louis Janssens, Gene Outka, Christine Gudorf, and others. It interprets neighbor love through the idea of equal regard. Loving your neighbor or spouse as yourself means loving him or her exactly as much as you love yourself. It means you must take the needs and claims of the spouse as seriously as your own. But this love ethic also means that you are obligated to take your own needs and claims seriously. It includes values from both the independence and the self-sacrificial model of love but avoids their excesses. The equal regard interpretation of neighbor love fits the needs of the postmodern family faced with a new range of issues around shared authority, more equal financial power, and more nearly equal roles in raising children and meeting each other's needs in the midst of the 80-hour work week.

Self-sacrifice and the demands of the cross are still required in this love ethic. Sometimes we must love even when circumstances do not permit us to be loved fully in return. But in this love ethic, sacrifice is not an end in itself. Its task is to unleash the energy required to return a marital or human relation to mutuality and equal regard. Sacrifice in this ethic cannot be manipulated to justify perpetual oppression, submission, vulnerability or inequality on the part of either the husband or wife, father or mother. Appeals to self-sacrifice cannot be used to justify physical or mental abuse. In fact, it is precisely the ethic of equal regard which gives a marital partner the right and responsibility to resist abuse. Love as equal regard should also leave the marital couple with an ethic of commitment sufficient to live together, raise children, meet hard times, confront misunderstandings and remain integrated in the relationship.

There are many concrete ways that the churches could teach such a love ethic. The most important focus is youth. Youth ministries, which have declined in the mainline churches, should be revived to help initiate youths into the love ethic of equal regard required for the postmodern family. Many families of church youth are still significantly traditional or modern. It will take explicit work, education, even rites of passage, to prepare the young for mutuality in the postmodern family. Outside of offering this new love ethic in a commanding way, initiating youth—especially boys—into this ethic is the single most important thing that churches can do to address the decline of families. Poet Robert Bly and psychoanalyst Robert Moore have called for new rites of initiation for young males. They have a point. We offer this love ethic to guide that initiation process.

The church should also discuss proposed legislation supporting the postmodern family. Government support for more and better day care will help the two-career family with children. Some experts, however, propose increasing tax exemptions for young children or offering a system of tax credits to help the many families who elect to have one parent stay home with the children during the preschool years. A new political coalition appears to be in the making between conservatives Phyllis Schafly and Gary Bauer and liberal Democratic Representative Pat Schroeder which is designed to advance these very proposals. The recent report from the National Commission on Children achieved unusual bipartisan support for a $1,000-per-child tax credit proposal. The influential Progressive Policy Institute's report *Putting Children First* has made a similar proposal but primarily for the poor. Such tax proposals would make a single income more nearly a family income. Although 57 percent of all wives are employed outside the home, it is also true that 33 percent of all mothers stay home full time for a few years with their preschool children before returning to outside employment. Another 13 percent work outside the home only part time during these early childrearing years. Nearly half of postmodern families are traditional for at least a few years during their children's preschool years. These tax proposals are ways the government can help families without taking over their child-care functions. The church needs to be part of the debate about the relative investments that society should make to day care and tax relief as means of supporting the postmodern family.

There are other radical proposals the churches need to debate. Should society try to cope with the growing epidemic of teenage pregnancies and single parents and with the feminization of poverty by requiring states to list the name of the father on the birth certificate of a child born out of wedlock? And should this father be forced by federal law, possibly through deductions from his paycheck, to support his child until it reaches maturity, regardless of whether or not he ever marries the mother? Should the church support stricter divorce laws or at least a more equitable treatment of women with regard to property settlements and child-care payments?

We cannot fully evaluate such proposals here, but a church supporting families, both modern and postmodern, must at least enter the public debate. The church's greatest contribution, however, will be in formulating its own vision of love as equal regard in the intimate affairs of the postmodern family.

Christianity against and for the Family
Nicholas Peter Harvey

The assumption seems widespread in the contemporary church that the institution of the family is unambiguously supported by the central thrust of Christian faith. It would of course be absurd to claim that Christianity is merely against the family. As we shall see, our ancient texts largely take the continuing existence of the family for granted. Yet for most of its history Christianity has called people out of their families into a quite different form of identity and self-definition.

This is exemplified in the commendation of martyrdom, in the cultivation of consecrated virginity, in the preeminence so widely given to monastic and eremitical life. Even as late as the immediately pre-Vatican II days of my childhood Catholicism, the constraints on contact between members of religious orders, particularly nuns, and their relatives were very severe. However crude and even cruel such restrictions are now adjudged to have been, their purpose was clear and in principle defensible: to foster a strong extra-familial identity.

Meanwhile my father, in this respect typical of the Protestant professional classes, took it for granted that what a man does is to marry and have children. He did not realize the extent to which our history fails to support so drastic a limitation of the range of possibilities for being human. He was innocent of the profound ambivalence of Christianity's connection with the family. The purpose of this paper is to attack not the family but the notion that the family is something given in nature and shown by revelation to be a divine ordinance.

From "Christianity against and for the Family," by Nicholas Peter Harvey, in *Studies in Christian Ethics,* 1996. Reprinted by permission.

Two major assumptions lie behind this claim. The first is that the tie of blood is of crucial significance in forming the basis of our most intimate and lasting relationships.[1] What seems at first sight to corroborate this is the well-attested fact that an adopted child reaches a point where it is of critical importance to seek the identity of and possible contact with one or both biological parents. Whatever the depth and richness of the adoptive relationship, ties of blood have to be somehow broached and negotiated if the person's development is to proceed.

But things are often far from what they seem. Consider in particular the case of so many children conceived in unspeakable circumstances: casually, brutally, fecklessly, in contexts where the relationship with the biological mother and father is without abiding significance. Reflection on such situations might lead to the conclusion that in relational terms ties of blood have no importance, and yet such children are liable to seek at least information about their progenitors. This, I suggest, can only be accounted for as an instance of the power of the human unconscious to endow some things, in this instance ties of blood, with vast symbolic import. Even the seemingly rational tendency to argue for the givenness of the family in terms of blood-ties is itself an example of this unconscious symbolising. One of the tasks of theology is to uncover such processes and give them critical scrutiny, lest we remain in idolatry. We have no business to add a theological tier to the unredeemed need to discover one's biological parents.

A second major assumption is that the Hebrew and Christian scriptures provide validation for the notion of the family as an institution with an explicitly theological warrant. First to be considered is the Genesis text so often cited to this effect. This text reflects a contemporary concern with a particular moment in the history of the family, when it begins to break up with the departure of the children. A man is to leave father and mother and cleave to his wife. The background is a society in which, like ours, exogamy was practised and incest frowned upon. There is nothing here about God setting up or sanctioning the institution of the family, which is already there.

As regards the gospel sayings about divorce and remarriage it is, as in Genesis, a particular moment in the history of the family which is being considered. Both texts presuppose the family rather than seeking to establish its originating credentials in some form of divine ordinance. In the gospel case it is especially odd that what is in fact an attack on superficial and dehumanising attitudes to divorce gets turned into a foundation charter for the idealised family unit. In face of the statement, 'What God has joined together let not man put asunder', has it occurred to you to wonder what is to happen if *God* is putting a particular relationship asunder?

A different angle on Christian faith in relation to the family is provided by Paul in 1 Corinthians 7. His correspondents are preoccupied with whether it is acceptable for a Christian to marry; or whether a Christian who is married should cease to be so in the interests of faith. Paul's reply is that these are not the important questions. If you are single, don't worry about being married. If you are married don't worry about being unmarried. Whether you are married or not is of no great moment, and changing your state is for most people a distraction from more important matters.

It has become commonplace to say that Paul wrote thus because he thought the world was about to come to an end: 'The time is short' and all that. The implication is that Paul's time-scale was mistaken, and that his views on the unimportance of the family need not be taken seriously. This has always seemed to me too easy an escape-route. Could it not rather be that Paul has an appropriate sense of urgency about being caught up in the mystery of life through death which is revealed to him in Christ, from which perspective questions which might otherwise loom large cease to occupy the foreground?

In any case it cannot be a matter of particular time-scales. Doubtless Paul did not have our sense of the possibility of an extended future for this universe, but once we are awake to reality the time is always short, for us as for him. My purpose here is not to insist that Paul was right about the unimportance of the family. It is to suggest that what leads him to this conclusion is his overwhelming sense that the crucified and risen Christ represents and empowers life in the new age. This new identity means possibilities for human living hitherto unimaginable, in the light of which the law is seen to have fulfilled its role as nursemaid and the family is, shall we say, relativised. . . .

This is a good moment to introduce Gregory of Nyssa to the discussion, not least because he sees the question of Christianity and the family as part of the wider picture of Christianity's relation to social institutions in general. These he sees as all having the same purpose, the denial of our mortality by attempting to blot out the sight of the grave. Marriage is for obvious reasons chief among such institutions. Gregory is thinking not primarily of individual choices but of a society braced against the onset of death.

This is very close indeed to the feminist view that marriage and the family are part of a particular social construction of reality rather than a given or divinely willed ordering of our relationships. Gregory concludes that Christians have no need to marry, for they are no longer ruled by that death-denying compulsion which originates marriage: they have the risen Jesus. Like Paul, though for different reasons, Gregory does not believe that for those identified with the risen Lord the existing pattern of social institutions is to remain undisturbed.[2]

The so-called hard saying of Jesus to the effect that hating your relatives is a necessary condition of discipleship has not received serious attention from theologians. Barth sought to marginalize these words by saying, without evidence, that they apply only to special and rare vocations.[3] Instead of staying with the strangeness of the text Barth thus distanced the saying by inventing a category for it, a familiar device of biblical commentators and theologians for dealing with texts which sharply confront something unregenerate in us.

What is Barth resisting? It is, I think, the insight that the very strength of the family unit contains seeds of destruction in the imposition of a static and ultimately regressive identity on individual members. This is vividly exemplified in the story of Jesus, and poignantly in the stories of an ancient and a modern martyr, Vibia Perpetua and Franz Jägerstätter. Jesus' relatives and friends from earlier days, thinking he was beside himself, set out to restrain him. They are not criticised for this, but their anxious concern is brutally dismissed in the name of his present reality. In other words two versions of who this person is collide here, and Jesus prefers his own version to that of his family. This is a matter of life and death for all humans, so the language of hatred is fitting.[4]

In Perpetua's case her father pleads with her in the interests of her family: 'Think of your brothers, think of your mother and your aunt; think of your child, who will not be able to live once you are gone . . . Give up your pride! You will destroy all of us.'[5] Visiting her in prison, her father begged her to give up the name Christian, but instead she gave up her familial name and proceeded with joy to martyrdom. The point about identity could hardly be more sharply made. If it is objected that martyrdom is a very extreme case remote from day-to-day life, the answer is that it was not so for Christians at that time.

Perhaps a modern martyr makes the point with even greater immediacy. When Hitler took over Austria, Franz Jägerstätter refused to serve in the army because he believed the war to be unjust, in accordance with traditional criteria. In prison he was visited by various church leaders, who all sought to dissuade him from the course on which he was embarked. Their cruellest move was to emphasise how he was hurting his wife, whom he dearly loved. A letter to her is extant in which he faces this question: 'Though I sit behind prison walls, I still believe I can build further on your love'.[6] Yet these counsellors implied that no burden of conscience could outweigh the obligation to keep the family together.

It is certainly true that some New Testament epistles give evidence of another tradition, which sought to play down the subversive implications of Christianity for the family. My point is that the subversive strand has been there from the beginning, has excellent credentials in scripture and elsewhere in the tradition, and suggests a theological critique which if taken seriously sets problems of marriage and family in a context quite different from the one which dominates current church debate.

Some tentative indications are in order as to how this critique might offer a refocussing of a range of contentious matters. In discussion of adoption, of gay and lesbian concerns, and of divorce and remarriage an idealised model of the family receives largely uncritical allegiance. In the case of adoption, is it wise to go to such lengths to ensure that children stay with or return to their biological parents? Is such an emphasis, at the price of other positive relational factors which may well be in play, really so crucial to a child's developing sense of identity? As regards lesbian and gay relationships I agree with Elizabeth Stuart, who writes from a lesbian viewpoint, that there is an incongruity in the present search for recognition of same-sex domestic partnerships on the analogy of marriage.[7] A theological critique of attitudes to the family would suggest a rethink here.

It is fashionable to deplore the decline of fidelity, as of family life generally, as if the facts are so obvious as not even to need careful statement. My concern would rather be to explore the forms which faithfulness is taking in our world. Where is faithfulness in evidence? What are the strengths and weaknesses of its present forms? We need to recognise that all our relationships entail faithfulness, and that marital breakdown is only one of a range of breaches in relationship which touch all our lives. Why do we allow an obsession with divorce to make us morally insensitive to this wider picture? If we can pursue these questions with disciplined, contemplative attentivity we might get somewhere. Wittgenstein apparently said, 'Don't say what must be, but look!'. . .

The idealised model of the family, so hard to fully eradicate from our thinking, has its roots in an unconverted need to receive our identity from the family. Unconversion, when unnoticed and therefore unattended to, issues in oppression. Someone said to me the other day, 'Whenever there is an appeal to family values we are only one step away from the knock on the door at midnight.'

Christianity for and against the Family: A Response to Nicholas Peter Harvey
Linda Woodhead

Nicholas Peter Harvey's 'Against and for the Family' can well be described as radically Christocentric. On the one hand, this is its great strength. It recalls us to the decisive revelation of God in Christ and reminds us that all human forms of living, the family included, are to be judged in its light. Harvey is properly critical of those Christians who simply assert that the family is given in creation, and seek no further justification or explanation in terms of the revelation in Christ. On the other hand, however, I believe that Harvey's particular brand of Christocentrism is the origin of some of the most questionable aspects of his article—in particular of its bleakly negative appraisal of the family. For, as I will argue in the second part of this paper, I think that the Christology which Harvey develops is in some ways a Spirit-Christology, a Christology which denies the reality of the Word made *flesh*. Before embarking on that criticism, however, I would like to begin on a more positive note by mentioning some of the many things I learnt from Harvey's article.

With his usual perspicacity, I believe that Harvey has identified one of the most pervasive idolatries of the modern church: 'family worship'. As I read Harvey's article, I take him to be suggesting that instead of taking Christ as the standard by which all forms of human relationship must be judged, the modern

From "Christianity for and against the Family: A Response to Nicholas Peter Harvey," by Linda Woodhead in *Studies in Christian Ethics,* 1996. Reprinted by permission.

church has often substituted the family. It is not in the light of Christ, but in the light of the family that different forms of intimate human relationship are being assessed. This may not be the official teaching of all the churches, but it is certainly the impression with which these churches leave many people today. Those whose lives are not lived within the context of a family often feel themselves judged and excluded by Christianity. . . .

'Against and For the Family' contains a clear-sighted recognition that the family can easily become no more than a licensed form of selfishness. Real hardness of heart may not be all that easy for an individual to sustain, but it can be very easy for a family to fall into. Too many families pull up the drawbridge on the 'heartless world' and refuse to open their hearts to anyone outside the family circle. Harvey is quite right to remind us that to allow love to be limited by the limits of blood relation in this way is to fail to understand the real implications of the gospel. Families ought to have fluid boundaries. Families which could admit people besides blood relations on equal terms—be they friends, servants, orphans, or adopted children—seem sadly to have become rarer today. So too does a strong sense of the duty of hospitality, a duty which could act as a powerful counterforce to the closed family. And the loss of a sense that we belong to other communities besides the family—local, political and ecclesial communities—has left the family as the sole claimant upon our ultimate loyalties.

As well as suggesting that 'family worship' may be a relatively recent phenomenon, Harvey suggests that a very different approach has been more characteristic of Christianity. He believes that this approach is one in which the family has been assessed extremely critically from a Christocentric perspective. There is clearly much evidence to support this. . . . He reminds us that Christianity has spawned other experimental social forms besides that of *ekklesia*— most notably, the various forms of monasticism. These, he rightly insists, were viewed throughout much of Christian history as much better able to sustain Christian lives than the family, and he reminds us of the brutal ways in which monasticism has often dismissed family ties. Though he does not do so, Harvey could also have drawn our attention to Christianity's eschatological relativisation of the family. Jesus' words: 'In the resurrection they neither marry nor are given in marriage' (Mt. 22:30) were to prove highly influential for the church's subsequent understanding and evaluation of marriage and the family. They were commonly taken to show that at best the family should be viewed as a 'holding operation'—part of the dispensation in which we await the Kingdom rather than part of the Kingdom itself.

There is much then that I find very valuable in Harvey's recalling us to a Christocentric starting-point, and I believe that he is right to insist that such a starting-point relativises the family. Yet I believe that there is more to be said. In particular, I believe that Harvey's rather bleakly negative judgement on the family is not the only possible outcome of a Christocentric approach. Indeed, I want to suggest that in an important sense Harvey's negative judgement on the family is the result of his failure to be Christocentric *enough*. For I believe that he neglects the importance of both the incarnation (in which the Word becomes

flesh) and of the resurrection (in which the flesh is redeemed). Taking these aspects of the revelation in Christ more seriously seems to me to lead to a rather
more positive Christian evaluation of the body, and so ultimately of the family.
Let me explain what I mean.[8]

Both the incarnation and the resurrection remind us that Christianity is not a
spiritualising gnosticism which would dismiss the body as base and irredeemable.
The Word was able to become flesh without ceasing to be God, and the flesh was
redeemed and restored in God's exaltation of Jesus Christ. Christians are therefore
right to believe that the body has value and importance and that it is a proper and
essential aspect of human-being. But if the Christocentric perspective thus involves taking the body seriously, then it must also involve taking bodily relatedness seriously. If bodies matter, then the following facts also matter: that a child is
produced by the bodily union of a man and a woman and the fusing of egg and
sperm; that a mother carries a child in her body; that the child shares some of its
parents' physical characteristics and bears their genetic inheritance. These facts
mean that parents and children have a bond in the flesh, and the importance of
the flesh means that this bond cannot be dismissed as insignificant.

Once the importance of bodily relatedness is acknowledged, I believe that
it is a short step to acknowledge the importance of the family—on properly
Christian grounds. For the family is simply that social unit which is organised
around the ties of bodily relatedness. At its minimum, the family is the social
group composed of parents and their immediate offspring; at its maximum it is
the widest group who are known to be related by blood ties. (Contrary to what
some would maintain, the fact that families come in different shapes and sizes
does not therefore problematize the notion of family.) The family thus finds a
proper justification in the Christocentric acknowledgement of the importance
of the body and of bodily ties.

Harvey does not agree with this stress upon the importance of the blood-
tie. The explicit reasons he gives for his disagreement seem weak. The real and
more weighty reason is surely that he believes that what may be called the 'ties
of the spirit' are far more important than those of the body. This, it seems, is the
truth which he believes Jesus' hard sayings about the family convey, and this is
the premise upon which he believes that new Christian forms of community
like church and monastery are founded. For Harvey, Christianity offers a vision
and a hope of humans bound by the bonds of free and gracious love rather than
by the bodily tie. The latter is, in his word, 'unredeemed'.

There is, I believe, much truth in Harvey's stress on the spiritual nature of
Christian community. There is even something to be said for his stress that
Christians are those bound by the Spirit of Christ rather than by bodily ties. But
I think that he is wrong to speak as if the latter two are mutually exclusive options. Are Christians really forced to choose between ties of blood or ties of the
spirit? Surely this is an unhelpfully dualistic way of conceiving things. It reminds
me of the problematic Christian insistence that the Old Israel, bound by ties of
blood, must be rejected in favour of the New Israel, bound by ties of the spirit.
Just as this way of drawing the distinction between *ekklesia* and *synagogue* is

crude and over-simple, so, I believe, is Harvey's oppositional juxtaposition of bodily and spiritualities, and his dismissal of the former in favour of the latter. There is much in the Christian tradition which should make us suspicious of Harvey's dualistic move. Let me mention just two things.

First, Harvey fails to mention that the overwhelming verdict of the church in all phases of its development has been that the family, alongside the church, is a legitimate context for the living of the Christian life. The condemnation of marriage was early identified as an heretical position—a heresy first identified with the Encratites and the Nicolatians. Since Tertullian also attributes this heresy to Marcion, it seems that it was closely bound up with the adoption of a gnostic style of dualism and a fierce rejection of the God of the Old Testament. Harvey mentions Gregory of Nyssa's views on procreation. He fails, however, to mention that these were extreme views which failed to win the mind of the church, a mind which was won instead by Augustine's definitive exposition of the virtue of marriage, an exposition in significant continuity with the earlier work of writers like Clement of Rome, John Chrysostom, and Tertullian. Of course, Augustine did not commend the family as the only—nor even as the best—context in which to live the Christian life. But he was clear nonetheless that it was a legitimate context.

Secondly, Harvey fails to acknowledge that, far from turning its back on bodily relationships, Christianity gives such relationships a privileged place in its understanding of the relationships within the Godhead, the relationship of God to His people, and the relationships between God's people. Thus the first and second persons of the Trinity are spoken of as Father and Son, Christ being the 'only begotten'. Thus, by being caught up into the body of Christ, Christians are also able to address God as 'Father' and become 'sons of adoption.' And thus the church is understood as the body of Christ, its members brothers and sisters of one another. (One could also add that it was a common Christian belief, spelt out, for example, in Augustine's commentaries on Genesis, that God created the human race from a single man and woman as a way of establishing the fundamental unity and relatedness of all people.)

Far from rejecting the bodily tie as unimportant, then, Christianity treats it as the model of the most unbreakable, intimate and lasting of bonds. Christianity's radical move is not the rejection of the blood-tie, but its suggestion that the strength and power of this tie can be extended beyond the family. By grace, human beings are allowed to become children of God, and brothers and sisters of one another—just as adoptive children may form a bond with their non-biological parents as strong as that with biological parents. But it is a strange logic which would conclude from this that the biological bond is now unimportant or irrelevant. Christianity wishes to throw open the boundaries of the family rather than to abolish it. The fact that the spiritual bond may be as strong as the natural bond gives no reason for saying that the latter no longer matters. The latter has been graciously extended, not abolished.

Harvey might object at this point that, on the contrary, if the spiritual bond is indeed as secure as the bodily, the Christian can happily leave the latter behind. We should leave behind marriage and giving in marriage and become like the angels in heaven, united by a pure spiritual love. But here Jesus is speaking about resurrection. About life restored under God's perfect reign. In insisting that we live thus here and now Harvey is guilty, I believe, of illicitly bringing the eschatological horizon forward into the present without remainder. It is because he makes this move that he is so hostile to any defence of the family that would appeal to the fallenness of the present age. To view the family as one of the 'orders' appropriate for this present, fallen age is, he says, 'to allow our ambition for promised transfiguration to be undermined before it gets going'. Of course, Harvey is right that Jesus insists that life now must be lived in the knowledge that God's reign has begun—but Jesus is also clear that the Kingdom has not yet come in its fullness. It is 'at hand'—present, and yet still to come. The Spirit, though active in the world, has not yet triumphed over the world.

Against Harvey, I believe that it is important to acknowledge that the Kingdom has not yet come. This involves acknowledgement of the reality of evil and sin in our world. And this in turn involves acknowledgement that human beings need to erect every defence against sin which may be available to them—precautions which will, of course, be unnecessary in the Kingdom. The marriage vow is one such defence. It defends us from our own fickleness and sin (but will be unnecessary in heaven). The bodily tie is another such defence. It binds generations together, and even binds parents together through their children (it too will be unnecessary in heaven). The bodily tie is not, of course, an unbreachable defence. But it is a strong one, as is shown by the undeniable strength of the love of a parent for a child. As Oliver O'Donovan explains so well in *Begotten or Made?* the bodily tie makes it harder to separate our existence from the one to whom we are related, and inhibits the sinful impulse to think of oneself as quite other than, and exalted over, another person. Of course, not all people who are related to one another through the body achieve loving relationships. But equally obviously, it is more common to find love between those who are thus related than between those who are not. Harvey's suggestion that we already live in the age of the spirit is therefore a dangerous one, because it would lead us to dismantle those dykes against sin which the angels and saints do not need, but which many of us in this present age still do....

SUGGESTIONS FOR FURTHER READING FOR PART 2

Chapter 3: Christian Perspectives on Sexual Intimacy

Cahill, Lisa Sowle. *Between the Sexes: Foundations for a Christian Ethics of Sexuality*. Philadelphia: Fortress Press, 1985.

Countryman, L. William. *Dirt, Greed, and Sex: Sexual Ethics in the New Testament and Their Implications for Today.* Minneapolis: Fortress Press, 1990.

Farley, Margaret. *Just Love: A New Christian Sexual Ethic.* New York: Crossroad/Continuum, 1997.

Fortune, Marie Marshall. *Sexual Violence: The Unmentionable Sin.* New York: Pilgrim Press, 1983.

Genovesi, Vincent J. *In Pursuit of Love: Catholic Morality and Human Sexuality.* Collegeville, MN: The Liturgical Press, 1996.

Gudorf, Christine. *Body, Sex, and Pleasure: Reconstructing Christian Sexual Ethics.* Cleveland: Pilgrim Press, 1994.

Harrison, Beverly. *Making the Connections: Essays in Feminist Social Ethics.* Boston: Beacon Press, 1985.

Nelson, James B. *The Intimate Connection: Male Sexuality, Masculine Spirituality.* Philadelphia: Westminster/John Knox Press, 1988.

Nelson, James B., and Sandra P. Longfellow, eds. *Sexuality and the Sacred: Sources for Theological Reflection.* Louisville, KY: Westminster/John Knox Press, 1994.

Timmerman, Joan H. *Sexuality and Spiritual Growth.* New York: Crossroad Publishing Company, 1992.

Whitehead, Evelyn Eaton. *A Sense of Sexuality: Christian Love and Intimacy.* New York: Doubleday, 1990.

Chapter 4: The Church and Family Values

Ammerman, Nancy Tatom, and Wade Clark Roof, eds. *Work, Family, and Religion in Contemporary Society.* New York: Rutledge, 1995.

Anderson, Ray S., and Dennis B. Guernsey. *On Being Family: Essays on a Social Theology of the Family.* Grand Rapids, MI: Eerdmans, 1986.

Boyer, Ernest. *Finding God at Home: Family Life as Spiritual Discipline.* San Francisco: Harper & Row, 1988.

Cahill, Lisa Sowle. *Sex, Gender and Christian Ethics.* NY: Cambridge University Press, 1996.

Cahill, Lisa Sowle, and Delmar Mieth, eds. *The Family.* Maryknoll, NY: Orbis Books, 1995.

Carr, Anne, and Mary Stewart Van Leeuwen, eds. *Religion, Feminism, & the Family.* Louisville, KY: Westminster/John Knox Press, 1996.

Erdman, Chris W. *Beyond Chaos: Living the Christian Family in a World Like Ours.* Grand Rapids, MI: Eerdmans, 1996.

Fishburn, Janet. *Confronting the Idolatry of Family: A New Vision for the Household of God.* Nashville: Abingdon Press, 1991.

Melton, J. Gordon, ed. *The Churches Speak on Sex and Family Life.* Detroit: Gale Research, 1991.

Patton, John. *Christian Marriage and Family.* Nashville: Abingdon Press, 1988.

Post, Stephen G. *Spheres of Love: Toward New Ethics of the Family.* Dallas: SMU Press, 1994.

Scott, Kieran, and Michael Warren, eds. *Perspectives on Marriage: A Reader.* New York: Oxford University Press, 1993.

Stackhouse, Max L. *Covenant & Commitments: Faith, Family, & Economic Life.* Louisville, KY: Westminster/John Knox Press, 1995.

Weems, Renita J. *Battered Love: Marriage, Sex and Violence in the Hebrew Prophets.* Minneapolis: Fortress Press, 1995.

PART 3

The Christian and Issues of Prejudice and Oppression

Chapter 5

RACISM: THE STRUGGLE CONTINUES

Virtually every Christian church around the globe agrees that racism is morally wrong and that all possible steps should be taken to eliminate racist attitudes and institutional racism. Despite this agreement, we in the United States and virtually every other nation are finding that racism has a long shelf life. The persistence of racism almost makes one believe in original sin; racism appears that deep-rooted in human nature.

The civil rights and equal opportunity movements of the 1960s and 1970s seem to be merely part of American history at times; at other times the burning of African-American churches or the systematic exclusion of Hispanic people from the United States or the institutional bias against women remind us that civil rights and equal opportunities remain threatened to this day.

While much has been accomplished, much remains to be done. From 1955–1968 central parts of the legal structure of racial discrimination were struck down in the United States. This was done through the principles and strategies of nonviolence, based in part on an appeal to the founding ideals of this country but also on the Judeo-Christian understanding of the equality of all persons under God. Martin Luther King, Jr., and a large group of other leaders—black and white—helped bring down the legal underpinning of discrimination against racial and ethnic minorities. Political offices have opened up; there are far more upper-middle class professionals from minority ranks; minority women have come a long way towards equality.

Every positive statistic can be matched by a negative one: worsening rates of infant mortality among minority families; high rates of minority unemployment and underemployment; high rates of crime for African-American and Hispanic male youth; disproportionately low income levels. Racism may have become more subtle, less political, and more economic over the years. Its more visible manifestations—whether in resurgent Ku Klux Klan and other hate group violence, church burnings, or job discrimination—all receive broad societal condemnation. The realities of discrimination and prejudice and their results, however, continue to take their toll. With the claims and quests for minority-group power muted by cultural indifference and by the variety of competing groups and positions (including Native Americans, Hispanics, Hmong, Laotian, and other Asian immigrants), together with the gradual shutdown of federal assistance programs in the past decade, the task of reassessing the nation's struggle with racism continues. In fact, it has taken on greater complexity and urgency. The questions include both how to understand racism and what to do about it.

The face of racism has changed somewhat. Income level and social class seem more significant now. There is evidence that the past 20 years have seen a decline in real income in the United States; many of the new jobs that have been added to the economy are minimum wage or only somewhat higher-paying; and the ranks of the middle class are thinning as more become downwardly mobile and few become upper class. This has aggravated the feeling among some disadvantaged white groups that women and minority group members have been given unfair advantages to the detriment of white and working or middle income men. The policy that has come under fire in particular is affirmative action, preferential treatment for those who have historically been discriminated against. This chapter will focus on the morality of affirmative action as a tool for combating racism.

The 1984 policy statement of the National Council of the Churches of Christ in the U.S.A. (the NCC's most recent full policy statement) is a good example of religious reflection on this continuing struggle. While it acknowledges the significant involvement of many denominations in opposing racism, it also devotes extensive attention to the churches' own participation in racial injustice. As other discussions of this issue have done, the statement concentrates on institutional forms of racism and holds both the churches and the nation accountable for the ways these institutional expressions are allowed to continue. It acknowledges that despite the good intentions of individuals, institutions and systems perpetuate the kinds of domination and exclusion that are identified by the term "racism." Its proposals for an adequate response, therefore, in parts of the document not included here, address institutional dimensions such as the structures of organizations, hiring practices, media images, educational materials and opportunities. Notice, however, that affirmative action is recommended in that statement as a compensatory practice. In pointing to the endemic quality of racism in the nation and the world, the document calls for both continued and long-term attention to this issue and argues that legislation by itself cannot be sufficient.

The continuing legacy of racism and the conflict over proposals to deal with it (especially with affirmative action) are central to Glenn Loury's perspective on ways to achieve "true equality." Despite a four-decade social transformation in race relations, there is substantial alienation, hopelessness, and despair among African-Americans. One significant problem, Loury believes, is the lack of meaningful political dialogue on the issue; instead, there are two divergent views, each of which has something important to contribute but by itself misses the important element represented by the other. The one blames racism for all the problems, while the other blames the actions of big government for creating a welfare culture and inhibiting ambition. If the first sees political responses as crucial, the second advocates personal and community-based "self-help" responses as the best way to counter dependency. Loury believes affirmative action policies have undercut self-development efforts and indeed painted all African-Americans as victims. Loury argues that both individual and social responsibility are important, and he urges the emergence of a broader moral leadership that will raise the issue of racial equality to the level of priority it deserves.

Cornel West, who calls Loury his "friend and fellow Christian" while disagreeing with him, appreciates the voices of black conservatives for calling the black liberal leadership to sharpen its arguments and positions rather than simply appeal to victimhood. However, he suggests that black conservatives have overlooked the fact that affirmative action policies were political responses to the refusal of most white Americans to judge black Americans on the basis of merit. For West, the fundamental problem in black America (and he might be willing to add many other racial and minority communities here) is "too much poverty and too little self-love." He appears to accept affirmative action only reluctantly, but does so "as part of a redistributive chain that must be strengthened if we are to confront and eliminate black poverty." The issue of redistributive justice and under what circumstances it is morally justified—rather than being mere reverse racism and unjust—is discussed in these selections. Clearly West believes affirmative action needs the complement affirmation of racial identity and value.

By contrast, Franklin Gamwell basically defends affirmative action against the charge of being reverse discrimination. Gamwell asks whether the concept of affirmative action violates an overriding moral commitment of our democratic society; namely, the 14th Amendment, which mandates "equal protection under the law." He argues that the U.S. Constitution itself was written to establish a certain kind of community or civil order, or the essential conditions of such an order. The democratic constitution holds that natural and historically created differences are irrelevant unless different treatment is justified by some overriding purpose that the democratic process assigns to the state—such as relieving the suffering of people who are victims of circumstances beyond their control. Whether the current form of affirmative action is substantively just and effective is beyond the scope of Gamwell's article. The Christian community, however, has reason to advocate effective forms of affirmative action because it is committed to a substantive principle of equality and to a society where the conditions for human happiness are equally available to all. The purpose of affirmative action, at least, is just in that it attempts to advance the common good by compensating for racial and gender discrimination.

On Racial Justice
National Council of the Churches of Christ in the U.S.A.

GOD'S CREATION

All humanity is created in the image of God. Christians are called to oneness in Christ which unites all particularities and reaffirms the Biblical image of God as a universal affirmation of faith.

Racism is an expression of idolatry, replacing faith in the God who made all people and who raised Jesus from the dead with the belief in the superiority of one race over another or in the universality of a particular form of culture. When this idolatry is expressed by those who possess economic and political power, it leads to a cruel and extensive repression of selected peoples and a negation of their identity and value as given by God.

THE CHURCH'S MISSION

The church is called to identify racism as sin against God and is summoned to eliminate it. As Christians hear and respond to the Gospel, they confess that all people are called into the fellowship of Christ, and through the Holy Spirit create such a fellowship. The grace of God is needed in this task because sin exerts its power over all people (Romans 3:23). Racism can be vanquished, finally, by nothing less than God's redemptive action to liberate both victims and victimizers from this evil.

The struggle against racial injustice continues to be waged by the Lord Jesus, confessed by Christians together as the Christ. In Christ, God challenges racism and promises its defeat. That challenge is part of the meaning of the Cross and is a part of the resurrection promise.

Through the Holy Spirit, God calls and gathers the church in obedience to the gospel of Jesus Christ. Although no one, not even those called by the name of Jesus Christ, can claim to be free from racism or its effects, those who have been baptized into the death and resurrection of Christ are called to walk in newness of life (Romans 6:4). In each generation the faithful of the church are to struggle against racial injustice. . . .

DEFINITIONS

Prejudice is a personal attitude towards other people based on a categorical judgment about their physical characteristics, such as race or ethnic origin.

From "On Racial Justice," National Council of the Churches of Christ in the U.S.A. Excerpted from the Policy Statement adopted by the NCCC U.S.A. in 1984 and published by the Racial Justice Working Groups of the Division of Church and Society.

Racism is racial prejudice plus power. Racism is the intentional or unintentional use of power to isolate, separate, and exploit others. This use of power is based on a belief in superior racial origin, identity, or supposed racial characteristics. Racism confers certain privileges on and defends the dominant group, which in turn sustains and perpetuates racism. Both consciously and unconsciously, racism is enforced and maintained by the legal, cultural, religious, educational, economic, political, and military institutions of societies.

Racism is more than just a personal attitude—it is the institutionalized form of that attitude.

Institutional Racism is one of the ways organizations and structures serve to preserve injustice. Intended or not, the mechanisms and function of these entities create a pattern of racial injustice.

Racism is one of several sub-systems of domination in the modern world. It interacts with these other sub-systems to produce broad patterns of oppression and exploitation that plague the world. Among these sub-systems are class and sexual oppression. Women who are victimized by racism face a compound burden. They not only have to deal with oppression due to their racial origin or identity, but they are also confronted with economic and political exploitation and oppression based on their sex and/or class.

RACISM IN U.S. HISTORY

The United States has prided itself on its grounding in religious values, especially its founding claim that "all [people] are created equal." Yet historically it has uncritically placed a priority on being white, male, and English-speaking.

Historically, people of European ancestry have controlled the overwhelming majority of the financial resources, institutions, and levers of power. Racism in the United Staes can therefore be defined as white racism: racism as promulgated and sustained by the white majority. White racism is not peculiar to the U.S.; it permeates much of the world. The complete dominance and institutionalization of white racism in the United States make "reverse racism" nearly impossible because the victims of racism lack power.

The colonists who invaded North America came with some preconceived notions of economic exploitation and white superiority. They institutionalized racism by the creation of dual economic, educational, social and political systems that made clear distinctions between Europeans and Africans, Asians, Hispanics, and Indigenous People. To the colonist, life was significant only if it was of European ancestry. Africans were enslaved, maimed, and killed. Asians and Hispanics were paid low wages, imprisoned, and slaughtered. Indigenous People were removed from their land and massacred.

From the early colonial years through the westward expansion, the general pattern of racial exploitation and oppression continued. This westward expansion did not end at the Pacific Ocean; it continued on with Western imperialism extending to the Hawaiian Islands, the Philippines, Samoa, Puerto Rico, the Caribbean, and Latin America. Even now racial exploitation is still clearly visible in U.S. international policies and practices towards Africa, the Caribbean, Latin America, Aisa, the Pacific Islands, and the Middle East.

RACISM IN THE CHURCH

During the early colonial years and through the westward expansion, in the U.S. the general pattern of most Christian traditions was either to condone, participate in and develop a religious rationale for racism, or to keep silent. Yet, at points in U.S. history, some national and local churches were exceptions to this pattern and championed the call for equality, human rights, and the dignity of all people.

Within many of the denominations, there have been prophetic streams which have advanced the cause of justice in the face of slavery, racial segregation, religious intolerance, racial violence, and human suffering. At other times, the church has been silent in the face of appalling injustice. For example, some congregations joined the "underground railroad" to rescue Africans from slavery while other congregations profited from slavery. During World War II, when Japanese-Americans were imprisoned in concentration camps, only a few Christian communions publicly protested. Some individual Christians, however, assisted in the resettlement of Japanese-Americans after the war.

At the national level, Christian denominations have recently failed to give adequate support to immigrants who are victims of racism, especially those who have migrated to the U.S. to escape political and economic oppression. A sign of hope has been that some churches have offered sanctuary to victims of persecution from Central America.

However, despite the significant involvement of some Christian denominations in attempting to combat racism, racial injustice still continues in both the church and society. Christians must no longer assume that racial justice is a matter of overcoming individual attitudes and personal bigotry, nor that well-intentioned and non-racist attitudes can, in and of themselves, effectively eliminate racism. Christians must acknowledge that, despite their good intentions, religious and societal structures, institutions and systems can and do perpetuate racism. They must confess that by its style of organization and management, the white institutional church excludes those who are victims of racism. . . .

RACISM IN SOCIETY

Christians share with people of good will a deep concern for the dignity of humankind and a profound respect for the inalienable rights with which we have been endowed by our Creator, including life, liberty, and the pursuit of happiness.

A responsible society is one in which freedom and social responsibility are practiced by all. Those who administer justice and public order and who hold political authority or economic power are accountable for its exercise to

God and to the people whose welfare is affected by that authority or power. The responsibility of the church is to call attention to the injustices of society and to empower the victims of injustice in their struggle against the systems and individuals that oppress them.

Since racism knows no boundaries and penetrates religious and secular communities throughout the world, we are compelled to monitor its evolution and destructiveness in its entirety and create strong and effective strategies for combatting it. . . .

RACISM IN THE UNITED STATES

As we see the connection between global racism and racism in the United States, we affirm that our public and private treatment of all of God's people should exemplify not only our commitment to racial justice, but also our vision of an inclusive and caring society. Our strategies should include resignation from racist professional, civic, service and social clubs, monitoring negative media stereotypes, and identifying racist legislation at all levels of government. Our public pronouncements and witness should also include promotion and financial assistance for racial justice education, compensatory programs, fair and non-discriminatory housing, and land rights. The following issues have been selected on the basis of their direct relationship to racial justice. But commitment in these areas should not exclude the many other areas of human life affected by racism.

ECONOMICS AND EMPLOYMENT

Economics is the heart of racism in the United States. We continue to challenge those of the nation's economic priorities which belie the established right of each and all to a job with an equitable wage. We note that discriminatory practices and the precarious nature of the labor market jeopardize adequate and substantial financial security for racial ethnic people, who continue to be the most adversely affected during times of economic crisis, decreases in government services, and labor management disputes.

We pledge support for the development and full implementation of aggressive social, economic, and employment policies that protect the economic well-being and job security of all people, mindful of the particular economic insecurities facing racial ethnic people. In view of the historic exclusion of racial ethnic people from full participation in society, we call for intentional efforts by societal institutions to include racial ethnic people in decision making and leadership. We support goals, quotas, and other remedies of affirmative action when used as *minimum,* but not *maximum,* measures of participation. We call for a restructured economic system based on a cooperative model in place of current competitive and comparative models that promote profit at the expense of others. (Acts 2:44) We commit ourselves to promoting the principles of Justice, Participation, and Sustainability.

CIVIL RIGHTS

We support the advances made in the area of civil and human rights, and in equal opportunity. We also affirm the protection of the essential liberties guaranteed by the Bill of Rights and the U.S. Constitution against efforts to undermine them. We reiterate our commitment to anti-racist efforts such as programs, policies and legislation that protect the civil rights of all people, their access to legal and social service, and their full participation in this country's political process.

We support a strong, independent U.S. Civil Rights Commission whose members are genuinely committed to racial justice, affirmative action and desegregation, and whose vigilance in defense of civil rights is not impaired by regressive or partisan manipulation. We call for a vital process of continuing liaison between the Civil Rights Division at the Department of Justice and citizen organizations working for racial justice.

EDUCATION

We believe that the nation should provide a system of quality education that is accessible and affordable to all of its people. Since property-tax financing does not provide sufficient resources for public education in many areas of this country, we call for new, more effective ways of financing public education. Because of this society's ethnic diversity, we also affirm the development and implementation of multicultural and multi-lingual education at all levels to meet the needs of racial-ethnic people, and to promote greater understanding of racial-ethnic communities. In assessing a variety of educational systems nationwide, we have determined that many private schools, especially many of the so called "Christian" academies, promote and practice racial segregation and instill racist value systems in their students. We find this type of instruction antithetical to Biblical precepts and extremely dangerous to the social and faith development of young people. We call for the elimination of these administrative and curriculum policies.

We commit ourselves to work for quality education for all people and to press for the financial resources necessary to support this vital system. We oppose all efforts to diminish the delivery of a variety of educational options, services, curricula, credentials, and degrees. We also commit ourselves to the development, distribution, and use of anti-racist materials and curricula that not only provide insights into racial justice, but also encourage people to unlearn racial stereotypes and to work towards the elimination of racism.

FAMILY

We recognize and deplore the negative impact that bigotry, racial stereotyping, and racial discrimination have on the quality of family life in this society. We also deplore the economic indignities that disproportionately affect the health and wholeness of family members, and that contribute to the growing infant-mortality rates especially within racial ethnic communities. We advocate full access to health care, nutrition, and preventive medicine for all people. We also commit ourselves to provide support, resources, and educational materials that clarify the variety of images and roles within racial ethnic families in an effort to correct the stereotypes and biases that have distorted public perception, eroded interpersonal relationships and destroyed family structures.

VIOLENCE AND THE ADMINISTRATION OF JUSTICE

We abhor the pervasiveness of violence in the U.S., and we are particularly concerned about the violence that is perpetrated against racial ethnic communities. We deplore the sinful appropriation of the cross of Jesus, a symbol of religious wholeness, for diabolical usage by the Ku Klux Klan. We commit ourselves to continue analyzing and responding to the systemic genocide of racial ethnic people and to continue investigation of violence by individuals, groups and even law enforcement agencies. We also commit ourselves to continue monitoring the administration of justice throughout the nation to determine if any miscarriage of justice is being inflicted upon racial ethnic people through the court systems or legal procedures such as bail-setting, sentencing, and incarceration.

We pledge ourselves to the eradication of the root causes of violence in this nation. . . .

BENEDICTION

From the beginning of human existence, justice has been a key element in God's revelation for human relationships. The Old Testament Prophets' words of condemnation and the need for repentance as well as their vision of the Kingdom of God, emphasize that peace and full life come from Justice. As churches of Jesus Christ, we acknowledge that we have not always shown leadership in issues of justice. At this time, God is calling us more strongly than ever to take a prophetic stance and move from powerful rhetoric to critical action. The call is to raise the banner against racial injustice and to make a significant impact on our nation and throughout the world. We commit our churches, our resources, and our lives to the cleansing of racism and genocide from our world. As we focus our attention upon the evils of national and international secular racism, we must also, emphatically and intentionally, focus equally upon the evil resident within ourselves.

In order to concretize this commitment, the National Council of the Churches of Christ in the U.S.A. commits itself and calls upon its member communions to commit themselves for the next decade to racial justice by eliminating racism from church structures and to initiate and support efforts to eliminate it from society. . . .

Black Dignity and the Common Good
Glenn C. Loury

. . . Beginning in the mid-1950s and culminating a decade later, the Civil Rights Movement wrought a profound change in American race relations. The civil rights revolution largely succeeded in its effort to eliminate legally enforced second-class citizenship for blacks. The legislation and court rulings to which it led effected sweeping changes in the structures of education, employment, and electoral politics. This social transformation represents a remarkable, unparalleled experience; in barely the span of a generation, and with comparatively little violence, despised and largely disenfranchised minority descendants from chattel slaves used the courts, the legislature, the press, and the rights of petition and assembly of the republic to force a redefinition of their citizenship. One can begin to grasp the magnitude of this accomplishment by comparison with the continuing turmoil that besets those many nations around the world suffering under long-standing conflicts among racial and religious groups.

Yet, despite this success, hopes that the Movement would produce true social and economic equality between the races remain unfulfilled. No compendium of social statistics is needed to see the vast disparities in economic advantage which separate the inner-city black poor from the rest of the nation. No great talents of social observation are required to notice the continuing tension, anger, and fear that shroud our public discourse on matters concerning race. When, in 1963, Martin Luther King, Jr., declared his "dream"—that we Americans should one day become a society where a citizen's race would be an irrelevancy, where black and white children would walk hand-in-hand, where persons would be judged not by the color of their skin but by the content of their character—this seemed to many Americans both a noble and attainable goal. Today, even after King's birth has been made an occasion for national celebration, this "dream" that race should become an irrelevancy seems naively utopian— indeed *that* dream is renounced even by those who no longer claim his mantle of leadership. . . .

THE CURRENT CHALLENGE

Today black Americans, and the nation, face a challenge different in character, though perhaps no less severe in degree, than that which occasioned the civil rights revolution. It is the challenge of making real for all of our citizens the American dream that, as King aptly put it, "every man is heir to the legacy of

Glenn C. Loury, "Black Dignity and the Common Good," *First Things,* June/July 1990, pp. 12–19. *First Things* is a monthly journal published by the Institute on Religion and Public Life in New York City.

worthiness." The bottom stratum of the black community has compelling problems that can no longer be blamed solely on white racism, that will not yield to protest marches or court orders, and that force us to confront fundamental failures in lower-class black urban society. This profound alienation of the ghetto poor from mainstream American life has continued to grow worse in the years since the triumphs of the Civi Rights Movement, even as the success of that movement has provided the basis for an impressive expansion of economic and political power for the black middle class.

There is no way to minimize the social pathologies that afflict the urban underclass, just as it cannot be denied that vast new opportunities have opened for blacks to enter into the mainstream of American life. In big-city ghettos, the black youth unemployment rate often exceeds 40 percent. According to one recent study, over one-quarter of young black men in the critical age group 20 to 24 have dropped out of the economy, in the sense that they are not in school, not working, and not actively seeking work. In the inner city far more than half of all black babies are born out of wedlock.

These statistics depict an extent of deprivation, a degree of misery, a sense of hopelessness and despair, a fundamental alienation that is difficult for that great majority of Americans who lack direct experience with this social stratum to comprehend. They pose an enormous challenge to the leadership of our nation, and to the black leadership. Yet we seem increasingly unable to conduct a political dialogue out of which might develop a consensus about how to respond to this reality. There are two common, partisan themes that dominate the current debate. One is to blame everything on racism, to declare that the situation proves the continued existence of old-style American racial enmity, only now in a more subtle and modernized form. This is the view of many civil rights activists. From this perspective the tragedy of the urban underclass is a civil rights problem, curable by civil rights methods. Black youth unemployment represents the refusal of employers to hire competent and industrious young men because of their race. Black welfare dependency is the inescapable consequence of the absence of opportunity. Black academic underperformance reflects racial bias in the provision of public education. Black incarceration rates are the result of the bias of the police and judiciary.

The other theme, regularly expressed by those on the right in our politics, is to blame everything on the failures of "Great Society liberals," to chalk the situation up to the follies of big government and big spending, to see the problem as the legacy of a tragically misconceived welfare state. A key feature of this view is the apparent absence of any felt need to articulate a "policy" on this new race problem. It is as though those shaping the domestic agenda of the government do not see the explicitly racial character of this problem, as if they do not understand the historical experiences that link, symbolically and sociologically, the current urban underclass to our long, painful legacy of racial trauma. Their response has been to promulgate a *de facto* doctrine of "benign neglect" on the issue of continuing racial inequality. They seem to think that it is enough merely to be right about liberals having been wrong on this question.

These responses feed on each other. The civil rights leaders, repelled by the Reagan and now Bush administrations' public vision, see increased social spending as the only solution to the problem. They characterize every question raised about the cost effectiveness or appropriateness of a welfare program as evidence of a lack of concern about the black poor; they identify every affirmative action effort, whether aimed at attaining skills training for the ghetto poor or securing a fat municipal procurement contract for a black millionaire, as necessary and just recompense in light of the history of racial oppression. Conservatives, for their part, repelled by the public vision of civil rights advocates and convinced that the programs of the past have failed prefer not to address racial issues at all; when they do, they talk in formalistic terms about the principle of "color-blind state action." Federal civil rights officials have absurdly claimed that *they* are the true heirs of Martin Luther King's moral legacy, by virtue of their having remained loyal to his "color blind" ideal—as if King's moral leadership consisted of this and nothing else. Conservative spokesmen have pointed to the "trickling down" of the benefits of economic growth as the ultimate solution to racial problems; they have at times seemed to court the support of segregationist elements; and they remain at this late date without a positive program of action aimed at narrowing the yawning chasm separating the black poor from the rest of the nation.

There is, many would now admit, merit in the conservative criticism of liberal social policy. It is clear that the Great Society approach to the problems of poor blacks has been inadequate. Intellectually honest people must now concede that it is not nearly as easy to truly help people as the big spenders would suggest. The proper measure of "caring" ought not be the size of budget expenditures on poverty programs, if the result is that the recipients remain dependent on those programs. Moreover, many Americans have become concerned about the indifference toward values and behavior that was so characteristic of the Great Society thrust, the aversion to holding persons responsible for those actions that precipitated their own dependence, the assumption that "society" is to blame for all the misfortune in the world. Characterizing the problem of the ghetto poor as a function of white racism is one variant of the "society is guilty" argument. It overlooks the extent to which values and patterns of behavior of inner-city black youths are implicated in the difficulty.

BEYOND THE CONSERVATIVE-LIBERAL DEBATE

Many Americans, black and white, have become disgusted with the way in which the underclass problem is exploited for political gain by professional civil rights and poverty advocates. . . .

Ironically, each party to this debate has helped make viable the otherwise problematic posture of the other. The lack of a positive, high-priority response from a series of Republican administrations to what is now a long-standing, continuously worsening social problem has allowed politically marginal and intellectually moribund elements to retain a credibility and force in our political life

far beyond what their accomplishments would otherwise support. Many are reluctant to criticize the marginal elements because they do not wish to be identified with a Republican administration's policy on racial matters. Conversely,
the shrill, vitriolic, self-serving, and obviously unfair attacks on administration
officials by the civil rights lobby has drained their criticism of much of its legitimacy. The "racist" epithet, like the little boy's cry of "wolf," is a charge so often
invoked that it has lost its historic moral force.

The result of this perverse symbiosis has been to impede the establishment
of a political consensus sufficient to support sustained action on the country's
most pressing domestic problem. Many whites, chastened by the apparent failures of 1960s-style social engineering but genuinely concerned about the
tragedy unfolding in our inner cities, are reluctant to engage the issue. It seems to
them a political quagmire in which one is forced to ally oneself with a civil rights
establishment no longer able to command broad respect. Many blacks, on the
other hand, who have begun to have doubts about the effectiveness of liberal social policy, are hindred in their articulation of an alternative vision by fear of being too closely linked in the public mind with a policy of indifference to racial
concerns. We must find a way to get beyond this partisan squabbling. A part of
our nation is dying. And if we fail to act, that failure will haunt us for generations.

I can personally attest to the difficulties that this environment has created.
I am an acknowledged critic of the civil rights leadership. There are highly partisan policy debates in which I have gladly joined on the conservative side—on
federal enterprise zones, on a youth opportunity wage, on educational vouchers for low-income students, on stimulating ownership among responsible
public-housing tenants, on requiring work from able-bodied welfare recipients, on dealing sternly with those who violently brutalize their neighbors. I
am no enemy of right-to-work laws; I do not despise the institution of private
property; I do not trust the capacity of public bureaucracies to substitute for
the fruit of private initiative. I am, to my own continuing surprise, philosophically more conservative than the vast majority of my academic peers. And I
love, and believe in, this democratic republic.

But I am also a black man; a product of Chicago's South Side; a veteran in
spirit of the civil rights revolution. I am a partisan on behalf of the inner-city
poor. I agonize at the extraordinary waste of human potential which the despair of ghetto America represents. I cannot help but lament, deeply and personally, how little progress we have made in relieving the suffering that goes on
there. It is not enough, far from being enough, for me to fault liberals for much
that has gone wrong. This is not, for me, a mere contest of ideologies, or a competition for electoral votes.

And it is because I see this problem as so far from solution, yet so central to
my own sense of satisfaction with our public life, that I despair over our government's lack of commitment to its resolution. I believe that such a commitment, coming from the highest levels of our government, without prejudice
with respect to the specific methods to be employed in addressing the issue but
involving a public acknowledgment of the unacceptability of the current state

of affairs, is now required. This is not a call for big spending. Nor is it an appeal for a slick public-relations campaign to show that George Bush "cares" as much as Jesse Jackson. Rather, it is a plaintive cry for the need to actively engage this problem, for the elevation of concern for racial equality to a position of priority on our government's domestic affairs agenda.

In some of my speeches and writing on this subject in the past, I have placed great weight on the crucial importance to blacks of "self-help." Some may see my present posture as at variance with those arguments. It is not. I have also written critically of blacks' continued reliance on civil-rights-era protest and legal strategies, and of the propagation of affirmative action throughout our employment and educational institutions. I have urged blacks to move "Beyond Civil Rights." I have spoken of the difference in the black community between the "enemy without"—racism—and the "enemy within"—the dysfunctional behavior of young blacks that perpetuates poverty and dependency. I have spoken of the need for blacks to face squarely the political reality that we now live in the "post-civil rights era"; that claims based on racial justice carry much less force in American public life than they once did; and that it is no longer acceptable to seek benefits for our people in the name of justice, while revealing indifference or hostility to the rights of others. Nothing I have said here should be construed as a retraction of these views. But selling these positions within the black community is made infinitely more difficult when my black critics are able to say, "But your argument plays into the hands of those who are looking for an excuse to abandon the black poor," and I find myself unable credibly to contradict them.

It is for this reason that the deteriorating quality of our public debate about civil rights matters has come to impede the internal realignment of black political strivings that is now so crucial to the interest of the inner-city poor and to the political health of the nation. There is a great existential challenge facing black America today—the challenge of taking control of our own future by exerting the requisite moral leadership, making the sacrifices of time and resources, and building the needed institutions so that black social and economic development may be advanced. No matter how windy the debate becomes among white liberals and conservatives as to what should be done in the public sphere, meeting this self-creating challenge ultimately depends upon black action. It is to make a mockery of the ideal of freedom to hold that, as free men and women, blacks ought nonetheless to wait passively for white Americans, of whatever political persuasion, to come to the rescue. If our people languish in dependency, while the means through which we might work toward our own advancement exist, then we have surrendered our claim to dignity and to the respect of our fellow citizens. If we are to be a truly free people, we must accept responsibility for our fate even when it does not lie wholly in our hands.

PUBLIC AND PRIVATE RESPONSIBILITIES

But to say this—and it is critical that blacks hear it—is not to say that there is no public responsibility. It is obvious that in the areas of education, employment training, enforcement of anti-discrimination laws, and the provision of minimal subsistence to the impoverished, the government must be involved. There are public programs—preschool education for one—that cost money, but that seem to pay even greater dividends. It is a tragic error that those of us who make the "self-help" argument in internal dialogue concerning alternative-development strategies for black Americans are often construed by the political right as making a public argument for a policy of "benign neglect." Expanded self-reliance is but one ingredient in the recipe for black progress, distinguished by the fact that it is essential for black dignity, which in turn is a precondition for true equality of the races in this country.

It makes sense to call for greater self-reliance at this time because some of what needs to be done cannot, in the nature of the case, be undertaken by government. Dealing with behavioral problems, with community values, with the attitudes and beliefs of black youngsters about responsibility, work, family, and schooling is not something government is well-suited to do. The teaching of "oughts" properly belongs in the hands of private, voluntary associations— churches, families, neighborhood groups. It is also reasonable to ask those blacks who have benefited from special minority programs—such as the set-asides for black businesses—to contribute to the alleviation of the suffering of poor blacks, for without the visible ghetto poor, such programs would lack the political support needed for their continuation. Yet such internal efforts, however necessary, cannot be a panacea for the problems of the inner city. This is, truly, an American problem; we all have a stake in its alleviation; we all have a responsibility to address it forthrightly.

Thus, to begin to make progress on this extremely difficult matter will require enhanced private and public commitment alike. Yet to the extent that blacks place too much emphasis on the public responsibility, we place in danger the attainment of true equality for black Americans. By "true equality" I mean more than an approximately equal material provision among the races. Also crucial, I maintain, is an equality of respect and standing in the eyes of one's fellow citizens. Yet much of the current advocacy of blacks' interests seems inconsistent with achieving equal respect for black Americans.

Leaders in the civil rights organizations as well as in the halls of Congress remain wedded to a conception of the black condition and to a method of appealing to the rest of the polity that undermine the dignity of our people. Theirs is too much the story of discrimination, repression, hopelessness, and frustration, and too little the saga of uplift and the march forward to genuine empowerment whether others cooperate or not. These leaders seek to make blacks into the conscience of America, even if the price is the loss of our souls. They require us to present ourselves to American society as permanent victims, incapable of advance without the state-enforced philanthropy of possibly resentful whites. By evoking past suffering and current deprivations experienced by the ghetto poor, some black leaders seek to feed the guilt, and worse, the pity of the white establishment. But I hold that we blacks ought not to allow ourselves to become ever-ready doomsayers, always alert to exploit black suffering by offering it up to more-or-less sympathetic whites as a justification for incremental monetary transfers. Such a posture seems to evidence a fundamental lack of confidence in the ability of blacks to make it in America, as so many millions of immigrants have done and continue to do. Even if this method were to succeed in gaining the support it seeks, it is impossible that true equality of status in American society could lie at the end of such a road.

Much of the current, quite heated, debate over affirmative action reveals a similar lack of confidence in the capabilities of blacks to compete in American society. My concern is with the inconsistency between the broad reliance on quotas by blacks and the attainment of "true equality." There is a sense in which the demand for quotas, which many see as the only path to equality for blacks, concedes at the outset the impossibility that blacks could ever be truly equal citizens. For aside from those instances in which hiring goals are ordered by a court subsequent to a finding of illegal discrimination, and with the purpose of providing relief for those discriminated against, the use of differential standards for the hiring of blacks and whites acknowledges the inability of blacks to perform up to the white standard.

So widespread has such practice become that, especially in the elite levels of employment, all blacks must now deal with the perception that without a quota, they would not have their jobs. All blacks, some of our "leaders" seem proud to say, owe their accomplishments to political pressures for diversity. And the effects of such thinking may be seen in our response to almost every instance of racially differential performance. When blacks cannot pass a high school proficiency test as a condition of obtaining a diploma, let us throw out the test. When black teachers cannot exhibit skills at the same level as whites, let us attack the very idea of testing teachers' skills. If black athletes less frequently achieve the minimal academic standard set for those participating in intercollegiate sports, then let us promulgate for them a separate, lower standard, even as we accuse of racism those suggesting the need for a standard in the first place. If young black men are arrested more frequently than whites for some criminal offense, then let us insist that police are disproportionately concerned about the crimes which blacks commit. If black suspension rates are higher than whites in a given school district, well, let's investigate that district for racist administrative practice. When black students are unable to gain admission at the same rate as whites to the elite public exam school in Boston, let's ask a federal judge to mandate black excellence.

The inescapable truth of the matter is that no judge can mandate excellence. No selection committee can create distinction in black scholars. No amount of circuitous legal maneuvering can obscure the social reality of inner-city black crime, or of whites' and blacks' fear of that crime. No degree of double-standard setting can make black students competitive or comfortable in academically exclusive colleges and universities. No amount of political gerrymandering can create genuine sympathy among whites for the interests and strivings of black people. Yet it is to such double-standard setting, such gerrymandering, such maneuvering that many feel compelled to turn.

Signs of the intellectual exhaustion and of the increasing political ineffectiveness of this style of leadership are now evident. Yet we cling to this method because of the way in which the claims of blacks have been most successfully pressed during the civil rights era. These claims have been based, above all else, on the status of blacks as America's historical victims. Maintenance of this claiming status requires constant emphasis on the wrongs of the past and exaggeration of present tribulations. He who leads a group of historical victims as victims must never let "them" forget what "they" have done; he must renew the indictment and keep alive the supposed moral asymmetry implicit in the respective positions of victim and victimizer. He is the preeminent architect of what British philosopher G. K. Minogue has called "suffering situations." The circumstance of his group as "underdog" becomes his most valuable political asset. Such a posture, especially in the political realm, militates against an emphasis on personal responsibility within the group and induces those who have been successful to attribute their accomplishments to fortuitous circumstance and not to their own abilities and character.

GETTING BEYOND "VICTIM" STATUS

It is difficult to overemphasize the self-defeating dynamic at work here. The dictates of political advocacy require that personal inadequacies among blacks be attributed to "the system," and that emphasis by black leaders on self-improvement be denounced as irrelevant, self-serving, dishonest. Individual black men and women simply cannot fail on their own, they must be seen as never having had a chance. But where failure at the personal level is impossible, there can also be no personal successess. For a black to embrace the Horatio Alger myth, to assert as a guide to *personal* action that "there is opportunity in America," becomes a *politically* repugnant act. For each would-be black Horatio Alger indicts as inadequate or incomplete the deeply entrenched (and quite useful) notion that individual effort can never overcome the inheritance of race. Yet where there can be no black Horatio Algers to celebrate, sustaining an ethos of responsibility which might serve to extract maximal effort from the individual in the face of hardship becomes impossible as well. . . .

Moreover, the fact that there has been in the U.S. such a tenuous commitment to social provision to the indigent, independent of race, reinforces the ideological trap. Blacks think we must cling to victim status because it provides the only secure basis upon which to press for attention from the rest of the polity to the problems of our most disadvantaged fellows. It is important to distinguish here between the socioeconomic consequences of the claims that are advanced on the basis of the victim status of blacks (such as the pressure for racially preferential treatment) and their symbolic, ideological role. For even though the results of this claiming often accrue to the advantage of better-off blacks, and in no way constitute a solution to the problems of the poor, the desperate plight of the poorest makes it unthinkable that whites could ever be "let off the hook" by relinquishing the historically based claims—that is, by a broad acceptance within the black community of the notion that individual blacks bear personal responsibility for their fate....

My point to conservatives should be plain. Rather than simply incanting the "personal responsibility" mantra, we must also be engaged in helping these people who so desperately need our help. We are not relieved of our responsibility to do so by the fact that Ted Kennedy and Jesse Jackson are promoting legislation aimed at helping this same population with which we disagree. Remember King's description of the animating idea of the Declaration of Independence: "*Every* man is heir to the legacy of worthiness." "Those people" languishing in the drug-infested, economically depressed, crime-ridden central cities—those people are *our* people. We must be in relationship with them. The point here transcends politics and policy. The necessity of being engaged with the least among us is a moral necessity. We Americans cannot live up to our self-image as a "city on a hill," a beacon of freedom and hope for all the world, if we fail this test.

My point to blacks should also be plain. We must let go of the past and take responsibility for our future. What may seem to be an unacceptable political risk is also an absolute moral necessity. This is a dilemma from which I believe we blacks can escape only by an act of faith—faith in ourselves, faith in our nation, and ultimately, faith in the God of our forefathers. He has not brought us this far only to abandon us now. . . . We must believe that our fellow citizens are now truly ready to allow us an equal place in this society. We must believe that we have within ourselves the ability to succeed on a level playing field, if we give it our all. We must be prepared to put the past to rest; to forgive if not forget; to retire the outmoded and inhibiting role of "the victim."

Embracing the role of "the victim" has unacceptable costs. It is undignified and demeaning. It leads to a situation where the celebration among blacks of individual success and of the personal traits associated with it comes to be seen, quite literally, as a betrayal of the black poor, because such celebration undermines the legitimacy of what has proven to be their most valuable political asset—their supposed helplessness. There is, hidden in this desperate assertion of victim status by blacks to an increasingly skeptical white polity, an unfolding tragedy of profound proportion. Black leaders, confronting their people's need and their own impotency, believe they must continue to portray blacks as "the conscience of the nation." Yet the price extracted for playing this role in incompletely fulfilled lives and unrealized personal potential amounts to a "loss of our own souls." As consummate victims, we lay ourselves at the feet of our fellows, exhibiting our lack of achievement as evidence of *their* failure, hoping to wring from their sense of conscience what we must assume, by the very logic of our claim, lies beyond our individual capacities to attain, all the while bemoaning how limited that sense of conscience seems to be. This way lies not the freedom so long sought by our ancestors but, instead, a continuing serfdom.

Race Matters
Cornel West

The impact of economic recessions on African-Americans was immense. Not surprisingly, they more deeply affected the black working poor and very poor than the expanding black middle class. Issues of sheer survival loomed large for the former, while the latter continued to seize opportunities in education, business, and politics. Most middle-class blacks consistently supported the emergent black political class—the black officials elected at the national, state, and local levels—primarily to ensure black upward social mobility. But a few began to feel uncomfortable about how their white middle-class peers viewed them. Mobility by means of affirmative action breeds tenuous self-respect and questionable peer acceptance for middle-class blacks. The new black conservatives voiced these feelings in the forms of attack on affirmative action programs (despite the fact that they had achieved their positions by means of such programs).

The importance of this quest for middle-class respectability based on merit rather than politics cannot be overestimated in the new black conservatism. The need of black conservatives to gain the respect of their white peers deeply shapes certain elements of their conservatism. In this regard, they simply want what most people want, to be judged by the quality of their skills, not the color of their skin. But the black conservatives overlook the fact that affirmative action policies were political responses to the pervasive refusal of most white Americans to judge black Americans on that basis.

The new black conservatives assume that without affirmative action programs, white Americans will make choices on merit rather than on race. Yet they have adduced no evidence for this. Most Americans realize that job-hiring choices are made both on reasons of merit and on personal grounds. And it is this personal dimension that is often influenced by racist perceptions. Therefore the pertinent debate regarding black hiring is never "merit vs. race" but whether hiring decisions will be based on merit, influenced by race-bias against blacks, or on merit, influenced by race-bias, but with special consideration for minorities and women, as mandated by law. In light of actual employment practices, the black conservative rhetoric about race-free hiring criteria (usually coupled with a call for dismantling affirmative action mechanisms) does no more than justify actual practices of racial discrimination. Black conservative claims about self-respect should not obscure this fact, nor should they be regarded as different from the normal self-doubts and insecurities of new arrivals in the American middle class. It is worth noting that most of the new black conservatives are first-generation middle-class persons, who offer themselves as examples of how well the system works for those willing to sacrifice and work hard. Yet, in familiar American fashion, genuine white peer acceptance still preoccupies—and often escapes—them. In this regard, they are still affected by white racism....

> *Institutionalized rejection of* difference *is an absolute necessity in a profit economy which needs outsiders as surplus people.*
>
> *As members of such an economy, we have* all *been programmed to respond to the human differences between us with fear and loathing and to handle that difference in one of three ways: ignore it, and if that is not possible, copy it if we think it is dominant, or destroy it if we think it is subordinate.*
>
> *But we have no patterns for relating across our human differences as equals. As a result, those differences have been misnamed and misused in the service of separation and confusion.*
>
> —AUDRE LORDE, *Sister Outsider (1984)*

The fundamental crisis in black America is twofold: too much poverty and too little self-love. The urgent problem of black poverty is primarily due to the distribution of wealth, power, and income—a distribution influenced by the racial caste system that denied opportunities to most "qualified" black people until two decades ago.

The historic role of American progressives is to promote redistributive measures that enhance the standard of living and quality of life for the have-nots and have-too-littles. Affirmative action was one such redistributive measure that surfaced in the heat of battle in the 1960s among those fighting for racial equality. Like earlier *de facto* affirmative action measures in the American past—contracts, jobs, and loans to select immigrants granted by political machines; subsidies to certain farmers; FHA mortgage loans to specific home buyers; or GI Bill benefits to particular courageous Americans—recent efforts to broaden access to America's prosperity have been based upon preferential policies. Unfortunately, these policies always benefit middle-class Americans disproportionately. The political power of big business in big government circumscribes redistributive measures and thereby tilts these measures away from the have-nots and have-too-littles.

Every redistributive measure is a compromise with and concession from the caretakers of American prosperity—that is, big business and big government. Affirmative action was one such compromise and concession achieved after the protracted struggle of American progressives and liberals in the courts and in the streets. Visionary progressives always push for substantive redistributive measures that make opportunities available to the have-nots and have-too-littles, such as more federal support to small farmers, or more FHA mortgage loans to urban dwellers as well as suburban home buyers. Yet in the American political system, where the powers that be turn a skeptical eye toward any program aimed at economic redistribution, progressives must secure whatever redistributive measures they can, ensure their enforcement, then extend their benefits if possible.

If I had been old enough to join the fight for racial equality in the courts, the legislatures, and the boardrooms in the 1960s (I *was* old enough to be in the streets), I would have favored—as I do now—a class-based affirmative action in principle. Yet in the heat of battle in American politics, a redistributive measure in principle with no power and pressure behind it means no redistributive measure at all. The prevailing discriminatory practices during the sixties, whose targets were working people, women, and people of color, were atrocious. Thus, an *enforceable* race-based—and later gender-based—affirmative action policy was the best possible compromise and concession.

Progressives should view affirmative action as neither a major solution to poverty nor a sufficient means to equality. We should see it as primarily playing a negative role—namely, to ensure that discriminatory practices against women and people of color are abated. Given the history of this country, it is a virtual certainty that without affirmative action, racial and sexual discrimination would return with a vengeance. Even if affirmative action fails significantly to reduce black poverty or contributes to the persistence of racist perceptions in the workplace, without affirmative action, black access to America's prosperity would be even more difficult to obtain and racism in the workplace would persist anyway.

This claim is not based on any cynicism toward my white fellow citizens; rather, it rests upon America's historically weak will toward racial justice and substantive redistributive measures. This is why an attack on affirmative action is an attack on redistributive efforts by progressives unless there is a real possibility of enacting and enforcing a more wide-reaching class-based affirmative action policy.

In American politics, progressives must not only cling to redistributive ideals, but must also fight for those policies that—out of compromise and concession—imperfectly conform to those ideals. Liberals who give only lip service to these ideals, trash the policies in the name of *realpolitik,* or reject the policies as they perceive a shift in the racial bellwether give up precious ground too easily. And they do so even as the sand is disappearing under our feet on such issues as regressive taxation, layoffs or takebacks from workers, and cutbacks in health and child care.

Affirmative action is not the most important issue for black progress in America, but it is part of a redistributive chain that must be strengthened if we are to confront and eliminate black poverty. If there were social democratic redistributive measures that wiped out black poverty, and if racial and sexual discrimination could be abated through the goodwill and meritorious judgments of those in power, affirmative action would be unnecessary. Although many of my liberal and progressive citizens view affirmative action as a redistributive measure whose time is over or whose life is no longer worth preserving, I question their view because of the persistence of discriminatory practices that increase black social misery, and the warranted suspicion that goodwill and fair judgment among the powerful does not loom as large toward women and people of color.

If the elimination of black poverty is a necessary condition of substantive black progress, then the affirmation of black humanity, especially among black people themselves, is a sufficient condition of such programs. Such affirmation speaks to the existential issues of what it means to be a degraded African (man, woman, gay, lesbian, child) in a racist society. How does one affirm oneself without reenacting negative black stereotypes or overreacting to white supremacist ideals?

The difficult and delicate quest for black identity is integral to any talk about racial equality. Yet it is not solely a political or economic matter. The quest for black identity involves self-respect and self-regard, realms inseparable from, yet not identical to, political power and economic status. The flagrant self-loathing among black middle-class professionals bears witness to this painful process. Unfortunately, black conservatives focus on the issue of self-respect as if it were the one key that would open all doors to black progress. They illustrate the fallacy of trying to open all doors with one key: they wind up closing their eyes to all doors except the one the key fits.

Progressives, for our part, must take seriously the quest for self-respect, even as we train our eye on the institutional causes for black social misery. The issues of black identity—both black self-love and self-contempt—sit alongside black poverty as realities to confront and transform. The uncritical acceptance of self-degrading ideals that call into question black intelligence, possibility, and beauty not only compounds black social misery but also paralyzes black middle-class efforts to defend broad redistributive measures.

This paralysis takes two forms: black bourgeois preoccupation with white peer approval and black nationalist obsession with white racism.

The first form of paralysis tends to yield a navel-gazing posture that conflates the identity crisis of the black middle class with the state of siege raging in black working-poor and very poor communities. That unidimensional view obscures the need for redistributive measures that significantly affect the majority of blacks, who are working people on the edge of poverty.

The second form of paralysis precludes any meaningful coalition with white progressives because of an undeniable white racist legacy of the modern Western world. The anger this truth engenders impedes any effective way of responding to the crisis in black America. Broad redistributive measures require principled coalitions, including multiracial alliances. Without such measures, black America's sufferings deepen. White racism indeed contributes to this suffering. Yet an obsession with white racism often comes at the expense of more broadly based alliances to effect social change and borders on a tribal mentality. The more xenophobic versions of this viewpoint simply mirror the white supremacist ideals we are opposing and preclude any movement toward redistributive goals.

How one defines oneself influences what analytical weight one gives to black poverty. Any progressive discussion about the future of racial equality must speak to black poverty and black identity. My views on the necessity and limits of affirmative action in the present moment are informed by how substantive redistributive measures and human affirmative efforts can be best defended and expanded.

Affirmative Action: Is It Democratic?
Franklin I. Gamwell

In 1971 Marco DeFunis was denied admission to the University of Washington Law School, even though his grades and aptitude test scores were superior to those of "virtually all the black students who were accepted." He sued. The Washington State Supreme Court upheld the university's action, and the U.S. Supreme Court agreed to hear DeFunis's appeal. Since the other eight justices were equally divided, William O. Douglas held the swing vote. Douglas's recently opened papers reveal uncharacteristic indecision. "He seemed genuinely torn," notes Nicholas Lemann in a perceptive essay on affirmative action.

On the one hand, Douglas opposed racial preferences; on the other, "he was a fiery liberal and champion of the downtrodden who had come down on the side of blacks in every landmark civil rights case." After several drafts that argued the matter to differing conclusions, his final draft opposed reverse discrimination but let the Washington court's decision stand. Douglas escaped the apparent contradiction by indicting the Law School Aptitude Test as racially biased, even though he had no evidence to support this claim. "So," Lemann concludes, "he went through every possible feeling one can have about affirmative action and wound up in effect throwing up his hands."[1]

Since its inception in the 1960s, "affirmative action" has come to mean many things. Originally a description of special efforts to solicit minority applicants, it now includes the favoring of women and minorities over men and whites who, as judged by test scores and other prevailing criteria, are better or equally qualified. In part, the practice has developed voluntarily, but its better-known forms occur by virtue of governmental mandates. Though it has provoked public controversy from time to time, on the whole affirmative action evolved with minimal public dissent. But the practice is now under heavy attack. Following the Republican triumphs in 1994, significant political power has massed to end virtually all that goes by the name affirmative action. For the first time the concept has become the object of extensive public debate.

Many attackers argue that specific affirmative action programs have allowed widespread abuse and that most have failed to serve their stated purpose: to correct the consequences of generations of institutional discrimination. But the criticism of results is almost invariably joined to a principled insistence that affirmative action, whatever its effects, is inherently unjust or unfair. This view holds that affirmative action commits the very kind of injustice whose consequences it is supposed to correct. Our public life should be blind to differences of religion, race, gender or ethnic origin. To defy this principle is always an offense to human dignity, and to justify its current violation on the grounds that it has been violated in the past is a practical contradiction. Even if some programs of affirmative action make an important difference, reverse discrimination is no less discrimination.

Attacks on the practice are sometimes a covert attempt to maintain established patterns of racial and gender advantage. But the fundamental moral vision of a society that is fair to all is profoundly important to many citizens. Even those who believe that minorities and women do not have equal access to the social conditions of human flourishing may nonetheless question affirmative action. Like Douglas, many of us are genuinely torn.

My intent here is to address this confusion. I take it as a given that the problems affirmative action is meant to remedy are both real and acute. I further assume that there are or could be forms of affirmative action (for instance, in employment decisions, governmental contract awards or higher education admissions) that have important positive effects. The question, then, is whether the very concept of affirmative action violates an overriding moral commitment of our democratic society. That commitment is expressed in the words of the 14th Amendment to the Constitution, which prescribes "equal protection of the law." To clarify the relevance of this provision to affirmative action, it will be instructive first to ask about the proper character of a democratic constitution.

If, as the Constitution says, the body politic is ordained and established by "we, the people," the sovereign ruler of the community is the entire community itself. Thus, the decisions or activities of the state are properly determined in the only way consistent with the sovereignty of the people—through full and free debate about what laws and policies are just. Justice is not properly defined by a privileged individual (a monarch) or group (a ruling class) or by any inherited institutional pattern or established religion. All activities of the state and all proposed norms and principles for deciding which activities are just are assessed by the people in a full and free discourse about what ought to be done. Nothing so well expresses the constitution of a democracy as do the singular words in Jefferson's "Act for Establishing Religious Freedom in Virginia": "Truth is great and will prevail if left to herself; . . . She is the proper and sufficient antagonist to error, and has nothing to fear . . . unless by human interposition disarmed of her natural weapon, free argument and debate, errors ceasing to be dangerous when it is permitted freely to contradict them."

It follows that a democratic constitution should establish the essential conditions of such a civil order. It should, for instance, stipulate freedom of religion, speech, assembly and the press; the right to the franchise; and legislative, executive and judicial offices that maximize the role of public debate. We might say that the proper function of a democratic constitution is to stipulate the *formal* conditions of justice, that is, to establish the architecture of a body politic in which all claims about justice, including those of the constitution itself, are open to full and free public assessment.

Because a discourse in which all participate is sovereign over every political prescription, even those of the constitution itself, one formal condition of justice is that all individuals in the political community are equal members of "we, the people." All natural and historically created differences (for instance, differences of race, gender or ethnicity) are constitutionally irrelevant. In a full and free discourse the only differences that matter are the validity of claims, the force of arguments and the commitments of individuals to the common pursuit of truth. "Equal protection of the law" belongs to the architecture of a democracy because it stipulates this equality. It means that no law can prescribe differential treatment of individuals solely because they exhibit some natural or historically created difference. For instance, no law can prescribe differential burdens or benefits solely on the basis of differences in race or gender or ethnicity. To do so is to assert their fundamental moral importance or to deny that all individuals are equal as participants in the democratic discourse.

This constitutional equality is what gives such apparent force to the criticism that affirmative action is inherently unjust. Laws that prescribe favorable treatment for women and minorities appear to violate the profound equality of those who ordain and establish the body politic. For many citizens this argument may be especially compelling because constitutional equality seems directly to reflect or express religious affirmations of the ultimate worth of every human life.

But to clarify the matter in this way is also to provide the terms for assessing the criticism. If we say that the constitutional principle asserts the formal equality of all as participants in the democratic discourse, does this mean that natural or historically created differences are never relevant to substantive political purposes, so that differential treatment on this basis is never constitutional?

Consider the implications of that interpretation. It would make it unconstitutional to exempt older people from military conscription or entitle them to special treatment, since differences in age are natural. Similarly, all statutes that prescribe differential advantage on the basis of physical circumstance (e.g., support for those who are physically handicapped or who are the victims of natural disasters) would violate the Constitution.

We would also have to question any law that requires difference in treatment based on difference in past performance or present abilities, since these differences are due at least in part to talents and opportunities that are naturally given or historically created. A law that prescribes admission to public law schools on the basis of past grades and LSAT scores or one that prescribes selection for governmental employment on the basis of civil-service examinations would be suspect. Though differences in ability may be due in part to people's efforts to develop their potentialities, how could institutions ever decide in what measure superior capacity may be credited to individual initiative rather than to beneficial conditions?

There are in fact many laws that discriminate on the basis of natural and historically created differences, and these laws are not thought to be unconstitutional because the differential treatment serves some political good. Formal or constitutional equality, in other words, is not equality with respect to all political purposes. On the contrary, it means that natural and historically created differences within the community cannot *in themselves* justify differences in treatment, as if these differences had some fundamental moral importance.

Constitutional principles which establish the essential conditions of a full and free discourse imply that there are other principles of justice by which the purposes of the state should be informed. The very reason for the discourse is to identify these other principles and to determine particular laws or policies accordingly. Democracy is committed to a twofold theory of justice. The *formal* or constitutional conception presupposes a *substantive* or comprehensive conception that the activities of the state should exemplify. A democratic constitution says that the people shall identify the common good. Hence, the formal equality stipulated in "equal protection of the laws" can only mean that natural and historically created differences are irrelevant *unless* differential treatment is justified by some substantive purpose that the democratic process assigns to the state—like raising an army, executing the laws in an effective manner, or relieving the suffering of people who are victims of circumstances beyond their control.

Citizens of a democracy must always keep clear the difference between what is unconstitutional and what is unjust. To be sure, everything that is unconstitutional is unjust, because the constitution stipulates formal conditions of justice; but not everything that is unjust is unconstitutional. When the Supreme Court concluded in 1954 that public school segregation is inherently unequal, the court could also have decided that the practice is unconstitutional because it served no purpose other than to assert the fundamental moral importance of differences in race. A law prescribing that academic record alone shall be relevant for admission to public universities (passed because the democratic process decided that meritocracy in this sense best serves the long-term welfare of the community) may or may not be unjust—but it is not unconstitutional, even if the differential treatment it prescribes is based on differences that are due in large part to naturally given talents and historically created opportunities.

By the same token, then, the debate about affirmative action is not properly understood as a constitutional debate and cannot be settled by appeal to the formal equality stipulated in the 14th Amendment. The purpose of affirmative-action programs is not to assert the fundamental moral importance of differences between individuals. On the contrary, their purpose is to correct the consequences of generations of institutionalized discrimination.

Whether or not affirmative action actually serves that purpose is certainly a relevant question. I have assumed that there are or could be forms of the practice that contribute to this end in order to highlight that the issue before us is misrepresented when affirmative action is said to violate the formal principle of democratic equality. To the contrary, the issue is whether the practice is substantively just, and the principle or set of principles proper to this debate is the one that identifies the comprehensive character of justice.

The Christian community, then, has reason to advocate effective forms of affirmative action. Since for Christians the source and end of all human life is the all-embracing love of God, it follows that human communities are meant to pursue a common good in which all share and to which all contribute. Accordingly, the comprehensive principle of justice that ought to inform all of the state's purposes prescribes giving all equal access to the common conditions of human flourishing. Christians are thereby committed not only to democracy but to a substantive principle of equality: the community should be so ordered politically that we maximize the measure in which common conditions of human happiness—for instance, educational and economic opportunities—are equally available to all.

This formulation of justice needs extended exposition before it can assist most of our political deliberations. Even in this summary form, however, it allows us to assert that the purpose of affirmative action is just. Unless we deny that discrimination against women and minorities, especially African-Americans, has resulted in acute inequality in the common conditions of human flourishing, we require policies that correct those consequences.

Perhaps some who seek to abolish affirmative action will contest the Christian conception of justice. If they do, the debate moves on to another level. But their appeal to the constitutional equality of "we, the people" remains a confusion of the issue. The only pertinent question is whether forms of affirmative action advance the common good.

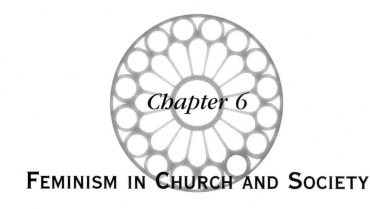

Chapter 6

FEMINISM IN CHURCH AND SOCIETY

Among the many liberation movements that began in the 1960s, the one that is most far-reaching and affects our whole society most directly is the women's movement. In terms of numbers alone, the reason is obvious enough. This movement has raised profound questions concerning what it means to be male and female and the place of the family in our society; it has compelled a male-dominated society to examine the assumptions of masculine superiority that are implicit in most forms of social organization. As with every movement intent on changing society, there is a fundamental moral character to "women's liberation" in its protest against inequality and injustice and its vision of a society in which women are better able to arrive at autonomy and self-realization.

However, when we turn from generalities to specifics, we find that the meaning of women's liberation is debated by women themselves. Such matters as economic equality (equal pay for equal work) are generally endorsed, but conservative support evaporates when some advocates of the movement speak of fundamental changes in family structure and reject the customary child rearing role of the mother. Some have even suggested that medical science should perfect the artificial womb and provide asexual reproduction as at least an option for those women who want to be freed from traditional sexual and family roles. Counterorganizations to the movement have been formed by women who argue that the goals of women's liberation actually deny the inherent distinctiveness of being feminine. They maintain that the women's movement glorifies the "male world"—that is, the world of economic production—as the ultimate place for feminine achievement as well. Much of the opposition to the Equal Rights Amendment in the 1970s from women reflected this concern that women could lose more than they might gain in their quest for equality.

One of the simplest expressions of this tension is among the most difficult to resolve: Are women the same as men, or are they different? Does biological determination imply social, cultural, intellectual, emotional, and professional differences? The feminist agenda from its earliest forms in the 19th century sought to break down discrimination against women in various areas, including education, voting, standing for and holding public office, marital and property rights, and employment. The goal behind these efforts was the equality of women and men at all levels of society. Changes obviously did not happen all at once, and the issues have received attention at different times since then. But one result of the latest round of consciousness-raising concerning the role and status of women has been a variety of legislation to promote a gender-blind world.

At the same time, different groups, including the feminist movement, have expressed the concern that our culture and laws be gender-sensitive, that is, alert to the different demands upon women compared to men. Though chiefly related to particulars like childbirth and child rearing (in such public policy issues as maternity leave, the right to resume one's job after leave, and day care), the possibilities are broadly extended when it is argued that "the woman's perspective" is needed to balance the dominant "male perspective" at all levels of society. This view calls not simply for equal access to opportunity but also for substantial representation of women in the workplace and in decision making. Although involving quite opposite goals, it is a position that actually bears close similarities to the arguments for "complementarity" between men and women made by conservative advocates like Phyllis Schafly. It was precisely those contentions of complementarity that allowed people to claim over the centuries that women should not seek to enter the world of men but should preserve their superiority, influence, and strength within their own appropriate sphere.

Whatever character this ongoing debate takes, one result of women's quest for equality in the last two decades is an increased number of women in the workplace. More than half of all women with dependent children, for example, now work outside the home. But this has not necessarily made them better off; many are in low-paying clerical positions where they continue to earn substantially less than men; and with a high incidence of divorce, they are more responsible than ever before for the sole maintenance of families. Language such as "the feminization of poverty" emerged in the 1980s to describe this reality. A chasm exists between this group and those women who, relatively speaking, are doing much better economically. Indeed, some regard feminism as a luxury of the middle and upper classes— exactly the opposite of what it was intended to be. Conflicts over abortion rights and over the moral beliefs of a more vigorous conservative religious movement have also divided women. Except for certain continuing pockets of support, it is not at all clear what the import of feminism in church and society is or should be.

Julie Polter highlights one foundation of the women's movement— women's experience itself—and explores the implications of this often neglected source of wisdom for theology and ethics. She argues that much traditional theology is androcentric. Misidentifying all human experience with the male experience results in the sanctification of patriarchy. While some feminists believe the church to be irredeemably sexist, others call for its radical reformation. Christian feminists believe that when reinterpreted in light of women's experience, significant strands of both the Bible and Christian tradition will prove liberating. Attention to the rich diversity of experience among women reveals the interconnection of many forms of oppression. Thus, present-day social justice agendas must move beyond concerns frequently perceived as "women's issues" and redress racism, classism, and heterosexism.

In articulating a conservative feminist philosophy and ethic, Katherine Kersten takes a clear step beyond those conservatives who are self-consciously antifeminist. But in basing her position on the Western tradition of justice and equality for all as well as on the concept of a universal human nature, she challenges a contemporary feminist philosophy that either argues for an essential gender difference or contends that difference is a result of the patriarchal oppression of women. By combining a conservative understanding of limitation (both of human nature and of society) with the classical feminist assertion that biology is not destiny, Kersten attempts to be realistic about possibilities for social change but also aware of the need for reform. Her primary focus is on the individual, which again connects her to the conservative tradition. Her understanding of happiness is shaped by the duties one moral being has to others and by the possibilities of personal fulfillment.

Quite the reverse of Kersten's individualistic emphasis is Jacqueline Grant's focus on black women's domestic service. Their distinctive, collective experience of servitude makes her wary of all facile attempts within Christianity to link servanthood with liberation. Grant's claim that "some folks are more servants than others" directly challenges the conservative premise that disparities in the workplace no longer stem from an individual's social location in particular groups. In addition, Grant works to unravel any theological warrants calling for the oppression of any group.

When Body Meets Soul
Julie Polter

Woman was defined as body only, historically. Man was, mind and soul, the "better" part. As body, woman was dangerous, the home of lust, the issuer of defil-

Reprinted with permission from *Sojourners*, 2401 15th St. N.W., Washington, DC 20009; (202) 328-8842; (800) 714-7474.

ing blood; she was chaos—like the sea, she only answered to the moon. She was without conscience and mind enough to know the way of righteousness on her own.

Yet women have always been mystics and preachers, prophets and teach-ers, servants and leaders, as well as whores, virgins, and mothers.

Women have talked about God—have sought, defied, laughed with, cursed, praised, wept for, and pondered God. But their knowledge has been divided up, boxed away, and ignored, except for glimmers in the story, in the tradition—the name of the house church leader, the writings of a mystic, the story of a girl raped and killed. And in that boxing up, creation itself has been divided, defiled. The full revelation of God has been packed away.

Feminist theology is, in part, the effort to reunite body and soul. It is the effort for women to reclaim the power of speech, the power to tell what they know about God, to question the tradition that tried to take away their God-given voice, to create new expressions of the life of faith. As with all passionate endeavors, it can be both controversial and a rich source of life and energy in the church.

Questions that are raised by feminist theology, even by women who fiercely claim the Christian tradition, can seem to strike at the very foundations of that faith. Alternative expressions of spirituality that emerge as women explore life with God on their own terms can seem too strange, new, different.

But we have to place theology in its proper context. It has never been an exact science or a world of once-and-for-all pronouncements. A theologian is always exploring the shifting places where revelation, tradition, his or her current circumstances, and mystery meet. Uncertainty is intrinsic to authentic theology; God cannot be caged.

In the same way, rituals aren't equations to be completed in just the right way to catch God's attention: they are hypotheses to be tested and adjusted, again and again. Deep, eternal truths will manifest themselves in changing circumstances, but some elements of tradition will fall away, take new forms, or return to their original intent. (In this way, the sinful church is called again and again to understand that the liberation of Exodus will always trump cultural justifications for slavery.)

Feminist theology brings feminist theory into the conversation about God. Just as there is not one "feminist position," there is not a single feminist theology, even if one focuses on the Christian faith. Rather, feminist theology is a stream of interpretations and emphases, welling up from some shared assumptions, but with different currents and streamlets, at many points feeding into or being fed by other traditions.

What insights does feminist theory offer? Feminism asserts that historically what has been called the human understanding of the world has more often than not been subsumed in *men's* understanding of the world. Human nature and the cosmos have been defined from the point of view of men's experience, and further, women's experience and perspectives have been suppressed. As Maria Riley has written (*Sojourners,* July 1987), "Patriarchy includes those symbols, language patterns, attitudes, structures, systems, and social and cultural mores that constantly impress upon all women their inferiority and dependency."

Feminism holds that women are, in contrast to the implications of patriarchy, fully human and fully equal. In light of this, women and men of conscience must name oppression, think about its sources, and claim their own understanding of reality. This counters the dualism that is dominant in much of human culture, which starts (consciously or not) from an assumption that authentic selfhood is male, with female being the "other," a deviant from the "norm."

Among the basic agreements and assumptions shared among feminist theologians is that most traditional theology is in fact patriarchal, created with men as its norm and men as its primary audience. (Although some women mystics and prophets in every age have been the exception to this patriarchal norm.)

Another commonly agreed upon understanding is that such theology is not only distorted and limiting of God's creation in theory, but helps to shape world views, culture and actions. Theology that denigrates women supports—even sacralizes—behavior, attitudes, and structures that do the same in society.

Finally, feminist theologians agree that women need to create theology. Women need to develop alternative interpretations of theological sources (such as scripture and tradition) that have been misused to oppress, and to seek other sources from the vantage point of women's experience.

There is not a single feminist theological method. A given Christian feminist theology, like any other specific example of Christian theology, may draw more heavily from some sources than others, and may hold different parts of tradition as more authoritative than others. The church tradition of a feminist theologian will often influence whether she or he concentrates more on, for example, church teaching, scripture, or the authenticity of new revelation through the Holy Spirit.

Most Christian feminist theologians fall within a broad range that has been called liberation feminism. Their primary interest is the liberation of women with the eventual goal of human liberation of all sorts. Such feminists may view scripture as their central authority or as just one of several (including tradition, other writings, and women's experience).

Others take women's experience as the primary norm for assessing theology: Is this theology credible to women's experience? In other words, if it can be used to promote the interests of a small group over those of the whole, if in any way it can be used to deem women non-persons, it is not credible, no matter what place it has held in Christian tradition.

Theologians who claim a Christian identity fall within the "reform" approach of feminist theology. Individually they may claim any number of the above criteria for authority (scripture; combination of scripture, tradition, and experience; or women's experience alone), but they have also made a primary affiliation or commitment to the Christian community of faith or the non-patriarchal vision demonstrated by Jesus. Other theologians have firmly decided that the Christian tradition can in no way be redeemed from patriarchy (what has been termed a "rejection-ist" approach) and now would be termed post-Christian.

While acknowledging the ways the Bible has been used as justification for women's subordination, some Christian feminists affirm that moving through-out scripture and proclaimed and demonstrated by Jesus Christ is an egalitarian, mutual, all-inclusive vision of what God calls creation to become. This biblical feminism takes the Bible as both the source for theology and the primary au-thority or norm for its authenticity.

Letha Scanzoni and Nancy Hardesty wrote *All We're Meant to Be* in the late 1970s, a landmark book based on an evangelical feminist, non-literal reading of the Bible. Using critical methods, research of tradition, and comparison of dif-ferent passages, biblical feminists assess it holistically. Some verses are then held to be less authoritative for our times because they reflect specific cultural cir-cumstances (such as 1 Timothy 2:11-12, "Let a woman learn in silence in full submission . . ."), rather than universal doctrinal statements.

Letty Russell, a Presbyterian minister (based in Harlem for many years) and theologian, argues (as has Rosemary Radford Ruether) that a "liberating tradition" located in the Bible's "'prophetic-messianic' message" serves as a self-critique of the Bible itself and critiques all structures of oppression. Russell emphasizes theology as action, relationship, and reflection—the shared work of communities (comprised of all different sorts of people) of struggle and faith. She sees the biblical story as "open-ended," being continued by those who struggle against oppression "in the light of hope in God's promise."

Others explore theology and ritual through gatherings of primarily (al-though often not exclusively) women for alternative worship ceremonies that explore symbols from both inside and outside of Christian tradition that speak to women. These include the member groups of the predominantly Catholic "Women-church" network, and a multitude of independent groups, affiliated with churches and not, ecumenical and interfaith, clergywomen groups and lay.

These broad approaches can serve as markers in the flow or range of Chris-tian feminist theology. It is best not to make idols of categories, however, for of-ten a theological position is really a hybrid of different approaches. For exam-ple, Sojourners has maintained a feminist position that is deeply rooted in the central authority of scripture. And active, concrete pursuit of liberation for all peoples also has been intrinsic to Sojourners' understanding of the Christian message.

Other approaches to feminist theological work arise to address the fact that the women's experience cited as key to feminism and feminist theology has of-ten meant white, middle-class women's experience. White women feminists can be racist and classist (actively or passively). Feminists have not always been aware that both their diagnosis of oppression and definitions of liberation have drawn from a dominant culture that might not have the same truth in the expe-rience of the African-American woman, the Latina woman, the Asian woman, the Appalachian woman, and so on.

But creating 'hierarchies of suffering' isn't especially helpful for anyone; neither is allowing those whose primary interest is the preservation of the status quo, not the elimination of sexism or racism, to pit women against one another. And as Susan Thistlethwaite, a theologian who also counsels domestic abuse victims, notes, patriarchy can kill racially and financially privileged women too.

Still, different experience draws forth different analysis and must claim different roots. Many black women have claimed the term "womanist" to describe themselves as black feminists, distinct from black males and white feminists. (For a review of three recent womanist works, see "Wading in the Water," by Cheryl J. Sanders, August 1994). Latina *mujerista* theologians such as Ada Maria Isasi-Diaz, Korean theologian Chung Hyun Chung, Chinese theologian Kwok Pui-Lan, and many, many others create new expressions of Christian faith that are specific to their culture and place.

White feminism has often talked of a sort of universal "sisterhood." Womanist theologian Jacquelyn Grant writes that "sisterhood" or "partnership" between black women and white might not be possible, since often it would be nothing more than reconciliation without liberation or repentance. But "coalition" might be the answer—"temporary alliance for some specific purpose." Various forms of oppression—racism, classism, sexism, and imperialism—are all interconnected, Grant contends. No one of them can be eliminated by challenging them separately. Black women cannot simply put aside two-thirds of their "triple burden" of race, sex, and class to engage in sisterhood.

These insights have been working their way throughout current feminist theology, with white theologians such as Thistlethwaite critiquing the lack of attention to difference in women's experience within the dominant white feminist movement. While a case could be made that feminism and feminist theology have always made some interconnection between systems of oppression, such connections—and the need for autonomy and acknowledgment of conflict among different groups of women—are becoming both more intrinsic to all feminist theology and more concrete.

Elizabeth Bettenhausen notes that while the naming and active work of resistance to oppression is now often trivialized and dismissed, people of faith are no less called to do justice. Multiple aspects of human existence are marginalized and designated as inferior in the United States: "Sex, race, class, sexual orientation, age, physical ability, mental condition—even this is the short list," Bettenhausen asserts. All subjugation is what those who would call themselves feminist must work to actively resist.

This interconnection of work for justice, among women of very different backgrounds and theological self-definitions, may be one of the most exciting and much-needed ways that feminist theological work can feed the church as it goes into the next century. Deep connections have already been made between environmental concerns and feminist theology (as both work to reunite spiritual understandings with the body, whether the human body or the body of creation).

Likewise, many feminist theologians are investigating (and working against) many edges of pain and brokenness in the world that have been neglected (and often implicitly sustained, via sexual repression and denial) by the church. Prostitution, the global sex trade, sexual abuse in the church, and child abuse are being treated seriously by theologians as places of deep pain and injustice that must be spiritually addressed, as places where God must be, and as places where previously unheard stories of faith and doubt, healing and crucifixion, are told.

Feminist theology usually evokes strong reactions, positive and negative, but often negative. An event like the November 1993 "Re-Imagining" conference, a gathering to explore women's concepts of God, Jesus, church, sexuality, and family, is still drawing angry fire from many members of the sponsoring denominations 10 months later, and has resulted in the forced resignation of at least one national Presbyterian staff person because of the controversy. Some of the tension about Re-Imagining has arisen from isolated incidents being pulled out of context to characterize the whole event negatively, and conversely, from inadequate dialogue about feminist theology with people in the pews.

But lurking beneath much of the strong emotion, the fear that arises around an event like the Re-Imagining conference, is the primal belief that woman is indeed inherently "pagan" or even "demonic." Some women, whether post-Christian or of other faith origins, have in fact freely claimed "pagan" roots or Goddess worship. Some might, as human beings are wont to do, assume that they have found the only true path and reject women who maintain ties to patriarchal religious traditions.

But this is a long way from the assumption bandied about by many critics of feminist theology that *all* woman-centered spiritual exploration, organizing, analysis, and challenge is inherently outside of the Christian tradition, or leading people to the door. It is also a long way from assuming that most women who have chosen to consider themselves post-Christian maintain a goal of drawing other women "away from the faith."

Many women have freely chosen to claim deep roots in Christian tradition and scripture *and* a firm commitment to challenging pervasive male domination. There can be very real contradictions in doing so. There are those (both from a Christian perspective and from a feminist perspective) who say it is impossible. But there is no such thing as a life of faith, a meeting of human being and mystery, that does not have contradictions, paradoxes, and questions.

Such women do not lack human conscience with which to discern the authenticity of their path and their experience of Spirit and God. (It must also be made clear that women who choose other faith explorations or traditions or no faith at all also make their choices from full human conscience as well.) Women who claim feminism are not somehow more or less vulnerable to idolatry than the priest who thirsts for power, the literalist who puts faith in a translation rather than God, or the church committee that favors the building fund over feeding the poor.

The title of a just-released book, *Defecting in Place,* describes the situation of many women. They are seeking out groups within which to explore women's spirituality, stretching their own creativity and skills, claiming responsibility for their spiritual lives and understandings—and remaining committed to their faith communities, congregations, and denominations, often in positions of lay or clerical leadership. While alienated in some ways from the church institutions, they are claiming church as the people of God and challenging the institutions to follow.

People have, almost from the beginning, tried to make the Christian church concrete and unchanging. While the institutions of the church have their dynamic moments, the community of faith, the body of Christ, is where the Spirit truly makes its home. If we do not open our eyes to the whole body, male and female, who can say what Pentecostal fire we will miss?

[handwritten margin notes: MANY FORMS OF Feminism — ALL the Same premise : PATRIARCHY is oppressive — seek justice for all women]

What Do Women Want? A Conservative Feminist Manifesto
Katherine Kersten

Am I a feminist? Like many American women, I have been uncertain for years how to respond. This might seem odd, for as a professional woman, I owe an incalculable debt to those who battled to open the voting booths, the universities, and the boardrooms to women. I believe that men and women are one another's equals, and that both sexes must be free to develop their potential unhampered by preconceptions about their abilities. Moreover, I know from personal experience that in many of their endeavors women continue to face greater obstacles to their success than men do.

Yet despite these convictions, I find I have little in common with most of the women I know who call themselves feminists. Reduced to its essence, their feminism often seems a chip on the shoulder disguised as a philosophy; an excuse to blame others for personal failures; a misguided conviction that rage is the proper response to a society that—try as it might—can't seem to arrange things so that everyone "gets it all." I sometimes feel an outright antipathy to women's organizations that claim to have an inside track on my "interests" and "perspectives," and purport to speak for me in the public arena. These organizations seem ill-equipped to advance women's happiness, for all too often their leaders appear neither to understand nor to respect the majority of American women. . . .

Reprinted with permission from the Spring 1991 issue of *Policy Review,* the flagship publication of The Heritage Foundation, 214 Massachusetts Avenue, N.E., Washington, DC 20002.

The conservative tradition incorporates a view of human nature, and of justice and equality, that offers a useful starting point to women who seek fulfillment in a world of limitation. The tradition of classical feminism takes a step beyond and teaches women that their horizons should be as limitless as men's.

FEMINISM'S FOUNDING PRINCIPLES

At the root of the American Founding is the notion of a universal human nature, which renders people everywhere more similar than different. This common humanity confers on all human beings certain natural and inalienable rights. In addition, it enables people of markedly different times and places to speak intelligibly to one another about questions of justice and virtue, of good and evil, and to enrich one another's understanding, despite the intervention of thousands of miles or thousands of years.

Yet, human nature, so noble in certain ways, is limited in its potential, as thinkers from James Madison to Thomas Sowell have reminded us. It is limited by passion and self-interest, by its finite capacity to gather and process information, and by its inability to realize its loftiest goals without provoking a host of unintended consequences. As a result of these limitations, and of human contingency on a natural world characterized by disease, disasters, and scarce resources, suffering and inequity are endemic to the human condition.

Perfect justice and equality, then, are beyond the grasp of any human society, present or future. However, justice and equality as *moral principles* must always animate the norms, institutions, and policies of a society that aspires to be good. As the political philosopher Charles Kesler has pointed out, conservatives differ from ideologies of both the Left and Right in according *prudence* a central role in determining how these principles can best be secured and honored in practice.

As Western, and specifically conservative, ideas about justice and equality have developed, a corollary line of thought has emerged. This is the tradition of classical feminism, which draws its inspiration from the Western belief in a universal human nature conferring inalienable rights on all who share it. Classical feminism holds that, because men and women participate equally in this nature, the application of uniform standards of justice and equality to both sexes is morally imperative.

EXCESSES OF CONTEMPORARY FEMINISM

Classical feminism embodies, in Cynthia Ozick's words, a vision of "aspiration and justice made universal, of mankind widened to humankind." Yet today many feminist leaders repudiate the concept of a universal human nature. In fact, as the philosopher Christina Sommers has observed, most contemporary feminist intellectuals regard human nature as "a myth invented by men to oppress women."

Contemporary feminists have little choice but to reject the concept of human nature, for it poses a fatal threat to the utopian yearnings at the heart of *their* feminist vision. Although this vision takes different forms, it tends to rely on two premises: first, that men's oppression of women is the governing principle of human social life, and second, that patriarchal social institutions are all that stand between women and a truly just and egalitarian world.

Feminists who repudiate the traditional notion of human nature have tried to replace it with one of two mutually inconsistent concepts, and have thereby plunged feminism into the intellectual schizophrenia that plagues it today. One camp—the "female chauvinists"—insists that men and women have radically *different* natures, which derive from their gender. These feminists tend to believe that men are naturally analytical, "logocentric," and obsessed with power and domination, while women are naturally intuitive, concrete, peaceful, and "life-affirming." Female chauvinists, of course, regard the female nature as superior to the male. They believe that because the two sexes lack a common nature, they have fundamentally different ways of experiencing the world, and find it difficult—if not impossible—to understand each others' perspectives.

On the other hand, feminists of the "unisex" school insist that men and women are essentially *identical.* This does not mean that they share a common nature; rather, it means that they have no discernible nature at all, but are infinitely plastic and malleable beings. Unisex feminists tend to attribute all differences in male and female behavior, preferences, and social roles to discrimination on the part of patriarchal males, or false consciousness on the part of hoodwinked women. Insisting like political scientist Richard Rorty that "socialization goes all the way down," these feminists maintain that—although men are oppressors now—re-education can eventually induce both sexes to want the same things and act in the same ways.

American women need conservatism, with its sense of the fundamental limitations of human nature and the value of the Western tradition, to temper the serious excesses that threaten contemporary feminism. But they need feminism, in its classical form, to elicit the best from conservatism. Because it starts from the premise that the world is imperfect, conservatism runs the risk of mistakenly concluding that we cannot, or need not, strive to make the world a more just place.

Conservatism, when it wavers in its active commitment to the ideas of justice and equality, too easily falls into a reflexive defense of the status quo, and a cramped and self-serving understanding of the dictates of prudence. Feminism provides a counterweight, asserting that when justice and equality are at issue, we must seek reform boldly as well as prudently. In the public sphere, conservative feminism aims to help women judge *when* change—and *which* change—is desirable, and to recognize the circumstances under which change is likely to produce unintended consequences that make matters worse, rather than better. On a personal level, conservative feminism aims to help women make choices that will render their own lives more productive and fulfilling.

OUR DUTIES, OUR SELVES

[handwritten: Components of happiness]

Conservative feminism holds that there are two essential components of happiness for both women and men. Human beings find happiness in fulfilling obligations to family, fellow citizens, and the larger human enterprise we call civilization. But they also have a deep-seated need to expand their personal horizons by turning their energies in whatever direction interest, talent, and thirst for adventure may lead.

If the conservative feminist becomes a mother, she accepts the need to make a host of sacrifices—personal, professional, and financial—for her children's sake. She expects her spouse to sacrifice as well, and decides together with him how each can best contribute to the family welfare. She believes that family roles are flexible: men can become primary caregivers, for example, while women can pursue full-time careers. But as she and her spouse make their choices about family responsibilities, they take one thing as a given: their primary duty is to ensure their children's physical and emotional well-being, to promote their intellectual development, and to shape their moral characters.

The conservative feminist sees the greatly expanded role of fatherhood as one of the most valuable legacies of classical feminism. But she is not surprised that women choose to become primary caregivers for their children more often than men do. She senses that many women *prefer* to spend time at home with their children, especially when the children are very young. She is joined in this view by as prominent a feminist as Simone de Beauvoir, who opposed allowing women to stay home and raise their children because "if there is such a choice, too many women will make that one." Unlike Beauvoir, however, the conservative feminist views the special bond of motherhood not as evidence of oppression, but as cause for thanksgiving.

[handwritten: Is it a consciousness issue]

DUTIES TO COMMUNITY AND TRADITION

The conservative feminist knows that her own good, and that of her family, are inextricably bound up with the good of the larger community. She believes she has a duty to promote the public welfare by strengthening the institutions that promote communal values, and by shaping her community's vision of justice and equality.

The conservative feminist strives to make time for voluntary organizations such as the church or synagogue, the PTA, and the service clubs, which provide her community's social glue and enhance its quality of life. If work-related constraints prevent her from contributing directly to community-building, she makes a special effort to acknowledge and support those who do give generously of their time. In her view, men and women who labor voluntarily to promote the common good deserve at least as much respect as men and women who are paid for their exertions.

Moreover, the conservative feminist seeks to develop a prudential understanding of the ways in which justice and equality, as moral principles, can best be realized in her own society. For guidance, she looks to the Western cultural tradition, with its legacy of democratic institutions and civil rights. Like the philosopher Alasdair MacIntyre, she views the Western tradition as "an historically extended, socially embodied *argument"* about good and evil, and about the nature of the good life. She believes that before she can contribute to this argument, she must study the great ideas and social forces that have shaped the Western heritage. By learning from the lessons of history, she hopes to develop a capacity for judgment that will clarify, as MacIntyre would say, "the future possibilities which the Western past has made available to the Western present."

IN PURSUIT OF HAPPINESS

For centuries women have carried out duties toward family and community, and have found satisfaction in doing so. Yet there is more to the pursuit of happiness than the performance of duties. Women's historical exclusion from whole fields of human endeavor has greatly restricted the dimensions of life in which they have been able to seek and find personal fulfillment. Until recently, women could not educate themselves broadly, express themselves politically or artistically, live independent of the authority of father or husband, or pursue most vocations with a locus outside the home.

The conservative feminist rejoices in the achievements of her era's most accomplished women: Jackie Joyner-Kersee; Barbara Tuchman; Sally Ride; Leontyne Price; Margaret Thatcher; Nobel prize-winning scientist Barbara McClintock; novelist and scholar Margaret Drabble. She seeks to ensure that women everywhere have the opportunity to participate in *all* aspects of the human enterprise: to develop their talents, to follow their interests to their natural conclusion, to seek adventure, to ask and answer the great questions, and to select from a multitude of social roles.

EQUAL RIGHTS, COMPARABLE WRONGS

Like other feminists, the conservative feminist sees the promotion of justice and equality as a primary goal of public policy. Yet she understands these principles quite differently than do most contemporary feminists. Specifically, the conservative feminist tends to see *individuals* as having rights to justice and equality, while other feminists tend to see *groups* as having such rights.

The conservative feminist understands justice in universal terms: she believes that its essence is fair treatment for *all* citizens. Justice requires that women have equal access to employment, education, housing, and credit, and—thanks to the civil rights legislation of the '60s and '70s—their rights to these things are now secure. But the conservative feminist believes that it is manifestly unjust to pass laws that create a privileged status for women, or that

attempt to remedy past wrongs done to women by imposing wrongs or disad- *Support*
vantages upon men. . . .

THE CONSERVATIVE FEMINIST AGENDA

The conservative feminist's political and social agenda differs markedly from
that of most contemporary feminists. Not surprisingly, she believes that there
are far more urgent threats to the average woman's well-being than the "glass
ceiling," the predominantly male composition of fire departments, or the possibility that state legislatures, rather than the Supreme Court, may someday decide matters related to abortion.

Of most concern to the conservative feminist are contemporary social
conditions that inflict disproportionate suffering and hardship on women, and
threaten their ability to grasp new opportunities. Other feminists also lament *unfair-*
these conditions, and some even take time out from raising funds for the
National Abortion Rights Action League to say so. But the sad fact is that many
feminists are prevented from effectively addressing fundamental threats to
women's welfare by their hostility to the "bourgeois" values and social institutions that ordinary women find meaningful.

Four pressing issues top the conservative feminist's agenda:

Crime: Rape and violence against women are naturally a major concern of
contemporary feminism. What most feminists overlook is the disproportionate impact of other sorts of crime on women. . . .

Cultural degradation: The popular culture increasingly shapes Americans' moral and cultural horizons. Unfortunately, it routinely degrades and
abuses women in ways that would have elicited universal cries of protest in
less liberated days.

Sex without commitment: A fundamental tenet of contemporary feminism is that women must become men's "sexual equals" if they expect to
become their political and social equals. Sex, many feminists insist, is
merely one component of a healthy, self-affirming lifestyle, and as such requires no serious commitment from either partner to be enjoyed. Feminists
often explain traditional restraints on women's sexual freedom in one-
dimensional terms, dismissing them as male attempts to wrest control of
women's vital reproductive functions.   *even this term*

The feminization of poverty: Illegitimacy and divorce—and the poverty
they engender—blight the lives of American women and their children to
an ever more appalling degree. One-quarter of American children are now
born out of wedlock, and most endure lives of privation as a result. The
sociologist Lenore Weitzman's finding regarding the economic effects of divorce has passed into American folklore: Divorced men experience an average 42 percent rise in their standard of living in the first year after the
divorce, while divorced women and their children experience a 73 percent
decline. Moreover, children whose fathers are absent from the home are far

more likely than others to be plagued by drug use, violent behavior, and dismal educational performance. Mothers frequently fight the uphill battle against these risks alone.

Contemporary feminists deplore the feminization of poverty, but they tend to see the answer solely in terms of increasing government spending, rather than in terms of encouraging behavior that would stabilize and strengthen the traditional family. After all, to acknowledge that marriage is women's best defense against poverty and despair, or that two-parent families generally serve children better than one-parent families do, is to admit that women need men more than fish need bicycles. Yet despite many feminists' reluctance to face this fact, 25 years of failed government programs seem to prove unequivocally to most observers that Uncle Sam can't fill Dad's shoes.

[handwritten margin note: this is wrong — if perhaps the programs were more generous]

PRIVATE SOLUTIONS

The conservative feminist maintains that women have largely won their battle for equality before the law. This does not mean that discrimination and harassment are likely to disappear soon. It does mean that women now have the tools they need to combat injustice of this sort, and that those who look to government for more comprehensive solutions risk creating other, more far-reaching problems. Reform is essential, however, in laws that affect family life. Divorce and child support legislation, in particular, must be altered if women and their children are to enjoy equal status with men.

But the conservative feminist is careful not to make the mistake of seeking exclusively political solutions to problems that are essentially social and cultural in nature. She believes that changing individual behavior is the key to reducing the ills that consign an increasing number of women to second-class citizenship. She knows, of course, that passing laws can be easy, while influencing behavior is notoriously difficult. Nevertheless, starting at home and in her immediate community, she attempts to do just that.

Addressing herself to young people, the conservative feminist seeks to define responsible behavior, and to articulate compelling arguments in its favor. She urges social institutions—schools, churches, and community leaders—to join in this effort and to stress in all their activities that public welfare depends on private virtue. She believes that the environmental movement, which has had a powerful effect on the imaginations of young people, provides a useful model in this respect. For that movement shares many of the premises that the conservative feminist wishes to promote: that citizenship entails responsibilities, that the actions of every person affect the good of the whole, that it is better to do what is right than what is convenient, and that careless actions now may have unforeseen deleterious consequences down the road.

[handwritten margin note: Yes! the role of individuals — very relevant to this kind of issue!]

The conservative feminist also attempts to influence, or at least to blunt the harmful effects of, the popular culture. She strives to convince parents of the fact—well known to social philosophers from Plato to Jane Addams—that young people's imaginations and moral reflexes are shaped as much by the stories and images of the surrounding culture as by the formal lessons taught in school. Children who spend their after-school hours watching MTV rock stars demean scantily clad women are, in a sense, being *educated* about society's expectations regarding conduct toward women. The conservative feminist lets entertainment executives and advertisers know how she feels about their products, and she supports concerted action to convince them that such products don't pay.

The conservative feminist attempts to provoke public scrutiny of the consequences of feminist policies for the average American woman. She makes clear that feminist leaders do harm every time they deride the traditional family as the hungup legacy of Ozzie and Harriet; demand the adoption of University of Beijing-style sexual harassment regulations; or burden the court system with yet another costly and ill-conceived class-action suit. Her objective is to persuade foundations and public bodies to rethink the resources they devote to the feminist establishment and to question the rhetoric and world view on which it is based.

Although she seeks to break their near-monopoly in the public policy arena, the conservative feminist encourages feminist organizations to use their resources and political clout in ways that truly benefit the majority of women. If these organizations devoted themselves to reversing the popular culture's degradation of women, for example, they might well do real good. And, if public or student demand were loud enough, the women's studies programs now firmly in the grip of academic feminists might be compelled to expand their "oppression studies" curriculum to include useful investigations of "real world" gender-related issues, like the causes and consequences of divorce and the realities of balancing a family and career.

ARCHITECT OF HER OWN HAPPINESS

As she carries out the tasks she has set for herself, the conservative feminist cultivates an intellectual outlook quite distinct from that of most contemporary feminists. The word "victim" does not trip easily off her tongue. She regards adversity as an inevitable component of human life rather than an aberration afflicting primarily her and her sex. When hard times come, she strives to face them with courage, dignity, and good humor—qualities often in short supply in the feminist camp. And when her own shortcomings lead to failure, she resists the temptation to blame a hostile "system."

The conservative feminist is the architect of her own happiness. She finds happiness in striving to fulfill her responsibilities, to cultivate wisdom, to develop her talents, and to pursue excellence in all her endeavors. The world being what it is she knows that excellence must sometimes be its own reward. But no matter how unfair or frustrating others' behavior may be, she refuses to seek solace in a life of rage and self-pity. Rage and self-pity, she knows, are hallmarks of the weak, not of the strong.

At the heart of the conservative feminist's vision is her conception of a universal human nature. Believing that men and women share equally in this nature, she rejects the contemporary feminist view of life as a power struggle, in which self-oriented "interest groups" contend relentlessly for advantage. The conservative feminist knows that it is possible to identify transcendent *human* interests that can mediate between the sexes' competing claims and thereby illuminate a truly common good.

In everything she does, the conservative feminist's watchword is "balance." In her private life, she strives to balance her obligations to others with her quest for personal fulfillment. In her public life, she seeks to promote justice and equality, but also to safeguard individual freedom. Her boldness in pursuit of reform is tempered by her respect for fundamental social values and institutions, which embody the collective wisdom of generations who sought the good life as fervently as she. Prudent in her expectations, tireless in her quest for knowledge, she seeks to explore—and to advance—the conditions necessary for human happiness.

The Sin of Servanthood and the Deliverance of Discipleship
Jacquelyn Grant

. . . Many contradictions stared me in the face a few years ago when I was in the midst of my dissertation process. The study, a comparative analysis of Black women's and white women's experiences of Jesus Christ, led me to exploring the lived realities of Black women and white women.[1] One theme that constantly emerged was that of "servanthood." Why is this the case? Could it be that women in general are believed to be, by nature, servants of men, and in the context of women's community, Black women are seen primarily as servants to all?

The theme "servanthood" was intriguing because of the contexts in which it was and is used. As critical components to Christianity, the notions of "service" and "servanthood," when seen against lordship, may be perceived as a necessary dialectical tension, but when viewed in light of human indignities perpetrated against those who have been the "maid servants" of the society, they represent contradictions. Indeed, we are all called to be "servants."

From "The Sin of Servanthood," by Jacqueline Grant in *A Troubling in My Soul,* edited by Emilie M. Townes, Orbis Books, Maryknoll, New York, © 1993, Orbis Books. Reprinted by permission of publisher and author.

It is interesting, however, that these terms are customarily used to relegate certain victimized peoples—those on the underside of history—to the lower rung of society. Consequently, politically disenfranchised peoples have generally been perceived as the servant class for the politically powerful. Nonwhite peoples, it is believed by many white people, were created for the primary purpose of providing service for white people. Likewise, in patriarchal societies, the notions of service and servant were often used to describe the role that women played in relation to men and children.

As I examined the words and work of nineteenth-century feminists, I found that white women were challenging the fact that they were relegated to the level of "servants of men." They were incensed because they were being treated as second-class citizens in the larger society, and second-class Christians in the church. Certainly, any perusal of history in general, and women's history in particular, validates their claim.

Further, an examination of Black women's reality reveals that they are further removed from the topside of history. In fact, African-American women have been the "servants of the servants." It was clear that one of the best entrées for comparing the lives of white and Black women was through the study of slavery and of domestic service. This kind of comparison would allow us to answer partially the old theodicy question in relation to Black women—because service has been basically a life of suffering for those "relegated" to that state, the question to be raised is, why do Black women suffer so? Or even more pointedly, why does God permit the suffering of Black women? Does God condone the fact that Black women are systematically relegated to being "servants of servants?"

It is said that confession is good for the soul. Let me therefore confess my problem, at that time, with this line of research inquiry. Given the nature of Black women's servanthood/servitude, I found it difficult to settle for the use of such terminologies to describe their relationship with God. Servanthood in this country, in effect, has been servitude. It (service) has never been properly recognized. Servants have never been properly remunerated for their services. One could possibly argue that by definition, one does not engage in services for monetary gains, but for benevolent reasons instead. However, if this is so, one could ask, why is it that certain people are more often than others relegated to such positions? Further, why is it that these positions are more often than not relegated to the bottom (or at least the lower end) of the economic scale? Why is it that those so-called service positions that are higher or high on the economic scale are almost always held by those of an oppressor race, class, or gender? For example, public officials claim to be public servants; they are most often of the dominant culture, white and male. The hierarchy of the church claims to be servants of God and the people, yet they are likewise most often of the dominant culture—white and/or male. Generally and relatively speaking, they are economically well-off, or at least adequately provided for. This is not often true for service/servants on the lower rung of society. Why are the real servants overwhelmingly poor, Black, and Third

World? Why is their service status always controlled by the upholders of the status quo?

These questions lead me to postulate that perhaps Christians, in the interest of fairness and justice, need to reconsider the servant language, for it has been this language that has undergirded much of the human structures causing pain and suffering for many oppressed peoples. The conditions created were nothing short of injustice and, in fact, sin.

FEMINIST REDEMPTION OF SERVANTHOOD

Feminists have attempted to redeem the notion of service, servant and servanthood. In explicating her position that Jesus is the representative for all, Letty Russell draws upon traditional phrases and words such as "Jesus is Lord" (*kyrios*) and "servant" (*diakonos*). Finding no problem with either of these terms, she emphasizes in her discussion that these functions are necessary. Recognizing the possible objection to the use of such metaphors as servant and Lord, Russell is quick to refer to the true meaning of servant, Lord, and lordship. Servant and Lord are defined not as the titles for the oppressed and oppressors, or inferior and superior persons, which they have come to mean in our unjust and oppressive church and society. But they are used to refer to "one divine *oikonomia*."...

Rosemary Radford Ruether prepares the way for her liberation approach to Christology when she poses the question, "Can Christology be liberated from its encapsulation in the structures of patriarchy and really become an expression of liberation of women?"[2] Ruether provides a positive response to the question. Two concepts are elevated, "service" and "conversion." Service must not be confused with servitude. In her view, "Service implies autonomy and power used in behalf of others."[3] We are called to service. Our conversion is to accept this call by abandoning previous, inaccurate notions of being called to hierarchical and oppressive leadership and power....

It seems that Ruether is getting at the real issue at hand, "power." Here, service is connected with empowerment. The question that remains is, in what way(s) is there mutual empowerment? Does this mutuality extend to all of humanity?

SOME FOLK ARE MORE SERVANTS THAN OTHERS

Both of these thinkers, Russell and Ruether, have provided reformulations that are helpful in making somewhat palatable a traditional Christian concept that is distasteful, to say the least, because of its history of misuse and abuse. They have articulated Christologies of which service, suffering, empowerment and Lordship are integral parts.

As I examined my discomfort with this, I felt that perhaps my problem was with the ease with which Christians speak of such notions as service and servant. Perhaps my discomfort stemmed from the experiential knowledge of the Black community vis-à-vis service and particularly the Black women vis-à-vis domestic service. Black people's and Black women's lives demonstrate to us that some people are more servant than others. In what ways have they been substantially empowered? Has there been social, political, or economic empowerment? Is the empowerment simply an overspiritualization of an oppressed and depressed reality?

Studies in the area of Black women's work—domestic service—demonstrate the point that is being made here. It enables us to see not only that some people are more servant than other, but more specifically, that relationships among women of the dominant culture and minority women merely mirror the domination model of the larger society....

Though legally emancipated, servants were still essentially (treated as) property. The life of servants was almost as controlled as it was during slavery. Domestic service is personal service related so much to the personal property of slavery times that it too was unregulated by law. Still under the conditions of servitude, Black women, as Black people, were considered subordinate property and unequal in pursuit of life, liberty, and happiness. Katzman credits racial stereotype as the justification of the subordination of Black women in the South. According to popular view, Blacks "were childlike, lazy, irresponsible, and larcenous." They were worthless, dirty, dishonest, unreliable, and incompetent.[4] In ruling over them, white women were only acting in the best "interest of all concerned." ...

These questions that Black women pose, then, coming out of women's experience, represent merely a microcosm of the larger society. What is the meaning of such conciliatory notions as "we are all called to be servants?" What is the significance of a distinction between service and servitude, when for Black women they have been one and the same? Service has not led to empowerment and liberation, but in fact has insured that they not happen. This leads to a theological dilemma.

SERVANTHOOD: A THEOLOGICAL DILEMMA

The dilemma for me is a theological one that can be expressed in two questions. The first question emerges out of white women's claim that *women's experiences* is the source for feminist theology. In light of the data presented vis-à-vis the servant relationship between two groups of women in this country, my question is, which women's experience is the source of theology? Further, one could ask, how do these experiences impact the direction taken in one's theological perspective? Is it the experience of the daughters of slaveholders or the experience of the daughters of slaves? These two experiences are irreconcilable as they stand. Certainly, servanthood is not the only dimension of women's experiences. But still, before we can realistically talk about reconciling the women of both groups, we must find that which is required for eradicating the pain and suffering inflicted by the one group upon the other. We must ask, how is the gulf bridged between two groups of people who, though they have lived in close proximity, have radically different lives?

Womanist theology acknowledges these experiences. They cannot be covered up or swept under the rug, so to speak; they must be confronted with intentionality. To speak of sisterhood prematurely is to camouflage the reality. We must begin to eliminate the obstacles of sisterhood—the hate, the distrust, the suspicion, the inferiority/superiority complex. The same can be said about humanity in general. Racism, classism, and other forms of oppression are still deeply embedded in the church and society. Until the relational issues are adequately addressed, it is premature (or at least not very meaningful) to speak of such things as reconciliation and community. In other words, we must seek salvation, for we've been living in a world of sin. That is, we've been perpetuating the sins of racism, sexism, classism and so forth.

Second, I am led to ask, how does one justify teaching a people that they are called to a life of service when they have been imprisoned by the most exploitative forms of service? Service and oppression of Blacks went hand in hand. Therefore, to speak of service as empowerment, without concrete means or plans for economic, social, and political revolution that in fact leads to empowerment, is simply another form of "overspiritualization." It does not eliminate real pain and suffering, it merely spiritualizes the reality itself. It's one thing to say that people spiritualize in order to "make it through the days, weeks, and months" of agony. But it is another to give the people a "pie in the sky" theology, so that they would concern themselves with the next world in order to undergird the status quo. The one can be seen as liberating while the other is oppressive.

The one begs respect; the other begs the question: how do you propose that we are called to service to Jesus, the one who has been sent by God to redeem us, when both God and Jesus have been principal weapons in the oppressors' arsenal to keep Blacks and Black women in their appropriate place? Both God and Jesus were portrayed as white and male and interested primarily in preserving the white patriarchal and racist status quo. In light of that then, do we simply answer Bill Jones' question—yes, God is white racist[5]— not only that, but God is also a male chauvinistic pig—an irredeemable sexist? Is God actually responsible for the systemic pain and suffering of Blacks and women? Does God condone the servanthood relationships between Blacks and women? If we are unwilling or unable to accept the proposition implied in an affirmative response to these questions, then how are the redeemers liberated from the oppressive structures of the oppressor? How do we liberate God? Bill Jones answers this inquiry by proposing that reality must be viewed from a humanocentric perspective. In other words, the conditions that existed have resulted from human beings' will for evil and not from God's will. Effectively, Jones has liberated the redeemers from the structure of oppression by locating them strictly in the human world. When applied to the notion of servanthood, one can squarely locate the problems with oppressive human beings. The sin of servanthood is the sin of humanity that results from the sociopolitical interests of proponents of the status quo and their attempts to undergird their intended goal through psychological conditioning that comes partially with the institutionalization of oppressive language, even theological language.

THEOLOGICAL LANGUAGE AND LIBERATION

[handwritten: Location of Theology]

The language that we use to talk about God more often than not says more about the speaker than about God. Understanding the context of the speakers, then, is critical for interpreting the language about God.... What is appropriate or adequate theological language? Language, including theological language, arises out of the context of the community, or the experiences of the people. The recent debate about inclusive versus exclusive language demonstrates not only how language emerges out of community situations, but also how powerful language really is. Those who are in control of the dominant culture are in control of the language and consequently, men have produced language that is advantageous to men and disadvantageous to women. Language functions the same in oppressive ideology and theology. For example, in racist ideology and theology, in color symbolism, Black is invariably evil and white is good....

A Black woman Ph.D. candiate in religious studies recently told of her experience in a northern seminary of constantly being presumed to be the maid by both professors and students. Serving is reserved for victims, while being served is the special privilege of victimizers, or at least representative of the status quo. These privileged servants are often served by servants who are in fact often treated as slaves. The process of euphemizing is often used to camouflage the real meaning of the language.

Clarice Martin, in her article "Womanist Interpretations of the New Testament," provides insights into the dangers of euphemizing and cautions us against it. To the tendency of some to interpret the Greek *doulos* as *servant,* Martin argues that the correct interpretation is *slave,* and to interpret it otherwise would be to camouflage the real injustice in relationships of biblical times and of today.... A language needs to be adopted or emphasized that challenges the servant mentality of oppressed peoples and the oppressive mentality of oppressors.

FROM DOUBLE CONSCIOUSNESS TO DELIVERANCE

African-American thinker W. E. B. DuBois is helpful, perhaps not in resolving the dilemma identified in this essay, but certainly in helping us to see more clearly the African-American reality. In articulating the spiritual struggle of Black people, DuBois speaks of a double consciousness.

> After the Egyptian and Indian, the Greek and Roman, the Teuton and Mongolian, the Negro is a sort of seventh son, born with a veil, and gifted with second-sight in this American world—a world which yields him no true self-consciousness, but only lets him see himself through the revelation of the other world. It is a peculiar sensation, this double-consciousness, this sense of always looking at one's self through the eyes of others, of measuring one's soul

by the tape of the world that looks on in amused contempt and pity. One ever
feels his twoness—an American, a Negro; two souls, two thoughts, two unrec-
onciled strivings; two warring ideals in one dark body, whose dogged strength
alone keeps it from being torn asunder.[6]

When I consider the "twoness" or "double" nature of the Black consciousness (and in fact the triple nature of Black women's consciousness), I am able to
reconsider my thesis that this servanthood theme in Christianity needs to be
eliminated from Christian theology for it has outlived its usefulness.

What we find instead is the capacity of Blacks to live in two or more worlds
at the same time. They understood what their relationship with the other
world—the white world—was to be. Even when they did not accept it, they understood it nonetheless. Survival made this a necessity.

For Black people the double-consciousness meant that Blacks, to some degree, functioned in the white world on terms defined by that world. In the white
world, Blacks were referred to as "uncle," "joe," "tom," "aunty," and "mammy." It
is also the case that Black people functioned in their own world based on their
own self-understanding. Black people in their churches knew themselves to be
"deacon," "trusty," "mrs.," "sister," and "brother." This point was perhaps not adequately expressed by DuBois, for Blacks indeed did not always see themselves
through the eyes of white people.

With this in mind it is possible to understand the birth of the Black church.
It was a public declaration that our self-understanding took precedence over
the definition of the other world or the external world. In this context we
can be truly servants of the living Christ. This brings me back to my original
problem regarding Black women and servanthood. What sense does it make to
rejoice in the service of a man (Jesus), who has been used not to save but to
exploit?

The triple consciousness of Black women makes it possible to see how
they were able to liberate redemption as they overtly and covertly challenged
the assumption of the racist and sexist status quo. That triple consciousness
gave them the possibility of experiencing a liberating Jesus even as they were
given a racist and sexist one. It enabled me to better understand how Black
women relegated to domestic service could go to church on Tuesday, Wednes-
day nights and Sunday morning and testify of being a better servant of the Lord
and Savior Jesus. What they were saying was perhaps what the early church
was saying to the Roman Empire when they professed Jesus Christ as Lord. Or
what Karl Barth and the confessing church of Germany were saying when they
gave their allegiances to Jesus rather than to Hitler, or what the Southern
African writers of *The Kairos Document* meant as they proclaimed a living and
just God.

Perhaps what these Black women were saying is that what "I am forced to
do on Monday through Saturday is redemptive only in the sense that it facilitates
survival." In this sense, then, Martin Luther King, Jr., was right, suffering is redemptive.[7] True redemption takes place when one experiences the redeemer

even as it is in the context of oppression. Their speaking of such titles as Lord and Master with regard to Jesus and God meant that the lords and masters of the white world were illegitimate.

The church and/or religious experience for African Americans allowed them the opportunity to express their spirituality freely—at least to a certain degree. For African-American women the third level of consciousness is accented as we consider the limitations placed upon women even within the church/religious sphere. This third consciousness level caused some women to challenge the church internally and in other instances it resulted in women leaving the church still in the pursuit of liberating themselves and Jesus.

When Jesus was liberated from the oppressive theology of the white church and the white consciousness, Black women were able to see themselves as "servants" of the Christ and not of the oppressive world. It was Jesus who befriended Sojourner Truth when no one else could or would; it was Jesus that made Jarena Lee preach anyhow. In more recent times, it was Jesus that provided guidance for Mary McLeod Bethune and Jesus that motivated activist Fannie Lou Hamer. Black women/African-American women were constantly liberating Jesus and Jesus was liberating them.

Where then is the dilemma? If I listen to Black women's communities I would say that the dilemma is at the point of having to live in two and sometimes three different worlds, their world and the world of oppressors (the white world and the male world). Womanist theology is committed to bringing wholism to Black women. Being a servant of the redeemer means joining in the struggle of the redeemer against oppression, wherever it is found. If the source is white women, that is, being consumed in the universal definition of women's experiences, then Black women must continue to challenge the oppressive notions. This may mean challenging traditional notions of servanthood and embracing a more liberal understanding of the self.

AN INVITATION TO CHRISTIAN DISCIPLESHIP

DuBois' notion of double consciousness is helpful in understanding how oppressed peoples are able to live in a world designed to keep them in an appointed place, and yet move beyond that world. Martin Luther King, Jr.'s notion of "suffering servant" explains how Black people and Black women were able to make sense out of, and possibly bring hope out of, apparently hopeless life situations.[8] Whereas both of these interpretations are helpful as a part of the survival strategies of Black people, they are unable to provide adequate substance for liberation. For liberation to happen the psychological, political, and social conditions must be created to nurture the processes. Servant language does not do this. What is the best way to create these conditions?

Susan Nelson Dunfee has suggested that we must move beyond servanthood, for traditional notions of service (and altruism) do not provide an adequate way of interpreting the Christian experience of liberation. The category that is most helpful for her is that of "friendship." Jesus, she argues, calls us to be friends, for "the freedom and authority grounded in the friendship of Jesus would empower women to our liberation."[9]

Though the category of "friendship" is helpful in undercutting the "domination/submission" model inherent in the servanthood model, I would suggest that the model of discipleship implies more of an empowerment model, particularly for a group of people, women, who have not been considered to be disciples. As a part of most church programs/services, there is usually an opportunity to "join church," as some would say, or to become Christian. It is often referred to as the "call to Christian discipleship." The truth of the matter, however, is that when women "join the church," they are not allowed to become full members, with all of the rights and privileges invested therein; rather, they are only permitted to become servants. Contrary to popular beliefs, women are not full members because they are not given opportunities for full participation at all levels of the church, particularly at the decision-making levels. Women must be invited into the power houses of the church and society to participate on all levels.

Given the overwhelming racial and gender politics that relegate Blacks, other third-world peoples and women to the level of mere servant, there stands a great need for a language of empowerment. Servanthood language has, in effect, been one of subordination. Perhaps, we need to explore the language of discipleship as a more meaningful way of speaking about the life-work of Christians. We are all called to be disciples. True, the "disciples' club" has been given to us as an "old boys' club." I'm not suggesting that the goal of women and minority men ought simply be to join the "old boys' club." What I am suggesting instead is that the club may need to be shattered, and the real discipling network must be restored.

Womanist theology seeks to foster a more inclusive discipleship. The kind of wholism sought in womanist theology requires that justice be an integral part of our quest for unity and community. I would suggest that the discussion above indicates that, minimally, three areas of concern must be addressed in theological reformulations.

First, we must resist the tendency of using language to camouflage oppressive reality, rather than eliminating the oppressive reality itself. My distaste for the use of such terms as "service" and "servant" is paralleled by similar suspicion in using such terms as "reconciliation," "covenant relationship," "unity" or "community." How can we realistically talk about these things when we are not yet seriously grappling with racism, sexism, classism, and other oppressive structures that plague our reality? It is tantamount to the concern for peace, without equal love for justice and liberation. The fact of the matter is that these terms—service, reconciliation, community, etc.—are apparently nonthreatening. Who can be against them? But just as service and servanthood have historically slipped into servitude, these concepts run the similar danger, if the conciliatory language is not given substance with actions of justice. . . .

For example, real concern for liberation may mean relinquishing our preoccupation with reconciliation and peace. Instead, our energies must be refocussed upon liberation and justice—after all, true liberation and justice include reconciliation and peace anyway. In the same way, this means that being a true "servant" may mean relinquishing the dubious honor of servanthood.

Second, we must resist the tendency of relegating some to the lower rung of society. Certainly, the data I have articulated above strongly indicates that some people are more servant than others. Any Christian relationship must eliminate the injustices of such relationships. In fact the kind of relationships that have existed between women (and men) of the dominant culture and third-world women (and men) must be destroyed. A few years ago, the argument of some feminists on the question of sin was that women needed to reexamine the question of sin as it has been interpreted traditionally within the context of patriarchal Christian community. When we examine women's experiences, we may discover, they argue, that perhaps pride—one of those old patriarchal sins—is not the sin of women, but instead, too much pride is sin. In the same vein, I would argue that perhaps, for women of color, the sin is not the lack of humility, but the sin is too much humility. Further, for women of color, the sin is not the lack of service, but too much service. The liberation of servants means that women will no longer shoulder the responsibility of service. Oppressed people, women of color, men of color will no longer be relegated to the place of servanthood and servitude. But, there will be justice in living the Christian life. Justice means that some will give up, and some will gain; but all will become disciples; that is, simultaneously, oppressors must give up or lose oppressive power, as oppressed people are empowered for discipleship.

Third, we must resist the tendency of devaluing the lives of people by virtue of who they are. The data strongly demonstrates that some people are victimized even to the extent of having their very humanity denied. How can justice be a reality when servants are considered less than human? The affirmation of humanity must move far beyond mere words to deeds of justice. This justice must be more than mere equality. Certainly, minimally it must include equality. Fannie Lou Hamer challenged us at this point when she challenged us to move beyond equality. The affirmation of humanity causes us to move beyond the mere acceptance and acknowledgement of societal and church structures—political, social, and theological. These oppressive structures that render and keep "some people more servant than others" must be eliminated. The church does not need servants, as oppressively conceived and experienced by many; the church needs followers of Christ—disciples.

Women have been invited to become disciples. In the historical records, women were left out of the inner circle of the disciples. Therefore, women must be empowered to become disciples. The language of discipleship for women provides the possibility of breaking down traditional stereotypical, exclusivistic understandings of discipleship. Overcoming the sin of servanthood can prepare us for the deliverance that comes through discipleship.

Chapter 7

HETEROSEXISM

Not too many years ago homosexuality was mentioned only on the fringes of polite or serious conversation regarding sexuality, and those with same-sex partners were harassed, condemned, and subjected to assaults from the law. The civil rights movement with its aim to empower African Americans and the parallel concern in the 1960s to guarantee rights for individuals each contributed to the growing visibility of the homosexual community and its own claims for "Gay Liberation." Not only did the tone of discussion begin to shift as a result of these pressures, but new terminology emerged as well, such as "homophobia" and "heterosexism" to describe a socially determined prejudice and system of discrimination that should be condemned as strongly as racism or sexism. The very act of shifting the guilt was a major transformation in itself.

The churches, along with other institutions in our society, participated in this transformation. The emergence of the Metropolitan Community Churches in 1968 was a testimony to the neglect or rejection of homosexual persons by established denominations as well as to the interest of many gays and lesbians to be part of a meaningful religious community. But it did not stop there. Several denominations continue to wrestle with the question of ordination to the ministry; most still declare that they will not ordain openly gay men and lesbians, but they have at the same time encouraged a ministry to and with homosexual Christians and defended (to some extent) their civil rights.

The fact is that Christian theologians and ethicists, as well as denominational leaders and members, hold sharply divergent views on the nature of homosexuality and on the appropriate response to it. Some maintain what can be called the "traditional" view, in which homosexuality is regarded as a perversion that warrants a clear negative judgment from the church. More recent writers who reflect this position are often careful about expressing condemnation; yet they emphasize the "natural" or God-ordained character of heterosexuality and the consequent aberration that is inherent in homosexual activity. Our "creatureliness" includes our heterosexuality, and it is in knowing the opposite sex that we come most fully to know ourselves. The homosexual person, for whatever reason, is caught in a deviant orientation that prevents him or her from attaining the fullness of that self-knowledge that belongs to our very being as heterosexual creatures.

A different approach begins with the empirical evidence concerning the nature of homosexuality. It takes issue with the way in which the traditional position makes such a firm distinction between hetero- and homosexuality, arguing that the evidence indicates that our maleness-femaleness is a continuum in each of us, rather than an exclusive duality. Thus, the picture is too ambiguous for us to make clear and decisive judgments. Representatives of this second group do regard a heterosexual orientation as morally preferable; at the same time they are willing to acknowledge that homosexual persons can and do maintain meaningful and life-building relationships that are justifiable. Rather than pronouncing judgment, these writers see a need for understanding and support in order to enable homosexual persons to make as satisfying an adjustment as possible in a world that is hostile to them.

A third viewpoint maintains that homosexuality is as acceptable an orientation as heterosexuality. Human beings display a variety of sexual expression and needs, and any normative judgment must be limited to rejecting exploitative sexual activity, whether heterosexual or homosexual. This is the position of the well-known English Quaker statement of 1963, which declared that homosexuality is no more to be deplored than left-handedness. Rather than attending to the division between hetero- and homosexuality, the question to be asked is whether persons can be loving and faithful in their sexual activity. Since there appears to be ample evidence that homosexual persons can be (a point disputed by others, however), their sexual activity should be regarded as morally neither better nor worse just because it is homophile in orientation.

We have noted in Chapter 2 the important—but often ambiguous—role that scripture plays for Christians in working out a response to social issues. What constitutes faithful interpretation of scripture has become a particularly contentious issue in regard to homosexuality. James B. Nelson argues that what scripture says about this topic is not as clear as many would have us believe. Indeed he argues the questions about homosexuality with which we wrestle are not directly addressed in the Bible. Insights from several additional sources of moral wisdom—tradition, reason, and experience—invite Christians to affirm homosexuality as a good gift of God.

In contrast, the Ramsey Colloquium argues against this celebration. Its members interpret human sexual differentiation in such a way that calls for the restraint of any sexual desires that do not draw people toward procreative and complementary unions. The claims of the gay movement are then refuted on the basis of this heterosexual norm.

In early 1991, the Centers for Disease Control reported that over the previous 10 years some 100,000 Americans had died of AIDS, with nearly a third of the deaths occurring the year before. Researchers were projecting as many as 215,000 would die over the next three years. AIDS is not "a gay disease," but the high proportion of gay persons who have been afflicted has intensified the moral and theological discussion concerning homosexuality. Ronald Sider challenges all those who fail to articulate moral judgment where it is called for. Rather than succumb to a "mushy relativism," Sider sees the need for both judging homosexual practice and extending the promise of forgiveness where there is repentance. However, to designate AIDS as divine punishment is Biblically and theologically irresponsible, he argues.

Sources for Body Theology: Homosexuality as a Test Case
James B. Nelson

It is not news that matters of sexual orientation for some years now have been the most debated, the most heated, the most divisive issues in American church life. . . . Protestants typically have asked, first and foremost, "What does the Bible say?" Roman Catholics typically have asked, "What does the church say?" Both questions are crucial. Neither is sufficient by itself.

One of John Wesley's legacies is the "quadrilateral" interpretation of authority, an approach with roots in Wesley's own Anglican tradition, and one still used by many persons in many communions. The quadrilateral formula reminds us that when we do our theological reflection, we must draw on more than one source. Wesley himself gave central weight to the scripture. But, over against the biblical literalizers and simplifiers, he argued that scripture must always be interpreted through the Spirit, with the indispensable aid of the church's tradition (which checks our own interpretation against the richness of past witnesses), reason (which guards against narrow and arbitrary interpretations), and experience (which is personal, inward, and enables us to interpret and appropriate the gospel).[1] Let us apply this approach to the subject of homosexuality, surely a test case for the church in our day.

SCRIPTURE

. . . When we approach scripture on the question of homosexual expression, or any other issue, we must always ask two questions.[2] First: What did the text mean? What was the writer trying to say? What questions was the writer addressing? What was the historical context? What literary form was being employed? Answering the question, What did it mean? requires our drawing upon the best insights of biblical scholars with their various forms of critical analysis.

Only after having struggled with the first question, can we proceed to the second: What does the text mean *for us today?* Whether a particular text has relevance for us now depends on our answer to two additional questions. First, Is the text consonant with our best understandings of the larger theological-ethical message of the Bible as interpreted through the best insights of the church's long tradition and our reason and experience? Second, Is the situation addressed by the biblical writer genuinely comparable to our own? When, but only when, these criteria are met, the text is ethically compelling for us.

Not many texts in scripture—perhaps seven at most—speak directly about homosexual behavior. We have no evidence of Jesus' teachings on or concern with the issue. The subject, obviously, is not a major scriptural preoccupation. Compare, for example, the incidence of texts on economic justice, of which there are many hundreds. In any event, what conclusions can we reach from careful assessment of the few texts in question?

My own conclusions, relying on the work of a number of contemporary biblical scholars, are several:

We receive no guidance whatsoever about the issue of sexual *orientation.* The issue of "homosexuality"—a psychosexual orientation—simply was not a biblical issue. Indeed, the concept of sexual orientation did not arise until the mid-nineteenth century. Certainly, biblical writers knew of homosexual acts, but they apparently understood those acts as being done by heterosexual people (they assumed everyone was heterosexual). Thus, when persons engaged in same-sex genital behavior, they were departing from their natural and given orientation. Regardless of our beliefs about the morality of same-sex expression, it is clear that our understanding of sexual *orientation* is vastly different from that of the biblical writers.

It is true, we do find condemnation of homosexual acts when they violate ancient Hebrew purity and holiness codes. We do find scriptural condemnation of homosexual prostitution. We do find condemnation of those homosexual acts which appear to be expressions of idolatry. We do find condemnation of pederasty, the sexual use of a boy by an adult male for the latter's gratification.

Note several things at this point. First, scriptural condemnation is also evident for similar *heterosexual* acts—for example, those that violate holiness codes (intercourse during menstruation), commercial sex, idolatrous heterosexual acts (temple prostitution), and the sexual misuse of minors. Further, the major questions that concern us in the present debate simply are not directly addressed in scripture. Those unaddressed issues are the theological and ethical appraisal of homosexual *orientation,* and the question of homosexual relations between adults committed to each other in mutuality and love.

On the other hand, we do find something in scripture that is frequently overlooked in the current discussions. There are clear biblical affirmations of deep love between same-sex adults. I am not implying genital relations in these instances. I simply note that in the instances of David and Jonathan, Ruth and Naomi, Jesus and "the beloved disciple," and others, the scripture seems to hold strong emotional bonding between members of the same sex to be cause for celebration, not fear.

Robin Scrogg's New Testament scholarship provides an example of the help we need on the biblical question. Looking closely at the cultural and religious contexts of the relevant New Testament passages, he discovers that in the Greco-Roman world there was one basic model of male homosexuality: pederasty, the sexual use of boys by adult males, often in situations of prostitution and always lacking in mutuality. He concludes that "what the New Testament was against was the image of homosexuality as pederasty and primarily here its more sordid and dehumanizing dimensions. One would regret it if somebody in the New Testament had not opposed such dehumanization."[3] In short, the specific New Testament judgments against homosexual practice simply are not relevant to today's debate about the validity of caring, mutual relationships between consenting adults. Nor does the Bible directly address today's question about the appropriateness of homosexuality as a psychosexual orientation.

However, the problem concerning direct guidance from scripture about specific sexual behaviors is not unique to homosexual behaviors. The same problem arises with a host of other forms of sexual expression. The scriptures are multiform and inconsistent in the sexual *moralities* endorsed therein. At various points there are endorsements of sexual practices that most of us would now reject: women as the sexual property of men; the "uncleanness" of menstrual blood and semen; proscriptions against intercourse during menstruation and against nudity within the home; the acceptance of polygamy, levirate marriage, concubinage, and prostitution. On these matters some would argue that the cultic laws of the Old Testament are no longer binding, and they must be distinguished from its moral commandments. Such arguments fail to recognize that most of the sexual mores mentioned above are treated as moral, not cultic, issues in scripture.

Those Christians who argue that, since Christ is the end of the law, the Hebraic law is irrelevant, must, if consistent, deal similarly with New Testament pronouncements about sexual issues. Even on such a major issue as sexual intercourse between unmarried consenting adults there is not explicit prohibition in either Hebrew scripture or the New Testament (which John Calvin discovered to his consternation). Indeed, the Song of Solomon celebrates one such relationship. I believe that our best biblical scholarship reaches Walter Wink's conclusion: "There is no biblical sex ethic. The Bible knows only a love ethic, which is constantly being brought to bear on whatever sexual mores are dominant in any given country, or culture, or period."[4]

This is by no means to suggest that these sources have little to say to us. Consider scripture. As L. William Countryman reminds us, the New Testament frames its particular sexual ethic in terms of purity and property systems that no longer prevail among us. Thus, we cannot simply take numerous New Testament injunctions and assume that they apply literally to significantly different contexts. On the other hand, scripture does for us something far more important. It radically relativizes our theological and ethical systems. It presses toward the transformation—the metanoia, the conversion—of the hearer. It presses us to do our ongoing theological-ethical work in ways that attempt faithfully to discern the inbreaking reign and grace of God in our present contexts. Even if many specific scriptural prescriptions and proscriptions regarding sex are not the gospel's word for today, there are still more basic and utterly crucial scriptural foundations for our sexual ethic.[5]

What are some of those foundations? Surely, they include such affirmations as these: the created goodness of our sexuality and bodily life; the inclusiveness of Christian community, unlimited by purity codes; the equality of women and men; and the service of our sexuality to the reign of God. That incorporation of our sexuality into God's reign means expression in acts shaped by love, justice, equality, fidelity, mutual respect, compassion, and grateful joy. These are criteria that apply regardless of one's orientation. Scripture also offers ample testimony that sexual acts that degrade, demean, and harm others and ourselves are contrary to God's intent and reign. But, for more specific application of such scriptural guidance to issues of homosexuality and same-sex expression, we need to read the scriptures in light of the other three sources.

TRADITION

G. K. Chesterton once counseled our taking out "membership in the democracy of the dead." To do so, in Chesterton's thought, is to refuse to submit to that small, arrogant oligarchy of those people whose only virtue is that they happen, at that moment, to be alive and walking about. When we join this democracy of the dead by taking our tradition seriously, we realize that our ancestors in faith and culture have relevant and important insights for us. Truth is not necessarily carried by the book with the latest copyright date.

However, the postbiblical tradition provides no more unambiguous guidance on specific sexual expressions than does scripture. Selective literalism in use of the tradition is almost as common as it is in the use of scripture itself. Most of us would fully endorse the tradition's movement toward monogamy and fidelity. Many of us would endorse the tradition's growth toward the centrality of love as the governing sexual norm. Many of us would celebrate those parts of the tradition that not only tolerate but positively affirm gays and lesbians, including lesbian and gay clergy. But few of us would endorse those elements of tradition which baptize patriarchal oppression, endorse violence against women, oppress lesbians and gays, exalt perpetual virginity as the superior state, or declare that heterosexual rape is a lesser sin than masturbation (since the latter is a sin against nature while the former, while also sinful, is an act in accordance with nature). As with scripture, it is impossible to find one consistent, coherent sexual ethic in the postbiblical tradition.

Of what use, then, is the long sweep of Christian tradition regarding homosexual orientation and expression? On this subject, I believe that tradition most helpfully poses a series of questions—challenges to much of our conventional Christian wisdom.

One question is this: Has the church's condemnation of gay and lesbian people been consistent throughout its history? As Yale historian John Boswell has demonstrated, a careful examination of tradition yields a negative answer. Indeed, for its first two centuries, the early church did not generally oppose homosexual behavior as such. Further, the opposition that did arise during the third to sixth centuries was not principally theological. Rather, it was based largely on the demise of urban culture, the increased government regulation of personal morality, and general churchly pressures toward asceticism. Following this period of opposition, however, ecclesiastical hostility to homosexuality largely disappeared once again. For some centuries there was no particular Christian antagonism toward homosexuality, and legal prohibitions were rare. Indeed, the eleventh-century urban revival saw a resurgence of gay-lesbian literature and leadership in both secular society and the church. Once again, though, hostility appeared late in the twelfth century now as part of the general intolerance of minority groups and their presumed association with religious heresies.

Our conventional wisdom has assumed that Christian history has been all of one piece, uniform in its clear disapproval of homosexuality. In fact, a closer look at the tradition tells us that there were periods of remarkable acceptance. Further, we are reminded to interpret the theological opposition that was, indeed, often present in the context of broader changes occurring in the surrounding society.

Another challenge to us, suggested by the tradition, is this: Has the church always agreed that heterosexual marriage is the appropriate sexual pattern? The answer is no. Singleness, particularly celibacy, was prized above marriage for much of the time from the church's beginnings to the sixteenth-century Reformation. Moreover, a careful look at tradition reveals that heterosexual marriage was not celebrated by Christian wedding services in church worship until perhaps the ninth century. We have no evidence of Christian wedding rites until that time. Obviously, many Christians married during these earlier centuries, but marriage was considered a civil order and not a rite of the church. Curiously, there is some emerging evidence that unions of gay or lesbian Christians were celebrated in some Christian churches earlier than heterosexual marriages. All of this suggests that heterosexual marriage has not always been central as the norm for Christian sexuality.

The tradition suggests a third question: Is it true that procreation has always been deemed primary to the meaning and expression of Christian sexuality? That is, if we do not use our sexuality with the intent to procreate or at least with the possibility of doing so, is there something deficient about it? It is an important question, for the procreative norm has often been used to judge lesbians and gays adversely: "Your sexuality is unfit to bless because your acts are inherently nonprocreative."

Once again, tradition casts large question marks on many current assumptions. In those times wherein celibacy was more highly honored than marriage, it is obvious that procreative sex was not the norm—it was second class on the ladder of virtue. But what of the centuries, particularly since the Reformation, when marriage has been blessed as the normative Christian calling?

Still the answer is no. In the seventeenth century, a number of Christians—especially among the Puritans, Anglicans, and Quakers—began to teach, preach, and write about a new understanding. It appeared to them that God's fundamental purpose in creating us as sexual beings was not that we might make babies, but that we might make love. It was love, intimacy, mutuality, not procreation, that were central to the divine intention for sexuality. Some Puritans, for example, declared that if children were born to a marriage, that was as "an added blessing," but not the central purpose of the marriage.

The centrality of love, companionship, and mutual pleasure in the meaning of sexuality has been embraced by most Protestants during the last three hundred years and, in practice, by numerous Catholics, even if not with Vatican approval. The proof in heterosexual relations is the use of contraception as a decision of conscience. Most of us do not believe we must be open to procreation each time we make love—in fact, we believe strongly to the contrary. The curious double standard still exists, however; the procreative norm has been smuggled in the back door and applied negatively to lesbians and gay men.

Thus, while the church's tradition may not give definitive answers to specific questions about homosexual orientation and same-sex expression, it raises questions—these and others—that challenge conventional wisdom and refocus our perspectives.

REASON

In searching for God's truth, theologically and ethically, we need to draw on the best fruits of human reason, a third source from the quadrilateral. Wesley put it this way: "It is a fundamental principle with us that to renounce reason is to renounce religion, that religion and reason go hand in hand, and that all irrational religion is false religion."[6]

One of the ways we honor our God-given reason is in striving for consistency and adequacy in our theological judgments. These two age-old tests of the philosophers are perennially relevant. Consistency eschews the use of double standard. Adequacy prods us to judgments that do justice to the widest range of data.

Reason is also expressed in the various sciences, our disciplined human attempts to understand creation. Biological, psychological, and social sciences can shed significant light on questions of sexual orientation. What, for example, might we learn?

In 1948 Alfred Kinsey and his associates jarred America with the first major study of the sexual behaviors of persons in this society. In his volume on the male, he presented two things that particularly caught the public eye regarding sexual orientation. One was the continuum on which orientations might be represented. Challenging either-or assumption (one is *either* homosexual *or* heterosexual), Kinsey introduced evidence suggesting that we might be "both/and." The other finding, widely reported in the press, was Kinsey's discovery that at least 50 percent of the male population had experienced homosexual genital relations at some time in their lives, and for 37 percent of them it was orgasmic behavior after puberty. This alone startled many, simply because it appeared to be evidence that same-sex attraction and expression were not just the province of a tiny minority.[7]

Though most of us tend toward one or the other side, it is probable that the vast majority of us are not exclusively either heterosexual or homosexual. Kinsey's conclusions were substantiated by his studies on the American female five years later and by subsequent research by others. Indeed, in recent decades, most sexologists have not only validated Kinsey's continuum but have also added other dimensions to it. While Kinsey was primarily interested in behaviors (genital experiences culminating in orgasm), later sexologists have argued that when other dimensions of orientation—such as fantasy, desire, social attraction, or emotional preference—are added to the picture, it is probable that none of us is exclusively one or the other. Most of us have more bisexual capacities than we have realized or than we have been taught in a bifurcating society. This recognition is of particular importance when we come to try to understand some of the dynamics of homophobia.

Another question on which the sciences shed some light is the origin of sexual orientation. While there is still much debate, at least two things seem clear. One is that our orientations are given, not freely chosen. The likelihood is that they arise from a combination of genetic and hormonal factors, together with environmental and learning factors—both nature and nurture. The other general agreement is that our sexual orientations are established rather early in life, most likely somewhere between the ages of two and five, and thereafter are largely resistant to any dramatic changes. "Therapies" that attempt to change persons from homosexual to heterosexual are now discredited by reputable scientists. Such procedures may change certain behaviors, they may make some people celibate, but they will not change deep feelings and most likely will produce great psychic and emotional confusion. These facts, too, are relevant to the theological-ethical questions.

Further, stereotypes about gay men and lesbians wither under scientific scrutiny. For example, the notion that homosexual males are more likely to abuse children sexually than are heterosexual males has been thoroughly disproved. Linking emotional instability or immaturity with homosexuality, likewise, is no longer scientifically tenable. Granted, lesbians and gay men suffer emotional distress from their social oppression, but this is far different from assuming that the cause of this distress lies in their orientation.

EXPERIENCE

The fourth and last area of insight comes from experience. Wesley was rightly suspicious of trusting all the vagaries of human experience. Experience by itself is not reliable, nor does it give a consistent picture. However, without the validation of scriptural insight by experience as well as reason and tradition, such insight remains abstract and uncompelling. The Spirit, Wesley believed, inwardly validates God's truth through our experience. I believe that is true. And

I also believe that we must expand the focus of "experience" to include the careful examination of both individual and common experience to find those things which nurture wholeness and those things which are destructive to our best humanity.

Our experience of *homophobia,* in careful examination, provides one key example. The term refers to deep and irrational fears of same-sex attraction and expression or, in the case of lesbians and gay men, internalized self-rejection. Though the word was coined only within recent decades, the reality has long been with us.[8] Another term, *heterosexism,* more recently has come into use. It too is helpful, for it reminds us that prejudice against gays and lesbians is not simply a private psychological dynamic but, like racism and sexism, is also structured deeply into our institutions and cultural patterns. While I clearly recognize the pervasive realities of heterosexism, in this illustration of the uses of experience in doing body theology I will focus on homophobia.[9]

I lived the first forty years of my life assuming that I was completely heterosexual. That had been my sexual experience, and that was my only awareness. Then, through some volunteer work in urban ministries I came into close interaction, for the first time that I consciously recognized, with a number of articulate gay men and lesbians. They challenged my stereotypes and my homophobia, and they launched me into a process of examining my own experience.

One thing I discovered was that homophobia was a particularly acute problem for males—it certainly was for me. For the first time I realized that my fear of lesbians and gays was connected to issues in my own masculine identity. Gay males seemed to have an ill-defined masculinity, a threat to any man in a society where one's masculinity seems never achieved once and for all and always needs proving. Lesbians threatened my masculinity simply because they were living proof that at least some women did not need a man to validate or complete them as persons.

Gay males were a problem for me also, I realized, because they threatened to "womanize" me (a threat to any male in a sexist society where men have higher status). The gay could treat me simply as a sexual object, a desirable body—not a full person. I had to admit that this was the way that men (myself included?) had treated so many women for so many years. Now the tables were turned.

Examining my experience made me aware, further, that I might be involved in what the psychologists call reaction formation and projection. If it is true that all of us are a mix of heterosexual and homosexual capacities (even though we happen to be considerably more of one than the other), and if it is true that we have been taught by a rigidly bifurcating society to deny the existence of anything homosexual, what do we do with any same-sex feelings that might arise? We vigorously defend against them in ourselves by projecting them onto others and blaming those others for having more obviously what we, to some extent, may also experience. Though I had not been conscious of same-sex desires, I needed also to examine this possibility in my experience, for some capacity was likely there.

Another factor I discovered was simply sexual envy. Looking at gays and lesbians through stereotypical lenses, I had been seeing them as very sexual people. That, in part, is what stereotyping does to the stereotyper—it gives us tunnel vision. I did not see them fundamentally and almost exclusively as sexual actors. The result was obvious: they appeared more sexual than I. And this was cause for envy, particularly to a male who has been taught that virility is a key sign of authentic masculinity.

Still another contribution to my homophobia, I discovered, was intimacy envy. As a typical man, I had difficulty making close, deep, emotionally vulnerable friendships, especially with other men. Yet, deep within, I sensed that I yearned for such friendships. Then I saw gay men closely bonding with each other, apparently having something in friendship that I too wanted—male-to-male emotional intimacy. I was pressed to look at my experience again, this time to see if my intimacy envy and consequent resentment were part of my homophobia.

Further, confronting my own fears meant confronting my fears of sexuality as such—my erotophobia. Though I had long enjoyed the sexual experience, I came to realize that, reared in a dualistic culture, I was more distanced from my sexuality than I cared to admit. Reared as a male and conditioned to repress most bodily feelings, reared as "a good soldier" and taught to armor myself against any emotional or physical vulnerability, I discovered I was more alienated from my body than I had acknowledged. Gay males and lesbians brought into some kind of dim awareness my own erotophobia because they represented sexuality in a fuller way.

The fear of death may sound like a strange contributor to homophobia, but it is likely there. Though in Christian community we are named people of the resurrection, our reassurances in the face of mortality are often grounded much more by children and grandchildren. The thought of childless persons awakens fear of death. And while many gays and lesbians have produced and parented children, they stand as a key symbol of nonprocreating people. In this way also, I realized, they caused me fear, but once again it was fear of myself.

Homophobia thrives on dualism of disincarnation and abstraction that divide people from their bodily feelings and divide reality into two opposing camps. As never before we need gracious theologies. Homophobia thrives on theologies of works-justification, wherein all persons must prove their worth and all males must prove their manhood. As never before we need erotic theologies. Homophobia thrives on erotophobia, the deep fear of sexuality and pleasure. Homophobia thrives on eros-deprived people because it grows in the resentments, projections, and anger of those whose own hungers are not met. As never before we need theologies of hope and resurrection. Homophobia thrives wherever there is fear of death, for then people try to dominate and control others to assure themselves of their own future. Homophobia thrives on bodily deadness, so deeply linked as it is with sexual fear and repression. Though its varied dynamics are complex, the root cause of homophobia is always fear, and the gospel has resources for dealing with fear.

These are a few of the dynamics of homophobia that I became conscious of in my own experience some years ago. Doubtless, there are others. I have focused particularly on the male experience both because that is my own and because I believe homophobia is a particularly severe problem for dominantly heterosexual males such as I. Nevertheless, it is a disease that affects all of us—female as well as male; lesbian, gay, and bisexual as well as heterosexual. Homophobia is an example of the experience that enters into our theological and ethical reflection on issues of sexual orientation (and many other matters as well). Our awareness of these dynamics in ourselves gives us heightened self-critical consciousness, an important ingredient of theological-ethical reflection.

I have not attempted here to present a fully developed theological-ethical perspective on sexual orientation. My attempt is far more limited. It has been to name and to illustrate some uses of the four major sources of interpretation—scripture, tradition, reason, and experience—so important to the churches' responses to the most troubling and divisive question facing them.

My own bias is evident. Just as homophobic fears are not principally about "them," but about myself and about us all, so also the basic issue is not homosexuality but rather *human* sexuality. Our sexuality, I believe, is a precious gift from God, critically important as part of a divine invitation. It is an invitation that we come together with each other and with God in relationships of intimacy and celebration, of faithfulness and tenderness, of love and justice. Our sexuality is a gift to be integrated fully and joyously into our spirituality. Our orientations, whatever they may be, are part of that gift—to be received with thanksgiving and honored by each other.[10]

The Homosexual Movement: A Response
The Ramsey Colloquium

I. THE NEW THING

. . . The new thing, the *novum*, is a gay and lesbian movement that aggressively proposes radical changes in social behavior, religion, morality, and law. It is important to distinguish public policy considerations from the judgment of particular individuals. Our statement is directed chiefly to debates over public policy and what should be socially normative. We share the uneasiness of most Americans with the proposals advanced by the gay and lesbian movement, and we seek to articulate reasons for the largely intuitive and

From "The Homosexual Movement: A Response," The Ramsey Colloquium, *First Things* 41 (March 1994): 15–20. *First Things* is a monthly journal published in New York City by the Institute on Religion and Public Life.

pre-articulate anxiety of most Americans regarding homosexuality and its increasing impact on our public life.

II. NEW THING/OLD THING: THE SEXUAL REVOLUTION

While the gay and lesbian movement is indeed a new thing, its way was prepared by, and it is in large part a logical extension of, what has been called the "sexual revolution.". . .

In light of widespread changes in sexual mores, some homosexuals understandably protest that the sexual license extended to "straights" cannot be denied to them.

We believe that any understanding of sexuality, including heterosexuality, that makes it chiefly an arena for the satisfaction of personal desire is harmful to individuals and society. Any way of life that accepts or encourages sexual relations for pleasure or personal satisfaction alone turns away from the disciplined community that marriage is intended to engender and foster. Religious communities that have in recent decades winked at promiscuity (even among the clergy), that have solemnly repeated marriage vows that their own congregations do not take seriously, and that have failed to concern themselves with the devastating effects of divorce upon children cannot with integrity condemn homosexual behavior unless they are also willing to reassert the heterosexual norm more believably and effectively in their pastoral care. In other words, those determined to resist the gay and lesbian movement must be equally concerned for the renewal of integrity, in teaching and practice, regarding "traditional sexual ethics." . . .

One reason for the discomfort of religious leaders in the face of this new movement is the past and continuing failure to offer supportive and knowledgeable pastoral care to persons coping with the problems of their homosexuality. Without condoning homogenital acts, it is necessary to recognize that many such persons are, with fear and trembling, seeking as best they can to live lives pleasing to God and in service to others. Confronted by the vexing ambiguities of eros in human life, religious communities should be better equipped to support people in their struggle, recognizing that we all fall short of the vocation to holiness of life.

The sexual revolution is motored by presuppositions that can and ought to be effectively challenged. Perhaps the key presupposition of the revolution is that human health and flourishing require that sexual desire, understood as a "need," be acted upon and satisfied. Any discipline of denial or restraint has been popularly depicted as unhealthy and dehumanizing. We insist, however, that it is dehumanizing to define ourselves, or our personhood as male and female, by our desires alone. Nor does it seem plausible to suggest that what millennia of human experience have taught us to regard as self-command should now be dismissed as mere repression.

At the same time that the place of sex has been grotesquely exaggerated by the sexual revolution, it has also been trivialized. The mysteries of human sexuality are commonly reduced to matters of recreation or taste, not unlike one's preferences in diet, dress, or sport. This peculiar mix of the exaggerated and the trivialized makes it possible for the gay and lesbian movement to demand, simultaneously, a respect for what is claimed to be most importantly and constitutively true of homosexuals, and tolerance for what is, after all, simply a difference in "lifestyle."

It is important to recognize the linkages among the component parts of the sexual revolution. Permissive abortion, widespread adultery, easy divorce, radical feminism, and the gay and lesbian movement have not by accident appeared at the same historical moment. They have in common a declared desire for liberation from constraint—especially constraints associated with an allegedly oppressive culture and religious tradition. They also have in common the presuppositions that the body is little more than an instrument for the fulfillment of desire, and that the fulfillment of desire is the essence of the self. On biblical and philosophical grounds, we reject this radical dualism between the self and the body. Our bodies have their own dignity, bear their own truths, and are participant in our personhood in a fundamental way.

This constellation of movements, of which the gay movement is part, rests upon an anthropological doctrine of the autonomous self. With respect to abortion and the socialization of sexuality, this anthropology has gone a long way toward entrenching itself in the jurisprudence of our society as well as in popular habits of mind and behavior. We believe it is a false doctrine that leads neither to individual flourishing nor to social well-being.

III. THE HETEROSEXUAL NORM

Marriage and the family—husband, wife, and children joined by public recognition and legal bond—are the most effective institutions for the rearing of children, the directing of sexual passion, and human flourishing in community. Not all marriages and families "work," but it is unwise to let pathology and failure, rather than a vision of what is normative and ideal, guide us in the development of social policy.

Of course many today doubt that we can speak of what is normatively human. The claim that all social institutions and patterns of behavior are social constructions that we may, if we wish, alter without harm to ourselves is a proposal even more radical in origin and implication than the sexual revolution. That the institutions of marriage and family are culturally conditioned and subject to change and development no one should doubt, but such recognition should not undermine our ability to discern patterns of community that best serve human well-being. Judaism and Christianity did not invent the heterosexual norm, but these faith traditions affirm that norm and can open our eyes to see in it important truths about human life.

Fundamental to human life in society is the creation of humankind as male and female, which is typically and paradigmatically expressed in the marriage of a man and a woman who form a union of persons in which two become one flesh—a union which, in the biblical tradition, is the foundation of all human community. In faithful marriage, three important elements of human life are made manifest and given support.

(1) Human society extends over time; it has a history. It does so because, through the mysterious participation of our procreative powers in God's own creative work, we transmit life to those who will succeed us. We become a people with a shared history over time and with a common stake in that history. Only the heterosexual norm gives full expression to the commitment to time and history evident in having and caring for children.

(2) Human society requires that we learn to value difference within community. In the complementarity of male and female we find the paradigmatic instance of this truth. Of course, persons may complement each other in many different ways, but the complementarity of male and female is ground in, and fully embraces our bodies and their structure. It does not sever the meaning of the person from bodily life, as if human beings were simply desire, reason, or will. The complementarity of male and female invites us to learn to accept and affirm the natural world from which we are too often alienated.

Moreover, in the creative complementarity of male and female we are directed toward community with those unlike us. In the community between male and female, we do not and cannot see in each other mere reflections of ourselves. In learning to appreciate this most basic difference, and in forming a marital bond, we take both difference and community seriously. (And ultimately, we begin to be prepared for communion with God, in Whom we never find simply a reflection of ourselves.)

(3) Human society requires the direction and restraint of many impulses. Few of those impulses are more powerful or unpredictable than sexual desire. Throughout history societies have taken particular care to socialize sexuality toward marriage and the family. Marriage is a place where, in a singular manner, our waywardness begins to be healed and our fear of commitment overcome, where we may learn to place another person's needs rather than our own desires at the center of life.

Thus, reflection on the heterosexual norm directs our attention to certain social necessities: the continuation of human life, the place of difference within community, the redirection of our tendency to place our own desires first. These necessities cannot be supported by rational calculations of self-interest alone; they require commitments that go well beyond the demands of personal satisfaction. Having and rearing children is among the most difficult of human projects. Men and women need all the support they can get to maintain stable marriages in which the next generation can flourish. Even marriages that do not give rise to children exist in accord with, rather than in opposition to, this heterosexual norm. To depict marriage as simply one of several alternative "lifestyles" is seriously to undermine the normative vision required for social well-being.

There are legitimate and honorable forms of love other than marriage. Indeed, one of the goods at stake in today's disputes is a long-honored tradition of friendship between men and men, women and women, women and men. In the current climate of sexualizing and politicizing all intense interpersonal relationships, the place of sexually chaste friendship and of religiously motivated celibacy is gravely jeopardized. In our cultural moment of narrow-eyed prurience, the single life of chastity has come under the shadow of suspicion and is no longer credible to many people. Indeed, the non-satisfaction of sexual "needs" is widely viewed as a form of deviance.

In this context it becomes imperative to affirm the reality and beauty of sexually chaste relationships of deep affectional intensity. We do not accept the notion that self-command is an unhealthy form of repression on the part of single people, whether their inclination be heterosexual or homosexual. Put differently, the choice is not limited to heterosexual marriage on the one hand, or relationship involving homogenital sex on the other.

IV. THE CLAIMS OF THE MOVEMENT

We turn our attention now to a few of the important public claims made by gay and lesbian advocates (even as we recognize that the movement is not monolithic). As we noted earlier, there is an important distinction between those who wish to "mainstream" homosexual life and those who aim at restructuring culture. This is roughly the distinction between those who seek integration and those who seek revolution. Although these different streams of the movement need to be distinguished, a few claims are so frequently encountered that they require attention.

Many gays argue that they have no choice, that they could not be otherwise than they are. Such an assertion can take a variety of forms—for example, that "being gay is natural for me" or even the "God made me this way."

We cannot settle the dispute about the roots—genetic or environmental—of homosexual orientation. When some scientific evidence suggests a genetic predisposition for homosexual orientation, the case is not significantly different from evidence of predispositions toward other traits—for example, alcoholism or violence. In each instance we must still ask whether it should be resisted. Whether or not a homosexual orientation can be changed—and it is important to recognize that there are responsible authorities on both sides of this question—we affirm the obligation of pastors and therapists to assist those who recognize the value of chaste living to resist the impulse to act on their desire for homogenital gratification.

The Kinsey data, which suggested that 10 percent of males are homosexual, have now been convincingly discredited. Current research suggest that the percentage of males whose sexual desires and behavior are exclusively homosexual is as low as 1 percent or 2 percent in developed societies. In any case, the statistical frequency of an act or desire does not determine its moral status. Racial discrimination and child abuse occur frequently in society, but that does not make them "natural" in the moral sense. What is in accord with human nature is behavior appropriate to what we are meant to be—appropriate to what God created and calls us to be.

In a fallen creation, many quite common attitudes and behaviors must be straightforwardly designated as sin. Although we are equal before God, we are not born equal in terms of our strengths and weaknesses, our tendencies and dispositions, our nature and nurture. We cannot utterly change the hand we have been dealt by inheritance and family circumstances but we are responsible for how we play that hand. Inclination and temptation are not sinful, although they surely result from humanity's fallen condition. Sin occurs in the joining of the will, freely and knowingly, to an act or way of life that is contrary to God's purpose. Religious communities in particular must lovingly support all the faithful in their struggle against temptation, while at the same time insisting that precisely for their sake we must describe as sinful the homogenital and extramarital heterosexual behavior to which some are drawn.

Many in our society—both straight and gay—also contend that what people do sexually is entirely a private matter and no one's business but their own. The form this claim takes is often puzzling to many people—and rightly so. For what were once considered private acts are now highly publicized, while, for the same acts, public privilege is claimed because they are private. What is confusedly at work here is an extreme individualism, a claim for autonomy so extreme that it must undercut the common good.

To be sure, there should in our society be a wide zone for private behavior, including behavior that most Americans would deem wrong. Some of us oppose anti-sodomy statutes. In a society premised upon limited government there are realms of behavior that ought to be beyond the supervision of the state. In addition to the way sexual wrongdoing harms character, however, there are often other harms involved. We have in mind the alarming rates of sexual promiscuity, depression, and suicide and the ominous presence of AIDS within the homosexual subculture. No one can doubt that these are reasons for public concern. Another legitimate reason for public concern is the harm done to the social order when policies are advanced that would increase the incidence of the gay lifestyle and undermine the normative character of marriage and family life.

Since there are good reasons to support the heterosexual norm, since it has been developed with great difficulty, and since it can be maintained only if it is cared for and supported, we cannot be indifferent to attacks upon it. The social norms by which sexual behavior is inculcated and controlled are of urgent importance for families and for the society as a whole. Advocates of the gay and lesbian movement have the responsibility to set forth publicly their alternative proposals. This must mean more than calling for liberation from established standards. They must clarify for all of us how sexual mores are to be inculcated in the young, who are particularly vulnerable to seduction and solicitation. Public anxiety about homosexuality is preeminently a concern about the vulnerabilities of the young. This, we are persuaded, is a legitimate and urgent public concern.

Gay and lesbian advocates sometimes claim that they are asking for no more than an end to discrimination, drawing an analogy with the earlier civil rights movement that sought justice for black Americans. The analogy is uncon-

[margin note: ISSUE OF "NATURAL"]

vincing and misleading. Differences of race are in accord with—not contrary to—our nature, and such differences do not provide justification for behavior otherwise unacceptable. It is sometimes claimed that homosexuals want only a recognition of their status, not necessarily of their behavior. But in this case the distinction between status and behavior does not hold. The public declaration of status ("coming out of the closet") is a declaration of intended behavior.

Certain discriminations are necessary within society; it is not too much to say that civilization itself depends on the making of such distinctions (between, finally, right and wrong). In our public life, some discrimination is in order—when, for example, in education and programs involving young people the intent is to prevent predatory behavior that can take place under the guise of supporting young people in their anxieties about their "sexual identity." It is necessary to discriminate between relationships. Gay and lesbian "domestic partnerships," for example, should not be socially recognized as the moral equivalent of marriage. We note again that marriage and the family are institutions necessary for our continued social well-being and, in an individualistic society that tends to liberation from all constraint, they are fragile institutions in need of careful and continuing support.

[margin note: But is this what is happening?]

V. CONCLUSION

We do not doubt that many gays and lesbians—perhaps especially those who seek the blessing of our religious communities—believe that theirs is the only form of love, understood as affection and erotic satisfaction, of which they are capable. Nor do we doubt that they have found in such relationships something of great personal significance, since even a distorted love retains traces of love's grandeur. Where there is love in morally disordered relationships we do not censure the love. We censure the form in which that love seeks expression. To those who say that this disordered behavior is so much at the core of their being that the person cannot be (and should not be) distinguished from the behavior, we can only respond that we earnestly hope they are wrong.

We are well aware that this declaration will be dismissed by some as a display of "homophobia," but such dismissals have become unpersuasive and have ceased to intimidate. Indeed, we do not think it is a bad thing that people should experience a reflexive recoil from what is wrong. To achieve such a recoil is precisely the point of moral education of the young. What we have tried to do here is to bring this reflexive and often pre-articulate recoil to reasonable expression.

Our society is, we fear, progressing precisely in the manner given poetic expression by Alexander Pope:

Vice is a monster of so frightful mien,
As to be hated needs but to be seen;
Yet seen too oft, familiar with her face,
We first endure, then pity, then embrace.

To endure (tolerance), to pity (compassion), to embrace (affirmation): that is the sequence of change in attitude and judgment that has been advanced by the gay and lesbian movement with notable success. We expect that this success will encounter certain limits and that what is truly natural will reassert itself, but this may not happen before more damage is done to innumerable individuals and to our common life.

Perhaps some of this damage can be prevented. For most people marriage and family is the most important project in their lives. For it they have made sacrifices beyond numbering; they want to be succeeded in an ongoing, shared history by children and grandchildren; they want to transmit to their children the beliefs that have claimed their hearts and minds. They should be supported in that attempt. To that end, we have tried to set forth our view and the reasons that inform it. Whatever the inadequacies of this declaration, we hope it will be useful to others. The gay and lesbian movement, and the dramatic changes in sexual attitudes and behavior of which that movement is part, have unloosed a great moral agitation in our culture. Our hope is that this statement will contribute to turning that agitation into civil conversation about the kind of people we are and hope to be.

[handwritten margin note: Seems to indicate all homosexual behavior is promiscuous.]

AIDS: An Evangelical Perspective
Ronald J. Sider

How should Christians respond to people with AIDS? Our Christian understanding of both creation and redemption tells us that people with AIDS are of inestimable worth, persons so important and precious in the sight of their creator and redeemer that God declares them indelibly stamped with the divine image. Indeed, people with AIDS are so special that the creator of the galaxies declares that his son's death on the cross was precisely for them. No matter how weak or frail, no matter how marginalized or despised, no matter how ravaged by wrong choices, people with AIDS enjoy the full sanctity of human life. So we offer them our love and support no matter how inconvenient or costly. That is the first, middle, and last thing to say.

To be sure, there are other things that must be added. But only secondarily. One crucial test of our commitment to the sanctity of human life in our time will be whether as a society we will spend the money, take the time, and run the risk required to treat people with AIDS as persons, down to the last painful gasp. That basic theological affirmation does not settle many complex issues of public policy, but it does provide an essential framework for grappling with them.

How should our response to the AIDS epidemic be influenced by the fact that in many places the primary transmitters of the disease are promiscuous male homosexuals and intravenous drug users? Answering this secondary question is more complex. It is a prejudicial untruth to call AIDS a homosexual disease. AIDS is a viral disease that affects heterosexuals and homosexuals. There is no evidence whatsoever to indicate that this new virus was originally produced by homosexual practice.

At the same time, however, it is dishonest and unwise to minimize the fact that much of the transmission of AIDS occurs because of promiscuous (especially homosexual) sexual intercourse. Regardless of one's view of either homosexuality or promiscuity, the facts are that the only truly safe intercourse is that within a lifelong monogamous relationship, and that AIDS is closely linked with homosexual promiscuity. The December 1986 Hastings Center Report indicates that "many AIDS patients report 1,000 sexual partners over a single life time."[11] One third of all male homosexuals, according to an authoritative national survey cited in the report, said that they had had more than 50-70 sexual partners in the previous year. Insisting, in our public-policy decisions, on the importance of the connection between homosexual promiscuity and the transmission of AIDS is not an instance of heterosexual homophobia.

AIDS AS GOD'S PUNISHMENT?

What about the charge that AIDS is God's punishment for gays? For many this question might not even arise, and it is not the most important question. But it is essential to deal with it at some length, first, because some evangelicals have made this charge; second, because the media have spread the charge far and wide; and third, because some religious people discussing AIDS seem to want to ignore the biblical teaching that there is a moral order in the universe and that wrong choices have consequences.

To begin with, it is wrong to suggest that God created AIDS as a special punishment for the sin of homosexual practice. Such a suggestion ignores, for one thing, much empirical data. Apparently the virus is new. Why would God wait for millennia to design this special punishment? Furthermore, many people who have not engaged in homosexual activity have AIDS. At least 500 babies have already been born with AIDS, and a minimum of 700 people have contracted the disease through blood transfusions. If AIDS is divine punishment for homosexual practice, why don't gay women get it? Are the radical feminists right that God is exclusively female? In parts of Africa, AIDS affects heterosexuals and homosexuals in approximately equal numbers.

Furthermore, there is no biblical basis for linking specific sicknesses with specific kinds of sin. Certainly sickness and death are the result, in biblical thought, of the fall, but a specific sickness is seldom related to a specific sinful act, and then only by special prophetic declaration. In the one situation where Jesus explicitly dealt with the question, he emphatically rejected the suggestion that blindness was caused by a man's sin or that of his parents (John 9:2–3). Rather, Jesus said that the reason for the blindness was to make manifest the works of God. If Christians today offer compassionate, costly care to people with AIDS, they will in a similar way bring glory to God.

Evangelicals should be able, however, to condemn homosexual practice as a sinful life-style without being charged with homophobia or blamed for many of the problems emerging in the AIDS epidemic. Almost all evangelicals consider homosexual practice (which must be carefully distinguished from homosexual orientation) to be sinful. And I agree, although I want to add that it is no more sinful than adultery, greed, gossip, racism, or materialism.

Ethicist James B. Nelson goes much too far when he argues that "we who call ourselves Christians bear major responsibility for the problems created by the AIDS crisis. . . . We have been the major institutional legitimizer of compulsory heterosexuality."[12] Evangelicals confess that they have been guilty of homophobia. But they reject the charge that their condemnation of homosexual practice somehow played a major role in creating the AIDS crisis. To the extent that there is a link between AIDS and homosexuality, the major point that must be made is that it is homosexual promiscuity that stands condemned, not evangelical belief that homosexual practice is wrong.

An argument similar to Nelson's is made by Dan Beauchamp in the *Hastings Center Report.* Beauchamp contends that religious prejudice against homosexuality impedes changes in gay promiscuity, and that if it is to end, society will have to permit permanent forms of gay association, including marriage. In the name of public health he calls on health officials to work for this kind of "sexual freedom." He concludes by pleading that we keep our eyes fixed on "the central issue—the many ways in which centuries of religious and social superstitions and prejudice stand in the way of improving public health."[13]

This is largely unacceptable special pleading. Certainly there has been homophobic and misguided public restriction of private sexual acts between consenting adults, and that must end. But to demand that Christians either give up a belief that homosexual practice is wrong and endorse government sanction of gay marriage, or else accept major responsibility for the AIDS crisis, is nonsense. Gay folk can stop being promiscuous and thus end the risk of infection any time they choose. They don't need to wait for others to affirm their sexual preference.

AIDS AND THE LAW OF GOD

My next comment on the issue of AIDS as punishment for homosexual practice may upset even more people than my previous point. The Bible throughout teaches that God is both loving and just, both merciful and holy, and therefore has established a moral order in the universe. Ignoring God's law structured into nature has consequences. A major article on AIDS in a religious periodical asserted that "The God of the Christian revelation is not a God who punishes people."[14] But that is not what the Scriptures say. In fact, nowhere in the Bible is there more discussion of punishment of sin than in the words of Jesus. Furthermore, St. Paul argues the general point about there being a moral order in the universe precisely with reference to male and female homosexual practice (Rom. 1:26–28). God has created free persons who may freely choose to reject God's law, but their choices have consequences both now and in the future.

This point is just as relevant, of course, to any type of self-destructive behavior, or to acts of economic injustice, as it is to homosexual practice. (Someone has quipped that if AIDS is divine punishment, then surely the people who bring us economic oppression, environmental pollution, and devastating wars should at least get herpes.) Oppressing the poor violates God's moral order and produces disruption, chaos and other evil consequences. (It is relevant to point out here that the unusually high proportion of blacks and Hispanics in the population of drug addicts, including intravenous drug users with AIDS, is surely related to the incredibly high unemployment rate for black and Hispanic teenagers, which in turn is related to racism and economic injustice. Similarly, the increasing number of female prostitutes with AIDS is related to female poverty and the tragedy of battered women.) Sexual sin is no worse than other varieties, and they all have consequences.

We cannot ignore this general truth when we come to the issue of AIDS. If the Bible teaches that homosexual practice is wrong, as I think it does, then it is right to suppose that violating God's law in this area will have negative consequences.

This is not to say that the AIDS virus is some supernatural divine creation to punish homosexual practice; I have emphasized that I reject that view. But I refuse to bow to today's widespread relativism and deny and ignore the clear biblical teaching that some actions are wrong no matter what Hollywood or Greenwich Village says. Ignoring the moral order of the universe has consequences.

As a citizen, I insist on the right to say that and to seek to shape public policy in ways consistent with that belief without being called a bigot. Evangelical Christians believe that one reason Western society today is in trouble is its widespread ethical relativism and accompanying sexual promiscuity (both heterosexual and homosexual). I do not ask that public policy enforce biblical sexual norms, but I do ask that public policy not undermine them.

It is important to add here that there are contexts in which it is appropriate, and other contexts in which it is inappropriate, to emphasize the link between actions and consequences. When a person is dying of lung cancer, one does not lecture her on the dangers of smoking. When a friend is struggling to survive a heart attack, one does not denounce him for poor eating patterns or failure to exercise. Nevertheless, warnings about smoking or overeating are entirely appropriate at other times.

I have been dismayed by failures to observe this very simple distinction. In his book on AIDS, John Fortunato quotes an evangelical chaplain who began every initial conversation with gay AIDS patients with a harsh denunciation of the sin of homosexual practice.[15] Such an approach is so far from Jesus' compassionate and forgiving relationship with the adulterous woman that one wants to scream. The first thing the Christian must say to an AIDS patient is that God loves him or her so much so that if it were necessary for Jesus to experience the cross again just for that person, he would gladly do it.

But just because one does not admonish and educate at the deathbed does not mean, to quote Episcopal Bishop John Walker of Washington, D.C., that "our calling is not that of judging but of serving." We must do both, albeit in different settings. Much depends, too, on what one means by "judging." Harsh, insensitive, self-righteous attitudes are never acceptable. But "not judging" in that sense is fully compatible with insisting that certain behavior is wrong. Jesus never supposed, as do some modern relativists, that his command to "judge not" means that we cannot condemn sin.

THE ROLE OF THE CHURCH

What should be the church's role in the AIDS crisis? It does not take long to say what the church should do; but actually doing it is quite another matter. One decisive test of whether the church is truly what it claims to be will be whether or not it can muster the obedience and courage to embody its teaching that all human life is sacred even in the midst of the racing panic of plague time.

The most basic role for the church is to set a good example. Thus far it has not batted 1,000. Members of one church in Florida not only led the fight to exclude three hemophiliac boys with AIDS from public school but also decided not to admit persons carrying the AIDS virus into Sunday school, worship, or other church activities. Many other churches, on the other hand, have exhibited a different spirit, recognizing that the AIDS virus cannot be spread by casual contact.

Second, the church should provide direct ministry, both pastoral and other services, to people with AIDS and their families. Third, the church can serve an indispensable role in education. Because people generally trust the church, it should be able to combat the irrational fears and rumors by presenting facts and respected counsel.

Fourth, the church should, as James Nelson suggests, engage in further theological reflection on the issues raised by the AIDS epidemic. It needs to rediscover and proclaim the full biblical understanding of the joy and boundaries of sexual expression, teach by word and example the goodness of the lifelong marriage covenant between a man and a woman, and learn better how to offer unlimited acceptance to everyone without succumbing to mushy relativism. Those four points take only three minutes to articulate. To incarnate them requires a lifetime of struggle.

Nelson is very helpful in calling for a careful balancing of individual rights and social good. The people who speak most often about the sanctity of human life should have been the very first to champion the right of people with AIDS to adequate healthcare rather than lobbying against government expenditure for AIDS research, as did the Moral Majority. And the people who speak frequently about democratic freedom and individuals' personal relationships with God ought to be among the most vigorous champions of the right to individual freedom and privacy. At the same time, Nelson rightly insists that these individual rights must be balanced by a concern for the public good so that we protect the blood supply, and the health of schoolchildren and health professionals, while wisely allocating scarce medical resources.

Finally, the topic of condom ads needs to be addressed, not because it is more important than (probably it is not even as important as) other public-policy questions such as mandatory AIDS testing or contact notification, but because it has provoked such extensive discussion among evangelicals. Some conservative Christians have vigorously, even viciously, denounced fellow evangelical Surgeon General C. Everett Koop for suggesting advertisements and education about condoms in the battle against AIDS. Koop insists that the only safe sex is that within a monogamous relationship, but he also demands that we deal with the real world where promiscuity persists and spreads the AIDS virus at a terrifying rate.

Koop is correct that we need a public education campaign that includes TV and print media encouraging people who choose to persist in high-risk behavior to use condoms. But I also find substance in the response of many people—from Sir Immanuel Jakobowits, the chief rabbi of Britain, to writers in *Christianity Today* to delegates at the 1987 Southern Baptist Convention— that the promotion of condoms could easily encourage promiscuity. If we are trying to warn adolescent youngsters about the dangers of promiscuity, I doubt we do it effectively by a TV ad featuring (to take one current example) a glamorous young woman who says she wants love but she is not willing to die for it.

There is a way to meet both sides' concerns. We could have TV spots featuring someone like Rock Hudson at a stage of the AIDS disease where its ravages are unmistakable. The text could read something like this:

> The only safe sex is within a lifelong monogamous relationship. I wish I had lived that way before I got AIDS. But if, in spite of today's harsh facts, you want to play Russian roulette with your life, then please use condoms. They are not fail-proof, but they do improve your chances.

Such TV spots would not glamorize promiscuity. But they would get the word out on condoms. It is highly unlikely that condom manufacturers would pay for such ads. But promoting their profits is not our agenda. (In fact, TV ads by condom manufacturers should be discouraged because their commercial interests will almost certainly override any concern for public-health education.) Rather, government agencies and private groups, including churches, should develop such spots, and stations should run them as public-service announcements.

Religious leaders today have the awesome task of helping to lead people through what may well become the most deadly epidemic in human history. I hope we will have the courage and faith to turn away from irrational fear, panic, and the temptation to place personal security above compassionate care for the marginalized and ravaged. I hope that instead we will be given the grace to incarnate the belief that all persons, including our sisters and brothers dying of AIDS, are stamped with the divine image and are thus of inestimable value.

SUGGESTIONS FOR FURTHER READING FOR PART 3

Chapter 5: Racism: The Struggle Continues

Barndt, Joseph. *Dismantling Racism: The Continuing Challenge to White America*. Minneapolis: Augsburg, 1991.

Carter, Stephen L. *Reflections of an Affirmative Action Baby*. New York: Basic Books, 1991.

Cone, James H. *A Black Theology of Liberation*. 2nd ed. Maryknoll, NY: Orbis Books, 1986.

D'Souza, Dinesh. *The End of Racism: Principles for a Multicultural Society*. New York: The Free Press, 1995.

Lynch, Frederick R. *Invisible Victims: White Males and the Crisis of Affirmative Action*. Westport, CT: Greenwood Press, 1989.

Mills, Nicolaus, ed. *Debating Affirmative Action: Race, Gender, Ethnicity, and the Politics of Inclusion*. New York: Delta Trade Paperbacks, 1994.

Morales, Rebecca, and Frank Bonilla, eds. *Latinos in a Changing U.S. Economy: Comparative Perspectives on Growing Inequality*. Newbury Park, CA: Sage, 1993.

Nieli, Russell, ed. *Racial Preference and Racial Justice: The New Affirmative Action Controversy*. Washington, D.C.: University Press of America, 1991.

Paris, Peter J. *Black Religious Leaders: Conflict in Unity*. Louisville, KY: Westminster/John Knox Press, 1991.

Schlesinger, Arthur M., Jr. *The Disuniting of America: Reflections on a Multicultural Society*. Knoxville, TN: Whittle Direct Books, 1991.

Stroupe, Nibs, and Inez Fleming. *While We Run This Race: Confronting the Power of Racism in a Southern Church*. Maryknoll, NY: Orbis, 1995.

West, Cornel. *Race Matters*. New York: Vintage Books, Random House, 1994.

Young, Iris Marion. *Justice and the Politics of Difference*. Princeton: Princeton University Press, 1990.

Chapter 6: Feminism in Church and Society

Adams, Carol J., and Marie M. Fortune, eds. *Violence against Women and Children: A Christian Theological Sourcebook*. New York: Continuum, 1995.

Andolson, Barbara Hilkert, Christine E. Gudorf, and Mary D. Pellauer, eds. *Women's Conscience: A Reader in Feminist Ethics*. San Francisco: Harper & Row, 1987.

Bloesch, Donald G. *Is the Bible Sexist?: Beyond Feminism and Patriarchalism.* Westchester, IL: Crossway Books, 1982.

Cannon, Katie G. *Black Womanist Ethics.* Atlanta: Scholars Press, 1988.

Carmody, Denise Lardner. *Virtuous Woman: Reflections on Christian Feminist Ethics.* Maryknoll, NY: Orbis Books, 1992.

Curran, Charles E., Margaret A. Farley, and Richard A. McCormick, eds. *Feminist Ethics and the Catholic Moral Tradition: Readings in Moral Theology.* No. 9. Mahwah, NJ: Paulist Press, 1996.

Daly, Lois K., ed. *Feminist Theology Ethics: A Reader.* Louisville, KY: Westminster/John Knox Press, 1994.

Fiorenza, Elisabeth Schüssler, ed. *The Power of Naming: A Concilium Reader in Feminist Theology.* Maryknoll, NY: Orbis Books, 1996.

Fiorenza, Elisabeth Schüssler, and M. Shawn Copeland, eds. *Violence Against Women.* Maryknoll, NY: Orbis Books, 1994.

Hunt, Mary E. *Fierce Tenderness: A Feminist Theology of Friendship.* New York: Crossroads, 1991.

Isasi-Díaz, Ada María. *En La Lucha (In the Struggle): A Hispanic Women's Liberation Theology.* Minneapolis: Fortress Press, 1993.

Parsons, Susan Frank. *Feminism and Christian Ethics.* New York: Cambridge University Press, 1996.

Patrick, Anne E. *Liberalizing Conscience: Feminist Explorations in Catholic Moral Theology.* New York: Continuum, 1996.

Townes, Emile M., ed. *A Troubling in My Soul: Womenist Perspectives on Evil and Suffering.* Maryknoll, NY: Orbis Books, 1993.

Van Leeuwen, Mary Stewart, ed. *After Eden: Facing the Challenge of Gender Reconciliation.* Grand Rapids, MI: William B. Eerdmans, 1993.

Chapter 7: Heterosexism

Brash, Alan A. *Facing Our Differences: The Christians and their Gay and Lesbian Members.* Geneva, Switzerland: WCC Publications, 1995.

Brawley, Robert L., ed. *Biblical Ethics & Homosexuality: Listening to Scripture.* Louisville, KY: Westminster/John Knox Press, 1996.

Cleaver, Richard. *Know My Name: A Gay Liberation Theology.* Louisville, KY: Westminster/John Knox Press, 1995.

Coleman, Gerald D. *Homosexuality: Catholic Teaching and Pastoral Practice.* Mahwah, NJ: Paulist Press, 1995.

Grmek, Mirko D. *History of AIDS: Emergence and Origin of a Modern Pandemic.* Princeton, NJ: Princeton University Press, 1990.

Hartman, Keith. *Congregations in Conflict: The Battle over Homosexuality.* New Brunswick, NJ: Rutgers University Press, 1996.

Hefling, Charles, ed. *Ourselves, Our Souls and Bodies: Sexuality and the Household of God.* Boston: Cowley Publishing, 1996.

Heyward, Carter. *Staying Power: Reflections on Gender, Justice and Compassion.* Cleveland: Pilgrim Press, 1995.

Jung, Patricia Beattie, and Ralph Smith. *Heterosexism: The Ethical Challenge.* Albany, NY: SUNY Press, 1993.

Meilaender, Gilbert. *Morality in Plague Time: AIDS in Theological Perspective.* St. Louis: Concordia Publishing House, 1989.

Mohr, Richard D. *Gays/Justice: A Study of Ethics, Society, and Law.* New York: Columbia University Press, 1990.

Peddecord, Richard. *Gay and Lesbian Rights, A Question: Sexual Ethics or Social Justice?* Kansas City: Sheed and Ward, 1996.

Pronk, Pim. *Against Nature? Types of Moral Argumentation Regarding Homosexuality.* Grand Rapids, MI: Eerdmans, 1993.

Scanzoni, Letha Dawson, and Virginia Ramey Mollenkott. *Is the Homosexual My Neighbor?: A Positive Christian Response.* San Francisco: Harper, 1994.

Sikes, Jeffrey S., ed. *Homosexuality in the Church: Both Sides of the Debate.* Louisville, KY: Westminster/John Knox Press, 1994.

Soards, Marion L. *Scripture and Homosexuality: Biblical Authority and the Christian Today.* Louisville, KY: Westminster/John Knox Press, 1995.

Stuart, Elizabeth. *Just Good Friends: Towards a Lesbian and Gay Theology of Relationships.* New York: Mowbray, 1995.

PART 4

The Christian and Issues of National Priority

Chapter 8

IMMIGRATION:

CAN WE HAVE OPEN BORDERS?

The inscription on the Statue of Liberty on Liberty Island reads "Give me your tired, your poor, your huddled masses yearning to breathe free." Over the years the United States has more or less lived up to that sentiment, that value. Every grade-school child learns the names of those immigrants who contributed to the creative and technological prowess of our country. The United States frequently celebrates its cultural diversity as one reason for its rich traditions in the arts, sciences, and history of democratic government.

However, in August of 1993, California governor Pete Wilson wrote an open letter to President Clinton asking him to address the issue of immigration. In the letter, published nationwide, Wilson complained that his state was paying a high price for the failure of the federal government—which holds sole authority for immigration—to control the nation's borders. In 1994, California passed Proposition 187, which denied education, health care, and incarceration to illegal immigrants.

Immigration has become a hot political topic. Some accused Wilson of adopting his stance as a manipulative means of garnering political support. Others consider Wilson's and California's stance part of a growing trend by the public to blame immigrants for society's ills and to punish them for problems that arose elsewhere. The immigrant rights group La Resistencia described Wilson's letter as "a lesson in scapegoating of the ugliest and most mean-spirited style."

While we in the United States may conceive of this as only a national or merely a domestic issue, others are claiming that this is already a global issue and threatens to become a matter of poor nations going to war with rich ones. Matthew Connelly and Paul Kennedy invite us to consider the latter prospect in an article "Must It Be The Rest Against the West?" (*Atlantic Monthly,* December 1994, not excerpted here). They call attention to "the key global problem of the final years of the twentieth century: unbalanced wealth and resources, unbalanced demographic trends, and the relationship between the two." (p. 62) The vision they put forward is of a world divided into two camps, in which the rich have to fight and the poor will have to die if mass migration is not to overwhelm us all. At risk are the traditional cultures of affluent nations who fear that Third World hordes will wipe out not only their culture, but also their standard of living and environment. And what if some affluent countries, such as France, restrict immigration severely and others, such as the United States, are relatively liberal in their immigration policy? Connelly and Kennedy quote the Federation for American Immigration Reform (FAIR) in its publication *Crowding Out the Future:*

> A traditional moralist may object, asserting, "I am my brother's keeper." We must ask him: "And what about your children? And your children's children? What about the children of your neighbors next door? Must we subdivide and distribute our patrimony among the children of all the world?" Americans are already outnumbered twenty-to-one by the rest of the world. Our grandchildren will be outnumbered even more. Must we condemn them to the poverty of an absolutely equal distribution? How would that benefit them or the descendants of other people?

The prospect that there will be wars of migration, with Fortress America or Fortress Japan protecting itself against teeming mobs, offers no hope of ameliorating the population and deprivation crises in the Third World. These global fault lines and the fact of global interconnectedness persuade Connelly and Kennedy that the only serious alternative is to recognize that everyone's future is implicated in this crisis and to devote every resource possible to slowing down the buildup of worldwide demographic and environmental pressures. This issue is one that shows every possibility of expanding into the future.

Dana Wilbanks is author of our first article in this chapter: "The Moral Debate Between Humanitarianism and National Interest About U.S. Refugee Policy: A Theological Perspective." To be sure, this is a special case of immigration policy, but one whose dimensions are useful in stimulating our thinking about this issue. Wilbanks writes that he finds the debate about U.S. refugee policy cast in terms of humanitarianism, which requires hospitality to refugees, and also in terms of national interest, which dictates a narrowly open door at best. He believes that national interest is on the playing field of refugee policy, while humanitarianism is like a perpetual bench-sitter. He uses the game analogy to describe the five different ways that refugee advocates construe the relationship between humanitarianism and national interest. The article offers some ideas about the future of the debate from the perspective of Christian ethics. The three contributions that Christians can make to the public moral ethos, he writes, are the attempt to understand things in relation to God's compassionate concern for the world, especially the world of the outcast; the way that Christian thought views the refugee as "stranger" or "other" that is to be shown hospitality; and the public significance of the church that is to publicly articulate an ethic of community.

In contrast to Wilbanks's careful reasoning, our next selection comes from an immigrants' rights advocate, Aurora Camacho de Schmidt, who is clearly viscerally engaged in this question. Camacho de Schmidt raises the spectre of a quasi-military closing of the border at El Paso and of the Clinton administration's returning Haitian boat people to "a murderous regime." Although borders are not open, they have become more meaningless as transnational labor forces develop in response to the "decapitalization of their countries of origin." This phrase suggests the contradiction of international economic agreements (NAFTA, GATT) that have the effect of wiping out national borders for trade purposes, while at the same time maintaining strict borders for purposes of immigration. One seems to dismantle national sovereignty, while the other seems to escalate its importance. The effect of these agreements has been to strengthen the wealthy and powerful. What can the community of faith do? Welcome immigrant peoples; hear their voices; espouse costly politics; trust in our own imagination and in the imagination of God. The older paradigms are fading; the new is not yet revealed. The people "who overcome the border patrol and the U.S. Coast Guard are not *bearers* of the good news; they themselves *are* the good news."

The third of our essays reveals just how difficult this question is by raising the hard nubs of issues. "The Coming Immigration Debate" is a portion of a review of the book *Alien Nation: Common Sense About America's Immigration Disaster* by Peter Brimelow. The reviewer, Jack Miles, correctly sees that this book is indispensable because Brimelow raises the right issues in making a powerful case against the status quo. Brimelow is worried that the projections are that by the year 2050 the percentage of whites (mostly EuroAmericans) in the U.S. will be only 53 percent. He also compares the immigration policies of various other fairly affluent (and not so affluent) countries with that of the United States, and declares ours a disaster. While the rest of the world is closing or has closed its doors, he suggests that those of the United States are wide open. Do we really want the consequences that will accompany this policy? Brimelow thinks not. He appeals to the self-interest of the United States, to its Anglo majority, and also to the relatively well-off of whatever race. The appeal appears to be quite in contrast to Wilbanks and Camacho de Schmidt's humanitarian values, but Brimelow might argue that his is the more profoundly humanitarian position in the long run.

The Moral Debate between Humanitarianism and National Interest about U.S. Refugee Policy: A Theological Perspective
Dana W. Wilbanks

THE POLARITIES OF HUMANITARIANISM AND NATIONAL INTEREST

As I have studied ethical perspectives on U.S. refugee policy in recent months, I find that often the discussion is framed by the polarities of humanitarianism and national interest. The debate goes something like this. Humanitarianism requires compassionate and generous responses on the part of peoples and governments to the desperate needs of today's refugees. Not only should we protect refugees according to the most strict international standards, we should expand the definition of refugee to include a far larger number of persons.

Yet, the world is organized into nation states with each claiming territorial sovereignty. The right to maintain and control national boundaries is a central feature in the exercise of sovereignty. Thus, national governments will necessarily make decisions about refugee admission on the basis of national self-interest. Considerations of national interest are in tension with humanitarian sentiments, indeed sometimes in outright conflict. Whereas humanitarianism requires hospitality to refugees, national interest dictates a narrowly open door at best. It is not an equal struggle or debate. In the end, national interest prevails.

How then shall refugee advocates argue the case for refugee admission in public discourse? Shall we seek to become more eloquent humanitarians? Or should we attempt to work more effectively within the narrow confines of national interest? Can religious perspectives contribute anything to the debate? In order to analyze the debate, I shall adopt the analogy of a game. Let me illustrate. National interest is on the playing field of refugee policy determination, but humanitarianism is like a perpetual bench-sitter. It is on the sidelines, not really on the field of play. National interest dominates the play. Humanitarianism is told that it is important, but in fact it is not really a player.

In my study of moral arguments I have discovered at least five different ways that refugee advocates construe the relation of humanitarianism and national interest. In the remainder of this essay, I shall use the game analogy to describe the options, identify the strengths and weaknesses of each and then offer some ideas about the future of the debate from the perspective of Christian ethics. It is important to emphasize that each of these types of humanitarianism/national interest relation has representatives who have strong moral commitments to the

From Dana Wilbanks, "The Moral Debate between Humanitarianism and National Interest about U.S. Refugee Policy: A Theological Perspective," Center for Migration Studies, *Migration World,* Vol. 21, No. 5, pp. 15–18. Reprinted with permission of the Center for Migration Studies.

well-being of refugees. The question has to do with the terms on which advocates present their arguments in public discourse. In my view, Christians and members of other religious communities should neither try to dominate nor withdraw from the public arena; rather they should communicate publicly how the moral resources of their traditions speak to the questions of refugee policy.

NATIONAL INTEREST

The first type is that only national interest should play. Humanitarianism does not belong on the field of refugee policy determination. According to this view, we should keep humanitarianism on the bench and national interest in the game. . . .

This first perspective makes the important point that humanitarianism should not necessarily be regarded as more moral than arguments based on national interest. Well-intentioned humanitarianism may in fact contribute to morally troubling consequences. But the chief problem with this view is that national interest becomes the taken-for-granted and functional moral absolute. Ethical supremacy is granted to the historical arrangement of the world into nation states. In a context of radically unequal power relations among states, might therefore determines right.

Moreover, the moral content of national interest is rarely acknowledged, justified and debated. National interest according to whom? Whose interests are touted as the nation's interests? National interest is often a platitude in public policy discussions, concealing much more than it reveals. It may serve primarily to legitimate the continuing dominance of nationalistic ethics in international relations.

HUMANITARIANISM

The second type reverses somewhat the first one. Here humanitarianism makes the rules and enforces them while national interest plays the game. Humanitarianism is the referee or umpire or judge of national refugee policy. National interest must play the game within legitimately humanitarian boundaries. . . .

The moral logic of this perspective seems incontestable. When persons are fleeing for their lives, seeking a place of safety from conditions of brutality and deprivation, elemental humanitarianism requires protection by another state and its peoples. Any resistances by governments pale in their claim beside the urgent needs of individual human beings who want only to find a place of refuge. There are very few considerations of national interest, perhaps none, that would be weightier than the basic human rights of individuals. It is morally required that states will protect such rights, especially the right to life and to protection from bodily harm.

Very rarely do national interest proponents disagree with humanitarians on substantive grounds. Instead they maintain that humanitarian norms are rather ineffectual in the real world. The difficulty in this second perspective is the wide gap between humanitarian ideals and government refugee practice. While giving a nod to international human rights standards in a formal or abstract sense, the U.S. government in fact maneuvers through definitional and procedural strategies to avoid their implications. The treatment of Haitian refugees is a clear example. While I believe in fact that humanitarian ethics has been more effective than cynics allow, we need a moral argument that will overcome this split between abstract ideal humanitarian norms and refugee politics.

SEPARATING NATIONAL INTEREST AND HUMANITARIANISM

A third type is that humanitarianism and national interest play separate games. It is a dualistic viewpoint. Each has its own field, its own characteristics and purposes. The relationship between the two games is essentially cooperative, though some tensions and conflicts are almost inevitable. . . .

Governments have their own legitimate national interests to protect. Humanitarianism seeks its own independent space to assist as many refugees as possible. The two are not incompatible, but they are different games.

There is much to commend this position. With the dominance of state politics in international relations, it is possibly dangerous to do anything that will undermine the political independence of humanitarian refugee work. Nichols wants to support effective ways to meet the basic needs of refugees within the dynamics of national and international politics. Yet he exaggerates the independence of refugee work from politics. And his ethical perspective is flawed because it does not address the conditions which produce refugees. His humanitarian ethic perpetuates the image of the refugee as recipient of assistance, dependent on the generosity of providers, rather than as a moral agent with a legitimate claim to justice.

COMBINING NATIONAL INTEREST AND HUMANITARIANISM

The fourth type is to find those elements of a refugee policy that satisfy both humanitarian and national interest considerations. To use the game analogy, the field of play is still in the hands of national interest, but both humanitarianism and national interest get to play. The assumption is that they are not necessarily in opposition. Where the requirements of each coincide, then one has a strong moral basis for refugee policy.

This perspective is frequently found among U.S. government officials. . . . Humanitarianism requires protection of Haitians whose basic rights to security and subsistence are threatened. But it is also in the national interest of the United States to manage Haitian migration in a fair and orderly way, and to use its influence to foster the protection of human rights by the Haitian government.

This perspective is an important one. It seeks to retain the contributions of humanitarianism within the presumed real world of practical politics. The task is to translate moral language into interest language in a way that effectively fuses them, thereby developing both a moral and realistic basis for policy. But it has its weaknesses also. That which is regarded as the national interest has the trump card. The discourse of "interest" is taken for granted without critical scrutiny. Moreover, one may wonder about the degree to which both are served when they presumably coincide or if, in fact, humanitarianism has been coopted to support a particular conception of national interest.

SUBORDINATING NATIONAL INTEREST TO HUMANITARIANISM

The fifth type is a slightly different version of the fourth one. It accepts the givenness of the national interest basis for refugee policy. But it seeks to define that interest in a humanitarian way. Or, again, to use the game analogy, the playing field is national interest. Both humanitarianism and national interest play, but the quality of play is substantially improved because of the participation of humanitarianism. . . .

In many ways this is a compelling option. It accepts the practicality of national interest discourse, yet it seeks to contest the interpretations of this discourse. And it seeks to do so not from an abstract idealistic perspective but from one that is rooted in the historical and moral experience of the United States. The critique is not so easy. One may question, though, if more humanitarian renderings of national interest have been any more effective in shaping U.S. policy than more explicitly idealistic ones. More basic, however, is the question of the national interest paradigm itself. To accept the givenness of this paradigm is to concede moral sovereignty to the nation state.

I want to argue here that to retain the duality of humanitarianism and national interest is an inadequate way for refugee advocates to communicate their moral views in the public arena. We need to invent another discourse game. Humanitarianism is regarded as marginal at best to the controlling norms of national interest and tends therefore to be regarded as politically impotent. Yet, national interest arguments acquiesce to the dominance of national perspectives over broader views of moral responsibility. Moreover, appeals to national interest do not replenish the reservoirs of moral conviction and imagination necessary to sustain a generous public response to the moral challenge of refugees. "What is needed is a public moral perspective that does not concede functional supremacy to the norm of national interest and that does represent the integral connection between moral values and political struggle in the formation of refugee policy."

One way to begin to shape such a public ethic is to draw on the particular moral convictions of specific religious communities (e.g., Christian, Jewish, Buddhist, Muslim, etc.), as well as non-religious communities. I am suggesting that it is legitimate for religious communities to display in public how their moral convictions inform their public policy positions. Not only this, it is important to a healthy public life that they do so. I shall briefly identify some of the theological and ethical contributions which Christians can make to the public moral ethos.

First, Christians seek to understand things in their relation to God and to God's compassionate concern for the world, especially the world of outcasts. The nation is necessarily de-centered in this perspective. Absolutizing claims of state sovereignty are rejected. The national interest cannot be the ultimate arbiter of morality. In fact, in theological language, the identification of God with the nation state or the absolutizing of the state is regarded as idolatry—the worship of false gods—and hence to be vigorously resisted.

To view human community in its relation to God moves persons away from more exclusive notions, such as nations, to ever greater inclusivity. It projects a vision of transnational interrelationship. The national community is viewed in relation to a wider community which includes other nations and peoples. National borders may serve necessary and useful purposes, but their moral claim is qualified and relativized by the universality of the human family.

The nation is replaced at the center of moral discourse with the refugee herself. The beginning point is the cry of distress, the story of suffering and hope, that is present in the refugee. It is the concrete reality of the refugee which is the occasion for moral response and the challenge to moral reflection. . . .

Another way of saying this is that for Christians the lives of refugees may be seen as sacred texts. That is, the most concrete way to encounter the living God is not through words on a page but in the personhood of the refugees. In the presence of the refugee one is summoned to responsibility. It is this most basic interpersonal character of the challenge of refugees that needs to be kept at the center of discussions about what kinds of policies to adopt.

Second, in a theological interpretation, how one views refugees determines how one responds to them. To view them as created in the image of God provides an orientation to refugees as persons which generates responses consistent with their divinely given value. They are not "objects" for receiving aid but subjects with whom to enter relationship. Christian responsibility to the refugee is to act in ways that ensures their lives are protected, their personhood is respected, and that therefore their own capacities are given opportunity to be expressed and to flourish.

Another important metaphor in Christian thought for viewing the refugee is the notion of "stranger," or "other." Christians have drawn from Hebrew Scriptures the conviction that God has special compassion for the stranger and sojourner. Jesus himself, traditionally regarded by Christians as the personal embodiment of God, identifies with the stranger. The refugee is stranger; the appropriate moral response is hospitality. In hospitality, the refugee stranger becomes neighbor, welcomed and loved as a member of the community, respected in her difference, protected from harm, invited to speak and to teach, supported and encouraged in her capacities as a moral agent.

According to some critics of the abstractness of human rights discourse, the problem to be addressed in refugee policy is not so much the violation of universal rights but the rejection of the personhood of the concrete other who addresses us as not so much similar as different. What, then, is needed in public discourse about refugee policy is a way of valuing difference rather than hating, fearing or scapegoating it. The notion of refugee as stranger contributes the sense that public and individual life may be viewed as a moral and social adventure.

To be sure, hospitality to refugees brings difficulties. There is no need to romanticize or sugarcoat the problems. But the point in public policy is not to rid life of difficulties, which will find us in any case. It is to ask which struggles and challenges human communities will undertake and how they will undertake them. A theological perspective can contribute the conviction that the challenges of vulnerability and diversity brought in the persons of refugees are ones worth meeting. The United States needs the refugee as much as the refugee needs admittance, as a valued ingredient of community change and revitalization.

The third theological contribution is ecclesiology. In Christian discourse this has to do especially with the church. The general point is to emphasize the public significance of the church and other voluntary associations that are activated by an ethics of personal responsibility and transnational human community. In Christian theology, ethics is not primarily the construction of a rational framework of thought about moral matters. Rather it is a vision of life in relation to God that is to be embodied historically in a community. The ethic is to be lived, not just refined, clarified and talked about.

In terms of U.S. refugee policy, I believe this implies the need to nourish and shape the moral resources of particular moral communities so they might model as well as advocate hospitality and justice for refugees. It is through the agency of mobilized constituencies that change in public policy is most likely to occur. The strategic focus in this refugee-centered perspective is less on convincing national officials about what is or is not in the national interest. It has more to do with morally energizing persons and communities to respond expansively to the challenge of refugees.

Another element in the moral significance of the church is that it is itself a transnational community. Frequently church related groups provide channels for hearing the voices of people in other countries outside the control of governments, breaking open the dominance of nationalistic view. The most profound interpretation of the importance of the church for refugee policy is provided by the Quaker agnostic and sanctuary leader, Jim Corbett. Corbett maintains that the way to achieve greater international implementation of rights for refugees is through the activism of "border transcending" communities that live according to human rights norms in their own localities.

A refugee centered moral discourse should not be viewed as just another version of impractical idealism. One must find effective ways to operationalize this ethic politically. But it is also important to nourish the moral ethos through enlivened public discussion about refugee policy. Religious communities can contribute to the revitalization of the moral and spiritual capacities of the society to undertake the challenges of refugee admission. Pitting national interest and humanitarianism against each other does not take us very far. Instead, the challenge is to thicken the moral resources that can motivate and sustain people's readiness to extend hospitality to refugees.

Mi Casa No Es Su Casa
Aurora Camacho de Schmidt

If the Statue of Liberty were to do her job now, she would stand somewhere along the U.S.–Mexico border, perhaps just outside El Paso, Texas, on terrain that was once Mexico, and before that part of the Spanish empire, and even before that inhabited by American Indians. She would be in a place with a long history. And she would be looking south.

I wonder if, from her new location, Lady Liberty would still welcome immigrants, the seeds of future U.S. citizens, or if she would lend her torch instead to the U.S. border patrol. Perhaps she would become part of the physical barrier built to save the integrity of U.S. borders. Quite possibly she would be armed to the teeth, the hopeful poem at her feet replaced by a nasty warning written in Spanish.

Many in the United States are troubled about the number of immigrants crossing our borders. *The New York Times* recently reported that on any given Sunday in the Los Angeles archdiocese, mass is celebrated in forty-six languages. *The Atlantic Monthly* described how a town in Wisconsin changed for the worse after the resettlement of Indochinese refugees. Eugene McCarthy's *A Colony for the World* charged that "ethnic groups" believe "immigration of their own is a virtual entitlement." The Federation for American Immigration Reform (FAIR) cautions that every ten years "a new state of Michigan" is added to the U.S. population through neglect of our borders. Pat Buchanan has warned us that "if present trends hold, White Americans will be a minority by 2050."

This roaring, anti-immigrant message is coming from many fronts. The governors of California, Florida, Texas, and New York have requested payment from the federal government for expenditures made on behalf of undocumented immigrants, because U.S. policy has failed to contain the flow of people. Last year, a quasi-military closing of the border at El Paso demonstrated that the Clinton administration is not above the prevailing mentality. Most Haitian boat people—men, women, and children—continue to be returned to a murderous regime, even after being interviewed aboard U.S. ships stationed in Jamaican waters.

Congress is swamped with bills addressing immigration, most of them designed to restrict the presence of immigrants or to make their lives here more

Reprinted with permission from *The Other Side,* a Christian magazine devoted to peace and social justice. For information call 1-800-700-9280.

difficult. In California, the gubernatorial campaigns have integrated the issue into their platforms: Governor Pete Wilson's television commercial features an infrared film of the California-Mexico border that shows people crawling like ants on the screen. Alan Nelson, former commissioner of the Immigration and Naturalization Service (INS), and Harold Ezell, former director of INS's western region, have launched the Save Our State (SOS) campaign in California, supporting a ballot initiative to exclude undocumented immigrants from public services, including education and health. Even the environmental movement has augmented the hysteria by portraying immigrants not only as threats to cultural unity, neighborhood safety, and labor stability, but also as out-of-control progenitors and pollutants.

There is fear in the land. Borders are not open, yet they have become more and more meaningless as transnational labor forces develop in response to the decapitalization of their countries of origin. Amidst the flow of peoples, immigrants' rights advocates are called to hear the pain of those who fear that new immigrants aggravate the situation of poor people in the United States.

Those who fear immigration, on the other hand, must realize that the injustice embodied in each human being who is forced to leave his or her home and survive in a hostile place parallels that suffered by each homeless, jobless, hungry, uneducated, sick, and neglected U.S. citizen.

The so-called new world order and "economic globalization" have territorialized labor in new ways. Far from providing the Third World with prosperity and freedom, the reorganization of investment, production, and consumption through initiatives such as the North Atlantic Free Trade Agreement (NAFTA) and the Caribbean Basin Initiative have strengthened transnational elites and further consolidated wealth and political power. As a result, the rich in Mexico and the rich in New York City have a lot in common; Haiti's poor and poor people in Denver are in the same boat.

Yet prevailing attitudes make it almost impossible for poor people across borders to unite in a common cause. They are instead pitted against each other: Koreans against African Americans, Mexicans against Vietnamese, Haitians against Chicanos. To working people of all races, immigrants are the enemy. Restrictionist organizations such as FAIR boast polls showing Latino support for radical measures of immigration control. Meanwhile, oppressive economic structures remain unchallenged.

What can people of faith do? Welcome immigrant women and men and support hearing their voices. Join their struggles for justice. Take seriously labor advocates who say that the inexhaustible supply of undocumented workers makes it easy for a sector such as agriculture to maintain abominable working conditions. Support neighborhood and labor organizations across ethnic and immigration-status lines. Support sound research in opposition to corrupt science disguised as demography, bioecology, and sociology. Make a commitment to profound change, not to easy legislative measures that eradicate "the problem" by eradicating people. Espouse *costly* politics and embrace a *costly* faith, not the ideology and religious fervor that leave lives untouched. In the words of Cornel West, we must adopt "not optimism, but audacious hope."

Christians in the United States have not trusted enough in our own imagination or in the imagination of God. But the God of history is surely at work. "Behold, I am doing a new thing" (Isa. 43:19). No one can yet see this new thing. The concepts of nation, community, and culture are being redefined, and the weakness of old paradigms makes it difficult to read the present. Can the faithful trust God through this time of questions without answers?

Refugees and undocumented workers feel the terrible sorrow of being uprooted. Even before the Haitian asylum-seeker or the Filipina undocumented nurse sets foot on U.S. soil, she has been expelled from a home and has suffered. The people of the United States need to help prevent such expulsions, but they must not thwart the search for shelter and survival.

Through this uprootedness and these enormous demographic changes, we must together forge a new society built on new visions and hopes. If immigrants and refugees can struggle with the people of this country for a more just nation and world, their presence here will fill a precious vocation. Then we will realize that those people—armed only with a jug of water and a foreign language—who overcome the border patrol and the U.S. Coast Guard are not *bearers* of the good news: they themselves *are* the good news.

Look them in the eyes. You will see what I mean.

The Coming Immigration Debate:
An Englishman Takes an Alarmed Look
at a Quintessentially American Issue
Jack Miles

ALIEN NATION: COMMON SENSE ABOUT AMERICA'S IMMIGRATION DISASTER, BY PETER BRIMELOW

In the late 1940s, when the Marshall Plan was being debated in Congress, Arthur Vandenberg, presenting the plan on the floor of the Senate, summoned up a vision of "270,000,000 people of the stock which has largely made America." He insisted, "This vast friendly segment of the earth must not collapse. The iron curtain must not come to the rim of the Atlantic either by aggression or by default." Nearly fifty years later Peter Brimelow, an Englishman by birth and a senior editor of *Forbes* magazine, has summoned up another vision of danger to the common European-American stock. Comparing himself to the Thomas Paine of *Common Sense,* he warns that the survival of the American nation-state is in peril to a degree scarcely seen since revolutionary days. Unless radical corrective measures are quickly taken, he says, unchecked Third World immigration will overwhelm the United States—its culture, its economy, and its ethnic identity—within a matter of a few decades. European-Americans will be just one more minority group in a nation that few of today's Americans, whatever their ethnicity, would any longer recognize. . . .

Peter Brimelow has written what may prove to be an indispensable book . . . because of the highly contentious form the book takes. Brimelow serves up imagined debaters, duels one after another, with the final thrust invariably delivered by the author's side. Consider, for example, the following:

> You hear a lot about Ph.D. immigrants working in California's Silicon Valley computer complex. Just under 3 percent of recent immigrants had Ph.D.s, as opposed to just over 1 percent of native-born Americans. But that's only, say, 30,000 immigrant Ph.D.s a year. And have you heard that surveys show some 10 percent of Mexican illegal immigrants . . . were *totally illiterate in any language?*
> You haven't? Oh.

Brimelow calls the contending parties, with polemical panache, "immigration enthusiasts" and "patriots." Others have used the more neutral terms "admissionists" and "restrictionists." But either party may profitably imbibe this bottled brio. One side will be confirmed, the other forearmed.

Some of Brimelow's claims seem unproved, however intriguing—for example, his observation that America's ethnic groups are sorting themselves out by region.

> California . . . is being abandoned by lower-income whites in particular, exactly the group that would appear to be most vulnerable to competition from unskilled immigrants. Much of this white flight is flocking to the intermountain West, which seems likely to emerge as part of America's white heartland.
> Less noticed, minorities are polarizing too. Asians move to California's Bay Area—they now make up 29.1 percent of San Francisco County—and to the Los Angeles megalopolis, even if they originally settled in other parts of the United States.

Brimelow might have added that some blacks are returning to the South. Still, if it is difficult to maintain the character of even an ethnic neighborhood in a highly mobile society, will it not be all the more difficult to establish and maintain an entire ethnic region?

A more serious issue, though amusing enough in Brimelow's telling, is immigration reciprocity. Brimelow formally inquired into the possiblity of emigrating to several of the countries that send the most immigrants to the United States, and shares with us what he was told. Here are some of the opening sentences:

China: "China does not accept any immigrants. We have a large enough population."

Mexico: "Unless you are hired by a Mexican company that obtains a temporary work permit, or a retiree older than sixty-five who can prove financial self-sufficiency, you must get a six-month tourist visa and apply in person to the Ministry of the Interior in Mexico City."

South Korea: "Korea does not accept immigrants."

Jamaica: "You cannot simply immigrate to Jamaica."

Egypt: "Egypt is not an immigrant country."

But if, as so many claim, immigrants contribute more to the economy than they cost, Brimelow asks, why are these countries not eager for immigration—particularly for a highly skilled, well-capitalized immigrant like him? The size of the population should have nothing to do with it.

One admissionist response might be that these countries should indeed encourage immigration and would be economically better off if they did so. A likelier admissionist response would be "America is different": these countries may rightly claim that they are not nations of immigrants, but America has a different tradition. Historically, however, as Brimelow effectively shows, the United States has experienced intermittent rather than continuous immigration. Twice in the past we have deliberately interrupted the flow. We could do so again.

Should we? This is the central question of the book and of the upcoming national debate. Before that question is asked, however, the mistaken belief that large-scale legal immigration to the United States is a purely natural phenomenon should first be corrected. Heavy immigration has not just happened. It has come about through political decisions. Many Americans remember the Civil Rights Act of 1964. Too we remember the Immigration and Nationality Act Amendments of 1965. At the time, proponents of the new law, which ended national quotas and introduced the family-reunification principle, confidently predicted that it would bring about neither any dramatic increase in immigration nor any significant change in the ethnic makeup of the United States. Had either change been predicted, the law would not have passed.

Both changes, however, are now accomplished fact. In 1990, Brimelow reports, a staggering 1.5 million *legal* immigrants were admitted, of whom only eight percent came from Europe, including some en route from Asia or the Caribbean by way of Europe. In 1960 the U.S. population was 88.6 percent white. By 1990 the percentage of whites had dropped to 75.6, and the Bureau of the Census forecasts a further drop, to 64 percent by 2020 and to 53 percent by 2050.

Without congressional action this would not have happened. Do we want it to continue happening?

> In other words: let's suppose that it would indeed be impolite to raise the question of ethnic balance—if a shift were occurring due to the unaided efforts of one's fellow Americans, resulting in different birthrates for different groups.
>
> But how can it be impolite to mention it when the shift is due to the arrival of unprecedented numbers of foreigners—arbitrarily and accidentally

selected by a government that specifically and repeatedly [in 1965] denied it was doing any such thing?

If by decision or inaction this process continues, then America will indeed be different—not just different from what it has been but different from every other nation in the world in its radical openness to immigration. No other nation, as Brimelow's queries about emigration make clear, permits immigration by the hundreds of thousands annually on criteria no more compelling than "family reunification." None would dream of countenancing a tremendous demographic transformation for that reason alone.

If the United States chooses to make itself truly the great exception, the implications are virtually endless, one of them being a potentially profound transformation of black-white relations, as "now, suddenly, there are new minorities, each with their own grievances and attitudes—*quite possibly including a lack of guilt about, and even hostility toward, blacks.*"

In this regard Brimelow may be saying more than he realizes. Within living memory virtually all who immigrated to the United States became citizens, and all who became citizens took on American history as their own. Numerous poems and stories have been written over the years about the comedy and poignancy of this process. But more-recent immigrants, by no means excluding immigrants from Europe, evince little enthusiasm for what Lincoln called the "unfinished work" of building a nation on "the proposition that all men are created equal." They hold or divest U.S. citizenship on the basis of tax-savings yield just as some native-born Americans have done. Their attitude bodes ill for the United States as other than a business arrangement and particularly ill for what Gunnar Myrdal called the "American dilemma" of race relations after slavery.

Perhaps a few Americans formally espouse the view that their country is not truly a nation but only a political system, a kind of inherited calculus for reconciling the interests of a group of nations (or ethnic groups, to use the domestic designation) occupying a single territory. But even if we wish the United States to be no more than that, can we get away with it? Can the American political system—the polity, the state—survive the demise of the American nation? The state has survived past peaks of immigration by relying on the nation to assimilate the immigrants culturally. But if the nation can no longer assimilate new groups because it has itself become no more than a group of unassimilated, contending cultures, how will the state survive a continuous heavy influx?

Assimilation itself has come into some disrepute. Proponents of multiculturalism want to preserve the immigrant cultures and even languages rather than see them absorbed by a host culture. Even the mutual assimilation or accommodation of native-born groups one to another, though it continues, is questioned. The melting pot, once celebrated, is now sometimes reviled. Other metaphors—the mosaic, the salad—are preferred. True, some foresee a less separatist, more mutually appreciative multiculturalism—a new cosmopolitanism, if you will—on the far side of multiculturalism as we now know it.

But will the new cosmopolitanism mature soon enough to guarantee the minimum cultural coherence that political coherence requires?

If there is any question about that, and, more important, if there is a serious question about whether immigration confers any economic benefits whatsoever, shouldn't the United States sharply curtail immigration, just to be on the safe side, given the other risks and stresses that accompany it?

Unsurprisingly, Brimelow believes that there is indeed a serious question about whether immigration confers any economic benefits. Surprisingly, however, and perhaps prudently, he goes no further than this. He attends to no single topic at greater length than he does to economics, but he concludes that the economic case against the status quo in American immigration must be built into the cultural case against it. In the last paragraphs of the second of his two chapters on the economic consequences of immigration, he summarizes as follows:

> It's a simple exercise in logic:
> *1. Capitalism (and no doubt every other economic system) needs specific cultural prerequisites to function;*
> *2. Immigration can alter the cultural patterns of a society.*
> THEREFORE—
> *3. Immigration can affect a society's ability to sustain capitalism.*
> Let's leave the last word with [the economist] George Borjas. . . : *"The economic arguments for immigration simply aren't decisive,"* he says. "You have to make a political case—for example, does the U.S. have to take Mexican immigrants to provide a safety valve?"

Brimelow is a financial journalist and a political conservative. He knows perhaps better than many liberal journalists that conservatives are divided about the economic consequences of immigration. Robert Bartley, the editor of *The Wall Street Journal,* notoriously favors open borders. Last November, William Bennett and Jack Kemp, conservatives who had campaigned against California's Proposition 187, gave the endorsement of their organization, Empower America, to an "Immigration Index" produced by the conservative Center for the New American Community. The index purports to show that, as Kemp put it, "immigrants are a blessing, not a curse."

Brimelow sees more curse than blessing. He observes, for example, that most Third World immigrant-sending countries are without income-redistributing social welfare. Accordingly, the ablest, richest people in those countries have little reason to move to highly redistributionist Europe or the moderately redistributionist United States. By the same token, the European poor have reason to stay home and the Third World poor have reason to come here.

Arguing against the importance of imported labor at any level of skill, Brimelow points out that Japan's extraordinary economic development has come about without the benefit of immigration. In a population of 125 million Japan has perhaps 900,000 resident foreigners; in a population of 260 million the

United States has 23.4 million. And rumors to the contrary notwithstanding, Japan is not about to change its policy. Here is the response Brimelow got to his inquiry about emigrating to Japan:

> Anonymous Japanese Official. (*complete surprise and astonishment*) "Why do you want to emigrate to Japan? . . . There is no immigration to Japan. (*Asked if there aren't political refugees or asylum seekers*) There might be three people a year who become Japanese (*chuckles*). And even they don't stay long, they try to emigrate elsewhere, like the U.S."

The Japanese have achieved economic success without immigration secondarily because their high savings rate has assisted capital formation but primarily, Brimelow says, because technical innovation is more important than either capital or labor.

Brimelow implies, however, and surely he is right, that Japan's immigration policy is ultimately dictated by cultural rather than economic considerations. When immigration policy comes down to dollars and cents alone, policy formulation may be postponed indefinitely. Each side will have its economists, and each month will provide new numbers to be crunched. Borjas (to whom Brimelow's intellectual debt is enormous) is probably right: what politics has done, politics must decide either to undo or to continue doing.

Brimelow himself is blunt about the political course he would have the nation follow. Here are some of his recommendations:

Double the size of the Border Patrol.

"Urgently" increase the size of the Immigration and Naturalization Service.

Institute a new Operation Wetback to expel illegal aliens.

If necessary, establish a national identity card.

Go beyond employer sanctions to the interdiction of money transfers by illegals to their home countries.

Make it clear that there will never again be an amnesty for illegal immigrants.

Discontinue immigration for the purposes of family reunification. If family reunification is permitted at all, confine it to the nuclear family.

Move the INS from the Justice Department to the Labor Department, and make an immigration applicant's skills the criterion for admission.

Institute an English-language requirement for immigrants.

Ban immigration from countries that do not permit reciprocal immigration from the United States.

Cut legal immigration from the current one million or more annually to 400,000 (the 1972 Rockefeller Commission recommendation), 350,000 (the 1981 Theodore Hesburgh Select Commission recommendation), or 300,000 (the recommendation of the Federation for American Immigration Reform), or to an annual quota set by the Labor Department in response to the perceived needs of the economy (the approach taken in Canada and Australia).

· Cut back such special categories as refugee and "asylee."

See to it that no immigrant is eligible for preferential hiring, set-aside college admission, or other forms of affirmative action aimed at historically excluded groups.

Replace the omnibus census category "Hispanic" with national-origin or racial classifications as appropriate.

Consider repealing the citizenship-by-birth rule and lengthening the time of legal residence before naturalization to five or ten years "or even to fourteen years, as it was from 1798 to 1801."

I strongly agree with Brimelow that American immigration law needs to be reformed severely and quickly. And many of his proposals make good sense. However, his call for a new version of Operation Wetback—the hated federal program that forced a million illegal Mexican immigrants to return to their homeland in the 1950s—is worse than reckless. In a 40 percent Hispanic, heavily armed city like Los Angeles, the mass expulsion of illegal Mexican immigrants could not come about without a violent disruption of civic, economic, and even religious order, and probably not without provoking a major international incident. Such an operation could be implemented only at gunpoint, and it would be resisted the same way. Its announcement would be a virtual declaration of civil war.

Since the American Revolution was a civil war, this Tom Paine redux may know only too well what he is calling for. Returning to his hero in his closing pages, he writes,

> It is simply common sense that Americans have a legitimate interest in their country's racial balance. It is common sense that they have a right to insist that their government stop shifting it. *Indeed, it seems to me that they have a right to insist that it be shifted back* [emphasis added].

In that passage the first two sentences may pass muster as common sense; the last is pernicious nonsense.

Immigration as a political issue changed the course of the last gubernatorial election in California, the nation's most populous state. In the next three most populous states—New York, Texas, and Florida—the issue is only slightly less salient. Among them, these four states virtually guarantee that the immigration debate will play a central role in the next presidential election.

President Clinton and the new Republican leadership in Congress are proposing different, rapidly evolving versions of a "National 187," imitating the California citizens' initiative that seeks to deny most government services to illegal aliens. Taking a further large step toward militant restrictionism, the American Immigration Control Foundation, whose honorary advisory board is heavy with retired military men, is distributing a questionnaire that includes the following:

America cannot control its borders because the U.S. Border Patrol has only 4,000 officers. That's not nearly enough manpower to control the flood of 3 MILLION illegals every year. Experts have proposed assigning 10,000 troops from military bases near our borders (out of a total armed services of nearly 2,000,000) to assist Border Patrol officers in stopping the invasion of illegals. *Do you favor such a proposal?*

Experts believe if Congress would assign as little as 2,000 military personnel who have been forced to retire early because of defense cuts, but who still want to serve our country, they could give tremendous assistance to our seriously undermanned Border Patrol. *If such legislation was introduced in Congress, would you favor passage of it?*

The Border Patrol itself would probably prefer to see the Armed Forces reduced slightly and its own forces enlarged. But the same huge California majorities that supported Proposition 187 would probably support the full militarization of the border if asked—particularly if the recent devaluation of the peso produces, as expected, a new flood of economic refugees from Mexico. But if such an armed force were to cross over from guarding the border to rounding up aliens for Brimelow's new Operation Wetback, I am confident that there would be armed resistance. . . .

I regret that, having thus brought the matter to a cultural point, he goes no further than he does in cultural analysis. But for all that, he makes a powerful—indeed, nearly overwhelming—case against the status quo. And if his book is at times uncomfortably personal, it is also painfully honest. Sometimes it takes a personal book to make a public debate finally and fully public. This could, just possibly, be one of those times.

Chapter 9

CARING FOR THE ENVIRONMENT

At this point in history it is difficult to find a cogent argument denying the reality of ecological problems. Differences among scientists lie how seriously they view these problems or how imminent a crisis appears to be, or what priority is given to different ecological stresses—not in whether there are ecological problems. The past decade has seen considerable movement in the scientific community and also in the public; both are persuaded that environmental hazards are real. As a matter of fact, though very few people celebrate the fact of environmental regulations, they do appear to have produced real gains in such areas as the quality of air and water. We have also become more sensitive to the environmental dimension of our actions.

Environmental problems cover a wide range of life and human activity. There are atmospheric problems that involve air pollution, the emission of chlorofluorocarbons (CFCs) that attack the protective ozone layer high above the earth, the rising earth temperature, greenhouse gases, and acid rain. There are also problems in the earth's life-support systems, including shrinking rainforests, expanding deserts, soil erosion, farm chemicals leaching into the water supply, and disappearing plant and animal life. There are problems related to the way we use energy resources; for instance, using fossil fuels builds carbon dioxide in the atmosphere, which leads to acid rain and the destruction of lakes and forests. We have become sensitive to the way that human development projects, either for housing or commercial space, put pressures on wild animal habitat, such as grizzly bears in the Grand Tetons Park, cougars in California, or timberwolves in Minnesota. And there is the population problem, with humans putting pressure on the habitat of other humankind and demands on the world's natural resources. In many ways advances in medical technology and the reduction of the death rate have exacerbated population problems.

The Earth Summit in Rio de Janeiro and other numerous ways that countries are beginning to cooperate testify to the interlocking character of these ecological problems and the necessity of global cooperation in tackling them. In order to attain the goal of a "sustainable" society—one that can satisfy its needs without diminishing the prospects for future generations—there has to be economic and political decision-making both on a worldwide scale and within each nation.

Gregg Easterbrook has written frequently about the progress that has been made in improving areas of the environment's health. The fact is that the quality of air in major U.S. cities has improved in the past decade and a half. Despite the occasional sense of "compassion fatigue" for the environment, solid gains have been made in pollution accountability, expanding forests, declining toxic emissions from automobiles, and improving water quality. Given these gains, Easterbrook asks, why is it that environmental liberals resist the glad tidings of ecological rebound? Why do they talk in the vocabulary of fashionable defeatism?[1]

Sometimes Christians fall prey to the same infatuation with the bad news about the environment. It is well to remember that ethics involves assigning both blame and credit. It is morally acceptable to praise the progress that government, private, and religious action has produced. Indeed, all Christians can rejoice in any restoring of God's creation.

In the first selection, James Martin-Schramm questions why social ethicists and environmental ethicists are not working together, despite the fact that most ecological threats present both social and environment aspects. "Toward an Ethic of EcoJustice" offers a way of inviting the two groups into discussion. Martin-Schramm articulates for us four norms that comprise the ethic of ecojustice. This reflects the consensus about norms that the World Council of Churches has been developing over its last three world assemblies. In describing each norm—sustainability, sufficiency, participation, and solidarity—the author reveals its Biblical rootage. The selection, published here for the first time, gives us a baseline for thinking about environmental issues that is ecumenically accepted, clearly Christian in its foundations, and accessible to all concerned citizens.

Thomas Sieger Derr challenges the emerging ethic of biocentrism, which is associated at one extreme with the "deep ecology" movement. He does so in defense of the traditional ethic of stewardship that maintains that God created the earth good and gave human beings stewardship over it. "We are trustees for that which does not belong to us," stewards who are accountable to their Master for their use of the earth. Derr sees a rejection of this ethic in the name of biocentrism, which finds the notion of stewardship hopelessly anthropocentric. He argues that rights cannot inhere in nature, but only in human beings. Furthermore, biocentrism confuses the interests of humankind and those of plants and animals so that it is impossible to adjudicate whose benefit should prevail. Indeed, biocentrists expand the notion of "neighbor" so far that all natural species have intrinsic value. Derr denies this in a way that confronts at least one interpretation of the norm of solidarity. The last section of "The Challenge of Biocentrism" considers what policy consequences would flow from its adoption; one claim is that many human beings must die in order to preserve certain species. Derr presents a considered, hard theological case against such environmentalists as Holmes Rolston and James Gustafson.

Certainly most ecofeminists are biocentrists; and that is the case particularly for Carol J. Adams whose piece here would drive Derr right up the wall. "Feeding on Grace: Institutional Violence, Christianity, and Vegetarianism" makes the case that eating the flesh of animals is a case of institutional violence. In a section of the essay only summarized here, Adams argues that eating animals does not respect their "inviolability." In fact, our treatment of animals before we eat them involves abuse and injury; here her description of factory farming methods is discomfiting. Disguising this institutional violence requires that we establish arrangements that deny that this is happening, and that render the animals only appropriate victims for our disposal. A logic of domination prevails; this logic of domination is the prime target for ecofeminists who understand the same dynamics of domination that have been applied to women also being applied to animals and the environment generally. Adams concludes her assessment of institutional violence against animals by identifying its detrimental effects on the society as a whole—the environment, human health, workers in the meat packing business, and consumers.

Adams's essay is additionally valuable because the warrants for her position are explicitly Christian and because she devotes considerable attention to interpretation of the verse that is the heart of the stewardship position Derr espouses (Gn. 1:26). Her argument is that the verse cannot be taken as justification of human superiority that ultimately results in exploitation or oppression, especially not if it is read in conjunction with Genesis 1:29, where God recommends a vegetarian diet. Adams concludes her argument with an appeal to a Christology of vegetarianism that challenges institutional violence.

Toward an Ethic of EcoJustice
James Martin-Schramm

It is clear that present and projected levels of human activity on Earth pose grave dangers not only to human communities and cultures but also to millions of other organisms, animals, species, and the ecological systems that support life on our planet. Unfortunately, to date, there has been comparatively little discussion between social ethicists and environmental ethicists about this nexus of issues. Taking global population growth as an example, most studies in social ethics have either focused narrowly on policy issues or they have focused generally on issues in reproductive ethics like abortion. In neither case have most studies in social ethics directly addressed ecological dimensions to population growth. The same can be said for the field of environmental ethics. Most work in this field has focused on establishing the value of other forms of life and how to preserve them. In general, the value of human life has been assumed and the perils posed by population growth have been left to the social ethicists.

This essay strives to bring these fields together and takes up both of the questions outlined above in an attempt to fashion an ethic of *ecojustice*. An ecojustice approach attempts to discern and adjudicate various responsibilities owed to the poor, to future generations, to sentient life, to organic life, to endangered species, and finally to ecosystems themselves.

For example, how are we to balance duties to the poor with duties to ecosystems and endangered species? Tropical forests and endangered species can be protected through "debt for nature" swaps, but these arrangements preclude access by the poor to land they desperately need. Similarly, if one accepts the argument that we owe reparations to species that have been substantially reduced through human actions in the past, do we also owe reparations to indigenous peoples who have been substantially reduced and impoverished by similar exploitative actions? To whom should reparations first be paid? Should reparations be paid to descendants of past generations if they serve to impoverish or endanger present generations?

Questions like these have forced Christian communities to engage in significant theological and moral reflection. In the course of this resurgent interest in the relationship of Christian theology to social and environmental ethics, many ethicists and others responsible for shaping the moral direction of Christian communities have more fully explored the concept of ecojustice. Rooted in the principles of equity and distributive justice, ecojustice is increasingly described in relationship to four specific moral norms. These norms are sustainability, sufficiency, participation, and solidarity. Grounded in the Bible and developed in Christian traditions, the World Council of Churches brought renewed attention to these norms through the themes of its last three world assemblies and related conferences.[2] Recently, the Presbyterian Church (USA) and the Evangelical Lutheran Church in America incorporated these norms into policy documents and social statements of their respective churches.[3] Both churches highlight the relation of these norms to the principles of equity and distributive justice and it is fair to say that these four norms provide the most substantial foundation to date for an ethic of ecojustice. The remainder of this essay outlines these norms and traces their biblical and theological foundations in Judeo-Christian traditions.

SUSTAINABILITY

In brief, the ecojustice norm of sustainability expresses a concern for future generations and the planet as a whole and emphasizes that an adequate and acceptable quality of life for present generations must not jeopardize the prospects for future generations. Sustainability precludes a short-sighted emphasis on economic growth that fundamentally harms ecological systems, but it also excludes long-term conservation efforts that ignore human needs and costs. Sustainability emphasizes the importance of healthy, interdependent communities for the welfare of present and future generations.

There are at least two significant biblical and theological foundations for the norm of sustainability in Jewish and Christian traditions. The doctrine of creation affirms that God as Creator sustains God's creation. Psalm 104 is a splendid hymn of praise which celebrates God's efforts at sustainability: "When you send forth your spirit . . . you renew the face of the ground" (Ps. 104:30). Similarly, Psalm 145 rejoices in the knowledge that God gives each their food in due season and "satisfies the desire of every living thing" (Ps. 145:15–16). The doctrine of creation also emphasizes the special vocation of humanity to assist God in this task of sustainability. In Genesis, the first creation account describes this responsibility of stewardship in terms of "dominion" (Gn. 1:28) and the second creation account refers to this task as God places Adam and Eve in the garden of Eden "to till it and keep it" (Gn. 2:15). In both cases, the emphasis is on humanity's stewardship of *God's* creation. The parable of the Good Steward in the Gospel of Luke exemplifies this perspective. The steward is not the owner of the house, but the steward manages or sustains the household so that all may be fed and have enough (Lk. 12:42).

The covenant theme is another important biblical and theological foundation for the norm of sustainability. The Noahic covenant celebrates God's "everlasting covenant between God and every living creature of all flesh that is on the earth" and demonstrates God's concern for biodiversity and the preservation of all species (Gn. 9:16). It is the Sinai covenant, however, which may best reveal the links between the concepts of covenant and sustainability. Whereas the prior covenants with Noah and Abraham were unilateral and conditional declarations by God, the Sinai covenant featured the reciprocal and conditional participation of humanity in the covenant. "If you obey the commandments of the Lord your God . . . then you shall live. . . ." (Dt. 30:16). Each of the Ten Commandments and all of the interpretations of these commandments in the subsequent Book of the Covenant were intended to sustain the life of the people of God in harmony with the well-being of the earth (Exodus 20–24).

At the heart of the Sinai covenant rested the twin ecojustice commitments of concern for the poor and stewardship of the earth. The "new covenant" in Christ is very much linked with this dual concern for the earth and its poor and vulnerable members. Sustainability is always linked to justice.

SUFFICIENCY

The ecojustice norm of sufficiency emphasizes that all of creation is entitled to share in the goods of creation. This means, most fundamentally, that all forms of life are entitled to those things that satisfy their basic needs and contribute to their fulfillment. As such, the norm of sufficiency represents one dimension of the distributive form of justice. The norm of sufficiency repudiates wasteful and harmful consumption, emphasizes fairness, and encourages virtues of humility, frugality, and generosity.

Biblically, this norm is emphasized in several places. As the people of God wander in the wilderness after the Exodus, Yahweh sends "enough" manna each day to sustain the community. Moses instructs the people to "gather as much of it as each of you needs" (Exodus 16).

The norm of sufficiency is also integral to the set of laws known as the jubilee legislation. These laws fostered stewardship of the land, care for animals and the poor, and a regular redistribution of wealth. In particular, the jubilee laws emphasized the needs of the poor and wild animals to eat from lands left fallow every seven years (Ex. 23:11). All creatures were entitled to a sufficient amount of food to live.

In the New Testament sufficiency is also linked to abundance. Jesus says, "I came that they might have life, and have it abundantly" (Jn. 10:10). Jesus rejects the notion that the "good life" is to be found in the abundance of possessions, however (Lk. 12:15). Instead, the "good life" is to be found in following Christ. Such a life results not in the hoarding of material wealth but rather in its sharing so that others may have enough. The book of Acts reveals that this became the model of the early Christian communities as they distributed their possessions to any "as they had need" (Acts 2:45). The apostle Paul also emphasized the relationship of abundance to sufficiency in his second letter to the Corinthians: "God is able to provide you with every blessing in abundance, so that you may always have enough" (II Cor. 9:8).

PARTICIPATION

The ecojustice norm of participation emphasizes that the interests of all forms of life are important and must be heard and respected in decisions that affect their lives. The norm is concerned with empowerment and seeks to remove all obstacles to participation constructed by various social, economic, and political forces and institutions. The norm places an importance on open debate and dialogue and seeks to hear the voices or perspectives of all concerned.

The norm of participation is grounded in several biblical and theological traditions. The two creation accounts in Genesis emphasize the value of everything in God's creation and the duty of humanity to recognize the interests of all by acting as good stewards. Through their emphasis on humanity's creation in the image of God, the stories also give unique emphasis to the value of human life and the equality of women and men (Genesis 1-2).

The prophets brought sharp condemnation upon the kings and people of Israel for violating the covenant by neglecting the interests of the poor and vulnerable. They repudiated actions which disempowered people through the loss of land, corruption, theft, slavery, and militarism. The prophets spoke out for those who had no voice and could no longer participate in the decisions that effected their lives (Am. 2:6-7; Is. 3:2-15; Hos. 10:12-14).

The ministry of Jesus not only condemned such unjust actions, it sought to change them. Throughout the gospels Jesus crosses social and physical boundaries to demonstrate his compassion for the outcast, healing their wounds and changing their lives (Lk. 17:11–19; Jn. 4:1–39). Rather than command obedience, Jesus invites others to pick up their cross and participate in the coming Reign of God (Mk. 8:34; Mt. 10:38; Lk 9:23).

 SOLIDARITY

The ecojustice norm of solidarity emphasizes the kinship and interdependence of all forms of life and encourages support and assistance for those who suffer. The norm highlights the fundamental communal nature of life in contrast to individualism and encourages individuals and groups to join together in common cause and stand with those who are the victims of discrimination, abuse, and oppression. Underscoring the reciprocal relationship of individual welfare and the common good, solidarity calls for the powerful to share the plight of the powerless, for the rich to listen to the poor, and for humanity to recognize its fundamental interdependence with the rest of nature. In so far as solidarity leads to the equitable sharing of burdens, the norm manifests the demand for distributive justice. The virtues of humility, compassion, courage, and generosity are all marks of the norm of solidarity.

Both creation accounts in Genesis emphasize the profound relationality of all of God's creation. These two creation accounts emphasize the fundamental social and ecological context of existence. Humanity was created for community. This is the foundation for the norm of solidarity. While all forms of creation are unique, they are all related to each other as part of God's creation.

Understood in this context, and in relationship to the concept of stewardship in the New Testament, the *imago dei* tradition also serves as a foundation for the norm of solidarity. Creation in the image of God places humanity not in a position over or apart from creation but rather in the same loving relationship of God with creation. Just as God breathes life into the world (Gn 2:7), humanity is given the special responsibility as God's stewards to nurture and sustain this life.

In their descriptions of Jesus' life and ministry, the gospels probably provide the clearest examples of compassionate solidarity. Throughout the gospels, Jesus shows solidarity with the poor and oppressed; he eats with sinners, drinks from the cup of a Gentile woman, meets with outcasts, heals lepers, and consistently speaks truth to power. Recognizing that Jesus was the model of solidarity, Paul utilized the metaphor of the Body of Christ to emphasize the continuation of this solidarity within the Christian community. Writing to the Christians in Corinth, Paul stresses that, by virtue of their baptisms, they are all "in Christ." Thus, "if one member suffers, all suffer together with it; if one member is honored, all rejoice together with it" (I Cor. 12:26). It would be hard to find a better metaphor to describe the character of compassionate solidarity.

FROM FOUNDATIONS TO METHOD

In addition to these reflections on the sources for a theological ethic of ecojustice, there are also some methodological commitments that are central to such an ethic. First and foremost is a commitment to the preferential option for the poor and the extension of this concept to all creatures and species whose existence is endangered and oppressed by others.

A second important methodological commitment and liberationist assumption of an ecojustice approach is a commitment to explore the linkages between patriarchy, social domination, and ecological degradation. At the heart of an ecofeminist critique rests the conviction that various injustices are the consequences of false dualisms rooted in a patriarchal mindset governed by a logic of domination.

Finally, a third methodological assumption of an ecojustice approach is that any effort to redress these injustices requires not only the cultivation of a new mindset but also the need to create structural change in the systems that perpetuate injustice. While we need new theological metaphors that will promote a new ecological sensibility, we also need to demonstrate how this new sensibility can change the structures of society. A mystical love of creation must be paired with the hard-eyed view of Christian realism that demands justice when efforts of love fail.

The Challenge of Biocentrism
Thomas Sieger Derr

At first glance I might appear to be an unlikely person to be critical of the environmental movement in any way. A sometime countryman, I usually know where the wind is and what phase of the moon we're in. I take good care of my small woodland, and I love my dogs. My personal predilections carry over into public policy, too. I champion the goals of reducing the waste stream, improving air and water quality, preserving the forests, protecting wildlife. I think of environmentalism as in some form a necessary and inevitable movement.

But by current standards that does not make me much of an environmentalist, for I am profoundly unhappy with the direction of current environmental philosophy, and most especially because I am a Christian. My trouble stems

"The Challenge of Biocentrism," by Thomas Sieger Derr from *Creation at Risk? Religion, Science, and Environmentalism,* edited by Michael Cromartie, © 1995, The Ethics and Public Policy Center. Used by permission of Wm. B. Eerdmans Publishing Co., Grand Rapids, Michigan.

partly from the determination of mainstream environmentalism to blame Christianity for whatever ecological trouble we are in. This is a piece of historical nonsense that apparently thrives on repetition. . . .

THE CHRISTIAN APPROACH TO NATURE

What is the *real* orthodox Christian attitude toward nature? It is, in a word, stewardship. We are trustees for that which does not belong to us. "The earth is the Lord's, and the fullness thereof; the world and they that dwell therein" (Ps. 24:1). The implications of this idea for environmentalism are profound and, I think, wholly positive. . . .

And in the past it has been common for even the ecological critics of Christianity to say that the Christians' problem is only that they did not take their own doctrines seriously enough.

What is new in our world today is a rejection of this semi- or pseudo-irenic view and its replacement by a root-and-branch attack on the doctrine of stewardship itself by that increasingly powerful and pervasive school of environmental thought known as biocentrism. There are many variations of biocentrism, of course, and one must be careful not to overgeneralize. But it is fair to say of nearly all varieties that they find the idea of stewardship repulsively anthropocentric, implying as it plainly does that human beings are in charge of nature, meant to manage it for purposes that they alone are able to perceive. Stewardship, says Richard Sylvan (ex-Routley), means "Man as tyrant."[4] May we think of ourselves as the earth's gardeners? Bad metaphor: gardening is controlling the earth's fecundity in a way that nature, left to its own devices, would not do. Human design is wrongly imposed.

The problem is simply compounded by Christian theism, which places human beings at the apex of nature by design of the ultimate giver of life. Made, as we say, in the image of God, we give ourselves license to claim that our interests as a species take precedence over those of the rest of creation; stewardship of the creation means mainly that we should manage it so that it sustains us indefinitely. Nature is made for us, as we are made for God. Here, say the biocentrists, is the bitter harvest of anthropocentrism: human selfishness, parochialism, chauvinism, "speciesism" (the awful term Peter Singer uses of those who reject animal rights), moral naïvete, a profanation of nature, selfimportance and pride carried to their extreme. Regarding humankind as of more inherent worth than other species is, says Paul Taylor, like regarding noblemen of more inherent worth than peasants. A claim to human superiority is "a deepseated prejudice, . . . a wholly arbitrary claim, . . . an irrational bias in our own favor."[5] Lynn White was right after all: it is simply arrogance.

RIGHTS IN NATURE

What do the biocentrists propose instead? Their most fundamental proposition is that nature itself, the life process as a whole, is the primary locus of value.

Within that process all species have value, intrinsic value, just because they *are,* because they would not *be* if they did not have an appropriate niche in the ecology of the whole. And if they have intrinsic value, we must say that they have rights of some sort, claims on us for appropriate treatment, an integrity of their own that is not available for our mere willful disposition.

INTRINSIC VALUE IN NATURE

Since the assertion that the natural world has rights we must honor begins with the claim that the natural world has intrinsic value, let us spend a moment on this prior claim. No one, to my knowledge, has worked harder or with greater care to establish this idea—that natural entities have value independent of human beings (or, for that matter, independent of God, whom he does not mention)—than Holmes Rolston. . . .[6]

Rolston does not like any account of value in natural things that depends on human psychology. He wants the value to emerge from nature directly, so that we can value the object "for what it is in itself." Value may increase with the attention of human beings, but it is present without them. Thus his theory is "biocentric."[7]

On the contrary, I argue that, with the important theistic exception noted below, we human beings *supply* the value, that nature is valuable because we find it so. There is no value without a valuer. Values are for someone or some thing. A thing can provide value to someone, and in that sense it possesses value, i.e., the capacity to provide value for someone. That is not the same as "intrinsic" value, which is value in and for the thing itself, whatever anyone makes of it. The mere fact that we value studying a particular thing does not make that thing intrinsically valuable; it makes it valuable *for us.* Someone may find it valuable for his peace of mind to finger worry beads, but that does not mean that we must accord those beads intrinsic value. Some elderly recluses have been known to save newspapers for years, valuing the accumulating mountain highly. But that does not make these old papers *intrinsically* valuable. Mosquitos or bacteria may have a goal or drive for themselves in perpetuating their life; but that is quite different from having an *intrinsic* value that other, conscious beings are required to acknowledge.

The attempt of Rolston and other biocentrists—J. Baird Callicott, for example—to distinguish between human appreciation of nature's intrinsic value, and the value that human beings add to nature by appreciating it, strikes me as hairsplitting. It is much more compelling and credible to say simply that a natural object may generate value for us not by itself but only in conjunction with our situation. We supply the value; the object contributes its being. Value is not a term appropriate to it in isolation, by itself. . . .

REINING IN RIGHTS

With all due respect to the intellectual strength and agility of the biocentric arguments, I would slice through their Gordian tangles by limiting "rights" to intrahuman affairs. "Rights" is a political and social term in the first instance, applicable only to human society, often enshrined in a fundamental document like a constitution, or embedded in the common law. As a metaphysical term, the transcultural phrase "human rights" applies to that which belongs to human beings by their very nature, i.e., not by their citizenship. Theologically, we guarantee human rights neither by our nature nor by our citizenship but by the radical equality of the love of God, the concept of "alien dignity," a grace bestowed on us that does not belong to our nature as such. In none of these forms has nature participated in rights.

Biocentrists sometimes seek to redress what to them are these deficiencies in the history of ideas by what I will call the argument from extension. "Rights," they point out, originally applied only to male citizens; but just as rights were gradually extended to women, to slaves, and finally to all other human beings, so it is a logical extension of this political liberalism to extend rights now to nonhuman creatures and even to agglomerations like ecosystems. Or, if the forum is not politics but Christian ethics, one could argue that the command to love our neighbors must now apply to non-human "neighbors," our "co-siblings of creation,"[8] or that the justice we are obliged to dispense to the poor and oppressed must now be extended to oppressed nature, or even that the enemies we are asked to love may include nature in its most hostile modes.

Although I appreciate the generous spirit of this line of argument, I think it involves a serious category mistake. Non-humans cannot have the moral status that only human beings possess, by our very natures. It is not irrelevant that the command to love our neighbors, in its original context, does in fact *not* apply to non-humans. An "extension" amounts to a substantial misreading of the text. Our obligations to the natural world cannot be expressed this way.

Another use of the idea of extension, one that occurs in Nash and in a different way in Paul Santmire,[9] is to argue that ultimate redemption is meant not only for humankind but also for the natural world, indeed the whole cosmos. That would imply much about our treatment of nature, our companion in cosmic redemption. The Incarnation confers dignity not only on us but on the whole material world: the divine takes on not only human flesh but material being in general. Certain New Testament passages are suggestive here— Romans 8:18–25, Colossians 1:15–20, Revelation 21:1—and Eastern Orthodox theology has formally incorporated this notion.

This is a theological idea of considerable gravity, and it deserves to be taken seriously. . . . The doctrine of eschatological renewal cannot tell us much about the care of nature beyond what we already know from our stewardship obligation, that we are to preserve this world as a habitat fit for humanity. The natural details of a redeemed environment are beyond our ken. Our trust in God for the Eternal Presence beyond death does not require the preservation of these rocks and rills, these woods and templed hills. Again we find ourselves behind the veil of ignorance: we simply do not know nature's divine destiny.

In short, and in sum thus far, I believe it would be more consistent, more logical, and conceptually much simpler to insist that nature has neither intrinsic value nor rights. And I believe this is true whether we are secular philosophers or Christian theologians, whether we speak with the tongues of men or of angels.

POLICY CONSEQUENCES OF BIOCENTRISM

It is time now to ask what is practically at stake in this disagreement. What are the policy consequences of the biocentrists' position, for which they seek the vocabulary of rights or other strong language? What is denied to us thereby that would be permitted from the viewpoint of Christian humanism?

Since the biocentrists will not allow us to use nature as we see fit for ourselves, but insist that it has rights or at least claims of its own against us, their general recipe is that it should be left alone wherever possible. There is of course disagreement about the details and the exceptions, but the presumption is in favor of a hands-off policy. That is the *prima facie* rule: Let nature take its course. The burden of proof is on us to show why we should be allowed to impose our wills on natural processes.

Concretely this means we should take the necessary measures to protect existing species for their own sakes, not because they might offer something to us in the form of, say, aesthetic pleasure or possible future medicinal benefits. The Endangered Species Act should be vigorously defended and enforced; and its conflicts with human desires—the spotted owl vs. the timber industry, the snail darter vs. the Tennessee dam—should be settled in favor of the species threatened. The state will have to intervene to protect the species and the land, which means limitations on a landowner's use of his own property. After all, the wild animals and plants on the land should have their freedom, too.

Especially should we preserve and expand wild lands, the necessary larger habitats needed for these species, even though human beings may desire the land for other purposes, like farming. When it comes to such conflicts, mankind ought to lose. Arne Naess, founder of the Deep Ecology school (which is a form of biocentrism tending to argue the equal worth of all natural entities), says with astonishing frankness, "If [human] vital needs come in conflict with the vital needs of nonhumans, then humans should defer to the latter."[10]

We should also leave alone those injured wild creatures that we are tempted to save—the baby bird fallen from its nest, the wounded animal we come upon in the forest, the whale trapped by the ice. Intervention in natural processes is wrong whether the motives are benevolent or not. The species is strengthened by the premature extinction of its weaker members. Respecting nature's integrity means not imposing our soft-hearted human morality upon it. We should let forest fires burn and have their way with the wild creatures.

We should not build monuments in the wild. No more Mount Rushmores, no Christ of the Andes, no railroads up Mount Washington, and probably no more wilderness roads or ski lifts.

We should suspend genetic engineering in agriculture and animal husbandry and not permit there anything we would not permit among human beings. We should not take animal lives in teaching biology or medicine, and certainly not in testing cosmetics. Zoos and botanical gardens are suspect; better that the species there displayed should live in the wild. We should not keep pets. (There go my Springers.)

What about recreational hunting or fishing? Some biocentrists frown upon it as human interference with nature and unnecessary to our diet besides; but others would permit it as simply a form of predation, which is a fact of nature and not subject to our moral scrutiny. And by this same token there would be no moral obligation for us to become vegetarians. In fact, and rather awkwardly, even plants have a "good of their own" in the biocentric theory, which leads to some mental agility to sort out their permissible uses. It is all right to eat them, of course, for that is nature's way; but "frivolous" uses (Halloween pumpkins? Christmas trees?) are questionable. One suspects that even flower gardens would be a dubious activity, which may be why the biocentric literature rarely if ever mentions them.

Although we are in principle to leave nature alone, we are obligated to restore that which we have harmed. This form of intervention is acceptable because it is guided by the principle that pristine nature, before human impact, is somehow ideal. Here again the calculus of permissibility has to be rather finely tuned. It might be wrong to plant trees in a natural desert, for example, but obligatory to plant them if human activity had contributed substantially to creating that desert. Obviously this principle can be carried to extremes. Paul Shephard has seriously suggested that we in this country all move to the coasts and restore the land between to its pre-human condition, in which we would be permitted only as hunter-gatherers, like our most primitive ancestors. Few biocentrists would go anywhere near this far, but the principle is there. The argument is about the movable boundaries. . . .

The practical problems with the theory are many and are mainly intractable. They are also mostly unnecessary. Inevitably, once rights for non-human entities are proposed, the situation becomes impossibly complex. Absent this proposition, matters become much clearer, though solutions are seldom completely evident. We are still in for a process of experiment, of trial and error, mistake and correction. We have a lot to learn, mostly from science. But with a focus on human welfare we will have a reasonably clear idea how to use our knowledge; the complexities will be simpler, the conflicts easier to resolve.

BIOCENTRIC FATALISM: MANY MUST DIE

There is one final, serious problem with biocentrism, and that is its fatalism. Biocentrists take their cues as to what *ought* to be from what *is,* and thus base their views of an acceptable future on what will happen if we let the natural world follow its own laws as far as possible. If an organism exists, the biocentrist presumes it has an important ecological niche and should be left alone. "Natural kinds are good kinds until proven otherwise."[11] If it is an ecological misfit it will perish naturally anyway, and we should not regret its demise. Death may be bad for individuals, but it is good for the system.

Should this ecological "wisdom," if that is the word, be applied to Homo sapiens? Because the whole direction of biocentric thought is to answer this question affirmatively, and because the consequences are so fearsome for most people's sensitivities, it is hard to find candid replies. When they do come out, ordinary ethical opinion, unenlightened by this new environmental realism, is apt to be appalled. Should we curtail medicine so that more of us may die "naturally" and earlier? Yes. Should we refrain from feeding the hungry, so that population will not exceed its boundaries? Yes, said the "lifeboat school," and especially its helmsman Garrett Hardin, whose bluntness is plainly an embarrassment to the current generation of biocentrists. Or consider J. Baird Callicott's rendering of William Aiken's questions as direct statements: "Massive human diebacks would be good. It is our duty to cause them. It is our species duty, relative to the whole, to eliminate 90 percent of our numbers."[12]. . .

To be sure, and to be fair, many biocentrists recoil from the social implications of their theory. It is only the biocentric egalitarians, for whom all life is of equal value, who are driven to these fearful antihuman conclusions. For the others, their schema of hierarchical differentiation allows them to claim a different level of moral behavior among human beings, different from that between human beings and the natural world, and certainly different from natural amorality. Callicott insists that "humanitarian obligations in general come before environmental duties." Rolston calls it "monstrous" not to feed starving human beings, though he would let overpopulated wild herds die. . . .

Without a secure anchor in humanism, Christian or otherwise, biocentrism risks great moral evils. At the extreme, it appears actually indifferent to human destiny. Paul Taylor says that as members of a biotic community we must be impartial toward all species, our own included: that in fact we are unnecessary to other species that would be helped by our extinction. Thomas Berry is similarly minded: "The human species has, for some thousands of years, shown itself to be a pernicious presence in the world of the living on a unique and universal scale."[13] Since species must be allowed their "evolutionary time" and then die, and because this process is "good," the human species, too, must expect to perish; and from nature's point of view, that will be normal. If nature were capable of regret, there would be no regret for our passing. The ecosystem will survive as well or better without us at the top of the food chain. But since nature is amoral, we must say that our extinction is of no moral significance in nature.

Would God care? The whole direction of our faith says that God would indeed care, which suggests strongly that we should oppose biocentrism and not anticipate the demise of our species with equanimity. I admit that this is a conviction of faith. What God really is about I would not dare to say I knew.

Whether such modesty is becoming or not, it eludes the biocentrists, who seem to know more than I do about the ultimate principles that rule the universe. Here, for example, is Carol Christ:

We are no more valuable to the life of the universe than a field [of flowers]. . . .
The divinity that shapes our ends is an impersonal process of life, death, and

transformation. . . . The life force does not care more about human creativity and choice than it cares about the ability . . . of moss to form on the side of a tree. The human species, like other species, might in time become extinct, dying so that other lives might live.[14]

Rolston is only moderately more hopeful: the evolutionary system is "not just a random walk" but "some kind of steady, if statistical heading.". . . Rolston is quite fatalistic about our destiny: recognizing that there is nothing necessary or inevitable about our appearance on earth, we will simply have to accept the overall course of evolution as good, no matter where it eventually goes.[15]

James Gustafson, a justly celebrated ethicist, has written similarly that we should not count on humanity's being at the apex of creation nor consider that human good trumps the good of non-human nature. Our disappearance would not be bad "from a theocentric perspective," which acknowledges that "the source and power and order of all of nature is not always beneficent in its outcomes for the diversity of life and for the well-being of humans as part of that." "The Divine . . . [is] the ultimate source of all human good, but does not guarantee it." Such ruminations have led Nash to characterize Gustafson's "God" as "a nonconscious and nonmoral ordering power without intention, volition, or cognition. . . . This power sustains the universe, apparently unintentionally, but lacks the purposive, benevolent, or redemptive qualities to seek the good of individuals, the human species, otherkind, or the whole cosmos. . . . This perspective seems close to atheism or pantheism."[16]

The ecological ethic emerging from biocentric fatalism, such as it is, is simply to enjoy the earth's fecundity, to laugh and weep and celebrate all life, whether it is our life or not. "Humanity's highest possibility is to bear witness to and participate in the great process of life itself."[17] And so the biocentrist love affair with a mysterious Natural Process cultivates, inevitably, indifference to the human prospect.

It is, of course, a bit odd for biocentrists to view humanity as just another species serving out its evolutionary time, when with the same voice they must also acknowledge that we are a very special species, endowed with enormous power over the environment. We cannot renounce this power, either. It is ours to use for good or ill, and so they urge us to use it in a self-limiting way to preserve the rest of the environment and to care for the other creatures of the earth. Notice that the message is anthropocentric in spite of itself: our great power engenders our great responsibility. But that, of course, is precisely the Christian ethic of dominion and stewardship.

I do not know where the human story will end. But, as I think William Faulkner, that great literary icon of my college generation, said in accepting the Nobel Prize, "I decline to accept the end of man." I think that my efforts ought to be bent to perpetuating human life, and that goal ought to be the overriding test of our ecological conduct. In arguing otherwise, large sections of the environmental movement are on the wrong track. In the name of its own humanistic faith, Christianity ought to criticize these environmentalists, rather than scramble to say, "Me, too." What is historic and traditional in our valuation of Creation is a perfectly sufficient guide to sound ecology.

Feeding on Grace: Institutional Violence, Christianity, and Vegetarianism
Carol J. Adams

Better a dish of vegetables if love go with it than a fat ox eaten in hatred. Proverbs 15:17 (NEB)

INTRODUCTION

The day after I arrived home from my first year at Yale Divinity School, an urgent knocking summoned me from my task of unpacking. It was a distressed neighbor reporting that someone had just shot one of our horses. We ran through the pasture to discover that indeed, one of my horses was lying dead, a small amount of blood trickling from his mouth. Shots from the nearby woods could still be heard. One horse lay dead and the other frantically pranced around him.

That night, upset and depressed, I sat down to a dinner of hamburger. Suddenly I flashed on the image of Jimmy's dead body in the upper pasture, awaiting a formal burial by backhoe in the morning. One dead body had a name, a past that included my sense of his subjectivity, and was soon to be respectfully buried. The other dead body was invisible, objectified, nameless, except in its current state as hamburger, and was to be buried in my stomach. At the time I realized the hypocrisy of my action. The question confronting me was: "If Jimmy were meat would I, could I, be his meat eater?" And the answer was "of course not." Having recognized his individuality, his subjectivity, having been in relationship with him, I could not render him beingless. So why could I do this to another animal, who, if I had known her, would surely have revealed her individuality and subjectivity? The invisible became visible: I became aware of how I objectified others and what it means to make animals into meat. I also recognized my ability to change myself: Realizing what meat actually is, I also realized I need not be a meat eater.

This experience in 1973 catalyzed the process by which I became a vegetarian slightly more than a year later. It also catalyzed a theoretical and theological search to understand why our society invests so many economic, environmental, and cultural resources into protecting the eating of animals. It is my

From Carol J. Adams, "Feeding on Grace: Institutional Violence, Christianity, and Vegetarianism," from C. Pinches and J. McDaniel, eds., *Good News for Animals?*, Orbis, 1993, pp. 142–159.

position that the eating of animals is a form of institutional violence. The corporate ritual that characterizes institutional violence deflects or redefines the fact that the eating of animals is exploitative. This is why conscientious and ethical individuals do not see meat as a problem. . . . We require an analysis of institutional violence to identify just why it is that Christians ought to reconceptualize meat eating. This essay offers such an analysis and reconceptualization.

THE INSTITUTIONAL VIOLENCE OF EATING ANIMALS

Through an understanding of institutional violence we will come to see the dynamics of exploitation vis-à-vis the other animals, and begin to recognize their suffering as morally relevant in determining our own actions.

For something to be *institutional* violence it must be a significant, widespread, unethical practice in a society. As an industry, meat production is the second largest in this country. It is both widespread and vitally important to our economy. Though meat eating is now the normative expression of our relationship with other animals, a close examination of the functioning of institutional violence will reveal why I call it unethical.

Institutional violence is characterized by:

1. An infringement on or failure to acknowledge another's inviolability
2. Treatment of physical force that injures or abuses
3. A series of denial mechanisms which deflect attention from the violence
4. The targeting of "appropriate" victims
5. Detrimental effects on society as a whole
6. The manipulation of the public (e.g., consumers) into passivity

Meat eating fits this definition of institutional violence. In fact, the word *"meat"* itself illustrates several of these components. It renders animals appropriate victims by naming them as edible and deflects our attention from the violence inherent to killing them for food. Because the word "meat" contributes to minimizing the implications of institutional violence, it will be enclosed in quotation marks in this essay. At times the more accurate term "flesh" will be used.

Institutional violence toward animals at its core denies their inviolability. Its function is to uphold and act upon the violability of animals. It works at the individual level by wrenching any notion of inviolability from one's sense of Christian ethics. Even if many children object to eating animals upon learning where "meat" comes from, this objection is rarely respected. And even if adults are discomforted by some form of flesh—whether it be because of the animal it is stolen from, a dog, a horse, a rat, or the part of the animal being consumed, the brain, the liver—they have no Christian ethical framework into which these objections might be placed. The absence of such a framework means that any reminders that animals have to be killed to be consumed, experienced by children explicitly and by adults implicitly, remain unassimilated and repressed. Institutional violence interposes an ethics of exploitation for any burgeoning ethic of inviolability.

We become firmly and persuasively convinced that the eating of animals is not only acceptable but necessary for survival. This deviates from the representation of our corporate beginning in Genesis as vegetarians, when God/ess says in Genesis 1:29: "Behold, I have given you every plant yielding seed which is upon the face of all the earth, and every tree with seed in its fruit; you shall have them for food."[18] This corporate and personal beginning as vegetarians seems to be confirmed by anthropological sources that indicate that our earliest hominid ancestors had vegetarian bodies. In the records of their bones, dental impressions, and tools, these anonymous ancestors reveal the fact that "meat," as a substantial part of the diet, became a fixture in human life only recently—in the past 40,000 years. Indeed, it was not until the past two hundred years that most people in the Western world had the opportunity to consume "meat" daily.

Our bodies appear better suited to digesting seeds and fruits than muscle and blood, suggesting again our personal origins as vegetarians. From this perspective, ingesting flesh is an act against our own body as well as against another animal's body, a double violation.

We have fallen from this state of grace with the other animals represented in Genesis 1:29 and substituted institutional violence for respect for their inviolability. . . .

CHRISTIANITY AND THE INSTITUTIONALIZED VIOLENCE OF EATING ANIMALS

I have demonstrated the nature of institutional violence and how it is that "meat" eating is a form of institutional violence. With this framework established, we can now turn to the Christian dimension to the institutional violence of eating animals.

One reason that many Christians do not see animals as inviolable is because they believe that only humans are in the image of God, and thus only humans are inviolable. Animals become the appropriate victims because they are not in God's image, but instead consumable entities: lambs of God, sacrificial lambs, fatted calves. The same passage that establishes the relationship of humans to God's image appears to bestow legitimacy on the exploitation of the other animals. Genesis 1:26 reads: Then God said, "Let us make man in our image, after our likeness; and let them have dominion over the fish of the sea, and over the birds of the air, and over the cattle, and over all the earth, and over every creeping thing that creeps upon the earth."

Genesis 1:26 is seen to be God's permission to dominate the other animals and make them instruments for human's interests, thus de facto allowing "meat" eating. By interpreting "dominion" to mean God gave us permission to exploit animals for our tastes, several denial mechanisms are enacted. We are deflected from concern about animals by believing that we are absolved from the action that has cast animals as "meat." The comforting nature of this belief derives from the fact that the onus of the decision to eat animals is shifted from individual responsibility to divine intent. (Someone, but not me, is responsible for these animals' deaths. If I am not responsible, I do not need to examine what I am doing and its consequences.) In this viewpoint, God as the author of and authority over our lives has created us as "meat" eaters. In one act of authorization two ontological situations are created simultaneously: "meat" eater and "meat." As Bowie, the commentator in *The Interpreter's Bible,* remarks on this passage: "Fish and fowl and animals have been his [*sic*] food."

This interpretation of Genesis 1:26 requires associating dominion with exploitation. Some believe that the clue to this association is found in the choice of words in this passage. Von Rad opines that "[t]he expressions for the exercise of this dominion are remarkably strong: *rada,* 'tread,' 'trample' (e.g., the wine press); similarly *kabas,* 'stamp'."[19] But others see a less harsh meaning to the concept of dominion. Barr suggests that *rada* was generally used about kings ruling over certain areas. "For instance in 1 Kings 5:4 the verb is used to express Solomon's dominion (expressly a peaceful dominion) over a wide area." He believes that *kabas,* "subdue," refers not to animals but to the tilling of the earth.[20] C. Westermann has suggested that the use of *rada,* "have dominion, govern," "can be compared with what is said in 1:16 about the sun and moon, which are to 'govern' the day and night."[21] According to this viewpoint, dominion carries no idea of exploitation, indeed, "man [*sic*] would lose his 'royal [*sic*]' position in the realm of living things if the animals were to him [*sic*] an object of use or of prey."[22]

When dominion is equated with exploitation, people are conferring their own preconceptions concerning their relationship with animals upon the Bible, for an exploitative interpretation of Genesis 1:26 cannot be reconciled with the vegetarian passage quoted above found in Genesis 1:29. *The Interpreter's Bible* notes the difficulty of reconciling these two passages when it exegetes Genesis 1:29: "Man [*sic*] is thus to be a vegetarian. This is something of a contradiction to verse 26, according to which he was to *have dominion over* all living creatures."[23] For others:

> the human "dominion" envisaged by Genesis 1 included no idea of using the animals for meat and no terrifying consequences for the animal world. Human exploitation of animal life is not regarded as an inevitable part of human existence, as something given and indeed encouraged by the ideal conditions of the original creation.[24]

Genesis 1:26 does not supersede the meaning of creation that extends to include Genesis 1:29. When severed from the meaning of creation and the direction to be vegetarian, the scriptures are used as a historically justificatory defense of actions. This a denial mechanism at the theological level.

These defenses continue when considering God's explicit permission to consume animals in Genesis 9:3, "Every moving thing that lives shall be food for you; and as I gave you the green plants, I give you everything." On a certain view of Genesis, one must argue that "meat" eating is a consequence of the fall. The end of vegetarianism is "a necessary evil,"[25] and the introduction of flesh eating has a "negative connotation."[26] In his discussion of the Jewish dietary laws, Samuel H. Dresner argues that "the eating of meat [permitted in Genesis 9] is itself a sort of compromise,"[27] "a *divine concession to human weakness and human need.*"[28] Adam, the perfect man, "is clearly meant to be a vegetarian."[29] In pondering the fact that Isaiah's vision of the future perfect society postulates vegetarianism as well, Dresner observes:

> At the "beginning" and at the "end" man [*sic*] is, thus, in his ideal state, herbivorous. His [*sic*] life is not maintained at the expense of the life of the beast. In "history" which takes place here and now, and in which man [*sic*], with all his [*sic*] frailties and relativities, lives and works out his [*sic*] destiny, he [*sic*] may be carnivorous.[30]

What is interposed between Genesis 1:29 and Isaiah is human history. In this sense, history is the concrete, social context in which we move. Moreover, history becomes our destiny.

We come to believe that because an action of the past was condoned by the ethical norms of the time, it may continue unchanged and unchallenged into our present time, history becomes another authority manipulating and extending our passivity. It allows us to objectify the praxis of vegetarianism: it is an ideal, but not realizable. It is out of time, not in time. When Genesis 9 is used to interpret backward to Genesis 1 and forward to our own practice of "meat" eating, history is read into creation, and praxis is superseded by an excused fallibility. History will then immobilize the call to praxis—to stop the suffering, end institutional violence, and side with the oppressed animals. If vegetarianism is out of time, in the Garden of Eden, then we need not concern ourselves with it.

Objectifying the praxis of vegetarianism makes it ahistorical, outside of history and without *a* history. This may explain why vegetarianism throughout the ages has been called a fad despite its recurrence. "Meat" eating has not constituted a large part of the diets of humankind and, I believe, each individual at some point experiences some discomfort with the eating of animals. In the light of what I have called "the sexual politics of meat"—i.e., women, second-class citizens, are more likely to eat what are considered to be second-class foods in a patriarchal culture, vegetables, fruits, and grains rather than "meat"—the question becomes who exactly has been eating the "meat" after Genesis 9? Consider, for instance, this terse comment on Leviticus 6 by Elizabeth Cady Stanton, a leading nineteenth-century feminist: "The meat so delicately cooked by the priests, with wood and coals in the altar, in clean linen, no woman was permitted to taste, only the males among the children of Aaron."[31]

Perhaps we should ask of Genesis 9 and the notion that we are unable to avoid eating flesh: Is this true for us now? In light of the health, environmental, and ethical consequences of eating animals, do we cling to such an authorization that some find in Genesis 9? Do we continue to believe that our relationship with God/ess endorses a clearly exploitative relationship with the other animals? Do we affirm God/ess and creation by denying relationship with terminal animals? And what then do we do about this? Isn't, rather, reconstructing these relationships the most authentic and ethical response available to us?

RESISTING INSTITUTIONALIZED VIOLENCE

We are estranged from animals through institutionalized violence and have accepted inauthenticity in the name of divine authority. We have also been estranged from ways to think about our estrangement. Religious concepts of alienation, brokenness, separation ought to include our treatment of animals. Eating animals is an existential expression of our estrangement and alienation from the created order.

Elisabeth Shüssler Fiorenza reminds us that "The basic insight of all liberation theologies, including feminist theology, is the recognition that all theology, willingly or not, is by definition always engaged for or against the oppressed."[32] To side with history and posit vegetarianism as unattainable is to side against the oppressed animals; to side with the praxis of vegetarianism is to side with the oppressed and against institutional violence. Insofar as Christians are called to live in the reign of God initiated by Jesus, they cannot legitimately take the "practical" fallen history of Genesis 9 as authority.

It is here, in the conflict between history and eschatology, that I would place a Christology of vegetarianism. This Christology is not concerned with whether Jesus was or was not a vegetarian just as feminist theology rejects the relevance of the maleness of the twelve disciples. This is not a quest for historical duplication but for the acquisition of an ability to discern justice-making according to the Christological revelation. With this perspective we should come to see that a piece of "meat" turns the miracles of the loaves and fishes on its head. Where Jesus multiplied food to feed the hungry, our current food-producing system reduces food sources and damages the environment at the same time, producing plant food to feed terminal animals.

A Christology of vegetarianism would argue that just as Jesus challenged historical definitions such as Samaritan, or undercut identities such as the wealthy man, so we are equipped to challenge the historical and individual identity of a food habit that fosters environmental and ethical injustice. We are not bound by our histories. We have been freed to claim an identity based on current understanding of animal consciousness, ecological spoilage, and health issues. A Christology of vegetarianism would affirm that no more crucifixions are necessary, and insist that animals, who are still being crucified, must be freed from the cross. The suffering of animals, our sacrificial lambs, does not bring about our redemption but furthers our suffering, suffering from preventable diseases related to eating animals, suffering from environmental problems, suffering from the inauthenticity that institutionalized violence promotes. In the following quotation feminist ethicist Beverly Harrison contributes important insights into this process of Christians resisting institutional violence, which can be readily connected to the eating of animals. (I add these connections in brackets.)

> Each of us must learn to extend a critical analysis of the contradictions affecting our lives in an ever-widening circle, until it inclusively incorporates those whose situations differ from our own [such as animals]. This involves naming

structures that create the social privilege we possess [to eat animals and make them appropriate victims] as well as understanding how we have been victims [manipulated into passivity so that we believe that we need to eat dead animals]. . . . Critical consciousness and, therefore, genuine social and spiritual transcendence, do not and cannot emerge apart from our refusing complicity in destructive social forces and resisting those structures that perpetuate life-denying conditions [including eating animals].[33]

Perhaps our greatest challenge is to raise the consciousness of those around us to see the institutional violence of eating animals as an ethical issue. But how does something become an ethical issue? Sarah Bentley has described the process by which wife beating has become an ethical concern.[34] She does so by drawing on Gerald Fourez's *Liberation Ethics* which demonstrates that "'concrete historical struggles'" are the basis for the development of "the discipline called 'ethics'." For something to become an ethical issue we need "'a new awareness of some oppression or conflict'." This is critical consciousness.

I would suggest that an example of this critical consciousness is the animal liberation movement and its identification of the eating of animals as inhumane and exploitative. As Bentley explains, after a time of agitation by a group living with the critical consciousness of this oppression, others besides the group with the critical consciousness begin to question the oppression as well. The social consciousness of a community or a culture is transformed by this agitation. "Ethical themes, therefore, are *historically specific,* arising from 'the particular questions that certain groups are asking themselves'."

Christians responding to the insights of the animal liberation movement must ask questions about the institutional violence that permits them the personal satisfaction of eating flesh. "In effect, the [particular] questions represent 'problems *raised by practices* that have to be faced'." Farming and slaughtering practices such as caging, debeaking, liquid diets for calves, twenty-four-hour starvation before death, transporting and killing animals are all troublesome practices. We must stop denying them. But of course, denial is necessary when concrete practices are challenged. Indeed, ethical statements "always evolve 'as particular ways of questioning in which people, individually or in groups, *stake their lives* as they decide what they want to do and what their solidarity is.'" Thus, *if no one questions,* if no *practical engagement* takes place, no problem exists."

This can be linked with the success of false naming and other denial mechanisms we have mentioned. They cannot be overcome at a merely theoretical level. Unless we acquaint ourselves with the *practice* of farming and slaughtering animals, we will not encounter the *problems* raised by these practices, such as the abuse of animals, the environment, our health, and workers in the "meat" industry. If the problem is invisible, in a sense mirroring the physical invisibility of intensively farmed animals, then there will be ethical invisibility.

A Christian ethics adequate to challenging the institutional violence of eating animals and modeled on this understanding of the evolution of an ethical stance involves three connected parts: certain practices raise problems; practical engagement and solidarity ensues when these problematic practices are perceived; an ethical position arises from this ongoing solidarity that forges critical community consciousness. As we become personally aware of the contradictions between Christianity and the practice of eating animals, we find that we must enter into a struggle regarding our own and this culture's practice.

To overcome our failure to acknowledge another's inviolability we need to find alternative ways of relating to animals rather than eating them. Beverly Harrison proposes that "We know and value the world, *if* we know and value it, through our ability to touch, to hear, to see."[35] We have not known and valued the domestic animals that are eaten because we have not touched, heard, or seen them. To most of us, animals are disembodied entities. Disembodied animals have little potential of being touched, heard, or seen, except as "meat."

Demonstrating Harrison's sensual understanding of how we know the world, Alice Walker describes what happens when she touches, hears, and sees an animal. With Blue the horse she sees the depth of feeling in his eyes and recalls something she feels adults fail to remember: "human animals and non-human animals can communicate quite well."[36] Shortly after having that insight, Walker experiences the injustice of a steak: "I am eating misery" she thinks. Walker touches, hears, sees, and describes interactions with very specific animals, and she is changed by this, called to authenticity.

We all have an option to dispense with the consumption of misery: We can feed instead on the grace of vegetables. Virginia de Araujó describes such a perspective, that of a friend, who takes the barrenness of a cupboard, filled only with "celery threads, chard stems, avocado skins" and creates a feast

& says, On this grace I feed, I wilt
in spirit if I eat flesh, let the hogs,
the rabbits live, the cows browse,
the eggs hatch out chicks & peck seeds.

The choice is institutionalized violence or feeding on grace. One cannot feed on grace and eat animals. Our goal of living in right relationships and ending injustice is to have grace *in* our meals as well as *at* our meals. Socially responsible persons, justice-oriented persons, must recognize that we are violating others in eating animals, and in the process wilting the spirit. There are no appropriate victims. Let the hogs, rabbits, cows, chicks live. In place of misery, let there be grace.

Chapter 10

Violence and War in a Post-Communist World

Those who lived through the Vietnam War and the cold war/nuclear confrontation with the Soviet Union may have thought the demise of the USSR in 1989 marked an end to war. However, a scant two years later, the U.S. and its UN allies were involved in the Persian Gulf War. Since then, U.S. ground troops have been deployed to Somalia, to Bosnia, and to Haiti. There has been a devastating tribal war between Huti and Tutu in Rwanda which spilled over into Zaire (now Congo). There have been numerous conflicts around the globe. Clearly there has been no end to war.

It may be that the nature of war has changed somewhat. While the world seems to have stepped back from the spectre of a worldwide nuclear conflagation—which cannot yet be ruled out, the sort of wars that have erupted in the past few years appear to be civil, intra-national conflicts that threaten to expand. War is of course a form of violence and it seems inconceivable that violence could be efficiently outlawed. Violence is too close to the marrow of who we human beings are. Thus, perhaps the hope that there would be no more wars was just an expression of transient optimism.

When one considers the tragic nature of war, with its wanton destruction of human life and property, it may be surprising that Christians have not been able to agree on their moral evaluation of war. Almost everyone would agree that war is always evil, but many Christians do not agree on whether participation in war is ever necessary and justifiable. The earliest Christian community may have had the highest degree of unanimity when they were a persecuted minority in the Roman Empire. *Pacifism* was the norm. Many Christians refused to serve in military forces, claiming to follow the Prince of Peace instead. However, even in that time there is evidence that Christians served in the Roman army.

With the Constantinian establishment of 312, the Christian faith became recognized as the legitimate official religion of the empire and Christians took a more open stance on the possibility of engaging in war. As

Augustine contemplated the ravaging of Roman civilization by the barbarians in the fifth century, it led him to articulate certain conditions under which war could be justified—the so-called *just war theory*. These conditions, with their subsequent development, are the following:

1. The cause for entering into war must be just.
2. The war must be declared and waged by a lawful authority.
3. War must be the only possible means of securing justice.
4. The right means must be employed in the conduct of war (no wanton disregard for life; respect for noncombatants).
5. There must be a reasonable hope of victory.
6. The good probably to be achieved by victory must outweigh the possible evil effects of the war (the norm of proportionality).
7. War must be a last resort, entered into only after all peaceful means have been exhausted.

Most Christian churches have espoused a just war position, arguing that the presence of evil in the world at times necessitates the use of force in order to protect the innocent and to ensure a just and humane order. One obvious question is whether criteria for a justifiable war have any relevance for the modern age. Nations no longer fight only on weekends or with the use of limited weapons as they did in the Middle Ages. Nuclear know-how has not yet been scrapped. However, the just war criteria appear more useful today than they did at the height of the nuclear buildup. Advocates argue that just war criteria assume at least a symbolic value in attempts to keep human concerns at the forefront in our consideration of war.

The third position that Christians have adopted is that war can be a *crusade*, in which the faithful aggressively carry out the will of God. The Crusades of the Middle Ages are the primary example of this view, inspired by Old Testament stories of God's people using the sword against nonbelievers. This position has often, if only momentarily, been expressed by those who believe that "God is on our side," as it was during World War II and occasionally during the Vietnam War or the war against the "evil empire."

The new realities of the collapse of the Communist threat in Eastern Europe have caused us to turn our attention from defense and protection to peacekeeping and police actions around the world. Can the United States be the police officer in this new world order? Should it?

The de-escalation of the immediacy of the threat of war has enabled us to turn our attention to the related question of violence. Can violence ever be justified? Our society has become well aware of the extent of violence in the home and in our institutions. To what extent is violence written into our national character? Though we do not take up the issue here, the question of gun control is very much related. Should we regulate the possession of handguns and rifles? There is considerable heat on both sides. Meanwhile we are considered by many the most violent nation on earth.

In some ways the article by Jack Nelson-Pallmeyer joins the issues of wars of intervention and violence. Nelson-Pallmeyer suggests that many Christians are asking whether nonviolent means of conflict resolution and pacifism render us impotent and irrelevant in the wake of the interventions in Bosnia and Somalia. "Some Christians reject recourse to violence under all circumstances while others see 'ethnic cleansing' in Bosnia as analogous to Hitler's death camps and/or the mass starvation in Somalia as unacceptable and avoidable through the prudent use of force." In short, there is at present a real challenge to Christian pacifism and nonviolent conflict resolution. The article proceeds to offer ten observations about the use of force, which remind us of just war criteria used in the service of a basically pacifist position. Nelson-Pallmeyer warns against letting frustration push us to the use of military force prematurely (before force is the last resort). We are reminded that each conflict has a history and is bred by the policy failures that preceded it. It should come as no surprise that our use of force is often in the interests of major U.S. corporations—such as the four oil companies which had a stake in the pacification of Somalia. Nelson-Pallmeyer points to the failure of international organizations, namely their weakness in confronting threats, to suggest that we need stronger organizations capable of promoting conflict avoidance and resolution. They must be free of domination by Western powers, he writes. Finally, the Christian response needs to be generated from within our Christian values. Though he comes out embracing nonviolent means of conflict resolution and judging it incompatible for Christians to serve in the military or kill, Nelson-Pallmeyer says that we Christians cannot sit by and act as though we have no complicity in such areas as Bosnia. Christians cannot rule out humanitarian intervention; we need, instead, to actively promote international organizations capable of nonviolent conflict resolution.

By way of contrast, John Langan, S.J., clearly represents the just war tradition as he assesses the current political, military, and moral climate of international intervention. Langan denies that we are speaking of "wars" in the instance of interventions though he claims that we should observe just war criteria for the use of force. Clearly Langan thinks that neither the U.S. citizenry nor the world at large is willing to accept the American government intervening for humanitarian purposes in every place where it could be justified. Instead, we should intervene only wherever there is need and possibility of rescue. Our priorities should include only those regions where the U.S. has a special interest (the Caribbean or Latin America) or a special responsibility to one or more of the parties in the dispute (Israel). As Langan discusses the way intervention should be carried out, his appeals to just war criteria clearly have informing power.

A brief response to the Langan piece by Kale Williams raises the question of how to mount a nonviolent strategy that might obviate the need for military intervention. Rather than military intervention, Williams suggests trying two related avenues: the social organization of nonviolent resistance such as that employed by Martin Luther King and Gandhi, and the extension of democratic values and principles. Williams wonders whether our own schools and civic associations are doing enough to produce citizens who will lobby their politicians to build creative ways of engaging the rest of the world.

The last essay in this section raises disturbing questions about whether violence is embedded in Christianity. Mary Ann Rossi documents the ways women have been perceived as less than human in the misogynistic assumptions of such thinkers as Aristotle, Plato, Augustine, and Aquinas. Through this or other dualistic conceptions of women, Christianity has legitimated if not promoted the violent abuse of women. It is the source of other injustices to women as well. The acceptance of wife abuse as a private matter, as not open to public debate, and as not often acknowledged from the pulpit—do these suggest that there are not fully examined roots of violence against women in Christian theology? If so, they give us pause as to what other sorts of violence Christian thought has promoted. This is related to the issue of whether we are deceiving ourselves with the assistance of just war or pacifist categories. Fortunately, we have the consolation that Christianity is self-critical enough to deal with these issues.

A final development that must be mentioned is the rise of urban gangs, senseless crime, and also the rise of often-rural hate groups who target the federal government or racial and ethnic minorities. The conglomerate of incidents like Waco, Ruby Ridge, Oklahoma City, and the Freemen of Jordan, Montana, reveal an intermixture of violence that seems merely the expressive tip of the volcano. How should the church respond to the frustrations and injustices which lead to violent striking out and equally violent reaction?

Wise as Serpents, Gentle as Doves? The Challenge to Nonviolence in the Face of Pleas for Intervention
Jack Nelson-Pallmeyer

The promised new world order is predictably a disaster. Nonetheless, the very magnitude of the disaster, graphically symbolized by Bosnia and Somalia, has many Christians asking whether nonviolent means of conflict resolution and pacifism render us impotent and irrelevant.

Reprinted with permission from *Sojourners*, 2401 15th St. NW, Washington, DC 20009; (202) 328-8842; (800) 714-7474.

The loose coalition that resisted U.S. interventionism is fracturing. The political landscape is hard to read as progressives such as Minnesota's Paul Wellstone advocate some form of military response to deter Serbian aggression and Jesse Jackson endorses the U.S. intervention into Somalia.

Divisions are common within the peace community. A secular peace organization in Minnesota invited a Yugoslavian expert and protester to brief its members on Bosnia and then withdrew the invitation when they learned the former pacifist favored bombing Serbian weapons arsenals.

It is also a time of deep soul-searching for Christian communities, including my own, for whom nonviolence is a defining feature. Some people reject recourse to violence under all circumstances while others see "ethnic cleansing" in Bosnia as analogous to Hitler's death camps and/or the mass starvation in Somalia as unacceptable and avoidable through the prudent use of force.

Debates about the legitimacy or illegitimacy of military or humanitarian interventions are emotionally charged because they challenge both our political wisdom and the spiritual foundation of many of our communities. As we struggle to find our way, I would urge that we neither expect nor seek consensus as to what constitutes a faithful response to crises such as Bosnia and Somalia. I hope we can share our views and the process and outcome of our discernment passionately but with humility.

Jesus' community challenged a destructive "holiness code" which in first-century Palestine allowed powerful groups to define themselves as faithful over against others whom they considered less worthy or sinful. The definers and enforcers of the "holiness code" were separatist, elitist, and self-righteous. Each of these sins is present in the past and present conduct of Christian peacemakers. It would be ironic if as we struggle to respond faithfully to crises, many of which are rooted in a politics of separation and religious intolerance, we should ourselves be guilty of similar intolerance.

What follows are 10 observations that I hope can help us assess present challenges to Christian pacifism and nonviolent conflict resolution.

First, legitimizing the use of military force to resolve international crises is dangerous. In the midst of problems that seem to defy solutions, there is a great temptation to believe in the utility of violence. In frustration, many people tend to see violence as a "last resort" without asking how many approaches have yet to be tried—and without recognizing a long historical record in which military "solutions" have failed to resolve fundamental conflicts that surface later with greater and more deadly force.

Militarization of our minds, economies, and approaches to conflict resolution threatens our world with destruction. By way of example, respected environmental groups estimate that we have approximately 40 years to make a difficult transition to sustainable societies. This transition depends on a solar-based energy future, alternatives to the consumer culture, overcoming poverty, and dramatic shifts away from military spending, military definitions of security, and military responses to international conflict.

Second, there is a history to and/or evolution of each crisis. The escalation of a crisis is preceded by a failure or lost opportunity to intervene nonviolently in ways that could diffuse a conflict. Each failure marks a turning point at which violence escalates and nonviolent resolution of a conflict becomes more costly, less likely, and perhaps impossible.

For example, Dietrich Bonhoeffer, a pacifist, concluded that opportunities for a nonviolent resolution of the conflict in Nazi Germany had passed. This was, among other things, a confessional issue for the churches. Lost opportunities placed Bonhoeffer in a situation with no good choices. At this point he prayed for the defeat of his country and joined the plot to murder Hitler.

Third, the pervasive violence and destruction in Iraq, Haiti, former Yugoslavia, Somalia, our nation's cities, and other major areas of conflict generally confirm rather than discredit the worldview, perspectives, and programs of Christian pacifists and others committed to nonviolent conflict resolution. Today's crises were born out of yesterday's policy failures. We should not allow those most responsible for present crises to tell us self-servingly that nonviolence doesn't work. A great deal of violence could have been avoided if the principles and programs of nonviolent peacemakers had been followed throughout the Cold War period.

Fourth, these principles and programs should remain central to the peace community's emerging agenda. They include: refusing to arm dictators; curbing weapons sales; forsaking destabilizing covert operations and deadly interventions; drastically cutting military expenditures; strengthening international institutions; obeying international law; and pursuing greater economic justice. These remain central pillars of a more peaceful world.

Fifth, serious challenges to our pacifism or nonviolent means of conflict resolution arise from many sources, including present events in Bosnia, Somalia, and Iraq. However, much of our soul-searching is in relation to misconduct by the United States, both historically and in terms of present U.S. goals and objectives. I do not mean to downplay the horrible conduct of Saddam Hussein or Slobodan Milosevic. I do mean to counter the serious effort under way to project U.S. military power as an essential vehicle for human rights and justice within the "new world order." Such a view is naive, dangerous, and ahistorical.

It is the United States that leads the world in weapons sales. Our nation has squandered and continues to squander vital human, economic, and technological resources on excessive military expenditures. Nonviolence and pacifism are viewed with suspicion by many oppressed peoples because of their experience of abusive U.S. military and economic power. Those who attribute moral purpose to U.S. military actions should remember Hiroshima and Nagasaki, the contras, murdered priests and religious workers, dictatorships supported, and democracies undermined.

In this context Somalia needs to be understood as a tragedy of the Cold War, including U.S. support for a repressive dictatorship. The United States acknowledges no need for repentance, and once again U.S. troops have been ordered into action through presidential decree.

Sixth, the U.S. "humanitarian intervention" into Somalia served many non-humanitarian purposes. These include, among others: defense of U.S. military interests, reinforcement of unilateral initiatives, and promotion of U.S. economic interests.

The U.S. military in the post-Cold War period, as documented in *Brave New World Order,* is fearful of budget cuts and eager for enemies. The Pentagon, for example, named Iraq a potential budget-enriching foe months before Iraq's invasion of Kuwait. It is instructive that within the Pentagon, Desert Shield was referred to as "budget shield." *The National Catholic Reporter* noted recently (12-18-92) that the "U.S. military [is] gung ho for humanitarian missions," including Somalia, because they help justify large military expenditures.

Unilateral intervention in Somalia served the military's institutional interests in another way as well. The United States is eager to legitimate such actions while preventing or distorting the formation of international institutions that might prove capable of challenging the world's lone military superpower.

Finally, can any of us be surprised that four U.S. oil companies have a major stake in the pacification of Somalia? *The Los Angeles Times* reports that U.S. firms "are sitting on a prospective fortune in exclusive concessions to explore and exploit tens of millions of acres of the [Somali] countryside."

Seventh, whether or not one believes intervention using force or threatened force can ever be justified in places like Somalia or Bosnia, the peace community should be principled in its opposition to any unilateral military initiatives by the United States. The United States has no moral legitimacy or legal right to intervene unilaterally in the affairs of another country.

Eighth, although internationally approved sanctions—including the use of force or threatened force—are preferable to unilateral initiatives, they are not without problems. The first problem is that by default we are talking about the United Nations. The present decision-making structure of the United Nations is undemocratic. This helps explain why although the United Nations condemned both the Iraqi invasion of Kuwait and the U.S. invasion of Panama, and although the World Court condemned U.S. support for the contras in Nicaragua, it is Iraq that is subject to bombings and sanctions and not the United States.

At a time when we desperately need international organizations to respond effectively to global economic, environmental, and political problems, the United States and its Western allies are using international institutions as vehicles for their power. This is a problem that goes well beyond the United Nations.

For example, the International Monetary Fund, the General Agreement on Tariffs and Trade, and the North American Free Trade Agreement are international organizations and/or agreements that are dominated by Western countries and enormously destructive to the lives of people throughout the Third World. We should be sobered by the fact that the same nations that claim the moral right to intervene militarily in other countries also direct the global economy—which, over the past decade, witnessed the largest transfer of wealth in human history from the Third World poor to the First World rich.

Ninth, Christian pacifists and other Christians committed to nonviolent conflict resolution should work to develop, strengthen, and/or reform international institutions and organizations capable of conflict avoidance and resolution. Analysts such as Randall Forsberg argue that U.S. military spending could be reduced up to 80 percent by the year 2000 if the United States would embrace a cooperative approach to security. A cooperative approach, Forsberg argues, would save huge quantities of money and resources, help stop the global proliferation of weapons and weapons industries, and reduce the incidence and scale of war.

We cannot afford to stand outside the arenas in which collective security is debated, shaped, or ignored. Nor can we write off the United Nations, which while often abused by powerful countries has demonstrated its potential for lessening violence in places like Namibia and El Salvador. We must insist that the United States both pay its debt to the United Nations and stop crippling international peacekeeping efforts.

As followers of Jesus many of us understand our obedience to the state as provisional and selective. This does not mean we are anarchists. We believe in law and in some form of enforcement authority. However, in word and deed we have demonstrated that our ultimate allegiance is to God. Our obedience to and participation in the laws and institutions of the state are determined by whether obedience and participation are consistent with our faith. I would suggest similar behavior relative to international organizations: We should seek to influence them through nonviolent action and make obedience to them provisional in light of our faith.

Finally, whether and under what conditions we accept "humanitarian intervention," including the use of force, will likely be determined by our understanding of Jesus and the cross. It is at this point that I and others agonize over what to say and do. Some people who may agree with most or all of what I wrote above may disagree with everything that follows. Some will point out, perhaps rightly, that what I am about to say is inconsistent and contradictory. I know that I do not have the "right" answers, but I feel I should share how I answer for myself these difficult questions concerning faith and violence.

The biblical prophets offer us the helpful insight that violence is rooted in systems, and that those of us who are relatively well-off are often beneficiaries of such violence. Amos, for example, condemns the wealthy in Israel who "store up violence and robbery in their strongholds" (3:10). This insight leads to a rightful condemnation of institutionalized violence.

However, it can also be used to legitimate violent means of confronting injustice. Because of our participation in violent systems, the argument goes, we are already stained with the sin of violence. Therefore, there is no pure choice between violence and nonviolence.

I confess that I find this argument convincing. However, the example of Jesus and my commitment to be a follower of Jesus leads me to reject its pervasive logic. Most killing in today's world is done in the name of God or gods. I worship a God that embraced redemptive suffering rather than inflict death on others. Therefore, I embrace nonviolent means of conflict resolution and believe it is incompatible for Christians to serve in the military or to take another person's life.

As Christians we are to embrace redemptive suffering in our own persons. It is inappropriate, however, for us to turn our eyes from the suffering of others or to label suffering imposed on others as redemptive. We cannot in the spirit of Jesus, for example, cite a principled commitment to nonviolence as a reason to do nothing about "ethnic cleansing." Nor can we condemn violent responses to ethnic cleansing if we are not challenging it through nonviolent means.

Pervasive violence challenges but is not a judgment against the way of Jesus. It is a judgment against unjust systems and against the ineffectiveness of my nonviolent peacemaking that results in great violence to others. Just as the tragedy of Somalia calls our complicit nation to repentance, so, too, our inability to muster appropriate nonviolent responses to conflicts of this kind calls us to repentance.

If we are unwilling or unable to intervene nonviolently, risking our own lives in defense of others, then Gandhi's insight seems correct that violence is better than cowardice. Or stated another way, our cowardice or lack of preparedness makes violence inevitable.

The nonviolent movement has often "spoken truth to power" through symbolic actions, stressing fidelity over effectiveness. I believe that in the context of Bosnia and Somalia symbolic actions of protest or solidarity are not enough. Symbolically pouring blood is a poor substitute for a real presence in Somalia or Bosnia where blood is flowing and where our actual blood may need to be shed.

It seems to me that Christian pacifists and others committed to nonviolent conflict resolution cannot rule out the use of military force to liberate detention centers in Bosnia unless we are actively seeking to dismantle such centers through nonviolent means. And while I condemn the unilateral U.S. intervention into Somalia, we cannot rule out the need for internationally sanctioned humanitarian intervention, including that which uses or threatens the use of force, because we are not there in sufficient numbers and with adequate organization working for nonviolent resolution of the conflict.

In the coming decade, we must build international organizations capable of nonviolent conflict resolution in places such as Bosnia and Somalia. The seed of what is needed is present in the examples of Witness for Peace, the Fellowship of Reconciliation, and other groups who literally stand with the victims of violence and train others in nonviolent conflict resolution.

However, our failure to have mechanisms in place, through the United Nations or agencies that we create, whereby we can move 20,000 or 100,000 nonviolent, international peacemakers into Somalia to distribute food and help negotiate a settlement, or to help liberate concentration camps in Bosnia, is a judgment against Christian pacifism and Christian nonviolent protest. With such mechanisms in place, we can delegitimize violence in all its forms. Until then our voices are necessarily muffled.

The task before us is therefore pastoral as well as organizational. The most precious resources we have for our journey into uncharted waters are the strength of our communities and the Spirit of God that implores us to move from violence to wholeness and healing.

To Intervene or Not to Intervene
John Langan, S.J.

. . .The collapse of the one power capable of sustained and massive hostilities against the United States and the eruption of numerous local conflicts in and around the borders of the former communist world have produced a new set of attitudes and questions about intervention. First, there is no general basis for linking various local disputes to U.S. interests. Second, as the shift in public opinion with regard to Somalia made plain, there is no politically reliable domestic consensus for anything more than providing immediate humanitarian relief. Politicians are more likely to exploit failures in the execution of interventionist policies for partisan advantage than to support a worthwhile but precarious effort to help divided and tormented societies.

Third, the natural basis of political support for intervention has shifted in a significant way. Republicans and conservative Democrats were historically ready to support military interventions if these were presented as required by our national security, and they understood national security along the expansive lines appropriate to the superpower struggle. Especially after the Vietnam period, Democrats on the left became progressively more skeptical about such cold-war justifications. But those are the Democrats who are most likely to respond to universalistic appeals for humanitarian intervention—appeals that stress the vulnerability of victims and the bonds of human solidarity without relying on considerations of national interest specified in economic and military terms. As a result, many of those who supported interventionist actions and attitudes when these formed part of the struggle against communism are now critical of intervention aimed at humanitarian, nation-building or order-establishing objectives. On the other hand, people who were critical of such earlier U.S. military interventions as Grenada because they reflected an imperially expansive view of U.S. interests are now willing to consider a more activist and interventionist role for the U.S. in such places as Somalia and Haiti. An illustration of this criss-crossing at work was Senator Robert Dole's call for withdrawing U.S. forces from Somalia and the demands of the Congressional Black Caucus for deploying troops in Haiti.

In addition to this shift in the base of support for intervention and the various special considerations which affect attitudes among key groups (e.g., concern for Israel, local fears about immigration, reactions to terrorist attacks, shift in media attention), there is a continuing division among policymakers and experts between those who stress the risk and cost of intervention and those who affirm its potential benefits and its moral worth. This division depends on temperament and institutional ties as well as on ideological orientation. Thus the military, which might once have welcomed interventions as opportunities to show its usefulness, protect its budget and advance the careers of its members, has been brought by the calamity in Vietnam to see intervention's costs and dangers. On the right, with the important exception of cases involving the Middle East, there has been a decline in support for overseas intervention.

This shifting pattern does not imply any great inconsistency on either side. The variety and complexity of the factors that need to be weighed in arriving at political and ethical assessments about intervention make it morally inauthentic consistently to favor or oppose intervention. But the debate over intervention raises questions of consistency on other issues. Thus, opponents of intervention have looked to public opinion and to Congress to restrain the executive from committing U.S. forces and resources overseas. Many of those who now oppose intervention will find that the procedural and separation-of-powers arguments which once seemed to limit the chief executive's ability to combat communism are now welcome means of preventing misguided and expensive interventions.

Critics may think that this way of looking at the problem betrays two dangerous preoccupations: with the politics rather than the ethics of intervention, and with the perceptions and needs of the U.S. and its leaders rather than with the terrors and sufferings of people in less fortunate lands. In some respects this line of criticism helps us to grasp the heart of the problem that confronts the U.S., its major allies and the United Nations. As we look at the most troubled regions of the world where internal order is not merely disrupted but seems to have collapsed, (Haiti before 1994, Rwanda, Bosnia, Somalia, Sudan, the Caucasus region, Liberia, Kurdistan), we see groups of people, sometimes numbering in the millions, who cry out for relief from famine and misery and for rescue from genocide, rape and torture. All these groups can make a prima facie case that the international system of states should not stand by idly while they are slaughtered and their human rights violated. This case is not merely plausible; through the images and interviews broadcast around the world, it becomes unbearably poignant and immediately persuasive.

Responding with effective commitments of military personnel and equipment, along with civilian relief workers and supplies, would impose a massive political and financial burden on the U.S. and the UN (though the expenses of several peacemaking expeditions would be unlikely to equal the costs of even one modest war). Even after we put aside areas where conflict and suffering have been intense but which now seem to be moving toward stability (southern Africa, Cambodia, Lebanon, El Salvador, Cyprus) as well as those areas where the prospect of bloody conflict is real but where active intervention is likely to be universally rejected (Algeria, Afghanistan), there are more than enough places where humanitarian intervention can be justified. If the U.S. universally responded to peoples in need and under threat it would be attempting to carry every burden and fight every struggle as a kind of policeman of the world in a time of instability. This is not a morally contemptible role, since the good order of society does indeed depend on an honest and competent police force. But neither U.S. citizens nor the world at large are ready to accept the American government in such a role—a role which is not supported by the realities of international law or politics.

Beyond the legal and conceptual difficulties inherent in such an overriding of sovereignty in the international system is a dilemma that confronts every effort to establish the U.S. in the role of universal policeman. Through its alliances and pursuit of its own interests, the U.S. either is already involved in many local or regional quarrels and so is lacking in impartiality and distance, or its interests in the area of conflict are not sufficiently engaged to provide a reasoned basis of support for sustained U.S. involvement. This is not a complete dilemma. In some conflicts, such as the longstanding war between Israel and its Arab neighbors, the U.S. might well be accused of a conflict of interest because of its close ties to Israel; but it also has a wider set of concerns in this area so that an important part of its own national interest requires that regional disputes be settled fairly for the sake of greater stability. As a result, the various parties have been willing (at least sometimes) to accept the U.S. role in resolving disputed issues and enforcing agreements.

A further problem is the enormous difficulty of consistently fulfilling a program of comprehensive intervention and global policing, both in practical political and in theoretical ethical terms. This has already become clear in the case of human rights policy, in which the U.S. government has tried to coordinate such considerations as trade opportunities and the need to control nuclear proliferation with its assessment of a nation's human rights performance. The task is to devise the right set of sanctions, pressures and inducements to persuade another government to improve its treatment of minorities, dissidents and the oppressed. Elaborating a comprehensive intervention policy requires bringing in a further set of variables and uncertainties about the likely effects and costs of military action. The debates on such a policy are likely to be even more intense than those over most-favored-nation status for China or over protest against human rights abuses committed by regimes whose cooperation we need for ensuring our national security and well-being.

The question, then, is where and on what basis the U.S. will decide to intervene. This gives rise to such further questions as: Why, when and under what auspices should we intervene? What factors should rightly limit U.S. interventions? All of us who are neither pacifists nor isolationists will need to examine these questions, since we presumably accept both the moral legitimacy of some possible interventions and the morally and politically significant connections between order in the larger world and U.S. security interests. Even some traditional pacifists supported a humanitarian intervention in Somalia, where in the beginning there was no clearly defined adversary and where many of the elements of war were missing.

It may seem strange to link a geographical question about where to intervene and a metaethical question about the justificatory basis for intervention. But this juxtaposition makes us focus on the essential tensions in the current inconclusive debate over intervention. Our main religious and philosophical approaches to ethics and to law contain a strong element of universalism. They require us to take into account the joys and hopes, the sufferings and fears of all people without regard to their nationality or political affiliations. This points us toward a comprehensive policy of intervening wherever there is need and possibility of rescue.

During the cold-war period, the shared political story of struggling against communism provided a justification for intervening in some humanitarian crises and passing by others with no more than a protest. In the post-cold-war period, we need to find a new basis for justifying a selective policy of intervention which will not lead to the overreach of universalism but which will keep us from the moral insensitivity of a nationalistic or self-righteous isolationism. We also need an approach which takes seriously the special history and position of the U.S. and draws on a wider range of considerations than appeals for the relief of suffering. The government and people of the U.S. are bound to act and to intervene as themselves, not simply as rational agents of universal law or as disciples of Christ obeying the command or the exhortations of the Master. We must ask what responsibilities flow from our location and from our prior commitments to other peoples.

If scarce political, financial and military resources make it impossible for us to respond to the whole range of calls for humanitarian intervention, rescue missions, and peacekeeping and peacemaking of various sorts, then we must draw up priorities. One essential element of determining those priorities is the relative importance of the location of crises to us and to other powers in the region. Interventions in areas close to other major powers, in what in the case of Russia is commonly called the "near abroad," are very unlikely. No matter how grievous the sufferings of the Chechens, the Armenians, the Azeris and the various factions in Tajikistan, it would be irresponsible to encourage them to expect the U.S. to come to their rescue. Something similar holds for the peoples of Sri Lanka and of East Timor because of their proximity to two major regional powers, India and Indonesia. The geographical factor has also been used by some defenders of U.S. inaction in Bosnia, who have argued that the crisis there primarily concerns Europeans. Something similar will probably be said if the ongoing civil war in Algeria reaches the point where there are demands for intervention to end large-scale slaughter. Such a weighting of geographical factors may not lead to morally superior outcomes, but it is a starting point for shaping a sustainable policy.

The U.S., for instance, will react to crises in the Caribbean more forcefully than in other parts of the world. The political perceptions and prejudices that produce such outcomes as the subsidizing of the contras in Nicaragua have to be seen as a continuing fact of national and international life, not simply as something to be denounced or wished away. In this search for a realistic basis for intervention, the key question is whether the U.S. has a special interest in the area or a special responsibility toward one or more of the parties in the dispute. So the areas where there is some possibility of intervention include the Caribbean (because of its proximity), the Middle East (because of oil and Israel), the Andean countries (because of the drug traffic), and the northern parts of Central Europe (the Baltics, Poland, the Czech and Slovak republics, and Hungary), an area that seeks to be included in the Western alliance. Regions where intervention is unlikely include Southeast Asia, because of the Vietnam precedent, Africa (with the possible exception of South Africa), because of the area's poverty and of a reluctance to enter into avoidable conflicts with Islam, and the states which formerly belonged within the Soviet Union.

The most morally weighty reason for military intervention is to prevent large-scale loss of innocent human life—through explicit and intentional massacres, famine induced by government decision or military stalemate, or ethnic cleansing. The U.S. and its allies should not attempt to terminate local civil wars as such. These are unlikely to come to an end until the local combatants are convinced that their side can gain nothing significant from prolonging hostilities. Human rights violations, even when massive and persistent, should be dealt with through diplomatic and economic pressures.

To be effective, intervention must be carried out on a scale that will convince wrongdoers to cease and desist. At the same time, it is morally suspect to kill large numbers of people in the name of humanitarian rescue. What seems most useful is a combination of massive and early deployment of troops and cautious and discriminating use of force. While the general norms of just war teaching governing the use of force should be observed, it is important to recognize that interventions are not wars, though the line separating the two may be difficult to establish. One of the prime purposes of intervention is to establish a secure and reliable order of law in the affected area. In this regard intervention resembles the exercise of police force in places threatened by rioting. In such situations, clear and unambiguous threats of force have their greatest usefulness early on. This point suggests some modification of the just war criterion of last resort so that those who are preparing to attack their neighbors do not do irreparable damage while outside powers are gradually coming to accept the necessity of force. The applicability of this point to the early stages in the disintegration of Yugoslavia is obvious.

In general, U.S. interventions should be carried out with authorization from the United Nations and with cooperation from other concerned powers. This is particularly true with regard to the Caribbean and Central America, where it is all too easy for U.S. interventions to fall back into the patterns of pre-cold-war imperialism. This point is in tension with the preceding one, since the time and persuasion necessary to develop a broad international consensus may well get in the way of a firm and rapid response.

Intervention is likely to be the major focus of policy and ethical debates. Our concern for developing moral and political norms for intervention should not be allowed to get in the way of our attempt to understand those parts of the world which are most divided by traditional hatreds. Intervention can never be more than one element in resolving crises of those troubled lands; a wider understanding of their cultures and economic needs and a readiness to provide

creative forms of help—ranging from introducing new forms of conflict resolution and negotiation to providing capital for economic development—will
become ever more necessary.

The Promise of Nonviolent Strategies:
A Response to John Langan
Kale Williams

John Langan carefully balances the moral appeal of and the practical impedi-
ments to U.S. military intervention in the many situations around the world in
which ethnic and religious rivalries have exploded into war and caused the
suffering of innocents. His masterful sketch of the major arguments is limited
by his almost exclusive focus on military intervention. I would begin where
Langan ends, with the recognition that military intervention "can never be
more than one element in resolving the crises of those troubled lands." What
are the other elements? Can nonviolent strategies better achieve a resolution?
Are there alternatives that involve neither military intervention nor acquiescence to ethnic cleansing—nonviolent alternatives to others' use of violence in
imposing their political will? Is there, for example, a good prescription for
U.S. policy in Bosnia?

Clearly the present answer is no. We either intervene militarily and ride the
tiger of war where it takes us or we bear the responsibility of not exercising our
great power and recognized leadership to attempt to prevent years of slaughter.
Neither answer is easy to accept. What new element would have to be in place
before better responses could emerge?

Too narrow a focus on military intervention deters us from addressing that
question. But the present interdependence not just of nations but of civilizations makes the development of means other than mass violence for resolving
conflict a central task for our generation—especially since we live in the
shadow of thousands of weapons of mass destruction. Yet neither pacifists nor
political realists are putting much energy into developing alternatives that go
beyond traditional diplomacy.

Langan is correct in implying that committed pacifists have little to contribute when large-scale military battles have been joined. Short of offering
heroic witness, which is beyond most of them, or humanitarian relief, pacifists
are limited to a cry of "Stop the killing." If this cry often appears futile, it at least
has the virtue of speaking for the voiceless victims caught in the maelstrom. But
pacifists have too often focused simply on opposition to military means. Rarely

has political realism been combined with a serious analysis of long-term non-violent strategies. Both pacifists and political realists have reason to join and contributions to make to that essential enterprise.

Two related roads are worth exploring. One involves the socially organized withdrawal of consent—the strategy that Gandhi and Martin Luther King Jr. used to initiate and force change despite the guns in their opponents' hands. The lessons from these and numerous other, smaller-scale movements could be applied to the prevention of armed conflict and to its termination. For example, one can imagine a different outcome in the former Yugoslavia if the early forays by pacifists to organize a nonviolent citizens' response had been accompanied by significant communications and logistical support.

The second road is the extension of democratic values, principles and processes. These lay the essential groundwork for developing a political community and the institutions of conflict resolution that are the alternative to war. Democracy's core belief in the dignity of persons has powerful appeal, an appeal strong enough to challenge the current emphasis on racial and ethnic identities.

In recognizing the lack of citizen support for U.S. intervention, Langan has his finger on more than just a growing reluctance to commit American troops abroad. Support for the development of nonviolent approaches to conflict resolution might rank even lower than military intervention with the American populace. This lack of interest reflects the failure of our schools and civic associations to develop enough informed, thoughtful and concerned citizens to sustain and guide elected leaders in developing a nonisolationist, productive engagement with the world. We seem unable even to frame an intelligible debate. Enhancing the understanding of international issues in our schools and civil society is a task that ought to engage all those concerned about moving away from mass organized violence toward a world of political solutions for the conflicts that will, inevitably, continue to arise.

The Legitimation of the Abuse of
Women in Christianity
Mary Ann Rossi

How could it have come about that a religion rooted in equality and mutuality should have been transformed into a man-centered cult with the basic tenet of

From Mary Ann Rossi, "The Legitimation of the Abuse of Women in Christianity," from *Feminist Theology: The Journal of the Britain and Ireland School of Feminist Theology,* No. 4, September 1993, pp. 56–63. Reprinted by permission of the Publisher, Sheffield Academic Press Ltd.

excluding half of the human race from full personhood? When women are perceived as less than human, the consequence is violent abuse, such as woman battering, a crime that was not even acknowledged in our legal codes as recently as two decades ago, let alone addressed as a significant social problem or as one that must be addressed from the pulpit. I am convinced that the misshapen society resulting today from this Christian mindset is adversely affecting the lives of both women and men who refuse to challenge injustice to all women inherent in Christianity. This injustice stems from the misogynistic assumptions of the Christian teachings derived from Augustine, Aquinas, Gratian, and other founders of Christian precepts grounded in the Aristotelian conviction that females are defective males. This paper will make the connection between these Christian teachings and the acceptance of wife abuse as a private matter, and not open to public debate, and certainly not to acknowledgment from the pulpit.

The crime of battering came to my attention nearly twenty years ago. I was confronted with the problem when Cathy, a 'good Christian woman', knocked on my door and asked me to help her. Thinking that her husband was drinking too much, she went to a tavern to ask him to come home; his response was to beat her in the parking lot so severely that she was taken to the emergency ward, where the doctor, whom she had never met, asked 'What did you do to provoke him this time?'. This case and many similar episodes led to my legislative work in Wisconsin as a member of the Battered Woman Task Force. It was in this capacity that I began to suspect a strong connection between Christian upbringing and the acceptance of battering by women and men. In particular, a strongly worded letter from a rural Wisconsin woman accused me of sinful ways in trying to urge women to leave a battering situation; as she put it, it was woman's God-given duty to submit to her husband and to suffer in silence as a good Christian woman. I was motivated to discover how this woman had received such a message from her Christian education: that is, that for the sake of keeping the family together, a woman had to sacrifice her own safety and that of her children. Furthermore, the wife who is battered is made to feel the cause of this abuse, and—like the guilty Eve—shares the guilt that accrues to all women from the verses of Genesis.

As legislative chair of the Governor's Commission on the Status of Women, I monitored new legislation making the crime of wife battering a felony in Wisconsin statutes. It had always been a legal prohibition to batter a stranger. But a man's home was his castle, and this mindset reflected (and often still does) the English law of coverture, the basis of our American laws: that is, in marriage the man and the woman become one, the man. Anyone who has attended a Christian wedding ceremony recently can testify to the strangle-hold of this perception in requiring a woman to 'obey' her husband, and in acknowledging and affirming the reading of the passage from Genesis relating to the fashioning of the guilty Eve from Adam's rib, which is the most pernicious myth perpetrated against women since the ancient Greeks contrived the myth of the birth of Athena from the head of Zeus. And the continuing presence of this myth of Eve still exerts a strong influence on woman's self-perception today.

Let us now consider the single most powerful and persistent model of the 'good Christian woman', Monica, the mother of St. Augustine (d. 430), the Father of the church, who was the most influential author of Christian doctrines regarding the inferiority of women. Although Monica is often the scapegoat of the psychoanalysts of Augustine's sexual hangups, she was abused by Patricius, her pagan husband, and her advice to battered women who came to her for help was to return to their husbands and suffer in silence. It was Monica's virtue as a good Christian woman never to speak of what she endured at the hands of her violent husband. The heritage of Monica's lesson is in the countless cases of wife battering, unrecorded, unprosecuted, unacknowledged by their ministers, priests and fellow parishioners.

Let us turn now to the attitude of the church towards sexuality. Those of us raised in the Roman Catholic faith cannot discuss the defilement of the body by sexual intercourse without tracing the root of this 'mindset' in the teachings of the Fathers of the church, of whom the most notable is Augustine. The early Christians as they chose their canonical texts excluded all writings that conceived of God as both male and female. The orthodox ('straight-thinking') God is exclusively male. Eve is created from Adam's side for his fulfillment. This is translated in society into the domination of men over women as the proper God-given order for the human race and for the Christian church.

In Augustine maleness is assimilated into monism; femaleness becomes the image of the lower corporeal nature, or carnality and sexuality. Male/female dualism is assimilated into soul/body dualism. Woman is seen ethically as dangerous to the male. Let me illustrate the persistence of this male suspicion of all women. In 1962 at the first ecumenical council convened by Pope John XXIII in Rome, an Anglican journalist and dear friend of mine, Ann Cheetham, having been invited to attend, was confronted by a cardinal who screamed: 'Leave this place immediately! Do not sully this conference with the presence of a woman.' Deeply humiliated, Ann Cheetham, a lifelong worker for the cause of women's equality in the church, left Rome in tears, women's only resort in the face of a hierarchy deaf to the voices of women.[1]

As a counterpart to the debasing of women as an embodiment of the lower, or corporeal, nature, we must look to the exclusion of women in the perception of deity. To regard God in anthropomorphic terms as an elderly white male is detrimental not only to other races, but to all women. The works of outstanding theologians like Elisabeth Schüssler Fiorenza, Rosemary Radford Ruether and Elaine Pagels have succeeded in recovering the female images and metaphors of God. The transforming of the female apostle Junia (Rom. 16:15) into the male name Junias in the sixth century illustrates one way the testimony of women leaders was purposely erased from church history.[2] This cover-up of women leaders in the early church fortified the male hierarchy in their consolidation of power; the exclusion of women from priesthood and the imposition of mandated celibacy by the canons of the fifth and sixth centuries were the capstones to this encapsulation of women's basic inferiority to men. Battered women today still suffer the effects of this androcentric perception of human nature.

Augustine locates the source of original sin in the male erection and
women are the cause of it. The depersonalization of women into whore, wife
or mother may be traced to his writings. Most damaging is his reiteration of the
precept that the wife must submit completely to her husband, even to the point
of physical abuse and death. Augustine formulated the idea that women were
good only for reproduction and unqualified for anything connected with mind
or intelligence. Thus Augustine was the inventor of what the Germans call the
three K's, Kinder, Küche, Kirche: that is children, kitchen and church, an idea
that still has life in it. In fact, as the German theologian Ute Ranke-Heinemann
notes, it continues to be the Catholic hierarchy's primary theological position
on women.[3]

In conjunction with this debasing of women in the conception of humanness, we must acknowledge the purposeful if often subliminal cover-up or
omission of female images in Scripture or commentaries on Scripture. For
example, a French Jesuit translator of the Bible replaces the Greek verb for
parturition—I am the God who gave you birth—with the phrase 'I am the God
who fathered you'.[4]

Augustine describes the Catholic Church as the 'true Mother of all Christians', as if it might be the mother of all humanity and the guarantor of all
existing social bonds: 'It is you who make wives subject to their husbands . . .
by chaste and faithful obedience; you set husbands over their wives'.[5] Peter
Brown sums up Augustine's influence: 'Augustine created a darkened humanism
that linked the pre-Christian past to the Christian present in a common distrust
of sexual pleasure'.[6]

If we believe, as Clifford Geertz states, that religion is the shaper of society,
we must acknowledge the potential for healing and reform that resides in the
decision-making bodies of the church. How can we effect change that will
bring women into the deliberations that will affect their lives and their future?
First of all, we must recognize and acknowledge an evil before we can confront
it and extirpate it whether from our consciousness or from the mores of our
society.

There are three ways of accomplishing this goal:

(1) Recognize the omission of women from the texts of early Christian
history. Thanks to feminist theologians such as Elisabeth Schüssler Fiorenza,
Rosemary Radford Ruether, Elaine Pagels and others, we have seen a proliferation of research on the presence of women in the early church, from Junia
the Apostle to priests like Leta, recovered by Otranto of Italy.[7] To such an
extent have women been erased from androcentric texts that we must resort
to archaeological clues, such as the catacomb painting of women celebrating
the eucharist (with a modern reproduction transforming the women into men),
and locating a Bishop Theodora in the church of St Prassede in Rome (with
the last part of her name scratched out).[8]

(2) Recognize the seeds of the biological construction of women's inferiority in two of the most influential Greek thinkers of all time: Plato and Aristotle.
In the *Laws* Plato concludes that a woman has less potentiality for virtue than

a man; he says further that it is women's weakness and timidity that make them sly and devious (781 b 2-4). Again Plato shows his contempt for women: 'Human nature being twofold, the better sort was that which should thereafter be called man' (*Timaeus* 42 e). And twice he says: 'Evil and cowardly men are reborn as women, that being the first step downward to rebirth as animals' (42 b3-c4; 90 e 6-91 a 4). Aristotle sees woman as a misbegotten male (*De Generationel* IV 6; *Metaphysics* X 9) perhaps caused by some adverse circumstance, such as a southeast wind that is moist. This Aristotelian conception is adopted with approbation by Augustine and Aquinas, and we might observe the effects of such a mindset in the pages of medical textbooks in the USA up to a few years ago; the anatomy of the male is treated as normal throughout, and the differing features of the female anatomy as anomaly or abnormality.[9] The Aristotelian conception of procreation as male begetting and woman conceiving (or receiving the seed) is so imbedded in our thinking that we retain these terms, even though the female ovum was discovered by Van Baer in 1827, the first time that the woman's equal role in conception was realized. Such is the influence of language on the shaping of our thoughts.

(3) We must reconstruct our historical perception of women's equal role in the ancient Christian church in order to conceive of a liberating praxis in our present crisis. Such a praxis, wherever it is being learned and disseminated, will inspire its adherents to three actions: first, to work for the solidarity of women within or outside of their Christian congregations in order to voice their consensus; secondly, to refuse to accept interpretations of the Bible or any canonical doctrine that demeans or diminishes the worth of women as human beings; and thirdly, to urge governments to enact legislation recognizing that violence motivated by gender is a violation of civil rights.[10]

We are more and more aware that the greatest and most profound shaper of our thoughts and our society is religion. Elisabeth Schüssler Fiorenza has pointed the way to the recovery of women's Christian past by a method she calls feminist critical hermeneutics.[11] Her works have inspired and directed my research into the formation of the female mindset in Western society, especially in woman's compliance with battery and subservience according to the dictates of her Christian faith.

Women and men working on the problem of battering conclude that the legal system alone cannot eliminate this problem, for it is rooted in the pernicious and misguided fallacies of Christian teachings.[12]

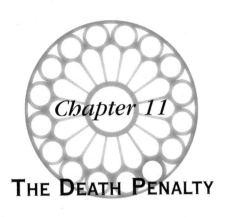

Chapter 11

THE DEATH PENALTY

Does the state have the right to take life in an act of retributive justice? People appealing to the Bible have responded both "Yes" and "No" to this question. Those who find support for the death penalty cite Genesis 9:6 ("Whoever sheds the blood of a human, by a human shall that person's blood be shed. . . .") as a sanction for this view. Others see this verse in relation to Genesis 4–6, which deals with corruption and taking vengeance, and thus argue that it states a fact and a limitation rather than advocates vengeance. The law of *talion* (legal retaliation), then, is understood to be a concession, rather than divine support for the taking of life. In the New Testament, support for capital punishment has often been seen in Paul's statement that the government "does not bear the sword in vain" (Romans 13:4). But whether this refers to the death penalty is strongly debated. Paul speaks of the state's right to govern, and some argue that his use of the word "sword" refers more broadly to judicial authority, not to the "sword" used to execute criminals (which is a different Greek word than the one Paul used).

Those arguing against the death penalty on biblical grounds note that the one direct reference to this subject is found in John 8, where Jesus addresses the woman guilty of a capital offense. He does not deny that the Mosaic law condemns her, but he questions the moral authority of those who would judge and execute her ("Let anyone among you who is without sin be the first to throw a stone at her") and introduces his authority to forgive sin. Incidents like this one illustrate the difficulty in attempting to find in a particular passage a direct answer to a social issue. If one were to take the primary message of the New Testament as the forgiving, reconciling love of God in Christ Jesus, how would one relate this message to the issue of capital punishment?

The problem becomes balancing the legitimate concern of the state to dispense justice with a higher vision of human relationships marked by love and reconciliation. In a criminal justice system, these ideals would presumably express themselves in the development of a system of rehabilitation that would reclaim the lives of offenders, not simply incarcerate or execute them. Many argue on utilitarian grounds for this rehabilitative approach, claiming that any added expense would be more than repaid in the long run when offenders are regained as productive members of society. The present system, in other words, does not really serve the best interests of society. Proponents of the death penalty, on the other hand, argue that those who take life have in effect forfeited the right to have their "ultimate welfare" taken seriously by the state. The state should take no risk in preserving the welfare of society by removing the offender for good.

In recent years the death penalty has become problematic in churches that have historically maintained its legitimacy. In the Roman Catholic church, for example, moral theologians have questioned the appropriateness of the death penalty in light of their church's position on abortion. Does not a "pro-life" position challenge other forms of life taking, as in war or capital punishment? This is an argument on grounds of principle, affirming the sanctity of life and its inviolate character. Others have raised questions on utilitarian grounds, looking at the effects of capital punishment in maintaining a society relatively free of violent crime. Here, the lack of evidence demonstrating that capital punishment serves as a deterrent to crime has raised further questions about its appropriateness. Another factor that has led to disenchantment with the death penalty is the apparent injustice of our whole system of criminal justice, which consigns to death row an inordinately large proportion of the poor and members of racial minorities. Evidence of this fact was established in an investigation of death row in North Carolina, a state with a large number of persons sentenced to die. Of those condemned, 65 percent were black and 62 percent were poor.

The legal setting for the current discussion was established in the 1970s with two Supreme Court decisions. The first one in 1972 *(Furman v. Georgia)* ruled that Georgia's death penalty system, as it was imposed and carried out, constituted "cruel and unusual punishment." In the second decision in 1976 *(Gregg v. Georgia),* the Court ruled that the sentence of death "does not invariably violate the Constitution." Many thought that the 1972 decision was a first step toward abolishing the death penalty, but the latter decision repudiated that assumption. It made clear that the issue was not the inherent cruelty of the death sentence, but the need for "objective standards to guide, regularize, and make rationally reviewable" the manner in which the death sentence is imposed. Since these decisions, the states have been busy establishing standards that would legitimate the death penalty, and in the decade following, 67 people were executed under these standards. Most of the states currently have capital punishment statutes, but in only about one-third of these has the death penalty been used.

Judge Richard L. Nygaard argues against the death penalty on three grounds. First he questions our killing those who commit murder or other heinous crimes; capital punishment is the killing of one whose sins Jesus said could be forgiven. His argument, second, surveys society's motivations for the death penalty and penological justification of it. He concludes that retribution—"getting even"—is both the motive and justification. He questions whether this could ever be a Christian motive. Turning from deontological grounds, Nygaard's third argument rests on consequentialist grounds: what institutionalized killing is doing to our society and ourselves. Most notably, he points to an increase in our desire for violence and vengeance rather than grace and mercy.

Ernest Van den Haag is one of the best-known advocates of the death penalty, writing widely in its defense. He accuses opponents of capital punishment of engaging in a sham argument when they point out inequalities in the administration of this penalty, for he maintains that this is not the essential moral question. The justice system, he argues, must continually be concerned with assuring equality before the law and preventing the punishment of the innocent, but any problems here should not be solved at the expense of justice itself. For Van den Haag, the essential moral question must revolve around the value put on life. He asks, "Does a social value system in which life itself, however it is lived, becomes the highest good enhance the value of human life or cheapen it?" To Van den Haag, vengeance in the form of taking the life of one who has taken life is not barbaric, but a means of affirming the value of human life.

Some opponents of the death penalty oppose it in principle, as Van den Haag suspects; thus, even if, in the language of Nygaard, it deterred crime, the opposition would not disappear. They, too, appeal to the value of human life and point to what they perceive to be a moral contradiction in taking a life in order to maintain the value of life. So, the parameters of the debate are wide.

'Vengeance is Mine' Says the Lord
Richard L. Nygaard

Perry Carris is dead. (This is not his real name.) I doubt, however, that many will mourn him. Indeed, even among those who did not want him to die, most

Reprinted with the permission of Judge Richard L. Nygaard and America Press, Inc., 106 West 56th Street, New York, NY 10019. Originally published in *America's* October 8, 1994, issue.

would readily admit that the world is a better place without him. He was a brutal killer and not one with whom anyone would easily sympathize. He and an accomplice entered the home of his friend's elderly uncle and aunt, then killed and robbed them. The uncle was stabbed 79 times, and the aunt, who weighed only 70 pounds, was stabbed 66 times. Carris and his friend had killed them with a bayonet.

But, you see; Perry Carris did not just die—we killed him. One night recently, officers of the prison where he spent his final hours injected him with lethal chemicals, and quietly he met eternity. And there are many more who are in like fashion scheduled to die. Moreover, the new federal crime bill imposes death as a penalty for 50 more crimes. Can Christians continue any longer to watch in passive silence? Is it not time to think about what society is doing—what we are doing? Carris's act was deliberate and fully planned. So was ours. Carris's motivation was a cruel disregard for life. What was ours? The first killing was clearly sinful, criminal and unjustified. But how about the second?

Punishment is a theme with which each of us must wrestle. The death penalty as the ultimate sanction brings punishment sharply into focus: It is the surrogate for society's frustration with its government's failures to protect the citizenry and maintain order. And as a form of punishment, the propriety of killing criminals is an issue with which Christians must also reconcile their beliefs. Many Christians, quick to condemn abortion because it kills an innocent being, just as quickly accept the death penalty, ostensibly because it kills a guilty being. Each is the killing of a human person. The first is one who Jesus said knows no sin; the second is one whose sins Jesus said could be forgiven. Is there a difference? Is this a paradox, or can we reconcile our ambivalent attitudes about death? Let us see.

It is important, first, to know why we punish and why we killed Perry Carris. American penology is really quite simple. We have just three means of criminal punishment: probation, incarceration and death. And we rely upon only four justifications: rehabilitation, deterrence, containment and retribution. How does the death penalty serve these ends? When we look at each possible justification, it becomes clear that both society's motivation and the penological justification for the death penalty are simply retribution—we are "getting even."

First, one can easily reject rehabilitation as an aim. If there is one thing the death penalty surely does not do, it does not rehabilitate the person upon whom it is imposed. It simply takes that person's life.

The second purpose, deterrence, is more problematic. Statistics uniformly show that the condemned on death row did not consider the possibility that they might die for their crimes. There may be others, of course, who thought of the consequences and did not kill. This possibility has been little researched, and as yet we simply do not know much about this aspect of deterrence. The incomplete data, however, indicate that of those disposed to kill, none seemed to fear the consequences. Hence, we cannot now conclude that by killing one person we deter others from killing. What we refer to as "general deterrence" does not philosophically justify the death penalty.

There is a second type of deterrence, "specific deterrence," which is directed toward the person we punish. In this instance none could deny that death works perfectly. Indeed, the person executed can never commit another crime. Death is permanent deterrence. The question here is whether death as a penalty is necessary. All current statistics indicate that it is, first of all, more expensive to execute a person than it is to imprison for life. Second, life imprisonment will protect society from further criminal acts by the malefactor. Consequently penological theorists reject both general and specific deterrence as legitimate justifications for the death penalty.

Containment too is philosophically problematic because it punishes one for something as yet not done. We use the crime already committed to project, sometimes without further data, that the criminal will do it again. Then we contain these people to prevent them from repeating. Unquestionably, although killing the offender does, in a grim and final sense, contain and thereby protect society from potential future criminal acts against it, one must ask again—is it necessary? It is not. Penologists recognize that one can be effectively and economically contained in a prison. Hence they also reject containment to justify the death penalty.

This leaves only retribution. Revenge. The ultimate payback. As a retributory tool, death works wonderfully. The desire for revenge is the dark secret in all of us. It has, I suppose, been so since the beginning of time. It is human nature to resent a hurt, and each of us has a desire to hurt back. Before there was law, the fear of personal reprisal may have been all that kept some from physical attacks and property crimes against others. But with law, cultures sought to limit personal revenge by punishment controlled and meted out in a detached fashion by the sovereign. Indeed, the Mosaic and the Hammurabic Codes, although severe, were the sovereign's attempt to temper and assuage personal vendettas by assuming the responsibility for punishment, thereby repudiating and curtailing personal reprisals.

The ideal citizen is not a feuding Hatfield or McCoy. Revenge between citizens is antithetical to civilized society. It invites a greater retaliation, which in turn invites counter-reprisal, which again invites more revenge. It contributes to a spiraling escalation of violence between society and the criminal culture. By exacting revenge upon criminals, society drops to the social stratum of its dregs. We are then playing on their terms; by their rules: and we cannot win. Leaders know, and have known for centuries, that civilization requires restraint and that open personal revenge is socially destructive, cannot be permitted and, indeed, must be renounced. Official revenge is no better, and the results are no less odious. By using revenge, by catering to the passions of society, government tells its citizens that vengeance is acceptable behavior—it is just that you, the individual, cannot exact it. Hence, when government does not control crime or is not vengeful enough to suit the demands of its citizens, they lust for more. Vengeance is our conditioned response to crime. It is also, after all, the official response to crime.

Unfortunately, although our government knows enough to do better, it is now ruled by the tides of public opinion and has deigned to respond politically to the base passions of society rather than act as a statesman upon the socio-logical necessities of civilization. Vengeance requires a victim; and in punish-ing a criminal, our government gives us one. Ignoring the conclusions reached over the centuries by philosophers, penologists, psychologists and theologians and the practical wisdom exercised by parents, our government has legitimated the notion of vengeance. "Paying back," although destructive to culture and fam-ily alike, is politically popular. Hence it is the law.

There is likewise a psychological overlay, and we as Christians must also confront what institutionalized killing is doing to our attitudes toward our-selves. As a judge, I have seen the defiant and unrepentant murderer and know how easy it is to identify only with the innocent and injured. Nonetheless, should we not as Christians strive to exemplify the grace and mercy of Jesus? And should we not desire this quality likewise in our society? In the hours lead-ing up to a recent execution, the newspapers and reporters hovered around like flies. One newspaper published the details of the condemned man's last meal and devoted three pages of its Sunday edition to such things as a full-color, front-page picture of the stretcher upon which he was to die. One television station gave death-watch "updates" every half-hour leading down to the execu-tion. An anchor-man was quoted as saying, "this is just the kind of break we needed for our ratings." Indeed it was—his station had won a lottery drawing to witness the execution.

It is difficult to feel pride in a culture that has become so inured to violence that death is an acceptable element of commercial value. Or worse. In Florida, on the eve of a scheduled execution, the crowds gathered outside the prison to await a condemned man's death, and at the fateful hour they cheered. The shameful truth is that society, by urging vengeful punishment, exposes its own desire for violence. Is it proper for government to give vent to this base desire? I seriously doubt that we, as a society, can kill without doing psychological damage to our culture.

The death penalty *is* constitutional and *is* legal. Moreover, Perry Carris re-ceived a fair trial and his full measure of due process on appeal. I know, because I was one of the judges on the court that declined to stay his execution. What, however, does all this mean to me or you, the Christian who must decide whether to support death as a penalty or endorse those who pass laws estab-lishing it? First, we are a government of the people, and are obliged to scruti-nize the reason why our society, and hence our government, behaves as it does. Indeed, if we are to support a society that kills, we must know why it does so and be satisfied that its reasons are reconcilable with the tenets of our faith. Are they—when society kills for revenge? "Vengeance is mine," says the Lord. What do you say?

The Collapse of the Case against Capital Punishment
Ernest Van den Haag

Three questions about the death penalty so overlap that they must each be answered. I shall ask seriatim: Is the death penalty constitutional? Is it useful? Is it morally justifiable?

THE CONSTITUTIONAL QUESTION

The Fifth Amendment states that no one shall be "deprived of life, liberty, or property without due process of law," implying a "due process of law" to deprive persons of life. The Eighth Amendment prohibits "cruel and unusual punishment." It is unlikely that this prohibition was meant to supersede the Fifth Amendment, since the amendments were simultaneously enacted in 1791.[1]

The Fourteenth Amendment, enacted in 1868, reasserted and explicitly extended to the states the implied authority to "deprive of life, liberty, or property" by "due process of law." Thus, to regard the death penalty as unconstitutional one must believe that the standards which determine what is "cruel and unusual" have so evolved since 1868 as to prohibit now what was authorized then, and that the Constitution authorizes the courts to overrule laws in the light of *new* moral standards. What might these standards be? And what shape must their evolution take to be constitutionally decisive?

Consensus. A moral consensus, intellectual or popular, could have evolved to find execution "cruel and unusual." It did not. Intellectual opinion is divided. Polls suggest that most people would vote for the death penalty.

If, however, there were a consensus against the death penalty, the Constitution expects the political process, rather than judicial decisions, to reflect it. Courts are meant to interpret the laws made by the political process and to set constitutional limits to it—not to replace it by responding to a presumed moral consensus. Surely the "cruel and unusual" phrase was not meant to authorize the courts to become legislatures.[2] Thus, neither a consensus of moral opinion nor a moral discovery by judges is meant to be disguised as a constitutional interpretation. Even when revealed by a burning bush, new moral norms were not meant to become constitutional norms by means of court decisions.[3] . . .

"Cruel" may be understood to mean excessive—punitive without, or beyond, a rational utilitarian purpose. Since capital punishment excludes rehabilitation and is not needed for incapacitation, the remaining rational-utilitarian purpose would be deterrence, the reduction of the rate at which the crime punished is committed by others. . . .

Justice, a rational but non-utilitarian purpose of punishment, requires that it be proportioned to the felt gravity of the crime. Thus, constitutional justice authorizes, even calls for, a higher penalty the graver the crime. One cannot demand that this constitutionally required escalation stop short of the death penalty unless one furnishes positive proof of its irrationality by showing injustice, i.e., disproportionality (to the felt gravity of the crime punished or to other punishments of similar crimes), as well as ineffectiveness, i.e., uselessness in reducing the crime rate. There is no proof of cruelty here in either sense.

"Unusual" is generally interpreted to mean either randomly capricious and therefore unconstitutional, or capricious in a biased, discriminatory way, so as particularly to burden specifiable groups, and therefore unconstitutional. (Random arbitrariness might violate the Eighth, biased artibrariness the Fourteenth Amendment, which promises "the equal protection of the laws.") Apart from the historical interpretation noted above (footnote 1), "unusual" seems to mean "unequal" then. The dictionary equivalent—"rare"—seems to be regarded as relevant only inasmuch as it implies "unequal." Indeed it is hard to see why rarity should be objectionable otherwise.

For the sake of argument, let me grant that either or both forms of capriciousness prevail[4] and that they are less tolerable with respect to the death penalty than with respect to milder penalties—which certainly are not meted out less capriciously. However prevalent, neither form of capriciousness would argue for abolishing the death penalty. Capriciousness is not inherent in that penalty, or in any penalty, but occurs in its distribution. Therefore, the remedy lies in changing the laws and procedures which distribute the penalty. It is the process of distribution which is capable of discriminating, not that which it distributes.

Unavoidable Capriciousness.   If capricious distribution places some convicts, or groups of convicts, at an unwarranted disadvantage,[5] can it be remedied enough to satisfy the Eighth and Fourteenth Amendments? . . .

Now, if possible without loss of other desiderata, accident and human capriciousness should be minimized. But, obviously, discretionary judgments cannot be avoided altogether. The Framers of the Constitution were certainly aware of the unavoidable elements of discretion which affect all human decisions, including those of police officers, of prosecutors, and of the courts. Because it always was unavoidable, discretion no more speaks against the constitutionality of the criminal justice system or of any of its penalties now than it did when the Constitution was written. . . .

Avoidable Capriciousness.   Capriciousness should be prevented by abolishing penalties capriciously distributed only in one case: when it is so unavoidable and so excessive that penalties are randomly distributed between the guilty and the innocent. When that is not the case, the abuses of discretion which lead to discrimination against particular groups of defendants or convicts certainly require correction, but not abolition of the penalty abused by maldistribution.

PRELIMINARY MORAL ISSUES

Justice and Equality.   Regardless of constitutional interpretation, the morality and legitimacy of the abolitionist argument from capriciousness, or discretion, or discrimination, would be more persuasive if it were alleged that those selectively executed are not guilty. But the argument merely maintains that some other guilty but more favored persons, or groups, escape the death penalty. This is hardly sufficient for letting anyone else found guilty escape the penalty. On the contrary, that some guilty persons or groups elude it argues for extending the death penalty to them. Surely "due process of law" is meant to do justice; and "the equal protection of the law" is meant to extend justice equally to all. Nor do I read the Constitution to command us to prefer equality to justice. When we clamor for "equal justice for all" it is justice which is to be equalized and extended, and which therefore is the prior desideratum, not to be forsaken and replaced by equality but rather to be extended.

Justice requires punishing the guilty—as many of the guilty as possible, even if only some can be punished—and sparing the innocent—as many of the innocent as possible, even if not all are spared. Morally, justice must always be preferred to equality. It would surely be wrong to treat everybody with equal injustice in preference to meting out justice at least to some. Justice then cannot ever permit sparing some guilty persons, or punishing some innocent ones, for the sake of equality—because othes have been unjustly spared or punished. In practice, penalties never could be applied if we insisted that they cannot be inflicted on any guilty person unless we can make sure that they are equally applied to all other guilty persons. Anyone familiar with law enforcement knows that punishments can be inflicted only on an unavoidably capricious, at best a random, selection of the guilty. I see no more merit in the attempt to persuade the courts to let all capital-crime defendants go free of capital punishment because some have wrongly escaped it than I see in an attempt to persuade the courts to let all burglars go because some have wrongly escaped imprisonment. . . .

The Essential Moral Question.   Is the death penalty morally just and/or useful? This is the essential moral, as distinguished from constitutional, question. Discrimination is irrelevant to this moral question. If the death penalty were distributed quite equally and uncapriciously and with superhuman perfection to all the guilty, but was morally unjust, it would remain unjust in each case. Contrariwise, if the death penalty is morally just, however discriminatorily applied to only some of the guilty, it does remain just in each case in which it is applied. Thus, if it were applied exclusively to guilty males, and never to guilty females, the death penalty, though unequally applied, would remain just. For justice consists in punishing the guilty and sparing the innocent, and its equal extension, though desirable, is not part of it. It is part of equality, not of justice (or injustice), which is what equality equalizes. The same consideration would apply if some benefit were distributed only to males but not equally to deserving females. The inequality would not argue against the benefit, or against distribution to deserving males, but rather for distribution to equally deserving females. Analogously, the nondistribution of the death penalty to guilty females would argue for applying it to them as well, and not against applying it to guilty males. . . .

However much each is desired, justice and equality are not identical. Equality before the law should be extended and enforced, then—but not at the expense of justice.

Maldistribution among the Guilty: A Sham Argument. Capriciousness, at any rate, is used as a sham argument against capital punishment by all abolitionists I have ever known. They would oppose the death penalty if it could be meted out without any discretion whatsoever. They would oppose the death penalty in a homogeneous country without racial discrimination. And they would oppose the death penalty if the incomes of those executed and of those spared were the same. Abolitionists oppose the death penalty, not its possible maldistribution. They should have the courage of their convictions.

Maldistribution between the Guilty and the Innocent: Another Sham Argument. What about persons executed in error? The objection here is not that some of the guilty get away, but that some of the innocent do not—a matter far more serious than discrimination among the guilty. Yet, when urged by abolitionists, this too is a sham argument, as are all distributional arguments. For abolitionists are opposed to the death penalty for the guilty as much as for the innocent. Hence, the question of guilt, if at all relevant to their position, cannot be decisive for them. Guilt is decisive only to those who urge the death penalty for the guilty. They must worry about distribution—part of the justice they seek.

Miscarriages of Justice. The execution of innocents believed guilty is a miscarriage of justice which must be opposed whenever detected. But such miscarriages of justice do not warrant abolition of the death penalty. Unless the moral drawbacks of an activity or practice, which include the possible death of innocent bystanders, outweigh the moral advantages, which include the innocent lives that might be saved by it, the activity is warranted. Most human activities—construction, manufacturing, automobile and air traffic, sports, not to speak of wars and revolutions—cause the death of some innocent bystanders. Nevertheless, if the advantages sufficiently outweigh the disadvantages, human activities, including those of the penal system with all its punishments, are morally justified. Consider now the advantages in question.

DETERRENCE

New Evidence.   Is there evidence for the usefulness of the death penalty in securing the life of the citizens? Researchers in the past found no statistical evidence for the effects sought: i.e., marginal deterrent effects, deterrent effects over and above those of alternative sanctions. However, in the last few years new and more sophisticated research has led, for instance, Professor Isaac Ehrlich to conclude that over the period 1933–1969, "An additional execution per year . . . may have resulted on the average in seven or eight fewer murders."[6] Other investigators have confirmed Ehrlich's tentative results. Not surprisingly, refutations have been attempted, and Professor Ehrlich has answered them. He has also published a new cross-sectional analysis of the data which confirms the conclusions of his original (time-series) study.[7] The matter will remain controversial for some time,[8] but two tentative conclusions can be drawn with some confidence by now. First, Ehrlich has shown that previous investigations, which did not find deterrent effects of the death penalty, suffer from fatal defects. Second, there is now some likelihood—much more than hitherto—of demonstrating marginal deterrent effects statistically.

The Choice.   Thus, with respect to deterrence, we must choose (1) to trade the certain shortening of the life of a convicted murderer for the survival of between seven and eight innocent victims whose future murder by others may be less likely if the convicted murderer is executed. Or (2) to trade the certain lengthening of the life of a convicted murderer for the possible loss of the lives of between seven and eight innocent victims, who may be more likely to be murdered by others because of our failure to execute the convicted murderer.[9]

If we were certain that executions have a zero marginal effect, they could not be justified in deterrent terms. But even the pre-Ehrlich investigations never did demonstrate this. They merely found that an above-zero effect cannot be demonstrated statistically. While we do not know at present the degree of confidence with which we can assign an above-zero marginal deterrent effect to executions, we can be more confident than in the past. It seems morally indefensible to let convicted murderers survive at the probable—even at the merely possible—expense of the lives of innocent victims who might have been spared had the murderers been executed.

Non-deterrence as a Sham Argument.   Most of the studies purporting to show that capital punishment produces no added deterrence, or that it cannot be shown to do so, were made by abolitionists, such as Professor Thorsten Sellin. They were used to show the futility of the death penalty. Relying on their intuition as well as on these studies, many abolitionists still are convinced that the death penalty is no more deterrent than life imprisonment. And they sincerely believe that the failure of capital punishment to produce additional deterrence argues for abolishing it. However, the more passionate and committed abolitionists use the asserted ineffectiveness of the death penalty as a deterrent as a sham argument—just as they used alleged capriciousness and maldistribution in application. They use the argument for debating purposes—but actually would abolish the death penalty even if it were an effective deterrent, just as they would abolish the death penalty if it were neither discriminatorily nor otherwise maldistributed.

Professors Charles Black (Yale Law School) and Hugo Adam Bedau (Tufts, Philosophy) are both well known for their public commitment to abolition of the death penalty, attested to by numerous writings. At a symposium held on October 15, 1977, at the Arizona State University at Tempe, Arizona, they were asked to entertain the hypothesis—whether or not contrary to fact—that the death penalty is strongly deterrent over and above alternative penalties: Would they favor abolition in the face of conclusive proof of a strong deterrent effect over and above that of alternative penalties? Both gentlemen answered affirmatively. They were asked whether they would still abolish the death penalty if they knew that abolition (and replacement by life imprisonment) would increase the homicide rate by 10 percent, 20 percent, 50 percent, 100 percent, or 1,000 percent. Both gentlemen continued to answer affirmatively.

I am forced to conclude that Professors Black and Bedau think the lives of convicted murderers (however small their number) are more worth preserving than the lives of an indefinite number of innocent victims (however great their number). Or, the principle of abolition is more important to them than the lives of any number of innocent murder victims who would be spared if convicted murderers were executed.

I have had occasion subsequently to ask former Attorney General Ramsey Clark the same questions; he answered as Professors Black and Bedau did, stressing that nothing could persuade him to favor the penalty—however deterrent it might be. (Mr. Clark has kindly permitted me to quote his view here.)

Now, Professors Black and Bedau and Mr. Clark do *not* believe that the death penalty adds deterrence. They do not believe therefore—regardless of the evidence—that abolition would cause an increase in the homicide rate. But the question they were asked, and which—after some dodging—they answered forthrightly, had nothing to do with the acceptance or rejection of the deterrent effect of the death penalty. It was a hypothetical question: If it were deterrent, would you still abolish the death penalty? Would you still abolish it if it were very deterrent, so that abolition would lead to a quantum jump in the murder rate? They answered affirmatively.

These totally committed abolitionists, then, are not interested in deterrence. They claim that the death penalty does not add to deterrence only as a sham argument. Actually, whether or not the death penalty deters is, to them, irrelevant. The intransigence of these committed humanitarians is puzzling as well as inhumane. Passionate ideological commitments have been known to have such effects. These otherwise kind and occasionally reasonable persons do not want to see murderers executed ever—however many innocent lives can be saved thereby. *Fiat injustitia, pereat humanitas....*

The Threat of Death Needed in Special Circumstances.   Another common sense observation. Without the death penalty, we necessarily confer immunity on just those persons most likely to be in need of deterrent threats: thus, prisoners serving life sentences can kill fellow prisoners or guards with impunity. Prison wardens are unlikely to be able to prevent violence in prisons as long as they give humane treatment to inmates and have no serious threats of additional punishment available for the murderers among them who are already serving life sentences. I cannot see the moral or utilitarian reasons for giving permanent immunity to homicidal life prisoners, thereby endangering the other prisoners and the guards, in effect preferring the life prisoners to their victims who *could* be punished if they murdered.

Outside prison an offender who expects a life sentence for his offense may murder his victim, or witnesses, or the arresting officer, to improve his chances of escaping. He could not be threatened with an additional penalty for his additional crime—an open invitation. Only the death penalty could deter in such cases.[10] If there is but a possibility that it will, we should retain it. But I believe there is *probability* that the threat of the death penalty will deter.

Reserved for the Worst Crimes.   However, effective deterrence requires that the threat of the ultimate penalty be reserved for the worst crime from which the offender may be deterred by that threat. Hence, the extreme punishment should not be prescribed when the offender, because already threatened by it, might feel he can add further crimes with impunity. Thus, rape, or kidnapping, should not incur the death penalty, while killing the victim of either crime should.[11] (The death penalty for rape may actually function as an incentive to murder the victim/witness.) This may not stop an Eichmann after his first murder; but it will stop most people before. To be sure, an offender not deterred from murdering one victim by the threat of execution is unlikely to be deterred from additional murders by further threats. The range of effective punishments is not infinite; on the contrary, it is necessarily more restricted than the range of possible crimes. Some offenders cannot be deterred by any threat. But most people can be; and most people respond to the size of the threat addressed to them. Since death is the ultimate penalty—the greatest threat available—it must be reserved for the ultimate crime even though it cannot always prevent it.

SOME POPULAR ARGUMENTS

Consider now some popular arguments against capital punishment.

Barbarization.   According to Beccaria, with the death penalty the "laws which punish homicide . . . themselves commit it," thus giving "an example of barbarity." Those who speak of "legalized murder" use an oxymoronic phrase to echo this allegation. However, punishments—fines, incarcerations, or executions— although often physically identical to the crimes punished, are neither crimes, nor their moral equivalent. The difference between crimes and lawful acts, including punishments, is not physical, but legal: crimes differ from other acts by being unlawful. Driving a stolen care is a crime, though not physically distinguishable from driving a car lawfully owned. Unlawful imprisonment and kidnapping need not differ physically from the lawful arrest and incarceration used to punish unlawful imprisonment and kidnapping. Finally, whether a lawful punishment gives an "example of barbarity" depends on how the moral difference between crime and punishment is perceived. To suggest that its physical quality, *ipso facto,* morally disqualifies the punishment is to assume what is to be shown.

It is quite possible that all displays of violence, criminal or punitive, influence people to engage in unlawful imitations. This seems one good reason not to have public executions. But it does not argue against executions. Objections to displaying on TV the process of violently subduing a resistant offender do not argue against actually subduing him.[12] Arguments against the public display of vivisections, or of the effects of painful medications, do not argue against either. Arguments against public executions, then, do not argue against executions.[13] The deterrent effect of punishments depends on their being known. But it does not depend on punishments being carried out publicly. The threat of imprisonment deters, but incarcerated persons are not on public display.

Crimes of Passion.   Abolitionists often maintain that most capital crimes are "acts of passion" which (a) could not be restrained by the threat of the death penalty, and (b) do not deserve it morally even if other crimes might. It is not clear to me why a crime motivated by, say, sexual passion is morally less deserving of punishment than one motivated by passion for money. Is the sexual passion morally more respectable than others? or more gripping? or just more popular? Generally, is violence in personal conflicts morally more excusable than violence among people who do not know each other? A precarious case might be made for such a view, but I shall not attempt to make it.

Perhaps it is true, however, that many murders are irrational "acts of passion" which cannot be deterred by the threat of the death penalty. Either for this reason or because "crimes of passion" are thought less blameworthy than other homicides, most "crimes of passion" are not punishable by death now.[14]

But if most murders are irrational acts, it would therefore seem that the traditional threat of the death penalty has succeeded in deterring most rational people, or most people when rational, from committing murder, and the fear of the penalty continues to deter all but those who are so irrational that they cannot be deterred by any threat. Hardly a reason for abolishing the death penalty. Indeed, that capital crimes are committed mostly by irrational persons and only by some rational ones would suggest that more rational persons might commit these crimes if the penalty were lower. This hardly argues against capital punishment. Else we would have to abolish penalties whenever they succeed in deterring people. Yet abolitionists urge that capital punishment be abolished because capital crimes are most often committed by the irrational— as though deterring the rational is not quite enough....

FINAL MORAL CONSIDERATIONS

The Motive of Revenge.   One objection to capital punishment is that it gratifies the desire for revenge, regarded as morally unworthy. The Bible has the Lord declare: "Vengeance is mine" (Romans 12:19). He thus legitimized vengeance and reserved it to Himself, probably because it would otherwise be disruptive. But He did not deprecate the desire for vengeance.

Indeed Romans 12:19 barely precedes Romans 13:4, which tells us that the ruler "beareth not the sword in vain: for he is the minister of God, a revenger to execute wrath upon him that doeth evil." It is not unreasonable to interpret Romans 12:19 to suggest that revenge is to be delegated by the injured to the ruler, "the minister of God" who is "to execute wrath." The Bible also enjoins, "The murderer shall surely be put to death" (Numbers 35:16–18), recognizing that the death penalty can be warranted—whatever the motive. Religious tradition certainly suggests no less. However, since religion expects justice and vengeance in the world to come, the faithful may dispense with either in this world, and with any particular penalties—though they seldom have. But a secular state must do justice here and now—it cannot assume that another power, elsewhere, will do justice where its courts did not.

The motives for the death penalty may indeed include vengeance. Vengeance is a compensatory and psychologically reparatory satisfaction for an injured party, group, or society. I do not see wherein it is morally blameworthy. When regulated and controlled by law, vengeance is also socially useful: legal vengeance solidifies social solidarity against lawbreakers and probably is the only alternative to the disruptive private revenge of those who feel harmed. Abolitionists want to promise murderers that what they did to their victims will never be done to them. That promise strikes most people as psychologically incongruous. It is.

At any rate, vengeance is irrelevant to the function of the death penalty. It must be justified independently, by its purpose, whatever the motive. An action, a rule, or a penalty cannot be justified or discredited by the motive for it. No rule should be discarded or regarded as morally wrong (or right) because of the motive of those who support it. Actions, rules, or penalties are justified not by the motives of supporters but by their purpose and by their effectiveness in achieving it without excessively impairing other objectives.[15] Capital punishment is warranted if it achieves its purpose—doing justice and deterring crime—regardless of whether or not it is motivated by vengeful feelings.

Characteristics.   Before turning to its purely moral aspects, we must examine some specific characteristics of capital punishment. It is feared above all punishments because (1) it is not merely irreversible, as most other penalties are, but also irrevocable; (2) it hastens an event which, unlike pain, deprivation, or injury, is unique in every life and never has been reported on by anyone. Death is an experience that cannot actually be experienced and that ends all experience. Actually, being dead is no different from not being born—a (non) experience we all had before being born. But death is not so perceived. The process of dying, a quite different matter, is confused with it. In turn, dying is feared mainly because death is anticipated—even though death is feared because it is confused with dying. At any rate, the fear of death is universal and is often attached to the penalty that hastens it—as though without that penalty death would not come. (3) However, the penalty is feared for another reason as well. When death is imposed as a deliberate punishment by one's fellow men, it signifies a complete severing of human solidarity. The convict is explicitly and dramatically rejected by his fellow humans, found unworthy of their society, of sharing life with them. The rejection exacerbates the natural separation anxiety of those who expect imminent death, the fear of final annihilation. Inchoate as these characteristics are in most minds, the specific deterrent effect of executions depends on them and the moral justification of the death penalty, and above and beyond the deterrent effect, does no less. . . .

The Value of Life.   If there is nothing for the sake of which one may be put to death, can there ever be anything worth risking one's life for? If there is nothing worth dying for, is there any moral value worth living for? Is a life that cannot be transcended by—and given up, or taken, for—anything beyond itself more valuable than one that can be transcended? Can it be that existence, life itself, is the highest moral value, never to be given up, or taken, for the sake of anything? And, psychologically, does a social value system in which life itself, however it is lived, becomes the highest of goods enhance the value of human life or cheapen it? I shall content myself here with raising these questions.[16]

Homo Homini Res Sacra.   "The life of each man should be sacred to each other man," the ancients tell us. They unflinchingly executed murderers.[17] They realized it is not enough to proclaim the sacredness and inviolability of human life. It must be secured as well, by threatening with the loss of their own life those who violate what has been proclaimed as inviolable—the right of innocents to live. Else the inviolability of human life is neither credibly proclaimed nor actually protected. No society can profess that the lives of its members are secure if those who did not allow innocent others to continue living are themselves allowed to continue living—at the expense of the community. To punish a murderer by incarcerating him as one does a pickpocket cannot but cheapen human life. Murder differs in quality from other crimes and deserves, therefore, a punishment that differs in quality from other punishments. There is a discontinuity. It should be underlined, not blurred.

If it were shown that no punishment is more deterrent than a trivial fine, capital punishment for murder would remain just, even if not useful. For murder is not a trifling offense. Punishment must be proportioned to the gravity of the crime, if only to denounce it and to vindicate the importance of the norm violated. Wherefore all penal systems proportion punishments to crimes. The worse the crime the higher the penalty deserved. Why not then the highest penalty—death—for the worst crime—wanton murder? Those rejecting the death penalty have the burden of showing that no crime ever deserves capital punishment[18]—a burden which they have not so far been willing to bear.

Abolitionists insist that we all have an imprescriptible right to live to our natural term: if the innocent victim had a right to live, so does the murderer. That takes egalitarianism too far for my taste. The crime sets victim and murderer apart; if the victim did, the murderer does not deserve to live. If innocents are to be secure in their lives murderers cannot be. The thought that murderers are to be given as much right to live as their victims oppresses me. So does the thought that a Stalin, a Hitler, an Idi Amin should have as much right to live as their victims did. . . .

One may object that the death penalty either cannot actually achieve the vindication of the violated norms, or is not needed for it. If so, failure to inflict death on the criminal does not belittle the crime, or imply that the life of the criminal is of greater importance than the moral value he violated or the harm he did to his victim. But it is not so. In all societies the degree of social disapproval of wicked acts is expressed in the degree of punishment threatened.[19] Thus, punishments both proclaim and enforce social values according to the importance given to them. There is no other way for society to affirm its values. There is no other effective way of denouncing socially disapproved acts. To refuse to punish any crime with death is to suggest that the negative value of a crime can never exceed the positive value of the life of the person who committed it. I find that proposition quite implausible.

SUGGESTIONS FOR FURTHER READING FOR PART 4

Chapter 8: Immigration: Can We Have Open Borders?

Barbour, Scott, ed. *Immigration Policy.* San Diego: Greenhaven Press, 1995.

Brimelow, Peter. *Alien Nation: Common Sense About America's Immigration Disaster.* New York: Random House, 1995.

Chavez, Leo R. *Shadowed Lives: Undocumented Immigrants in American Society.* Orlando: Harcourt, Brace, Jovanovich, 1992.

Cogswell, James A. *No Place Left Called Home.* N.Y.: Friendship Press, 1983.

Fox, Robert W. and Ira H. Mehlman. *Crowding Out the Future: World Population Growth, U.S. Immigration, and Pressures on Natural Resources.* Washington, DC: Federation for American Immigration Reform, 1992.

Mieth, Dietmar, and Lisa Sowle Cahill, eds. *Migrants and Refugees.* Maryknoll, NY: Orbis Books, 1993.

National Conference of Catholic Bishops, The. *Together a New People: Pastoral Statement of Migrants and Refugees.* Washington, D.C.: United States Catholic Conference, 1987.

Simon, Julian L. *The Economic Consequences of Immigration.* Cambridge: Blackwell, 1989.

Wattenberg, Ben J. *The First Universal Nation.* New York: Maxwell Macmillan International, 1991.

Wilbanks, Dana. *Re-Creating America: The Ethics of U.S. Immigration and Refugee Policy in a Christian Perspective.* Nashville: Abingdon Press, 1996.

Chapter 9: Caring for the Environment

Austin, Richard C. *Reclaiming America: Restoring Nature to Culture.* Abingdon, VA: Creekside Press, 1991.

Berry, Thomas. *Befriending the Earth: A Theology of Reconciliation between Humans and the Earth.* Mystic, CT: Twenty-third Publications, 1991.

Devall, Bill, and George Sessions. *Deep Ecology: Living as if Nature Mattered.* Salt Lake City: Gibbs Smith Publishing, 1985.

Ehrlich, Paul R., and Anne H. Ehrlich. *The Population Explosion.* New York: Simon and Schuster, 1990.

Hessel, Dieter T., ed. *After Nature's Revolt: Eco-Justice and Theology.* Minneapolis: Augsburg Fortress, 1992.

Jung, L. Shannon. *We Are Home: A Spirituality of the Environment.* Mahwah, NJ: Paulist Press, 1993.

Kinsley, David. *Ecology and Religion: Ecological Spirituality in Cross-Cultural Perspective.* Englewood Cliffs: Prentice-Hall, 1995.

McDaniel, Jay. *Of God and Pelicans.* Louisville, KY: Westminster/John Knox Press, 1989.

Nash, James A. *Loving Nature: Ecological Integrity and Christian Responsibility.* Nashville: Abingdon Press, 1991.

Pinches, Charles, and Jay McDaniel, eds. *Good News for Animals?: Christian Approaches to Animal Well-Being.* Maryknoll, NY: Orbis Books, 1993.

Robb, Carol, and Carl Casebolt, eds. *Covenant for a New Creation: Ethics, Religion and Public Policy.* Maryknoll, NY: Orbis Books, 1991.

Santmire, H. Paul. *The Travail of Nature.* Philadelphia: Fortress Press, 1988.

Chapter 10: Violence and War in a Post-Communist World

Allen, Joseph L. *War: A Primer for Christians.* Nashville: Abingdon Press, 1991.

Bell, Linda A. *Rethinking Ethics In the Midst of Violence: A Feminist Approach to Freedom.* Lanham, MD: Rowman & Littlefield, 1993.

Cahill, Lisa Sowle. *Love Your Enemies: Discipleship, Pacifism, and Just War Theory.* Minneapolis: Fortress Press, 1994.

Fox, Thomas C. *Iraq: Military Victory, Moral Defeat.* Kansas City: Sheed and Ward, 1991.

Geyer, Alan, and Barbara Green. *Lines in the Sand: Justice and the Gulf War.* Louisville, KY: Westminster/John Knox Press, 1992.

Gwyn, Douglas, George Hunsinger, Eugene F. Roop, and John Howard Yoder. *A Declaration on Peace.* Scottdale, PA: Herald Press, 1990.

Johnson, James Turner. *The Quest for Peace.* Princeton: Princeton University Press, 1987.

Mayhew, Peter. *A Theology of Force and Violence.* Philadelphia: Trinity Press International, 1989.

Miller, Richard B. *Interpretations of Conflict: Ethics, Pacifism, and the Just-War Tradition.* Chicago: University of Chicago Press, 1991.

Nardin, Terry, ed. *The Ethics of War and Peace: Religious and Secular Perspectives.* Princeton: Princeton University Press, 1996.

Shriver Jr., Donald W. *An Ethic for Enemies: Forgiveness in Politics.* NY: Oxford University Press, 1995.

Simon, Arthur. *Harvesting Peace: The Arms Race and Human Need.* Kansas City: Sheed and Ward, 1990.

Wink, Walter. *Engaging the Powers: Discernment and Resistance in a World of Domination.* Minneapolis: Fortress Press, 1992.

Chapter 11: The Death Penalty

Baird, Robert M., and Stuart E. Rosenbaum, eds. *Punishment and the Death Penalty: The Current Debate.* Buffalo, NY: Prometheus Books, 1995.

Bedau, Hugo Adam, ed. *The Death Penalty in America.* 3rd ed. New York: Oxford University Press, 1982.

Endres, Michael E. *The Morality of Capital Punishment: Equal Justice Under the Law?* Mystic, CT: Twenty-third Publications, 1985.

House, H. Wayne, and John Howard Yoder. *The Death Penalty Debate: Two Opposing Views of Capital Punishment.* Irving, TX: Word Publishing, 1991.

Prejean, Helen. *Dead Man Walking: An Eyewitness Account of the Death Penalty in the United States.* New York: Random House, 1993.

Redekop, Vernon W. *A Life for a Life? The Death Penalty on Trial.* Scottdale, PA: Herald Press, 1990.

Simmons, A. John, Marshall Cohen, Joshua Cohen, and Charles R. Beitz, eds. *Punishment: A Philosophy and Public Affairs Reader.* Princeton: Princeton University Press, 1995.

Van den Haag, Ernest, and John Phillips Conrad. *The Death Penalty: A Debate.* New York: Plenum Press, 1983.

Van Ness, Daniel W. *Crime and Its Victims.* Downers Grove, IL: InterVarsity Press, 1985.

Zehr, Howard. *Changing Lenses: A New Focus for Crime and Justice.* Scottdale, PA: Herald Press, 1990.

PART 5

The Christian and Economic Issues

Chapter 12

CHRISTIANITY AND CONSUMER LIFESTYLES

The place where many Christians experience economic issues is at the shopping mall. In the United States the mall has come to symbolize a cornucopia of material abundance and choice. In a very similar way, the grocery store, with its variety of fruits and vegetables in the dead of winter and its array of 14 different types of shampoo, represents a similar array of abundance and choice. Even visitors from other affluent countries report that they are most astounded by our grocery stores.

Some would say that Christianity's primary competitor as the religion of choice in the United States is consumption. They would claim that our values are shaped at least as much by consumer choice as they are by any formal, organized religion. Consumption has an organized structure with many of the trappings of religion—rituals, values, beliefs, and even high priests! Thus the consumer lifestyle functions as a religion, shaping our values and beliefs in a very powerful way.

It is also true that many of the moral issues discussed in other chapters of this book come together around the issue of lifestyle. Clearly there is an environmental impact to the level of our consumption; population theorists would say that the real threat to the carrying capacity of the planet comes not from the number of human beings, but from their consumption levels. Lifestyles are also tied into the economic system that has evolved in our country; in some ways, it is difficult to disentangle system from lifestyle. Even the issue of immigration has become complex because the affluent, consumptive lifestyle we enjoy is attractive to many people. Advertising and other media generate demand for many goods; the reach of these two is clearly global in its impact. Other issues in which consumption plays a role are sexuality, racism, and global justice.

Two ways of thinking about moral issues are joined in this chapter: the ethics of character and the ethics of moral decision-making. Because men and women are formed in an affluent society in the United States and are educated in consumer desires and values, their characters are shaped by the values of consumption in a way that is not subject to conscious choice. So James Nash writes that the reasons behind overconsumption are not "always or even usually morally contemptible; they are often merely mournful, revealing the hollowness and stress of many affluent lives. They reflect the quest for self-esteem, social acceptance, personal satisfaction, and ultimate meaning, while being culturally conditioned to follow paths that frustrate these hopes." (*Annual of the Society of Christian Ethics* 1995, p. 142) Nash is saying that Americans have been socialized into consumption and our characters have been shaped by that practice.

Another way of thinking about ethics pays attention more to rational or conscious decision-making than to the formation of our character traits or virtues. Pursuing a lifestyle of moderation in which one chooses the middle way between overconsumption and asceticism is a conception of ethics as old as Aristotle. Making conscious decisions not to own two or three cars, to raise some of one's own food, and not having to buy the top-of-the-line shoes or upscale clothes are all decisions about consumption. Perhaps the best example of choosing a simple lifestyle is the Amish way, but there are many less holistic degrees of simplicity that people are opting for today. In this section we see examples of both models of ethics—character and rational choice—because lifestyles into which we have been unconsciously formed also present us with issues requiring conscious choice for Christians.

Robert Roberts presents a clear example of the ethics of character. The subtitle of his article, "Greed and the Malling of our Souls," suggests from a conservative Christian perspective the dangers of a consumptive lifestyle. He suggests that greed is a serious vice for Christians even if it is commonly considered either trivial or a prime motive behind capitalism. One of greed's cousins is covetousness, which is prohibited by the Tenth Commandment. Roberts presents the antidote to these vices of exaggerated attachment to possessions in the virtue of generosity and even offers ways of becoming more generous. There is a hint in Roberts's article that the lifestyle of consumption is self-defeating, that it is based on disrespect for the fullness of ourselves and the purposes for which we were created. This article has the additional asset of being a good example of "divine command" ethics and clearly based on Biblical warrants.

While Roberts focuses on the effect of consumption on individual character, the next essay considers the social implications of consumption and economic growth. Allen Hammond treads a middle course between the extremes of Malthusian alarmism, which foresees the end of resources, and the Cornucopian position, which trusts in human ingenuity to surmount all obstacles. Hammond focuses especially on environmental impacts and sees few "limits to growth" in the area of nonrenewable resources. He does warn that unless we use our renewable resources responsibly they could become nonrenewable. The appeal here is that if human beings will change our consumption patterns, there is no reason to think that we cannot enjoy economic growth, consumption, and environmental health. Much depends on human beings' willingness to act responsibly and reasonably; Hammond thinks that is possible.

In the third essay Jay McDaniel poses the question "Can Americans and others who belong to the rich world morally justify living in a way, or consuming at a rate, which it would be impossible for the rest of the world to enjoy?" In contrast to Hammond, McDaniel thinks such patterns cannot continue and asks what changes of attitude and lifestyle are required. The selection poses an alternative, relational understanding of reality that presents wealth as a richness of experience living in harmony with all creatures and God. True Christian affluence or wealth mirrors the relational wealth of God's own life. This model of wealth as the experiential well-being of an individual-in-community, he further claims, is in fact what genuine human well-being or happiness is. This is what God created human beings to be.

This issue of consumer lifestyles is one with which every American can identify in some way. It is not one to be ignored, since we all have to consume to survive; the question is that of overconsumption. Clearly God intended the material well-being of all creatures; where does that cross the line into a materialism, which is ultimately at odds with human happiness?

Just a Little Bit More: Greed and the Malling of Our Souls
Robert C. Roberts

If you go to your psychotherapist complaining of depression, anxiety, a sense of emptiness in your life, a collapsing marriage, uncontrollable children, headaches, and ulcers, one thing he probably won't say to you is: "Herb, you're greedy. You need to change your whole attitude about money, turn your mind to healthier objects. The therapy I would suggest, for starters, is that you give away something that is of great value to you, and that you volunteer for a couple of weeks at the Salvation Army soup kitchen."

Our culture is little inclined to see greed as a major source of human troubles. Rather, it is seen as what makes the world go 'round. It's not a vice but a virtue.

Still, we have the apostle's words, "The love of money is the root of all evils" (1 Tim. 6:10). As a form of idolatry (Col. 3:5), the love of "goods" cancels out faith in God, since no one can have two absolute masters (Luke 16:13). Greed can create the anxiety, depression, and loss of meaning that often comes

"Just a Little Bit More: Greed and the Malling of Our Souls," Robert C. Roberts, *Christianity Today,* April 8, 1996, pp. 29–33. Reprinted with permission of Robert C. Roberts.

in middle age after a "successful" life of acquiring the "goods" of this world. Greed tempts us to other forms of corruption, such as lying, swindling, cheating clients, and cheating the government.

The psalmist says the righteous will hold in contempt those who trust in abundant riches (Ps. 52:6–7). A camel slips more easily through the eye of a needle than a rich person into the kingdom (Luke 18:25). To a wealthy man who has kept the law but still seeks salvation, Jesus says he must give his riches to the poor and follow him (Luke 18:18–22). A rich man who builds bigger barns so that he can use his agricultural fortune to secure himself is called a fool (Luke 12:15–21).

James puts the point more strongly than any: "Come now, you rich people, weep and wail for the miseries that are coming to you. Your riches have rotted, and your clothes are moth-eaten. Your gold and silver have rusted, and their rust will be evidence against you, and it will eat your flesh like fire. You have laid up treasure for the last days" (5:1–3; the following Bible references are all from the NRSV). No wonder rich people who believe in the authority of Scripture are so alarmed!

WHY WE GO TO MALLS

Why are shopping malls so popular? Why are they a place not just to make purchases, but to be entertained without even buying anything?

One answer is greed. Greedy people seek out stimulations that arouse and titillate their acquisition fantasies, just as lustful people seek out stimulations that arouse them sexually. If lust finds a certain frustrated gratification in perusing the pages of *Playboy* or *Playgirl*, greed finds similar satisfaction in ogling stylish clothes, computers, furniture, and kitchen appliances.

Greed and stinginess are twin vices concerned with the taking and giving of things of value. The greedy take too much, the stingy give too little. Greed is not just the behavior of taking too much and giving too little. The heart of greed is certain attitudes, thoughts, and emotions concerning things of value.

The importance of attitudes can be brought out by thinking of one of greed's cousins, covetousness. Covetousness is not just wanting lots and lots of something, but wanting, in an improper way, something that belongs to another. Imagine a farmer who covets his neighbor's rich land. For 20 years his mind swells on it, turning over schemes to get it for himself, but none of his plans ever comes to the point of execution, and finally he dies. Even though he never took a single thing unlawfully from this neighbor, his coveting corrupted his spiritual attitude toward his neighbor, preventing love and friendship, and it filled his heart and mind with this futile and unworthy wish.

It is not vicious to want to acquire things. Having possessions is as natural as eating and sexual relations. It would be a sign of ill health if we took no interest at all in these things. Desire is not by itself vicious; it becomes vicious when disordered, when the desire for food or sex becomes obsessive, for example, or directed toward improper gustatory or sexual objects.

A sure sign of greed (the disordered desire for wealth) is that your wanting things always outruns your having them. Greed is the successful business person who tells you, without blinking, that he is on the brink of poverty. It is the middle-class couple who say they cannot afford to have another child. It is "upward mobility," the climb that ends not in satisfaction and peace, but in exhaustion, disappointment, and emptiness. "Sweet is the sleep of [poor] laborers, whether they eat little or much; but the surfeit of the rich will not let them sleep," says the Preacher (Eccles. 5:12). Greed in its advanced stages will not let us rest content.

Jesus connects greed with anxiety: "Be on your guard against all kinds of greed.... Do not worry about your life ..." (Luke 12:13-34). Anxiety about our "security" drives us into a pattern of acquiring more and more, but the acquiring of more also leads to anxiety: the more we have to protect, and the higher the "standard of living" we must maintain, the more fragile we become, the more vulnerable to changes of circumstance.

THE ANTIDOTE

If greed, covetousness, and stinginess are the vices of exaggerated attachment to possessions, generosity is the proper disposition. The generous person is loosely attached to goods and wealth and more deeply and intensely attached to God and his kingdom. Stinginess is not just a pattern of bad behavior, but a bad attitude, a bad state of the heart. Generosity, likewise, is not just giving away one's goods, but having a certain mind about them. The generous person acquires goods in a different spirit from the greedy, and unlike the stingy, she does not cling to the ones she has. She sees her possessions differently, because she sees both herself and other people in a different light.

When Paul wrote to the Corinthians about their contribution to the church in Jerusalem (2 Cor. 8-9), he told them to give not reluctantly, or under compulsion, but gladly. Paul saw that the Corinthians might give lavishly but still not be generous. They might give to avoid embarrassment when Paul visited them, or in a spirit of competition with other givers. But God is unimpressed with such giving, "for God loves a cheerful giver" (9:7).

What is this gladness that goes with generosity? Not just any cheerfulness will count: God takes no special joy in the toothpaste manufacturer who cheerfully gives out lots of free samples in hopes of future profits. The generous person is glad that her beneficiary is being benefited, and glad for the beneficiary's sake. It pleases her that the gift will help the recipient out of some trouble, or will give him some pleasure, or be useful to him in some way. She has the good of the other in view.

The generosity of a believer is a response to Jesus Christ and never merely a "human" virtue. The gospel is about the generosity of God: God owed us nothing, and yet, out of sheer enthusiasm for us and desire for our well-being, God sent Jesus Christ to dwell among us, to reconcile us to God, and to usher us into God's fellowship. Through the influence of this welcoming word, our minds are renewed, and we come to see all things in a new light: God is our benefactor, our neighbor is a precious brother or sister, and our possessions are good, in large part, because they are things with which we can serve God and bless our neighbor. When the Holy Spirit has written this word of grace on our hearts, we become generous.

The generous person is not indifferent to possessions. He does not say, like the Stoic, that possessions are of no real importance. But they do not have the same importance for him as they have for the greedy person.

Consider someone's attitude toward a car. To the stingy person, the importance of the car is strongly tied up with its being her possession at her disposal. She will not be inclined to let other people use it, unless they pay her for its use. For the generous person, the value of the car is not nearly so tied up with its being his. So when it would be helpful or pleasurable for someone else to use his car, he is glad to have it so used. He takes pleasure in someone's getting some good out of it, even if loaning it out is inconvenient.

The generous person also has a distinctive attitude toward the recipients of her generosity. She sees them as fellow travelers on life's way, or as brothers and sisters in the Lord. She has a sense of being in some sort of community with these people with whom she shares. They are not alien to her, but united with her in bonds that make their pleasures, convenience, and safety important to her.

Christians do not have a monopoly on generosity, but generosity is very characteristic of the Christian who has taken the gospel to heart. At the center of that rebirth of self is the perception that fellow Christians are brothers and sisters in the Lord, and that even the non-Christian and the enemy are our neighbors whom God loves with the same concern with which he loves us.

The idea of a "Christian" who sees some other humans as aliens, whose well-being is of no interest to him, is a contradiction. And the idea of a greedy Christian does not make sense, though, of course, many people are struggling to be Christians, and part of their struggle is the battle against their own greed.

There is a difference in self-concept between the greedy and the generous person. The self-concept of a greedy person is very tied up with her possessions, which make her feel secure. Such a person sees herself as weak or vulnerable to the extent that she is short of possessions, and strong and secure if she has them.

The generous person, by contrast, does not think of herself as built up or secured by what she possesses. Her security and her substance come from elsewhere, so she can give away her material goods and do so cheerfully. Again, Christianity has no monopoly on generosity, for there are a number of different ways the self can be conceived as secure and substantial independent of possessions. But the truly converted Christian thinks of herself as a spirit, secured and made real by her relationships in a world of spirits. She trusts God for her security and is made real by God's loving intention. And she finds her substance as a person, her integrity and solidity, precisely in those acts of sharing her possessions, time, attention, and concern that most express the Christian virtue of generosity.

It is in giving to others that we find ourselves; it is in letting go of the ordinary securities of life that we find our true security. . . .

GENEROSITY 101

How can we become more generous and less greedy? Jesus said: "The good person out of the good treasure of the heart produces good, and the evil person out of evil treasure produces evil" (Luke 6:45).

The influence of thinking on greed was argued in a study conducted by Cornell University researchers. In a survey of U.S. college professors, they found that, despite having relatively high salaries, economists, most of whom assume that self-interest drives behavior, were more than twice as likely as those in other disciplines to contribute no money to private charities. In responding to public television appeals, their median (and most common) gift was zilch. In laboratory monetary games, students behave more selfishly after taking economics courses. These researchers concluded that economists need an alternative model of human behavior, one that teaches the benefits of cooperation. (The study, conducted by economist Robert Frank and psychologists Thomas Gilovich and Dennis Regan, is entitled, "Is the Self-interest Model a Corrupting Force?" [ms., Cornell University, 1991]).

If we can get greedier by digesting the selfish ideology of some economic theories, we might become more generous by taking to heart the Word of God: "For those who live according to the flesh set their minds on the things of the flesh, but those who live according to the Spirit set their minds on the things of the Spirit" (Rom. 8:5).

Christians have an "alternative model of human behavior" and of the universe; setting our minds on certain aspects of that "model" is a discipline by which to root out greed. In trying to become more generous, Christians are trying to change not just their behavior, but their minds. What are some things we might do to cultivate a Christianly generous mind?

First, we might think about possessions. What is a house, a car, a wardrobe, a library, a television set, a well-equipped kitchen, a computer? As useful and pleasant as they may be, are they what life is about? Would life be desperate without them? Do they improve a life that is not otherwise in good order? In the Christian "model," such things are good but optional. Life without them would be different—more difficult in some ways, but also perhaps more deeply meaningful.

Mission workers in primitive circumstances attest that the lack of possessions and conveniences is not all loss; it is also gain. They can identify with Paul when he said, "I know what it is to have little, and I know what it is to have plenty. In any and all circumstances I have learned the secret of being well-fed and of going hungry, of having plenty and of being in need" (Phil. 4:12). His secret seemed to be his life in God, which relativized these goods, making them good but not necessary.

Jesus thought it easier for a camel to get through the needle's eye than for the rich to enter the kingdom of God; God's reign is foreign to those who think their possessions are necessary. So Jesus prescribed radical therapy for the rich ruler: that he give away his possessions. Nothing short of experiencing the absence of possessions could make him see their true significance.

We can try setting our minds on the biblical concept of possessions by contemplating people whose lives are happy without them. But in all likelihood we will not put material possessions in proper perspective until we start giving them away. Try this exercise. Look among your possessions for something that is quite meaningful or useful to you, something you're inclined to think you can't do without and that you can't easily replace. Then give it away. The experience that will follow may help you to see possessions in gospel terms.

Second, try thinking about others' needs in connection with what you have. Imagine how some of your money would help a school in the Sudan, or some of your time would bless the elderly man down the street. Put yourself in the shoes of those who could profit from these goods; imagine the convenience or opportunity or comfort they may mean to these people.

Thinking changes us most when it's put into action, when we deliberately "go out of our way" to do something for someone else. Doctors can volunteer for short-term assignments in Third World clinics; teachers can give special attention, after hours, to certain students; husbands can take an afternoon off from "their" work to prepare a festive dinner for the family.

I am such a stingy person that taking some real care in selecting a birthday gift expands my horizons! I once helped paint a house being built by Habitat for Humanity. Seeing that house, working on it hands-on, meeting the people who were to own it, and experiencing a bit of their joy in the prospect of having a nice place to live gave me a very different perspective on my contribution. It made my mind more generous, more willing to give, and more cheerful in the giving.

If we are deeply stingy, we'll resist the imagining and experiencing that makes us perceive others as our neighbors. We won't want to open ourselves emotionally to their needs and pleasures, lest the appeal to our minds costs us time and goods! So it may take some courage to undertake this second discipline.

The third and last discipline is to think about yourself. Who are you? What is your mind like? Does your life consist too much in the abundance of your possessions? What kind of life do you want? What kind of person do you wish to be? We need to get very clear about how empty a life is if it consists in the abundance of our possessions—and then measure our actual abundance against this standard.

To see the beauty of generosity and the ugliness of greed, it helps to have models like Jean Vanier, Mother Teresa, or some saint in your congregation, people who find joy, fulfillment, and selfhood in God through giving themselves to others. Meditating on these persons as models for life helps us to see what a real, substantial, abundant self is like, and to yearn for that kind of personality.

Limits to Consumption and Economic Growth: The Middle Ground
Allen L. Hammond

All too many discussions of consumption and related issues tend toward the extremes: the Malthusian position that we are about to exceed the Earth's carrying capacity, to run out of resources, or to exceed the Earth's capacity to absorb pollution; or the Cornucopian position that the Earth's bounty, coupled with human ingenuity and markets, will surmount all obstacles and provide an ever-rising stream of economic goods, food, technologies, and so on. These positions—stated in their most general and sweeping terms—are suspect on basic principles, as we shall shortly illustrate. The Malthusian argument suffers an additional burden; historically, it has been demonstrably wrong, so far.

The fallacy of both extreme positions is perhaps most easily exposed by considering what is meant by the term "consumption." When economists use the term, they have in mind all the economic value that is produced by human activity, less only that which is saved; all else is, in this usage, "consumed," even intangibles such as legal services or television shows. By this definition, economic growth automatically implies growth in consumption. This is true but meaningless, at least with respect to the environment. If the additional economic activity imposes no environmental burden, then neither does the consumption that results.

Physical scientists, on the other hand, use "consumption" to mean conversion of matter or energy to an altered state, as in the consumption of iron ore to produce steel or the consumption of coal to produce electric power. Whether economic growth implies rising consumption in this sense depends on the precise nature of the economic activity which is increasing, that is to say, on the pattern of consumption. Rising sales of software need not imply any increase in the consumption of iron or of coal; indeed, they may imply a decrease, if software contributes to more efficient use of electricity. Thus economic growth may or may not face resource limits or place additional burdens on the environment— the case remains open, pending closer investigation.

Biological scientists, to give a third usage of the term, often focus on the consumption of food or other biologically produced resources and on carrying capacity—the presumed limit of the Earth's ability to produce such resources. This third sense of consumption does have a certain resonance with today's circumstances: overharvesting of many marine fisheries has led to a peak in the world's fish catch, and overuse is visibly degrading some other biological resources. But it is worth remembering that carrying capacity is dependent on

Reprinted with permission from *Ethics of Consumption: The Good Life, Justice, and Global Stewardship,* edited by David A. Crocker and Toby Linden (Rowman and Littlefield, 1997).

technology and social organization and hence changes over time. England supports far more people today than Malthus believed possible, and American farmers (less than 3 percent of the U.S. population, compared with 30 to 40 percent a century ago) feed a much larger population and regularly produce surpluses. It is increasingly possible, in principle, to decouple food production from the environment, wholly or partially (consider aquaculture, the source of the most rapidly growing portion of the world's fish catch). For all these reasons, the relation of economic growth to consumption, and of consumption to environmental harm, is more complex, and more context-specific, than might first appear.

I suggest that a careful examination of actual "consumption" patterns and their environmental effects supports a middle position. We are not, the evidence suggests, running out of subsoil or "nonrenewable" resources—minerals, fuels, and so on. Proved reserves have increased over the past twenty years, and commodity prices are down. Substitution (of optical fibers made from abundant silicon for copper wires, for example) is occurring, recycling is rising, and markets appear to be performing their allocative function. No apparent "limits to growth" can be seen in this direction.

But—Cornucopians, please take note—we are encountering scarcities of many "renewable" resources and degradation of the biological systems which produce or support them. In effect, we are "mining" many biological resources in ways that render them nonrenewable. Thus fish and fisheries, wood and the forests which produce it (wood is the one basic commodity for which prices have risen over the past twenty years), water and watersheds or aquifers (in many but not all regions), and fertile soils are all showing signs of stress and decreasing per capita availability. Even fresh air, the most basic of renewable resources, is becoming an endangered resource in some urban areas, where the scale of human activity overwhelms natural renewal processes.

Close examination of the pattern of degradation shows that some of it is associated with consumption by the wealthy. It is high-tech fishing boats from industrialized countries that are stripping the marine fisheries, and it is industrial use of oil and coal that is priming the Earth's atmosphere with greenhouse gases. Such consumption may rise with economic growth, if human society does not take measures to prevent it; unaided, the market will not.

Some of the degradation, however, is associated with the unplanned "consumption" of the world's poorest populations, who must depend directly upon natural ecosystems for most of their food, fiber, fuel, and often shelter. Markets cannot work for the 20 percent or more of the world's population who have no money to buy and who live a subsistence existence. Economic growth here, if it raised populations out of absolute poverty and gave them economic choices, might actually reduce consumption from—and degradation of—the most overstressed portions of the biological resource base. If they could afford it, people might burn kerosene or use electricity, rather than burn trees. And it is trees (and the watersheds and forests they anchor) and other renewable resources that appear the most threatened.

THE FUTURE OF GROWTH

What of the future? Suppose that we can reduce poverty, and the environmental damage associated with it, through jobs and economic growth. Such development would stabilize biological resources that are now at risk. But can a global industrial system expand indefinitely? Will economic growth and expanding human populations not rapidly "consume" all available energy and material resources, and produce more pollution than living things can tolerate?

Perhaps. But notice that in the industrial countries, per capita use of materials and energy has not grown significantly in twenty years. Indeed, structural shifts under way in the economy—toward services and knowledge-based activities rather than manufacturing and materials-based activity as the primary source of economic value—coupled with rapidly advancing information (and other) technologies make it plausible, if not at all certain, that per capita "consumption" of materials and energy could decline radically over the next fifty years. Knowledge workers do not generate the same consumption patterns as steel workers: production and consumption of software worth $100 has a far smaller environmental impact than production and consumption of an equivalent value of steel.

Set against these optimistic trends, however, is the reality that per capita consumption of energy and materials in developing countries—now far lower than in the developed world—will inevitably rise, even as population continues to grow. So global consumption, and many kinds of environmental problems, will rise, at least in the short term. Use of fossil fuels—and emissions of greenhouse gases—may double or even triple by the middle of the next century, so that we are likely to find out the real environmental consequences of global warming. Other forms of pollution, concentrated by swelling urban populations, will cause increasing local and regional degradation.

Such trends will continue until population growth stabilizes and the basic infrastructure for urban and industrialized societies is built in developing countries. Progress toward these goals is occurring at different rates in different regions and, on current prognosis, is unlikely to be complete before the middle of the next century. How rapidly the process goes forward, and the extent to which developing countries can make use of emerging technologies to build more energy-efficient, less resource-intensive infrastructures and economic patterns, will determine the overall environmental impact of global development. Here explicit policies, and the leadership example (or lack of it) in the industrial countries, will certainly play a crucial role.

The consequences of global warming and the resulting changes in climate are not known with any certainty; they may well be quite significant. But human societies have adjusted to other significant changes in climate; we are very adaptable creatures, especially over a half-century or more. And even though local and regional pollution may get worse before it gets better, the evidence suggests that as people's living standards rise, so do their demands for clean air, clean water, and other environmental amenities—things we do know how to achieve, after all. Indeed, just such demands have resulted in reductions in pollution in most industrial countries over the past twenty-five years, even with economic growth. So the prospect that, over the next half-century, India and China may achieve living standards and consumption patterns of a typical European country today (Spain, for example) is hardly the end of the world. This is especially true if we continue to use energy and materials ever more efficiently, which is the trend in both the advanced countries and in many newly industrialized countries as well. Eventually, if we are to stabilize the climate, all human societies will have to depend largely on energy sources other than fossil fuels.

THE SOURCES OF WEALTH

One way to consider what human societies might aspire to is to inquire into the sources of wealth in the broadest sense of that term. A recent and unusually bold study by the World Bank dares to provide estimates of the real wealth of nations—that is, not just their material possessions or "built" capital, but also the "natural" capital represented by biological and mineral resources and the "social" and human capital represented by people, their abilities, and their social organizations. The Bank finds that by far the greatest portion of national wealth, in all but the poorest nations, comes from human capital, and that developed nations differ from developing ones primarily in having a greater proportion of their wealth in the form of human capital.

Consider each form of wealth separately. We are gradually depleting some of the Earth's natural capital, such as oil deposits, but there are potential substitutes (solar energy, for example). And the Earth replenishes other forms of natural capital, such as trees (provided we do not clear the forests faster than they can regrow). Built capital can continue to accumulate, but it appears that we have already seen a saturation point in the more industrialized countries—limits to the demand for more consumption of this type rather than limits to material growth. For human and social capital, however, there appear to be no limits— no limits to the knowledge we can accumulate, to aesthetic achievement, to the desirability of more effective social organizations. If we can organize our economies so that their consumption patterns favor accumulation of human capital rather than material capital, then the human future would appear to be unbounded. It may even be worth trading some of our original inheritance, natural capital, for increased human capital, if that is the cost of redeeming human assets out of poverty and degradation.

So I assert that the relation between economic growth, consumption, and the environment is neither clearly an unalloyed good nor a proven evil. Basic principles and the available evidence both suggest a rather more complex—and mixed—assessment. Meanwhile, our consumption patterns *are* changing. More than 70 percent of U.S. economic activity is already based on services, rather than on manufacturing, and the percentage is climbing in virtually all countries. By means of vigorous policy, consumption patterns can be induced to change even further, in ways that would secure a more environmentally promising future. Note, however, that I do not predict such a future—the issue is still in doubt, and depends on decisions and actions still to be taken, separately, in many regions of the world.

Christianity and the Pursuit of Wealth
Jay McDaniel

"Can Americans and others who belong to the rich world morally justify living in a way, or consuming at a rate, which it would be impossible for the rest of the world to enjoy?" The question is posed by John B. Cobb, Jr., a North American theologian, and L. Charles Birch, an Australian biologist, in their recent work at the interface of process and liberation theology, *The Liberation of Life.*[1] They answer in the negative; if they are right, the implications for us are unmistakable. In the interests of a just and sustainable world, we must learn to live more simply.

Of course, much hinges on what is meant by "just" and "sustainable." Let us assume, along with Birch and Cobb, that a "just" world is one in which significant degrees of economic equality, political participation, and personal freedom are realized.[2] And let us assume that a "sustainable" world is one in which ecological limits are recognized: a world in which, for example, world population does not exceed the global carrying capacity, the need for renewable and nonrenewable resources is held within check, the emission of pollutants is minimized, manufactured goods are built to last, recycling is encouraged, and planned obsolescence is discouraged.[3] Indeed, let us assume, as Birch and Cobb do, that "justice" and "sustainability" are the primary social goals toward which we, middle- and upper-income Christians in the prosperous West, rightly strive in the interests of Christian love.[4]

If we make these assumptions, as I will in this essay, the problem becomes obvious. When viewed in a global context, our own lifestyles are neither just nor sustainable. Given the finitude of the earth's natural resources and the limits of the earth to absorb pollution, it would be impossible for all humans on the planet to live in the style to which many of us are accustomed. If all the people of the world were to consume resources at the rate of middle-income Americans, for example, total known reserves of petroleum would be used up in six years and the annual consumption of timber, copper, sulfur, iron, and water would exceed available known reserves. While technological innovation might diminish the effects of environmental limits in the short run, it cannot offset

From "Christianity and the Pursuit of Wealth," by Jay E. McDaniel, *Anglican Theological Review,* October 1987, pp. 349–361. Reprinted by permission of the author.

these limits in the long run. In the coming centuries, "the only way the poor world can grow is for the rich world to curb its growth."[5]

Thus, if the world is to become more just and sustainable, substantial changes in attitude and lifestyle are required. These changes can be provoked by the exigencies of circumstance: by shortages of needed resources, by international conflicts that result therefrom, and by government decree in light of these conflicts. In the process many will suffer, chiefly the poor. But the changes might also be produced by voluntary shifts in our ways of thinking, accompanied by actions that mirror these shifts. The purpose of this essay is to describe the shifts in thinking—about reality in general and wealth in particular—that might help move us toward a more just and sustainable future, and then to note some of the practical implications of these shifts for our lifestyles.[6]

At the level of thought, I focus on what Birch and Cobb call the "ecological" paradigm of process or Whiteheadian thought. By virtue of the rigor with which this conceptual framework has been articulated by thinkers such as Cobb and Birch, it constitutes the best available alternative among contemporary Christian perspectives to the "mechanistic" paradigm that currently informs a great deal of public policy in industrialized and developing nations, and that underlies aspects of our own individual lifestyles. In the first two sections of the essay, I show how process understandings of reality (Section I) and wealth (Section II) exemplify the very kind of thinking toward which middle- and upper-income Christians need to move at this stage in history in the interests of justice and sustainability. In the third and final section I discuss the difference this way of thinking might make for contemporary lifestyles.[7]

I. FROM MECHANISM TO ECOLOGY

In a Whiteheadian context the adjective "mechanistic" is assigned to (1) a deterministic worldview in which present happenings are understood to be utterly determined by causative powers from the past, (2) a utilitarian worldview in which the value of living things is understood to be purely instrumental rather than intrinsic, (3) a devitalized worldview in which the depths of physical matter are understood to be lifeless and inert rather than lifelike and creative, (4) a reductionistic worldview in which living wholes are understood to be utterly reducible to nonliving parts, and, when joined with religion, (5) a dualistic worldview in which sharp dichotomies are drawn between spirit and matter, supernatural and natural, mind and body, thought and feeling, or self and world....

What, then, is the alternative "ecological" perspective posed by process thinkers? It is a *relational* point of view in which emphasis is placed on the reality of internal relations. One entity is "internally related" to others if the entity's relations to those others are partly constitutive of the entity's own essence. In process theology these relations are not abstract spatial properties such as "above" and "below"; they are concrete acts of "taking into account" or "prehending" the other entities from the point of view of the entity at issue.

Even as living beings have a power for independent creativity and sentience in the present, so process thinkers argue, and even as they have intrinsic value as realities for themselves, they are internally related to the past and to the surrounding world. Either consciously or unconsciously they "take into account" the past and the surrounding world from a particular experiential perspective, and in so doing they are dependent upon that past and that world. In many instances and respects the specific character of their relations to others are imposed upon them; in some respects they are chosen; but in all respects the relations are part of, rather than apart from, the identities of the entities at issue. Living beings are individuals-in-community rather than individuals-in-isolation.

In process thought, relationality also applies in a more general way to communities.[8] A "community" may be an atom, molecule, living cell, animal body, ecosystem, bioregion, or, in its more distinctively human manifestations, a family, neighborhood, town, city, ethnic tradition, or nation. Its members will include human and nonhuman individuals that are voluntarily or involuntarily bound together as mutual participants in one another's destinies. Indeed, the human family is a community of sorts, as is the earth itself or the cosmos as a whole. To say that relationality applies to communities is to say that communities are what they are in relation to other communities, and that, particularly at this stage in history with reference to life on earth, their destinies are interdependent. The web of life is best conceived as a collective "we" in which, ontologically speaking, there are no "they's". . . .

The process emphasis on relationality extends also to God. As has often been emphasized in trinitarian modes of thought, there are internal relations even in the divine life. Process thinkers will emphasize, along with many strands of the biblical heritage, that these relations are not simply a matter of God's relations to Godself; they are also a matter of God's relations to the world. As events occurring in the world occur, they are prehended or "taken into account" by God, and God's feelings of them are partly constitutive of God's own essence. God "feels the feelings" of living beings, suffering with the sufferings and enjoying with the joys, and in so doing God's own life is affected. God then responds to these events by availing the world of possibilities for wholeness and growth relative to the situations at hand: for justice in times of injustice, for love in times of indifference, for hope in times of despair. It is in light of such relationality, characteristic even of God, that process thinkers invite the contemporary Christian to ask: What is an appropriate Christian understanding of wealth?[9]

II. WEALTH AS RICHNESS OF EXPERIENCE

Clearly a process perspective implies that wealth, as something to be rightly sought, must be understood relationally rather than atomistically. If wealth yields isolated egotism rather than a sense of connectedness with the world, we–they thinking rather than inclusive care, unnecessary exploitation of nature rather than a reverence for life, or, as all these problems imply, forgetfulness of

God rather than faithfulness to God, then it is not "wealth" in the normative, Christian sense. Rather, it is spiritual poverty. The task of the contemporary Christian is to re-vision "wealth" in light of relational thinking, therein moving beyond an understanding of wealth that has captivated industrial civilizations since the dawn of the modern era.

The dominant point of view is well captured by the late nineteenth- and early twentieth-century Austrian economist Karl Menger. "Wealth," Menger said, "is the entire sum of economic goods at an economizing individual's command."[10] A good is "economic" if it has monetary or exchange value. It is "at an individual's command" if the individual "is in a position to employ it for the satisfaction of his needs." If "either physical or legal obstacles" prevent a good from being at one's command, then the good is not a part of one's wealth.

Two things are to be noted about Menger's definition. First, wealth is seen as an attribute of material goods rather than as a quality of lived experience. As is implied by Menger's insistence that the goods at issue be "economic," wealth is something that can be measured and quantified by numerical indicators. Subjective qualities such as a sense of dignity, a capacity for creativity, and depth of compassion for others are not part of a person's wealth, because they are nonmeasurable. Second, wealth is understood as an attribute which, at least in principle, can belong to an individual quite apart from the quality of his or her relationships with the surrounding world. As long as a person has goods at his or her disposal by which to satisfy individual needs, he or she is wealthy.

As a working definition of wealth within the discipline of economics, Menger's definition may or may not be acceptable. But as a social ideal for individuals and groups to follow, "wealth" as defined by Menger is inadequate. If the Christian is to seek wealth for others, or for herself or himself, it cannot be "wealth" in the Mengerian sense. Rather it must be "wealth" in an earlier and more original meaning of the term: wealth as welfare, well-being, and weal. The Christian must affirm that one is "wealthy," not necessarily when one has an abundant stock of material goods, but rather when one fares well in relation to the world, when one embodies a state of well-being in community with others, when one prospers, or exhibits weal, in one's openness to the world. In this context, well-being involves the two properties so conspicuously absent from Menger's definition: nonquantifiable and subjective qualities such as a sense of dignity, a capacity for creativity, and a depth of compassion; and, equally as important, an affirmation of relationality. When wealth is defined as well-being, a person is said to be wealthy to the extent that both objectively and subjectively he or she embodies life-affirming relations with the surrounding world. The shift is from wealth as *the stock of goods at an individual's command* to wealth as *the experiential well-being of an individual-in-community.*

Process theologians speak of experiential well-being as "richness of experience." Generally speaking, richness of experience consists of *harmony* in an individual's relations to self, body, other human beings, nonhuman nature, and God, and *intensity* in his or her embodiment of this harmony. The word "harmony" suggests identification with, or solidarity in relation to, other beings; the word "intensity" suggests freedom and creativity, zest and vitality, openness to novelty, and a sensitivity to the entire range of human experience, including suffering. Richness of experience is not the same as pleasure or comfort, and indeed it may include displeasure and discomfort. Its value lies in its depth of feeling, its love of life, its sensitivity to what is, and its openness to what can be.

Given their emphasis on relationality, process theologians do not at all intend to imply by "richness of experience" a state of existence in which one is closed to the world. Rather, they intend precisely the opposite. This means among other things that a person's capacity for richness of experience depends in part on his or her personal decisions, and in part on the community in which he or she is situated. Certain community contexts—namely contexts of oppression—can and do restrict people's opportunities for richness of experience. It is difficult for political prisoners to enjoy the intensity of creative self-expression, for abused children to enjoy the harmony of a healthy family life, for disenfranchised women to enjoy the intensity of political involvement, and for victims of racism to enjoy the harmony of inter-racial cooperation. Alternative community contexts can increase opportunities for richness of experience, and therein increase the world's wealth. From a Christian perspective the call of God can indeed be conceived as a call toward wealth for each and for all, if wealth is understood as richness of experience, and if the pursuit of wealth is conjoined with a love of justice.

As a paradigm instance of wealth, Christians can look to Jesus, or at least to the pictures we have of him in the Gospels. Jesus was wealthy, not because he had an abundant stock of material goods, but rather because he embodied a harmony within himself concerning his mission and priorities, a harmony with the world as manifest in his love for the outcasts and thirst for justice, and a harmony with God as exemplified in responsiveness to God's will. He lived this harmony with an intensity expressed as free and zestful action (e.g., in his overturning the tables in the temple), creative self-expression (e.g., in his imaginative use of parables), and depth of feeling (e.g., in his passion on the cross). His wealth was what he called "abundant living": a way of being rich in its creative harmony with the world and with God, and potentially actualizable by those "who have ears to hear."

Other examples of such richness can be found both within and outside the Christian tradition. To one degree or another a Christ-like richness is evident in Francis of Assisi, Mother Teresa, Martin Luther King, Jr., Thomas Merton, Dom Helder Cámara, Dorothy Day, and Mohandas Gandhi. At least as we mythicize them, people such as these disclose a qualitative depth to us—an image of how life can be and should be lived—that seems rich in its own right. The claim of traditional Christianity is that this kind of wealth—wealth as richness of experience in creative harmony with the world—mirrors the wealth of God's own life. Christians are called to be wealthy, not as the advertising model on North American television is wealthy, but rather as God is wealthy.

In many contexts, of course, the call toward wealth involves a quest for quantity as well as quality. If one is to live in harmony with one's own body, for example, one must have adequate food, clothing, shelter, health care, and health education. Jesus, too, ate and washed. Stated more abstractly, richness of experience—understood as experiential well-being in community with others—includes rather than excludes physical well-being. The pursuit of wealth can rightly involve a quest for material goods that help satisfy the need to survive.

For middle- and upper-income Christians in the "First World," of course, the question is, Where do survival needs end and greeds begin? Many Christians in affluent societies have plenty of food, clothing, and shelter—indeed, much more than they actually need to survive. Often for these people the problem is not underconsumption, with its attendant problems of malnutrition and brain damage, but rather overconsumption, with its attendant problems of heart disease, cancer, and alcoholism. Even their basic psycho-social needs—the needs for safety, security, a sense of belongingness, and positive self-regard—have been met several times over. In light of God's call to be wealthy, God's call toward "abundant living," can they justify seeking even *more* goods and services?

If wealth is understood in the Mengerian sense as "the stock of goods at an individual's command," then of course they can. The call toward wealth is a call to increase the stock. If, however, wealth is understood as richness of experience, that is, an experiential well-being in creative harmony with the world, then the answer is no. This is because the very possession of an excessive stock of material goods, paralleled by the habits of consumption that usually accompany such possession, obstructs one's capacity to be in creative harmony with the world.

This is the case for at least three reasons. First, being in harmony with the world involves living in a way which, in principle, all human beings could enjoy. The rates of consumption characteristic of Americans and others in the rich world could in no way be enjoyed by all humans on the planet. The resource limits and pollution absorption capacities of the earth would not allow it. Already the greenhouse effect precipitated for the most part by affluent industrial nations brings potentially dangerous tidings to the planet as a whole. If Christians are to live in harmony with the world, and therein enjoy a richness of experience in relation to the world, they must adjust their lifestyles to a standard that, in principle, all can embody into the indefinite future given ecological limits.

Second, being in harmony with the world involves solidarity with present generations. For the Christian who follows Jesus' call to serve the poor, such solidarity must be particularly directed toward those who struggle on a daily basis to survive. If one is affluent, the excess goods that one possesses have usually been made from materials that can and should have been used to meet the basic survival needs of the poor. In buying them one becomes implicated in the system that has oppressed the poor. Moreover, the organizations of which one has taken advantage in order to accrue this stock are often the very organizations that keep the poor and oppressed in check. In taking advantage of these systems, and therein accruing an excessive stock, one keeps the systems going and therefore keeps the poor in their place. Inasmuch as one's objective relation with the poor is one of disharmony rather than harmony, one is like the rich young ruler in Jesus' parable. One has forsaken the kingdom of God, and the particular type of wealth it offers, for gods of fame, fortune, and power.

Finally, being in harmony with the world involves allegiance to future generations. Accumulating an excessive stock of material goods robs future generations of raw materials and energy sources necessary for basic survival. Here as well, one's objective relation with the world, in this instance the world of the future, is one of disharmony rather than harmony. Conspicuous consumption has been substituted for commitment to life.

My argument, then, is (a) that the God revealed in Jesus calls each and every person toward a "wealth" that is "experiential well-being in creative harmony with the world," and (b) that the ownership of too many material possessions and the indulgence of excessive habits of consumption actually obstructs such wealth. While it might be objected that this redefinition of the word "wealth" is but a subterfuge to encourage ethical commitments, the claim of the Christian, I believe, is that the life of creative harmony with the world actually is richer, and in that sense wealthier, than affluent alternatives. To live a life of creative harmony with the world is not simply to fulfill ethical obligations; it is to live well. Such living may not be more comfortable or pleasurable, but it is deeper and more meaningful. Indeed, it is the abundant living that Jesus promised.

III. SOME IMPLICATIONS FOR THE MIDDLE- AND UPPER-INCOME CHRISTIAN

If the argument posed above is correct, the question naturally and rightly emerges: What can we do?

In some sense the lifestyle changes toward which we are called must be relative to our contexts and capacities. In discussing the concrete ways in which middle-class Christians can change their habits of living, neither legalism nor purism will do. Nevertheless suggestions are in order, and Birch and Cobb point us in the right direction. Affluent Christians, they say, "can opt out of the system to some extent."

> Most can live more frugally than they do. They can be more intentional about avoiding support for some of the worst abuses of the system. They can experiment with new, more communal, life-styles; with more true partnership in living together; with more support for the current movements of liberation of women and minorities; with the sun or wind as sources of energy; with organic gardening; with driving cars less or even doing without them; and with spending more time in supporting grass-roots movements they believe in instead of making money or establishing status in the present system.[11]

Birch and Cobb recognize that such lifestyle changes alone cannot directly alter global problems of social injustice and ecological unsustainability. Parallel to lifestyle changes must come changes in public policy and social systems: changes to which a good deal of the discussion in their book is devoted. But lifestyle changes of the sort they propose are nevertheless important because they pave the way for the needed changes in policy and system, and because they manifest the kind of solidarity with the world toward which Christians are called by God. Even if such changes produce no visible effects in the global system, they still embody the kind of creative harmony with the world that is at the heart of Christian wealth....

My argument has been that, if such changes occur, middle-income Christians will find themselves "wealthier" than before. The life of intentional living in harmony with the world is in fact richer from an experiential perspective than that of a self-enclosed, affluent alternative. In addition, so I have argued, it is more Christian. The wealth toward which God calls the middle-class Christian, and all Christians for that matter, is a wealth that mirrors God's own.

Chapter 13

CAPITALISM AND CHRISTIAN VALUES

What features would a Christian want to see in an economic system? One obvious concern would be the success of that system in providing for the economic needs of the population. Any society that enjoys a high level of freedom from poverty and is able to meet its economic needs will have reason to be satisfied with its economic system. There are two dimensions to this feature: the level of protection from economic want and the extent to which that protection exists throughout the population. In other words, both production of wealth and equitable distribution of wealth are features that Christians desire in an economic system.

Capitalism, as we understand it today, is a fairly recent phenomenon in world history, dating back to the late 18th century. It can be defined as a privately financed competitive market economy in which the dynamic of supply and demand fuels production. Capitalism is based on the assumption that an economic system will function most adequately if it allows human needs to generate production to meet those needs, without imposing government requirements based on goals or ideals that people think an economic system should meet. Its advocates note that its emergence in the Industrial Revolution correlated with the beginnings of rapid economic growth and consequent upswing in the economic fortunes of the Western world. Capitalism has been credited for the achievement in the United States of a remarkable standard of living, and most Americans would likely defend it against any of its competitors.

While critics do not contest the success of capitalism as a system that facilitates the production of wealth, they are less satisfied with the distribution of wealth in the United States. Here they see more disparity between the rich and the poor than our citizens should be willing to accept. Studies from several sources that compare the United States with other leading industrialized nations reveal significantly more economic inequality in this nation. This situation in fact worsened noticeably during the decade of the 80s. For many millions of citizens, the comforts and opportunities associated with the middle-class style of life are hopelessly beyond reach.

This disparity between rich and poor, accentuated by the opulence of the rich in a society as affluent as our own, has always been a source of discontent among Christians. From a biblical perspective, Christians are called to place themselves on the side of the poor and the oppressed. Theologian Karl Barth put it succinctly in his *Church Dogmatics:* "God always takes his stand unconditionally and passionately on this side and this side alone: against the lofty and on behalf of the lowly; against those who already enjoy right and privilege and in behalf of those who are denied it and deprived of it." The primary questions for Christians evaluating an economic system thus become: How well does it provide for the poor? How oppressed are those at the bottom of the economic ladder? What kind of opportunity and support are provided for the disadvantaged?

It is not surprising that many Christians have been attracted to the ideal of equality that has been identified with socialism, an economic system that is intent on removing the vast distance between rich and poor. However, the viability of socialism in the West and elsewhere has been compromised by the recent political and economic transformations in eastern Europe. In this "post-communist era," socialism is routinely discounted as unworkable. It is also true that some form of capitalism in which the excesses of a market economy are tempered by governmental control appears most appealing to the majority of the world population.

How then can capitalism be humanized? The issue, as posed by British historian Paul Johnson, is whether it is possible "to harness the power of market capitalism to moral purposes without destroying its dynamism." The answer to Johnson lies in the realm of public policy that can establish certain ground rules for society. Two of those ground rules Johnson believes essential are equality before the law and equality of opportunity, including equal access to quality education. Capitalism would also be morally enhanced if there were greater access to public ownership of corporations through the purchase of stock. On the international scene, encouraging free trade and narrowing the gap between rich and poor countries by spreading the skills of market capitalism are morally commendable policies. This is the way the power of market capitalism can be harnessed. Even though he recognizes that many people will fail in spite of the fairness and opportunity these policies promote, Johnson believes that the wealth-creating power of capitalism has the potential to overcome poverty in the world.

Oliver Williams proposes that Roman Catholic social teaching, especially the encyclical *Centesimus Annus,* endorses a communitarian democratic capitalism that is a "humane and ethical alternative to the present state of affairs." Basically he is endorsing the reform of democratic capitalism. The major difference between Johnson's proposal and Williams's is that Johnson, in saying that one should not try to give capitalism a moral purpose, views capitalism as a system separate from public policies. Thus he is much less sanguine than Williams about the role of regulation and the way in which other systems impinge upon the economic. Williams is endorsing a moderate form of communitarianism in which human rights, the market, and the state operate in conjunction with private institutions toward building moral character in a way that will contribute to public virtue and "the good to be pursued in common." The moral grounds for Williams's view are anchored in the Christian values of solidarity and the pursuit of human community for all.

The article by Michael Lind suggests that both Johnson and Williams are too idealistic. Lind argues that inequality in the United States is a direct result of the present system of political economy, and that in fact the economy and our system of government are designed to enhance and promote the wealth of a tiny fraction of citizens. Lind argues that the real form of political economy in the United States is oligarchy, which the elite spare no effort in disguising. There is a two-class society that maintains only the façade of democratic elections. Our tax system is designed to protect the ability of the wealthy to become wealthier, and the corporate elite use global free trade as a means of driving down American wages. From Lind's point of view the debate between Johnson and Williams is delusional; indeed, he might call it part of the façade that the overclass has erected. Lind's article alerts us to the significance of reality and the way in which our interpretations of "reality" (the understanding of reality we accept) feed into our ethics and politics.

The Capitalism and Morality Debate
Paul Johnson

The decade of the 1980s has proved to be an ideological watershed. It has been marked by a huge resurgence of the power and efficacy of the capitalist market system and a corresponding collapse of confidence in the capacity of socialist "command economies." This loss of confidence in collectivism is the culmination of many decades of trial and misfortune. The truth is that, during the twentieth century, large parts of the world have given the collectivist alternative to capitalism a long, thorough, and staggeringly costly trial, and it seems to have failed absolutely everywhere. It was during the 1980s that this realization dawned even in the quarters most reluctant to admit it—among the rulers of the socialist-style states. Many of them are turning back—in despondency, almost in despair—to the despised market disciplines they had rejected.

From "The Capitalism and Morality Debate," by Paul Johnson. *First Things*, March 1990, pp. 18–22. *First Things* is a monthly journal published by the Institute on Religion and Public Life in New York.

Meanwhile the capitalist world is racing ahead and is creating wealth on a scale never before dreamed of. It is clear that capitalism, being a natural force rather than a contrived ideology, springing from instincts deep in our human natures, is modifying itself all the time, and we cannot foresee how it will evolve over the next century. But I am willing to predict, as a result of our experiences in this one, that never again will any considerable body of opinion seriously doubt its wealth-producing capacity or seek to replace it with something fundamentally different. We are near the end of an historical epoch in which capitalism has survived the collectivist assault and is now firmly reestablished as the world's primary way of conducting its economic business.

So where does this leave us? It leaves us, I suggest, with a considerable moral dilemma. I can state the dilemma in one sentence: how do we give a moral dimension to this triumphant reassertion of capitalism? For one thing we know: whereas wealth creation is essential to men's well-being, especially in a world where population is expanding so rapidly, it cannot in itself make men and women happy. We are creatures of the spirit as well as of the flesh, and we cannot be at ease with ourselves unless we feel we are fulfilling, however vaguely or imperfectly, a moral purpose. It is in this respect that capitalism, as such, is inadequate.

THE MORAL NEUTRALITY OF CAPITALISM

It is not that capitalism is immoral. Clergymen who insist that it is and preach against it are themselves confused, as were their predecessors a hundred years ago who insisted that any form of socialism was immoral. One can be a good Christian and a capitalist, just as one can be a good Christian and practice collectivism.

The trouble with capitalism is quite otherwise. It lies in its moral neutrality, its indifference to the notion of moral choices. Capitalism and the market system which gives it its efficiency and its power is single-minded in its thrust—that is why it is so productive. It is blind to all other factors: blind to class, race, and color, to religion and sex, to nationality and creed, to good and evil. It is materialist, impersonal, and nonhuman. It responds with great speed and accuracy to all the market factors. In a way it is like a marvelous natural computer. But it cannot make distinctions for which it is not programmed. It does not and cannot possess a soul and it therefore lacks a moral inclination one way or the other.

Indeed it is precisely because capitalism is morally indifferent—and so productive of great miseries as well as great blessings—that many idealists early in the nineteenth century saw it as evil, rejected it entirely, and sought to replace it. We have come to the end of that line of argument. We have discovered there is no effective substitute for the market. We have to accept capitalism as the primary means whereby wealth is produced and begin the process of moralization within its terms of reference. I say "begin," but in a sense we have been doing it for two hundred years—by factories acts, mines acts, by monopoly and fair-trading legislation, and by all the countless laws we devise to restrict ways in which the market system can be distorted by man's cupidity.

But these are merely negative attempts to correct the excesses of capitalism. They do not in themselves give capitalism a positive moral purpose. That is a quite different and much more difficult matter. The moment you start trying to give capitalism a moral purpose, you risk interfering with the basic market mechanism which provides its wealth-creating power. If, for instance, you try to use capitalism to promote greater equality of wealth by imposing on it a steeply progressive, redistributive system of taxation, you frustrate the way in which it rewards its chief dynamic force, the acquisitive impulse, and you are liable to end by making everyone poorer. Or if, to take another example, you try to redistribute power within capitalism by balancing managerial authority by trade union privileges, you either choke the entrepreneurial spirit or you eliminate profits—the system's lifeblood—or, as a rule, you do both, and so again you end by making everyone poorer.

Almost all efforts to provide capitalism itself with a positive moral purpose run into the same difficulty. Great Britain, between 1945 and the end of the 1970s, was a classic case where repeated and often ingenious attempts were made to cudgel capitalism into a system of national redistribution of wealth. It was part socialism, part corporatism, and wholly inefficient. It was baptized by the moral-sounding name of "the mixed economy." In fact, by the end of the 1970s, it had come to resemble an ancient piece of do-it-yourself machinery, constructed by amateurs, held together by adhesive tape, and emitting old-fashioned steam from every joint. The British economy had become one of the least efficient and productive in the Western world. In 1979 Mrs. Thatcher and her government began the return to true capitalism, but even after a decade of common sense reforms and rapid improvements in productivity, we calculate it will still take us another ten years or so to catch up with Germany and France, while the United Sates and Japan are still further beyond our reach.

That is the price of trying to make capitalism do something which is not in its nature to do—promote equality. The price is paid in the shape of reduced national wealth and income—lower general living standards, inadequate health care, a run-down transport system, impoverished social services, underfunded schools. These results have been repeated, in varying degrees, everywhere else in the world where attempts to invest capitalism with positive moral functions have been made. We have to accept that the market system, while exceedingly robust when left to itself, rapidly becomes sick and comatose once you try to force it to do things contrary to its nature. The more you interfere with its mechanism by imposing moral objectives the less efficiently it works. Indeed, under a sufficient weight of moral obligation, it will collapse altogether.

STEERING CAPITALISM IN A MORAL DIRECTION

How do we escape from this difficulty? How can we practice capitalism, with its unrivaled capacity to produce wealth, within the framework of a society that recognizes moral objectives? To put it another way: is it possible to harness the power of market capitalism to moral purposes without destroying its dynamism? That is the real, practical question that faces humanity. And I often wish our Christian theologians would address themselves to it, instead of peremptorily dismissing capitalism as intrinsically evil, as so many of them thoughtlessly do.

I do not pretend the problem is easily solved. On the other hand, I think it is defeatist to regard it as inherently insoluble. It is a mistake to try to turn capitalism itself into a moral animal. But I think it is possible to run it in tandem with public policies that make use of its energy while steering it in a moral direction. Let me indicate a number of ways in which I believe this can happen.

First, and in some ways the most important, is to provide the capitalist economy with an overall legal framework which has a moral basis. This can only be done if we accept that a fundamental object of the just society is to establish, so far as is humanly possible, absolute equality before the law. Equality of wealth is a utopian fantasy whose hopeless pursuit usually leads to tyranny. But equality before the law is a reasonable objective, whose attainment—albeit in an imperfect form—is well within the reach of civilized modern societies. Moreover, this form of equality responds to a strong human need: for whereas few of us really want equality of possessions, or believe it possible, all of us want fairness. The notion of a fair society is an attractive concept, and one toward which progress can undoubtedly be made. Moreover, equality before the law is a necessary adjunct to the competitive nature of capitalism: the end result cannot be equality, but from start to finish the rules must apply equally to all.

What do we mean by equality before the law? We mean that the law must make no distinction of birth or caste, race or color, sex or tribe, wealth or poverty. It must hold the scales of justice blindfolded. In a curiously paradoxical way, the capitalist system similarly makes no distinction about the nature of men and women. Hence for the law so to distinguish is a gross interference with the market mechanism and makes it less efficient. Equality before the law reinforces the natural power of capitalism, so that in this case moral purpose and wealth creation go hand in hand. Inequality before the law takes many forms, some of them grotesque, as in the Republic of South Africa or the Soviet Union, some more subtle. Even in advanced Western societies like the United States, where the principle is well understood and established, the ability to buy more law than your neighbor is a ubiquitous source of inequality. In no society that I know is full equality before the law established in practice, and I do not say that it can be realized perfectly and overnight anywhere. But it is one form of equality that can be broadly attained without destructive side-effects, and systematic progress toward it is an esssential object of any society that wishes to place capitalism in a context of justice.

Another way to combine capitalism with moral purpose is for society to endorse the related but broader concept of equality of opportunity. It is one of the miracles of the human condition that all of us, however humble, possess talents of one kind or another, waiting to be of service. The notion that all of us have something to contribute is God-given and stands at the heart of the Judeo-Christian tradition. The range of talents is as infinite as human variety itself, and the society that is swiftest to identify them in each, and put them to use, will certainly be the most efficient (as well as just). Here again, capitalism and justice pursue the same ends, for capitalism thrives on meritocracy—one of the prime functions of the market is to identify and reward objective merit— and it creates wealth most rapidly when all obstacles to equality of opportunity, social and historic as well as purely legal, are removed. This aspect of equality is a vital element in the moral legitimation of capitalism, for an economic structure in which every man and woman, in theory at least, can progress from the lowest to the highest place cannot be held to be intrinsically unjust.

I say "in theory." What about in practice? It is unrealistic to talk of equality of opportunity without taking drastic measures to make high-quality education generally available to those who can profit from it. I know that in practice we are not going to get a society where all will be able to benefit from the standards of the best schools and colleges. To begin with, throughout human history the most gifted teachers have always been in limited supply—there are never enough to go around. In any case, the culture and habits of industry, which parents transmit to their children, make absolute equality of opportunity unattainable. But it is one thing to concede the difficulties, quite another to accept the present system of educational inequality, which exists to some degree in every country in the world. There is no single way, in my view, more likely to make capitalism morally acceptable, to anchor its functions in justice, than by giving the poor access, by merit, to high-quality education of every kind and at every stage. And it is implicit in this objective that we identify merit, of every variety, at the earliest possible age—another respect in which we tend to be woefully inept.

Of course, to educate the poor, according to aptitude, to the highest standards is enormously expensive. But it is the great merit of capitalism that it does produce wealth in immense quantities for such necessary purposes; and the more people we educate efficiently, the more wealth the system will produce. The matter is increasingly urgent for, as capitalism advances itself, it demands ever more refined skills at each level. If training in them is not available for all who can benefit, inequalities—both within societies and between them—will increase instead of diminish, and the moral credentials of the system will inevitably be subjected to growing challenge. We have, in short, to educate ourselves into justice, and to do so with all deliberate speed.

But we must not stop at access to education. We must see to it that there is more readiness of access to the capitalist system itself. I believe that the notion of "democractic capitalism" is a genuine one, and that its realization, to some degree at least, is within our grasp. There are many ways in which it can be brought about. Some are old. Some we have only recently discovered. Some are yet to be devised.

DEMOCRATIC CAPITALISM

In the last half-century and more, we have found that to take an industry into public ownership in no way democratizes it—quite the contrary. Nationalization, whether in the form of a monolithic public corporation, as in the old British system, or through so-called "workers' control," as in Yugoslavia, for example, merely puts the business firmly into the hands of bureacratic or union elites, or indeed both. But it is now possible, as has been found in Britain and elsewhere, to float public corporations so that they become the property of millions of small stockholders.

Let us not deceive ourselves that this conveys control of them to the masses. But it does spread ownership widely, and it does introduce an element of mass financial participation in the system that is new and healthy. It gives millions of humble, ordinary people a sense that they are no longer entirely victims of the system: that they act, as well as are acted upon; that to some small degree they have a stake in society. It is a source of pride, of reassurance, even of security, and it is thus morally significant.

Democratic capitalism also lends itself to the old but unrealized idea of co-ownership by giving the workforce easy entry into the purchase of stock. Over 90 percent, for instance, of those who work for the recently privatized British corporation British Telecom now hold stock in the firm—thus bridging the destructive and needless chasm that separates owners and workers and that promotes class warfare. In any great capitalist enterprise, the community of interest between those who own, run, and work for it is, or ought to be, far greater than any conflict of interest. Access of workers to stock is the surest way of demonstrating this fundamental truth, which is often obscured by political sloganeering. This is particularly important in industries where the work is hard and dangerous and the profits high, such as mining and offshore oil extraction, to give two obvious examples. Democratic capitalism, and especially the worker-stock ownership aspect of it, serves to refute one of the gravest charges against capitalist practice—that it is, by its very nature, exploitative.

Stock ownership is not, however, the only or even the best way in which the notion of democratic capitalism can be pursued. One of the most important but least understood disadvantages of the so-called "mixed economy" is that, in its inevitable drift to corporatism, it involves tripartite deals between government, labor unions, and large-scale capital. Such deals invariably leave out small businesses. In Britain, for instance, it is only since we have begun to dismantle mixed-economy corporatism that the needs of small businesses, and equally important, of those wishing to start them, have played any part in the formation of government policy.

Why have we been so remiss? Now that most of the world is necessarily turning its back on the soil, to start one's own business has replaced that fundamental human urge to farm one's own land—it is an expression of the natural creativity in man, and as such a profoundly moral impulse. Sensible, practical assistance in helping people to set up their own businesses, and to ensure a climate of fairness in which they operate, is the best way to promote, at one and the same time, equality of opportunity, democratic capitalism, and, not least, the efficiency and acceptability of the system as a whole. There is almost invariably a strong correlation between the number of small business starts and soundly based economic expansion. So here again the interests of justice and the process of wealth creation coincide.

Popular access to capitalism at a national level has its international counterpart in access to markets. The vigorous promotion of free trade is an important way in which capitalism is legitimized morally. Protectionism in any form tends to undermine capitalist efficiency by creating privileged industries and it is unacceptable morally because it deprives the consumer of the full fruits of the market. It always appears to have advantages for new, small, and weak economies—or for old established ones meeting new and ruthless competition. But in the long term, and often in the short term too, these advantages are greatly outweighed by the drawbacks. Equally objectionable are barter deals between states, or deals between states and big international corporations. All these attempts to escape the rigors of competition invariably produce corruption and fraud, and bring out the worst aspects both of big government and of capitalism itself. One might put it this way: International free trade is the global version of equality of opportunity.

But just as equal opportunities within a society are unlikely to become reality without general access to high-quality education, so free trade will not in practice be generally accepted, especially among the poorer countries, until the huge discrepancies between nations in technical and commercial skills are diminished. I do not think that the normal workings of the international market will be recognized as just and reasonable until we narrow this gap, so much more important in the long run than any more obvious gap in living standards or financial resources. Yet here, perhaps, is the best way in which richer nations can effectively help the poorer ones.

Old-style aid is now discredited, and I think rightly so, for certainly there are few more foolish things than for a rich nation to salve its conscience by transferring cash to the government of a poor one, thus as a rule keeping an inefficient and unpopular tyranny in power. But it is another matter to use our resources to train the disadvantaged masses of the Third World—and indeed the emerging ex-communist world too—in the skills of market capitalism. By widening the availability of such skills, we do many things simultaneously: we benefit the poorer countries by enabling them to compete; we benefit ourselves by making it possible for them to open their markets to us; we strengthen the system by giving it universality as well as fairness; and consumers everywhere find goods cheaper as competition increases. Here again, the process of placing capitalism in a moral context has the additional advantage of adding to its wealth-creating power. To sum up my case: doing the right thing morally usually proves to be commercially the right thing to do as well.

THE PERSISTENCE OF POVERTY

However, I willingly concede that there is an important flaw in my argument. And it applies whether one looks at individual societies or at the global community—within nations and between them. However thoroughly one applies the principle of equality before the law, however ingeniously one provides equality of opportunity and universal access to high-quality education, bitter experience seems to show that a great many people remain in deprivation, misery, and hopelessness. It is not enough to provide individuals with an exit from this underclass. Its very existence, as a class, perpetuating itself from generation to generation, is, or at least seems to be, a categorical indictment of the capitalist market system itself.

In fact it does not truly reflect upon the market. The market can be made fair—to give it moral legitimacy it *must* be made fair—but what it cannot be made to do, at least not without wrecking it, is to discriminate in favor of failure. And we have to face the fact that many human beings, in any society, will fail however fair the rules and however wide the opportunities. There is overwhelming evidence that market capitalism can conquer mass want and create a very general affluence anywhere in the world. What we now have to demonstrate is that the societies in which capitalism is the energizing force can cope with the minority problem of failure. It is, in my judgment, the biggest single task our societies face today: a problem which is at one and the same time moral, economic, and political.

It is *moral* because we cannot accept, on a permanent basis, the exclusion of perhaps a fifth of society from a life of modest decency. Earlier ages had to reconcile themselves to permanent mass poverty. We *know* a solution can be found, and we have an inescapable moral obligation to find it.

It is *economic* because it is waste on a colossal scale. Often up to 50 percent of budgets are absorbed by coping with poverty. And it is not just material waste but waste of minds and hearts.

It is *political* because the percentage involved is too small to effect change through the democratic process. Thus, there is an inherent tendency to resort to violence, often with racial overtones—and a violence which possesses a kind of moral authority all its own.

The solutions tried up to now have been collectivist ones, so they have all failed. I believe we must now turn to entrepreneurial solutions and seek to use the problem-solving mechanism of market capitalism, which has never failed us yet, to provide the answers.

The need is urgent, because the problem is already reproducing itself at the international level. It is right, as I have argued, to press steadily for the expansion of free trade, and for the richer nations to finance training programs and other devices to make such expansion fair and profitable to all. The majority of the global population can be progressively drawn into such a system.

But it would be misleading to suggest that all the nations are at present eligible. Indeed an underclass of nations, mainly but not exclusively in Africa, is developing too. What we observe in large parts of Africa is what might be called the Haiti Syndrome: entities nominally classified as states which have virtually fallen out of the international economy and which seemingly cannot provide for their citizens elementary justice or allow them to provide for themselves the basic necessities of life. In many cases, the miseries of these underclass nations are envenomed by civil war and frontier disputes among themselves. As they are at present organized and governed, there is nothing that capitalism can do for them—and socialism, to which most have resorted, merely compounds their problems. Indeed such underclass states seem inevitably to attract the worst exponents both of capitalism at its most unscrupulous and socialism at its most destructive. Where lies the remedy? Indeed, is there a remedy?

Certainly there is no obvious remedy within the common assumptions of the late twentieth century—that all states, whatever their origins and nature, are equally sovereign. In the nineteenth century, the existence of such failed societies, with abysmally low and falling living standards exacerbated by chronic violence, would have attracted the attentions of one or other of the colonial powers. Sooner or later a colonial power would have moved in, from moral motives as well as from hope of commercial and political gain. That would be inconceivable now.

Or would it? Has not the failure of decolonization, in some areas at least, been as spectacular and tragic as the general failure of collectivism? And is it unthinkable to revive the notion of national trusteeship, once so important a part of the League of Nations' work in the 1920s and 1930s? And if trusteeship is a valid concept, worth discussing in the international context, is it, or something like it, a useful idea to mull over in the context of the intractable problem of the internal underclass?

What I am suggesting is that in exploring the future potentialities of the capitalist market system and in devising ways in which society can consolidate its moral acceptability, we should keep an open mind to fresh ideas. We are at the end of one ideological era, the era in which collectivism was tried and found wanting. One thing history surely teaches is that when old ideas die, others rush in to fill the vacuum. For men and women need ideas as much as they need food and drink. If sensible and creative ideas are not forthcoming, we can be certain that dangerous and destructive ones will emerge to exert their spell. It is essential that those of us whose roots are still within the Judeo-Christian system of ethics, who value freedom, who strive for the just society, and who recognize the enormous productive potential of market capitalism should be fertile in ideas in the coming battle for minds. For if we get the ideas right, the opportunities for mankind in the next century are almost without limit.

Catholic Social Teaching: A Communitarian Democratic Capitalism for the New World Order
Oliver F. Williams, C.S.C.

Harvard Business School professor George C. Lodge has long championed what he calls communitarianism, and he believes that this position is implicit in Catholic social teaching, especially in the writings of John Paul II.[1] In presenting communitarianism to the business community, Lodge proceeds as follows:

> The community—New York City, for example—is more than the sum of individuals in it; the community is organic, not atomistic. It has special and urgent needs as a community. The survival and the self-respect of the individuals in it depend on the recognition of those needs. . . . In the complex and highly organized America of today, few can live as Locke had in mind."[2]

This article will argue that contemporary Catholic social teaching, in particular, the most recent document, *Centesimus Annus,* offers a vision of a new communitarian democratic capitalism that is a humane and ethical alternative to the present state of affairs. It will outline the central communitarian features of Catholic social teaching and some of their implications for the reform of democratic capitalism.

COMMUNITARIANISM

Centesimus Annus (CA) was issued on May 16, 1991, the 100th anniversary of *Rerum Novarum,* a treatise generally considered the church's first formal reflection on the social and political implications of the biblical teaching. Catholic social teaching has consciously developed its positions in opposition to that of the influential philosopher John Locke (1632–1704) and the school of thought known as "liberalism." In "liberal" thought, society is understood as a collection of individuals who have come together to promote and protect their private rights and interests. For Locke[3] the law of nature is the basis for commutative justice which provides the norms for contractual and exchange relationships between atomistic individuals. . . .

Communitarianism, on the contrary, holds that the person is by nature social, not by choice. The need for others, for community, is a constitutive dimension of the person. Thus the "law of nature" grounds not only a commuta-

From Oliver F. Williams, C.S.C., "Catholic Social Teaching: A Communitarian Democratic Capitalism for the New World Order," from *The Journal of Business Ethics* 12 (1993): 919–32. Reprinted by permission.

tive justice but also a distributive and a social justice as well. *Centesimus Annus* is based on this premise.

Even prior to the logic of a fair exchange of goods and the forms of justice appropriate to it, there exists something which is due to man because he is man, by reason of his lofty dignity. Inseparable from that required "something" is the possibility to survive and at the same time to make an active contribution to the common good of humanity.[4]

This passage goes on to note that many developing countries still have not realized the basic communitarian vision of *Rerum Novarum* and lack such important safety net policies as unemployment insurance and social security (par. 34). While much of the developed world enjoys these benefits, there are many who still slip through the cracks and go without adequate food, shelter and healthcare. It is this group that is the focus of much of the religious social teaching. . . .

In my view, *Centesimus Annus* offers an account of "moderate communitarianism" which does justice both to the individual and the community and which holds much promise for a more humane democratic capitalism, especially as a New World Order is taking shape. To make this case, four features of Catholic social teaching that clearly embody moderate communitarianism are outlined below. The features identified, while not an exhaustive description, are the core of what many communitarians espouse.[5]

1. *Rights, while important, are not always viewed as absolute but are seen in the context of their role of promoting and protecting human dignity in community.*

Catholic social teaching has always understood that, while the right to private property is important, the worker's right to a "just wage" takes precedence over an employer's right to bargain for the cheapest wages possible. Setting wages below a just or living wage simply because the market will tolerate it is censured as "thoroughgoing individualism . . . contrary to the twofold nature of work as a personal and necessary reality" (par. 8). . . .

Catholic social thought is ever vigilant against the sort of collectivist tendencies which tend to stifle individual freedom and obliterate legitimate mediating structures. This defense of personal rights is clearly evident in the *Centesimus Annus* where Pope John Paul II vigorously defends the solidarity of workers and their right to come together in organizations to defend common interests as well as numerous other rights. Eschewing the model of interest-group pluralism in democratic politics which tends to view the world exclusively through the prism of one set of interests, Catholic social thought repeatedly returns to the notion of the common good as the appropriate context in which to consider one's own interests.

The sort of society envisioned by Catholic social teaching is one where private property is respected. Following the medieval scholar, Thomas Aquinas, the church assumes that private property enables the human development intended by the Creator. Yet the teaching has always insisted that private property has a social dimension which requires that owners consider the common good in the use of property.[6] This vision of society assumes that some persons will have more material goods than others but that the affluent will provide for the less fortunate, either through the channels of public policy or other appropriate groups of society. The emphasis is always on respect for the human dignity of the poor, even in their unfortunate situation. The ideal is to structure society so that all those who are able might provide for themselves and their families by freely employing their talents.

2. *The market has an important though limited function in society.*

Catholic social teaching has a teleological understanding of human institutions and so the constant refrain is to ask the *purpose* of the market economy in society. The key premise is that development entails much more than producing goods and services; development is a matter of enabling people to follow their unique personal vocation, to be creative, to participate and to work and thus "to respond to God's call" (par. 29). The market, in this vision, plays an important role in that it provides the material conditions for all these moral, spiritual and political ideals to be realized. It is not, however, the be all and end all.

While the writings of Catholic social teaching have not always seemed to understand the market system,[7] *Centesimus Annus* marks a dramatic change and explicitly endorses the value of a market economy, although with one important caveat, that is, that the market should not become an idol (par. 40). The significant point, however, is that while heretofore economic self-interest was largely equated with greed in church teaching, *Centesimus Annus* explicitly recognizes the virtues of a market economy in harnessing self-interest for the material betterment of society....

One way to view church statements which reflect on and offer guidance to capitalist economies is as an attempt to provide a religious vision. The church strives to influence the institutions of society so that they might be the moral force assumed by Adam Smith ensuring that a market economy does not so blind a people that it becomes an acquisitive society. This blindness happens when the *means* of developing the good society, wealth creation, becomes an *end* in itself. Moral institutions can influence minds and hearts and thus individual choices. The point is not to eliminate consumer sovereignty but rather to strengthen it. The goal is growth with all having some share and the perennial target of condemnation by Catholic social teaching is materialism, acquisitiveness for its own sake. Church teaching has never seen fit to condemn capitalism as intrinsically evil, although some theologians have,[8] but rather has aimed its guidance at the reform of institutions, structures and personal life involved with the free market economy. The key criticism of capitalism focuses on what it does to people.

It is not wrong to want to live better; what is wrong is a style of life which is presumed to be better when it is directed toward "having" rather than "being" and which wants to have more not in order to be more, but in order to spend life in enjoyment as an end in itself. It is therefore necessary to create lifestyles in which the quest for truth, beauty, goodness and communion with others for the sake of common growth are the factors which determine consumer choices, savings and investments (par. 36).

3. *The state has an important though limited function in society.*

Paragraph 42 of *Centesimus Annus* is the strongest affirmation of a market economy that Catholic social teaching has ever made. Yet within this affirmation there are qualifications which go to the core of the church's tradition on economic matters. The paragraph notes that now that communism is a failure, the question arises as to what economic system should be recommended as the model for all those developing countries struggling for economic and political progress. Clearly the answer is a market economy, but only the sort of mixed economy with government regulation that strives to cushion the inevitable destructive side of the market. While the concern for people is not new in Catholic social teaching, what is new is an *explicit* recognition that this concern is best exercised by taking into account the basic dynamic of the market system.

Paragraph 42 reflects the central concerns found throughout the history of Catholic social teaching since the publishing of *Rerum Novarum* in 1891. Catholic social teaching offers a vision of this world that is religious and ethical, it is a world where a huge gap between the rich and the poor is seen as a problem and where all, especially the poor in developing countries, ought to have the opportunity of earning a living wage;[9] the implicit assumption here is that some version of capitalism can narrow this gap.[10] It is a vision of society where the state has a role in influencing the economy toward the common good, but one where the state is not all powerful in the economic realm; in fact, the goal is for the state to encourage and enable "mediating institutions," those groupings between the individual and the state that foster freedom and initiative, such groups as professional associations, churches, corporations, trade unions, universities, families and so on.[11] While some communitarians would advocate a more comprehensive role for the state, for example Bellah calls for a "global New Deal,"[12] most are concerned that state power be limited. The fear is that inordinate power concentrated in either the market or the state will stifle initiative and freedom and generally not serve the human community....

This vision underpins all the economic teaching of the church. While accepting the value of a market economy, religious social thought argues that one must have a conscious concern for the common good of all, and not depend on unconscious workings of the market, the "hidden hand" to solve all problems. Some disciples of Adam Smith believed in God's providence working to ensure the common good, a self-regulating economy. Religious social thought says, in effect, that we must make God's work our own, that we must have a conscious care for the common good. This sometimes requires government regulation of the market. To be sure, regulation is tricky business and the good consequences sought are often elusive. For religious social thought, failure in a particular regulation is no argument against regulation, however, but rather one for better regulation. We must learn how to do it right is the continual refrain of Catholic social teaching. Deciding on appropriate social regulation entails much debate and often trial and error.[13]

4. *Individuality is shaped by social institutions and institutions that corrupt people's character need to be reformed while those engendering desirable character traits ought to be strengthened....*

In the area of economic ethics, the church has had much to say in the last century. While it is true that the skill of producing wealth is a relatively new one in the history of the human race, and that this skill has the potential to create a more humane life and hence advance the plan of God, the church insists that wealth creation always be carried out in the context of the end of life on this earth, *the formation of virtuous persons.* Economic activity is only a means, and it must be guided by reference to the moral ends. This is the heart of the teaching of Thomas Aquinas (1225–1274), and it continues to form the basis of Church documents. Some 700 years later, the Second Vatican Council decree, "The Church in the Modern World,"[14] restates the point clearly: "...economic activity is to be carried out according to its own methods and laws but within the limits of morality so that God's plan for humankind can be realized" (par. 64).

The insight of Catholic social teaching, applied in various circumstances throughout the last century, is that capitalism without a context in a humane community seems inevitably to shape people into greedy and insensitive human beings. Thus the church teaching accepts the market economy but with a key qualification, that the state intervene where essential to promote and protect the human dignity.

A major theme of the criticism of capitalism by the church is summed up well by Pope John Paul II in speaking of alienation. He notes that the Marxist analysis of alienation is false, but there is a type of alienation in our life today. The point is that it is quite possible for people in a market economy to lose touch with any real meaning or value in life (par. 4). This can happen in two ways, the first is called "consumerism," an easily misunderstood term.... Consumerism refers to that aberration where people are led to believe that happiness and self-fulfillment are found solely in acquiring material goods. The values of friendship, music and beauty, for example, come to pale in importance and because basic, nonmaterialistic needs are not met, there is alienation....

Alienation can also be traced to the workplace when the workers perceive their work as meaningless and have no sense of participation (par. 41). There is considerable research in this area of job satisfaction and the quality of work life and most find that worker productivity hinges on experienced meaningfulness. It is significant that it is only in the most advanced market economies that this research is being conducted and that the workplace is beginning to be humanized, a point that religious social teaching often overlooks....

One of the roles of the state, according to this religious perspective, is to facilitate the growth of desirable character traits and mute those that are less noble. Yet there is a confidence in the goodness, the cooperative dimension of the person, so that the social constraints of the state and the shape of institutions, including a market economy, are designed to enhance human freedom and curtail selfishness for the common good....

A key concern of communitarians is to strengthen the character-forming institutions that provide the discipline that develops the traits so essential for civic life and public trust. Institutions such as the family, the church, the neighborhood and the school are all eroded when the market dominates life in society. Catholic social teaching is clear in distinguishing its social doctrine from socialism where the social nature of the person is "completely fulfilled in the state."...

Catholic social teaching is particularly concerned that the family be supported and strengthened by social policies of the state. The role modeling in the family is taken to be the primary vehicle for developing the character essential for the good society.

In order to overcome today's widespread individualistic mentality, what is required is a concrete commitment to solidarity and charity, beginning in the family with the mutual support of husband and wife and the care which the different generations give to one another (par. 49).

Contemporary liberal philosophers are understandably concerned that communitarians, especially the religious variety, will strive in dogmatic fashion to reorient the society and ignore individual rights in the process. Catholic social teaching holds that both individual rights and the requirements of the community have equal moral status but that rights must be viewed in the light of community and the community in the light of individual rights. For example, in the case of the "living wage" discussed above, there is agreement that the employer has the right of private property but also that the community should have the power to protect and promote the human dignity of the worker and his or her family by shaping a just social system with its background institutions or, in developing countries, by regulating a just wage. Thus, the community is charged to protect this substantive good, human dignity.

Crucial to the moderate communitarian position of Catholic social teaching is the conviction that while individuals ought to shape their institutions in ways that form fulfilling communities, this shaping ought to be a product of rational public discussion. This is true whether the issue be curtailing individual rights to ensure competition in the market place or to control pornography or illicit drug traffic or the changing of unjust governments. For example, in discussing unjust governments Catholic social teaching tries to steer a course between simply supporting the status quo, where it may be unjust or corrupting, and unabashedly encouraging violent revolution. To the rich and the powerful, it counsels concern for the poor and the environment that nurtures them. To the poor, it preaches "solidarity," taking a stand and collectively reacting to exploitative situations and systems....

MODERATE COMMUNITARIANISM: REALIZING THE VISION

In the area of economic ethics, Catholic social teaching today is trying to develop a moral consensus and establish and strengthen those institutions which foster morally constrained behavior. The teaching calls the church to be a community that calls people to higher values and obligations. It offers an integrative vision, but it is not naive about the power of economic rationality in the workplace. The recent spate of hostile takeovers and plant closings serve as a reminder of the power of economic rationality. Catholic social teaching realizes that to have compelling power, its teaching must be matched by concrete proposals for institutional arrangements which might overcome the distrust inherent in the dynamic of self-interest in the market. Thus, for example, *Centesimus Annus* "recognizes the legitimacy of workers' efforts to obtain full respect for their dignity and to gain broader areas of participation in the life of industrial enterprises . . ." (par. 43). Institutional changes that may overcome distrust and harness greed and selfishness are suggested. . . .

The U.S. Bishops' 1986 Pastoral Letter on the economy, *Economic Justice for All,* is more specific than *Centesimus Annus* in making suggestions for new institutional arrangements that might enhance a communitarian democratic capitalism. The rationale is stated as follows:

> The virtues of good citizenship require a lively sense of participation in the commonwealth and of having obligations as well as rights within it. The nation's economic health depends on strengthening these virtues among all its people, and on the development of institutional arrangements supportive of these virtues (par. 296).

While recognizing that there are strengths and weaknesses to each of these proposals, the documents suggest some trial and error experimentation. The proposals include, among others, the following: new structures of accountability so that not only stockholders but all the stakeholders ("workers, managers, owners or shareholders, suppliers, customers, creditors, the local community, and the wider society") are considered in important decisions; cooperative ownership of a firm by all workers; and participation of workers in plant closing decisions or decisions on movement of capital. The U.S. Bishops' document, as well as *Centesimus Annus,* also champion the United Nations as an indispensable international agency which can serve to overcome distrust among nations and move the world toward a global community. While some of the above suggestions may prove wanting, the point is still valid. That is, a new vision is not feasible without new structures that will help overcome distrust and facilitate the birth of a communitarian democratic capitalism. A communitarian democratic capitalism could blossom from a vision that respects both individual rights and a virtuous community, values an essential but not all-powerful role for the state and the market, and supports a conscious effort to sustain and enhance those institutions that develop and support character. While this vision is far from realized, it is the vision of contemporary Catholic social teaching.

What is clearly revealed from the texts cited in this article is that Catholic social teaching now supports a market economy and understands the values and virtues entailed with participation in such an economy. Before the publication of *Centesimus Annus* such support and understanding was not entirely clear to many, particularly those in the business community.

The texts cited above also reveal that Catholic social teaching strongly supports a socially regulated capitalism. Of course, the mixed economy of the United States and many other nations has much social regulation. The great debate today concerns how much and what sort of new social regulations is appropriate. Here *Centesimus Annus* is not particularly helpful. It offers general principles on the role of government but few specifics on what constitutes "good" or "bad" government. Although partisans on both sides of the aisle quote the document to bolster their case, most scholars would argue that the role and function of the teaching is to offer a vision for believers and people of good will, not to offer concrete particulars.

On the one hand, the encyclical makes a shocking proposal: "sacrificing the positions of income and power enjoyed by the more developed economies" to aid the economies of the less developed countries (par. 52). On the other hand, the teaching is very cautious about advocating big government as the answer to social problems, even to the point of harshly criticizing the "welfare state" (par. 48). The encyclical displays an understanding of the tradeoff between efficiency and equity and constantly reminds decision-makers to focus on the dignity of the person. It does not, however, enter into specifics, leaving the prudential decisions about social regulation to those qualified to make them. The thrust of the encyclical, however, is to be unyielding on basic moral objectives such as concern for the poor and less fortunate. Those sympathetic with Arthur Okun's thesis in *Equality and Efficiency: The Big Tradeoff* (1975) will find much that is congenial in Catholic social teaching.

In my view Catholic social teaching and all religious and moral teaching play an important role in society. Perhaps Max Weber (1864–1920) said it best. In the final pages of his classic *The Protestant Ethic and the Spirit of Capitalism*, he candidly expressed doubts that capitalism could survive once it lost religious roots.[15]

> Where the fulfillment of the calling cannot be directly related to the highest spiritual and cultural values, or when, on the other hand, it need not be felt simply as economic compulsion, the individual generally abandons the attempt to justify it at all. In the field of its highest development, in the United States, the pursuit of wealth, stripped of its religious and ethical meaning, tends to become associated with purely mundane passions. . . . For of the last stage of this cultural development, it might well be truly said: 'Specialists without spirit, sensualists without heart.'[16]

From this perspective, religious social thought that reminds us of the plight of the poor and the powerless in society are capitalism's best friend. Its appeal to the consciences of people of good will keep alive the vision of a just and wholesome community, and consequently put the roles of business and government in their proper perspective.

If people without are ever to have the quality of life—food, housing, jobs, participation, etc.—envisioned by the encyclical, it will be because the highly skilled managers of today's complex institutions directed their time and talent to this challenge. . . . The pressing need is for cooperation, so that together visionaries and managers might begin to lay the groundwork for a more just world. If the encyclical can bring people together for discussion and action on this matter, in my view it will go down in history as a great success.

To Have and Have Not: Notes on the Progress of the American Class War
Michael Lind

Judging by the headlines that have been leading the news for the last several years, public debate in the United States at the end of the twentieth century has become a war of words among the disaffected minorities that so often appear on the never-ending talk show jointly hosted by Oprah, Larry King, Jenny Jones, and the McLaughlin Group. Conservatives at war with liberals; Christian fundamentalists at odds with liberal Jews; blacks at war with whites; whites at war with Hispanic immigrants; men at war with women; heterosexuals at war with homosexuals; and the young at war with the old. A guide to the multiple conflicts in progress would resemble the Personals pages in *The Village Voice,* with "versus" or "contra" substituted for "seeking" (Pro-Sex Classicists versus Anti-Sex Modernists).

The noise is deceptive. Off-camera, beyond the blazing lights, past the ropy tangle of black cords and down the hall, in the corner offices (on Capitol Hill as well as at General Electric, The Walt Disney Company, and CBS News), people in expensive suits quietly continue to go about the work of shifting the center of gravity of wealth and power in the United States from the discounted many to the privileged few. While public attention has been diverted to controversies as inflammatory as they are trivial—Should the Constitution be amended to ban flag-burning? Should dirty pictures be allowed on the Internet?—the American elites that subsidize and staff both the Republican and Democratic parties have steadfastly waged a generation-long class war against the middle and working classes. Now and then the television cameras catch a glimpse of what is going on, as they did last year during the NAFTA and GATT debates, when a Democratic President and a bipartisan majority in Congress collaborated in the sacrifice of American labor to the interests of American corporations and foreign capital. More recently, with a candor rare among politicians, House Speaker Newt Gingrich argued against raising the minimum wage in the United States—on the grounds that a higher minimum wage would handicap American workers in their competition with workers *in Mexico.*

The camera, however, quickly returns to the set and the shouting audience, while assistant producers hold up placards with the theme for the day: the Contract with America, the New Covenant, Affirmative Action, Moral Renewal. It's against the rules to talk about a rapacious American oligarchy, and the suggestion that the small group of people with most of the money and power in the United States just *might* be responsible to some degree for what has been happening to the country over the last twenty years invariably invites the news media to expressions of wrath and denial. Whenever a politician proposes to speak for the many—whether he is on the left (Jerry Brown), right (Patrick Buchanan), or center (Ross Perot)—the Op-Ed pages in the nation's better newspapers *(The Washington Post, The New York Times, The Wall Street Journal)* issue stern warnings of "demagogy." Yes, the pundits admit, economic and social inequality have been growing in the United States, with alarming results, but the ruling and possessing class cannot be blamed, because, well, there is no ruling and possessing class.

The American oligarchy spares no pains in promoting the belief that it does not exist, but the success of its disappearing act depends on equally strenuous efforts on the part of an American public anxious to believe in egalitarian fictions and unwilling to see what is hidden in plain sight. Anybody choosing to see the oligarchy in its native habitat need do nothing else but walk down the street of any big city to an office tower housing a major bank, a corporate headquarters or law firm, or a national television station. Enter the building and the multiracial diversity of the street vanishes as abruptly as the sound of the traffic. Step off the elevator at the top of the tower and apart from the clerical and maintenance staff hardly anybody is nonwhite. . . .

Amounting, with their dependents, to about 20 percent of the population,[17] this relatively new and still evolving political and social oligarchy is not identified with any particular region of the country. Homogeneous and nomadic, the overclass is the first truly national upper class in American history. In a managerial capitalist society like our own, the essential distinction is not between the "bourgeoisie" (the factory owners) and the "proletariat" (the factory workers) but between the credentialed minority (making a living from fees or wages supplemented by stock options) and the salaried majority. The salaried class—at-will employees, lacking a four-year college education, paid by the hour, who can be fired at any time—constitutes the real "middle class," accounting, as it does, for three-quarters of the population. . . .

There is rather a two-class society. The belated acknowledgment of an "underclass" as a distinct group represents the only exception to the polite fiction that everyone in the United States, from a garage mechanic to a rich attorney (particularly the rich attorney), belongs to the "middle class." Over the past decade the ghetto poor have been the topic of conversation at more candlelight-and-wine dinner parties than I can recall, but without looking at the program or the wine list it is impossible to tell whether one is among nominal liberals or nominal conservatives. The same kind of people in the same kind of suits go on about "the blacks" as though a minority within a 12 percent minority were taking over the country, as if Washington were Pretoria and New York a suburb of Johannesburg. Not only do the comfortable members of the overclass single out the weakest and least influential of their fellow citizens as the cause of all their sorrows but they routinely, and preposterously, treat the genuine pathologies of the ghetto—high levels of violence and illegitimacy—as the major problems facing a country with uncontrollable trade and fiscal deficits, a low savings rate, an obsolete military strategy, an anachronistic and corrupt electoral system, the worst system of primary education in the First World, and the bulk of its population facing long-term economic decline. . . .

During the past generation, the prerogatives of our new oligarchy have been magnified by a political system in which the power of money to buy TV time has become a good deal more important than the power of labor unions or party bosses to mobilize voters. Supported by the news media, which it largely owns, the oligarchy has waged its war of attrition against the wage-earning majority on several fronts: regressive taxation, the expatriation of industry, and mass immigration. Regressive taxes like the Social Security payroll tax and state sales taxes shift much of the tax burden from the rich to middle-income Americans. After the Reagan-era tax reforms, 75 percent of the American people owed more taxes than they would have owed had the 1977 tax laws been left untouched; only the wealthiest 5 percent of the public received any significant benefit from the tax cuts. . . .

Owing in large part to the bipartisan preference for regressive over progressive taxation, and despite the cries of anguish from Senator Phil Gramm and the editorial writers employed by *The Wall Street Journal,* the United States now stands second to last among the major industrialized countries in the rate of taxation on income—and dead last in terms of economic equality. The replacement of progressive income taxation by a flat tax, along with the adoption of national sales taxes (reforms favored by many conservative Democrats as well as Republicans), would further shift the national tax burden from the credentialed minority to the wage-earning majority. Average Americans have not only been taxed *instead* of the rich; they have been taxed to *repay* the rich. Borrowing, which accounted for only 5.3 percent of federal spending in the 1960s, increased to 29.9 percent in the 1990s. Interest payments on the debt (which last year amounted to $203 billion) represent a transfer of wealth from ordinary American taxpayers to rich Americans and foreigners without precedent in history.

On the second front of the class war, corporate elites continue to use the imperatives of global free trade as a means of driving down American wages and nullifying the social contract implicit in both the New Deal and the Great Society. U.S. corporations now lead the world in the race to low-wage countries with cheap and politically repressed labor forces. Concentrated in "export-processing zones" in Third World countries, and usually not integrated into the local economy, much of the transnational investment brings together foreign capital and technology with inexpensive and docile labor to manufacture consumer electronics, shoes, luggage, or toys. The export-processing zone is nothing new; it used to be called the plantation. In the nineteenth and early twentieth centuries, plantations owned by American, British, and European investors produced raw materials and agriculture for export; modern technology now permits factory work to be done in the same countries. The banana republic is being replaced by the sweatshop republic as national, middle-class capitalism gives way to global plantation capitalism.

Many advocates of free trade claim that higher productivity growth in the United States will offset any downward pressure on wages caused by the global sweatshop economy, but the appealing theory falls victim to an unpleasant fact. Productivity *has* been going up in America, without resulting wage gains for American workers. Between 1977 and 1992, the average productivity of American workers increased by more than 30 percent, while the average real wage *fell* by 13 percent. The logic is inescapable. No matter how much productivity increases, wages will fall if there is an abundance of workers competing for a scarcity of jobs—an abundance of the sort created by the globalization of the labor pool for U.S.-based corporations.[18]

Even skilled production often can be done more cheaply elsewhere. Software research and design is now being done by local computer specialists in India, in Russia, and in Poland. Since 1979, the real wages of high school dropouts have declined by 20 percent, while the incomes of workers with more than four years of college have risen by 8 percent....

Not all nonprofessional jobs can be expatriated to Mexico or Malaysia, and a great many low-skilled services—from truck driving to nursing and sales and restaurant work—still must be performed in America. Accordingly, on a third front of the class war, the American gentry support a generous immigration policy. Enlarging the low-skill labor pool in the United States has the same effect as enlarging the labor pool through the expatriation of American-owned industry. From the point of view of members of the white overclass, of course, this is good news—if mass immigration ended tomorrow, they would probably have to pay higher wages, fees, and tips. In the 1980s, during the "Massachusetts Miracle," the state's unemployment rate fell to half the national average, 2.2 percent. As a result of a tight labor market, wages for workers at McDonald's rose to more than $7 an hour. So unfortunate a development prompted a study from the Twentieth Century Fund in which author Thomas Muller took note of the awful consequences: "In many areas of the Northeast, a scarcity of clerks in the late 1980s caused a noticeable deterioration in service.... This is not an argument that long lines or *flip behavior by salespeople* will fundamentally affect America's well-being, but they do constitute an irritant that can diminish the quality of our life [emphasis added]." In a seller's market for labor, it seems, there is a danger that the help will get uppity.

"As the number of working mothers increases," Muller wrote, "such [household] help, once considered a luxury, is becoming more and more a necessity. Were it not for recent immigrants, nannies, maids, and gardeners would be a vanishing breed...." Although the vast majority of Americans still do not consider the employment of "nannies, maids, or gardeners" to be a necessity rather than a luxury, the 1 percent of the population that employs live-in servants ... cannot enjoy an appropriate degree of comfort without a supporting cast of deferential helots....

The Wall Street Journal, ever mindful of the short-run interests of the overclass, has called for an amendment to the U.S. Constitution consisting of five words: "There shall be open borders." If the United States and Mexican labor markets were merged (together with the capital markets already integrated by NAFTA), then American investment would flow south to take advantage of cheap labor, and tens of millions of Mexican workers would migrate north to better-paying jobs, until wages stabilized somewhere above the contemporary Mexican level (between $4 and $5 a day) but below the current American minimum wage of $4.25 an hour. The numbers of the white overclass would remain fixed, while the pool of cheap labor expanded, and Muller's dream of heaven would come true: every American who is not a maid or gardener might be able to afford one.

Although the inequalities of income in the United States are now greater than at any time since the 1930s, and although numerous observers have remarked on the fact and cited abundant statistics in support of their observations, the response of the American overclass has been to blame everybody but its nonexistent self—to blame the ghetto, or the schools, or the liberal news media, or the loss of family values. In a characteristic argument that appeared in early April on the Op-Ed page of *The Washington Post* ("Raising the Minimum Wage Isn't the Answer"), James K. Glassman dismissed the idea that public policy can help the majority of workers whose real wages continue to fall: "[T]he ultimate answer lies with workers themselves. . . . Government can help a bit through tax breaks for education, but ultimately the cure for low working wages may be nothing more mysterious than high personal diligence."

In any other democracy, an enraged citizenry probably would have rebelled by now against a national elite that weakens unions, slashes wages and benefits, pits workers against low-wage foreign and immigrant competition—and then informs its victims that the chief source of their economic problems is a lack of "high personal diligence." But for whom could an enraged citizen vote? The American overclass manages to protect itself from popular insurgencies, not only through its ownership of the news media but also by its financial control of elections and its use of affirmative-action patronage.

Of the three defenses, the uniquely corrupt American system of funding elections is by far the most important, which is no doubt why campaign finance reform was left out of the Contract with America. The real two-party system in the United States consists not of the Democrats and the Republicans but of the party of voters and the party of donors. The donor party is extraordinarily small. Roughly 10 percent of the American people make political contributions, most of them in minimal amounts. The number of large political donors is even smaller. Citizen Action, an independent consumer group, found that in the 1989–90 election cycle only 179,677 individual donors gave contributions equal to or greater than $200 to a federal candidate: "Thirty-four percent of the money spent by federal candidates was directly contributed by no more than one tenth of one percent of the voting age population." One may reasonably doubt that this one tenth of one percent is representative of the electorate or the population at large. . . .

Unified along the lines of economic interest, the wealthy American minority hold the fragmented majority at bay by pitting blacks against whites in zero-sum struggles for government patronage and by bribing potential black and Hispanic leaders, who might otherwise propose something other than rhetorical rebellion, with the gifts of affirmative action. The policy was promoted by Richard Nixon, who, as much as any American politician, deserves to be acknowledged as the father of racial preferences. . . .

The bipartisan white overclass, secure behind urban fronts and suburban walls, as well as the metaphorical moats of legacy preference, expensive schooling, and an impregnable interest rate, has neither reason nor incentive to moderate its ruthless pursuit of its own short-term concerns. In a more homogeneous society, the growing concentration of power and wealth in the hands of a privileged minority might be expected to produce a strong reaction on the part of the majority. In present-day America, however, no such reaction is likely to take place. Although heavily outnumbered, the unified few rest secure in the knowledge that any insurgency will almost certainly dissipate in quarrels among the fragmented many rather than in open rebellion; during the 1992 Los Angeles riots, black, Hispanic, and white rioters turned on Korean middlemen rather than march on Beverly Hills. The belligerent guests on the never-ending talk show, urged on by the screaming audience, will continue to enact allegorical conflicts, while, off-camera and upstairs, the discreet members of the class that does not exist ponder the choice of marble or mahogany for the walls of the executive suite from which they command.

Chapter 14

SEEKING JUSTICE BETWEEN
NORTH AND SOUTH

As the conflict between the United States and the Soviet Union recedes in our memory, along with it goes the support that capitalist and communist countries offered developing countries. Certainly there is less urgency about providing assistance to countries that might align themselves with one system or the other. To be sure, there are wars of intervention and even some—the Gulf War—where the vital interests of the United States are threatened. There no longer appears to be a competition between systems of economic organization or systems of government. Does the United States care about the plight of those "developing" countries? Reports from Africa would suggest that the situations in many nations there, and also in Central America, are sliding backward with increases in unemployment and declining per capita incomes.

It is relations between affluent and poor nations that we are speaking of when we speak of a North–South conflict. While there currently is little ideological debate or hostile political engagement, there is nonetheless a serious issue that becomes increasingly ominous: the widening economic imbalance between rich nations (usually in the Northern Hemisphere) and poor ones (usually in the Southern). While the North has perceived the primary needs of the South to be technological advancement and industrial growth, one could well argue that the needs are more fundamental than that: the needs for education, for their own scientific establishment, and for some control over the forces of production within their borders. And then there is the question of whether affluent nations should be promoting development along the same lines as they have enjoyed, via the policies of such organizations as the World Bank and the International Monetary Fund. It is extremely improbable that all the earth's inhabitants could sustain the consumption and production levels that people in the United States have come to need, enjoy, and experience. We simply don't have the resources as a planet.

There is of course a long history in the relations of North and South, with the economic disparity between them getting worse rather than better.

Sometimes it appears that the chasm between the affluent nations, which include those on the Pacific Rim, and the poor nations of the Southern Hemisphere is widening. In 1900 the gap between rich and poor nations in per capita income was 2:1. Today it is closer to 20:1. One must acknowledge that many factors within the poor nations contribute to this situation, including poor soil and poor climate, exploding populations and an absence of capital and technology, social inequalities that feature a few land-owning families of great wealth and the masses of landless peasants, and the lack of effective political leadership. At the same time, however, the impact of the rich countries on the poor has been critical. Colonization of these countries in the 19th and 20th centuries resulted in the transfer of their mineral wealth to the rich countries. This created a continuing economic dependence on the North, since the colonized economies were geared toward providing raw materials for the industrialized nations. This arrangement places a stranglehold on the attempts of nations in the South to develop economic independence and direct their productive efforts toward meeting the needs of their own populations. This economic inequity probably will only grow worse as the Information Age makes rapid access to information and instantaneous reaction more significant. The Information Age threatens to leave poor nations out in the economic cold.

While the international community has organized to address these problems, such responses as have been mounted have met with only limited success. The so-called G-8 industrial nations of Western Europe, North America, and Asia seem to concentrate on strengthening their own economies more than those of nations in the South. International trade agreements have not operated to the benefit of developing economies; if anything, they have further disadvantaged poor people in both affluent and poor nations. The world debt crisis continues. Efforts by developing nations to organize themselves have produced little relief. Despite the frequent acknowledgment that the era ahead of us will be one of increasing global interdependence, especially in terms of the environment, it is clear that the countries of the North continue to maintain economic hegemony over the South.

While it is not clear what the response of the United States should be in regard to developing nations, it is more clear what goals the Christian church should support. Our selections center on the question of how we as a nation and a church should respond to this situation.

The first essay comes to us from the South; Gnana Robinson is principal of the United Theological College, Bangalore, India. He addresses the goals of human development from a Christian perspective. Of special concern to him is how currently dominant theories of development, which equate development with economic growth, feed into the problems of developing nations. Modern development assumes a consumer society, which system "aggravates the acquisitive and aggressive instincts of people." By way of contrast, Robinson develops a Christian concept of development that focuses on just relations where distributive justice will replace economic growth as the center of development. Self-reliance should be the goal of development from the New Testament point of view. Holistic development rests on these twin principles of self-reliance and concern for the welfare of all.

Peter L. Berger addresses this issue of societal responsibility in a "post-socialist world" from a Northern point of view. The three questions he raises carry a very different tone from that of Robinson. First he deals with the issue of the sequence in which developing nations adopt a market economy and also a democratic regime. The real issue here is human rights and whether there is an interim period in which the violation of human rights can be more nearly justified. He secondly raises the question of the range and nature of political redistribution, to what extent and when governments should intervene to redistribute wealth—here he seems to be in some conflict with the perspective Robinson articulates. Berger's final moral issue concerns the cultivation of cultural values that contribute to economic development. What sorts of values should be cultivated—Japanese industry, corporations being *mater et magistra,* Puritan asceticism? The tone and the issues Berger considers, while quite familiar and even serious political issues to us in the United States, may strike a theologian from the South as effete. This raises the question of how Christians from one country can begin to make judgments about people in other cultures, and whether they should be concerned about more than how their nation's actions affect others.

Mark Lewis Taylor clearly thinks so; his essay "Transnational Corporations and Institutionalized Violence" presents "A Challenge to Christian Movements in the United States." Understanding the final section of the essay, which is presented here, requires some summary of its first three parts. Taylor begins by juxtaposing the voices of Rigoberta Menchu, a Guatamalan peasant whose book reports her life, and Fred Sherwood, a U.S. businessman operating in Guatemala. In essence, North and South are put into conversation with each other. Taylor then draws out the interwoven dimensions of that encounter: the Guatemalan in relation to the North Atlantic economy; the Guatemalan elite in relation to Guatemalan laborers; corporate power in relation to Guatemalan women; and corporate power in relation to land. Transnational corporations embody a dynamic of "abstraction," which is crucial to each of these dimensions. By "abstraction" Taylor will refer to both distancing and destructive functions that lie at the heart of institutionalized violence—international imperialism, local class exploitation, gender injustice, ethnic oppression, and environmental destruction. One wonders whether Taylor would label Berger's arguments "abstractions." Surely abstractions can operate in moral arguments from us Northerners. The selection presented here expresses Taylor's view of the contribution that Christian movements can make to Third World realities. He sees this as a "third system" and takes some pains not to fall into abstraction himself. One of the more interesting of his suggestions is that "strategic practices for global justice include a *celebration of the peoples' arts.*"

This moral issue seems as intractable as any; in fact, the environmental issue and the issue of economic systems are a complex of Gordian knots. Immigration and the manner of war and peace are issues with implications in this one as well. If we were to project a global future, then nothing seems more important in determining its shape than the manner in which North and South learn to live together with some measure of equality and peace. Pragmatically that seems important; to Christians it seems imperative.

Christian Theology and Development
Gnana Robinson

HUMAN DEVELOPMENT: A CONCERN OF THEOLOGY

Theology, the *logos* about God—the reason, knowledge and understanding of the being of God and his activities—has to do with the whole of creation, because Christians believe that the God who created order out of disorder created the universe with a purpose, and this purpose has to do with the welfare of human beings. . . .

Thus we see that the focus of God's concern is the holistic development of the human, the holistic development of every human person in the total human community, including both present and future generations. Any development discussion must therefore take into account both ecological and futuristic concerns.

MODERN DEVELOPMENT THEORIES

Modern discussions on development started at the end of the second World War, drawing on the theories of Adam Smith, David Ricardo and Thomas Malthus.[1] Development was understood in terms of "national growth" and "per-capita income,"[2] and the concepts of development and economic growth were considered to be synonymous.

Under economic growth, different shades of development theories could be identified. One is the *pyramid* or "Taj Mahal" type of economic growth, which perpetuates the pattern of dominance and dependence which characterized colonialism and now neo-colonialism. A second image is that of the *ladder*—a type of development which suggests that the under-developed, poor countries must chase after the so-called developed, rich countries, imitating their patterns of development and adopting their values and style of life with a view to "catching up" with them. Those who are unable to catch up are left

Reprinted by permission from Gnana Robinson, "Christian Theology and Development," *The Ecumenical Review* 463 (July 1994), pp. 316–321. Copyright © 1994, World Council of Churches.

behind, destined to remain poor forever. A third symbol is that of the *life-boat.* Here the rich nations of the world are to pick up, by a careful process of selection, on their own terms and according to their own criteria, those who can be saved (developed), leaving behind the hopelessly poor as beyond salvation. A fourth image of economic development is that of everyone trying to grab the largest *piece of the development pie.* This type of development is obsessed with ever-increasing production and overlooks the need for just distribution and the limitations of the earth's resources. As Somen Dhas from India rightly points out, "this is the kind of thinking and attitude that has created a consumer society which is compulsive and conspicuous in character. Such a system aggravates the acquisitive and aggressive instincts of people."[3]

Modern development is based on modern technology, which is capital-intensive. It gravitates towards the organized urban sector to the near exclusion of the traditional, rural agricultural sector. The costs which the people pay for such development are high. In the personal and social realms, life becomes fragmented and dehumanized. Extreme individualism increases and the sense of wholeness is lost. The marginalization of some people in society becomes normal. The intrinsic value of the human person is lost; instead, people are regarded for their "cash value." If they are not able to contribute to the production process, by input of either capital or labour, they are pushed aside. In the economic realm, this type of development leads to unemployment, under-employment and foreign debts. Rather than mobilizing the production potential of their people, poor nations import foreign know-how and technology, exhausting national resources and building up foreign debts. Since this type of development is geared to maximum profit in the shortest time, it is accompanied by enormous waste, leading to severe ecological and environmental damage.[4]

Development theories which are based merely on economic growth have to be subjected to criticism by Christian theology, which is, as we have seen, concerned for the holistic development of the whole human community. We are here concerned with the development of all people, all ethnic communities—black, white, brown and yellow, high-caste and low-caste, male and female. Holistic development focuses on the material, physical, psychological, emotional and spiritual needs of every person in the community, not only the present generation but also future generations. Stewardship of the resources of nature therefore becomes very important. Waste has to be avoided; and nothing should be done that will disturb the ecological balance of nature. Thus, as the eminent Indian Christian economist C.T. Kurien notes, "Development is complex as life. . . . All the ingredients of life find reflection the moment we talk about development—economics, sociology, religion, ethics—all these and more will come into account; and hence it is indeed a very complex issue."[5]

JUST RELATIONS: THE FOCUS OF DEVELOPMENT

If holistic development of the human community is the focus of Christian theology, "justice" is the means of achieving that goal. "Let justice roll down like waters, and righteousness like an everflowing stream," says God (Amos 5:24).

Development is a matter of human relations, and justice, according to the Bible, is a relational concept which raises the question of right relationship with God and with God's people. Wherever Old Testament prophets found irregularities in the society, wherever they found abnormal relations such as dominance, oppression and exploitation, they immediately raised the question of justice. "Learn to do good; seek justice, rescue the oppressed, defend the orphan, plead for the widow," says Isaiah (1:17)....

> It is no longer growth but "distributive justice" that has become the centre of discussion in development debates today. Thus, "development becomes liberation and the narrow or limited concern for development will have to be enlarged to take into account liberation in the economic sense, the social sense and the spiritual sense"....[6]

According to M.M. Thomas, true development is development of people, "the release of people from their enslaved conditions so that they can have the rightful dignity of participating in the process of making decisions which affect their life and labour."[7] Therefore he rejects the Taj Mahal or pyramid concept of development, which is based on brutalizing exploitation and forced labour.

Today we talk of North–South and First World–Third World relationships. Here again it is the question of justice we are concerned with. How far are these relationships just politically, economically and culturally? In every respect we see hegemony, dominance and exploitation from the side of the rich. Countries in the South which have suffered heavily under colonialism now suffer under neo-colonialism. The principle that the rich and the powerful dictate and dominate has characterized such relationships, and the question of justice has never been taken seriously. It is therefore important that the question of distributive justice is raised at all levels of our development discussions, both globally and locally.

Christian theology demands that all people enjoy the God-given blessings of creation equally, because all are created in the image of God and all are given the privilege of enjoying this creation equally. The biblical account of the Fall holds that the tension in the human's relationship with fellow human beings and with the animal world and nature result from the human's marred relationship with God. The right relationship with God, the right relationship with fellow human beings and the right relationship with nature all belong together. The right relationship with God is basic to all other just relationships—just human relationships as well as just relationships to nature—and these just relationships are the integral part of holistic development. Removal of unjust conditions and unjust structures in the relationships between countries and peoples is therefore basic to any process of development.

SELF-RELIANCE AS THE GOAL OF DEVELOPMENT

Describing the ideal state of life under messianic rule, the prophet Micah speaks of all humans sitting under their own vines and their own fig trees, "and no one shall make them afraid" (4:4). The idea of "dependence" is alien to the biblical understanding of human development, because dependence implies inequality, which is against the will of God. The Old Testament prophets condemn those people who use unjust means to deprive people of their freedom and force them to become dependent on others (cf. Amos 8:4–6; Micah 2:22). Inter-dependence is an essential aspect of human life; because God has intended humans to live in community, not in isolation (Genesis 2:18).

The New Testament also speaks for the self-reliant development of every human being. If we analyze the accounts of the healing miracles of Jesus, we see that they were meant to restore the sick and the suffering to normal humanity so that they might live as free people. He healed the disabled and the lepers in order to reintegrate them into society. The miracle performed by Peter and John at one of the gates of the temple in Jerusalem points to the same purpose. Peter says to the man born lame, "I have no silver or gold, but what I have I give you: in the name of Jesus Christ of Nazareth, stand up and walk" (Acts 3:6). Peter removes the condition which was responsible for the man's dependency on others: he can now stand on his own feet and walk. Development is thus essentially the removal of the conditions of dependency on others.

In the Eurocentric, growth-oriented understanding of development, unjust relations have created conditions of dependency. Under-development is not the original condition of any society, as some proponents of growth-oriented development theories would have us believe. Under-development is the condition created by the growth-oriented, exploitative, capitalistic development process. As an example of this, A.G. Frank points to the British de-industrialization in India, the destructive effects of the slave trade on African societies and the obliteration of the Indian civilization in Central and South America.[8] As Theotonio Dos Santos of Brazil points out, dependence is "a situation in which the economy of certain countries is conditioned by the development and expansion of another economy to which the former is subjected."[9] According to Dos Santos, "the concept of 'dependence' cannot be formulated outside the boundaries of the theory of imperialism, but should be seen as a complement to the term imperialism, since 'dependency' is the internal face of imperialism."[10] Factors that contribute to the condition of dependency have therefore to be resisted and countered.

The Cocoyoc Declaration, adopted by a UN symposium in Mexico in 1974, presents a development strategy of self-reliance: "We believe that one basic strategy of development will have to be increased national self-reliance. It does not mean autarchy. It implies benefits from trade and co-operation and a fairer redistribution of resources satisfying basic needs. It does mean self-confidence, reliance primarily on one's own resources, human and natural, and the capacity for autonomous goal-setting and decision-making. It excludes dependence on outside influences and powers that can be converted into political pressure."[11] Genuine development should be a socio-economic and political process in which all people who produce goods and render services become aware of the nature of existing power-structures, structures of dominance, and try to change them by creating "a countervailing power of the masses, thereby unleashing the full productive power of the people for total human development."[12]

Two principles of authentic development, according to Gandhi, were self-reliance (*swadeshi*) and welfare to all (*sarvodaya*), and here Gandi has drawn much from the teachings of Jesus. By contrast, the world in which we live today is one of great disparities. Much of the world's population lives in abject poverty, and the gap between rich and poor widens day by day. At the international level a few rich countries continue to increase their dominance over the poor countries, thus increasing dependency; at the national level poor and marginalized people, such as the aboriginals and the dalits in India, are dominated and exploited by the rich in their own country. In such a situation, all those who participate in development activities have to work towards removing the shackles of dominance by the rich and contributing to the self-reliance of the poor and the marginalized. They have to work towards creating a condition in which every human sits under his or her own vine and fig tree, and none shall make them afraid. This is what holistic development involves.

Social Ethics in a Post-Socialist World
Peter L. Berger

The title of these observations contains two assumptions—that now is indeed a post-socialist era and that there is such a thing as social ethics. It may be worthwhile to examine both assumptions with at least a measure of skepticism.

Is this a post-socialist era? One might reply yes on two grounds.

First, empirically: There is precious little socialism left—"real existent socialism," in the old Marxist phrase—for anyone who may want to reply no. This is not only because of the spectacular collapse of, first, the Soviet empire in Europe, and then of the Soviet Union itself, though that collapse is surely the single most dramatic event of this moment in history. There is also the rapid conversion to capitalist policies (even if not always capitalist rhetoric) of formerly socialist regimes and movements almost everywhere in the world. Populist politicians in Latin America, African dictators, Communist Party officials in China and Vietnam, Swedish social democrats—more and more they all sound like economics graduates of the University of Chicago, at least when they talk about the economy. "Real existent socialism" survives in a few countries, every one a disaster (North Korea and Cuba are prime cases), and in enclaves where one has the feeling of being in a time-warp (among, for example, academics in India or in the English-speaking universities of South Africa, or in some church agencies in the United States).

"Social Ethics in a Post-Socialist World," by Peter L. Berger, *First Things,* February 1993, pp. 9–14. Reprinted by permission of *First Things.*

Second, one might view this as a post-socialist era for theoretical reasons: Given the historical record of socialism in this century, one can say with some assurance that all the claims made for it have been decisively falsified—be it in terms of economic performance, of political liberation, of social equality, or of the quality of life. Similar falsification has befallen every major proposition of Marxism as an interpretation of the modern world. As a theory, then, socialist ideology today impresses one as being akin to a stubborn assertion that, despite everything, the earth is flat.

Why, then, the skepticism? In this particular instance it is not very difficult to imagine scenarios in the not-too-distant future in which there might occur resurgences of socialist policies and ideals: the failure of neo-capitalist regimes in developing societies and/or the formerly communist countries in Europe to achieve economic take-off; the insight granted to sundry dictators and despots that, while socialism invariably immiserates the masses, it is a very good recipe for enriching those who claim to hold power as the vanguard of the masses; the "creeping socialism" (still an aptly descriptive term) brought on by massive government intervention in the economy in the name of some societal good, e.g., there could be an environmentalist road to socialism, or a feminist one, or one constructed (perhaps inadvertently) with some other building blocks of politically managed regulations and entitlements; or, last but not least, the actual restoration of socialism, by coup or by voting, in a number of countries, beginning with Russia. For the last three years or so it has been fashionable to say that socialism is "finished." Let us not be so sure. Certainly, a rational mind has cause to conclude that socialism belongs on the scrapheap of history. But, alas, history is *not* the march of reason on earth.

With respect to our second question—Is there such a thing as social ethics? —the answer is obviously yes. . . . Leaving aside the far from simple issue of the relation between faith and ethics, and hewing strictly to the line of social science, we have to say that blueprints for a just society have typically been one of two things—either a set of propositions so abstract that they could be filled with just about any concrete content or a set of propositions that could indeed be practically applied, which applications have led to some of the great human catastrophes of the modern age. Put as an empirical statement: Beware of the prophets of a just society!

Socialism has been attractive to many social ethicists precisely because it is clearly of the second type—a concrete blueprint, based on an allegedly scientific understanding of the forces of history and providing some reasonably clear guidelines for action. Marxism, in all its variants, has provided the most coherent blueprint of this type, that is, an exhaustive analysis of the present, a fairly clear vision of the future, and on top of all that (especially in its Leninist version), a practical method of getting to that future. All of it, of course, has been a gigantic delusion—the analysis was false, the vision was deeply flawed, and the experiments of realizing the vision have exacted horrendous human costs. . . .

But the most intense infatuation with socialism in the churches came with the cultural earthquake of the late 1960s and early 1970s in the West. By then, there were many socialist societies scattered all over the globe, many of them with minimal or no connection with the Soviet Union. There followed a long and ever-changing list of socialist experiments, most of them in the Third World, each of which, we were told in turn, embodied some bright hope for a just and humane society—China, North Vietnam, Tanzania, Cuba, Nicaragua. The facts about these societies—facts about massive terror, repression, and economic misery, and, need it be said, about the persecution of Christians—were systematically ignored, denied, or explained away. . . .

If, in this thoroughly unmessianic spirit, we turn to the moral issues of contemporary capitalism, it is possible to distinguish two sets of issues, broadly definable as macro- and micro-dimensional. The macro-issues are those that involve the society or the economy as a whole; the micro-issues concern individual sectors or organizations within the economy, such questions as business ethics and corporate culture generally. The latter are naturally of great importance, and do in the aggregate affect the larger society. But our interest here will be the macro-level. Now, on this level, it would be easy right off to draw up a very long list of moral issues faced by capitalist societies today. For virtually no problems faced by and politically debated within these societies are without a moral dimension, including very technical economic problems (such as, say, the prime lending rate or rates of exchange between national currencies). A few specific examples of such issues follow.

First, there is the question of the sequencing of marketization and democratization.

For the time being at least, much of the world is moving toward a market economy and toward democracy. Among those who participate in the post-socialist mood of triumphalism, these two processes are commonly seen more or less as two sides of the same coin. Alas, they are not. There is, to be sure, a measure of validity to the identification. It is empirically correct, for instance, that a successful market economy releases democratizing pressures—the children of hungry peasants, once they have forgotten the hunger, become politically uppity. It is also empirically correct that a market economy is the necessary, though not sufficient, condition for democracy—there have been no socialist democracies, for reasons that can be explained sociologically. But it is *not* valid to say that one cannot have a market economy without democracy. The empirical evidence appears to suggest that, while a market economy tends eventually to generate democracy (put differently, dictatorships tend not to survive a successful capitalist development), a market economy need not have democracy in order to take off.

Indeed, it usually doesn't. None of the post-World War II success stories in East Asia took off under democratic regimes, except for Japan. And Japan's original take-off was almost a hundred years earlier, under the Meiji regime—and *that* was certainly not a democracy. Two recent success stories in other parts of the world, Spain and Chile, replicate the marketization-before-democratization pattern. And if one looks at the formerly socialist societies in Europe, one may well conclude that an important reason for their present difficulties is that they are attempting to undertake both transitions simultaneously. Nor does the earlier history of capitalism offer much comfort to the reverse-sides-of-the-same-coin viewpoint. England, where it all began, could hardly be described as a democracy in the eighteenth century; neither could France or Germany in the nineteenth. The United States may be the comforting exception. There are also some comforting cases in the more recent period—for example, Sri Lanka, or Pakistan in the 1960s. But on the whole, there is enough evidence at least to suggest that, if one wants to have both a market economy and democracy, it is better to have the former precede the latter—if you will, to have *perestroika* before *glasnost* (it being understood, of course, that Gorbachev had something other than full capitalism in mind with the former term, and something less than full democracy with the latter).

The reasoning behind such a hypothesis is not difficult to explain. It is safe to say that no economic takeoff can occur without pain. The pain, inevitably, will not be equitably distributed throughout the population. Initially, very likely, only a minority will benefit from economic growth. In a democracy, this minority is easily outvoted, especially if populist politicians agitate the majority that either feels the pain or, minimally, does not see any tangible benefits as yet. Mancur Olson has coined the useful term "distributional coalitions." By this he means vested interests that organize in order to get their slice of the economic pie by means of government actions. Olson argues that economic growth is slowed when these coalitions mature. In a wealthy, developed society such slowdowns are economically tolerable; in a poor, less-developed society a slowdown can abort the takeoff. Democracy, of course, gives distributional coalitions the free space to organize, to grow, and to influence government. By contrast, a dictatorship can more easily control those vested interests that seek to slow down or dismantle the government's economic policies.

The case of present-day China sharply illustrates both the empirical processes at issue and the resultant moral dilemma. It is not altogether clear whether what is now happening in China represents a deliberate policy of the Deng Xiao-ping regime or whether in fact the regime has lost control over what happens. In any case, what is happening is a capitalist revolution, especially in the south, unfolding rapidly under a regime that continues to spout Marxist rhetoric and that has, so far successfully, curbed any moves toward democracy. Ironically, this situation strongly resembles the situation in Taiwan when the authoritarian Kuomintang regime launched the capitalist takeoff there. The China story, of course, has not ended and the present economic course could yet be arrested. In large parts of the country, though, such a reversal would be very difficult. Guangdong province (a territory, by the way, that has some eighty million inhabitants) is rapidly becoming an economic extension of neighboring Hong Kong, registering one of the highest growth rates in the world. The prosperity generated by this economic transformation is creeping up the coast toward Shanghai. It is not unreasonable to suppose that eventually some kind of political liberalization will follow the economic one.

The moral problem in a case of this kind concerns the interim period, the duration of which cannot be predicted. One need not necessarily be troubled by the delay in the advent of democracy per se; though it is terribly un-Wilsonian to do so, one can, and in fact ought to, remain open to the possibility of the benevolent autocrat. The trouble, once again, is empirical—the aforementioned correlation between democracy and human rights. Put simply, dictatorships, much more than democracies, are likely to violate human rights. The key question for the sort of "interim ethic" called for here (New Testament scholars will please forgive the term) is how many and what sorts of violations one is prepared to accept. It is not all that difficult to swallow the absence of elections (or the absence of *honest* elections, which amounts to the same thing) as the price for spreading prosperity soon and widespread prosperity eventually (especially as democracy is likely to appear as the latter occurs). But on the other hand, genocide is certainly not an acceptable price. The real question is, where are the limits? Using tanks against unarmed civilians? Using them once only? Regularly? What about a network of political prison camps? What about the use of torture by the security forces? Occasionally? Regularly? And so on. The *real* moral dilemmas almost always get lost in current debates over human rights, especially if either democracy or the market or both of these are proposed as panaceas.

The second macro-level question concerns the range and the nature of political redistribution. It is clear that a market economy, once it has reached a certain level of affluence, can tolerate a considerable amount of governmentally managed redistribution. This, of course, is the basic lesson to be learned from the coexistence of capitalism with the welfare state. It should also be clear that this tolerance is not without limits. If political redistribution reaches a certain level, it must either send the economy into a downward spin (wealth being redistributed faster than it is produced) or dismantle democracy (to prevent those whose wealth is to be redistributed—a population which, as redistribution expands, will be very much larger than the richest group—from resisting). Now, it would be very nice if economists and social scientists could tell us just where this level is—one might call it the social-democratic tolerance threshold. Right-of-center parties in Western democracies perceive a very low threshold (each piece of welfare state legislation another step on "the road to serfdom"); left-of-center parties believe in a very high threshold, and some in that camp seem to think that there is no limit at all. What evidence there is clearly does not support either the disciples of Hayek or Swedish social democrats; but neither, unfortunately, does the evidence locate the tilting-point. Once again, a sort of "interim ethic" is called for, full of uncertainties and risks.

Paradoxically, the choices here are simpler in a poor society, where the amount of wealth available for redistribution is quite small. Perhaps a more accurate statement would be that in a poor society the choices should be simpler, if policies were to be decided upon rationally and with the general well-being of society as the goal. In fact, of course, all sorts of irrational motives are at work in every society, and what is bad for the whole society may be very good indeed for whatever clique of "kleptocrats" (Peter Bauer's term) is in charge of government. Still, the so-called "Uruguay effect," i.e., an expansive welfare state ruining the economy, becomes visible rather quickly in a poor society (though at that point it is very difficult to repair the damage). In a rich society the process of economic ruination is likely to take more time and to be less visible, with the consequence that the available choices may seem more free than they in fact are.

The moral problem here is, rather simply, to find a balance between economic prudence and the desire to meet this or that social need. Leave aside here the fact that some needs are artificially created and do not really arise out of genuine deprivation. Even when full allowance is made for this, there remain enough cases of real deprivation in any society to leave the moral problem in place. How much of a welfare state can a successful capitalist economy afford? How much of government intervention in the economy, not just for the sake of redistribution, but for any alleged societal good? Even if one is not a true disciple of Hayek, one must concede that the road to economic disaster (with all its ensuing human costs) is frequently paved with good intentions.

The moral problem becomes even more complicated. There are not only potential *economic* costs to political redistribution; there are costs in terms of democracy and in terms of the liberties of individuals, as well. The welfare state brings about an expansion of government power into ever more areas of social life, with government bureaucrats and governmentally authorized social workers peeking and poking into every nook and cranny of the lives of individuals. The purpose of all these interventions is almost always noble-sounding—to protect the public health, to assist children, the old, or the handicapped or some other underprivileged group, to safeguard entitlements, to watch over the expenditure of taxpayers' money, and so on and so forth.

The sum total of all these interventions, though, is what Bernard Levin has called "the nanny state," which reached its climax in the social democracies of northern Europe and which, of course, brought about a backlash even there, not only from irate taxpayers but from a lot of people who were fed up being interfered with at every turn by the agents of benevolent government. At what point, then, does well-meaning political intervention become tyrannical? How can specific social needs be met without aggrandizing state bureaucracy and depriving people, those with the putative needs, of more and more control over their own lives? In poor societies the question can be put this way: How can the most pressing social needs be met without risking the "Uruguay effect"? In richer societies the question becomes: How can one maintain a reasonably effective welfare state without succumbing to the "Swedish disease"?

Third, there is the issue of the relation between economic development and cultural values.

Max Weber was wrong about many things, and he may even have been wrong about the strategic place he gave to the "Protestant ethic" in the development of modern capitalism. But he was almost certainly right in his assumption that some form of what he called "inner-worldly asceticism," that is, a collection of values that led to worldly activism and to delayed gratification, was necessary before a modern economic takeoff could occur. The Puritan entrepreneur was indeed a prototypical figure embodying such values. Contemporary evidence about the economic cultures of East Asia, of successful ethnic groups in different countries, or of the mobility of immigrants to this country all seems to point in the same direction: self-denial and discipline are virtues that are the condition *sine qua non* of early capitalist development.

Christian ethicists usually have no great difficulty in admiring and even recommending these virtues, even in cases where they do not fully or even partially endorse the theological and philosophical presuppositions of people who evince them (such as, for instance, Latin American Pentecostals, Muslim fundamentalists, or neo-Confucian businessmen). At the same time, Christian ethicists often decry the absence or the decline of these values in Western societies today and go on to suggest that, unless we return to the old virtues, we will go under economically; and in this they may very possibly be mistaken.

Contemporary Western societies, with America in the lead, are anything but self-denying and disciplined. They are governed by values of self-gratification and untrammeled individual freedom. From a Puritan viewpoint, of course, such values will be seen perjoratively—as expressing greed, selfishness, irresponsibility. From a different perspective, one may perceive them as joyful and liberating. Be that as it may, in this century there has been an ongoing progression in Western cultures away from the older asceticism. A quantum leap in this development came with the cultural revolution that began in the 1960s. The culture has become even more liberating in terms of the wants of individuals, more libidinally positive, if you will "softer," more "feminized." This cultural change has by now invaded significant sectors of the business world, of the bastions of capitalism. Thus far there is no evidence that this has a negative effect on economic productivity, at least as one reads the actual evidence.

This obviously poses a moral problem for those who remain committed to the older virtues. Hard work, postponing enjoyments, discipline, sobriety—all these components of the "Protestant ethic" may have been held to be good in themselves, but it certainly helped when one could credibly argue that adhering to these virtues not only pleased God but worked to one's economic advantage in this world, here and now. Conversely, there would be some embarrassment to many ethicists if putative vices like self-indulgence, sloth, and lechery could be happily practiced without visible ill-effects in the economic progress of individuals or of society.

But there is another moral problem if one takes the view that our "softer" culture will indeed harm us economically, both as individuals and, more importantly, as an entire society. This point of view regularly recurs in discussions of our competitiveness vis-à-vis East Asia in general and Japan in particular. We must change, it is said, or we will lose out in the international competition. Usually it is not so much our hedonism that is being chastised in this way (though that comes in for some invidious comparisons too) as our alleged "excessive individualism." By way of contrast, we are asked to contemplate the wonderful loyalty of the Japanese to their company and their fellow-employees.

Now, never mind how accurate this picture of East Asian economic culture is; let it be stipulated, for the sake of the argument, that the Japanese are all they are here assumed to be and that this does indeed give them a comparative cultural advantage over us. Do we really want to become more like them? Do we want the corporation to become an all-embracing *mater et magistra?* Do we want people to submerge their aspirations for self-realization in loyalty to an organization? Do we want employees to put the company before family? And most basically, are we prepared to say that the whole history of Western individualism, including its expressions in the American political creed, can be looked at as a great mistake? And, if we say no to all these questions (as most of us surely would), how much of an economic price are we willing to pay for this position?

There are no definitive or unambiguous solutions to these or any other moral dilemmas of society. There is not, and cannot be, a design for a just society prior to the coming of the Kingdom of God. Moreover, when we start to act in society, the overwhelming probability is that our actions will either fail or will lead to consequences that we did not intend. Sometimes these consequences will be terrible. For this reason, the first and last principle of any Christian social ethics must be the forgiveness of sins. But that is a story for another time.

Transnational Corporations and Institutionalized Violence: A Challenge to Christian Movements in the United States

Mark Lewis Taylor

In the Guatemala of 1991, you could still see Mayan peoples proceeding to bury their dead children in small boxes, not all, of course, so startlingly stamped with a corporation label. An equally striking juxtaposition occurs if you happen to be driving a main highway to see what Guatemalan newspapers report daily: tortured and mutilated adult bodies, sometimes rolled into a ditch, lodged against wooden poles stretching upward to display the goods of corporate giants: Shell, CocaCola, Bank of America, Mitsubishi.

What would it mean for theology to think about the connection between a dead child and General Electric, between tortured bodies and transnational corporations (TNCs)? Can it be done without producing only the dismissable rhetoric of jeremiad and hyperbole? In this essay, I attempt that exercise in thought, beginning with a Guatemalan encounter of violence. Then in the second section, I identify the interwoven dimensions operative in that encounter.

A third section presents "abstraction" as a key dynamic in the institutionalized violence embodied in transnational corporations. Against the backdrop of this approach to "corporate evil," the fourth and final section then seeks to present Christian movements as a kind of "corporate grace," issuing in strategic practices of resistance and hope. . . .

UNLEASHING THE "THIRD SYSTEM": THE CONTRIBUTION OF CHRISTIAN MOVEMENTS

The pervasive institutionalized violence that TNCs often embody can work numbing despair once it is exposed and lamented. As powerful as this structural violence is, however, there do exist communities and dynamics of resistance and hope. In spite of the despair and ennui that knowledge of such violence can breed, in this final section I think in reliance upon the presence of such resistance and hope.[13]

MOVEMENTS AND THE "THIRD SYSTEM"

In considering the present global political situation, Richard Falk has distinguished three systems of political action. The "first system" is what this essay has characterized as diversified institutionalized violence. It is the system of power in governing structures of territorial states:

> . . . in short, the state system, including its supporting infrastructure of corporations, banks, media; a system that is hierarchical, fragmented and in which war and violence are accepted as discretionary options for power-wielders and in which armies, weapons, police and military doctrines play a crucial role within and among states.[14]

A "second system" of power consists of the United Nations and various "regional international institutions." Falk sees this as basically an extension of the first system with only a nominal verbal mandate, decrying first-system violence, lessening hierarchy and fragmentation.

Notable achievements of the second system rarely occur without linkages to a third system. This is a system of power consisting of "people acting individually or collectively through social movements, voluntary institutions, associations, including churches and labor unions. . . ." It is the primary embodiment of new values, demands, and visions. Hence, it can be co-opted, subverted, and repressed by the first system (or sometimes by the second system, too).[15]

Christian movements are obviously not the only contributors to this third system; but they, like others in the system, make their contribution by prompting the second-system agents into normative initiatives with structural consequences. Christian movements' contributions may, as Falk suggests of the third system generally, often be latent, potential, or symbolic, but precisely as such they can be catalysts and tools for needed social change.[16]

In the following two subsections, I present the Christian movement as contributing a distinctive mythos of emancipation, and a set of strategic practices. I emphasize that for the third system that needs to be unleashed against TNC institutionalized violence, it will need to be a coalition of diverse religious and nonreligious communities. In fact, religious communities in North Atlantic contexts may often *not* be the most vital contributors, or, at least, they will require the goading of other contributors in the third system. If I here discuss the contribution of Christian movements, I do so to clarify the nature of that contribution for Christians, and to initiate, from the side of Christian vision, a coalition-building dialogue with other third-system practitioners.

A MYTHOS OF RECONCILIATORY EMANCIPATION

Christian movements are first and foremost movements for emancipation. They are a distinctive kind of freedom-making movement. To be sure, we know well how from its earliest times, especially when consolidated with Constantinian rule, Christianity has served up obstacles to freedom. It has licensed repression, implemented inquisitional terror, and still reinforces systems of the worst sort with the power of its religious myth and ritual.[17] The use of Christian language and cult in South Africa is a clear recent example.[18]

In its formative years, however, when Christianity is perhaps best described as the "Jesus movement" or "early Christian movement," the primary value was one of emancipation and liberation—in the senses of both *from* every kind of oppressive dynamic and also *to*, or *into*, structured communities that sustain emancipation. As also a Jewish movement, it drew from the Exodus and prophetic traditions a stress on a kind of freedom–making, which, though worked by divine power, was nevertheless historical and human. Moreover, this movement of emancipation grew in the structurally dangerous time of imperial Roman domination and in a territory under especially ruthless, religiopolitical Hasmonean and Herodian rule.

There are, of course, the often-mentioned limits to how politically revolutionary one can present the historical Jesus movement. As Richard Horsley has emphasized, however, these constraints are no license for Christian scholars to screen out the political and emancipatory nature of the movement. Horsley well summarizes Jesus' position and the spirit of the emancipatory movement:

> Jesus would appear to have believed that God had already begun the political revolution even though it was hardly very far along. But in the confidence that it was underway, it was his calling to proceed with the *social revolution* thus made possible by God's rule, to begin the transformation of social relations in anticipation of the completion of the political revolution.[19]

Proceeding with the social revolution, therefore, it was fueled not only by the fact of oppression, but also by the sense that a sacrally enacted political revolution was already in motion. With this kind of fusion of grace and politics, the early Christian movement featured a unity of spirituality and human action. The social revolution meant the thriving of the movement especially among local peasant cultures and others suffering double taxation (local and imperial), increasing indebtedness, and loss of land. At times, the movement exacerbated class conflict. It moreover sought renewal through embodiment of a "new family." In rejecting rank and prestige, its communal aims were more egalitarian, seeking to be "an extended, non-patriarchal 'family' of 'siblings.'"[20] Based on these many dimensions of the early movement, the Christian movement may be understood as a multidimensional movement of emancipation and has been interpreted as such by contemporary Christian activists and thinkers.

The key qualifier here is signaled by this very word, "multidimensionality." Without forfeiting the primacy of its emancipation motif, it seeks to unify a manifold of emancipatory needs. In this sense its emancipatory interest is "reconciliatory," that is, it seeks to make unity along with, or in the wake of, making freedom from oppression. In the present setting, this would mean insisting on emancipation that orchestrates the claims of different groups (victims of class exploitation *and* ethnic oppression, *and* gender injustice *and* homophobia and heterosexism, etc.). The reconciliatory qualifier also means that Christian emancipatory action ultimately aims at a community that includes even the enemy-oppressor. Thus, as in the liberation theology of Peruvian Gustavo Gutiérrez, a "universality of Christian love" is extended even to the adversary. Such "love of the enemy" is compatible with both a preferential option for the poorest and most oppressed, and with a sustained adversarial stance toward the enemy.[21]

Enough has been said of the nature of the Christian movement's mythos of reconciliatory emancipation to enable an identification of the strategic practices mandated by the crises of corporate culture's institutionalized violence. For theologians, the relevant point is this: the praxis of Christian movements arises within an emancipative mythos that envisions sacral power as having already set in motion the political revolution that is capable of freeing Third World peoples from the institutionalized violence often embodied in the TNCs and other parts of the "first system." It remains now to identify certain strategic practices in which representatives of the Christian movement might now participate to embody a revolutionary praxis of reconciliatory emancipation. The mythos of reconciliatory emancipation does not romanticize any human structure or movement; but it does foster particular values and hopes needed for mobilizing strategies of resistance and restructuring.

AGAINST ABSTRACTION: FOUR STRATEGIC PRACTICES

When considering the institutionalized violence of corporate culture, the practices of Christian movements especially need to move against and model alternatives to the distancing and destructive functions of abstraction. In this regard, four kinds of practice are strategic. They constitute part of Christian movements' contribution to unleashing the third system of coalitional forces needed for resisting first-system destruction.

First, Christian movements entail the local, on-site organizing of people in distress. There is enormous empowerment for resistance and hope just in this organizing, which hears the cries of specific people in need and then brings them together. The hearing and the gathering are significant even without considering the also necessary agendas that may later emerge.

I use the term *organizing* intentionally, to suggest an effort at the grassroots level that structures relations among the oppressed. In Third World settings, those most victimized by structural adjustment policies or TNC firm actions do precisely this: they gather together and organize, not only to lament together but also to strategize for survival and change. U.S. Christians need to organize among populations on North American terrain those whose cries of distress can be linked to abusive TNC policies. A prime example here might be those without health insurance coverage who, through organizing, can begin to see the links between their deprivation and the exploitative practices of medical technology corporations.

By the stress on locality, grassroots, and the concrete organizing of local groups, the Christian movement begins to construct a countervailing dynamic to corporate abstraction. The emphasis on the local is a dynamic resisting the remoteness and distancing function of abstraction in institutionalized violence. Christian movements cannot simply engage in high-level corporate policies to resist institutionalized violence. Such macrolevel policy-making is essential, as I will suggest below. But without redressing the distancing function of corporate remoteness, substantial change will be less likely to occur; or, at least, less will be known about which "high-level" changes are needed for the cultural-material needs of the people "below."

Second, Christian movements must nurture, move out from, and return to distinctive kinds of social interaction: communities of the face. As applied to Christian movements, this phrase comes from the philosophy of Jewish thinker Emmanuel Levinas through Christian theologian Edward Farley. These are communities featuring a kind of embodied relationality that constantly rehearses its members, at the level of the concrete, in a sense of "species-being" (awareness of "the universal face") and in a sense of the unsubstitutable distinctiveness of each being (awareness of "the particular face"). Both the more universal reminder and the particular presentation are developed from Levinas's meditations on experiencing the face in relation. The universalizing impetus emerges from the fact that the face always points beyond regional loyalties and obligations, and thus communities that heed the face are oriented to the species as a whole, indeed to all life forms.[22] The face, however, has a special particularizing power, too. "It is the 'infinitely strange' and 'mysterious presence' of something that always contests my projecting meanings of it. . . ."[23] Thus, communities of the face inspire at once a universal sense or "species consciousness,"[24] but also a sense of each individual's particularity. Though Christian traditions have regularly compromised with, had their ideals kidnaped by, proponents of regional loyalties, Christian movements taking their cue from the reconciliatory emancipation of the Christian movement manifest the universal and particular senses of the face. The species consciousness is crucial for effecting a collective emancipation from structural evil and institutionalized violence, while the sense of the particular in the face is needed for developing that "reconciliatory" posture that acknowledges the many different types of emancipation needed, and seeks to orchestrate their particular, often conflicting, claims.

Perhaps a concrete example of the power in communities of the face can be taken from reflection on the practices of interrogation and torture. Victims frequently report (among them Jennifer Casolo, a U.S. citizen not tortured but interrogated and threatened in El Salvador in 1989) that wielders of intimidation often prefer their victims blindfolded, their faces somehow obscured. This is because face-to-face encounter or eye contact tends to break down the dehumanizing process. Is it any wonder, then, also that members of corporate cultures in Third World areas rarely cultivate sustained, face-to-face contact with the rural or barrio poor? In the course of her own interrogation, Casolo connived to get her interrogator to remove her blindfold and this mitigated the harshness of the interrogation. Christian movements have as a second strategic practice, then, this search to be in relation as communities of the face, nurturing face-to-face contact, indeed celebrating this contact. As such, they are forging a hedge against the distancing and destructive functions of abstraction in which the TNCs and institutionalized violence excel.

Third, Christian movements cannot avoid the strategic practice of global networking and institutional formation. Crucial as are the above two strategic practices for resisting and providing communal alternatives, especially to the "distancing function" of institutionalized violence, the global structures of transnational corporate culture will not be halted without countervailing structures of international scope and complexity. Global corporate culture has achieved a systemic power that also has the "destructive function," and this requires a countervailing, structuring response. With theologian Friedrich Schleiermacher of the nineteenth century, we might emphasize today that a "corporate evil" requires acknowledging and activating a "corporate grace,"[25] and this requires global networking and institutional formation.

Throughout the Third World today is evidence that locally organized modes of Christian movement and communities of the face (for example, "base ecclesial communities") are engaged in global networking now, to establish working connections with Christians suffering exploitation by corporate cultures on all continents.[26]

These efforts are still largely on the level of theological discourse. Christian movements still need to embody themselves in struggles supporting political-structural transformation. Many Third World countries and thinkers are now questioning second-system correctives to TNCs, such as the voluntary code of conduct sponsored by the United Nations. This voluntary code of conduct for regulating TNC practices leaves Third World countries in little better position than before the code.[27]

Hence, meaningful structural resistance to TNC culture requires the formation of "Third World only" organizations (sectoral, subregional, regional, interregional) for controlling the TNCs.[28] This entails an enormously complex task of institutional construction. Of course, Christian movements are themselves not the locus of such institutional arrangements, but if such movements take resistance seriously they need to support and incarnate themselves to some degree in such efforts.

For U.S. Christians, the special challenge of this strategic practice of global networking and institutional formation is no less demanding. There already exist significant organized resistances. The World Council of Churches and various ecclesiastical denominations have, for example, denounced the merely voluntary codes of conduct, have called for lobbying and pressuring of corporation shareholders, denouncing oppressive corporate policies, organizing boycotts of corporation products, etc.[29]

All these are important, but what really needs doing and what many in the established churches of the North are often reluctant to do is to work for radical structural changes in the present system of the global economy. Christian movements committed to participating in the emergence of a "corporate grace" to counter corporate institutionalized violence would do well to seek alliance with any of the following exemplary kinds of organizations working for radical structural transformation.

1. There are a number of environmental groups which have launched major campaigns, several of which have contributed tangibly to the education of development groups, and have addressed the World Bank and the IMF on the entrenchment of poverty around the world. . . .

2. In addition to environmental groups, there are other nongovernmental organizations (NGOs) working throughout North Atlantic states, which have carried on a variety of important third-system operations. . . .

3. Another kind of effort, perhaps a most important one, requires support of Christian movements. Since 1968, the World Order Models Project has been explaining the need for global structural change. Its recent work has focused on a Global Civilization Project (GCP) that seeks to mobilize scholars and activists of all levels and from different countries (the United States, the United Kingdom, Russia, Yugoslavia, Portugal, the Philippines, India, Japan, Egypt, and others). The effort is to organize a global civil society which, contrary to abstracting dynamics of destructive corporate culture, seeks a "rooted international society that emphasizes its normative moorings in law and human rights, and its practical urgency in relation to general peace and ecological sustainability."[30] . . .

4. Finally, strategic practices for global justice include a *celebration of the peoples' arts.* Strategic practices are notorious for fostering burnout, using up volunteers, and draining vision. That which sustains a dynamic Christian movement, perhaps any movement, is also a spirit of celebration and symbolic vision.

Christian movements may have a fundamental contribution to make to efforts to resist corporate cultures, because of their mythos of reconciliatory emancipation, and their rituals and liturgies of worship—sacred art forms, we might say, from which practice drinks from visionary power. Christian communities, however, even if they have a lively liturgical tradition—and often in North Atlantic Christendom they do not[31]—have regularly allowed their liturgies and art forms to become ecclesiocentric sedimentations that are abstracted from people in struggle. Such ecclesiocentric abstraction only reinforces the political-economic abstraction of corporate culture.

Christian movements in the United States need to find their way into relation with the arts of people engaged in struggle. This may mean including those art forms somehow in the regular meetings of Christian communities. More significantly, however, it may mean that representatives in Christian movements lead their communities into artistic movements already mobilized for structural change. This may mean participation of Christian movements in local arts and crafts, in music concerts, and in alliance especially with popular music developments which have the potential for yoking youth's desire in music to issues of structural change. Christian movements honor their own defining impulses when they see themselves in alliance with musicians—whether Public Enemy rapping that today "the Ku Klux Klan wears a three-piece suit," Bonnie Raitt giving concert proceeds to battered women's shelters, Jackson Browne singing against U.S. corporation and government involvement in Central America drug running, Bruce Springsteen saying "No thanks, mister" to Lee Iacocca's eight-million-dollar offer to buy his "Born in the U.S.A." song for Chrysler Corporation commercials and then singing for the Christic Institute instead, Neil Young mocking the capitalism of the corporate-controlled music channel MTV, or Michael Stipe of R.E.M. lecturing from the stage about limitations in NBC's reporting because of its connection to the General Electric Company. Whether we think of these musicians in the United States or Chinese rock star Cui Jian in the 1980s, Chilean folksinger Victor Jara of the 1970s, the experimental absurdist rock of *The Plastic People* in Czechoslovakia of 1976, of Thomas Mapfumo's *chimurenga* music in the Zimbabwe revolution or the musical-theatrical group Dos Que Tres in Guatemala of 1989—in all these contexts popular music played a key role in destabilizing tyrannies and repressive systems.[32]

Not only music, but all the arts are resources for the Christian movement and the unleashing of the third system generally. Maybe this is especially true of poetry, about which Audre Lorde has said, "Poetry is not a luxury, it is a vital necessity of our existence. It forms the quality of the light from which we predicate our hopes and dreams toward survival and change, first made into language, then into idea, then into more tangible action."[33]

Thus, I close with words from the Guatemalan poet Otto René Castillo, who in 1967, along with his *compañera*, Nora Paiz, was captured, tied to a tree, tortured, and burned alive in Guatemala.[34] His voice:

From
my bitter darkness
I go beyond
my own hard times
and I see
at the end of the line
happy children!
only happy!
they appear
they rise
like a sun of butterflies
after the tropical cloud-burst.

I'm happy for the children
of the world to come
and I proclaim it
at the top of my lungs,
full of universal rejoicing.[35]

SUGGESTIONS FOR FURTHER READING FOR PART 5

Chapter 12: Christianity and Consumer Lifestyles

Ewen, Stuart. *All Consuming Images.* New York: Basic Books, 1988.

Kavanaugh, John F. *Still Following Christ in a Consumer Society: The Spirituality of Cultural Resistance.* Maryknoll, NY: Orbis Books, 1991.

Moog, Carol. *Are They Selling Her Lips: Advertising and Industry.* New York: William Morrow, 1990.

Novak, Michael. *The Spirit of Democratic Capitalism.* New York: Simon & Schuster, 1982.

Schumacher, E. F. *Small is Beautiful.* New York: Harper & Row, 1974.

Chapter 13: Capitalism and Christian Values

Bellah, Robert N., Richard Madsen, William M. Sullivan, Ann Swidler, and Steven M. Tipton. *The Good Society.* New York: Knopf, 1991.

Clouse, Robert G., ed. *Wealth and Poverty: Four Christian Views of Economics.* Downers Grove, IL: InterVarsity Press, 1984.

Copeland, Warren R. *Economic Justice: The Social Ethics of U.S. Economic Policy.* Nashville: Abingdon Press, 1991.

Funiciello, Theresa. *Tyranny of Kindness: Dismantling the Welfare System to End Poverty in America.* New York: Atlantic Monthly Press, 1993.

Gay, Craig M. *With Liberty and Justice for Whom? The Recent Evangelical Debate over Capitalism.* Grand Rapids, MI: Eerdmans, 1991.

Griffiths, Brian. *The Creation of Wealth: A Christian's Case for Capitalism.* Downers Grove, IL: InterVarsity Press, 1984.

Korten, David. *When Corporations Rule the World.* West Hartford, CT: Kumarian Press, 1995.

MacEoin, Gary. *Unlikely Allies: The Christian-Socialist Convergence.* New York: Crossroad/Continuum, 1990.

Meeks, M. Douglas. *God the Economist.* Minneapolis: Augsburg Fortress, 1989.

Wogaman, J. Philip. *Economics and Ethics: A Christian Inquiry.* Louisville, KY: Westminster/John Knox Press, 1986.

Chapter 14: Seeking Justice between North and South

Berger, Peter L., and Michael Novak. *Speaking to the Third World.* Washington, D.C.: American Enterprise, 1985.

Evans, Robert A., and Alice Frazier Evans. *Human Rights: A Dialogue between the First and Third Worlds.* Maryknoll, NY: Orbis Books, 1983.

Lebacqz, Karen. *Justice in an Unjust World.* Minneapolis: Augsburg, 1987.

Nelson-Pallmeyer, Jack. *Brave New World Order.* Maryknoll, NY: Orbis Books, 1992.

Nichols, Bruce, and Gil Loescher, eds. *The Moral Nation: Humanitarianism and U.S. Foreign Policy Today.* Notre Dame, IN: University of Notre Dame Press, 1990.

Presbyterian Church (USA). *Hope for a Global Future: Toward Just and Sustainable Human Development.* Louisville, KY: Office of the General Assembly, 1996.

Shue, Henry. *Basic Rights: Subsistence, Affluence, and U.S. Foreign Policy.* Princeton: Princeton University Press, 1991.

Sider, Ronald J. *Evangelicals and Development: Toward a Theology of Social Change.* Louisville, KY: Westminster/John Knox Press, 1982.

Vallely, Paul. *Bad Samaritans: First World Ethics and Third World Debt.* Maryknoll, NY: Orbis Books, 1990.

PART 6

The Christian and Bioethical Issues

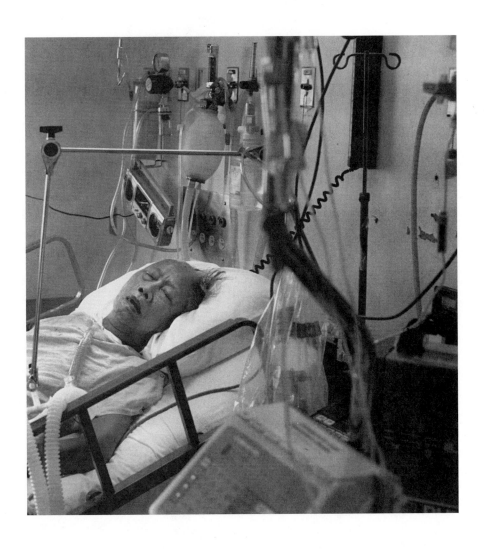

Chapter 15

GENETIC ENGINEERING AND CLONING

The impact of technology on the biological and medical sciences during the last few decades has been dramatic; what it promises for the future both stretches the imagination and sobers the mind. Some of the most exciting and beneficial developments are in biomedicine, where there is also uneasiness over the double-edged character of these advances. Our capacity to help people is accompanied by the possibility of misuse. Consider, for example, the possibilities of cloning human beings.

The term "biomedicine" indicates that the changes taking place are not restricted to medicine as such, but apply to larger issues involving the future development of the human race. Biomedicine involves gene splicing or genetic "engineering," diagnosing and treating genetic defects *in utero*, manipulating the reproductive process, transplanting organs, prolonging life, and modifying or altering behavior.

Concern over the genetic health of society reflects a certain irony, in that the concern is directly related to the success of modern medicine. This success has enabled vast numbers of genetically handicapped people to survive and live essentially normal lives, marry and have children. As a result, genetic defects are multiplied in the human gene pool, prompting some biological scientists to raise questions about whether we should be taking measures to improve the race's genetic health. Some would argue that our society needs to take direct action on the matter, while others are not convinced that we are in any imminent danger.

One suggestion currently receiving attention may appear frivolous to many, but is a serious matter for eugenics enthusiasts. They recommend the use of sperm and ova banks, where couples interested in having a child can go to select a superior genetic heritage for their offspring rather than reproduce their own. Such a prospect obviously raises some serious moral issues about procreation and the parent-child relationship. What is happening to a society in which parents "order" the kind of children they want? Moreover, are scientists correct when they predict that an improved genetic heritage will be necessary to survival, and is this the way to attain it? Some would regard the whole issue as simply another expression of elitism (and possibly racism), based on questionable apprehensions over the higher birth rate among the poor and racial minorities.

Another more recent development in this area relates directly to genetic engineering, or the surgical manipulation of genetic material. The article by James Walter offers us two very helpful sets of handles on these issues. First, Walter suggests that there are four possible types of genetic manipulation that one could defend morally: somatic cell therapy—splicing out a cell defect and splicing in a healthy gene; germ-line gene therapy—correcting a genetic defect in a patient's reproductive cells; third—enhancement genetic engineering in which genes could be manipulated to produce a desired trait; and finally, eugenic genetic engineering in which genes could be inserted to design the entire human subject. The first two of these are therapeutic— designed to correct a defect; the latter two are enhancements of specific traits. Walter suggests that there are theological warrants that could be used to justify all of these human genetic manipulations or to prohibit most, if not all, of them. The body of the article indicates how the position one takes on divine agency—how God acts—and on who human beings are in relation to God and nature influences the moral position one takes on genetic engineering. Walter does not take a particular stance but is content to demonstrate how theological presuppositions enter into the marrow of one's position on this issue.

The article by W. French Anderson affirms the principle of individual human dignity and asserts that "a line should be drawn between somatic cell therapy [Walter's first type of manipulation] and enhancement genetic engineering [Walter's third]." On the basis of beneficence and human dignity, Anderson supports the first form of intervention and argues against enhancement engineering. His position is that genetic engineering should be limited to the realm of treating disease, correcting hereditary defects and alleviating suffering. Such genetic diseases as ADA (an immune deficiency disease afflicting children), sickle cell anemia, hemophilia, some types of cancer, and viral diseases (such as AIDS) are appropriate targets for genetic treatment. To go beyond this kind of engineering raises two concerns: it could be medically hazardous because our knowledge is incomplete and we do not foresee all the consequences that could occur in future generations; and morally, even if our knowledge were complete, we might be plagued with problems of discrimination and abuse of power.

Ted Peters points to one such problem of discrimination: the same genetic research which promises to locate genetic defects makes it possible for private insurance companies to deny coverage to those born with genetic susceptibility to those defects. Needed steps to curb such a problem revolve around how the government can protect the privacy of one's genetic makeup and alleviate genetic discrimination in general. However, maintaining such privacy regarding one's genome prevents the possibility of intervening in therapeutic ways. Peters seems to accept the morality of somatic cell therapy, just as Anderson does, and introduces an "enhancement" issue: the possibility that parents will get caught up in the "perfect-child syndrome" and take steps to abort a fetus with defects or cancel an adoption of a child with defects. "Can we forecast a connection between genetic discrimination and selective abortion?" Peters thinks so. We are moving, he feels, toward a selective abortion scenario. A social byproduct of this may be increased discrimination against people with disabilities. The prospects that Peters presents are disconcerting to many because they make the possibility of totalitarian eugenics more real. Finally, the choice of genetic manipulation for Peters rests on rejecting the "commodification" of children and on genetic therapy serving God's love for all people, regardless of their genetic makeup.

The issue of cloning becomes less science fiction and more imaginable after Dolly. Dolly is the cloned sheep who raised all sorts of issues for the make-up and meaning of human families. Allen Verhey's article investigates those issues, using Paul Ramsey's responses to Joshua Lederberg, a proponent of human cloning. What would it mean for children to be made rather than begotten?

Presuppositions to Moral Judgments on Human Genetic Manipulation
James J. Walter

The U.S. government is currently funding the Human Genome Initiative, which is a fifteen-year scientific project to map the entire human genome. This monumental project, which began somewhat modestly in 1988, expanded to $200 million a year in 1993, and its estimated budget today is almost $3 billion. The goal is to identify and to map the 100,000 genes that are found in three billion base pairs on the 46 human chromosomes. In December 1993 the French reported that they had already completed a full, albeit very rough, map of the human genome. It is estimated that the French achievement will speed up by a factor of ten the final mapping of the human genetic blueprint.

Scientists could conceivably develop four different types of genetic manipulation from the results produced in the Human Genome Initiative. First, there is somatic cell therapy in which a genetic defect in a body cell of a patient could be corrected by splicing out the defect and by splicing in a healthy gene. Second, there is germ-line gene therapy in which a genetic defect in the reproductive

Reprinted from *Chicago Studies* (November 1994), Civitas Dei. Published by Liturgy Training Publications. Used with Permission.

cells—egg or sperm cells—of a patient could be corrected so that the patient's future offspring would also be free of the defect. Next is enhancement genetic engineering. In this form of genetic manipulation a particular gene could be inserted to improve a specific trait, for example, either by adding a growth hormone to increase the height of a patient or by genetically enhancing a worker's resistance to industrial toxins. Finally, there is eugenic genetic engineering in which genes would be inserted to design the entire human subject. The first two types of genetic manipulation are therapeutic in nature because their intent is to correct some genetic defect. The other two types are not therapies but are concerned with improving or enhancing either various aspects of the patient or with changing the whole patient, including even his or her genetic progeny.[1]

The purpose of this article is not to discuss, much less to settle, the morality of each of these four types of genetic manipulation. Rather, the purpose is to demonstrate that any informed moral judgment about the genetic manipulation of the human genome is always shaped within a context. This context for many religious people is a complex set of theological and anthropological presuppositions that operate in the background but inform one's moral thinking and judgment about genetic research on human subjects. These two sets of presuppositions form a coherent context in that each issue is related not only to other issues in its set—theological or anthropological—but is also interrelated to issues in the other set. Now, if one decides most if not all of these theological and anthropological presuppositions in a certain way, then the chances are high that many of the four types of genetic manipulation mentioned above might be judged as morally justified. On the other hand, if one decides these sets of presuppositions in the opposite way, then one would tend morally to prohibit most, if not all, human genetic manipulation.

THEOLOGICAL PRESUPPOSITIONS

There are two basic theological presuppositions that form the context for one's moral position on human genetic manipulation. The first presupposition is concerned with interpretations of: (1) who God is, (2) divine providence, and (3) how God acts in the world and in history. The second general presupposition is concerned with eschatology, that is, with one's view of the relation between human history and God's absolute future in the kingdom. Thus, the first presupposition deals with the general relation between divine and human agency, and the second deals with whether or not the future is already determined and with who has responsibility for the direction of the future.

VIEWS OF GOD AND OF DIVINE AGENCY

Two different views on the first theological presupposition are particularly important for determining the morality of genetic manipulation. In one perspective God is viewed as the one who has created the material universe and humanity and the one who has placed universal, fixed laws into the very fabric of creation. As sovereign ruler over the created order, God directs the future through divine providence. As Lord of life and death, God possesses certain rights over creation, which in some cases have not been delegated to humans and their authority. When humans take it upon themselves to usurp God's rights, for example, those rights to determine the future and to change the universal laws that govern biological nature, they act from a lack of a right *(ex defectu juris in agente)* and thus they act in a sinful manner. If one adopted the positions held in this perspective, then one would probably judge the scientist's attempt to change the genetic structure of the human species, especially any attempt to engineer the entire human person, as human arrogance. This conclusion is confirmed in a TIME/CNN poll on people's reaction to genetic research. Not only were many respondents ambivalent about this type of research but a substantial majority of the respondents (58%) thought that altering human genes in any way was against the will of God.[2]

In the second perspective, God is interpreted as the one who creates both physical nature and humanity but who does not place universal, fixed laws into the fabric of creation. God's actions in creation and in history are to continue to influence the world process, which itself is open to new possibilities and even spontaneity. Divine providence is understood as God providing ordered potentialities for specific occasions and responding creatively and in new ways to the continually changing needs of history.[3] Though there is some stable order in the universe, creation is not finished and history is indeterminate. Consequently, God continues to act to influence the final outcomes of both creation and history and to respond to the historical embodiments of human freedom. Contrary to the first view that construes God as acting in a physical "place" in nature, in this view God's action is understood as primarily persuasion, that is, persuading humans in the depths of their freedom to act responsibly. If one thinks that God has left most of material nature unfinished and believes that the future is mainly indeterminate, then one would be more inclined morally to justify attempts at genetic manipulation, including possibly limited nontherapeutic attempts at genetic enhancement and eugenic engineering.

ESCHATOLOGY

Harvey Cox has identified three strains of eschatology that traditionally have been used in Judeo-Christian theologies: the apocalyptic, the teleological and the prophetic.[4] All three can be found both in ancient religious traditions and in modern secularized forms. Each strain has a different understanding of God's future, which itself is grounded outside human history, and how God will inaugurate that future. Consequently, each strain will construe quite differently the relation of humanity's historical future to God's absolute future, and each will variously formulate what our moral responsibilities are for making sure human history turns out right.

The apocalyptic eschatology, which Cox traces to the influence of ancient near-eastern dualism, always judges the present as somehow unsatisfactory. In both its religious and secularized forms, this eschatology negatively evaluates this world and its history and it foresees imminent catastrophe. The religious form of this eschatology always draws a sharp distinction between God's absolute future in the kingdom and the conditions of our human history; and thus it generally argues for a great discontinuity between this world and the next. On the other hand, the teleological eschatology, which was derived principally from the Greeks but was adopted by Christians, views the future as the "unwinding of a purpose inherent in the universe itself or in its primal stuff, the development of the world toward a fixed end."[5] All creation, then, is moving toward some final end, for example, beatific vision with God; and thus there is some continuity between present human history and God's future. In its contemporary secularized form, this strain understands the world and humanity as evolving. Because humans cannot believe that the cosmos and all that is within it can possibly be devoid of all meaning and purpose, they project onto the cosmos their own purposive style. Of course, humans inevitably assign themselves a crucial place in the very *telos* of the universe. Finally, the prophetic strain of eschatology, which is characteristically Hebrew in nature, views the future as the open area of human hope and responsibility. In the Hebrew scriptures, the prophets did not foretell the future; rather, "they recalled Yahweh's promise as a way of calling the Israelites into moral action in the present."[6] In its biblical form, then, the future is not known in advance, but it is radically open and its actualization lies in the hands of humans who must take up responsibility for it. In its modern secularized form, the prophetic eschatology places great hope in human responsibility for the future, and it views the future with its manifold possibilities as unlocking the determinations of the past.

One of the most notable theologians of this century who adopted the apocalyptic eschatology and then applied it to issues in genetic research was the late Paul Ramsey. He regularly emphasized the discontinuity between this world and the next, and thus he always urged us to remain faithful to God's future as that is represented in the divine covenant between humanity and God. Ramsey did not believe that we have any moral obligation to safeguard the future of humanity through genetic research because "[R]eligious people have never denied, indeed they affirm, that God means to kill us all in the end, and in the end He is going to succeed."[7] It is this apocalyptic view, which sees human history coming to an abrupt end through divine activity, that determines Ramsey's interpretation of both our general moral responsibilities for the future and his specific moral prohibitions against genetic research.

If one adopted either a teleological or a prophetic eschatology, then one would be more inclined morally to accept certain genetic interventions into the human subject. Both strains emphasize human responsibility for the future, albeit each does this differently. Both understand that the future is open and somewhat indeterminate. Consequently, these eschatologies, in either their religious or secularized forms, could lead one to justify morally some types of genetic manipulation, for example, somatic cell therapy. However, because the prophetic eschatology in particular places the strongest emphasis on human responsibility for the future, it is possible that this strain would be very cautious about approving any form of genetic enhancement or germ-line eugenic engineering of the human subject due to the unforeseen deleterious consequences associated with such genetic manipulation.

ANTHROPOLOGICAL PRESUPPOSITIONS

There are three important anthropological presuppositions that shape the contextual background of one's moral position on genetic manipulation. The first is a specifically theological set of anthropological issues that are concerned both with how we view ourselves as created in the image of God *(imago dei)* and with our interpretations of the fall of humanity. The second presupposition is concerned with the various models of material nature. Finally, most of us approach issues in genetic research with some prior understanding of what we believe is the normatively human, that is, what we believe is distinctively human and thus what we ought to value about the human. Though there is not space here to address other issues, it is important to realize that one's evaluation of modern technology, one's understanding of the nature and role of medicine, and one's views of human sexuality and parenthood also affect a moral assessment of genetic engineering of ourselves and of our progeny.

THEOLOGICAL VIEWS OF THE *IMAGO DEI* AND OF THE FALL

There are two different interpretations of the doctrine of the image of God that shape moral judgments on genetic manipulation. The first interpretation defines humanity as a steward over creation. Our role is to protect and to conserve what the divine has created. Stewardship is exercised by respecting the limits that were placed by God in the orders of biological nature and society.[8] This view is consistent with the understanding of God as the creator who has placed universal, fixed laws into the very fabric of creation. If we are only stewards over both creation and our own genetic heritage, then our responsibilities do not include the alteration of what the divine has created. Our principal moral duties are to remain faithful to God's original creative will and to respect the laws that are both inherent in creation and function as limits to human intervention.

The second interpretation of the *imago dei* defines humans as co-creators with God in the continual unfolding of creation. As created co-creators we are both utterly dependent on God for our very existence and simultaneously responsible for creating the course of human history. Though we are certainly not God's equals in the act of creating, we do play a significant role in bringing creation and history to their completion.[9] Karl Rahner argues that we are not simply the products of material nature but beings who have been commissioned by God to further the divine work of creation. Thus, this view is consistent with an understanding of God who has begun the act of creation but who has not yet brought it to a final end. Both creation and history are open-ended, and their fulfillment partially requires the responsible exercise of human freedom. Furthermore, Rahner argued that humanity has been handed over to itself, and in this sense humanity as the *imago dei* must manipulate itself. For him this planned self-manipulation means self-determination. The conclusion Rahner drew from this perspective was that genetic self-manipulation did not automatically imply a morally repugnant act. There are obviously limits to how far humanity can genetically manipulate itself, but based on his anthropology Rahner did not prohibit outright all forms of genetic alteration of the human subject.[10]

The Christian tradition has consistently taught the doctrine of the fall. However, there have been different interpretations of the depth of human depravity. One view, which was adopted by many of the early Protestant reformers and continues in the thought patterns of some contemporary theologians, is that all aspects of the human are deeply fallen into sinfulness. This interpretation has led some to distrust that humanity will ever use modern technology for moral ends. Consequently, proponents of this view regularly seek to limit the extension of human control over the genetic heritage of individuals and of their progeny.

At the opposite end of the spectrum on this doctrine proponents almost entirely forget the fall of humanity. They see only the possibilities open to human ingenuity and rational control, and thus they regularly support efforts to manipulate the human genome. By down-playing the effects of the fall on humanity, these proponents extol human freedom and control over physical nature and the future.[11]

An alternate view to these two extremes, which is historically consistent with Catholic thought, could be described as a moderately optimistic assessment of the human condition. Though fallen, humanity remains essentially good and capable of knowing and doing the moral good with the grace of God. Proponents of this interpretation are not as quick to prohibit or to limit all forms of genetic manipulation as those who subscribe to the first view of the fall. However, unlike the excessively optimistic view in the second interpretation, these proponents recognize that the human capacities to reason and to will the moral good continue to be affected by sin. Consequently, they are cautious about putting too much trust in humanity's ability to use modern technology for moral ends. However, they are willing morally to endorse some limited forms of genetic manipulation, for example, somatic cell therapy, but they tend to prohibit all types of genetic engineering of the human person. They believe that all such attempts to engineer the person genetically will probably result in disastrous consequences for the human race due either to human error or to human arrogance and self-deception.

MODELS OF NATURE

There are three different models of material nature that shape one's moral position on genetic manipulation. Each model attempts not only to interpret the nature of material reality but also to understand the extent to which we can use human freedom to change our biological nature, especially our genetic heritage. Implicitly, each model entails a view of the relationship between body and spirit.

Daniel Callahan has argued that one of the most influential models of nature that operates in contemporary bioethics is the power-plasticity model. In this view, material nature possesses no inherent value, and it is viewed as independent of and even alien to humanity and its purposes. All material reality is simply plastic to be used, dominated and ultimately shaped by human freedom.[12] Thus, the fundamental purpose of the entire physical universe, including human biological nature, is to serve as the instrument for human purposes. Self-mastery, self-development and self-expression through the exercise of freedom are what are truly valuable and important. The body is subordinated to the spiritual aspect of humanity, and humans view themselves as possessing an unrestricted right to dominate and shape not only the body but also its genetic heritage.

Callahan has also described the opposite model of nature as the sacral-symbiotic model in which material nature is viewed as created by God and thus sacred. As created, human biological nature is static and normative in this understanding, and it must be respected and heeded. We are not the masters over nature but the stewards who must live in harmony and balance with our material nature. Because biological nature is our teacher that shows us how to live within the boundaries established by God at creation, our spiritual aspect is subordinated to our body in the moral order. Since physical nature is considered sacrosanct and inviolate, any alteration of the human genetic code, except possibly to cure a disease, would be absolutely prohibited. Thus, either germ-line genetic enhancements or forms of eugenic engineering would be viewed as playing God because these acts would be pretending to possess the rights over fixed, biological nature that only God possesses as Lord of life and death.

The final model interprets material nature as evolving. Unlike the first model, biological nature is not like plastic that can be twisted and molded into whatever shape and configuration humans desire. On the other hand, nature is not absolutely fixed and normative, as the second view postulates. There is some stability to nature and there are some laws that do govern material reality, but neither this stability nor these laws are considered absolutely normative. Change and development are considered more normative than other aspects of nature, and history is seen as linear rather than cyclic or episodic.[13] The relation between material nature and human freedom appears as a dialogue that dynamically evolves over time. It is within this dialogue that humans learn how to use material reality responsibly as the medium of its own creative self-expression.[14] The relation between body and spirit is not one of subordination; rather, humans are viewed as embodied spirits who are, and do not simply possess, their bodies. Though in this model we are not morally permitted to plan or to manipulate ourselves totally at the genetic level of our biological existence, nonetheless we do possess the freedom and the responsibility to intervene into our biological nature. Many who adopt either this model or one similar to it appear to limit genetic manipulation only to therapeutic measures at this point in our understanding of genetic medicine.[15]

VIEW OF THE NORMATIVELY HUMAN

Our capacities to control our biological nature raise an important issue about what we consider the normatively human to be. James Gustafson has recently argued that this issue contains four interrelated questions: (1) How do we adequately describe and explain what we believe to be distinctively human? (2) What do we value about the human? (3) What ought we to value about the human? and (4) How are our descriptions and explanations related to our evaluations?[16] We will be concerned here only with the first three questions.

Several answers could be given to the first question. One could argue that what is distinctive about humans is their biological genotype. One might also point to the fact that humans create culture, and this is what is descriptively distinctive about humans. If we point to the first answer, Gustafson believes that we could be led toward biological determinism, if not reductionism, and all genetic research could be halted. If we respond to the question with the second answer, then we will tend to stress human freedom, spirit, responsibility, and creativity. In any case, Gustafson argues that any answer to this question implies a view of both who God is and how we are made in the image of the divine.[17]

The second question is empirical in that we could take an inventory of what people say they value about the human. Some would say that they value life; others no doubt would say that they value happiness or well-being. Though this question cannot simply be answered by opinion polls, Gustafson maintains that individuals or communities should have the freedom and right to value what they choose to value.[18]

The third question concerns what we ought to value about the human, and it is the most important of the four questions. Several proposals have been offered as responses to this question. Joseph Fletcher originally suggested fifteen positive human criteria—for example, minimal intelligence and self-control—and five negative criteria—for example, humans are not essentially parental—to define what we ought to value about the human.[19] Later, he reduced his list to four essential traits that we ought to value: neocortical function, self-consciousness, relational ability, and happiness.[20] To adopt criteria similar to Fletcher's, especially criteria that stress human control, could be used to justify various forms of genetic enhancement and eugenic engineering. At the opposite extreme, there might be a minimalist criterion that determines what we ought to value about the human, such as the mere possession of a human biological genotype. To adopt a criterion of this sort probably would severly limit, if not absolutely prohibit, any genetic manipulation of the human subject. Of course, a number of middle positions on this question could be articulated. For example, a position might value not only our biological nature but also our capacities for free and responsible action. Consequently, this position might morally permit some limited genetic interventions, for example, somatic cell therapy, but prohibit all forms of genetic enhancement and eugenic engineering of the germ-line cells.

The purpose of this article has been to demonstrate that moral judgments about any form of intervention into the human genome are shaped within a complex context. This context involves an interrelationship of specific theological and anthropological issues that pertain to the question of human genetic manipulation. Future discussions about our moral responsiblities either to permit or to prohibit intervention into the human genome will be fruitful only to the extent that these theological and anthropological issues are explicitly acknowledged and adequately addressed with the discussion.

Genetics and Human Malleability
W. French Anderson

Just how much can, and should we change human nature by genetic engineering? Our response to that hinges on the answers to three further questions: (1) What *can* we do now? Or more precisely, what *are* we doing now in the area of human genetic engineering? (2) What *will* we be able to do? In other words, what technical advances are we likely to achieve over the next five to ten years? (3) What *should* we do? I will argue that a line can be drawn and should be drawn to use gene transfer only for the treatment of serious disease, and not for any other purpose. Gene transfer should never be undertaken in an attempt to enhance or "improve" human beings.

WHAT CAN WE DO?

In 1980 John Fletcher and I published a paper in the *New England Journal of Medicine* in which we delineated what would be necessary before it would be ethical to carry out human gene therapy.[21] As with any other new therapeutic procedure, the fundamental principle is that it should be determined in advance that the probable benefits outweigh the probable risks. We analyzed the risk/benefit determination for somatic cell gene therapy and proposed three questions that need to have been answered from prior animal experimentation: Can the new gene be inserted stably into the correct target cells? Will the new gene be expressed (that is, function) in the cells at an appropriate level? Will the new gene harm the cell or the animal? These criteria are very similar to

© The Hastings Center. Reprinted by permission from *The Hastings Center Report,* January/ February 1990. W. French Anderson is chief of the Laboratory of Molecular Hematology of the National Heart, Lung and Blood Institute, National Institutes of Health, Bethesda, MD.

those required before use of any new therapeutic procedure, surgical operation, or drug. They simply require that the new treatment should get to the area of disease, correct it, and do more good than harm.

A great deal of scientific progress has occurred in the nine years since that paper was published. The technology does now exist for inserting genes into some types of target cells.[22] The procedure being used is called "retroviral-mediated gene transfer." In brief, a disabled murine retrovirus serves as a delivery vehicle for transporting a gene into a population of cells that have been removed from a patient. The gene-engineered cells are then returned to the patient.

The first clinical application of this procedure was approved by the National Institutes of Health and the Food and Drug Administration on January 19, 1989.[23] Our protocol received the most thorough prior review of any clinical protocol in history: It was approved only after being reviewed fifteen times by seven different regulatory bodies. In the end it received unanimous approval from every one of those committees. But the simple fact that the NIH and FDA, as well as the public, felt that the protocol needed such extensive review demonstrates that the concept of gene therapy raises serious concerns.

We can answer our initial question, "What can we do now in the area of human genetic engineering?" by examining this approved clinical protocol. Gene transfer is used to mark cancer-fighting cells in the body as a way of better understanding a new form of cancer therapy. The cancer-fighting cells are called TIL (tumor-infiltrating-lymphocytes), and are isolated from a patient's own tumor, grown up to a large number, and then given back to the patient along with one of the body's immune growth factors, a molecule called interleukin 2 (IL-2). The procedure, developed by Steven Rosenberg of the NIH, is known to help about half the patients treated.[24]

The difficulty is that there is at present no way to study the TIL once they are returned to the patient to determine why they work when they do work (that is, kill cancer cells), and why they do not work when they do not work. The goal of the gene transfer protocol was to put a label on the infused TIL, that is, to mark these cells so that they could be studied in blood and tumor specimens from the patient over time.

The TIL were marked with a vector (called N2) containing a bacterial gene that could be easily identified through recombinant DNA techniques. Our protocol was called, therefore, the N2-TIL Human Gene Transfer Clinical Protocol. The first patient received gene-marked TIL on May 22, 1989. Five patients have now received marked cells. No side effects or problems have thus far arisen from the gene transfer portion of the therapy. Useful data on the fate of the gene-marked TIL are being obtained.

But what was done that was new? Simply, a single gene was inserted into a population of cells that had been obtained from a patient's body. There are an estimated 100,000 genes in every human cell. Therefore the actual addition of material was extremely minute, nothing to correspond to the fears expressed by some that human beings would be "reengineered." Nonetheless, a functioning piece of genetic material was successfully inserted into the human cells and the gene-engineered cells did survive in human patients.

WHAT WILL WE BE ABLE TO DO?

Although only one clinical protocol is presently being conducted, it is clear that there are several applications for gene transfer that probably will be carried out over the next five to ten years. Many genetic diseases that are caused by a defect in a single gene should be treatable, such as ADA deficiency (a severe immune deficiency disease of children), sickle cell anemia, hemophilia, and Gaucher disease. Some types of cancer, viral diseases such as AIDS, and some forms of cardiovascular disease are targets for treatment by gene therapy. In addition, germline gene therapy, that is, the insertion of a gene into the reproductive cells of a patient, will probably be technically possible in the forseeable future. My position on the ethics of germline gene therapy is published elsewhere.[25]

But successful somatic cell gene therapy also opens the door for enhancement genetic engineering, that is, for supplying a specific characteristic that individuals might want for themselves (somatic cell engineering) or their children (germline engineering) which would not involve the treatment of a disease. The most obvious example at the moment would be the insertion of a growth hormone gene into a normal child in the hope that this would make the child grow larger. Should parents be allowed to choose (if the science should ever make it posisble) whatever useful characteristics they wish for their children?

WHAT SHOULD WE DO?

A line can and should be drawn between somatic cell gene therapy and enhancement genetic engineering.[26] Our society has repeatedly demonstrated that it can draw a line in biomedical research when necessary. The Belmont Report illustrates how guidelines were formulated to delineate ethical from unethical clinical research and to distinguish clinical research from clinical practice. Our responsibility is to determine how and where to draw lines with respect to genetic engineering.

Somatic cell gene therapy for the treatment of severe disease is considered ethical because it can be supported by the fundamental moral principle of beneficence: It would relieve human suffering. Gene therapy would be, therefore, a moral good. Under what circumstances would human genetic engineering not be a moral good? In the broadest sense, when it detracts from, rather than contributes to, the dignity of man. Whether viewed from a theological perspective or a secular humanist one, the justification for drawing a line is founded on the argument that, beyond the line, human values that our society considers important for the dignity of man would be significantly threatened.

Somatic cell enhancement engineering would threaten important human values in two ways: It could be medically hazardous, in that the risks could exceed the potential benefits and the procedure therefore cause harm. And it would be morally precarious, in that it would require moral decisions our society is not now prepared to make, and it could lead to an increase in inequality and discriminatory practices.

Medicine is a very inexact science. We understand roughly how a simple gene works and that there are many thousands of housekeeping genes, that is, genes that do the job of running a cell. We predict that there are genes which make regulatory messages that are involved in the overall control and regulation of the many housekeeping genes. Yet we have only limited understanding of how a body organ develops into the size and shape it does. We know many things about how the central nervous system works—for example, we are beginning to comprehend how molecules are involved in electric circuits, in memory storage, in transmission of signals. But we are a long way from understanding thought and consciousness. And we are even further from understanding the spiritual side of our existence.

Even though we do not understand how a thinking, loving, interacting organism can be derived from its molecules, we are approaching the time when we can change some of those molecules. Might there be genes that influence the brains' organization or structure or metabolism or circuitry in some way so as to allow abstract thinking, contemplation of good and evil, fear of death, awe of a 'God'? What if in our innocent attempts to improve our genetic make-up we alter one or more of those genes? Could we test for the alteration? Certainly not at present. If we caused a problem that would affect the individual or his or her offspring, could we repair the damage? Certainly not at present. Every parent who has several children knows that some babies accept and give more affection than others, in the same environment. Do genes control this? What if these genes were accidentally altered? How would we even know if such a gene were altered?

My concern is that, at this point in the development of our culture's scientific expertise, we might be like the young boy who loves to take things apart. He is bright enough to disassemble a watch, and maybe even bright enough to get it back together again so that it works. But what if he tries to "improve" it? Maybe put on bigger hands so that the time can be read more easily. But if the hands are too heavy for the mechanism, the watch will run slowly, erratically, or not at all. The boy can understand what is visible, but he cannot comprehend the precise engineering calculations that determined exactly how strong each spring should be, why the gears interact in the ways that they do, etc. Attempts on his part to improve the watch will probably only harm it. We are now able to provide a new gene so that a property involved in a human life would be changed, for example, a growth hormone gene. If we were to do so simply because we could, I fear we would be like that young boy who changed the watch's hands. We, too, do not really understand what makes the object we are tinkering with tick.

In summary, it could be harmful to insert a gene into humans. In somatic cell gene therapy for an already existing disease the potential benefits could outweigh the risks. In enhancement engineering, however, the risks would be greater while the benefits would be considerably less clear.

Yet even aside from the medical risks, somatic cell enhancement engineering should not be performed because it would be morally precarious. Let us assume that there were no medical risks at all from somatic cell enhancement engineering. There would still be reasons for objecting to this procedure. To illustrate, let us consider some examples. What if a human gene were cloned that could produce a brain chemical resulting in markedly increased memory capacity in monkeys after gene transfer? Should a person be allowed to receive such a gene on request? Should a pubescent adolescent whose parents are both five feet tall be provided with a growth hormone gene on request? Should a worker who is continually exposed to an industrial toxin receive a gene to give him resistance on his, or his employer's request?

These scenarios suggest three problems that would be difficult to resolve: What genes should be provided; who should receive a gene; and, how to prevent discrimination against individuals who do or do not receive a gene.

We allow that it would be ethically appropriate to use somatic cell gene therapy for treatment of serious disease. But what distinguishes a serious disease from a "minor" disease from cultural "discomfort"? What is suffering? What is significant suffering? Does the absence of growth hormone that results in a growth limitation to two feet in height represent a genetic disease? What about a limitation to a height of four feet, to five feet? Each observer might draw the lines between serious disease, minor disease, and genetic variation differently. But all can agree that there are extreme cases that produce significant suffering and premature death. Here then is where an initial line should be drawn for determining what genes should be provided: treatment of serious disease.

If the position is established that only patients suffering from serious diseases are candidates for gene insertion, then the issues of patient selection are no different than in other medical situations: the determination is based on medical need within a supply and demand framework. But if the use of gene transfer extends to allow a normal individual to acquire, for example, a memory-enhancing gene, profound problems would result. On what basis is the decision made to allow one individual to receive the gene but not another. Should it go to those best able to benefit society (the smartest already)? To those most in need (those with low intelligence? But how low? Will enhancing memory help a mentally retarded child?). To those chosen by a lottery? To those who can afford to pay? As long as our society lacks a significant consensus about these answers, the best way to make equitable decisions in this case should be to base them on the seriousness of the objective medical need, rather than on the personal wishes or resources of an individual.

Discrimination can occur in many forms. If individuals are carriers of a disease (for example, sickle cell anemia), would they be pressured to be treated? Would they have difficulty in obtaining health insurance unless they agreed to be treated? These are ethical issues raised also by genetic screening and by the Human Genome project. But the concerns would become even more troublesome if there were the possibility for "correction" by the use of human genetic engineering.

Finally, we must face the issue of eugenics, the attempt to make hereditary "improvements." The abuse of power that societies have historically demonstrated in the pursuit of eugenic goals is well documented.[27] Might we slide into a new age of eugenic thinking by starting with small "improvements"? It would be difficult, if not impossible, to determine where to draw the line once enhancement engineering had begun. Therefore, gene transfer should be used only for the treatment of serious disease and not putative improvements.

Our society is comfortable with the use of genetic engineering to treat individuals with serious disease. On medical and ethical grounds we should draw the line excluding any form of enhancement engineering. We should not step over the line that delineated treatment from enhancement.

In Search of the Perfect Child: Genetic Testing and Selective Abortion
Ted Peters

The triumphs of genetic research include the discovery of disease-related genes. The gene for cystic fibrosis, for example, has been found on chromosome 7. Huntington's chorea was discovered lurking on the end of chromosome 4. Inherited breast cancer was traced to chromosome 17, early-onset Alzheimer's disease to chromosome 14 and colon cancer to chromosome 2. Disposition to muscular dystrophy, sickle-cell anemia and 5,000 or more other diseases is being tracked to genetic origins. The search goes on as well for the DNA switches that turn such genes on and off, and for genetic therapies that will turn the bad genes off and keep the good genes on. Such discoveries could improve medical diagnosis, prevention and therapy, thus advancing the quality of health for everyone.

Yet this apparent good news comes as bad news to those born with genetic susceptibilities to disease, because medical care is funded by private insurance companies and medical insurance is tied to employment. An identifiable genetic predisposition to disease counts as an existing condition, and insurance companies are beginning to deny coverage to people with existing conditions. As new techniques for prevention and therapy become available, the very people who could benefit may be denied access to them.

Paul Billings, a genetics researcher and ethicist at Stanford University Medical School, has collected anecdotal evidence of genetic discrimination. Testifying before Congress, Billings told of a woman who, during a routine physical spoke to her physician about the possibility of her mother having Huntington's disease. Later, when the woman applied for life insurance, her medical records were reviewed and she lost all her insurance.

In another case, a 14-month-old girl was diagnosed with phenylketonuria through a newborn screening program. A low phenylalanine diet was prescribed, and her parents followed the diet rules. The child has grown up to be a normal and healthy person. Her health care at birth was covered by a group insurance policy associated with her father's employment, but when he changed jobs the new carrier declared her ineligible for coverage. Once a genetic predisposition for an expensive disease becomes part of one's medical record, insurance carriers and employers connected to them find it in their best financial interest to minimize or deny health coverage.

In a report by the Committee on Government Operations, U.S. Representative John Conyers (D., Mich.) responded to Billings and others: "Like discrimination based on race, genetic discrimination is wrong because it is based on hereditary characteristics we are powerless to change. The fear in the minds of many people is that genetic information will be used to identify those with 'weak' or 'inferior' genes, who will then be treated as a 'biological underclass.'"

Until recently, the federal government has been slow to respond to testimonies made on behalf of the next generation. In an effort to draw attention to the issue, researchers in the Working Group on Ethical, Legal, and Social Implications of the Human Genome Project at the National Institutes of Health and the Department of Energy created a task force that included geneticists, ethicists and representatives from the insurance industry. The central message of their 1993 report is that information about past, present or future health status—especially health status due to genetic predispositions—should not be used to deny health care coverage or services to anyone.

Some officials are listening. The Kassebaum-Kennedy health insurance reform bill passed in August prohibits categorizing a genetic predisposition as a disqualifying precondition.

Another change occurred when U.S. Marines John Mayfield and Joseph Vlacovsky refused to allow their DNA to be deposited in a Pentagon data bank. The two men were court-martialed, but later the Pentagon dropped its original plan to keep DNA information for 75 years. Fearing that genetic information could be used to discriminate, it now restricts the use of DNA to the identification of human remains on the battlefield. Donors may request destruction of their gene samples when they leave Defense Department service.

Late last year the Genetic Privacy Act was introduced in Congress as well as six state legislatures. The proposal governs collection, analysis, storage and use of DNA samples and the genetic information obtained from them. The act would require explicit authorization to collect DNA samples for genetic analysis and limit the use of information gained from them. The aim is to protect individual privacy by giving the individual the right to authorize who may have access to his or her genetic information.

This is a good start, but it is not enough. Laws to protect genetic privacy appeal to our sense of autonomy, to our desire to take control of what appears to be our own possession, our genome. But privacy protection in itself will not eliminate the threat of genetic discrimination. First of all, it probably will not work. Genetic information as well as medical records are computerized. Computers are linked. In the world of the Internet, someone who wants to penetrate the system will eventually find a way to do so. Any attempt to maintain control over genetic information is likely to fail.

Second, privacy regarding one's genome is undesirable. Knowledge of one's genome could improve preventive health care. The more our physicians know about our genetic predispositions the more they can head off difficulties before they arise. Rather than privacy, what we want is the use of genetic information that does not discriminate against people because of their genetic makeup.

A few years ago my 23-year-old godson Matthew was rushed to the hospital for emergency surgery. He was diagnosed with familial polyposis, a colon cancer in an advanced stage. In a heroic effort, the surgeon's team managed to remove all malignancy. Afterward the surgeon asked the parents if there were any cases of colon cancer in Matthew's family. "We don't know," the parents answered, explaining that Matthew had been adopted as an infant and his records were closed.

"Well," said the doctor, "this kind of cancer is genetic. Had we known that Matthew had a predisposition, we could have monitored him from age ten and removed precancerous polyps. He would never have come to this crisis situation." This case shows the value of computerized and shareable genomic information.

At some point in the future a simple blood test will reveal each of our individual genomes, and we may be able to use this knowledge to great benefit. Laws promoting genetic information without discrimination will contribute to better health care rather than deny it.

A number of states have laws allowing genetic information to be secured from birth parents and made available to adopting parents. In this way, one can learn the frequency of a disorder in a family but not the identity of the family. As genetic testing becomes more sophisticated, DNA tests will provide the same information.

But if adopting parents view adoptable children as commodities to be consumed, such genetic testing could inadvertently lead to discrimination. If the child tests positively for a genetic defect, the adopting parents may think of the child as defective and refuse to adopt him or her. They may be caught up in the "perfect-child syndrome" and want nothing less than a perfectly healthy child. Or they may cancel the adoption because they fear that they'll lose their family health care insurance and become stuck with unpayable medical bills. The first problem is cultural or ethical, the second economic.

Can we forecast a connection between genetic discrimination and selective abortion? Yes. A couple in Louisiana had a child with cystic fibrosis, a genetic disorder leading to chronic lung infections and excruciating discomfort. When the wife became pregnant with the second child, a prenatal genetic test revealed that the fetus carried the mutant gene for cystic fibrosis. The couple's health maintenance organization demanded that they abort. If they refused to abort, the HMO would withdraw coverage from both the newborn and the first child. Only when the couple threatened to sue did the HMO back down and grant coverage for the second child.

With the advance of prenatal genetic testing, both parents and insurance carriers can find out whether a child may be prone to having a debilitating and expensive disease. It is not unrealistic to imagine the insurance industry publishing a list of disqualifying genetic predispositions. If one of the predispositions were found in a fetus, the industry would mandate an abortion under penalty of loss of coverage. This would outrage pro-life parents, and even pro-choice parents would find this financial pressure to be the equivalent of a compromise on choice.

We are moving step-by-step toward this selective abortion scenario. In addition to feeling pressure from the privately funded insurance industry, parents themselves will likely develop criteria for deciding which fetuses will be brought to term and which will be aborted. Genetic criteria will play a major role. Prenatal testing to identify disease-related genes will become routine, and tests for hundreds of deleterious genes may become part of the prenatal arsenal. Parents wanting what they believe to be a perfectly healthy child may abort repeatedly at each hint of a genetic disorder. Choice and selection will enter the enterprise of baby making at a magnitude unimaginable in previous history.

Most families will confront the issue when they find themselves in a clinic office talking with a genetic counselor. Although a genetic analysis of heritable family traits can help immensely in planning for future children, talking with a genetic counselor too often begins when a pregnancy is already in progress. The task of the genetic counselor is to provide information regarding the degree of risk that a given child might be born with a genetic disorder, and to impart this information objectively, impartially and confidentially (when possible) so that the autonomy of the parents is protected.

What is surprising and disconcerting to mothers or couples in this situation is that genetic risk is usually given statistically, in percentages. The parents find themselves with difficult-to-interpret information while facing an unknown future. Conflicting values between marital partners or even within each of them will increase the difficulty—and the anxiety.

Both genetic endowment and degree of disability are relative unknowns. For a recessive defective gene such as that for cystic fibrosis, when both parents are carriers the risk is 50 percent that the child will also be a carrier and 25 percent that the child will contract the disease. With this information parents decide to proceed toward birth or to terminate the pregnancy. Later in the pregnancy the specific genetic makeup of a fetus can be discerned via amniocentesis and other tests.

In cases of Down's Syndrome, for example, which is associated with trisomy (three copies of chromosome 21), eight out of every ten negative prenatal diagnoses lead to the decision to abort. Even though the genetic predisposition can be clearly identified in this way, the degree of mental retardation that will result is unknown. Mild cases mean near-average intelligence. Yet the choice to abort has become the virtual norm. The population of Down's Syndrome people in our society is dropping, making this a form of eugenics by popular choice.

In only 3 to 5 percent of cases does a positive prenatal diagnosis reveal the presence of a genetic disorder so severe that the probable level of suffering on the part of the child warrants that a parent consider abortion. In making this judgment I am invoking a principle of compassion—what bioethicists dub the principle of nonmaleficence or reducing human suffering whenever possible. In situations where such a diagnosis is made and where prospective parents strongly desire to bring a child into the world, a number of things happen.

First, genetic counselors report that parents automatically refer to the child as a "baby," never as a "fetus." They clearly think of the life growing in the womb as a person. Second, when confronted with the bad news, they experience turmoil. The turmoil usually leads to a decision to terminate the pregnancy but not always. It is not the job of the genetic counselor to encourage abortion; even advocates of choice on abortion defend the parents' right to decide to bring such a child to birth. Third, even when the decision to terminate is made, the grieving parents see their decision as an expression of their love, not a denial of love. It is an act of compassion.

The distinction between convenience and compassion is ethically significant here. As the practice of prenatal genetic testing expands and the principle of autonomy—the responsibility for choice—is applied to the parents and not to the unborn child, the total number of abortions will increase, perhaps dramatically. Each pregnancy will be thought of as tentative until the fetus has passed dozens or hundreds of genetic tests. A culturally reinforced image of the desirable child—the perfect-child syndrome—may lead couples to try repeated pregnancies, terminating the undesirables and giving birth only to the "best" test passers. Those born in this fashion risk being commodified by their parents. In addition, those who might be born with a disability *and* with the potential for leading a productive and fulfilling life might never see the light of day.

A social byproduct of selective abortion might be increased discrimination against people living with disabilities. The assumption could grow that to live with a disability is to have a life not worth living. Persons with disabilities fear that the medical establishment and its supportive social policies will seek to prevent "future people like me" from ever being born. The inference is: "I am worthless to society." The imputation of dignity to handicapped persons may be quietly withdrawn as they are increasingly viewed as unnecessary and expensive appendages to an otherwise healthy society.

This would be a tragedy of the first order. Disabled persons deserve dignity and encouragement. Such people frequently gain victory in their difficult life struggles. Most disabled people report that while the disability, the pain, and the need for compensatory devices and assistance can produce considerable inconvenience, the inconveniences become minimal or even forgotten once individuals make the transition to living their everyday lives.

Whether we like it or not, the advancing frontier of genetics, with its impact on reproductive technology thrusts us back into the abortion debate. *Roe vs. Wade* (1973) did not answer the questions we will be asking in 2003. The Supreme Court decided that a woman has the right to abort during the first trimester. Genetic discrimination raises an additional question: by what criteria might a fetus be considered abortable? *Roe vs. Wade* focuses on the woman's right to decide what to do with her body; now we focus on the fetuses and the criteria by which some will live and others will not. A skeptic might say that as long as the woman has the right to choose, it is a moot point to talk of criteria of choice. I believe that while a woman's right to choose is a legal matter, the criteria for choosing are an ethical matter.

Even though abortion on request is legal, not all grounds for requesting it are ethical. In the case of selective abortion, a decision based solely on the desires of the parents without regard for the child's well-being is unethical. As Martin Luther said, "Even if a child is unattractive when it is born, we nevertheless love it."

Most Christians are not ethically ready for the era of selective abortion. We are unprepared for the kind of decisions that large numbers of prospective parents will be confronting. We have thought about the issue of abortion on request and the question of when human dignity begins, but now we need middle axioms to guide the choices that will confront the next generation of parents.

First, we need to identify defective or undesirable genes prior to conception rather than after. Whether or not the conceptus has full personhood and full dignity comparable to living adults, ethicists agree that the fertilized zygote deserves a level of respect and honor that resists brute manipulation or irreverent discarding. Genetic selection in the sperm or ovum prior to fertilization, prior to the DNA blueprint of a potential person, seems more defensible.

Second, the choice for selective abortion should be the last resort. Prefertilization selection should be given priority when possible, as should prenatal gene therapy.

Third, the motive of compassion that seeks to minimize suffering on the part of children coming into the world should hold relative sway when choosing for or against selective abortion. Compassion, taken up as the principle of nonmaleficence in bioethics, constitutes the way that parents show love toward children-to-be. In rare cases (3 to 5 percent of prenatal diagnoses), the genetic disorder is so severe that no approximation to a fulfilling life is possible. The decision to abort can be understood as a form of caring for the baby as well as self-care for the parents. Yet it is still a judgment call. No clear rule tells us exactly when the imputed dignity of the unborn child may be trumped by a compassionate decision to abort.

Fourth, we should distinguish between acts of eugenics and acts of compassion. The goal of eugenics is to reduce the incidence of a certain genetic trait, usually an undesirable trait. Eugenics is social in scope and derives from some social philosophy. At this point, bioethicists tend to oppose eugenic policies because, if practiced on a large scale, they could reduce biodiversity. More important, eugenics connotes the political totalitarianism of the Third Reich. The compassion or nonmaleficence principle, when limited to the concrete situation of a family making a decision regarding a particular child, is much more acceptable. The line between eugenics and compassion is not a clear one, however. Some will argue that the attempt to eliminate a recessive gene for something like cystic fibrosis in future branches on a family tree is an act of compassion.

Fifth, we should distinguish between preventing suffering and enhancing genetic potential. Genetic selection to help reduce suffering is an act that, in at least a minimal sense, is directed toward the well-being of the child. In the future, when genetic selection and perhaps even genetic engineering make possible designer babies with higher-than-average intelligence, good looks or athletic prowess, then we will move closer to embracing the perfect-child syndrome. The risk of commodifying children and evaluating them according to standards of quality control increases when parents are "buying." The risk of commodification does not in itself constitute a reason to reject all genetic therapy, but it does call us to bolster a sound, biblically defensible principle: God loves people regardless of their genetic makeup, and we should do likewise.

Cloning and the Human Family:
Theology after Dolly
Allen Verhey

Some 30 years before the birth of Dolly, the cloned sheep, and sometime near the beginnings of bioethics, Nobel laureate Joshua Lederberg wrote an article for the *American Naturalist* (September–October 1966) commenting on the prospects for cloning a human being. Frogs, toads, salamanders and fruit flies had been cloned, and Lederberg was hospitable to the prospect of cloning a human being. The article prompted a reply by several theologians, including Princeton's Paul Ramsey.

Some of the reasons Lederberg gave 30 years ago for cloning a human being have been reiterated in recent weeks since we first said Hello to Dolly: We might clone individuals of great intelligence or athletic ability or beauty as a service to society. We might clone a sick child to provide that child a twin who could supply materials for transplant. Or we might clone a child who had accidentally suffered a severe brain injury, thereby giving the parents an identical twin of the child for whom they will shortly grieve. Lest we like sheep follow Dolly down this path, we might revisit Ramsey's reply to Lederberg (later published in *Fabricated Man*).

Perhaps the most persistent argument in favor of cloning a human being is simply that some people will want to do it and should be free to do so. To refuse them such freedom looks to some people like an unwarranted intrusion into the privacy of procreative decisions and a violation of reproductive rights and freedoms. The argument makes some sense if freedom is regarded as a sufficient principle and if it is understood as the capacity of neutral agents to will whatever they will, unconstrained and uncoerced. Then reproduction is a right, and the only "warranted" limit on that right is the requirement that it be exercised by "consenting adults."

Ramsey, like a good Protestant, did not deny the moral significance of freedom. But he insisted that freedom is not a sufficient moral principle. "There are more ways to violate man-womanhood than to violate the *freedom* of the parties," he said, and "something voluntarily adopted can still be wrong." He insisted that people are always more than their rational autonomy, and that we must regard and respect others always as *embodied* and as *communal* beings, members of covenants and communities, some of which at least are not of their own choosing.

If freedom is regarded as a sufficient principle, then family relationships are necessarily diminished, turned into merely contractual relationships between autonomous individuals. If one admits that freedom is insufficient for an account of the good life in a family—let alone for nurturing and sustaining it—then one may surely ask whether freedom is sufficient for considering ways of becoming a family, including cloning.

Moreover, Ramsey suggested, respect for freedom and for the struggle of the young for their own identity should itself caution us against cloning a human being. Cloning would manipulatively establish an identity for a child in the choice to have one: to design a human being—whether to be a good scientist or a good pianist—establishes an identity for the child which is not only not freely owned by the child but which does not invite anyone to nurture or even to engage the child's capacities for individual agency.

If, for example, one were to take seriously Joseph Fletcher's suggestion that we clone "top-grade soldiers," and if the procedure ended up producing a brilliant pacifist instead of a good soldier, then the procedure would be judged to have "failed." In such a procedure, the child's freedom will not be nurtured; it will be—and must be considered to be—a threat to the success of the reproductive procedures. The illustration need not be so fanciful; if one were to "replace" a dying child with its clone, the clone would have to live with the identity of the lost child and its "promise." A concern for freedom itself, then, should prohibit us from cloning a human being.

A second kind of argument about cloning is quite candidly utilitarian: the test for cloning is simply whether it maximizes happiness. Ramsey, who was not a utilitarian, vigorously rejected the reduction of moral discernment to the calculation of consequences and the reduction of the good to the maximizing of happiness or preference satisfaction.

Relationships in a family are not simply contractual, nor are they instrumental relationships designed to achieve some extrinsic good. Maximizing happiness is not what family is all about. Again, if utility calculations are insufficient to account for the good life in a family—let alone to nurture and sustain it—then it may be asked whether they are sufficient to justify new ways of becoming a family, including cloning.

Moreover, calculations of utility often ignore what is for Ramsey a basic moral question, the question of distributive justice. It is not enough to count up the costs and benefits. It is necessary also to ask: Who bears the costs? Who stands to benefit? And is this distribution of costs and benefits fair? Ramsey consistently opposed the imposition of risks and harms upon those who could not voluntarily assume them, and who would not be able to share in any possible benefits. He tried to speak for the voiceless, for the "mishaps"; he urged protection of the weak, of embryos, even if such protection meant that a great number of others would not be benefited. Ramsey could be quite nonchalant about good consequences, at least compared to the seriousness with which he took the moral responsibility to protect and nurture "the least of these."

Even if we want to identify and weigh costs and benefits, Ramsey reminds us that these tasks are not simply technical assessments; they inevitably express and form our profoundest convictions concerning our relationships with our bodies, with nature and with children. And on these matters, too, Ramsey's reply to Lederbeg is instructive.

Ramsey repudiated "the combination of *boundless determinism* with *boundless freedom*" in Lederberg's proposal. He refused to reduce "the person" to capacities for understanding and choice, to something altogether different from the body, something over and over against the body. And he refused to reduce the body to a mere object to be measured, mastered and manipulated for the sake of "personal" choices. He insisted instead on our embodiment and claimed again and again that the person is "an embodied soul or ensouled body."

Because the sexual person is "the body of his soul as well as the soul of his body," procreation (and intercourse) may not be reduced either to mere physiology or to simple consent to a technology. Because of our embodiment Ramsey refused to reduce baby-making (or love-making) to a technical accomplishment or to a matter of contract.

Our culture has sat at the feet of Francis Bacon. We take knowledge to be power over nature, and we assume that it leads (almost) inevitably to human well-being. Ramsey was deeply suspicious of the Baconian vision. He sat, instead, at the feet of C.S. Lewis. Ramsey saw that technology always involves the power of some people over other people; it provides no remedy for greed, envy or pride, and can be co-opted into their service. Such an account of technology may have its epitome in cloning.

The relationship of parents and children may be at stake in our response to the proposal to clone a human being. Ramsey worried not only that "replication" or "'reproduction' (itself a metaphor of a machine civilization)" would depersonalize and disembody acts of begetting, but that technological reproduction—and especially cloning—would tempt us to view our children as human and technical achievements rather than as gifts of God.

If we see children as achievements, as products, then the "quality control" approach appropriate to technology will gradually limit our options to choosing either a perfect child or a dead child. Our capacity as parents to provide the sort of uncalculating care and nurture that evokes the trust of children will be diminished. If we could cherish children as begotten, not made, as gifts, not products, then we will not be hospitable to cloning.

Chapter 16

REPRODUCTIVE TECHNOLOGIES

In this chapter we focus on reproductive technology, an area of biomedicine in which recent developments have raised some particularly troublesome moral dilemmas. Reproductive technology includes such topics as artificial insemination by husband (AIH) or by donor (AID), *in vitro* fertilization (IVF) and embryo transfer, surrogate mothers, sperm and egg banks with gender and trait selection, and embryo adoption. This technology allows us to intervene in the natural way in which procreation occurs, involving human manipulation and even human substitution at one point or another in the procreative process. The moral concerns raised most often about reproductive technology relate to parents who are not the usual heterosexual, married couple. For example, recently there seems to have been a lesbian baby boom. Consider the case of a lesbian couple, one of whom was artificially inseminated with the sperm of a friend who is gay. The two women plan to raise the child in cooperation with the father and his lover. There would in effect be two sets of parents, two of the four are the biological father and mother but not living as husband and wife. Certainly one of the moral issues involved in this decision is the effect upon the child in terms of its personal identity and relations with all four parents. There is also the problem in a consumer society of treating children as commodities (a concern raised in Ryan's article). Imagine the following scenario: (1) A single male decides to have a baby; (2) he selects his future child at the local sperm and egg bank, giving careful consideration to those personality traits and physical characteristics that he regards as most desirable; (3) he has the egg fertilized *in vitro;* (4) he negotiates a contract with a woman to bear the child; (5) nine months later he is a happy "father"! As in the case of IVF, the idea of using a surrogate mother was prompted by the situations of infertile married couples—in this case, where the woman is incapable of *bearing* the child. Because this practice involves a third party, there are peculiar legal as well as ethical problems. The Baby M case in New Jersey in 1987 was the first in the nation to involve a woman who agreed to bear a child and then refused to give up the baby. While the judge's decision favored the biological father, thus upholding the validity of the surrogacy contract, it remains to be seen whether state legislatures will be inclined to pass legislation that encourages or outlaws the practice. Some ethical issues involved are whether the process of gestation constitutes a bonding experience for the woman that ought not to be destroyed; whether the child's identity should not be assaulted by its intentional removal from its biological mother; and whether the practice will encourage the commercial exploitation of poor women by the rich. Lisa Cahill reviews traditional natural law arguments about sexual morality and traces the implications of this normative framework for the evaluation of various new reproductive technologies. She is not opposed in principle to the fertilization of ova outside of the womb (a position that is argued by the Roman Catholic Church). But she is morally apprehensive about all donor methods because they involve third parties in the procreative process. Though the teachings she reviews are not specifically religious, they are understood to be based on human experience, reasonably interpreted.

Ryan's essay examines in detail three versions of the warning that new reproductive technologies (NRTs) tempt us to "play God." Each of these objections highlights important concerns about the moral significance of life, death, and being human. Nevertheless, Ryan demonstrates that in order to win the debate about any particular technology, each requires further development.

The impact of technology is always a mixed blessing. Some are particularly alert to its dehumanizing features, while others are enamored with its possibilities to the point that technology is regarded as the panacea for every conceivable human problem. There is, in any event, a fascination with technological progress that gives credence to the notion that if we are technically *capable* of doing something, then for the sake of progress we *ought* to do it. Whether it is progress or not, technological developments carry considerable weight and momentum, necessitating careful consideration of their social consequences and a strong and discriminating moral judgment. This pervasive dimension of our life presents one of the most serious challenges we face as a society.

The New Reproductive Technologies: A Catholic Perspective
Lisa Cahill

Over two decades ago, the nation's attention was riveted by the well-publicized struggle over the fate of "Baby M," born to surrogate mother Mary Beth Whitehead

From Lisa Cahill, "The New Reproductive Technologies: A Catholic Perspective," *Santa Clara Magazine,* Winter 1989, pp. 10–13. Updated by author July 1997. Reprinted with permission.

in New Jersey (March, 1986). Ms. Whitehead had been artificially inseminated with sperm from Willam Stern, whose wife could not bear a child because of health risks. But when the baby was born, her mother refused to give her up to the father and his wife. After a prolonged court battle, the case eventually was resolved in favor of shared custody by the biological parents. The drama highlighted the pain of the Sterns, a couple for whom "natural" pregnancy and childbirth were out of the question. Mary Beth Whitehead's struggle for her baby also raised in a visible and personal way the question whether contributing genes, giving birth, or forming a social attachment to a child most constitutes "true" parenthood. There have been more recent reminders that decisions about unusual reproductive arrangements need a good deal more prudent consideration in our society. It has been known for mothers and daughters to donate ova or gestate babies for one another, resulting, for instance, in children whose mothers were their sisters or grandmothers.

There are less dramatic illustrations of the degree to which reproductive innovations have moved into the scenario of infertility. One common possibility is the artificial insemination of a fertile woman either with the concentrated sperm of her otherwise infertile husband (AIH), or with that of an anonymous donor (AID). A more expensive and less successful, but nonetheless expanding, technique is *in vitro* fertilization (IVF) accompanied by embryo transfer (ET), usually a remedy for female infertility such as blocked fallopian tubes. In IVF, the ovum is extracted from the body of the woman and united in the laboratory with sperm, usually that of her husband. The resulting embryo, after a brief period of growth, is implanted in her body in the hope that a successful pregnancy will ensue.

The success rate of IVF is difficult to calculate, since various programs implant different numbers of embryos in the hope that at least one will survive (the implantation of three is sometimes considered optimal). Most implanted embryos are not successful in instigating a pregnancy, and many pregnancies initiated do not result in live births. The chance that a woman who undergoes implantation on any one occasion will give birth is quite low. The procedure is expensive for the consumer, but extremely profitable for the provider. In 1993, a single *in vitro* cycle cost, on average, $6,200. In 1994, 18.6 percent of *in vitro* patients gave birth, many after multiple cycles.

Sperm donation to compensate for male infertility is a well-entrenched practice in wealthier countries, including the United States. Ovum donation programs are catching up. Typically, healthy young women are paid to undergo drug-induced hyperovulation and a surgical procedure, in order to provide ova for fertilization with the sperm of the husbands or partners of infertile women. These women can carry a pregnancy to term once the embryo has been created with a donated ovum. Because both ova and resulting healthy embryos to be reimplanted are scarce resources, clinics usually recommend aiming to fertilize the largest number of ova obtainable. Yet sometimes clinics and their clients must then make decisions about freezing, disposing of, or donating (for research or to other couples) "spare" embryos. Since many embryos do not survive to birth even after they are implanted in the mother, infertility programs often recommend implanting several—more than it would be healthy to bring to term and birth. This is now resulting in a new problem. Sometimes more embryos implant and grow than is expected. Then parents face a desperate choice: the birth of "supertwins" (three or more babies born at once) or "pregnancy reduction" (the abortion of some healthy fetuses so that their same-age siblings can have a better chance). Another emerging practice is the use of IVF and ovum donation to allow postmenopausal women to become pregnant. To date, two 63-year-old women have been known to give birth in this way, one in Italy, and one in the U.S. And the cloning in 1997 of Dolly the sheep from a mammary cell of an ewe makes it even possible to envision that children in the future could have only one genetic parent, rather than both a mother and a father.

Although the use of these technologies is a relatively recent phenomena, it provides a testing ground for some basic principles of Catholic sexual ethics. In March 1987, The Vatican's Congregation for the Doctrine of the Faith released its *Instruction on Respect for Human Life in Its Origin and on the Dignity of Procreation: Replies to Certain Questions of the Day (Donum vitae)*. This document attempted to give guidance regarding reproductive technologies and addressed four key concerns: the status of the embryo, the use of techniques that unite the gametes of a married couple (homologous techniques), the use of techniques that involve donor gametes (heterologous techniques), and the role of public policy in controlling or banning reproductive technologies. To summarize, the *Instruction* asserted that manipulation of the embryo in the laboratory manifests disrespect for its human identity, especially when "extra" embryos are permitted to die or are used for experimentation; that both heterologous and homologous techniques are immoral; and that civil laws should prohibit the use of these technologies.

On the issue of civil law, it is enough to say that the Vatican—like anyone else—is justified in encouraging the state to protect citizens by barring socially dangerous or harmful practices. If reproductive methods can be judged harmful by objective criteria, for an ecclesial body to lobby for their prohibition cannot be dismissed as a matter of imposing its peculiarly "religious" beliefs on a pluralistic public. The key, however, is the existence or non-existence of objective arguments against the condemned practices. If the Vatican, or any other group exercising political influence, cannot demonstrate the persuasiveness of its position and form a consensus around it adequate to put in place and enforce a law, then that position will not and should not prevail in the public forum in a democratic society. The task of the Catholic Church, then, is to convince the American public that its views of marriage, parenthood, and the family are indeed reasonable and deserve to help shape policy.

Perhaps the Vatican's prohibition of AIH or IVF for married couples (using only their own gametes) gave the average Catholic layperson (or theologian, for that matter) the greatest difficulty. The ongoing Baby M case had, by the time of the publication of the *Instruction,* made the U.S. public sensitive to the problematic aspects of involving a partner from outside a marriage in the couple's attempt to produce a child genetically related to at least one of them. To many, it does make sense to avoid the involvement of third parties, such as surrogate mothers, sperm donors, and egg donors, in a couple's efforts to become parents. Thus, there was less resistance in the press, among theologians, and (as I perceived it) by the laity generally, to the Vatican *Instruction's* idea that donor methods raise serious moral questions. Though the issue of the status of an embryo is a difficult one, it is not necessarily a moral barrier to artificial reproduction. In order to resolve the problem of "wastage" or of disposal of "extra" embryos, programs of IVF have been devised in which a limited number of ova are fertilized, and all healthy embryos are transferred back to the mother, and so given a chance of survival. So why should the use of reproductive techniques by a wife and husband in such a program be forbidden?

In the background of the 1987 document is the 1968 encyclical of Paul VI, *Humanae Vitae* (On Human Life), known primarily for its widely disputed prohibition of artificial birth control. On the more positive side, that encyclical also affirmed a "duty of responsible parenthood" (to be exercised by "natural" means, such as rhythm), and the unity of procreation and love as values that jointly should characterize all sexual acts. It is notable that Paul VI, following the Second Vatican Council *(The Pastoral Constitution on the Church in the Modern World),* treated love and procreation as equal values. Procreation is not today to be understood as the only or most important meaning of sex—as was once taught even as recently as 1930 (by Pius XI in *Casti Connubii*)—but is on a par with the marital love that sexual intercourse should express. Thus, a new framework for the analysis of sexual morality emerges. From the contemporary Roman Catholic viewpoint these three values are inseparable: sex, love, and procreation.

It is important to note that the Vatican does not teach this inseparability as a specifically "religious" teaching, but as deriving from the experiences of sex, marriage, and parenthood themselves. These are "natural" values. This does not mean, of course, that people always do in fact respect their unity, or that unity always does characterize human sexual behavior. Rather, to call the unity of sex, love, and procreation "natural" is to imply that it *should* be respected in order for human sexuality to be experienced as fulfilling and responsible. "Natural law" ethical teaching is normative, not simply descriptive.

Reproductive technologies add a new twist to the standard picture. It has always been possible for sex to take place without love or procreation or either; now science presents us with the prospect of procreation without sex, and in some cases without either sex or love on the part of the couple which reproduces. Mary Beth Whitehead and William Stern are a case in point, but so are the many couples who use donated sperm or ova. Can cooperative endeavors such as these ever be justified? Under what circumstances? What are the limits? The Vatican *Instruction* answered these questions simply by applying the rule of *Humanae Vitae:* Procreation, love, and sexual intercourse must be retained together as "inseparable." Hence, not only the donor methods, but even "artificial" conception by committed married persons, is said to be immoral if accomplished by a technological sex-substitute such as AID or IVF.

Interestingly, the document also notes that "homologous IVF and ET fertilization is not marked by all that ethical negativity found in extra-conjugal procreation." This slight qualification within the prohibition is offered precisely on the grounds that in techniques used by a committed couple in uniting their own gametes "the family and marriage continue to constitute the setting for the birth and upbringing of the children." Nonetheless, the Vatican authors felt constrained by "conformity with the traditional doctrine" to call homologous fertilization "*in itself illicit and in opposition to the dignity of procreation and of the conjugal union. . . .*" Some readers of the argument have perceived here a substitution of the authority of past teaching for a present connection with the experience of married persons. That experience almost came to the surface and controlled the argument in the Vatican's brief suggestion that heterologous methods, with their setting in the family, might not be so negative as to be ruled out absolutely. In the end, however, it was conformity with past teaching, especially the principle of *Humanae Vitae,* that became the dominant interest of the Vatican authors.

It was indicated above that the moral teaching of the Roman Catholic Church is based, according to the Church's own teaching, not on Scripture alone nor on revelation, but on human experience reasonably interpreted. This "natural law" morality, with its roots in Thomas Aquinas, may find in the Church an interpreter, but it finds its real grounding and strength in shared human values, tested in experience. A question to raise now is whether, on these difficult reproductive issues, the experience of married persons, of parents, and of would-be parents has been adequately interpreted as a basis for Church teaching. A criticism which has been offered against the *Instruction* since its publication is that more extensive consultation both with theologians and laypersons would have been appropriate. The *Instruction* makes a valuable move in trying to articulate the fundamental "natures" of marital sexuality and parenthood, and their implications for the morality of reproductive technologies. Yet it may fall short in asserting *for* married couples that their love would be violated in some radical way were they to resort to IVF or comparable techniques in their effort to give birth to the child who would be the extension of their life together.

Certainly every couple would agree that the ideal reproductive scenario involves one couple, an act of intercourse, one normal conception, one successful pregnancy, and a healthy birth. Yet what can legitimately be done to compromise when realization of this ideal is simply not a possibility for particular persons? It seems to many that if a couple expresses their love sexually over the entire course of a marriage, then a substitution for sex as a means of reproduction on an isolated occasion does not in any radical way violate the "unity" of sex, love, and procreation in their relationship. In fact, it succeeds in realizing the procreative value of their love, and so makes that unity even more visible. On these grounds, many commentors on the document, even those committed to Roman Catholic moral principles, disagree with its conclusion on homologous reproductive technologies. AIH or IVF in marriage need not disrupt the *fundamental* unity of love, sex, and procreation, even though they may be separated temporarily in a given act of laboratory conception.

(Perhaps of much more practical and moral significance is the great expense and low success rate of IVF, especially in view of the fact that there are many basic health needs to which society should devote more resources. It is also important to ask what social pressures on women make them so "desperate" to give birth—even when they are well past the normal years of childbearing—that they subject their bodies, psyches, and savings to such duress.)

What then of the justifiability of donor methods—which for some may be the only pathway to a genetically related child? We have seen that surrogate motherhood can pose pressing psychological and social problems for all involved. But there exist less socially visible forms of donorship, especially of sperm and ova. The resulting asymmetrical parental relationship might indeed cause psychological difficulty for the one spouse who would not be genetically realted to the child. But there are no doubt cases in which this imbalance has been accepted successfully as a small price to pay for the rewards of parenthood. The Vatican's condemnation of donor methods is far from having been accepted without controversy, even though it has met with less resistance than the condemnation of methods used in marriage.

In my view, and, I believe, in that of most Roman Catholic moral theologians, donor methods are much more morally questionable than those used within marriage. The central issue here, and again it is one that must be tested in the crucible of experience, is the nature of the solidarity to which spouses commit themselves in undertaking marriage. Does their partnership set the parameters for their procreative activity as well as for their sexual activity? I believe the answer must be affirmative. Sexual expression and procreative partnership constitute the physical aspects of the love commitment which is marriage. Just as the human person is constituted by the unity of body and spirit, so fundamental human relationships such as marriage and parenthood are constituted both by bodily and by psychic dimensions. Both the bodily and the spiritual or psychological must in some way be respected in moral decisions about marriage and parenthood.

Granting that it is the psychic or spiritual dimensions of life that are more distinctively human and thus more important (e.g., the love of spouses for one another and for the child they receive), the physical still needs to be integrated into the parental relationship in some basic and meaningful way just as sexuality is a part of marriage. This integration is accomplished by a couple creating a child who is the genetic offspring of both, even though the child is not conceived through sexual intercourse. When a married couple conceives a child, the physical dimensions of spousehood and of parenthood are joined. Although some loving married couples do not have children, they still preserve the basic procreative unity of their marriage when they agree or assume that if they were to procreate they would do so together.

The unity of the physical and spiritual is important from the standpoint of the parent-child relationship, as well as from that of the husband-wife relationship. Even the immense interest of many adopted persons in locating their biological parents indicates the role that intergenerational kinship plays in an individual's identity and self-image. The unity of the physical with the affective and social aspects of procreation and parenthood is gravely interrupted when the biological relation to the child is deliberately and completely set aside. In AID, the donor is willing to separate completely his or her biological contribution from any social relation to his or her child. Moreover, one spouse sees his or her own desire to procreate biologically as more important than solidarity with the spouse who is unable to procreate in that way.

I do not want to overstate the case, much less to minimize the plight of childless couples who very likely have tried long and hard to achieve a shared biological relation to a child before resorting to donorship. This relationship is undoubtedly valued by them. However, the decisive moral question is what constitutes adequate recognition of the value of shared biological parenthood in any reproductive venture that a couple chooses to undertake. Although in homologous techniques this relationship is concretely and enduringly realized, in heterologous methods it is not.

Of course, we readily justify and even praise the adoption of children, although there is no biogenetic relationship between parents and children. However, heterologous reproduction is in a crucial way not like adoption, even adoption by one spouse of the pre-existing biological children of the other. Donor reproductive methods differ from adoption in that they *create* children outside of the marital relationship *for the purpose* of allowing would-be parents to fulfill their need for a child. Adoption, on the other hand, is an after-the-fact decision on the part of adoptive parents and often birth parents that a child already in existence would be better off to be raised in a loving adoptive family, because of unfortunate circumstances which now must be remedied. But it would be certainly immoral, even for the worthy purpose of adopting a child, to create deliberately those circumstances—extramarital pregnancy, death of parents, abandonment, extreme poverty, child neglect or abuse.

Thus, it can be argued that donor methods of reproduction cross the boundary of the morally acceptable. They depend on a willingness to produce children completely outside the contexts of physical marital partnership and of biological kinship. Although the goals of birth and parenthood are worthy, the means—going outside the bond of marriage in order to join in reproduction with a third party, seen solely as a personally uncommitted provider of physical reproductive material—are objectionable.

If we stand back from the immediate discussion for a moment, the debate over reproductive technologies can yield some valuable lessons about the nature of Roman Catholic ethics and moral teaching. The greatest asset of Catholic moral tradition is that it is based on reasonable interpretation of universal human realities and values, such as love, sexuality, and parenthood. One of its nagging limitations is a tendency to neglect the importance of constantly bringing past teaching back into contact with the relevant human experiences, where that teaching can be reshaped and reinvigorated for continuing use. In the area of sexuality, Church teaching has kept pace with the modern consciousness of sexuality as an important interpersonal reality by changing the old priority of procreation to a new emphasis on love as of equal value. The development of reproductive technologies offers us another opportunity to give the realities of spousehood and parenthood a thoughtful examination, and to find ways to express the value of love, sex, and procreation in ways true to contemporary experience. The Church has given an important message to our culture by insisting that having children belongs in a loving marriage: hence third party reproductive methods are excluded. However, it is the view of many, including theologians, physicians, and married persons, that current teaching on the new reproductive techniques needs further refinement, because most couples would not experience such techniques used within the marriage bond as a violation of their love for one another, but as a fulfillment of that love and of its link to shared parenthood. ·

The *Instruction,* in fact, does not close the door to further discussion of the topic. It ends with an exhortation to theologians to "study more deeply" these questions, and cautions that its own conclusions, far from being meant "to halt the effort of reflection," are intended "rather to give it a renewed impulse." Continued examination of the teachings and the arguments of the document, particularly if carried out in close contact with parents and infertile couples, will be vital to the development of Church teaching on the ethics of reproductive technologies.

The New Reproductive Technologies: Defying God's Dominion?
Maura Anne Ryan

The Evangelist Luke tells us that when Elizabeth conceived John the Baptist very late in her life, all who heard the news responded with joy. Indeed, this improbable pregnancy is recorded as a testament to the fact that "with God *nothing* will be impossible."[1] But when sixty-two year old Rossana Dalla Corte gave birth to a son in July, 1994, the announcement generated more heated controversy than murmured wonder. The "miracle maker" in this modern-day pregnancy is Italian fertility specialist Severino Antinori. His use of donor-assisted *in vitro* fertilization therapy in post-menopausal women such as Dalla Corte has been called everything from "morally unsettling" to "border[ing] on the Frankenstein syndrome."[2] In an editorial in the Vatican newspaper

Kluwer Academic Publishers, *The Journal of Medicine and Philosophy* 20 (1995), pp. 419–438, "The New Reproductive Technologies: Defying God's Dominion," by Maura Anne Ryan. Copyright © 1995 with kind permission from Kluwer Academic Publishers.

L'Osservatore Romano, theologian Gino Concetti denounced the practice as "violating biological rhythms," accusing participants of "putting [themselves] above the laws of nature, . . . replacing God Himself by presuming to be the demi-urge[s] of what is to be made and the arbiter[s] of ethics and the law."[3]. . .

But what is really being said when the charge of "playing God" is levied? More important, in debating the appropriateness of a proposed course of action (e.g., extending *in vitro* fertilization therapy to post-menopausal patients), what weight should be given to objections that we are testing—or defying— accepted limits of human agency? In what follows, I examine three forms of the argument that the new reproductive technologies[4] create problematic opportunities for "playing God;" in turn, I consider objections that these technologies: 1) usurp God's rightful dominion in human reproduction (i.e., take us "above the laws of nature"); 2) allow us to "make" what should be received as a gift; and 3) involve us in a denial of human finitude. Although these three forms are intertwined in practice, I treat them separately in order to raise up the three distinct concerns they reflect: in the first, that these technologies promote wrong relationship with God or God's authority; in the second, that they promote wrong relationship with offspring, and in the third, that they promote wrong relationship with ourselves.

I show that none of these objections to medically assisted reproduction is persuasive by *itself;* each rests on either an insufficient or a weak foundation. Nonetheless, I acknowledge that "playing God" objections are both persistent and rhetorically powerful because of the immense importance of the questions they raise. Taken seriously, they challenge us to articulate the right relationship between divine authority and human responsibility in reproduction, they force us to discern the meaning of creatureliness and co-creativity under new circumstances. Thus, warnings not to play God can have an important parenetic function in the debate over reproductive technologies, even if the case against medically assisted reproduction requires more careful argument.

DEFYING GOD'S PLAN FOR HUMAN REPRODUCTION

The warning against "usurping God's dominion in reproduction" has rarely been stated more powerfully than by Paul Ramsey in *Fabricated Man.* "[W]e should not play God," he argues, "before we have learned to be men, and as we learn to be men we will not want to play God."[5] And when are we "playing God?" When we fail to honor the "parameters of human life," when we forget that we are essentially "creatures of flesh" born of other creatures "in the midst of love."[6] In ordaining that it should occur in "the marital embrace," God endows human reproduction with a distinct dignity and with a capacity to witness to the generative covenant which defines God's primary relationship with creation. When procreation is detached from its unitive or conjugal context (e.g., when it is accomplished through *in vitro* fertilization or with the use of donated gametes) it fails to be what it is destined to be: a creaturely reflection of the mystery that "God created nothing apart from His Love; and without the divine love was not anything made that was made."[7]. . . Altering the structures of reproduction is wrong because we risk losing the means through which we, as a species, correctly perceive our condition as graciously created and faithfully loved by God. Still, there is more than religious piety or "right relation" at stake in resisting the new reproductive technologies. There are predictable personal and social dangers in legitimizing procreation beyond the sphere of love or removing sexual love from the sphere of responsible reproduction.[8] Ramsey warns of several. Once the biological and personal dimensions of procreation are separated, he argues, there are no apparent limits to the possibilities for recombination.[9] "Hatcheries" and "designer babies" are not mere science fiction, but the logical outcome of making reproduction a union of *intentions* rather than of *bodies.* He dismisses the objection that a natural regard for children as human beings will prove a limit in itself to what reproductive options a society will permit. Our ability to regard children properly is based precisely on our understanding of how "human parenthood is a created covenant of life."[10] That ability is compromised with the first "breach" of two-in-one-flesh unity.[11]

Moreover, scientific self-modification (or self-creation) is inherently dangerous. Those who propose radical alterations in the form of human reproduction cannot know for certain whether their interventions will prove to be of sufficient benefit to justify the risk. By the time experience reveals what effects *in vitro* fertilization has had on offspring or on the institutions of marriage and the family, children may already have been harmed and the institutions at issue irretrievably altered. Since we human beings have not proven especially wise or responsible in our domination of the earth, Ramsey sees no strong reason to believe that we will do any better with "species domination."[12] "Only God knows, or . . . only God could know enough to hold the future in His hands";[13] thus, only God's wisdom should direct human choices at a place where the future of humanity as humanity is being determined.

Finally, Ramsey warns that while the new reproductive technologies promise to make us all masters over nature, they will deliver only control of the many by the few. Echoing C.S. Lewis's observation that the "power of Man to make himself what he pleases means, as we have seen, the power of some men to make other men what *they* please,"[14] Ramsey sees in these technologies unprecedented opportunities for a scientific "manifest destiny." Once essential human nature becomes raw material, those who control reproductive and genetic technology control human destiny.[15] Eventually, "[w]e the manufactured [will] be everybody and we the manufacturers a minority of scientists and technicians."[16] For Ramsey, to permit a "morally blind" science—science without an anchor in the wisdom of God or nature—to define the future of humanity is a chilling prospect.

What should we make of the charge that procreation "outside the conjugal act . . . sets creation asunder?" . . .

What is really important in assessing medically assisted reproduction is whether it "entails an *inappropriate* involvement of the person," whether, for example, such methods deny the spiritual or psychic good of the individual or a spousal relationship. Put another way, the limits of co-creation or cooperation emerge at the point where the proposed action would distort or destroy the nature of the good at issue (e.g., human reproduction as a biological *and* relational partnership). Cahill has argued persuasively that a line can be drawn on these grounds between homologous and donor-assisted methods of assisted reproduction.[17] Homologous intervention is a morally admissible exception to the ideal (or norm) for procreation and parenthood as "there remains a shared biological relation to a child, of two people whose committed union is expressed sexually (even if acts of sexual expression do not lead directly to conception and childbirth)."[18] . . .

We have to ask whether the consequences voiced by Ramsey and others (however likely to come to pass) follow directly from "laying our indefinitely tampering hands on reproduction," that is, from procreating outside of the conjugal act. We can easily acknowledge that the new reproductive technologies have the potential to endanger the health of women and children and to alter certain core human relationships negatively. But the institution of "hatcheries" or the adoption of consumer attitudes toward children are not obvious consequences of separating the unitive and procreative dimensions of reproduction. They are more likely to result from two other factors: the abstraction of reproduction from the context of procreative responsibility, and the shift from a medical to a social rationale for reproductive therapy. That is, hatcheries will result not from our coming to think that procreative acts need not be sexual, but our coming to think that procreation need not occur in the context of a committed and responsible partnership. Likewise, it is when no normative distinction can be made in reproductive medicine between treating infertility and satisfying a desire for a child that legitimate concerns about "designer babies" arise. One might argue, of course, that these two moves follow directly from the original breach of the "one-flesh-unity" of sexual expression, but an intermediate step is needed to show why this must be the case.

Admittedly, a great deal is unknown about the long-term physical and psychosocial effects of medically assisted reproduction on offspring. Even less is known about the long-term effects of fertility treatment on women's health and well-being. Available information suggests that the use of therapies such as *in vitro* fertilization does not pose *unacceptable* risks to women and children, although certain features of medically assisted reproduction (e.g., higher rates of Cesarean section deliveries) raise legitimate doubts about its safety.[19]

But suppose we concede that complete information regarding the consequences of utilizing assisted reproduction is unavailable, and that some of the information that is available suggests caution and on-going evaluation. . . . To respond this way is not to dismiss the dangers of human and scientific hubris or to deny the limits of human wisdom. It is merely to argue that the proper response to these human factors is not helplessness but ongoing self-critique vis-à-vis the goods which we seek or the purposes we pursue. . . .

It should by now be clear why the objection that the new reproductive technologies necessarily involve a wrong and dangerous defiance of God's plan for reproduction fails to be persuasive. We need not deny some parameters set for human action by the knowable intentions of God—indeed we can appreciate the importance of seeking an understanding of reproduction as co-creation under new circumstances—to argue that a more careful analysis of medically assisted reproduction is needed to distinguish interventions which would distort or destroy the meanings of human reproduction from those which can legitimately serve them. In the same way, we can acknowledge the harmful potential of these technologies without concurring that disastrous consequences follow from an original defiance.

BEGOTTEN, NOT MADE?

Some readers will object that the problem with the new reproductive technologies is not (or not only) that they place us in a wrong relationship with God or nature but that they place us in a wrong relationship to potential offspring. The important distinction between Elizabeth's story and the stories of "grandmother" births coming from modern fertility clinics is that in the latter the "miracle" has been planned or executed rather than witnessed. An event which ought to be blessing, gift, or grace becomes in medically assisted reproduction the intended outcome of a scientific process. Those who should be gifts bestowed upon their parents' love, the natural fruit of their parents' two-in-one-flesh unity, and the symbols of God's continued hope in the future of humanity become merely the products of a skilled technician's labor.

Oliver O'Donovan's critique of medically assisted reproduction illustrates this position well.[20] He does not object to the new reproductive technologies on the grounds that they breach the inseparability of relational and procreative ends in the sexual act. Indeed, he thinks it quite possible to see homologous *in vitro* fertilization as "not the making of a baby apart from the sexual embrace, but the aiding of the sexual embrace to achieve its proper goal of fruitfulness."[21] Rather, his concern is that the new reproductive technologies transform reproduction from "begetting" to "making." . . .

The appeal of this objection to medically assisted reproduction is obvious. Treating children as mere "commodities," products, or "parental need satisfactions" is morally distasteful. Concerns that the new reproductive technologies promote such behaviors appear frequently in both theological and secular commentaries on the new reproductive technologies.[22] They appear frequently enough, in fact, to suggest that this may be a decisive issue for many people.

But is the child of *in vitro* fertilization "made, not begotten"? . . . Does technical intervention into the reproductive process destroy in parents a proper sense of wonder at "how God has called [their child] out of nothing into personal being"? It is not obvious that it does. Couples who undergo medically assisted reproduction often endure many disappointments and wait a very long time with no medical guarantees; for them the sense of wonder when they finally do give birth may be even greater than for others. Nor is it obvious that childbearing in the ordinary fashion cannot be undertaken as a project.

Would-be parents have long tried various means (from choice of partner to conduct of gestation) to influence reproductive outcomes. Moreover, there is no reason to think that receiving a child "along the order of a gift" guarantees that parents will regard him or her with appropriate love and respect.

Nonetheless, O'Donovan's point is terribly important: children ought not be thought of as products or commodities, as something owed to their parents or amenable to design, as existing to fulfill their parents' desires or round out their possessions. We ought to resist whatever forces would erode our societal awareness of offspring as fully, equally, and uniquely human, and we ought to resist the new reproductive technologies insofar as they are such a force.

But resistance to a "production mentality" does not lie in continuing to see our offspring as "gifts"; it lies in continuing to see reproduction as a *trust*. . . . What we need to understand is that each new human life is entrusted to us, individually and communally, for our care; insofar as it is possible, each human life ought to be brought forth under conditions which honor that trust. Children ought to be brought forth by people who will attend to their well-being, take interest in their development, respect them as ends in themselves, and equip them for independent life beyond childhood. . . .

In sum, objections are often raised of the new reproductive technologies on the grounds that they involve acquiring or "making" children. We "play God" when we cease to wait for a child (for a miracle) and turn to medicine for assistance. Behind these objections are legitimate concerns about the effects of medically assisted reproduction on our attitudes toward children. But admonitions that children ought to be "begotten, not made" do not account sufficiently for the complexity of human reproduction, whether medically assisted or not. Rather, we ought to view reproduction as a trust. By so doing, we attend to the limits of co-creativity without negating the place of appropriate human agency in reproduction.

A SENSE OF LIMITS?

Still, someone might argue that I am neglecting the most subtle and insidious of the temptations held out to us by the new reproductive technologies: the temptation toward self-deception. Like so many medical advances, these technologies give welcome solutions to long-suffered human problems. At the same time, they raise social expectations. Too easily we begin to slip over the line from asking medicine to help some people solve some problems to asking it to solve all problems for all people.[23] And when we finally demand that we be "saved from our human condition," we have done more than simply invest medicine with divine powers. We have lost sight of what is most true about us: our finitude, our creatureliness, our ultimate dependence upon God.

Two features of medically assisted reproduction make it a particularly vulnerable site for the limitless duel of promise and demand. First, patients seeking medically assisted reproduction are typically healthy adults who are highly motivated and committed to seeing the treatment process through to a successful outcome. The ordinary limits of time, physical stamina or capacity for discomfort which often serve to signal the appropriate end of a therapeutic process do not function well here. Each new ovulatory cycle presents a new possibility of conceiving; as long as their resources hold out, many patients cannot "quit" for this next time might be the time.[24]

Second, reproductive services are delivered primarily on a fee-for-service basis. Because resources have usually determined access to therapy, there has been little attention to developing general therapeutic criteria for treatment. Thus, fertility clinics differ widely as to whether they admit as patients only "clinically infertile individuals," or only married couples, or whether they admit any patient who seeks procreative services. Because these therapies often function more like consumer goods than health care goods, there is no universal agreement over whether it is *infertility* reproductive specialists should be treating or any form of involuntary childlessness. Since there is often no normative clinical distinction made between seeking medically assisted reproduction to satisfy a desire and seeking it to overcome a disability, it then becomes difficult to draw boundaries around legitimate desires. If the access category is simply a generalized "involuntary childlessness," for example, there is no obvious basis on which to distinguish "involuntary childlessness resulting from natural menopause" from "involuntary childlessness resulting from absence of a partner," from "involuntary childlessness resulting from a blocked fallopian tube." Therefore, in the context of medically assisted reproduction, the temptation to collapse "needs" and "desires" in determining appropriate care is even greater than in health care generally since the working assumption that therapy should address illness or disability is absent from the start.

But what difference does it make if we bring unlimited expectations and demands to reproductive medicine and if reproductive medicine attempts to offer satisfaction? Setting aside questions concerning the conditions under which it is appropriate to bring forth new life, are there discernible risks or losses incurred by a reproductive medicine which is motivated by the willingness to satisfy any and all human desires? We can identify at least three: First, a promise to overcome all human limitations is inherently illusory. To expect medicine to solve all human problems assumes that energy, time, and skill will eventually transcend all limitations, even those of death and disability. This is no less a lie in reproductive medicine than anywhere else. . . .

Moreover, infertility is to some extent a socially constructed impairment. The availability of technology increases the burden many patients feel to pursue all methods of conceiving a genetically related child; now, not even menopause releases the infertile woman from the "obligation" to continue trying! When reproductive medicine denies finitude, when it denies "the law of the body," it fails patients in the area where they most need assistance: in discerning what is an appropriate pursuit of fertility.

Finally, the expectations we bring to medicine help define our social priorities. As the current health care situation in the United States attests, when we invest medicine with God-like expectations, we give it an unlimited budget.

While we are waiting to be "saved from the human condition," we are diverting moneys from the pursuit of a wide variety of goods and projects. The third risk in denying the reality of procreative finitude, therefore, lies in its contribution to this wider problem. Reproductive care is only one area in which we do not have a clear sense of what needs and desires medicine ought to be addressing. However, where large investments are being made in the pursuit of a complex combination of needs and desires, and the technology is still comparatively new, it is a logical candidate for critical assessment in light of social needs. How to go about such an assessment is too complex a question to address here. The important thing is simply to acknowledge the problematic relationship between expectations and investments.

So, there is something important to be taken from the suggestion that reproductive medicine may be caught up in an unhealthy denial of human limitation. . . .

But as we saw earlier, acknowledging the reality or necessity of parameters (or in this case the value of charity) merely *initiates* reflection. What remains to be offered is 1) some framework for distinguishing when reproductive medicine is "assisting in the courageous effort to conceive," and when it is "encouraging self abuse"; 2) some means for defining the proper scope of reproductive medicine (e.g., by drawing a line around "unjust" or "untimely" reproductive impairments); 3) some principle for interpreting the "laws of the body" in this context, and 4) some suggestion concerning how procreative services might be weighed against societal needs and interests. . . .

CONCLUSION

. . . I have shown that Ramsey's objection that procreation outside the conjugal act "plays God" fails to be persuasive without some further argument, as do other sorts of claims about "playing God." Nonetheless, the exhortation not to exceed creaturely limits appears for good reason in debates over the new reproductive technologies. We can doubt whether the parameters of human responsibility are as clearly marked out or the obligations of co-creativity so obvious in the area of assisted reproduction as Ramsey or O'Donovan assume. And we can disagree on the conditions under which medicine ceases serving and begins violating those parameters or breaching those obligations. Still, the warning that there are some things we ought not do continues to surface and garner support precisely because of the importance of what it seeks to preserve: a sense of boundaries drawn by respect for offspring as human persons, the character of parenthood as a reproductive trust, and the natural limits of our bodily and psychic natures. We need not accept admonitions about "playing God" as conclusions about the permissibility of medically assisted reproduction to welcome the persistent challenge they issue: that in whatever possibilities for reproduction we consider, we continue to ask what it means to be created by God and entrusted with the responsibility for furthering that creation.

Chapter 17

ABORTION

When does life begin? When does it end? The two topics of abortion and euthanasia express the moral issues at stake in these questions which we will address in the two concluding chapters. Debates about abortion and euthanasia have been intense because of the advances in medical technology and the new medical practices created by these advances in the treatment of both nascent life and the terminally ill or severely diminished.

The subject of abortion has been particularly divisive in our society. At one extreme in this debate are those who maintain that the fetus is essentially tissue belonging to the woman, having no independent humanity of its own. On the opposite side are those who argue that the fetus is a human being, innocent and totally dependent upon us, whose rights to life must be weighed against the rights of the woman. The first view absolutizes the rights of the woman, the second view does the same for the fetus. Each of these positions denies that there is a moral issue in terms of competing values; there is simply a clear-cut answer to the question of abortion (either for or against) without any need to consider the circumstances of each particular case. Between the advocates of these two positions stand those who are compelled to find a more nuanced point of view. They believe that one cannot give an absolute answer covering every case of contemplated abortion. On the contrary, each case must be considered in light of its own circumstances.

In order to gain a picture of the present situation in the abortion debate, a brief view of the legal setting is necessary. Abortion had been governed by state laws in this country, which uniformly prohibited it. In 1959 the American Law Institute proposed that abortion be legalized in cases where, upon certification of two physicians, an interruption of the pregnancy was required for the "physical or mental health" of the mother. In 1962 the American Bar Association suggested the liberalizing of abortion laws, allowing abortion in cases of incest, rape, and in those instances where the physical and mental well-being of the woman was at stake (just what constitutes a meaningful threat to mental health or well-being was clearly destined to become an issue). With Colorado taking the lead in 1967, a number of states liberalized their abortion laws according to the model suggested by the American Bar Association. Some statutes were changed to the point that women could receive an abortion with no questions asked— "abortion on demand."

The legal struggle that ensued soon reached the Supreme Court. The cases of *Roe v. Wade* and *Doe v. Bolton* (January 22, 1973) marked an important turning point in the abortion debate. In these decisions the Court struck down both the older, more restrictive legislation operative in 30 states and the more lenient legislation of 16 other states. By a 7–2 vote the Court affirmed the right of a woman to have an abortion in the first trimester of her pregnancy; it also declared that the state's interest in the health of the mother and in the potentiality of human life may lead it to regulate abortion procedures in the second trimester and to regulate and possibly proscribe abortion after viability of the fetus. Even after viability, however, abortion must be permitted if there would be danger to the life or health of the mother.

Justice Harry Blackmun's majority opinion tried to skirt the complicated moral questions concerning abortion. "We need not resolve the difficult question of when life begins," he wrote, stating that the Court could not resolve an issue on which those who work in the disciplines of medicine, theology, and philosophy do not agree. Instead, the Court based its decision on four supports: (1) It noted that historically there has been no consistent opposition to abortion because of differing judgments concerning the time when the fetus developed into a person; (2) it observed that the late nineteenth-century laws establishing a clear pattern of opposition to abortion were frequently motivated by the danger of abortion to the health of the mother, a factor that has been altered by modern technology; (3) it determined that the rights of privacy guaranteed by the Fourteenth Amendment protect a woman's decision to have an abortion in the first stage of pregnancy, but do not eliminate state interest in later stages out of concern for the woman's health and for the "potentiality of life"; and (4) it declared that the word "person" in the Fourteenth Amendment cannot be used to include the unborn. However, by its legal discussion and its preference for the phrase "potentiality of life," the Court took a clear position on the question of when personhood begins, the issue it claimed to avoid.

Anti-abortionists, having lost the judicial battle, turned to Congress in an effort to create legislation that would make abortion illegal. A "Human Life Amendment" to the Constitution never got out of the Senate, and other efforts to define life as beginning at conception have not been successful. With the recent conservative tilt of the Supreme Court, the hopes of anti-abortionists have been renewed concerning the possibility that *Roe v. Wade* may be overturned. These hopes were not realized with the Supreme Court decision of June 1992 (*Planned Parenthood of Southeastern Pennsylvania v. Casey*), which upheld *Roe v. Wade* and affirmed the right of a woman to have an abortion, but also allowed states to pass more restrictive legislation as long as such restrictions did not pose an "undue burden" on the woman. What constitutes an "undue burden" should now become a critical legal issue.

The two initial articles are by feminists: Beverly Harrison and Shirley Cloyes articulate a pro-choice stance, and Sidney Callahan a pro-life or anti-abortion one. Harrison provides a historical perspective on the practice of abortion and the equation of any effort to control procreation with homicide. Even so, the anti-abortion tradition has not been universal. The article then makes two moral responses to the claim that the fetus in early stages of development is a human person. Harrison concludes her forceful argument by considering the social policy dimensions of abortion and, in doing so, asserts that we need to separate our reflection on the morality of specific acts from questions of how to express moral values within social institutions and systems. The argument suggests that patriarchal bias has led to prohibition of abortion, and that a reconsideration of feminist theological grounds would support the position that abortion should be a matter of choice.

Providing a fascinating counterpoint is the article by Sidney Callahan, which argues a pro-life position on a feminist basis and concludes that "women can never achieve the fulfillment of feminist goals in a society permissive toward abortion." She advocates a more inclusive ideal of justice that does not exclude human life in its beginning stages. Concerning the injustice of not letting women themselves decide on abortion, Callahan asks whether it has not always been recognized that justice is not served when an interested party (and the more powerful party in this case) is able to decide on his or her own case when there may be a conflict of interest. Rather than being simply the victim of a male-dominated society, Callahan argues that women are in danger of adopting a male-dominated sexual ethic that assumes a permissive, erotic view of sexuality and consequently a permissive attitude toward abortion. The results, according to Callahan, are already proving to be destructive of women's best interests.

The final article in this chapter demonstrates how both scientific advances and medical practices can influence moral choices in the area of abortion. While the issue of abortion itself seems so ancient as to be primordial, medical science has transformed the date of viability from 30 weeks to 21 or 22 weeks in a way that Tom Shannon labels as "simply stunning." The fetus can now be removed from the uterus, undergo a surgical procedure, and then be replaced in the uterus for the duration of the pregnancy. Furthermore, medical science has contributed to the development of chemical abortions, which make abortion totally private rather than "semi-public." Shannon suggests that "we need to focus on the underlying standing of the fetus" in ways that bear on the abortion debate but also on such issues as fetal research. While it is difficult to prove that the pre-implantation embryo is a person, Shannon argues that it is living, it possesses the human genome, and has a biological and developmental teleology that lead it eventually to become a person.

Theology and Morality of Procreative Choice
Beverly Wildung Harrison with Shirley Cloyes

Much discussion of abortion betrays the heavy hand of misogyny, the hatred of women. We all have a responsibility to recognize this bias—sometimes subtle—when ancient negative attitudes toward women intrude into the abortion debate. It is morally incumbent on us to convert the Christian position to a teaching more respectful of women's concrete history and experience. . . .

Although I am a Protestant, my own "moral theology"[1] has more in common with a Catholic approach than with much neoorthodox ethics of my own tradition. I want to stress this at the outset because in what follows I am highly critical of the reigning Roman Catholic social teaching on procreation and abortion. I believe that on most other issues of social justice, the Catholic tradition is often more substantive, morally serious, and less imbued with the dominant economic ideology than the brand of Protestant theological ethics that claims biblical warrants for its moral norms. I am no biblicist; I believe that the human wisdom that informs our ethics derives not from using the Bible alone but from reflecting in a manner that earlier Catholic moral theologians referred to as consonant with "natural law."[2] Unfortunately, however, all major strands of natural law reflection have been every bit as awful as Protestant biblicism on any matter involving human sexuality, including discussion of women's nature and women's divine vocation in relation to procreative power. And it is precisely because I recognize Catholic natural law tradition as having produced the most sophisticated type of moral reflection among Christians that I believe it must be challenged where it intersects negatively with women's lives. . . . Given the brevity of this essay, I will address the theological, Christian historical, and moral theoretical problematics first and analyze the social policy dimensions of the abortion issue only at the end, even though optimum ethical methodology would reverse this procedure.

ABORTION IN THEOLOGICAL CONTEXT

In the history of Christian theology, a central metaphor for understanding life, including human life, is as a gift of God. Creation itself has been interpreted primarily under this metaphor. It follows that in this creational context procreation itself took on special significance as the central image for the divine blessing of human life. The elevation of procreation as the central symbol of divine benevolence happened over time, however. It did not, for instance, typify the very early, primitive Christian community. The synoptic gospels provide ample evidence that procreation played no such metaphorical role in early Christianity.[3] In later

Christian history, an emergent powerful antisexual bias within Christianity made asceticism the primary spiritual ideal, although this ideal usually stood in tension with procreative power as a second sacred expression of divine blessing, and procreation has since become all but synonymous among Christians with the theological theme of creation as divine gift. It is important to observe that Roman Catholic theology actually followed on and adapted to Protestant teaching on this point.[4] Only in the last century, with the recognition of the danger of dramatic population growth in a world of finite resources, has any question been raised about the appropriateness of this unqualified theological sacralization of procreation. . . .

The problem, then, is that Christian theology celebrates the power of human freedom to shape and determine the quality of human life except when the issue of procreative choice arises. Abortion is anathema, while widespread sterilization abuse goes unnoticed. The power of man to shape creation radically is never rejected. When one stops to consider the awesome power over nature that males take for granted and celebrate, including the power to alter the conditions of human life in myriad ways, the suspicion dawns that the near hysteria that prevails about the immorality of women's right to choose abortion derives its force from the ancient power of misogyny rather than from any passion for the sacredness of human life. An index of the continuing misogyny in Christian tradition is male theologians' refusal to recognize the full range of human power to shape creation in those matters that pertain to women's power to affect the quality of our lives.

In contrast, a feminist theological approach recognizes that nothing is more urgent, in light of the changing circumstances of human beings on planet Earth, than to recognize that the entire natural-historical context of human procreative power has shifted.[5] We desperately need a desacralization of our biological power to reproduce[6] and at the same time a real concern for human dignity and the social conditions for personhood and the values of human relationship.[7] And note that desacralization does not mean complete devaluation of the worth of procreation. It means we must shift away from the notion that the central metaphors for divine blessing are expressed at the biological level to the recognition that our social relations bear the image of what is most holy. An excellent expression of this point comes from Marie Augusta Neal, a Roman Catholic feminist and a distinguished sociologist of religion:

> As long as the central human need called for was continued motivation to propagate the race, it was essential that religious symbols idealize that process above all others. Given the vicissitudes of life in a hostile environment, women had to be encouraged to bear children and men to support them: childbearing was central to the struggle for existence. Today, however, the size of the base population, together with knowledge already accumulated about artificial insemination, sperm banking, cloning, make more certain a peopled world.
>
> The more serious human problems now are who will live, who will die and who will decide.[8]

A CRITICAL HISTORICAL REVIEW OF ABORTION: AN ALTERNATIVE PERSPECTIVE

Between persons who oppose all abortions on moral grounds and those who believe abortion is sometimes or frequently morally justifiable, there is no difference of moral principle. Pro-choice advocates and antiabortion advocates share the ethical principle of respect for human life, which is probably why the debate is so acrimonious. I have already indicated that one major source of disagreement is the way in which the theological story is appropriated in relation to the changing circumstances of history. In addition, we should recognize that whenever strong moral disagreement is encountered, we simultaneously confront different readings of the history of a moral issue. The way we interpret the past is already laden with and shaped by our present sense of what the moral problem is.

For example, professional male Christian ethicists tend to assume that Christianity has an unbroken history of "all but absolute" prohibition of abortion and that the history of morality of abortion can best be traced by studying the teaching of the now best-remembered theologians. Looking at the matter this way, one can find numerous proof-texts to show that some of the "church fathers" condemned abortion and equated abortion with either homocide or murder. Whenever a "leading" churchman equated abortion with homicide or murder, he also *and simultaneously* equated *contraception* with homicide or murder. This reflects not only male chauvinist biology but also the then almost phobic antisexual bias of the Christian tradition. Claims that one can separate abortion teaching into an ethic of killing, separate from an antisexual and antifemale ethic in the history of Christianity, do not withstand critical scrutiny.[9]

The history of Christian natural law ethics is totally conditioned by the equation of any effort to control procreation with homicide. However, this antisexual, antiabortion tradition is not universal, even among theologians and canon lawyers. On the subject of sexuality and its abuse, many well-known theologians had nothing to say; abortion was not even mentioned in most moral theology. An important, untold chapter in Christian history is the great struggle that took place in the medieval period when clerical celibacy came to be imposed and the rules of sexual behavior rigidified.

My thesis is that there is a relative disinterest in the question of abortion overall in Christian history. Occasionally, Christian theologians picked up the issue, especially when these theologians were state-related, that is, were articulating policy not only for the church but for political authority. Demographer Jean Meyer, himself a Catholic, insists that the Christian tradition took over "expansion by population growth" from the Roman Empire.[10] Christians opposed abortion strongly only when Christianity was closely identified with imperial state policy or when theologians were inveighing against women and any sexuality except that expressed in the reluctant service of procreation.

The Holy Crusade quality of present teaching on abortion is quite new in Christianity and is related to cultural shifts that are requiring the Christian tradition to choose sides in the present ideological struggle under pressure to rethink its entire attitude toward women and sexuality. My research has led me to the tentative conclusion that, in Protestant cultures, except where Protestantism is the "established religion," merging church and state, one does not find a strong antiabortion theological-ethical teaching at all. At least in the United States, this is beyond historical debate.[11]...

In concluding this historical section, I must stress that if present efforts to criminalize abortion succeed, we will need a state apparatus of massive proportions to enforce compulsory childbearing. In addition, withdrawal of legal abortion will create one more massively profitable underworld economy in which the Mafia and other sections of quasi-legal capitalism may and will profitably invest. The radical right promises to get the state out of regulation of people's lives, but what they really mean is that they will let economic activity go unrestrained. What their agenda signifies for the personal lives of women is quite another matter.

An adequate historical perspective on abortion recognizes the long struggle women have waged for some degree of control over fertility and their efforts to regain control of procreative power from patriarchal and state-imperial culture and institutions. Such a perspective also takes into account that more nearly adequate contraceptive methods and the existence of safe, surgical, elective abortion represent positive historic steps toward full human freedom and dignity for women. While the same gains in medical knowledge also open the way to new forms of sterilization abuse and to social pressures against some women's use of their power of procreation, I know of no women who would choose to return to a state of lesser knowledge about these matters.

There has been an objective gain in the quality of women's lives for those fortunate enough to have access to procreative choice. That millions upon millions of women as yet do not possess even the rudimentary conditions—moral or physical—for such choice is obvious. Our moral goal should be to struggle against those real barriers—poverty, racism, and antifemale cultural oppression—that prevent authentic choice from being a reality for every woman. In this process we will be able to minimize the need for abortions only insofar as we place the abortion debate in the real lived-world context of women's lives.

ABORTION AND MORAL THEORY

The greatest strategic problem of pro-choice advocates is the widespread assumption that pro-lifers have a monopoly on the moral factors that ought to enter into decisions about abortion. *Moral* here is defined as that which makes for the self-respect and well-being of human persons and their environment. Moral legitimacy seems to adhere to their position in part because traditionalists have an array of religioethical terminology at their command that the sometimes more secular proponents of choice lack. But those who would displace women's power of choice by the power of the state and/or the medical profession do not deserve the aura of moral sanctity. We must do our homework if we are to dispel this myth of moral superiority. A major way in which Christian moral theologians and moral philosophers contribute to this monopoly of moral sanctity is by equating fetal or prenatal life with human personhood in a simplistic way and by failing to acknowledge changes regarding this issue in the history of Christianity. . . .

In any case, there are two responses that must be made to the claim that the fetus in early stages of development is a human life, or more dubiously, a human person. . . . First, the historical struggle for women's personhood is far from won, owing chiefly to the opposition of organized religious groups to full equality for women. Those who proclaim that a zygote at the moment of conception is a person worthy of citizenship continue to deny full social and political rights to women. Whatever one's judgment about the moral status of the fetus, it cannot be argued that that assessment deserves greater moral standing in analysis than does the position of the pregnant woman. This matter of evaluating the meaning of prenatal life is where morally sensitive people's judgments diverge. I cannot believe that any morally sensitive person would fail to value the woman's full, existent life less than they value early fetal life. Most women can become pregnant and carry fetal life to term many, many times in their lifetimes. The distinctly human power is not our biologic capacity to bear children, but our power to actively love, nurture, care for one another and shape one another's existence in cultural and social interaction.[12] To equate a biologic process with full normative humanity is crass biologic reductionism, and such reductionism is never practiced in religious ethics except where women's lives and well-being are involved.

Second, even though prenatal life, as it moves toward biologic individuation of human form, has value, the equation of abortion with murder is dubious. And the equation of abortion with homicide—the taking of human life—should be carefully weighed. We should also remember that we live in a world where men extend other men wide moral range in relation to justifiable homicide. For example, the just-war tradition has legitimated widespread forms of killing in war, and Christian ethicists have often extended great latitude to rulers and those in power in making choices about killing human beings.[13] Would that such moralists extended equal benefit of a doubt to women facing life-crushing psychological and politicoeconomic pressures in the face of childbearing! Men, daily, make life-determining decisions concerning nuclear power or chemical use in the environment, for example, that affect the well-being of fetuses, and our society expresses no significant opposition, even when such decisions do widespread genetic damage. When we argue for the appropriateness of legal abortion, moral outrage arises.

The so-called pro-life position also gains support by invoking the general principle of respect for human life as foundational to its morality in a way that suggests that the pro-choice advocates are unprincipled. I have already noted that pro-choice advocates have every right to claim the same moral principle, and that this debate, like most debates that are morally acrimonious, is in no sense about basic moral principles. I do not believe there is any clear-cut conflict of principle in this very deep, very bitter controversy.

It needs to be stressed that we all have an absolute obligation to honor any moral principle that seems, after rational deliberation, to be sound. This is the one absolutism appropriate to ethics. There are often several moral principles relevant to a decision and many ways to relate a given principle to a decisional context. For most right-to-lifers only one principle has moral standing in this argument. Admitting only one principle to one's process of moral reasoning means that a range of other moral values is slighted. Right-to-lifers are also moral absolutists in the sense that they admit only one possible meaning or application of the principle they invoke. Both these types of absolutism obscure moral debate and lead to less, not more, rational deliberation. The principle of respect for human life is one we should all honor, but we must also recognize that this principle often comes into conflict with other valid moral principles in the process of making real lived-world decisions. Understood in an adequate way, this principle can be restated to mean that we should treat what falls under a reasonable definition of human life as having sanctity or intrinsic moral value. But even when this is clear, other principles are needed to help us choose between two intrinsic values, in this case between the prenatal life and the pregnant woman's life.

Another general moral principle from which we cannot exempt our actions is the principle of justice, or right relations between persons and between groups of persons and communities. Another relevant principle is respect for all that supports human life, namely, the natural environment. As any person knows who thinks deeply about morality, genuine moral conflicts, as often as not, are due not to ignoring moral principles but to the fact that different principles lead to conflicting implications for action or are selectively related to decisions. For example, we live in a time when the principle of justice for women, aimed at transforming the social relations that damage women's lives, is historically urgent. For many of us this principle has greater moral urgency than the extension of the principle of respect for human life to include early fetal life, even though respect for fetal life is also a positive moral good. We should resist approaches to ethics that claim that one overriding principle always deserves to control morality. Clarification of principle, for that matter, is only a small part of moral reasoning. When we weigh moral principles and their potential application, we must also consider the implications of a given act for our present historical context and envision its long-term consequences. . . .

Two other concerns related to our efforts to make a strong moral case for women's right to procreative choice need to be touched on. The first has to do with the problems our Christian tradition creates for any attempt to make clear why women's right to control our bodies is an urgent and substantive moral claim. One of Christianity's greatest weaknesses is its spiritualizing neglect of respect for the physical body and physical well-being. Tragically, women, more than men, are expected in Christian teaching never to honor their own well-being as a moral consideration. I want to stress, then, that we have no moral tradition in Christianity that starts with body-space, or body-right, as a basic condition of moral relations. (Judaism is far better in this regard, for it acknowledges that we all have a moral right to be concerned for our life and our survival.) Hence, many Christian ethicists simply do not get the point when we speak of women's right to bodily integrity. They blithely denounce such reasons as women's disguised self-indulgence or hysterical rhetoric.[14]...

Only when people see that they cannot prohibit safe, legal, elective surgical abortion without violating the conditions of well-being for the vast majority of women—especially those most socially vulnerable because of historic patterns of oppression—will the effort to impose a selective, abstract morality of the sanctity of human life on all of us cease. This is a moral battle par excellence, and whenever we forget that we make it harder to reach the group most important to the cause of procreative choice—those women who have never suffered from childbearing pressure, who have not yet put this issue into a larger historical context, and who reverence women's historical commitment to childbearing. We will surely not reach them with pragmatic appeals to the taxpayer's wallet! To be sure, we cannot let such women go unchallenged as they support ruling-class ideology that the state should control procreation. But they will not change their politics until they see that pro-choice is grounded in a deeper, tougher, more caring moral vision than the political option they now endorse.

THE SOCIAL POLICY DIMENSIONS OF THE DEBATE

Most people fail to understand that in ethics we need, provisionally, to separate our reflection on the morality of specific acts from questions about how we express our moral values within our social institutions and systems (that is, social policy). When we do this, the morality of abortion appears in a different light. Focusing attention away from the single act of abortion to the larger historical context thrusts into relief what "respect for human life" means in the pro-choice position. It also illuminates the common core of moral concern that unites pro-choice advocates to pro-lifers who have genuine concern for expanding the circle of who really counts as human in this society. Finally, placing abortion in a larger historical context enables proponents of pro-choice to clarify where we most differ from the pro-lifers, that is, in our total skepticism that a state-enforced antiabortion policy could ever have the intended "pro-life" consequence they claim.

We must always insist that the objective social conditions that make women and children already born highly vulnerable can only be worsened by a social policy of compulsory pregnancy. However one judges the moral quality of the individual act of abortion (and here, differences among us do exist that are morally justifiable), it is still necessary to distinguish between how one judges the act of abortion morally and what one believes a societywide policy on abortion should be. We must not let those who have moral scruples against the personal act ignore the fact that a just social policy must also include active concern for enhancement of women's well-being and, for that, policies that would in fact make abortions less necessary. To anathematize abortion when the social and material conditions for control of procreation do not exist is to blame the victim, not to address the deep dilemmas of female existence in this society. . . .

If we are to be a society genuinely concerned with enhancing women's well-being and minimizing the necessity of abortions, thereby avoiding the danger over time of becoming an abortion culture,[15] what kind of a society must we become? It is here that the moral clarity of the feminist analysis becomes most obvious. How can we reduce the number of abortions due to contraceptive failure? By placing greater emphasis on medical research in this area, by requiring producers of contraceptives to behave more responsibly, and by developing patterns of institutional life that place as much emphasis on male responsibility for procreation and long-term care and nurturance of children as on female responsibility.

How can we reduce the number of abortions due to childish ignorance about sexuality among female children or adult women and our mates? By adopting a widespread program of sex education and by supporting institutional policies that teach male and female children alike that a girl is as fully capable as a boy of enjoying sex and that both must share moral responsibility for preventing pregnancy except when they have decided, as a deliberative moral act, to have a child.

How would we reduce the necessity of abortion due to sexual violence against women in and out of marriage? By challenging vicious male-generated myths that women exist primarily to meet the sexual needs of men, that women are, by nature, those who are really fulfilled only through our procreative powers. We would teach feminist history as the truthful history of the race, stressing that historic patterns of patriarchy were morally wrong and that a humane or moral society would be a fully nonsexist society.

Technological developments that may reduce the need for abortions are not entirely within our control, but the sociomoral ethos that makes abortion common is within our power to change. And we would begin to create such conditions by adopting a thoroughgoing feminist program for society. Nothing less, I submit, expresses genuine respect for human life.

Abortion and the Sexual Agenda
Sidney Callahan

The abortion debate continues. In the latest and perhaps most crucial development, pro-life feminists are contesting pro-choice feminist claims that abortion rights are prerequisites for women's full development and social equality. The outcome of this debate may be decisive for the culture as a whole. Pro-life feminists, like myself, argue on good feminist principles that women can never achieve the fulfillment of feminist goals in a society permissive toward abortion.

These new arguments over abortion take place within liberal political circles. This round of intense intra-feminist conflict has spiraled beyond earlier right-versus-left abortion debates, which focused on "tragic choices," medical judgments, and legal compromises. Feminist theorists of the pro-choice position now put forth the demand for unrestricted abortion rights as a *moral imperative* and insist upon women's right to complete reproductive freedom. They morally justify the present situation and current abortion practices. Thus it is all the more important that pro-life feminists articulate their different feminist perspective.

These opposing arguments can best be seen when presented in turn. Perhaps the most highly developed feminist arguments for the morality and legality of abortion can be found in Beverly Wildung Harrison's *Our Right to Choose* (Beacon Press, 1983) and Rosalind Pollack Petchesky's *Abortion and Woman's Choice* (Longman, 1984). Obviously it is difficult to do justice to these complex arguments, which draw on diverse strands of philosophy and social theory and are often interwoven in pro-choice feminists' own version of a "seamless garment." Yet the fundamental feminist case for the morality of abortion, encompassing the views of Harrison and Petchesky, can be analyzed in terms of four central moral claims: (1) the moral right to control one's own body; (2) the moral necessity of autonomy and choice in personal responsibility; (3) the moral claim for the contingent value of fetal life; (4) the moral right of women to true social equality.

THE MORAL RIGHT TO CONTROL ONE'S OWN BODY

Pro-choice feminism argues that a woman choosing an abortion is exercising a basic right of bodily integrity granted in our common law tradition. If she does not choose to be physically involved in the demands of a pregnancy and birth, she should not be compelled to be so against her will. Just because it is *her* body which is involved, a woman should have the right to terminate any pregnancy, which at this point in medical history is tantamount to terminating fetal life. No one can be forced to donate an organ or submit to other invasive physical procedures for however good a cause. Thus no woman should be subjected to "compulsory pregnancy." And it should be noted that in pregnancy much more than a passive biological process is at stake.

From one perspective, the fetus is, as Petchesky says, a "biological parasite" taking resources from the woman's body. During pregnancy, a woman's whole life and energies will be actively involved in the nine-month process. Gestation and childbirth involve physical and psychological risks. After childbirth a woman will either be a mother who must undertake a twenty-year responsibility for child-rearing, or face giving up her child for adoption or institutionalization. Since hers is the body, hers the risk, hers the burden, it is only just that she alone should be free to decide on pregnancy or abortion.

This moral claim to abortion, according to the pro-choice feminists, is especially valid in an individualistic society in which women cannot count on medical care or social support in pregnancy, childbirth, or childrearing. A moral abortion decision is never made in a social vacuum, but in the real life society which exists here and now.

THE MORAL NECESSITY OF AUTONOMY AND CHOICE IN PERSONAL RESPONSIBILITY

Beyond the claim for individual *bodily* integrity, the pro-choice feminists claim that to be a full adult *morally,* a woman must be able to make responsible life commitments. To plan, choose, and exercise personal responsibility, one must have control of reproduction. A woman must be able to make yes or no decisions about a specific pregnancy, according to her present situation, resources, prior commitments, and life plan. Only with such reproductive freedom can a woman have the moral autonomy necessary to make mature commitments, in the area of family, work, or education.

Contraception provides a measure of personal control, but contraceptive failure or other chance events can too easily result in involuntary pregnancy. Only free access to abortion can provide the necessary guarantee. The chance biological process of an involuntary pregnancy should not be allowed to override all the other personal commitments and responsibilities a woman has: to others, to family, to work, to education, to her future development, health, or well-being. Without reproductive freedom, women's personal moral agency and human consciousness are subjected to biology and chance.

THE MORAL CLAIM FOR THE CONTINGENT VALUE OF FETAL LIFE

Pro-choice feminist exponents like Harrison and Petchesky claim that the value of fetal life is contingent upon the woman's free consent and subjective acceptance. The fetus must be invested with maternal valuing in order to become human. This process of "humanization" through personal consciousness and "sociality" can only be bestowed by the woman in whose body and psychosocial system a new life must mature. The meaning and value of fetal life are constructed by the woman; without this personal conferral there only exists a biological, physiological process. Thus fetal interests or fetal rights can never outweigh the woman's prior interest and rights. If a woman does not consent to invest her pregnancy with meaning or value, then the merely biological process can be freely terminated. Prior to her own free choice and conscious investment, a woman cannot be described as a "mother" nor can a "child" be said to exist.

Moreover, in cases of voluntary pregnancy, a woman can withdraw consent if fetal genetic defects or some other problem emerges at any time before birth. Late abortion should thus be granted without legal restrictions. Even the minimal qualifications and limitations on women embedded in *Roe v. Wade* are unacceptable—repressive remnants of patriarchal unwillingness to give power to women.

THE MORAL RIGHT OF WOMEN TO FULL SOCIAL EQUALITY

Women have a moral right to full social equality. They should not be restricted or subordinated because of their sex. But this morally required equality cannot be realized without abortion's certain control of reproduction. Female social equality depends upon being able to compete and participate as freely as males can in the structures of educational and economic life. If a woman cannot control when and how she will be pregnant or rear children, she is at a distinct disadvantage, especially in our male-dominated world.

Psychological equality and well-being is also at stake. Women must enjoy the basic right of a person to the free exercise of heterosexual intercourse and full sexual expression, separated from procreation. No less than males, women should be able to be sexually active without the constantly inhibiting fear of pregnancy. Abortion is necessary for women's sexual fulfillment and the growth of uninhibited feminine self-confidence and ownership of their sexual powers.

But true sexual and reproductive freedom means freedom to procreate as well as to inhibit fertility. Pro-choice feminists are also worried that women's freedom to reproduce will be curtailed through the abuse of sterilization and needless hysterectomies. Besides the punitive tendencies of a male-dominated healthcare system, especially in response to repeated abortions or welfare pregnancies, there are other economic and social pressures inhibiting reproduction. Genuine reproductive freedom implies that day care, medical care, and financial support would be provided mothers, while fathers would take their full share in the burdens and delights of raising children.

Many pro-choice feminists identify feminist ideals with communitarian, ecologically sensitive approaches to reshaping society. Following theorists like Sara Ruddick and Carol Gilligan, they link abortion rights with the growth of "maternal thinking" in our heretofore patriarchal society. Maternal thinking is loosely defined as a responsible commitment to the loving nurture of specific human beings as they actually exist in socially embedded interpersonal contexts. It is a moral perspective very different from the abstract, competitive, isolated, and principled rigidity so characteristic of patriarchy.

How does a pro-life feminist respond to these arguments? Pro-life feminists grant the good intentions of their pro-choice counterparts but protest that the pro-choice position is flawed, morally inadequate, and inconsistent with feminism's basic demands for justice. Pro-life feminists champion a more encompassing moral ideal. They recognize the claims of fetal life and offer a different perspective on what is good for women. The feminist vision is expanded and refocused.

FROM THE MORAL RIGHT TO CONTROL ONE'S OWN BODY TO A MORE INCLUSIVE IDEAL OF JUSTICE

The moral right to control one's own body does apply to cases of organ transplants, mastectomies, contraception, and sterilization; but it is not a conceptualization adequate for abortion. The abortion dilemma is caused by the fact that 266 days following a conception in one body, another body will emerge. One's own body no longer exists as a single unit but is engendering another organism's life. This dynamic passage from conception to birth is genetically ordered and universally found in the human species. Pregnancy is not like the growth of cancer or infestation by a biological parasite; it is the way every human being enters the world. Strained philosophical analogies fail to apply: having a baby is not like rescuing a drowning person, being hooked up to a famous violinists's artificial life-support system, donating organs for transplant—or anything else.

As embryology and fetology advance, it becomes clear that human development is a continuum. Just as astronomers are studying the first three minutes in the genesis of the universe, so the first moments, days, and weeks at the beginning of human life are the subject of increasing scientific attention. While neonatology pushes the definition of viability ever earlier, ultrasound and fetology expand the concept of the patient in utero. Within such a continuous growth process, it is hard to defend logically any demarcation point after conception as the point at which an immature form of human life is so different from the day before or the day after, that it can be morally or legally discounted as a non-person. Even the moment of birth can hardly differentiate a nine-month fetus from a newborn. It is not surprising that those who countenance late abortions are logically led to endorse selective infanticide.

The same legal tradition which in our society guarantees the right to control one's own body firmly recognizes the wrongfulness of harming other bodies, however immature, dependent, different looking, or powerless. The handicapped, the retarded, and newborns are legally protected from deliberate harm. Pro-life feminists reject the suppositions that would except the unborn from this protection.

After all, debates similar to those about the fetus were once conducted about feminine personhood. Just as women, or blacks, were considered too different, too underdeveloped, too "biological," to have souls or to possess legal rights, so the fetus is now seen as "merely" biological life, subsidiary to a person. A woman was once viewed as incorporated into the "one flesh" of her husband's person; she too was a form of bodily property. In all patriarchal unjust systems, lesser orders of human life are granted rights only when wanted, chosen, or invested with value by the powerful.

Fortunately, in the course of civilization there has been a gradual realization that justice demands the powerless and dependent be protected against the uses of power wielded unilaterally. No human can be treated as a means to an end without consent. The fetus is an immature, dependent form of human life which only needs time and protection to develop. Surely, immaturity and dependence are not crimes....

It also seems a travesty of just procedures that a pregnant woman now, in effect, acts as sole judge of her own case, under the most stressful conditions. Yes, one can acknowledge that the pregnant woman will be subject to the potential burdens arising from a pregnancy, but it has never been thought right to have an interested party, especially the more powerful party, decide his or her own case when there may be a conflict of interest. If one considers the matter as a case of a powerful versus a powerless, silenced claimant, the pro-choice feminist argument can rightly be inverted: since hers is the body, hers the risk, and hers the greater burden, then how in fairness can a woman be the sole judge of the fetal right to life?

Human ambivalence, a bias toward self-interest, and emotional stress have always been recognized as endangering judgment. Freud declared that love and hate are so entwined that if instant thoughts could kill, we would all be dead in the bosom of our families. In the case of a woman's involuntary pregnancy, a complex, long-term solution requiring effort and energy has to compete with the immediate solution offered by a morning's visit to an abortion clinic. On the simple, perceptual plane, with imagination and thinking curtailed, the speed, ease, and privacy of abortion, combined with the small size of the embryo, tend to make early abortions seem less morally serious—even though speed, size, technical ease, and the private nature of an act have no moral standing.

As the most recent immigrants from non-personhood, feminists have traditionally fought for justice for themselves and the world. Women rally to feminism as a new and better way to live. Rejecting male aggression and destruction, feminists seek alternative, peaceful, ecologically sensitive means to resolve conflicts while respecting human potentiality. It is a chilling inconsistency to see pro-choice feminists demanding continued access to assembly-line, technological methods of fetal killing—the vacuum aspirator, prostaglandins, and dilation and evacuation. It is a betrayal of feminism, which has built the struggle for justice on the bedrock of women's empathy. After all, "maternal thinking" receives its name from a mother's unconditional acceptance and nurture of dependent, immature life. It is difficult to develop concern for women, children, the poor and the dispossessed—and to care about peace—and at the same time ignore fetal life.

FROM THE NECESSITY OF AUTONOMY AND CHOICE IN PERSONAL RESPONSIBILITY TO AN EXPANDED SENSE OF RESPONSIBILITY

A distorted idea of morality overemphasizes individual auotonomy and active choice. Morality has often been viewed too exclusively as a matter of human agency and decisive action. In moral behavior persons must explicitly choose and aggressively exert their wills to intervene in the natural and social environments. The human will dominates the body, overcomes the given, breaks out of the material limits of nature. Thus if one does not choose to be pregnant or cannot rear a child, who must be given up for adoption, then better to abort the pregnancy. Willing, planning, choosing one's moral commitments through the contracting of one's individual resources becomes the premier model of moral responsibility.

But morality also consists of the good and worthy acceptance of the unexpected events that life presents. Responsiveness and response-ability to things unchosen are also instances of the highest human moral capacity. Morality is not confined to contracted agreements of isolated individuals. Yes, one is obligated by explicit contracts freely initiated, but human beings are also obligated by implicit compacts and involuntary relationships in which persons simply find themselves. To be embedded in a family, a neighborhood, a social system, brings moral obligations which were never entered into with informed consent.

Parent-child relationships are one instance of implicit moral obligations arising by virtue of our being part of the interdependent human community. A woman, involuntarily pregnant, has a moral obligation to the now-existing dependent fetus whether she explicitly consented to its existence or not. No pro-life feminist would dispute the forceful observations of pro-choice feminists about the extreme difficulties that bearing an unwanted child in our society can entail. But the stronger force of the fetal claim presses a woman to accept these burdens; the fetus possesses rights arising from its extreme need and the interdependency and unity of humankind. The woman's moral obligation arises both from her status as a human being embedded in the interdependent human community and her unique lifegiving female reproductive power. To follow the pro-choice feminist ideology of insistent individualistic autonomy and control is to betray a fundamental basis of the moral life.

FROM THE MORAL CLAIM OF THE CONTINGENT VALUE OF FETAL LIFE TO THE MORAL CLAIM FOR THE INTRINSIC VALUE OF HUMAN LIFE

The feminist pro-choice position which claims that the value of the fetus is contingent upon the pregnant woman's bestowal—or willed, conscious "construction"—of humanhood is seriously flawed. The inadequacies of this position flow from the erroneous premises (1) that human value and rights can be granted by individual will; (2) that the individual woman's consciousness can exist and operate in an *a priori* isolated fashion; and (3) that "mere" biological, genetic human life has little meaning. Pro-life feminism takes a very different stance to life and nature.

Human life from the beginning to the end of development *has* intrinsic value; which does not depend on meeting the selective criteria or tests set up by powerful others. A fundamental humanist assumption is at stake here. Either we are going to value embodied human life and humanity as a good thing, or take some variant of the nihilist position that assumes human life is just one more random occurrence in the universe such that each instance of human life must explicitly be justified to the universe such that each instance of human life must explicitly be justified to prove itself worthy to continue. When faced with a new life, or an involuntary pregnancy, there is a world of difference in whether one first asks, "Why continue?" or "Why not?" Where is the burden of proof going to rest? The concept of "compulsory pregnancy" is as distorted as labeling life "compulsory aging."

In a sound moral tradition, human rights arise from human needs, and it is the very nature of a right, or valid claim upon another, that it cannot be denied, conditionally delayed, or rescinded by more powerful others at their behest. It seems fallacious to hold that in the case of the fetus it is the pregnant woman alone who gives or removes its right to life and human status soley through her subjective conscious investment or "humanization." Surely no pregnant woman (or any other individual member of the species) has created her own human nature by an individually willed act of consciousness, nor for that matter been able to guarantee her own human rights. An individual woman and the unique individual embryonic life within her can only exist because of their participation in the genetic inheritance of the human species as a whole. Biological life should never be discounted. Membership in the species, or collective human family, is the basis for human solidarity, equality, and natural human rights.

THE MORAL RIGHT OF WOMEN TO FULL SOCIAL EQUALITY FROM A PRO-LIFE FEMINIST PERSPECTIVE

Pro-life feminists and pro-choice feminists are totally agreed on the moral right of women to the full social equality so far denied them. The disagreement between them concerns the definition of the desired goal and the best means to get there. Permissive abortion laws do not bring women reproductive freedom, social equality, sexual fulfillment, or full personal development.

Pragmatic failures of a pro-choice feminist position combined with a lack of moral vision are, in fact, causing disaffection among young women. Middle-aged pro-choice feminists blamed the "big chill" on the general conservative backlash. But they should look rather to their own elitist acceptance of male models of sex and to the sad picture they present of women's lives. Pitting women against their own offspring is not only morally offensive, it is psychologically and politically destructive. Women will never climb to equality and social empowerment over mounds of dead fetuses, numbering now in the millions. As long as most women choose to bear children, they stand to gain from the same constellation of attitudes and institutions that will also protect the fetus in the woman's womb—and they stand to lose from the cultural assumptions that support permissive abortion. Despite temporary conflicts of interest, feminine and fetal liberation are ultimately one and the same cause.

Women's rights and liberation are pragmatically linked to fetal right because to obtain true equality, women need (1) more social support and changes in the structure of society, and (2) increased self-confidence, self-expectations, and self-esteem. Society in general, and men in particular, have to provide women more support in rearing the next generation, or our devastating feminization of poverty will continue. But if a woman claims the right to decide by herself whether the fetus becomes a child or not, what does this do to paternal and communal responsibility? Why should men share responsibility for child support or childrearing if they cannot share in what is asserted to be the woman's sole decision? Furthermore, if explicit intentions and consciously accepted contracts are necessary for moral obligations, why should men be held responsible for what *they* do not voluntarily choose to happen? By pro-choice reasoning, a man who does not want to have a child, or whose contraceptive fails, can be exempted from the responsibilites of fatherhood and child support. Traditionally, many men have been laggards in assuming parental responsibility and support for their children; ironically, ready abortion, often advocated as a response to male dereliction, legitimizes male irresponsibility and paves the way for even more male detachment and lack of commitment.

For that matter, why should the state provide a system of day-care or child support, or require workplaces to accommodate women's maternity and the needs of childrearing? Permissive abortion, granted in the name of women's privacy and reproductive freedom, ratifies the view that pregnancies and children are a woman's private individual responsibility. More and more frequently, we hear some version of this old rationalization: if she refuses to get rid of it, it's her problem. A child becomes a product of the individual woman's freely chosen investment, a form of private property resulting from her own cost-benefit calculation. The larger community is relieved of moral responsibility.

With legal abortion freely available, a clear cultural message is given: conception and pregnancy are no longer serious moral matters. With abortion as an acceptable alternative, contraception is not as responsibly used; women take risks, often at the urging of male sexual partners. Repeat abortions increase, with all their psychological and medical repercussions. With more abortion there is more abortion. Behavior shapes thought as well as the other way round. One tends to justify morally what one has done; what becomes commonplace and institutionalized seems harmless. Habituation is a powerful psychological force. Psychologically it is also true that whatever is avoided becomes more threatening; in phobias it is the retreat from anxiety-producing events which reinforces future avoidance. Women begin to see themselves as too weak to cope with involuntary pregnancies. Finally, through the potency of social pressure and force of inertia, it becomes more and more difficult, in fact almost unthinkable, *not* to use abortion to solve problem pregnancies. Abortion becomes no longer a choice but a "necessity."

But "necessity," beyond the organic failure and death of the body, is a dynamic social construction open to interpretation. The thrust of present feminist pro-choice arguments can only increase the justifiable indications for "necessary" abortion; every unwanted fetal handicap becomes more and more unacceptable. Repeatedly assured that in the name of reproductive freedom, women have a right to specify which pregnancies and which children they will accept, women justify sex selection, and abort unwanted females. Female infanticide, after all, is probably as old a custom as the human species possesses. Indeed, all kinds of selection of the fit and the favored for the good of the family and the tribe have always existed. Selective extinction is no new program.

THE NEED TO FEMINIZE SEXUALITY

There are far better goals for feminists to pursue. Pro-life feminists seek to expand and deepen the more communitarian, maternal elements of feminism—and move society from its male-dominated course. First and foremost, women have to insist upon a different, woman-centered approach to sex and reproduction. While Margaret Mead stressed the "womb envy" of males in other societies, it has been more or less repressed in our own. In our male-dominated world, what men don't do, doesn't count. Pregnancy, childbirth, and nursing have been characterized as passive, debilitating, animal-like. The disease model of pregnancy and birth has been entrenched. The female disease or impairment, with its attendant "female troubles," naturally handicaps women in the "real" world of hunting, war, and the corporate fast track. Many pro-choice feminists, deliberately childless, adopt the male perspective when they cite the "basic injustice that women have to bear the babies," instead of seeing the injustice in the fact that men cannot. Women's biologically unique capacity and privilege has been denied, despised, and suppressed under male dominations; unfortunately, many women have fallen for the phallic fallacy.

Childbirth often appears in pro-choice literature as a painful, traumatic, life-threatening experience. Yet giving birth is accurately seen as an arduous but normal exercise of lifegiving power, a violent and ecstatic peak experience, which men can never know. Ironically, some pro-choice men and women think and talk of pregnancy and childbirth with the same repugnance that ancient ascetics displayed toward orgasms and sexual intercourse. The similarity may not be accidental. The obstetrician Niles Newton, herself a mother, has written of the extended threefold sexuality of women, who can experience orgasm, birth, and nursing as passionate pleasure-giving experiences. All of these are involuntary processes of the female body. Only orgasm, which males share, has been glorified as an involuntary function that is nature's great gift; the involuntary feminine process of childbirth and nursing have been seen as bondage to biology.

Fully accepting our bodies as ourselves, what should women want? I think women will only flourish when there is a feminization of sexuality, very different from the current cultural trend toward masculinizing female sexuality. Women can never have the self-confidence and self-esteem they need to achieve feminist goals in society until a more holistic, feminine model of sexuality becomes the dominant cultural ethos. To say this affirms the view that men and women differ in the domain of sexual functioning, although they are more alike than different in other personality characteristics and competencies. For those of us committed to achieving sexual equality in the culture, it may be hard to accept the fact that sexual differences make it imperative to talk of distinct male and female models of sexuality. But if one wants to change sexual roles, one has to recognize pre-existing conditions. A great deal of evidence is accumulating which points to biological pressures for different male and female sexual functioning.

Males always and everywhere have been more physically aggressive and more likely to fuse sexuality with aggression and dominance. Females may be more variable in their sexuality, but since Masters and Johnson, we know that women have a greater capacity than men for repeated orgasm and a more tenuous path to arousal and orgasmic release. Most obviously, women also have a far greater sociobiological investment in the act of human reproduction. On the whole, women as compared to men possess a sexuality which is more complex, more intense, more extended in time, involving higher investment, risks, and psychosocial involvement.

In pro-choice feminism, a permissive, erotic view of sexuality is assumed to be the only option. Sexual intercourse with a variety of partners is seen as "inevitable" from a young age and as a positive growth experience to be managed by access to contraception and abortion. Unfortunately, the pervasive cultural conviction that adolescents, or their elders, cannot exercise sexual self-control, undermines the responsible use of contraception. When a pregnancy occurs, the first abortion is viewed in some pro-choice circles as a *rite de passage*. Responsibly choosing an abortion supposedly ensures that a young woman will take charge of her own life, make her own decisions, and carefully practice contraception. But the social dynamics of a permissive, erotic model of sexuality, coupled with permissive laws, work toward repeat abortions. Instead of being empowered by their abortion choices, young women having abortions are confronting the debilitating reality of *not* bringing a baby into the world; *not* being able to count on a committed male partner; *not* accounting oneself strong enough, or the master of enough resources, to avoid killing the fetus. Young women are hardly going to develop the self-esteem, self-discipline, and self-confidence necessary to confront a male-dominated society through abortion.

The male-oriented sexual orientation has been harmful to women and children. It has helped bring us epidemics of venereal disease, infertility, pornography, sexual abuse, adolescent pregnancy, divorce, displaced older women, and abortion. Will these signals of something amiss stimulate pro-choice feminists to rethink what kind of sex ideal really serves women's best interests? While the erotic model cannot encompass commitment, the committed model can—happily—encompass and encourage romance, passion, and playfulness. In fact, within the security of long-term commitments, women may be more likely to experience sexual pleasure and fulfillment....

The pro-life feminist position is not a return to the old feminine mystique. That espousal of "the eternal feminine" erred by viewing sexuality as so sacred that it cannot be humanly shaped at all. Woman's *whole* nature was supposed to be opposite to man's, necessitating complementary and radically different social roles. Followed to its logical conclusion, such a view presumes that reproductive and sexual experience is necessary for human fulfillment. But as the early feminists insisted, no woman has to marry or engage in sexual intercourse to be fulfilled, nor does a woman have to give birth and raise children to be complete, nor must she stay home and function as an earth mother. But female sexuality does need to be deeply respected as a unique potential and trust. Since most contraceptives and sterilization procedures really do involve only the woman's body rather than destroying new life, they can be an acceptable and responsible moral option.

With sterilization available to accelerate the inevitable natural ending of fertility and childbearing, a woman confronts only a limited number of years in which she exercises her reproductive trust and may have to respond to an unplanned pregnancy. Responsible use of contraception can lower the probabilities even more. Yet abortion is not decreasing. The reason is the current permissive attitude embodied in the law, not the "hard cases" which constitute 3 percent of today's abortions. Since attitudes, the law, and behavior interact, pro-life feminists conclude that unless there is an enforced limitation of abortion, which currently confirms the sexual and social status quo, alternatives will never be developed. For women to get what they need in order to combine childbearing, education, and careers, society has to recognize that female bodies come with wombs. Women and their reproductive power, and the children women have, must be supported in new ways. Another and different round of feminist consciousness-raising is needed in which all of women's potential is accorded respect. This time, instead of humbly buying entrée by conforming to male lifestyles, women will demand that society accommodate to them.

New feminist efforts to rethink the meaning of sexuality, femininity, and reproduction are all the more vital as new techniques for artificial reproduction, surrogate motherhood, and the like present a whole new set of dilemmas. In the long run, the very long run, the abortion debate may be merely the opening round in a series of far-reaching struggles over the role of human sexuality and the ethics of reproduction. Significant changes in the culture, both positive and negative in outcome, may begin as local storms of controversy. We may be at one of those vaguely realized thresholds when we had best come to full attention. What kind of people are we going to be? Pro-life feminists pursue a vision for their sisters, daughters, and granddaughters. Will their great-granddaughters be grateful?

Fetal Status: Sources and Implications
Thomas A. Shannon

I. INTRODUCTION

In the United States, the debate about abortion, the moral status of the fetus, and the use of fetal tissue and organs for various therapeutic interventions continues to rage. Within this debate, however, there seems to be some emerging consensus on issues of critical note. First, there is a growing recognition that fertilization is a process that takes about a day to complete rather than being a sharply defined moment. Thus the beginning of a particular human life is not as clearly demarcated as previously thought. Additionally there seems to be growing consensus around the fact that individuality—the inability of an organism to be divided into whole other organisms—comes after the process of restriction—which commits each cell to becoming a particular body part— occurs. There is about a two-week time period in which the pre-implantation embryo, while manifesting a unique genetic code, is not an individual for it can be divided either naturally into twins or triplets or artificially into individual cells each of which can become a whole other being. Third, there is a degree of consensus that while not necessarily a person in the full sense, the pre-implantation embryo is entitled to some measure of respect because it is living, shares the human genome, and has a strong potential (though not a present reality) for personhood.

Parallel to these developments, which provide some moral room for maneuvering, are others which seemingly want to take this moral inch and stretch it to the proverbial mile. Thus fetal cells are sought for therapeutic procedures, or fetuses for experimentation. Some have proposed the developments of embryos explicitly for the sake of research. Others have proposed fetuses as sources for organs. These and other social practices make contradictory contributions to the debate on fetal moral status. The small gains in moral coherence suggested above are in danger of being lost because of practices that seem to contradict any moral status the fetus may have. At present we have in our country a kind of undiagnosed and, therefore, untreated cultural schizophrenia with respect to fetal standing.

In this essay, then, I will examine four social contexts which contribute to these differing views of fetal status: the fetus in the context of developments in technology and medicine; fetal usefulness; the fetus in prenatal diagnosis; the fetus in the abortion debate. I will conclude that we must go beyond the procedural issues primarily related to the presence or absence of rights with which we typically resolve fetal standing. This in turn argues to some recognition of the moral status of the fetus in itself, independent of its uses or social or medical valuing.

II. THE SOCIAL CONTEXT OF THE FETUS

A. TECHNICAL AND MEDICAL DEVELOPMENTS

The rapidly developing field of Artificial or Assisted Reproduction (AR) has had a profound, though unrecognized, impact on views of the pre-implantation embryo and the early fetus. In AR, this entity is the prize of a quest that begins with a desire for a child and ends in a laboratory at the cost of enormous psychological and physical strain and at least tens of thousands of dollars. The parents, as well as the health care providers, are heavily invested in this quest. The pre-implantation embryo is valued and clearly seen and experienced as a child-to-be.

Another medical basis for the valuing of the fetus is the growing practice of fetal surgery. While still experimental, surgeons can remove the fetus from the uterus, perform a surgical procedure, and replace the fetus in the uterus for the duration of the pregnancy. It is also possible to perform procedures on the fetus within the uterus. Again the perception conveyed is that the fetus not only has some degree of worth based on the willingness to intervene for therapeutic purposes, but can be a legitimate patient. But patients have rights, and so the question is: if the fetus is a legitimate patient, does it have rights? Then we need to consider the implications for abortion of the answer to this question.

A final medical and technical dimension that places the fetus in a different light is the amazing developments in the Newborn Intensive Care Units (NICU). These units have been in full operation for about two decades and the progress is simply stunning. Viability for premature newborns has shifted from about 30 weeks to somewhere around 21 to 22 weeks, depending on the technology available in the unit and the skill of the staff. The NICU functions essentially as an artificial uterus. But this progress comes at a high price. The average stay in such a unit can easily run into the hundreds of thousands of dollars. But NICUs are expanding, not contracting. Whether this will continue given constraints on health care financing is not clear, but presently such costs are considered worthwhile because of high survival rates of such mid-term fetuses.

Two related practices, which are not as prominent as they were several years ago, also speak to perceptions of fetal value. Criminal charges have been brought against women who used illegal drugs during pregnancy. Whether prosecution is a way of telling the larger community that "we are serious about drug abuse," or whether it is a way of further victimizing women in desperate circumstances, the practice makes a strong statement about the value of the fetus. Moreover, there have been a number of well publicized instances of involuntary Caesarean sections performed on the basis of fetal well being. While these cases seem to be diminishing, or at least not publicized if performed, the basis for such court-justified involuntary surgical procedures was fetal well-being, which again suggests a perception of fetal value.

B. FETAL USEFULNESS

Fetal tissue can be quite useful in various medical procedures. It is important in research which seeks to understand the process of fertilization, to discover the causes of developmental anomalies during early gestation, and for alleviating the symptoms of individuals with Parkinson's Disease. A borderline case is the debate over the use of fetuses with anencephaly, an extremely severe brain trauma which results in very early death, as organ donors. In some cases organs were sought from infants already born, but in other cases there was discussion over whether to induce birth so the organs would be more useful.

Such practices see the pre-implantation embryo or fetus as valuable, but the value is seen in utilitarian terms, i.e., as a means to an end. That is, in practices such as fetal tissue transplantation, the pre-implantation embryo or fetus is not experienced as having some value in itself but as valuable because it is useful. It serves the needs or purposes of others such as physicians involved in research, patients who benefit through symptomatic relief of their disease, or the recipients of organ transplantation. Such practices suggest the fetus is an object at the disposal of others and that its value is derived from its instrumental utility. It is a means, rather than an end.

C. PRENATAL DIAGNOSIS

The last several decades have seen remarkable developments in the area of prenatal diagnosis. We have moved from amniocentesis which provides samples of fetal cells which can then be examined for genetic anomalies, to various visualization technologies, such as ultrasound and fetoscopy. These allow quite clear, occasionally technicolor, images of the fetus, both internally and externally. In the newly developed field of pre-implantation diagnosis, a cell or cells are taken from the pre-implantation embryo so its genetic profile can be ascertained before implantation. Such practices, with the exception of pre-implantation diagnosis, are standard obstetric care. Because these technologies are widely used and because of the practice of defensive medicine, one has to make a very active and firm decision not to utilize these diagnostic technologies.

The still definitive study of prenatal diagnosis by Barbara Katz Rothman, *The Tentative Pregnancy,* highlights the tensions raised by such technologies. On the one hand, if a pregnancy continues to the stage where prenatal diagnosis is recommended, it is clear that it is essentially a desired pregnancy, or at least has not been rejected by means of abortion. On the other hand, the fetus still must pass an acceptability test. It must have an acceptable genetic profile to continue to be valued and desired.

While I do not want to minimize, trivialize, or dismiss the genuine ethical dilemmas surrounding prenatal diagnosis and selective abortion, its practice does raise fundamental questions about the perception of the fetus. First, what is the problem the practice is to solve; whose problem is it: the woman's, the couple's, or the fetus's? Second, how is the problem to be resolved? The practice of prenatal diagnosis seems to put the fetus in the category of being a patient because it is a diagnostic procedure. But, more often than not, the disease or the disposition to one has no cure. This leads to other problematic choices: abortion, avoiding future pregnancies, using artificial insemination with a donor for future pregnancies, having the child and letting the disease run its natural course with appropriate interventions. Whose interests should govern the selection of any of these alternatives—those of the fetus or child-to-be, the parents, the extended family, or society? And on what basis are these interests determined? Again how these questions are answered reveals much about the fetus's standing.

D. ABORTION

The practice of abortion continues to be at the center of national politics, religious debate, and difficult individual decisions. While there is a decrease in the abortions performed annually, there are still over one million abortions per year performed in the United States. The majority of these are performed on women under 20 years of age. There have been numerous challenges to *Roe v. Wade* but its core claim of abortion's being an issue of privacy and, therefore, constitutionally protected appears to be secure. While there has been some fraying at the edges of this right with respect to issues such as information presented, waiting periods, and parental notification, the core of *Roe* remains intact. Chemical abortions such as RU 486 could replace the surgical methods now used. These will make abortion totally private or hidden as part of routine obstetric care for the procedure will occur in a physician's office and no one will know the reason for the visit. Abortion would no longer be the semi-public event it is now, which could significantly impact social, moral, and legal perspectives on abortion and fetal standing.

Finally, there is a point of conflict brought about by modern technology and the timing of abortion articulated in *Roe* which defined viability as the time when the state might assert an interest in regulating abortion. At the time of *Roe,* viability was about 28 weeks but now, given technological developments, viability is around 22–24 weeks. Some hospitals and clinics are reluctant to perform mid-second trimester abortions because, depending on the method used, the fetus might be viable. Thus while an abortion at the gestational age of 24 weeks is legal, such a fetus is potentially viable. Technology has injected a note of tension between law, medicine, morality, social practice, and women's choices.

III. CONCLUSIONS

Where does all of this leave us? If my analysis is correct, we have been engaging simultaneously in several practices that reveal a mixed picture of the fetus. Legally, we rely on a procedural analysis that tends to sideline the ethical issues and values which extend beyond privacy and freedom of choice. The procedural analysis focuses on the questions of individual rights, who has them, and which take priority. The limits of this practice are evident from the many legal battles over abortion as well as continued attempts to insert other moral issues into the debate. We need to come to terms with the underlying standing of the fetus—a standing which cannot be resolved by procedural appeals.

Two factors are crucial in reconsidering the moral status of the pre-implantation embryo or the fetus as we consider new medical and social practices which involve it.

First, few would dispute that the pre-implantation embryo is a living entity. It engages in cell division and metabolizes. True, it is dependent, but so are most other living creatures, including human infants. Second, this entity has the human genome. That is, it has a biological program from its DNA which ensures its development into a human being, not a horse or a tree. This outcome is neither a possibility nor a random occurrence. Given its DNA, we know what this organism will become.

On the one hand, these developmental directions are matters of biological fact. That is, if one presented a pre-implantation human embryo to a biologist or embryologist, he or she would make these observations: it is living, has the human genome, and has a development program. On the other hand, these factors raise, if not force, certain moral issues: the fact that this entity is living and shares in the human genome is a basis for differential treatment.

Second, there are some claims I think are extremely difficult to make about the pre-implantation embryo. It is arguably not an individual, for example, until the process of restriction is completed. That is, until the cells become restricted to becoming a particular part of the body and that part only, the pre-implantation embryo is divisible into parts, each of which can become a whole. After restriction, at around two weeks, the capacity of the cells to become any body part is "turned off" and the pre-implantation embryo becomes indivisible. Because the pre-implantation embryo is not an individual during this time, it cannot be a person for individuality is a necessary, though not sufficient, condition of being in that state. While the potential for personhood is inherent in the ongoing developmental process, this is not actualized and the pre-implantation embryo is not morally a person.

These two sets of observations leave us in a morally complicated position. It is difficult, if not impossible, to argue that the pre-implantation embryo is a person because it lacks individuality. Yet it is living, possesses the human genome, and has a biologically grounded, developmental teleology that eventuates in a person and only a person. The pre-implantation embryo thus has a value related to the value of human personhood—even though this is difficult to define precisely. However, this is not the value associated with actualized personhood. Nonetheless, these factors force us to move beyond primarily procedural considerations of the pre-implantation embryo and the fetus. Such moves make us, in my judgment, address the very difficult issue of the value of the pre-implantation embryo and fetus in itself and to consider that such a value might place constraints on its use.

Yet, because the value of the pre-implantation embryo is not that associated with personhood, there is also an opening for justifying its use in other settings. Does appropriate "respect for" and "protection of" the pre-implantation embryo necessarily preclude its use in research, for example? The critical issue is a balancing of the genuine value of the pre-implantation embryo against the actual benefits and significance of the research, considered as a means of contributing to the well-being of individuals whose personhood is established and not merely tentative. These and other dilemmas can be resolved only through painful, but honest, public debate which could eventuate in policies which balance the actual value of the pre-implantation embryo against the values to be achieved through an abortion or the potential benefits to be obtained by, for example, a research project or the use of such tissue in medical therapy to benefit another.

Chapter 18

EUTHANASIA/ASSISTED DEATH/SUICIDE

In recent years our country has witnessed a growing campaign on behalf of the right of each individual to a "death with dignity." This expression means that people who are terminally ill should have the right to choose death rather than to have their lives prolonged at great expense and often with considerable suffering. Today, patients who would otherwise die can be kept "alive" through machinery that maintains their vital functions. Proponents of euthanasia argue that the medical profession's attempt to do all in its power to maintain life imposes "life" upon the dying when it is no longer meaningful and even constitutes an indignity. In such a case "letting a person die" is usually called "passive" euthanasia, and doctors and ethicists generally agree that there comes a time when any further treatment is inappropriate—an imposition upon the dying.

But the argument for euthanasia (from the Greek, meaning "a good death") goes beyond this situation, and then the ethical issue becomes acute. For example, should an elderly person who is afflicted with a terminal illness and who wants to die be given a pain-killing drug, which would be increased until the dosage reaches the lethal stage? Such an act is called "active" euthanasia and at the present time would be legally judged as murder. A continuing debate among ethicists is whether there is a significant moral difference between active and passive euthanasia, between the overt act that causes death and the act of omission in which one lets death take its course without attempting to combat it.

Traditionally Christians have resisted any argument for actively terminating the life of a person, whatever the circumstances, because they believe that life is a gift of God and not something to be taken away by human decision. Many are concerned that if our society lifted this prohibition—even in limited circumstances in the hospital wards of terminally ill patients—the door would be open to a growing sense of human autonomy over life and a consequent cheapening of life. The view of life as a gift is tied to the view of life as a mystery not wholly capable of our comprehension. This sense of mystery is allied with our sense of the sanctity of life, which Christians have seen as an important bulwark in maintaining a humane social order. Some religious thinkers such as Albert Schweitzer have related this sense of reverence to all forms of life.

Most people would likely agree that it is not humane to work heroically to prolong the life of a patient who is lying in a coma with no hope of recovery. But the threat of lawsuits has often caused doctors and hospitals to connect such patients with intensive-care, life-preserving equipment. Once this has been done, medical personnel are understandably cautious about removing this equipment, even in cases that appear utterly hopeless. With the gradual recognition that our medical technology has actually created a new situation for us by this artificial maintenance of the dying, various groups have been lobbying in behalf of legislation that would legalize withdrawing equipment or the decision not to use such equipment. Often called a "living will," this legislation provides an instrument for persons to sign in the presence of witnesses affirming their desire that heroic measures not be taken to keep them alive when responsible medical judgment clearly indicates no hope of recovery. Over forty states have now passed such legislation.

Canada is undergoing considerable controversy around the question of assisted death or euthanasia. The article by Hanns Skoutajan focuses attention on the case of Tracy Latimer, a twelve year old whose cerebral palsy was severe. She had the mind of a three month old, weighed 38 pounds, and experienced frequent seizures. Tracy's father, Robert, enabled her to die. Or did he kill her? Or was this a case of euthanasia? The article describes the nature of the dilemma facing Canadian courts and also recognizes the values that come into play when parents, physicians, ministers, and others face this issue. In June 1997 the U.S. Supreme Court unanimously concluded, in the words of Chief Justice Rehnquist "that the asserted right to assistance in committing suicide is not a fundamental liberty interest protected by the due process clause" of the Constitution.

Margeret Farley untangles many of the distinctions that surround these cases. Her article identifies some of the larger issues that underlie decisions that people make regarding their own or others' deaths. She reviews some of the ethical boundaries and distinctions that have been important in the Christian tradition in helping people make such decisions. She also probes arguments both for and against changes in the law that would broaden individual choice regarding our dying.

Both Skoutajan and Farley avoid politicizing this issue. Though one catches a sense that their positions differ, both assist us in seeing beyond simple polarities. Farley's careful work especially enables her to make some telling recommendations.

Euthanasia Debate in Canada: Post-Sacred Society
Hanns F. Skoutajan

Angel of darkness or angel of light? The name Jack Kevorkian evokes a variety of responses from people across the United States. At one end of the spectrum, the name signals revulsion and fear. Some, including handicapped people, feel that assisted suicide will lead to the elimination of those whom society finds too cumbersome to accommodate. On the other end are those who see assisted suicide as a light at the end of a tunnel of terrible suffering, a dignified end to a life of tubes and pain, semiconsciousness and fear.

Between these two poles there are probably as many opinions as there are people. We all face an unknown future; none of us are immune to suffering. Among us are people who care deeply about life and believe in the value of the gift, but are at the same time perplexed by the conditions under which some endure this life. Although Kevorkian already faces possible prosecution for murder in his right-to-death campaign, in June he was present at another suicide, the 24th. "Present" implies that as a medical doctor he has in some way facilitated a terminal patient's passage from this life. In May John Evans died in Kevorkian's company. He was a retired Unitarian minister and longtime peace activist who wrote that he had once considered carrying out his suicide inside a church because "the finality of this act has a religious quality."

The U.S. is not the only country in which citizens have contended with this question. A number of wrenching situations have placed the issue of life and death on the front page of the Canadian conscience. Indeed, a Senate committee has struggled with the question of euthanasia, assisted suicide and related matters in recent months. The committee has requested deadline extensions, an indication of its difficulty in reaching a consensus.

Recently, Canadians have been struggling with the emotional and controversial issue of mercy killing in the case of Robert Latimer, a Saskatchewan farmer who ended the life of his 12-year-old daughter, Tracy. A jury of six women and five men found Latimer guilty of second-degree murder; he was sentenced to the minimum sentence—life imprisonment without eligibility for parole for ten years.

Tracy was declared clinically dead when she was born and had to be resuscitated. Her mother said, "We grieved for her when she was born." A severe form of cerebral palsy affected her entire body. At 12 she had the mind of a three-month-old baby; she could not walk or talk, but only smile, laugh or cry. She weighed only 38 pounds and experienced frequent seizures. In her last few months she suffered extreme pain from a dislocated hip, and was scheduled to have it removed.

Her parents, who live on a farm near Wilkie, Saskatchewan, had cared for her ever since her birth except for a few months when her mother went through a difficult pregnancy. Although the Latimer household includes three other children, life revolved around Tracy. "Her father rocked her on his knees for hours and hours," said Mrs. Latimer in defense of her husband. After his conviction Robert Latimer told the court, "I still feel I did what is right. I don't think you people [the jury] are being human."

Although at first he reported Tracy's death as a natural occurrence, Latimer soon told the police the full story. He had put the child in the cab of his pick-up and driven her out into the country. He had carefully constructed a tube that transferred carbon monoxide from the exhaust system into the cab. Tracy died very peacefully. "If she had cried I would have removed her," Latimer told the court.

The trial attracted national media attention. It was the first case of mercy killing involving a parent and child to be handled by Canadian courts. It came at a time when euthanasia is very much under discussion. In 1994, Sue Rodriguez, a terminally ill woman in Victoria, British Columbia, committed a doctor-assisted suicide after the Supreme Court of Canada refused to allow her to end her life legally. Rodriguez suffered from amyotrophic lateral sclerosis (Lou Gehrig's disease). No charges have been made, and the assisting physician has not been found. Two years earlier the Quebec Supreme Court allowed Nancy B. (her name has not been revealed) to be disconnected from the life-support system that had kept her alive.

In December 1994 a case of murder-suicide in Hamilton, Ontario, claimed Cathy Wilkinson, 43, and her son Ryan, 16. Both were found dead of carbon monoxide poisoning in a garage. Ryan suffered from cerebral palsy, was partly deaf and blind and could barely speak. With a great deal of help, he graduated from eighth grade last year. The family received assistance at home as well as financial help from a government agency, but were recently refused additional assistance; this disappointment may have precipitated the murder-suicide.

In each case there is an underlying theme: Does the sacredness of life override any justification to terminate it no matter how painful, difficult and hopeless that life may be? In the Latimer case, advocates have lined up on opposing sides of the question. Karen Schwier of the Saskatchewan Association for Community Living said, "The verdict [of the court] sends an unmistakable message to the Canadian public that the lives of the disabled are valuable." Elke Kluge, University of Victoria professor, a member of British Columbia's special advisory committee on ethical issues in health care, predicted that "this case may end up changing Canadian law."

Committing suicide is not a crime in Canada, but helping someone to commit suicide is. A debate at McGill University addressed the question, "Should the law be changed to incorporate the 'right to die'?" Margaret Somerville, director of the McGill Centre for Medical Ethics and Law, opposed any legislation condoning euthanasia, denying that it could be seen as a strictly individual moral issue. "It involves another person, usually a physician and society itself."

To allow physicians to administer lethal injections, Somerville said, is "to put the very soul of medicine on trial" and "to change arguably the most fundamental norm on which our society is based . . . that we do not kill one another . . . even for reasons of the utmost compassion and mercy." She labeled today's society as "post-sacred" and charged that "we have lost a sense of mystery—the mystery of life and death. We're frightened by mysteries, and to deal with this fear, we convert mysteries to problems, because we can control problems."

On the other side of the spectrum was Svend Robinson, a longtime member of Parliament who had been with Sue Rodriguez when she died. He made an eloquent argument in favor of euthanasia. He upheld the right of individuals to self-determination and echoed the words of Rodriguez: "If I cannot give consent to my own death, then whose body is this? Who owns my life?"

Robinson went on to point out that 16 percent of terminally ill patients fail to respond to palliative measures. "These patients can be rendered into a state of pharmaceutical oblivion, but there are people who do not want to die that way and who don't want to live that way."

John Williams, director of the ethics and legal affairs department of the Canadian Medical Association, stated that he preferred to contribute to the debate by "helping other people to make the right decisions." He identified "natural rights," which are inherent to every human being, and "posited rights," which are acquired through legislation or other communal agreements. "I don't think that the natural rights approach to assistance in dying is fruitful, mainly because it would be very difficult to reach a consensus on this. I think we would be better off looking for a posited right to such assistance."

Marcel Boisvert, a specialist in palliative care at Montreal's Royal Victoria Hospital, called for legislation that would give a mentally competent person in severe pain the right to die. Euthanasia should be regarded as a "special case" in law, he said. It cannot be considered like murder, because it is not murder. "The role of the physician is to find the medical means and offer the medical opportunity so that patients can realize their preferences and destinies, not their physician's preferences."

Robinson recounted a true story told by Balfour Mount, perhaps the best-known Canadian physician in the field of pain control, who visited a patient who was suffering from a brain tumor. He could no longer speak but managed to scribble on a piece of paper the words: "I horse." Mount sought to help him. "Do you want a horse?" he asked. The patient shook his head. "Are you saying," Mount suggested, "that if you were a horse, we would put you out of your suffering?" The patient nodded.

One of the vexing questions is how to offer support to families coping with severely handicapped people. Many feel isolated, financially ruined, and stressed beyond endurance. Often health and marriages are broken. In many cases families are unwilling to place the handicapped into institutional care even if it is available.

Walter Farquharson, former moderator of the United Church of Canada, stated in a report that "in my travels across the country I have found that church members are dissatisfied with the church's apparent failure to address concerns such as the use of life-support systems, living wills and euthanasia."

After exploring various aspects of these concerns, he concluded, "We believe that it is appropriate to withdraw medical treatments that are not benefiting the patient and that are prolonging suffering and dying when the competent patient decides and when . . . firm evidence of disease irreversibility exists. . . . We do not believe, however, that legalization of assisted suicide is justified."

The Saskatchewan Court of Appeal, the highest court in the province, turned down Robert Latimer's appeal in July. The judges writing the decision placed the responsibility on the Canadian Parliament to "modify the existing law by appropriate legislation that establishes sentencing criteria for 'mercy' killing. In the meantime, it is not for the court to pass judgement on the wisdom of Parliament with respect to the range of penalties to be imposed on those found guilty of murder." The matter will now be referred to the Supreme Court of Canada, which will decide this fall whether it will hear the case.

In the meantime Latimer has been released from prison on bail and confined to his farm pending an appeal. He is positive that the law will exonerate him, but others are less sure. The Council of Canadians with Disabilities and its member organization, the Saskatchewan Voice of the Handicapped, will intervene in any appeal. "We cannot support Mr. Latimer's claim that he had the legal right to decide to commit suicide for his daughter. The verdict of the jury and sentence of the court are just and appropriate. To do otherwise is to say that the life of a person with a disability is not equal to that of someone nondisabled," said Francine Arsenault, chairperson of the council.

Neighbors of the Latimers have supported the family. One farmer put up his farm as guarantee for Latimer's bail. Members of their United Church congregation have sent letters of condolence and encouragement as well as money—at the end of 1994, $32,000 had accumulated in a special fund to help with legal costs. Many have petitioned the Governor General of Canada to grant Latimer pardon. Legal authorities, however, fear that leniency may set a precedent for other acts of mercy killing.

An anonymous writer in the *Globe and Mail* (a national Canadian newspaper) commented: "I can easily understand what Robert Latimer was thinking the day his daughter died. He had helped to keep her alive for 12 years. Perhaps it seemed to fall within some greater natural law to help her die." Jerry Shepherd of Emmanuel College (United Church of Canada) suggested that "it is possible that God can smile on an action that contravenes his/her commandments."

Undoubtedly Somerville is right: we are living in a "post-sacred" society in which we seek to convert mysteries into problems. In a society that prides itself on living by the rule of law, we will need laws. Yet those laws cannot form an ethic. And they will not get us off the hook if we believe we stand before the God of love.

Issues in Contemporary Christian Ethics: The Choice of Death in a Medical Context
Margaret A. Farley

All religious and cultural traditions have incorporated moral assessments of choices regarding human death. These choices appear in contexts of individual self-defense, war, criminal sanctions, debility and old age, and a variety of other situations where life and death appear to conflict and the balance between them threatens to tilt in the direction of death.

Though clear norms have governed many of these contexts, ambivalence and ambiguity have not always been overcome. Jewish and Christian traditions, so profoundly influential in Western culture, have not escaped ambiguity and internal controversy regarding some questions of human life and death.

Ambivalence in the Christian tradition, for example, has in some respects increased over the centuries. In the first three hundred years of the life of the church, there was a strong prohibition against taking any human life, even in self-defense (though one could lay down one's life in martyrdom, for there was not a corresponding absolute obligation to preserve life in every circumstance).[1] The attitude toward war was generally one of pacifism. Justin Martyr could write confidently that "The Christian must not resist attack." Origen maintained that the Christian lawmaker must not allow killing at all. Ambrose, in the fourth century, taught that the Christian could not take the life of another even to save his own life. By the time Saint Augustine was writing and preaching, however, the prohibition against killing was less absolute. The fifth commandment still yielded a prohibition against private individuals killing either themselves or another; but now there could be justification for a Christian's engaging in warfare. With the beginning of a Christian version of "just war" theory, Christians could be not only soldiers but magistrates leading armies to war; and they could be hangmen performing as agents of justifiable capital punishment. In the middle ages, the prohibition against murder (taking the life of innocent persons) was clear, as was a prohibition against suicide; but the right of the state to wage war and to impose capital punishment, and the right of individuals to self-defense, were now formulated and accepted. Indeed, gradually there developed a full-scale casuistry regarding the meaning and application of the right to self-defense.

Today, questions about death and dying have become more than ever before complex and troubling. Apart from issues of war, revolution, capital punishment, and abortion, almost all of us in western culture are faced with multiple options regarding our own and our loved ones' dying. My topic focuses primarily on issues regarding death in a medical context—issues that are raised

Santa Clara Lecture Series, Religious Studies Dept., Santa Clara University.

for us in large part by developments in medical technology, technology whose possibilities have fueled a cultural need and pressure to expand the horizons of death through scientific power.

The range of moral options in response to the use of medical technology near the end of life perhaps needs no detailing here. It includes everything from preserving life as long as possible no matter what the cost, to ending life by our own hand before it becomes what we fear will be intolerable; from agreeing to Do Not Resuscitate orders in hospital settings, to specifying orders for Limitation of Treatment that extends to the use of ventilators, artificial modes of nutrition, etc.; from formulating Living Wills to granting Medical Durable Power of Attorney so that we will not be left without an arm of agency in the midst of the medical world. These options are all too familiar to us; we know them through various communications media and through direct experience in our personal lives and our professions.

To focus our considerations, I am going to try to do three things: 1) to identify some of the larger issues that underlie the choices we may make regarding our own and others' deaths; 2) to indicate some of the ethical boundaries and distinctions that have traditionally been important in evaluating specific choices in relation to human death; 3) to probe arguments both for and against changes in the law that would extend the range of individual choices regarding our dying. In addressing these three tasks, I have a concern to resist the polarization and politicization of the issue of euthanasia in the manner we have experienced with the issue of abortion.

UNDERLYING ISSUES

The issues I have in mind here are philosophical (and medical and legal) but finally religious (and hence theological) issues. They are issues deep within both Judaism and Christianity, and they have analogues in other world religions. A way to identify them briefly is to reflect on two convictions that are lodged in our attitudes toward human dying. On the one hand, life is a fundamental good. It is a gift from God, to be held as a gift is held, with reverence and respect; it is to be stewarded, cared for as something that is our own yet not only our own to be done with simply as we please. A sign that life is this kind of a value for us, this kind of a gift, is God's command to us: "Thou shalt not kill" (Exodus 20:13). The command appears in legal and prophetic traditions in the Hebrew scriptures and in the teachings of Jesus in the Christian scriptures, articulated along with imperatives neither to kill or to be angry, and not to despair in the face of suffering. We interpret this command not only as a negative prohibition against killing but as a positive prescription—so that, for example, as Karl Barth expresses it: Thou shalt will to live, and even will to be healthy.[2] "The freedom for life to which the human is summoned by the command of God is the freedom to treat as a loan both the life of all persons with one's own and one's own with that of all human persons."[3] Or, as the American Catholic bishops put it in their document on the provision of artificial nutrition and hydration:

> The Judeo-Christian tradition celebrates life as the gift of a loving God and respects the life of each human being because each is made in the image and likeness of God. As Christians we also believe we are redeemed by Christ and called to share eternal life with him. . . . Our church views life as a sacred trust, a gift over which we are given stewardship and not absolute dominion.[4]

The value of human life, then, and its ultimate ownership, is revealed in God's command and in the story of God's relationship to humanity. And there are other indications that life is a fundamental value and a gift, our own but not only our own—that is, indications not provided directly through God's special revelation. For example, some have recognized in human "nature" itself a basic drive toward life, a desire to live, indicative of a moral "law," an obligation to preserve human life. Others have found this good of life in their love for one another, experiencing in relation to a beloved a revelation of the value of life such that an intention to kill cannot be a part of what love requires. Others have maintained that life is valuable at least as the necessary condition for human persons to have and to enjoy other values. Still others have argued that respect for the life of each individual is necessary for the common good of the human community. On all of these counts, life is to be preserved—as a good that is precious to God, to the community, and to each person.

But if this is one conviction, religiously and philosophically affirmed, that human life is a fundamental good, there is a second: Life is not an absolute good, not the supreme value for humans. Thus, Karl Barth can qualify the command, "Thou shalt will to live," with the paradoxical formulation, "[but] not will to live unconditionally, . . . rather will to stake and surrender [one's life], and perhaps be prepared to die."[5] And the Catholic bishops can write: "As conscientious stewards we have a duty to preserve life, while recognizing certain limits to that duty."[6] So that, as the ethicist and legal theorist Richard Stith has put it: There are these two intuitions: Life must not be destroyed, but it need not always be preserved. Every person is utterly valuable, and each one's life is utterly valuable, yet things other than life are sometimes more valuable. Human life deserves respect; it even has sanctity; but death may sometimes be welcomed.[7]

We are therefore faced with serious questions: What are the limits to our obligation to preserve life? And, is the prohibition against taking life, against intending death, absolute? When we begin to reflect on these questions, we tend to do at least two things. First, we identify limits, boundaries, to our obligations regarding human life. In order to do so, we ask what are the conditions under which life must always be preserved? If physical life in this world is not an absolute good, to what other goods is it relative? What other values might, under what circumstances, take priority over life? And second (though relatedly), we consider distinctions. We differentiate between kinds of choices in order to see whether some of them may be morally justified though others may not. We distinguish, for example, between choices to kill and choices to let die. Let me say something briefly about each of these two strategies.

LIMITS AND DISTINCTIONS

LIMITS TO THE OBLIGATION TO PRESERVE LIFE

While my focus is on choices in a medical context, it is helpful to consider more generally the limitations that have been proposed or acknowledged regarding the obligation to preserve human life. None of these is without controversy, but they indicate the willingness of most persons to relativize in some way the value of human life. It is, actually, difficult to find anyone who finally wants to make of life in this world an absolute value. For example, when it comes to questions of war, those who think that some wars can be justified are willing to relativize the lives of their enemies; those who are absolute pacifists are willing to relativize their own lives.

Some of the candidates for limits to the obligation to preserve life (which is not to be equated with limits to the obligation not to kill) include the following:

1. Personal integrity and moral or religious witness: For the martyr, life is less valuable than the integrity of her or his faith or moral commitments; it may also be of less value than witnessing to what is believed to be right and true.

2. Conflict between human lives: There are situations in which the value of one or more individuals' lives comes into conflict with the value of another's. Criteria have been developed to justify the limiting of efforts to preserve some lives when all cannot be preserved. Examples of situations where these apply include self-defense; scarcity of resources (as when triage methods are used or more general policies are developed for rationing access to medical treatments); conflict between individual and common good (as when capital punishment is justified as a deterrent to crime).

3. Individual autonomy: The free choice of an individual sets some limits to the obligation of another to preserve that individual's life, as when an individual's refusal of medical treatment takes priority over the beneficent wishes and actions of medical caregivers.

4. Quality of life: A conflict of values can occur for and within an individual person for whom there is a "totality" of value. Physical life is a condition for every other value enjoyed by the individual in this life, but as a condition it is for the sake of the person as a whole. Thus, the loss of present and future conscious awareness, of the ability to relate with others, of the possibility of a life free from intractable and personality-changing pain, etc., may relativize the value of ongoing sheer biological existence and limit the obligation to preserve one's own or another's life under such circumstances.

5. Medical futility: The ineffectiveness of some forms of activity (for example, medical treatment) to extend the life of a patient (or to extend it with a reasonable quality of life for the person as a whole) sets a limit to the obligation to attempt to preserve that life.

To identify limits to the obligation to preserve life helps us see how life is a value but a relative value; it is a way of gaining clarity on what life is relative to; it provides us with a perspective from which we may ask whether or not we are truly obliged to preserve a particular life, our own or another's. Yet categories of "limits" in this sense do not by themselves resolve the questions about preserving life (and staving off death) that arise for us in the concrete. They are necessary but not sufficient for our moral discernment in this regard. We need additional conceptual tools such as descriptions of moral actions in terms of their intentions and their circumstances. Descriptions allow distinctions, and distinctions serve discernment.

DISTINCTIONS AMONG CHOICES REGARDING DEATH

Some choices regarding death can be morally justified, some cannot; and among the choices that are potentially justifiable, some are more easily justified than others. So general a statement is hardly controversial, but a great deal of controversy surrounds every effort to specify it. Prior to its specification, therefore, a preliminary comment may be in order.

There is an ironic twofold problem with distinguishing the moral status of different choices regarding death. On the one hand, relying too strongly on such distinctions to solve our moral questions regarding death can obscure the real problems we face. I hope to show this in what follows. But on the other hand, blurring the distinctions among these choices can compound the problems we face. This is most dangerous when we lump together all sorts of choices regarding death (in a medical context) under one category and call it "euthanasia."

This, I am afraid, is a temptation for advocates of the left and of the right on these issues. Even those who otherwise take distinctions seriously, such as the writers of official documents for the Roman Catholic community, contribute to confusion when they define euthanasia as "an action or omission which of itself or by intention causes death, in order that all suffering may in this way be eliminated."[8] Important distinctions are contained in this definition (based on concepts such as "intention" and "cause"), but they are all too often invisible under the large umbrella of the oversimplified category, euthanasia.

The kinds of distinctions I have in mind appear at three levels. (1) The first is a distinction between so-called active and passive euthanasia, or more accurately, actively taking life (killing) on the one hand, and letting someone die (omitting what would otherwise preserve someone's life), on the other. (2) The second is a distinction that further divides the possibilities of passive euthanasia (or letting die); it is a distinction based on the circumstances of the patient, and it has traditionally been referred to in considerations of ordinary versus extraordinary means. (3) Finally, there is a distinction that divides the possibilities of active euthanasia; it is the distinction between what has traditionally been called direct versus indirect active causing of death. All of these distinctions have been in the tradition of Roman Catholic moral theology for a long time, and they have also functioned significantly in contemporary medical ethics. What can be given, then, to preserve the distinction between active and passive euthanasia?

The key elements in a distinguishing description of these two options are that to let die (as opposed to actively killing) need not be to intend death or actively to cause it, though it is to accept it (for the consequences of not-doing will indeed be death in most instances) and to be the occasion of it. A sign that one need not be intending death is that should the patient continue to live, despite the withholding or withdrawal of treatment, one would not consider one's aims frustrated; and the active cause of the death when it does take place is not immediately one's omission of treatment but the underlying disease process that brings the person to the brink of death in the first place.

But why would these distinguishing features change the moral status of one's choices? Here disagreement runs deep. Nonetheless, those who want to maintain this distinction (including myself) argue that to accept death, to allow it and provide an occasion for it by removing unreasonable barriers,[9] is not to violate the value of human life—not to violate it as a divine gift, a fundamental drive within the heart of the human individual, a good of great importance to the human community. It is indeed to accept the inevitable process of dying that is a part of human living.

The descriptive difference between active and passive euthanasia is not trivial, even though each represents a choice whose consequence is death and each requires morally justifying reasons. Indeed, because the consequence (foreseen if not intended) of each is death, there can be no avoidance of moral responsibility for omitting treatment, any more than there can be for actively and directly killing someone. In other words, there must be justifying reasons if a choice to let someone die is to be a morally good choice. These reasons emerge in the further distinction to be drawn between ordinary and extraordinary means.

This second distinction has been signaled with a variety of terms ordinary/extraordinary, obligatory/optional, beneficial/burdensome, medically indicated/not indicated, etc.[10] The point of the struggle for appropriate terminology is to express most clearly a concrete situational difference that yields either an obligation, or not an obligation, to treat in a particular way. The distinction is not one of customary versus unusual treatment, nor is it one that can be captured by identifying general categories, kinds, of treatments. Its meaning is circumstantial, situational, in that it refers to the proportionate benefit and burden of a particular treatment relative to a particular patient. It is a matter of medical and personal discernment as to what counts morally as an "excessive" burden or what counts morally as an acceptable benefit.[11] The point of the distinction, however, is that some discernment of this sort is required if one is to justify omitting (withholding or withdrawing) some form of medical treatment.

To maintain that passive euthanasia can be justified in some situations is not to suggest that active euthanasia cannot also be justified. The third distinction I have noted, between direct and indirect active euthanasia, has offered a traditional way to allow for a morally justified limited form of action to hasten death. The distinction is often a subtle one, and it is not helpful in many cases. Its clearest application is in cases where action is taken to alleviate pain even though the medication given may hasten the process of dying. Here, too, the distinction rests upon clarification of what is directly intended (relief from pain) as opposed to what is foreseen as a consequence and hence held in a complex act of choice only by indirect intention (death).[12]

As I have said, it is not possible for me here to provide a full account of the meaning of these distinctions or the controversy that presently surrounds them. I am assuming some familiarity with them and raising them up because I believe in their continued importance for ethical discernment and for the forging of policies regarding choices of death. But let me here return to the question of why a distinction between active and passive euthanasia remains morally significant, and along with this, the question of why a distinction between direct and indirect active euthanasia is significant morally. The answer has two parts. First, there is a profound difference (at least for many persons) in the moral experience of letting someone die and the moral experience of actively killing someone; and there is a profound difference (at least for some persons) in the moral experience of giving an individual medication to alleviate pain and giving an individual medication with the precise and direct intention of killing her. It will not do to dismiss these differences in experience (in the perception, the judgment, the self-determined goal, of what one is doing) as illusory or self-deceptive, as the residue of a taboo morality that will disappear under critical scrutiny. Granted that omission must have justifying reasons (as commission must), and that indirect causing of death must be justified by grave reasons (in some sense, just as direct killing must be), there is nonetheless a profound difference in the moral experience of letting life go and actively, directly, taking it. The grounds of this experience may be several, but it can be rationally described and supported.[13] To reject it out of hand may be to change drastically the moral sensibilities of individuals and a culture. This is why disagreement about these moral experiences, experiences of moral obligation, run so deep. It is also why our debates about them require such respect and such care.

This leads me to the second part of an answer to the question of why the distinctions between active and passive euthanasia and between direct and indirect active euthanasia, remain morally significant. They play an important role in our assessment of options in the realm of public policy. If the line is drawn against the active, direct, taking of life in a medical context, it secures a line against expanding the population of those for whom decisions of death can be made. It prevents us from making decisions of death for persons who are vulnerable by reason of poverty, age, race, mental acuity, or whatever status makes their life appear to be of less value to society than the lives of others. It limits our choices of death to populations whose death is inevitable when medical treatment is deemed unreasonably burdensome to them, and populations for whom the obligation to care in a medical context focuses on providing them comfort in the face of terrible pain.

I am, therefore, prepared to argue that choices for death may be more easily justified when they are choices to let a life go, under circumstances in which the burdens of preserving life outweigh the benefits (for the one who is dying);

passive
indirect
ordinary
voluntary

and when the hastening of death is the secondary and not directly intended result of reasoned decisions to provide positive remedies for pain. These choices need not be made in the kind of "bad faith" that slips out from under true moral responsibility. They require moral justification; they are the result of discernment; they draw on legitimate and significant distinctions among moral choices; they ratify the value of human life as gift and as responsibility.

Yet, as I have said, the application of such distinctions does not finally resolve all of our quandaries regarding the welcoming of death in the context of sickness and debility. There remains the question of whether or not direct and active intervention with the intention to kill can ever be justified. Indeed, one of the most urgent issues that faces us as a society now is the issue of directly ending lives marked by great suffering and caught in a prolonged process of dying—issues, that is, of active euthanasia and of assisted suicide. Widespread and growing public support of the decriminalization of these options reflects a general cultural (and religious) shift in evaluations of suicide;[14] it also represents deep fears in anticipation of the circumstances of sickness and death.

In large part, our fears are of being given too much medical treatment, being kept alive too long, dying not at peace but in a wild frenzy of efforts to give us a little more time to live. The radical possibilities introduced by modern medicine lead ironically to scenarios of dying that have become unacceptable to many individuals. To more and more persons, it appears that the only way to retain some control over our death—to die a death marked by conscious self-awareness, with knowledge of our ending, surrounded by those we love—is to take our death into our own hands. It begins to make sense that while science has made death an enemy to be fought on the battlefield of medicine, so science must come to befriend death, to assist us scientifically in dying as we choose. This is part of the point of proposals for physician-assisted suicide and for voluntary active euthanasia.

The debate surrounding these proposals intensifies weekly in almost every state of our nation, and the polarization of positions threatens to become as intractable as our polarization over the issue of abortion. It is not possible for me to address what is at stake in anything like an adequate manner; hence, it will not be surprising if what I offer is unsatisfying to persons presently on either side of the question. There may also be dissatisfaction on all sides because I will not shape what I say as an advocacy position for or against the proposals before us. What I want to do, briefly, is to reflect on the major arguments that surround these proposals and to do so against the background of the underlying principles and moral distinctions that I have just outlined.

ACTIVE TAKING OF LIFE IN A MEDICAL CONTEXT

The issues that surround the active taking of life in the context of sickness and dying are most often joined, it seems to me, in three ways. First, individual choice (or individual autonomy) competes with community interests (or with perceptions of the common good). What is frequently identified as a "right to die" conflicts with a concern to protect society from a "slippery slope" of abuses that will ultimately violate the clearer and prior rights of the majority of citizens. Second, arguments for the moral legitimacy of a choice to die (by an active taking of life) conflict with arguments for a strong prohibition against such a choice. In other words, the issue is not joined merely over the right of the individual versus the good of the community, but over the evaluation of the moral goodness or evil intrinsic to active euthanasia and assisted suicide. Third, the issue is joined over competing assessments (competing predictions) of the social consequences of the legalization of a right to choose death. These three ways of joining the issues are obviously closely related.

I will not attempt here to adjudicate the three conflicts, but only to reflect in a particular way on the second and third. (This does not signal a judgment that the first issue—regarding the sheer right of choice on the part of the individual to choose death—is unimportant, but only that I am limited here in time. Moreover, the second and third sets of arguments have significant implications for adjudicating the first.) I will address the second and third within the context of a particular faith community, the Roman Catholic community. I do so both because of my audience here this evening and because the Catholic community is one whose voice promises to be significant in our national debate on these questions.

MORAL ELEMENTS IN THE CHOICE TO TAKE LIFE

Let me, then, consider for a moment arguments for and against the moral legitimacy of a choice to die. I have already pointed to the major reasons for maintaining that we ought not to take our own life or to ask another to take it for us. To repeat them quickly: (1) Our life is not our own; it belongs to God; it is God's prerogative to decide when our life must end in this world. (2) It is the law of nature to preserve our life as long as we are able; while there are limits to our power to do so and to our reasonable obligation to do so, we must not give in too quickly to the forces of death, not refuse the burdens of our whole life or cut off prematurely its possibilities. (3) We are essentially social beings, and to take our life by our own decision is to injure the community (our family, our friends, and the wider communities to which we belong).

On the other side of this issue, specific counterarguments are mounted— for example, to characterize the free agency of the one who is to die as the only morally significant feature of the choice to die; to deny that God holds (or wants) complete control over our dying; to reject a notion of "natural law"; to construe community on the model of an ecosystem where the demise of some is nature's way of making room for others. Perhaps most frequently it is argued that the suffering of the one dying overrides all other considerations that otherwise would make the active taking of human life immoral. All of these are extremely important arguments to assess, even within the Catholic tradition. But within this context they suggest questions of a particular sort, questions through which the issues may be seriously joined and strongly pressed either to resolution or to deeper levels of conflict.

For example, for those who believe that God is their ultimate destiny—their beginning and their end, their holder in life and savior in death—is it not conceivable that profound "acceptance" of death, acknowledgment of an ending that is indeed God's will, can be expressed through action as well as through passion, through doing as well as being done unto? For those who believe that they are called to resist the forces of diminishment and death as long as they can, and to surrender in the end not to evil (or even to sickness) but to God, can this never take the form of an active decision to die? Or better, does it not always, at its most profound and radical level, take this form? But can "yielding" ever be expressed through an active ending of life by one's own hand or another's? Dying holds the mystery and the hope that (as Teilhard de Chardin put it[15]) our death will be truly a "communion" with God. But in communion, action and passion, giving and receiving, embracing and letting go, become two sides of the same reality.

I recently stood at the bedside of a young man dying of AIDS. He had fought his disease long and hard, with extraordinary intelligence and courage. The day came, however, when it was clear that no more could be done. Aggressive treatments, even technologies of sheer life support, were finally being overwhelmed by the forces of death. As his family, friends, and physician were telling him of this dire situation, he said in what he could manage of a whisper, "You mean it's time to concede?" For him, conceding was an active surrender to God, and it entailed a decision to stop the technologies that were keeping him alive. He took no direct action (nor requested any) to end his life, though he chose to accept death and to cease prolonging his dying. Without erasing the difference between his form of letting go and a more active taking of his life, is it nonetheless possible that all the elements of religious acceptance could have been incorporated into one or the other?

Moreover, is it not possible, at least in exceptional circumstances, that the law of one's nature, the law of one's being, presses one to self-preservation in a manner whereby the whole of one's being must be saved? If it is possible that an individual can be in such dire straits that her very integrity as a self is threatened (by intractable pain, ravaging the spirit as well as the body), is it not justifiable in such circumstances to end one's life, to surrender it while it is still whole?

Finally, for those who believe in the Communion of Saints, is there a way in which membership in community is sustained no matter how death is accepted? Is it possible that, when death becomes inevitable and surrender to God is made in the face of it, then communal bonds can be preserved and not violated in an active as well as a passive dying-into-life?

I raise these questions not to suggest that it makes no moral difference if we refuse treatment or ask for a lethal dosage of medicine; for I am convinced that in most circumstances it does make a difference. I raise the questions, rather, in order to probe the possibility of exceptions to a rule. I raise them also in order to expand our understanding of perspectives on these issues that may be different from our own.

Now, however, let me move to the third set of issues I identified earlier. That is, let me consider competing assessments of the consequences of legalizing voluntary active euthanasia and assisted suicide.

SOCIAL CONSEQUENCES OF CHANGES IN THE LAW

There are many persons who argue against a change in policy and law in these matters not because active euthanasia or suicide are intrinsically wrong (wrong "in principle") but because they will be injurious to society. Holders of this position point to several factors: We will soon be on a very slippery slope, where what began as respect for some individuals' right of private choice becomes a violation of others' right to medical care; where we create an ethos in which individuals are pressured, socially coerced, to choose to die rather than to live as a burden to others; where voluntary active euthanasia slips into involuntary active euthanasia (as it has, according to some reports, in the Netherlands[16]); where the "easy way out" short-circuits the possibility of an individual and his or her family's resisting death to the end, companioning one another to the end, and only then surrendering into God. Moreover, risks of error, and pressures to expand the practice of euthanasia, are greater in a society such as ours where medical care is inequitably distributed according to factors of race, economic status, geography, gender, etc.; and where there is already a massive breakdown in trust between patients and physicians and a crisis of professional identity among medical care providers. In this view, then, the negative social consequences of decriminalizing voluntary active euthanasia and/or assisted suicide are serious indeed, and they weigh against any change in the law. The interests of society, not as a collectivity but as a community of many, finally should take priority over the interests of a few.

There are, however, responses to these concerns. For example, potential abuses may be limited if we craft careful safeguards against them (as has been attempted in legislative proposals for assisted suicide that require three requests, both oral and written, medical consultation, communication with family members, etc.). Besides, it is not as if we are currently invulnerable to abuses (for physicians are sometimes even now asked to write prescriptions or to provide injections that will, in a hidden way, end a patient's life; and if they respond out of compassion, there is no public scrutiny of their choices and actions).

Then, too, loss of spiritual depth among individuals in society is not inevitable should active direct taking of life in limited circumstances become possible; and in any case, one person's way to spiritual wisdom and courage is not necessarily the same as another's. There are other ways, besides holding the line against new legislation, for religious traditions to promote reverence for life, courage in the face of suffering, and religious meaning in death.

Moreover, of central importance to the good of society is tolerance and respect for differing moral perceptions. If a prohibition against active euthanasia can only be sustained "in principle" by appeals to a certain belief in God, or a particular interpretation of the natural law, then it is sustained on sectarian appeals, not on reasons grounded in a universal morality. Insofar as this is the case, the basic values of a democratic pluralistic society may be violated—by the imposition of this prohibition on all without a sufficient achievement of moral or religious consensus. Hence, in this view, the negative social consequences of changes in the law are not grave enough to support an absolute prohibition against the active taking of life in a medical context, and there may be some consequences that argue positively for change.

SOME RECOMMENDATIONS

How shall we weigh these arguments, these analyses, and the many more that I have not had time to identify? My goal, as I have said, has not been to reach a conclusion or to advocate a position. I have been, on this occasion, more concerned about the process of our societal and religious discourse than on its ending. Still, I will jump ahead of where I have come in my analysis thus far— for the sake of honesty—to signal four provisional conclusions and directions that seem to me defensible and important.

(1) The concerns on all sides about dying point to some things that can be done without moving to active voluntary euthanasia or assisted suicide. What we must do, first and foremost, is to clarify the meaning and the effectiveness of refusal of treatment. If this is truly legally safeguarded, and if there is wide and deep understanding of its medical as well as its moral and religious possibility and power, we shall be able to recognize that: (a) We do have decisions to make regarding our death, choices to live but choices finally to surrender to what must be and what can even be welcomed. And (b) as Paul Ramsey once wrote, "If the sting of death is sin, the sting of dying is solitude. . . . Desertion is more choking than death, and more feared. The chief problem of the dying is how not to die alone."[17] To choose in the end to let go is a choice we should make with others. In the medical context, the most pressing need and the most effective safeguard against all that we fear is communication. It is to be structured by policy and nurtured by those who share our life.

(2) What we must also do is to press for medical progress in the management of pain. Along with this must come a clearer focus in the clinical setting on the goals of care for each individual patient—goals that are appropriate to the individual's medical condition and personal values. Only so can we determine whether aggressive treatments should be continued or withheld; only so can we be clear about the requirements of care and the possibilities of alleviating suffering. If we can manage these things, the situations in which there appears no way out but through active killing—situations that are already rare— will be almost nonexistent.

(3) Yet I do not dispute that there are and will be rare circumstances, exceptional cases, in which intractable suffering may threaten the very soul of the person, and in which the active taking of life may be justified. Such decisions must remain the exception, however, and not become the rule. Whatever we must do, in law and in policy, to allow but to limit these actions is worthy of our discernment and our efforts at agreement.

(4) The process of our discernment, whether in the political arena or in our own faith communities, is a process that holds a moral requirement of mutual respect. We must find the ways to secure this respect, and through it the hope for the fruits of a discernment that will ultimately injure neither the individual or society.

I end where I began. Human life has profound value, it is even holy. It therefore deserves utter respect. Yet death may sometimes be welcomed—if it is welcomed in a way that does not ignore or violate the requirement to respect and to value each person. The questions before us are questions of what that way means and what, from all of us, it demands.

SUGGESTIONS FOR FURTHER READING FOR PART 6.

Chapter 15: Genetic Engineering and Cloning

Annas, George A., and Sherman Elias, eds. *Gene Mapping.* New York: Oxford University Press, 1992.

British Medical Association. *Our Genetic Future: The Science and Ethics of Genetic Technology.* New York: Oxford University Press, 1992.

Cole-Turner, Ronald. *The New Genesis Theology and the Genetic Revolution.* Louisville, KY: Westminster/John Knox Press, 1993.

Glover, Jonathan. *What Sort of People Should There Be? Genetic Engineering, Brain Control and Their Impact on Our Future World.* New York: Penguin Books, 1984.

Gustafson, James M. *Genetic Engineering and Humanness: A Revolutionary Process.* Washington, D.C.: Washington National Cathedral, 1992.

Nelson, J. Robert. *On the New Frontiers of Genetics and Religion.* Grand Rapids, MI: Eerdmans, 1994.

Neuhaus, Richard John, ed. *Guaranteeing the Good Life: Medicine and the Return of Eugenics.* Grand Rapids, MI: Eerdmans, 1990.

Peters, Ted. *Playing God: Genetic Determinism and Human Freedom.* New York: Routledge, 1996.

Reiss, Michael J. *Improving Nature?: The Science and Ethics of Genetic Engineering.* New York: Cambridge University Press, 1996.

Shannon, Thomas. *What Are They Saying about Genetic Engineering?* New York: Paulist Press, 1985.

Wekesser, Carol. *Genetic Engineering: Opposing Viewpoints.* San Diego: Greenhaven Press, 1996.

Chapter 16: Reproductive Technologies

Andrews, Lori B. *Between Strangers: Surrogate Mothers, Expectant Fathers, and Brave New Babies.* New York: Harper & Row, 1989.

Blank, Robert H. *Human Reproduction: Emerging Technologies and Conflicting Rights.* Washington, D.C.: CQ Press, 1995.

Corea, Gena, et al., eds. *Man-Made Women: How New Reproductive Technologies Affect Women.* Bloomington: Indiana University Press, 1987.

Lauritzen, Paul. *Pursuing Parenthood: Ethical Issues in Assisted Reproduction.* Bloomington: Indiana University Press, 1993.

O'Mahony, Patrick J. *A Question of Life: Its Beginning and Transmission: A Moral Perspective of the New Genetics in the West, the USSR, Poland, and East Germany.* Westminster, MD: Christian Classics, 1990.

Peters, Ted. *For the Love of Children: Genetic Technology and the Future of the Family.* Louisville, KY: Westminster/John Knox Press, 1996.

Raymond, Janice G. *Women as Wombs: Reproductive Technologies and the Battle Over Women's Freedom.* San Francisco: Harper, 1993.

Rea, Scott B. *Brave New Families: Biblical Ethics and Reproductive Technologies.* Grand Rapids, MI: Baker Books, 1996.

Spallone, Patricia, and Deborah Lynn Steinberg, eds. *Made to Order: The Myth of Reproductive and Genetic Progress.* Oxford: Pergamon, 1987.

Vaux, Kenneth L. *Birth Ethics: Religious and Ethical Values in the Genesis of Life.* New York: Crossroad, 1989.

Warren, Mary Ann. *Gendercide: The Implications of Sex Selection.* Totowa, NJ: Rowman & Allenheld, 1986.

Chapter 17: Abortion

Baird, Robert M., and Stuart E. Rosenbaum, eds. *The Ethics of Abortion: Pro-Life vs. Pro-Choice.* Rev. ed. Buffalo, NY: Prometheus Books, 1993.

Burtchaell, James T. *Rachel Weeping: The Case against Abortion.* New York: Harper & Row, 1984.

Callahan, Daniel, and Sidney Callahan, eds. *Abortion: Understanding Differences.* New York: Plenum Press, 1984.

Cornell, Drucilla. *The Imaginary Domain: Abortion, Pornography, & Sexual Harrassment.* New York: Routledge, 1995.

Dworkin, Ronald. *Life's Dominion.* New York: Knopf, 1993.

Jung, Patricia B., and Thomas H. Shannon, eds. *Abortion and Catholicism: The American Debate.* New York: Crossroad/Continuum, 1988.

Kamm, Frances Myrna. *Creation and Abortion: A Study in Moral and Legal Philosophy.* New York: Oxford University Press, 1992.

Larson, David R., ed. *Abortion: Ethical Issues and Options.* Loma Linda, CA: Loma Linda University, 1992.

Pojman, Louis J., and Francis J. Beckwith, eds. *The Abortion Controversy: A Reader.* Boston: Jones and Bartlett, 1994.

Schwarz, Stephen D. *The Moral Question of Abortion.* Chicago: Loyola University Press, 1990.

Steinbock, Bonnie. *Life before Birth.* New York: Oxford University Press, 1992.

Tickle, Phyllis, ed. *Confessing Conscience: Church Women on Abortion.* Nashville: Abingdon Press, 1990.

Thomasma, David C. *Human Life in the Balance.* Louisville, KY: Westminster/ John Knox Press, 1991.

Tribe, Lawrence H. *Abortion: The Clash of Absolutes.* New York: Norton, 1990.

Chapter 18: Euthanasia/Assisted Death/Suicide

Donnelly, John, ed. *Suicide: Right or Wrong?* Buffalo, NY: Prometheus Books, 1990.

Droge, Arthur J., and James D. Tabor. *A Noble Death: Suicide and Martyrdom among Jews and Christians in the Ancient World.* San Francisco: Harper, 1991.

Gorovitz, Samuel. *Drawing the Line: Life, Death, and Ethical Choices in an American Hospital.* New York: Oxford University Press, 1992.

Gula, Richard M. *Euthanasia: Moral and Pastoral Perspectives.* Mahwah, NJ: Paulist Press, 1994.

Hamel, Ron, ed. *Choosing Death: Active Euthanasia, Religion, and the Public Debate.* Chicago: The Park Ridge Center, 1991.

Hamel, Ronald P., and Edwin R. DuBose, eds. *Must We Suffer Our Way to Death?* Dallas: SMU Press, 1996.

Kevorkian, Jack. *Prescription—Medicine: The Goodness of Planned Death.* Buffalo, NY: Prometheus Books, 1991.

Miller, John, ed. *On Suicide.* San Francisco: Chronicle Books, 1992.

Rachels, James. *The End of Life: Euthanasia and Morality.* New York: Oxford University Press, 1986.

Steinbock, Bonnie, and Alastair Norcross, eds. *Killing and Letting Die.* Rev. ed. New York: Fordham University Press, 1994.

Veatch, Robert. *Death, Dying, and the Biological Revolution.* Rev. ed. New Haven, CT: Yale University Press, 1988.

Walter, James J., and Thomas A. Shannon. *Quality of Life: The New Medical Dilemma.* New York: Paulist Press, 1990.

Wennberg, Robert N. *Terminal Choices: Euthanasia, Suicide, and the Right to Die.* Grand Rapids, MI: Eerdmans, 1989.

NOTES

Chapter 2

1. Rudolf Schnackenburg, *The Moral Teaching of the New Testament* (New York: Herder and Herder, 1965), 83; Dodd, *Gospel and Law,* 14.
2. Harmon L. Smith and Louis W. Hodges, *The Christian and His Decisions* (Nashville: Abingdon, 1969), 31.
3. J. Robertson McQuilkin, "The Behavioral Sciences Under the Authority of Scripture," *Journal of the Evangelical Theological Society* 20, no. 1 (1977): 42.
4. Joseph Fletcher, *Situation Ethics: The New Morality* (Philadelphia: Westminster Press, 1966), 69.
5. Ibid., 78.
6. Emil Brunner, *The Divine Imperative* (Philadelphia: Westminster Press, 1947), 134.
7. Harmon L. Smith, *Storm over Ethics* (Philadelphia: United Church Press, 1967), 100.
8. Paul L. Lehmann, *Ethics in a Christian Context* (New York: Harper and Row, 1963), 138.
9. James M. Gustafson, *Protestant and Roman Catholic Ethics* (Chicago: University of Chicago Press, 1978), 44.
10. For an early (1970) attempt to state my position on the use of scripture in the discussion of contemporary issues, see "Tradition, Freedom, and the Abyss," now in *The Text and the Times: New Testament Essays for Today* (Minneapolis: Fortress Press, 1993), 5–19.
11. The definition of "authority" is notoriously difficult, and theologians have given many sophisticated treatments throughout the centuries. I operate in this paper with a fairly simple definition, which I think is taken as correct by the majority of church people, however much theologians would add caveats. It is basically a "legal" understanding. When I use the term "authority" in relation to the Bible, I mean the view that the statements of the texts, both ethical and theological, are binding on believers of all times. A Christian is obligated to believe what the Bible says is essential to faith and to perform what the Bible says one must do or not do. The term "authority" is, of course, used in many other ways in relation to the Bible. The Bible can be said to have evocative and persuasive power, and this could be called its authority. In this sense, my own position could be said to operate within a broad understanding of the authority of the Bible. Given the prevailing legal understanding, however, I think it wise to remove the term from our discussion.
12. Cf. my brief comments in "The Bible as a Weapon in Evangelical-Liberal Warfare," in *The American Religious Experiment: Piety and Practicality,* ed. Clyde L. Manschreck and Barbara Brown Zikmund (Chicago Exploration Press, 1976), 62–63, and the survey by Ernest R. Sandeen, *The Roots of Fundamentalism* (Chicago: University of Chicago Press, 1970).
13. Cf. e.g., W. G. Kümmel, *The New Testament: The History of the Investigation of Its Problems* (Nashville: Abingdon Press, 1972), 120–205.
14. Cf., e.g., Rudolf Bultmann in *Kerygma and Myth,* ed. H. W. Bartsch (New York: Macmillan Publishing Co., Inc., 1953).
15. Theologians have retreated to positions that claim the ethical (normative) is separated from the ritual (disposable), with the ethical divided into those injunctions only appropriate to the time of the Bible (disposable) and the "weightier matters" (normative); finally, only the injunction to love seems to remain. But if this is the final outcome, it is clear that the Bible as authoritative ethical norm has disappeared. One hardly need read the Bible to affirm that love is, or should be, a guiding rule.

16. I do not wish to call into question what seems to be an obvious fact: that many believers do begin from the Bible as an authoritative statement and adjust their own views accordingly. In general, however, I believe that my position is justified by the logic of the arguments.

17. Rudolf Bultmann, *Theology of the New Testament* (New York: Scribner's, 1955), esp. Part IV.

18. A fascinating contemporary example of this kind of argument with regard to the issue of male and female in the New Testament is found in Paul Jewett, *Man as Male and Female* (Grand Rapids, MI: Wm. B. Eerdmans Publishing Co., 1975).

19. *Not Every Spirit: A Dogmatics of Christian Disbelief* (Valley Forge, PA: Trinity Press International, 1994). Cf. esp. chaps. 4 and 6.

20. Ibid., 92-93.

21. Ibid., 93-94.

22. "Biblical Authority in the Post-Critical Period," under "Scriptural Authority," *The Anchor Bible Dictionary,* ed. D. N. Freedman (New York: Doubleday, 1992), V, 1049-56.

23. Ibid., 1050 (col. 2).

24. Ibid., 1052 (col. 1).

25. Ibid., 1051 (col. 2).

26. This is in no way a denial of the reality of the Holy Spirit or its influence upon our thinking. To invoke the Spirit in public debate as the source of our interpretation of the Bible, however, is nonproductive and should be avoided.

27. This signals my disagreement with the use of a "deconstructionist" approach, which solves the problems by forcing the text to fit contemporary sensibilities. The problem is that anybody can play this game. Sensibilities differ and there is no criterion by which to evaluate one revision as better than an opposing one. For all its inadequacies, the scholarly approach, which self-consciously attempts—and therefore exercises some control over meaning assigned—to limit itself to what the text meant in its own time and place, seems still the best and primary way to try to read the texts.

28. Cf. Robin Scroggs, "New Being: Renewed Mind: New Perception. Paul's View of the Source of Ethical Insight," in *The Text and the Times,* 167-183.

29. Here I follow Hans-Georg Gadamer, *Truth and Method* (New York: The Crossroad Publishing Co., 1979), 333-41, where he argues that the purpose of a text is primarily to engage the interpreter in a dialogue with the *questions* that lie behind the answers given by the text itself.

30. The position I am suggesting is similar to David Tracy's description of the Bible as a religious classic (*The Analogical Imagination: Christian Theology and the Culture of Pluralism* [New York: The Crossroad Publishing Co., 1981]). A classic has evocative power to impress and influence people in different times and places. The New Testament as "classic" serves as "the normative, more relatively adequate expressions of the community's past and present experience of the Risen Lord, the Crucified One, Jesus Christ" (*Analogical Imagination,* 248).

31. While I am not close to the details concerning the "Re-Imagining" conference, I suspect that the frightening response of many church people to what they understood were the ideas expressed in the Conference is due to their fear that Christianity is being redefined out from under their feet. I would hope that this controversy will have the positive effect of causing a genuine dialogue about what counts as legitimate parameters to, and definition of, the Christian religion.

32. My position comes closer, perhaps, to the Roman Catholic views of scripture *and* tradition than to the classical Protestant notion of *sola scriptura*. I go beyond the Roman position (as I understand it), however, in that I suggest that the Bible not be taken to be qualitatively different from tradition, except—and it is a significant exception—that, as foundational document, *it is the one part of the tradition that must always be taken into account.*

33. The difficulty with putting the matter this way is it makes it appear that theology is a first-order enterprise when in fact the work of the theologian is parasitical on faithful practice of Christian people. That does not mean theologians reflect on what most Christians are currently doing, but what Christians have done through the centuries. Such an appeal to the "past" does not mean that Christians will be faithful today by doing what was done in the

past, but by attending to how Christians did what they did in the past we hope to know better how to live now. Of course, since we believe in the communion of saints it is a comfort to know that our past forebearers are present with us.

As one as critical as I am of the Christian complicity with the order of violence that in shorthand is call "Constantinianism," the significance of this I hope will be duly noted. I do not believe that God ever abandons the church even in its unfaithfulness. So the "Constantinian" church remains "my" church as I know, even in the Constantinian strategies, that within it lie aspects of the Gospel. After all, behind the Constantinian attempt to rule lay the presumption that all is God's good creation. I am well aware that in many ways my theology is no less imperialistic than are many forms of Constantinianism. I certainly would, if I could, have as many be nonviolent as possible. The problem, of course, is that since I am committed to nonviolence, I cannot coerce anyone to so live.

34. Pacifism no more names a position that one can assume than does the name Christian. Both name a journey that is ongoing and never finished in this life. For the pacifist, nonviolence is not a "given," but an activity that hopefully helps us discover the violence that grips our lives in ways we had not noticed. Such discoveries require the use of the art of causistrical comparison through which descriptions are tested by analogy. Though I find it tiresome to be constantly subjected to "But what would you do if . . ." by those convinced that violence and war are moral necessities, I still must count them blessed insofar as they help me see what I may have missed.

35. Of course, there are all kinds of conversions. I want my reader to submit to the discipline of the church, but that means they first will have to be converted from being a liberal. In *Whose Justice? Which Rationality?* (Notre Dame, IN: University of Notre Dame Press, 1988), MacIntyre characterizes the liberal self as "the person who finds him or herself an alien to every tradition of enquiry which he or she encounters and who does so because he or she brings to the encounter with such tradition standards of rational justification which the beliefs of no tradition could satisfy. This is the kind of post-Enlightenment person who responds to the failure of the Enlightenment to provide neutral, impersonal tradition-independent standards of rational judgment by concluding that no set of beliefs proposed for acceptance is therefore justifiable" (395). MacIntyre rightly observes that only "by a change amounting to a conversion, since a condition of this alienated type of self even finding a language-in-use, which would enable it to enter into dialogue with some tradition of enquiry, is that it becomes something other than it now is, a self able to acknowledge by the way it expresses itself in language standards of rational enquiry as something other than expressions of will and preference" (396–97).

36. For example, Ronald Thiemann in *Constructing a Public Theology: The Church in a Pluralistic Culture* (Louisville, KY: Westminster/John Knox Press, 1991) suggests that the challenge before Christians is to "develop a public theology that remains based in the particularities of the Christian faith while genuinely addressing issues of public significance. Too often, theologies that seek to address a broad secular culture lose touch with the distinctive beliefs and practices of the Christian tradition. On the other hand, theologies that seek to preserve the characteristic language and patterns of Christian narrative and practice too often fail to engage the public realm in an effective and responsible fashion. [He means Hauerwas.] Either they eschew public discourse altogether in order to preserve what they see as the uniqueness of Christian life, or they enter the fray with single-minded ferocity, heedless of the pluralistic traditions of our democratic polity. [He means fundamentalist.] If Christians are to find an authentic public voice in today's culture, we must find a middle way between these two equally unhappy alternatives" (19). The rhetorical strategy of this paragraph would take an essay to analyze, but note that Thiemann assumes that there is a "public discourse" that is simply "out there." Christians cannot eschew the use of that discourse if we are to work within the "pluralist traditions of our democratic polity." It is unclear to me from where the justifications for such descriptions come. They probably sound a good deal more convincing at Harvard—namely, that institution dedicated to producing the people who would rule the world in the name of "freedom." I find the language of pluralism

particularly puzzling, since it would seem if we really value pluralism, then I do not see why those who enter the fray with "singleminded ferocity" are doing anything wrong. Thiemann later says my attacks on liberalism blind me "to the resources that liberalism might provide for the reconstruction of a political ethos that honors the pluralism of contemporary public life" (24). I simply have no idea what it means or why Christians have a stake in honoring "the pluralism of contemporary public life." Why should we call this social world "pluralistic?" and if we do in what sense is it "public?" From my perspective "public" and "pluralism" are simply words of mystification that some people use when their brains are on automatic.

37. In their recent book, *Fullness of Faith: The Public Significance of Theology* (New York: Paulist Press, 1993), Michael Himes and Kenneth Himes, O.F.M. go to great lengths to show that the Christian belief in the Trinity, which "is the summary grammar of our most fundamental experience of ourselves," is not incompatible with a commitment to human rights (59). They do try to distance themselves from liberal theories of rights by suggesting that rights gain their intelligibility from our capacity of self-gift. Yet even with such a qualification the conceptual relations between their considerations of the Trinity and human rights are vague at best. Even more puzzling is why they think it matters. Who are they trying to convince? Liberal rights theorists could care less. Are they trying to convince Catholics who may believe in the Trinity that they also ought to support human rights? Do they think American Catholics need to be convinced of that? One cannot help but feel the pathos of such projects as they strive to show that Catholics too can be good liberals. For example, consider their suggestion that "in his teaching Jesus emphasized the value his Father placed on human life and the extent of God's concern which embraced all people irrespective of distinctions such as class, race, gender or nationality" (92). We needed Jesus to reveal that God is the great liberal bureaucrat? I leave without comment that the cover of the book has a picture of the White House with the Washington Monument in the background. I assume they did not choose the cover.

38. For those anxious for an adequate characterization of liberalism, I can do no better than that offered by Ronald Beiner in his *What's the Matter with Liberalism?* (Berkeley: University of California Press, 1992). The interrelation between liberal political, social, and ethical theory is complex. MacIntyre in *Whose Justice? Which Rationality?* has presented that complexity as well as anyone.

39. Liberalism as a politics and morality has been made possible by its continued reliance on forms of life it could not account for within its own presuppositions. There is nothing wrong about it having done so except the power of liberal practices has increasingly undermined just those forms of life for which it could not account—such as why we have children. For example, T.M. Scanlon recently noted in a review of Ronald Dworkin's *Life's Dominion: An Argument about Abortion, Euthanasia, and Individual Freedom* that "if, as most contemporary moral philosophy suggests, morality can be simply identified with the sphere of rights, interests, duties, and obligations (i.e., with 'what we owe to others') then there is no distinctive morality of sex. Sexual activity is judged to be right or wrong by the same categories that apply to every other sphere of life, categories such as deception, coercion, consent, and injury" ("Partisan for Life," *New York Review of Books*, 15 July 1993, 46). The problem is that such a view of morality is insufficient to account for why such everyday activities such as friendship and having children make any sense at all.

The influence of liberal moral theory can be seen insofar as some now think that murder is wrong because it robs the one killed of his or her rights. Such accounts derive from the presumption that you need a theory to tell you what is wrong with murder. I have no doubt that liberals do need such a theory, which is but an indication why they are in such desperate need of retraining.

40. No doubt many people are oppressed as well as victimized in this society as well as in others, but the current cult of victimization has clearly gotten out of hand. I attribute this development to liberal egalitarianism, which creates the presumption that any limit is arbitrary and thus unjust. As a result, we are all victims who must compete to show who has been more decisively victimized. The difficulty with such a process is that nothing more victimizes us than accepting the description that we have been victimized.

41. I am in the process of writing a book that will tell the story of the rise and fall of Christian ethics as a discipline in the United States. My way of putting the matter is to have the book ask the dramatic question: How did a tradition that began with Walter Rauschenbusch's *Christianizing the Social Order* end with a book by James Gustafson entitled *Can Ethics Be Christian?* My answer is simple: Just to the extent that we got the kind of society the Social Gospel wanted, that outcome made Christianity unintelligible. An overview of this story can be found in my *Against the Nations: War and Survival in a Liberal Society* (Notre Dame, IN: University of Notre Dame Press, 1992), 23–50. For a very different account of this development, see Harlan Beckley, *Passion for Justice: Retrieving the Legacies of Walter Rauschenbusch, John A. Ryan, and Reinhold Niebuhr* (Louisville, KY: Westminster/John Knox Press, 1992). Susan Curtis's account of the Social Gospel rightly argues: "With their focus on the improvement of society in the here and now, social gospelers had helped lay the ideological and moral foundations of a society and culture dominated by secular institutions, standards, and values. The evolution of the social gospel and of American culture occurred simultaneously, each influencing the nature of change in the other. By 1920 the message of the social gospel had helped create and legitimize a new culture in the United States that effectively marginalized historical Protestantism. Social gospelers, in their effort to be part of the changing culture they served, adopted the secular language, methods, and standards of commerce in their religious belief and practices. The success of the social gospel writers in articulating a new social understanding of work, family and polity also had the ultimate effect of undermining its originating religious impulse" (*A Consuming Faith: The Social Gospel and Modern American Culture* [Baltimore: John Hopkins University Press, 1991], 228–29).

42. For more extensive reflection on how preaching as a truthful practice might look, see William Willimon and my *Preaching to Strangers* (Louisville, KY: Westminster/John Knox Press, 1992).

43. I have no "theory" about the secular. All I mean by the "secular" is that many, including many who count themselves "religious," are quite capable of living lives of practical atheism. If pressed for an account of this development I certainly think that by Charles Taylor in *Sources of the Self: The Making of Modern Identity* (Cambridge: Harvard University Press, 1989) tells much of the story. People obviously still "believe in God," but the relation of that "belief" to any "sources" of that belief is the problem. From my perspective the problem in modernity is not that people are not religious, but they are too religious. Secularists too often think when Judaism and Christianity are destroyed that people will then learn to live "rationally." Rather what happens is people live religiously in the most dangerous ways—romanticism, as depicted by Taylor, being one form of such religious resurgence. As a Christian I confess I think we live in a very frightening time religiously. For a more critical perspective on Taylor's account see David Matzko and my "The Sources of Charles Taylor," *Religious Studies Review* 18 (October 1992): 286–89.

As one who has a reputation as an unapologetic Enlightenment basher, I am quite well aware that the enlightenment in many ways grew from Christians' presuppositions. Indeed, I think Leszek Kolakowski is right to suggest that the Enlightenment emerged from a reconsidered Christian heritage, but in order to take root, crystallized and ossified forms of that heritage had to be defeated. "When it does begin to take root, in an ideological humanist or reactionary shape, that is, in the shape of the Reformation, it gradually drifts away from its origins to become non-Christian or anti-Christian. In its final form the Enlightenment turns against itself: Humanism becomes moral nihilism, undergoes a metamorphosis that transforms it into a totalitarian idea. The removal of the barriers erected by Christianity to protect itself against the Enlightenment, which was the fruit of its own development, brought the collapse of the barriers that protected the Enlightenment against its own degeneration, either into a deification of man and nature or into despair. It is only today that a spiritual movement on both sides is taking shape: Christianity and the Enlightenment, both gripped by a sentiment of helplessness and confusion, are beginning to question their own history and their own significance. From this doubt a vague and uncertain vision is emerging, a vision of new arrangement of which, as yet, we know nothing" (*Modernity on Endless Trial* [Chicago: University of Chicago Press, 1990], 30). There is no question of excepting or rejecting the

Enlightenment *in toto.* I have no idea what that would even look like. That I often seem to side with the "nihilistic, deconstructionist, relativist," should not be surprising, however, as they are the kind of "atheist" only the Enlightenment could produce. Christians are also "atheist" when it comes to humanism, but our atheism is, of course, Trinitarian.

For the account of "the secular" I think most compelling, see John Milbank, *Theology and Social Theory: Beyond Secular Reason* (Cambridge: Basil Blackwell, 1990). My general indebtedness to Milbank's argument I hope is obvious.

44. For a rejection of the category genius to characterize theologians as well as an answer to the question, "where have all the great theologians gone?" see William Willimon and my, "Why *Resident Aliens* Struck Such a Chord," *Missiology: An International Review* 19 (October 1991): 419–29.

45. John Howard Yoder, *The Politics of Jesus* (Grand Rapids, MI: Eerdmans, 1972).

46. Ibid., 132.

47. Eccentric he may be, but I believe Harold Bloom is closer to the truth than many wish to believe when he argues that American Christianity is actually a form of gnosticism—that is, the American religion "is a knowing, by and of an uncreated self, or self-within-the-self, and the knowledge leads to freedom, a dangerous and doom-eager freedom: from nature, time, history, community, other selves. I shake my head in unhappy wonderment at the politically correct younger intellectuals, who hope to subvert what they cannot begin to understand, an obsessed society wholly in the grip of a dominant Gnosticism" (*The American Religion: The Emergence of the Post-Christian Nation* [New York: Simon and Schuster, 1992], 49). What Bloom misses, I think, is how this kind of "gnosticism" is almost endemic in Protestantism once salvation is freed from the church. Niebuhr, of course, would be aghast at being identified with Bloom's heroes, the Mormons and the Southern Baptists, but that simply makes him all the more interesting as an exemplification of Bloom's narrative.

48. This interpretation of Niebuhr is obviously controversial, though I think it is less so as Niebuhr's theological liberalism is increasingly recognized. Only a liberal culture could have identified Niebuhr as "neo-orthodox" because of his emphasis on sin. Niebuhr had a much better self-understanding, as he was aware he stood squarely in the heritage of Protestant liberalism. For Niebuhr's most explicit account of the "symbolism" of the cross, see *The Nature and Destiny of Man* (New York: Charles Scribner's Sons, 1949), 70–76.

49. Fredric Jameson, *Postmodernism, or the Cultural Logic of Late Capitalism* (Durham, NC: Duke University Press, 1991), 390.

Chapter 3

1. *Canons on the Sacrament of Marriage,* Canon 10, November 11, 1563.

2. Christine E. Gudorf, *Body, Sex, and Pleasure: Reconstructing Christian Sexual Ethics* (Cleveland: The Pilgrim Press, 1994).

3. Sandra M. Schneiders, *Women and the Word: The Gender of God in the New Testament and the Spirituality of Women,* 1986 Madeleva Lecture in Spirituality (New York/Mahwah: Paulist Press, 1986), 35.

4. Judith S. Wallerstein and Sandra Blakeslee, *The Good Marriage: How & Why Love Lasts* (Boston & New York: Houghton Mifflin Company, 1995).

5. *San Francisco Chronicle,* January 7, 1990, Sunday Punch section.

6. Marie Marshall Fortune, *Sexual Violence: The Unmentionable Sin* (New York: Pilgrim Press, 1983), 22.

7. The National Institutes of Health and *Ms.* magazine recently conducted a study of six thousand college students; their findings are reported in the videotape *Against Her Will: Rape on Campus,* narrated by Kelly McGillis. The study established that one out of four women had been raped or had been the victim of attempted rape on campus. These statistics reflect only those who experienced attack on campus and do not reflect child sexual abuse, marital rape, or other attacks that raise the average.

8. Dianna Russell, *Rape in Marriage* (New York: Collier Books, 1962) reported in Linda A. Moody, "In the Search of Sacred Spaces," *American Baptist Quarterly* 8, no. 2 (June 1989): 109–110.

9. *Against Her Will: Rape on Campus.*

10. Menachem Amir, "Forcible Rape," *Federal Probation* 31, no. 1 (1967): 51, reported in Diane Herman, "The Rape Culture," in *Women: A Feminist Perspective,* ed. Jo Freeman (Palo Alto, CA: Mayfield, 1979), 50.

11. Indeed, Andre Guindon notes that half the crimes in North America are perpetrated within the heterosexual family and suggests that images of man as the violent one contribute not only to these crimes but also to those perpetrated outside the heterosexual family. See *The Sexual Creators: An Ethical Proposal for Concerned Christians* (New York: University Press of America, 1986), 173.

12. It is hard to overestimate the long-term effects of rape, especially when the victim is a young child or girl or when the rape is the victim's first sexual experience. Most rapes are in fact perpetrated on very young victims.

13. Carole R. Bohn, "Dominion to Rule: The Roots and Consequences of a Theology of Ownership," in *Christianity, Patriarchy and Abuse: A Feminist Critique,* ed. Joanne Carlson Brown and Carole R. Bohn (New York: Pilgrim Press, 1989), 109.

14. Beverly Wildung Harrison, "Theology and Morality of Procreative Choice," in *Making the Connections: Essays in Feminist Social Ethics,* ed. Carol S. Robb (Boston: Beacon Press, 1985), 123.

15. Indeed, I am convinced that the treatment of sexual ethics is inadequate because it fails to represent the concrete experience of women, including both our experiences of pain and our experiences of erotic joy. The feminist literature has begun to reflect both of these concerns.

16. While this is not explicit in the quotation above, it is both implicit and explicit elsewhere in Harrison's work.

17. Legal definitions of rape vary from state to state. In the past, in some jurisdictions rape has been defined in such a way that attack of one's spouse would *not* have fit the definition of rape. Most states today have definitions along the lines of that proposed by Fortune (*Sexual Violence,* 7): "forced penetration by the penis or any object of the vagina, mouth, or anus against the will of the victim."

18. These statistics are reported in Fortune, *Sexual Violence,* 2. They are taken from Laurel Fingler, "Teenagers in Survey Condone Forced Sex," *Ms.,* February 1981, 23.

19. Carol Turkington, "Sexual Aggression Widespread," *APA Monitor* 18, no. 13 (1987): 15, quoted in Polly Young-Eisendrath and Demaris Wehr, "The Fallacy of Individualism and Reasonable Violence against Women," in *Christianity, Patriarchy and Abuse,* ed. Brown and Bohn, 136.

20. Camille E. LeGrand, "Rape and Rape Laws: Sexism in Society and Law," *California Law Review* 61, no. 3 (1973): 927, reported in Herman, "The Rape Culture," in *Women: A Feminist Perspective,* ed. Freeman, 57.

21. Herman, "The Rape Culture," in *Women: A Feminist Perspective,* ed. Freeman, 57.

22. Herman argues that this attitude reflects the clear understanding of women as the property of men. In this regard, L. William Countryman's *Dirt, Greed, and Sex: Sexual Ethics in the New Testament and Their Implications for Today* (Philadelphia: Fortress Press, 1988) is instructive.

23. It is often difficult to see this, because we think of the erotic dimension as personal, private, or biological. In *Intimate Matters: A History of Sexuality in America* (New York: Harper and Row, 1988), John D'Emilio and Estelle B. Freedman demonstrate that the assumption that sexuality is oriented toward erotic and personal pleasure is itself a modern development.

24. Fortune, *Sexual Violence,* 16.

25. While there is no single definition of pornography, I take Marianna Valverde's to be consonant with that of most other feminist thinkers. Valverde proposes that pornography is characterized by (1) the portrayal of men's social and physical power over women as sexy, (2) the depiction of aggression as the inevitable result of power imbalances, such that we

expect the rape of the powerless by the powerful, and (3) the idea of sex as having a relentless power to cut across social barriers and conventions, so that people will do things to others that would not normally be expected (e.g., rape a nun). See Marianna Valverde, *Sex, Power and Pleasure* (Philadelphia: New Society Publishers, 1987), 129f. Particularly important in Valverde's analysis, however, is her recognition that pornography cannot be defined solely by the content of the material, but must also be defined by its *use*—e.g., the commercialization of sex. See also Mary Hunt, "Theological Pornography: From Corporate to Communal Ethics," in *Christianity, Patriarchy and Abuse,* ed. Brown and Boh.

26. Nancy C. M. Hartsock, *Money, Sex and Power: Toward a Feminist Historical Materialism* (Boston: Northeastern University Press, 1985), 168.

27. The Professional Ethics Group of the Center for Ethics and Social Policy at the Graduate Theological Union has had a grant from the Lilly Endowment to conduct studies of pastors. These studies suggest that many men find a woman's tears or other signs of vulnerability very sexually arousing. We had one pastor in our study who claimed that he was addicted to pornography.

28. Pornography often depicts group attacks on a woman. Similarly, rape itself is often done by gangs or in the presence of other men. See Herman, "The Rape Culture," in *Women: A Feminist Perspective,* ed. Freeman, 47.

29. Andrea Dworkin, *Pornography: Men Possessing Women* (London: The Women's Press, 1981), 24-25. Dworkin argues (69) that pornography reveals an inextricable link between male pleasure and victimizing, hurting, and exploitation of women: "sexual fun and sexual passion in the privacy of the male imagination are inseparable from the brutality of male history." I think that to claim that male pleasure is "inextricably" tied to hurting the other is too strong. Nonetheless, the prevalence and power of pornography in our midst demonstrates that much pleasure for both men and women has been tied to having power to make another person do what is humiliating.

30. The roots of violence need further exploration. In *Touching Our Strength* (San Francisco: Harper and Row, 1989), 13-15, Carter Heyward notes that the recent work of the Stone Center for Developmental Services and Studies at Wellesley College, Massachusetts, suggests that the roots of violent abuse lie in socialization for separation, in which we are cut off from the possibilities of mutuality and joy in our most important relationships.

31. Herman, "The Rape Culture," in *Women: A Feminist Perspective,* ed. Freeman, 47.

32. Hunt, "Theological Pornography," in *Christianity, Patriarchy, and Abuse,* ed. Brown and Boh, 95.

33. Valverde, *Sex, Power, and Pleasure,* 62.

34. In *Office Romance: Love, Power, and Sex in the Workplace* (New York: Rawson Associates, 1989), 159, Lisa A. Mainiero quotes one executive woman as saying, "The combination of power and business judgment can be a real turn-on. It's sexy as hell."

35. Nancy Friday, *My Secret Garden: Women's Sexual Fantasies* (New York: Pocket Books, 1973), 110.

36. Lonnie Barbach and Linda Levine, *Shared Intimacies: Women's Sexual Experiences* (New York: Bantam Books, 1980), 123.

37. Two caveats need to be entered here. First, Marianna Valverde (*Sex, Power and Pleasure,* 47) charges that, due to the wide range of heterosexual experiences, we cannot speak confidently about heterosexuality in general. Second, Harrison, et. al. ("Pain and Pleasure," 148) charge that in the sexual arena more than in any other, feminists tend to impose their own morality on others. My intention is neither to label all heterosexual men or women, nor to impose an ethic on them, but rather to lift up dimensions of experience that have been neglected, in hope that those dimensions might assist at least some women in the effort to create a Christian sexual ethic that takes their experience seriously. I am also keenly aware that what I will describe here is culture-bound and may not speak as helpfully to those from different backgrounds.

38. Shere Hite, *The Hite Report* (New York: Dell Publishing Co., 1976), 461-62. One woman said, "I felt like hell—angry and unhappy." Another "hated" herself for being afraid to say no.

Another thought she was not "supposed" to say no since she was married; she "faked orgasms."

39. Barbach and Levine, *Shared Intimacies,* 125.The responses also make clear that women do not always feel that they can say no and that women will tend to blame themselves instead of the man—hating their own passivity or "weakness."They further make clear that women will fake orgasm rather than confront their partner with the truth of their dislike. Deception is a technique commonly used by those with little power against their oppressors.

40. Hite, *The Hite Report,* 419.

41. Ibid., 420.Whether men are in fact getting what they want is, of course, also an issue. My own interpretation would be that in an oppressive society, most men also do not get what they really want.

42. Nel Noddings, *Women and Evil* (Berkeley: University of California Press, 1989), 198.

43. In *Talking Back:Thinking Feminist, Thinking Black* (Boston: South End Press, 1989), 127, Bell Hooks argues that labeling men "the enemy" in the early stages of the feminist movement was an effective way to begin the critical separation that women needed in order to effect rebellion, but that as the movement has matured, we have seen the error in such separation and have come to appreciate the need for the transformation of masculinity as part of the feminist movement.

44. In so doing, I will no doubt stretch and possibly misuse their insights; if so, I offer my most genuine apologies. Nothing could prove better how socially constructed all of our realities are than the difficulties experienced by a white person of some privilege in trying to utilize insights drawn from black experience.

45. King, *Strength to Love,* 34.

46. Ibid.

47. Paul Lauritzen, "Forgiveness: Moral Prerogative or Religious Duty?"*Journal of Religious Ethics* 15, no. 2 (Fall 1987): 150. Lauritzen does not argue (151), however, that in the context of religious belief, forgiveness can be given without repentance on the other's part because the forgiveness itself takes away the character of the sin.

48. Ibid., 143. Forgiveness is then akin to "jubilee justice"; see Karen Lebacqz,*Justice in an Unjust World: Foundations for a Christian Approach to Justice* (Minneapolis:Augsburg Press, 1987).

49. Katie G. Cannon, *Black Womanist Ethics* (Atlanta: Scholars Press, 1988), 6-7.

50. Hartsock,*Money, Sex and Power,* 177.

51. In this regard, I have not found the literature on love of enemies as helpful as I wished. Most of it is focused on instances where we clearly recognize our enemy, whereas I am trying to deal with a situation where we do not recognize that we are in fact dealing with an enemy and where recognition is the first step (see Lebacqz, *Justice in an Unjust World,* 108f.).Also, the literature focuses on attitudes rather than roles; its primary concern is reducing enmity (Cf. Stephen C. Mott, *Biblical Ethics and Social Change* [New York: Oxford University Press, 1982], 37). If "enemy" is understood as a culturally constructed role, then the task is not to reduce hatred but to ask how one loves the person who stands in a particular role, just as one might ask about love of mother, sister, teacher, etc.

Chapter 4

1. See Linda Woodhead,"Faith, Feminism and the Family," in *Concilium:The Family* (1995), 43-52.

2. See Peter Brown, *The Body and Society* (Winchester, MA: Faber and Faber, 1990), 297-301.

3. Karl Barth, *Church Dogmatics* (Herndon,VA:T&T Clark, 1961). III.4 chapter XIII Section 54.2, pp. 265-85.

4. See Nicholas Peter Harvey, *The Morals of Jesus* (Darton, Longman and Todd, 1991), chapters 11 and 12.

5. Quoted in Elaine Pagels, *Adam, Eve and the Serpent* (New York: Penguin, 1988), 33.

6. Geoffrey Bould, "A Martyr's Witness," in *The Tablet*, 11 August 1984, 773.
7. Elizabeth Stuart, *Just Good Friends: Towards A Lesbian and Gay Theology of Relationships* (Lincoln, RI: Mowbray, 1995), 117.
8. I have developed this argument at greater length in my article "Faith, Feminism and the Family," in *Concilium, The Family* (1995/4), 43–52.

Chapter 5

1. Nicholas Lemann, "Taking Affirmative Action Apart," *New York Times Magazine*, 11 June 1995.

Chapter 6

1. Jacquelyn Grant, *White Women's Christ and Black Women's Jesus* (Atlanta: Scholars Press, 1989).
2. Ruether, *To Change the World: Christology and Cultural Criticism* (New York: Crossroad, 1981), 47.
3. Ibid., 5.
4. David Katzman, *Seven Days a Week: Women and Domestic Service in Industrializing America* (New York: Oxford University Press, 1978), 186, 188. The irony of these beliefs is that these were the people that whites had care for their children and their homes.
5. William Jones, *Is God a White Racist?* (New York: Anchor/Doubleday, 1973).
6. William E. B. DuBois, *The Souls of Black Folks* (New York: A Signet Classic, New American Library, 1969), 49.
7. Martin Luther King Jr., "Suffering and Faith" in *A Testament of Hope,* ed. James Washington (New York: Harper & Row, 1986), 41.
8. Ibid.
9. Susan Nelson Dunfee, *Beyond Servanthood: Christianity and the Liberation of Women* (New York: University Press of America, 1989), 159.

Chapter 7

1. An excellent discussion of Wesley's quadrilateral can be found in Colin W. Williams, *John Wesley's Theology Today* (Nashville: Abingdon Press, 1960), chap. 2.
2. Robin Scroggs has formulated these questions succinctly in his important study, *The New Testament and Homosexuality* (Philadelphia: Fortress Press, 1983), 123. The entire volume is a persuasive illustration of the application of these questions.
3. Ibid., 126.
4. Walter Wink, "Biblical Perspectives on Homosexuality," *The Christian Century,* 7 December 1979, 1085.
5. L. William Countryman, *Dirt, Greed, and Sex* (Philadelphia: Fortress Press, 1988).
6. John Wesley, in *The Letters of John Wesley,* ed. John Telford, Standard Edition, vol. 5 (London: Epworth Press, 1931), 364. Commenting on 1 Corinthians 14:20, Wesley also said, "Knowing religion was not designed to destroy any of our natural faculties, but to exalt and improve them, our reason in particular." Cf. Williams, *John Wesley's Theology Today,* 30.
7. See Alfred C. Kinsey et al., *Sexual Behavior in the Human Male* (Philadelphia: W. B. Saunders, 1948). See also his *Sexual Behavior in the Human Female* (Philadelphia: W. B. Saunders, 1953).
8. George Weinberg, a psychotherapist, is usually credited with popularizing the term. See his *Society and the Healthy Homosexual* (Garden City, NY: Doubleday & Co., Anchor Press, 1972), chap. 1.
9. For a fuller discussion of the dynamics of homophobia, see Nelson, *The Intimate Connection,* chap. 3, n. 3, and 59ff.

10. For a review of literature on the subject of this chapter, see my article "Homosexuality and the Church: A Bibliographical Essay," *Prism* 6, no. 1 (Spring 1991): 74-83.

11. Carol Levine, Deborah Jones Merritt, Daniel M. Fox, Ruth Macklin, Larry Gostin, William J. Curran, Dan E. Beauchamp, "Aids: Public Health and Civil Liberties," *Hastings Center Report,* December 1986.

12. James B. Nelson, "Responding to, learning from AIDS," *Christianity & Crisis,* 19 May 1986, 179.

13. Levine, et. al., 35.

14. David James Randolph, "Aid for Persons with Aids," *Engage/Social Action,* February 1986, 43.

15. John Fortunato, *AIDS, the Spiritual Dilemma* (San Francisco: Perennial Library, 1987).

Chapter 9

1. Gregg Easterbrook, *The New Yorker,* 10 April 1995, 38-43.

2. The Fifth Assembly of the World Council of Churches in 1975 emphasized the need to create a "just, participatory, and sustainable society." A follow-up conference in 1979 entitled "Faith, Science and the Future" gave explicit attention to the norms of sustainability, sufficiency, participation, and solidarity. In 1983, the Sixth Assembly of the WCC challenged all of its member communions to strive for the integration of "justice, peace, and the integrity of creation." This emphasis continued with the theme of the Seventh Assembly in 1990, "Come Holy Spirit—Renew Your Whole Creation."

3. See, Presbyterian Eco-Justice Task Force, *Keeping and Healing the Creation* (Louisville, KY: Committee on Social Witness Policy, Presbyterian Church [USA], 1989); and Evangelical Lutheran Church in America, *Caring for the Creation: Vision, Hope, and Justice* (Chicago: Division for Church in Society, 1993). The term is also being utilized by various groups including the Eco-Justice Working Group of the National Council of Churches and the Eco-Justice Project and Network of the Center for Religion, Ethics, and Social Policy at Cornell University.

4. Richard Sylvan, "Is There a Need for a New, an Environmental Ethic?" in Michael Zimmerman, *Environmental Philosophy: From Animal Rights to Radical Ecology* (Englewood Cliffs, NJ: Prentice-Hall, 1993), 13-14.

5. Paul Taylor, "The Ethics of Respect for Nature," in Zimmerman, *Environmental Philosophy,* 78-80.

6. Systematically in Holmes Rolston, *Environmental Ethics: Duties to and Values in the Natural World* (Philadelphia: Temple University Press, 1988).

7. Ibid., 112-116.

8. Larry Rasmussen's phrase, defending the extension of neighbor love even to inorganic nature; in Wesley Granberg-Michaelson, ed., *Tending the Garden: Essays on the Gospel and the Earth* (Grand Rapids, MI: Eerdmans, 1987), 199. For an anti-theological version of the extension argument, see J. Baird Callicott, following his hero, the much-cited Aldo Leopold, *In Defense of the Land Ethic* (Albany: State University of New York, 1989), 80-82.

9. H. Paul Santmire, *The Travail of Nature: The Ambiguous Ecological Promise of Christian Theology* (Philadelphia: Fortress, 1985). James A. Nash, *Loving Nature: Ecological Integrity and Christian Responsibility* (Nashville: Abingdon, 1991), 124-133.

10. Arne Naess, "The Deep Ecological Movement: Some Philosophical Aspects," in Zimmerman, *Environmental Philosophy,* 203. George Sessions is less severe but, as a "biocentric egalitarian," will give us no more than equality with nature: non-human entities have "equal inherent value or worth along with humans" ("Deep Ecology and Global Ecosystem Protection," in Zimmerman, *Environmental Philosophy,* 236).

11. Rolston, *Environmental Ethics,* 103.

12. Hardin's essay "The Tragedy of the Commons" (*Science,* 13 December 1968) is still routinely cited and anthologized, as are the conclusions he drew from it in another essay, "Living on a Lifeboat" (*Bioscience* 24, 1974). But harshest of all is *Exploring New Ethics for Survival: The Voyage of the Spaceship Beagle* (Baltimore: Penguin, 1973), which is virtually invisible today. The quotation from William Aiken is from his essay "Ethical Issues in Agriculture," in Tom

Regan, ed., *Earthbound: New Introductory Essays in Environmental Ethics* (New York: Random House, 1984), 269; cited in Callicott, *In Defense of the Land Ethic*, 92. This is not Aiken's position, though Callicott's alterations make it appear to be so. Aiken says that these statements, which in his essay are questions, would be those of a position he calls "eco-holism," an extreme stance that he suggests may be ascribed to Paul Taylor among others, and which he rejects in favor of a more humanistic one. On p. 272 he outlines a scale of comparative value much like Nash's, one that favors human beings.

13. Taylor, "Ethics of Respect for Nature," 71, 81. Berry, in Zimmerman, *Environmental Philosophy,* 174.

14. Carol Christ, "Rethinking Theology and Nature," in Irene Diamond and Gloria Feman Orenstein, eds., *Reweaving the World: The Emergence of Ecofeminism* (San Francisco: Sierra Club, 1990), 68.

15. Rolston, *Environmental Ethics,* 344–45.

16. James Gustafson, *A Sense of the Divine: The Natural Environment from a Theocentric Perspective* (Cleveland: Pilgrim Press 1995), chaps. 1 and 3. Nash, *Loving Nature,* 233–34, no. 10, commenting on Gustafson's *Theocentric Ethics,* vol. 1 (Chicago: University of Chicago Press, 1981), 106, 183–184, 248–50, 270–73.

17. Michael Zimmerman, "Deep Ecology and Ecofeminism: The Emerging Dialogue," in Diamond and Orenstein, *Reweaving the World,* 140. Zimmerman, like Naess and Sessions, is a "biocentric egalitarian"; thus: "Humanity is no more, but also no less, important than all other things on earth" (Ibid.).

18. Rosemary Radford Ruether, *New Woman, New Earth* (New York: Seabury Press, 1975), 46. I use the term God/ess after Rosemary Radford Ruether in *Sexism and God-Talk: Toward a Feminist Theology.* Ruether explains: "when discussing fuller divinity to which this theology points, I use the term God/ess, a written symbol intended to combine both the masculine and feminine forms of the word for the divine while preserving the Judeo-Christian affirmation that divinity is one.... [I]t serves here as an analytic sign to point toward that yet unnameable understanding of the divine that would transcend patriarchal limitations and signal redemptive experience for women as well as men."

19. Gerhard Von Rad, *Genesis: A Commentary* (Philadelphia: The Westminster Press, 1961, 1972), 60.

20. James Barr, "Man and Nature—The Ecological Controversy and the Old Testament," *Bulletin of the John Rylands University Library of Manchester* 9, no. 32 (1972): 22.

21. Ibid., 23. James Barr adds parenthetically, "a different Hebrew word indeed, but there is no reason to suppose that this makes much difference."

22. Ibid.

23. Cuthbert Simpson and Walter Russell Bowie, *The Interpreter's Bible (Genesis)* (New York and Nashville: Abingdon Press, 1952), 486. Cuthbert Simpson's explanation is that verse 29 may have been an addition to P's original narrative, containing the classical conceptualization of the Golden Age—which was seen as vegetarian and peaceful between humans and animals—and so it is more linked to the visions of Isaiah 11:6–8; 65:25, Hosea 2:18. Thus it posits potentiality rather than reality.

24. Jean Soler, "The Dietary Prohibitions of the Hebrews," *The New York Review of Books,* 14 June 1979, 24; Barr, 21. Soler agrees with Barr's conclusion, stating "meat eating is implicitly but unequivocally excluded" and that the reason for this has to do with the way that God and humans are defined in Genesis 1:26 by their relationship to each other.

25. Anthony Phillips, *Lower than the Angels: Questions Raised by Genesis 1–11* (The Bible Reading Fellowship, 1983), 48.

26. Soler, 24; Abraham Isaac Kook, "Fragments of Light: A View as to the Reasons for the Commandments," *Abraham Isaac Kook: The Lights of Penitence, The Moral Principles, Lights of Holiness. Essays, Letters and Poems,* Trans. Ben Zion Bokser (New York: Paulist Press).

27. Samuel H. Dresner, *The Jewish Laws* (New York: The United Synagogue of America, 1957), 21.

28. Ibid., p. 26.

29. Ibid., p. 22.
30. Ibid., p. 24.
31. Elizabeth Cady Stanton, *The Woman's Bible: Part I* (New York: European Publishing Co.; Seattle: Coalition Task Force on Women and Religion, [1898], 1974), 91.
32. Elisabeth Schüssler Fiorenza, *In Memory of Her: A Feminist Theological Reconstruction of Christian Origins* (New York: Crossroad, 1984), 6.
33. Beverly Harrison, *Making the Connections: Essays in Feminist Social Ethics,* ed. Carol S. Robb (Boston: Beacon Press, 1985), 235-36.
34. The quotations which follow about the development of an ethical issue are from Sarah Bentley, 16-17. Those quotations with both single and double quotation marks are Bentley's references to Gerard Fourez's *Liberation Ethics* (Philadelphia: Temple University Press, 1982), 93, 108-109. Italicized words within the quotation marks contained this emphasis in the original source.
35. Harrison, 13.
36. Alice Walker, *In Search of Our Mother's Gardens: Womanist Prose* (San Diego: Harcourt Brace Jovanovich, 1983), 5.

Chapter 10

1. At a meeting of older religious women in April, a letter was sent by the group to the Archbishop to protest the exclusion of women from a Synod on religious life. The exclusion of women from decision making in regard to their own lives continues in the church to this day and punctuates the failure of the hierarchy to acknowledge the full humanity and personhood of women, often recognized in society, but not in the Catholic Church, in this last decade of the twentieth century.
2. Cf. E. Schüssler Fiorenza, *In Memory of Her: A Feminist Theological Reconstruction of Christian Origins* (New York, 1989).
3. U. Ranke-Heinemann, *Eunuchs for the Kingdom of Heaven* (New York, 1990).
4. Deuteronomy 32:14.
5. P. Brown, *The Body and Society* (London: André Deutsch, 1988), 426.
6. Brown, *The Body and Society*, 426.
7. 'Priesthood, Precedent, and Prejudice: On Recovering the Women Priests of Early Christianity' (English trans. G. Otranto's 'Notes on the Female Priesthood'), *Journal of Feminist Studies in Religion* 7, no. 1 (1991): 73-94.
8. D. Irvin, 'The Ministry of Women in the Early Church: The Archaeological Evidence,' in *Duke Divinity School Review* 45, no. 2 (Spring 1980): 76-86.
9. For these and other citations, cf. M. Horowitz, 'Aristotle and Woman,' *Journal of the History of Biology* 9 (1976): 183-213.
10. E.F. Defeis, 'An International Human Right: Gender Equality,' *Journal of Women's History* 3, no. 1 (1991): 90-107.
11. E. Schüssler Fiorenza, *In Memory of Her.*
12. S. Brooks Thistlethwaite, "Every Two Minutes: Battered Women and Feminist Interpretation," in L. Russell, ed., *Feminist Interpretation of the Bible,* 96-107.

Chapter 11

1. Apparently the punishment must be both—else cruel *or* unusual would have done. Historically it appears that punishments were prohibited if unusual in 1791 *and* cruel: the Framers did want to prohibit punishments, even cruel ones, only if already unusual in 1791; they did prohibit new (unusual) punishments if cruel. The Eighth Amendment was not meant to apply to the death penalty in 1791 since it was not unusual then; nor was the Eighth Amendment intended to be used against capital punishment in the future, regardless of

whether it may have come to be considered cruel: it is neither a new penalty nor one unusual in 1791.

2. See Chief Justice Burger dissenting in *Furman:* "In a democratic society legislatures not courts are constituted to respond to the will and consequently the moral values of the people."

3. The First Amendment might be invoked against such sources of revelation. When specific laws do not suffice to decide a case, courts, to be sure, make decisions based on general legal principles. But the death penalty (as distinguished from applications) raises no serious legal problem.

4. Attention should be drawn to John Hagan's "Extralegal Attributes and Criminal Sentencing" (*Law and Society Review,* Spring 1974), which throws doubt on much of the discrimination which sociologists have found.

5. I am referring throughout to discrimination among those already convicted of capital crimes. That discrimination can be tested. However, the fact that a higher proportion of blacks, or poor people, than of whites, or rich people, are found guilty of capital crimes does not *ipso facto* indicate discrimination, any more than does the fact that a comparatively high proportion of blacks or poor people become professional baseball players or boxers.

6. "The Deterrent Effect of Capital Punishment: A Question of Life and Death," *American Economic Review,* June 1975. In the period studied capital punishment was already infrequent and uncertain. Its deterrent effect might be greater when more frequently imposed for capital crimes, so that a prospective offender would feel more certain of it.

7. See *Journal of Legal Studies,* January 1977; *Journal of Political Economy,* June 1977; and (this is the cross-sectional analysis) *American Economic Review,* June 1977.

8. *Per contra* see Brian Forst in *Minnesota Law Review,* May 1977, and *Deterrence and Incapacitation* (National Academy of Sciences, Washington, D.C., 1978). By now statistical analyses of the effects of the death penalty have become a veritable cottage industry. This has happened since Ehrlich found deterrent effects. No one much bothered when Thorsten Sellin found none. Still, it is too early for more than tentative conclusions. The two papers mentioned above are replied to, more than adequately in my view, in Isaac Ehrlich's "Fear of Deterrence," *Journal of Legal Studies,* June 1977.

9. I thought that prudence as well as morality commanded us to choose the first alternative even when I believed that the degree of probability and the extent of deterrent effects might remain unknown. (See my "On Deterrence and the Death Penalty," *Journal of Criminal Law, Criminology, and Police Science,* June 1969). The probability is more likely to become known now and to be greater than was apparent a few years ago.

10. Particularly since he, unlike the person already in custody, may have much to gain from his additional crime (see note 14).

11. The Supreme Court has decided that capital punishment for rape (at least of adults) is "cruel and unusual" (*Coker v. Georgia,* 1977). For the reasons stated in the text, I welcome the decision—but not the justification given by the Supreme Court. The penalty may indeed be as excessive as the court feels it is, but not in the constitutional sense of being irrationally or extravagantly so, and thus contrary to the Eighth Amendment. The seriousness of the crime of rape and the appropriateness of the death penalty for it are matters for political rather than judicial institutions to decide. I should vote against the death penalty for rape—and not only for the reasons stated in the text above; but the Court should have left the matter to the vote of the citizens.

   The charge of racially discriminatory application was most often justified when the penalty was inflicted for rape. Yet I doubt that the charge will be dropped, or that the agitation against the death penalty will stop, once it is no longer inflicted for rape. Discrimination never was more than a pretext used by abolitionists.

12. There is a good argument here against unnecessary public displays of violence. (See my "What to Do about TV Violence," *The Alternative,* August/September 1976.)

13. It may be noted that in Beccaria's time executions were regarded as public entertainments....

14. I have reservations on both these counts, being convinced that many crimes among relatives, friends, and associates are as blameworthy and as deterrable as crimes among strangers. Thus,

major heroin dealers in New York are threatened with life imprisonment. In the absence of the death penalty they find it advantageous to have witnesses killed. Such murders surely are not acts of passion in the classical sense, though they occur among associates. They are, in practice, encouraged by the present penal law in New York.

15. Different motives (the reason why something is done) may generate the same action (what is done), purpose, or intent, just as the same motive may lead to different actions.

16. Insofar as these questions are psychological, empirical evidence would not be irrelevant. But it is likely to be evaluated in terms depending on moral views.

17. Not always. On the disastrous consequences of periodic failure to do so, Sir Henry Maine waxes eloquent with sorrow in his *Ancient Law* (408-9).

18. One may argue that some crimes deserve more than execution and that the above reasoning would justify punitive torture as well. Perhaps. But torture, unlike death, is generally rejected. Therefore penalties have been reduced to a few kinds—fines, confinement, and execution. The issue is academic because, unlike the death penalty, torture has become repulsive to us. (Some reasons for this public revulsion are listed in chapter 17 of my *Punishing Criminals*, Basic Books, 1975.) As was noted above the range of punishments is bound to be more limited than the range of crimes. We do not accept some punishments, however much deserved they may be.

19. Social approval is usually not unanimous, and the system of rewards reflects it less.

Chapter 12

1. John B. Cobb Jr., and L. Charles Birch, *The Liberation of Life* (Cambridge: Cambridge University Press, 1981), 247.

2. Ibid., 325-39.

3. Ibid., 244f.

4. Translating these terms into the language of those in Europe and North America who are currently active in the peace movement, justice and sustainability might be treated as dual prerequisites for, and aspects of, a lasting peace. A lasting peace is one in which international tensions resulting from injustice and unsustainability are minimized, such that the desire or need to build, deploy, or use nuclear weapons is itself minimized. The authentic pursuit of peace in a contemporary setting thus involves a concomitant pursuit of justice and sustainability.

5. Ibid., 262.

6. Of course, changes in individual lifestyle are not enough. Changes in public policy and social system are also necessary. Much of the content of *The Liberation of Life* deals with the latter changes. Concrete proposals are made for more just and sustainable forms of agriculture, energy production, public transportation, urban design, and economic development.

7. Whether or not the prevailing habits of thought that I criticize are more characteristic of affluent Christians in capitalist contexts than in socialist contexts, or vice versa, is a question left open. Birch and Cobb suggest, and perhaps rightly, that socialist systems are as captivated in their own ways by mechanistic habits of thought as are capitalist systems. Both systems are in need of creative transformation. I have chosen not to enter into a more sustained debate between capitalism and socialism because (a) such is not within the scope of this essay and (b) the relation between the two is extensively discussed by Birch and Cobb in *The Liberation of Life*. See Chapter 9 on "Economic Development in Ecological Perspective" in *The Liberation of Life*, 265-95.

8. The word used in process philosophy is usually "society" rather than "community." I am using the two words interchangeably. Relationality applies to communities "in a more general way" because, for process thinkers, societies *per se* do not prehend or experience. Relations between communities are mediated by the individuals composing them.

9. Process thinkers are not alone among liberation thinkers to emphasize relationality even in respect to God. For a contemporary expression of relational thinking in North American black theology, see Archie Smith Jr., *The Relational Self: Ethics and Therapy from a Black Church Perspective* (Nashville: Abingdon, 1982), 51.

10. Karl Menger, *Principles of Economics,* trans. James Dingwall and Bert F. Hoselitz, with an Introduction by F. A. Hayek (New York: New York Univ. Press, 1981), 109.
11. Birch and Cobb, *Liberation of Life,* 329.

Chapter 13

1. G. C. Lodge, *The New American Ideology* (Alfred A. Knopf, New York, 1976). G. C. Lodge, "Managers and Managed: Problems of Ambivalence," in Houck, John W. and Williams, Oliver F. eds., *Co-Creation and Capitalism: John Paul II's Laborem Exercens* (Washington, D.C.: University Press of America, 1983), 229-53.
2. J. Locke, *Two Treatises of Government,* edited by Peter Laslet (New York: Cambridge University Press, 1963), 245.
3. Ibid.
4. Unfortunately, exclusive language prevails throughout papal encyclicals. Since it is a reminder of justice issues yet to be tackled, I have let it stand. All citations of *Centesimus Annus* are to the text published by the United States Catholic Conference, Washington, DC.
5. See R. Bellah, *The Good Society* (New York: Alfred A. Knopf, 1991); M.A. Glendon, *Rights Talk: The Impoverishment of Political Discourse* (New York: The Free Press, 1991).
6. For the view of Thomas Aquinas on private property, see *Summa Theologica* II-II, 66, 2. For a summary of the tradition, see Duff, E. 'Private Property,' *New Catholic Encyclopedia* 28, pp. 49-55.
7. See J.A. Pichler, "Business Competence and Religious Values—A Trade-Off?," in John W. Houck and Oliver F. Williams, eds., *Co-Creation and Capitalism: John Paul II's Laborem Exercens* (Washington, D.C.: University Press of America, 1983), 101-123; J.A. Pichler, "Capitalism and Employment: A Policy Perspective," in John W. Houck and Oliver F. Williams, eds., *Catholic Social Teaching and the U.S. Economy: Working Papers for a Bishops' Pastoral* (Washington, D.C.: University Press of America, 1984), 37-76.
8. See G. Baum, *The Priority of Labor* (New York: Paulist Press, 1982).
9. J. G. Hehir, "John Paul II and the International System," in Oliver F. Williams and John W. Houck, eds., *The Making of an Economic Vision* (Washington, D.C.: University Press of America, 1991), 67-73; E. J. Bartell, "John Paul II and International Development," in Oliver F. Williams and John W. Houck, eds., *The Making of an Economic Vision* (Washington, D.C.: University Press of America, 1991), 217-39; D. Vogel, "The International Economy and the Common Good," in Oliver F. Williams and John W. Houck, eds., *The Common Good and U.S. Capitalism* (Washington, D.C.: University Press of America, 1987), 388-409.
10. C. K. Wilber, and K. P. Jameson, "Goals of a Christian Economy and the Future of the Corporation," in Oliver F. Williams and John W. Houck, eds., *The Judeo-Christian Vision and the Modern Corporation* (Notre Dame, IN: University of Notre Dame Press, 1982), 203-17; C. K. Wilber and K. P. Jameson, *An Inquiry into the Poverty of Economics* (Notre Dame, IN: University of Notre Dame Press, 1983).
11. P. Berger, "In Praise of Particularity: The Concept of Mediating Structures," *Review of Politics,* July 1976, 130-144.
12. Bellah.
13. See R.T. DeGeorge, "Ethics and the Financial Community: An Overview," in Oliver F. Williams, Frank K. Reilly, and John W. Houck, eds., *Ethics and the Investment Industry* (Savage, MD: Rowman & Littlefield, 1989), 197-216; and C. C. Walton, "Investment Bankers from Ethical Perspectives," in Oliver F. Williams, Frank K. Reilly, and John W. Houck, eds., *Ethics and the Investment Industry* (Savage, MD: Rowman & Littlefield, 1989), 217-32; and D.W. Schriver, "Ethical Discipline and Religious Hope in the Investment Industry," in Oliver F. Williams, Frank K. Reilly, and John W. Houck, eds., *Ethics and the Investment Industry* (Savage, MD: Rowman & Littlefield, 1989), 233-50 for a discussion of appropriate regulation in the investment industry.
14. D. M. Byers, *Justice in the Market Place: Collected Statements of the Vatican and the U.S. Catholic Bishops on Economic Policy, 1891-1984* (Washington, D.C.: United States Catholic Conference, Inc., 1984).

15. Max Weber, *The Protestant Ethic and the Spirit of Capitalism,* trans. Talcott Parsons (New York: Charles Scribner's, 1958).
16. Ibid., 182.
17. Defined as individuals with professional or graduate education (which is roughly correlated with high income), and without counting dependents, the members of the overclass account for no more than 5 percent of the U.S. population.
18. According to Common Cause, the leading first-time contributor to the Republican National Committee since the 1994 congressional elections, Fruit of the Loom, gave $100,000 to the RNC in February 1995, three days before the House Ways and Means trade subcommittee held hearings on a bill to ease quotas on low-wage Caribbean countries in which the corporation has commerical ventures. The subcommittee approved the measure.

Chapter 14

1. Magnus Blomstrom and Bjorn Hettne, *Development Theory in Transition: The Dependency Debate and Beyond,* (London: Zed Books, 1988), 8.
2. C.T. Kurien, "Widening Our Perspective on Development," *Bangalore Theological Forum,* July–September 1987, 135.
3. Somen Dhas, "A Theological-Ethical Critique of Modern Development," *Bangalore Theological Forum,* July–September 1987, 199–202.
4. Ibid., 202–204.
5. *Loc. cit.,* 138.
6. Ibid., 137.
7. M.M. Thomas, *Response to Tyranny,* New Delhi, Forum for Christian Concern for People's Struggle, 88.
8. Cited by Blomstrom and Hettne, *op. cit.,* 52.
9. Ibid., 65.
10. Ibid., 66.
11. Ibid., 106.
12. Jose George, "Organization and Mobilization of Peasants and Agricultural Labourers in Kerala: An Alternative Development Strategy," *Bangalore Theological Forum,* July–September 1987, 162.
13. The fact of the presence and persistence of such dynamics may be the starting point for a theology of grace in contemporary contexts, especially a theology of grace that thinks it has a requisite gift for resisting political oppression and not simply, as so often in the history of Western theology, an unmerited favor given to relieve individuals' guilt-consciences.
14. Richard A. Falk, "Normative Initiatives and Demilitarization: A Third System Approach," in *World Order Models Project,* Working Paper No. 13 (New York: Institute for World Order, 1992), 6.
15. Ibid., 8.
16. Ibid., 7–8. Falk also discusses various limitations of the third system: its frequent fragmentation, its lack of autonomy, the lack of coordination among its different participants, its failures to achieve structural expression beyond utopian projection, etc.
17. See the commentary and challenge concerning right-wing Christians in the seven nations of Namibia, South Africa, Guatemala, Nicaragua, South Korea, the Philippines, and El Salvador in *The Road to Damascus: Kairos and Conversion* (Washington, D.C.: Center of Concern, 1989).
18. John DeGruchy and Charles Villa-Vicencio, eds., *Apartheid Is a Heresy* (Grand Rapids, MI: Eerdmans, 1983).
19. Richard Horsley, *Jesus and the Spiral of Violence* (Minneapolis: Fortress Press, 1993), 114.
20. Richard Horsley, *Sociology and the Jesus Movement* (New York: Crossroad, 1989), 106, 111, 113, 130. Compare Elisabeth Schüssler Fiorenza, *In Memory of Her: A Feminist Reconstruction of Christian Origins* (New York: Crossroad, 1983), 118–154.
21. Gustavo Gutiérrez, *A Theology of Liberation: History, Politics and Salvation,* Sister Caridad Inda and John Eagleson, trans. and eds., 15th anniversary ed. (Maryknoll, NY: Orbis Books, 1988), 160.

22. Edward Farley, *Good and Evil: Interpreting a Human Condition* (Minneapolis: Fortress Press, 1991), 291.

23. Ibid., 39.

24. On this notion, see Robert Jay Lifton and Eric Markusen, *The Genocidal Mentality: Nazi Holocaust and Nuclear Threat* (New York: Basic Books, 1990), 258-77.

25. Friedrich Schleiermacher, *The Christian Faith*, H.R. Mackintosh and J.S. Stewart, eds. (Philadelphia: Fortress Press, 1976), 282-304.

26. For example, see the fruit of ongoing negotiations among theologians participating in the Ecumenical Association of Third World Theologians, in K.C. Abraham, *Third World Theologies: Commonalities and Divergences* (Maryknoll, NY: Orbis Books, 1990).

27. Kwamena Acquaah, *International Regulation of Transnational Corporations: The New Reality* (New York and London: Praeger, 1986), 191.

28. Ibid., 162-173.

29. Ulrich Duchrow, *The Global Economy: A Confessional Issue for the Churches?* (Geneva: WCC, 1987), 77-78.

30. Richard Falk, *World Order Models.*

31. On the issue, see Nicholas Wolterstorff, *Until Justice and Peace Embrace* (Grand Rapids, MI: Eerdmans, 1983), especially chap. 5.

32. Jefferson Morley and Nathaniel Wice, "Fear of Music," *SPIN,* November 1991, 53-54, 56-59.

33. Audre Lorde, *Sister Outsider: Essays and Speeches* (Trumansburg, N.Y.: Crossing Press, 1984), 36-39.

34. See John Beverley and Marc Zimmerman, *Literature and Politics in the Central American Revolutions* (Austin: University of Texas Press, 1990), 154-160.

35. Susanne Jonas, *The Battle for Guatemala* (Boulder, CO: Westview Press, 1991), ix.

Chapter 15

1. W. French Anderson, "Genetics and Human Malleability," *Hastings Center Report* 20 (1990): 21-24.

2. A TIME/CNN poll on people's reaction to genetic research, *Time,* 17 January 1994, 48.

3. Ian G. Barbour, *Issues in Science and Religion* (New York: Harper & Row, 1966), 449.

4. "Evolutionary Progress and Christian Promise," in *Concilium Vol. 26: The Evolving World and Theology,* ed. Johannes B. Metz (New York: Paulist Press, 1967), 35-47.

5. Ibid., 38.

6. Ibid.

7. Paul Ramsey, *Fabricated Man: The Ethics of Genetic Control* (New Haven, CT: Yale University Press, 1970), 27.

8. Thomas A. Shannon, *What Are They Saying About Genetic Engineering?* (New York: Paulist Press, 1985), 21.

9. Ann Lammers and Ted Peters, "Genethics: Implications of the Human Genome Project," in *Moral Issues & Christian Response,* eds. Paul T. Jersild and Dale A. Johnson (New York: Harcourt Brace Jovanovich College Publishers, 1993), 302.

10. Karl Rahner, "The Problem of Genetic Manipulation," *Theological Investigations,* Vol. 9 (New York: Crossroad, 1972), 225-52. Also see his "The Experiment with Man" in Ibid., 210-23.

11. Joseph Fletcher, "Ethical Aspects of Genetic Controls: Designed Genetic Changes in Man," *The New England Journal of Medicine,* 285 (30 September 1971), 776-83.

12. Daniel Callahan, "Living with the New Biology," *Center Magazine* 5 (1972): 4-12.

13. Shannon, 37.

14. W. Norris Clarke, S. J., "Technology and Man: A Christian Vision," in *Science and Religion: New Perspectives on the Dialogue,* ed. Ian G. Barbour (New York: Harper & Row, 1968), 287-88.

15. LeRoy Walters Jr., "Ethical Issues in Human Gene Therapy," *The Journal of Clinical Ethics* 2 (Winter 1991): 267-74.